SONGWRITERS ON SONGWRITING

Paul Zollo

DA CAPO PRESS

A Member of the Perseus Books Group

Cataloging-in-Publication data for this book is available from the Library of Congress

Second Da Capo Press edition 2003
Reprinted by arrangement with the author.
ISBN 0–306–81265–7

This Da Capo Press paperback edition of *Songwriters on Songwriting* is a greatly expanded and
revised version of the edition published in Cincinnati, Ohio, in 1991, incorporating interviews
previously published in *SongTalk* magazine.

The following page constitutes an extension of this copyright page.

Published by Da Capo Press
A Member of the Perseus Books Group
http://www.dacapopress.com

Da Capo Press books are available at special discounts for bulk purchases in the U.S. by
corporations, institutions, and other organizations. For more information, please contact the
Special Markets Department at the Perseus Books Group, 11 Cambridge Center, Cambridge,
MA 02142, or call (800) 255–1514 or (617) 252–5298, or e-mail j.mccrary@perseusbooks.com.

1 2 3 4 5 6 7 8 9——07 06 05 04 03

Credits

All interviews herein were conducted by Paul Zollo and published originally in *SongTalk*, the journal of the National Academy of Songwriters. NAS is a non-profit organization dedicated to assisting, educating and supporting all songwriters. For information about *SongTalk* or N.A.S., call toll-free 800-826-7287 outside of California, 213-463-7178 inside of California, or write to the National Academy of Songwriters, 6255 Sunset Boulevard, Suite 1023, Hollywood, California 90028.

The only exception is the second interview with Loudon Wainwright III, which was combined with the original *SongTalk* interview. It was conducted for *Acoustic Guitar* magazine, and is used with permission.

All of the following photographs were taken by Henry Diltz: Jimmy Webb, P. F. Sloan, Harry Nilsson, Frank Zappa, Leonard Cohen, Neil Young, Graham Nash, David Crosby, Carlos Santana, Jackson Browne, Walter Becker, Dan Fogelberg, Lindsey Buckingham, Todd Rundgren, Tom Petty, Bob Dylan, Richard Thompson, Bruce Cockburn. They are reprinted courtesy of Henry Diltz Photography, North Hollywood, California. Henry's website can be found at www. Hyper-Active.

The photos of Livingston & Evans, Willie Dixon, Brian Wilson, Carole King & Gerry Goffin, Randy Newman, Van Dyke Parks, Janis Ian, and Mose Allison were all taken exclusively for *SongTalk* by Carl Studna, and are used courtesy of Carl Studna Photography, Los Angeles.

The photo of Yoko Ono is by Jayne Wexler and is used courtesy of the Lenono Photo Archive, New York.

The photo of Paul Simon is by Robert Mapplethorpe. The photo of Rickie Lee Jones is by Deborah Feingold. The photo of R.E.M. is by Frank Ockenfels. The photo of Joan Baez is by Matthew Rolston.

The photo of David Byrne is by Bonnie Schiffman. The photo of k.d. lang is by Greg Allen. The photo of Stan Ridgway is by Ed Colver. The photo of Townes Van Zandt is by Steve Salmieri. The photo of Pete Seeger is by Curt Koehler.

Permission to reprint song lyrics are as follows:

"Talking Union" by Pete Seeger, Lee Hays and Millard Lampell. Copyright 1947, Storm King Music, Inc. All rights reserved. Used by permission.

"Graceland" and "Under African Skies" by Paul Simon. Copyright 1986, Paul Simon. Used by permission of the publisher.

"Hurdy Gurdy Man" by Donovan Leitch. Copyright 1968, Donovan (Music) Ltd. Sole selling agent: Peer International Corporation. International copyright secured. All rights reserved. Used by permission.

"Save The Last Dance For Me" by Doc Pomus and Mort Shuman. Copyright 1960, Unichappell Music, Inc. All rights reserved. Used by permission.

"Political Science" and "God's Song" by Randy Newman. Copyright 1969, January Music Corp., Six Continents Music & Unichappell Music. All rights administered by Unichappell Music, Inc. All rights reserved. Used by permission.

"Season Of Glass" by Yoko Ono. Copyright 1981, Yoko Ono. All rights reserved. Used by permission.

"Sky Blue and Black," "Before The Deluge," by Jackson Browne, copyright 1993, Swallow Turn Music. Used by permission.

Credits for the 2003 edition:

The interviews with Mark Knopfler and Roger McGuinn were originally conducted for *SongTalk*, the former publication of the National Academy of Songwriters. The interview with John Fogerty was originally conducted for *Musician* magazine. The interviews with Steely Dan, Alanis Morissette, Lou Reed, Merle Haggard, and Lenny Kravitz were originally conducted for *Performing Songwriter* magazine. The interview with MeShell NdegeOcello was combined from two interviews with her, conducted for *Musician* magazine and *Performing Songwriter*. The interview with John Hiatt was also combined from two interviews with him, conducted for *SongTalk* and for *Performing Songwriter* magazine.

The photos of John Hiatt, Merle Haggard, Alanis Morissette, John Fogerty, Lou Reed, and Becker & Fagen of Steely Dan, were all taken by Henry Diltz, the world's greatest photographer. The photo of MeShell NdegeOcello was taken by David Fenton. The photo of Mark Knopfler was taken by Brian Aris.

Thanks to Ben Schafer and Da Capo Press for your ongoing support of this ever-expanding book of interviews, and to all songwriters everywhere, for doing what you do.

Dedicated to Leslie
For All the Things You Are

Acknowledgments

This book has been ten years in the making, and I'd like to thank all of those who have supported and encouraged me through these years, especially my wife Leslie, who helped edit everything here, and my parents, Burt & Lois Zollo, my sister Peggy Miller, my brother Peter Zollo, all the Millers and Zollos, Howard Diller, Nancy & Bruce Robbins and Purlie Olloz.

Many thanks to Yuval Taylor and Da Capo Press for sharing my vision for this book, to my agent Ronnie Schiff for persisting on my behalf, to my lawyer Al Schlesinger, to the world's finest photographer Henry Diltz, and to two truly great teachers, Judd Sager and Camille Bertagnolli, who encouraged and inspired a budding songwriter when he needed it the most.

Thanks also to Janet Heaney, Miriam Corrier, Sharon Robinson, Jean Stawarz, Sean Heaney, Jeff Gold, Bert Saper, Wayne Boon, Andrew Kurtzman, Anne Kurtzman, Beatrice Pfister, Holly Goldsmith, Michael Diller, Mark Salerno, *Arshile*, Parthenon Huxley, Tricia Flannick, Mark Sanchez, Mark Dubrow, Steve Schalchlin, Daniel "Woody" Woodington, Tomas Ulrich, Jill Freeman, Art Garfunkel, Allan Rich, Holly Schak, Dan Kirkpatrick, Rik Lawrence, Scott Eyerly, William "Jerome" Holab, Timothy Emmons, Renato Medina, Carl Kraines, Mark Spier, Roger Rose, Peter Scheff, Sherban Cira, Randy Sharp, Steve Goodman, Rich Kerstetter & *Sing Out!*, David Lusterman, Jeffrey Pepper Rodgers & *Acoustic Guitar*, Ben Sidran, John Bettis, Helen King, Peter Luboff, Michael Smith, Mason Daring, Raspin Stuwart, Bob Gibson, Terre Roche, Tom Bowden, Mark Rowland, Bill Flanagan, *Musician*, Richard Barron, Leah Really, David Bloom, Lucy's El Adobe, Rich & Leslie Brenner & *Highland Grounds*, Severin Browne, James Coberly Smith, Randy & Pamela & Raphael Dreyfuss, MeShell NdegeOcello, Marco West, T Bone Burnett, Kevin Odegard, Spirit & Pearl, Brett Perkins, Jeff Barry, Peter Case, George Burakowski, Musso & Frank, Michael Greene, NARAS, Arthur Hamilton, The Blues Heaven Foundation, Madeleine Smith, EJ Doyle, Verno Urquiza, Phil Sloan, Abigail Bram, Alfred Johnson, Linda Smith, Bill DeMain, Bill Ede, Rooster Mitchell, Roy Halee, Peter Plath, Suzan Rivera, Gordon Pogoda, Lucy Hagan, The Arkie & Snarkie Show, Areepong Bhoocha-Oom, Bliss, Melody Daniels, Murdoch McBride, Marjorie Guthrie, Brian May & *Malibu Folk*, Canary Kahn & Franceska, Glory, John Silber and Nelson Strickland.

I'd also like to extend my sincerest appreciation to all the managers and publicists who enabled me to arrange these interviews over the years, especially Bill Bentley, Ian Hoblyn, Dolores Lusitana, Bob Merlis, Mary Klauzer, Liz Rosenberg, and Elliot Mintz.

And special thanks to all the songwriters I have been privileged to interview, for sharing so much of your time and wisdom, and for writing the songs that have added so much beauty and magic to our lives.

"If I knew where the good songs came from,
I'd go there more often. It's a mysterious condition.
It's much like the life of a Catholic nun.
You're married to a mystery."
—Leonard Cohen

Preface

I started writing songs the summer I turned eleven. Like most beginning song-writers, I knew little about music except for a handful of chords. My first attempt at songwriting was not a real song but a set of lyrics for an existing melody, Paul Simon's "The Sound of Silence." Mine was called "The Look of Absence"—masking my influences was evidently not a major concern at that age. My first real song—words and music—lifted surreal lyrics from "Fixing A Hole" and other Beatles songs. For my third song I inadvertently ripped off the tune of the Monkees' "I'm A Believer," rendered unrecognizable to me by my melodramatic choice of an especially slow tempo.

But this is precisely the way that all songwriters learn to write songs, imitating and emulating that which inspires us until our own styles gradually emerge. Through the years I've hoped to find some formula, some trick or method, that would make songwriting simple. But there is none. Unlike magicians who create the illusion of magic, writing a great song is genuine magic, miraculous even to those making the miracles. Most of the songwriters interviewed for this book are in awe of the great songs that came through them, and not one can offer an easy answer how to do it because there are no easy answers. "That's what makes it so attractive," Bob Dylan said. "There's no rhyme or reason to it. There's no rule."

Yet there is a lot of collective wisdom to be found in the ways that these songwriters have sought that magic. As the editor since 1987 of *SongTalk*, the journal of the National Academy of Songwriters, I've preserved much of that wisdom by interviewing scores of songwriters, always with the assurance that my focus is strictly on songwriting and the creative process, as opposed to the celebrity-oriented queries often directed to them by the press. With few exceptions, they were genuinely grateful for this rare opportunity to talk about the subject closest to their hearts: songwriting. And many said that reading about how other songwriters write songs helped them persist through what can be a very solitary, even lonely undertaking. Van Dyke Parks said, "What I get [from these interviews] is this sense of courage. . . . This is infectious, and highly contagious. And confirmational. It's as helpful as belonging to some religious sect. Hearing someone say, 'Amen.' "

For me, among the most confirmational aspects of conducting these interviews was to realize that these songwriters, all of whom have created extraordinary work, are regular folks who dwell in our ordinary world. And it's a peculiar kind of realization because their songs are infinite and eternal—everywhere at once, untouched by time. Yet the songwriters themselves are as finite and earthbound as the rest of us, sitting in the same room, drinking coffee, talking songs. It underscores the knowledge that all songwriters are in the same boat, and that even the most enduring and magical of their songs began where all songs begin—with a single spark of inspiration that is balanced with the mastery of craft that comes from years of work.

Regardless of genre or generation, all songwriters are connected by this singular pursuit of merging music and language to create songs. As Pete Seeger says in the opening chapter of this book, "All songwriters are links in a chain." It's a foundational truth that is verified by the rich reflections and remembrances recorded here. Songwriters are forever united in this delicate balancing act of discovering words that seamlessly match the mandate of music, and music that enhances that lyric with a sense of resonance and organic grace.

How that has been achieved has varied enormously over the years, as the nature of popular songs has evolved. Much of this evolution can be traced throughout the work of the songwriters interviewed here, each of whom started with the forms created by previous writers and created new ones. From Sammy Cahn to Bob Dylan, for example, is a profound leap forward in the potential of the popular song, although it comprises only a short span of years. And from Dylan onward, songwriting has never been the same.

No book like this one can ever be truly complete because of the links in that chain that are missing. I am gratified, however, that since 1991, when the first edition of this book was published, I've been able to interview many more of the world's most significant songwriters, including Dylan, Leonard Cohen, Laura Nyro, Neil Young and more. I've also conducted further interviews with many of my original subjects, allowing me to considerably expand and update the interviews with Paul Simon, Randy Newman, Rickie Lee Jones, Los Lobos, Janis Ian, Jimmy Webb, and Van Dyke Parks. My gratitude to Da Capo Press is immense for publishing what is an enormous tome of a book, and one that preserves the original substantial nature of these discussions.

These are not interviews about how to break into or exist within the music business, although they do touch on the necessary struggle in modern songwriting between art and commerce. These are interviews about how songwriters have succeeded in creating something timeless and lasting within an industry that emphasizes new product over all other concerns.

For songwriting is much more than a mere craft. It's a conscious attempt to connect with the unconscious; a reaching beyond ordinary perceptions to grasp images that resonate like dreams, and melodies that haunt and spur the heart. Many songwriters said that their greatest songs were written in a flash, words and music arriving simultaneously, like uncovering something that was already there. Even those who scoffed at the suggestion of a spiritual source of songs admitted that the process is mysterious and can't be controlled. Rickie Lee Jones said that inspiration is like a distant rumbling she hears coming from far away. Paul Simon said, "Mostly it's a lot of waiting—waiting for the show to begin."

How does one get in to see that show? How do you get to the place where those distant rumblings can be heard? These are the questions at the heart of this book, and although the answers offered contradict each other as often as they concur, one truth remains constant: the writing of a song is a sublime achievement, a "triumph of the spirit," as Van Dyke Parks put it. What follows is a celebration of those victories, a search for the source of songs, and an exploration into the wonders of creation. As Dylan said, "It's a magic thing, popular song. It's not a puzzle. There aren't pieces that fit. It doesn't make a complete picture that's ever been seen. But you know, as they say, thank God for songwriters."

Table of Contents

SONGWRITERS
ON
SONGWRITING

Pete Seeger

Westwood, California 1988
Beacon, New York 1988

Pete Seeger's songs are some of the most heartfelt a country has heard, songs that seem to have been born with the earth because we grew up not only hearing them but singing them, songs such as "Where Have All the Flowers Gone?" and "If I Had a Hammer." He's written songs of protest and outrage, like "Last Train to Nuremberg" and "Waist Deep in the Big Muddy"; songs of love and simplicity, like "Turn, Turn, Turn" and "Rainbow Race"; and he's introduced us to songs that are enduring anthems for humanity, such as "We Shall Overcome."

He was born in 1919 in New York City, the third son of Charles Seeger, a musicologist, and Constance de Clyver Edison, a violinist. His love of folk music began when he was sixteen. He attended the Asheville Folk Festival in North Carolina, and from that day on he stopped playing pop songs on his banjo and switched to folk.

He could have followed his father's scholarly path, and he did go to Harvard for a few years, but he was impatient to see the world. His goal at the time was to be a journalist, not a musician. So he dropped out of Harvard to get his writing career under way, but soon found himself spending more time with his banjo than his typewriter. Meeting a young songwriter named Woody Guthrie taught him that he could still collect facts like a journalist, but by putting them into a song rather than a newspaper, he could give them more power.

He rode the rails and hitchhiked with Woody across America, gaining wisdom he never could have picked up in Harvard Yard—such as that a banjo's neck can easily break if you use it to cushion your fall from a moving train. He also learned that there are few better ways to earn a meal than by singing a song. And that there is no better way to unite people than by getting them to sing together, a talent he has always possessed in abundance.

His entire career attests to the power of song; many of his first songs were written for the unions, with the precise intention of bringing people together. But while the workers were united, the bosses were incensed by the blatant truth contained in songs like "Talking Union," which was based on the age-old talking blues he learned from Woody:

"Now you know you're underpaid but the boss says you ain't.
He speeds up the work until you're bound to faint.
You may be down and out but you ain't beaten;
Pass out a leaflet, call a meeting, talk it over,
Speak your minds.
Decide to do something about it."

Whether playing solo or with either of the two bands he has belonged to (the Almanac Singers and the Weavers), Pete has used the power of song to unite people in a rainbow of ways—from singing "We Shall Overcome" with Martin Luther King, Jr. and thirty thousand other marchers en route from Selma to Montgomery, Alabama, in 1965; to singing "Golden River" while sailing down the Hudson with a crew of musicians on the mighty Sloop Clearwater, which inspired people to join in the cleaning of the river. But while one sector of the population was united and empowered by his songs, another was scared and threatened by them.

So the same guy who has been called "America's tuning fork" and a "living saint" (by Bob Dylan) has also been called "un-American" and "Kruschev's songbird." He's been blacklisted and kept off radio and TV through much of his career. The one time that the network machines let down their guard enough to let him sing on TV, he came on the "Smothers Brothers Show" in 1968 and sang "Waist Deep in the Big Muddy," an indictment of LBJ's Vietnam policy. ("And the big fool says to push on.") The Smothers quickly lost their show and Seeger was kept off the airwaves for another decade. Such is the power of song.

Pete doesn't bemoan the blacklist. "I always made a living," he said. These days he's still very busy making that living—touring with Woody's son Arlo Guthrie, recording albums, writing a column for *Sing Out!* magazine, lecturing at UCLA and other places, sailing the Clearwater, learning, collecting, and writing new songs, and keeping up an enormous correspondence with friends new and old the world over.

This interview was conducted in two parts. The first part was in Pete's dark hotel room early in the morning, just down the street from UCLA. He told me that I could accompany him on his morning walk if I arrived at his hotel by eight. Prepared as I was to interview this living legend in motion, I was happy when he reconsidered and talked to me while sitting on his unmade bed, his banjo and twelve-string guitar on the floor beside us. A week later we spoke again, thanks to his generous and journalistic spirit, over the phone from his home in upstate New York.

Do you remember writing your first song?

I wrote poems as a kid. My uncle was a poet and there was a tradition of poetry in our family. My grandfather wrote light verses and one of my brothers and I, from time to time, would try to write a poem.

But I didn't really start writing songs till I met Woody Guthrie. And I suddenly learned something that was *awful* important. And that was: Don't be so all-fired concerned about being original. You hear an old song you like but you'd like to change a little, there's no great crime in changing a little.

I saw Woody doing it with song after song. It wasn't long before I heard him sing, [*sings*] "T for Texas, T for Tennessee . . ." It was the fall of 1940 so I sang, [*sings*] "C for conscription, C for Capitol Hill, C for the Congress, pass that goddamn bill . . ."

So that, you might say, was one of my first songs. I used the same melody, which Woody had copied from Jimmie Rodgers, and the same verse which I heard Woody sing from Jimmie Rodgers. And I built on it.

Did you and Woody discuss songwriting?

No, we didn't discuss it theoretically. We just went out and did it. And we didn't always agree. I was influenced by Caribbean music. And in 1942 I made up a song about a woman who had organized a domestic worker's union in Harlem, New York. And the melody I used was a distinctly Caribbean pattern. Woody was furious. He said, "Oh, that's not our kind of music. Let those people sing that kind of music. They know how to do it well." And he refused to sing the song and eventually I stopped—it wasn't that great a song.

But this is true with most songs you write. You have to assume that you write dozens if not hundreds of songs and you're lucky if one out of ten is worth singing a year later.

Was Woody a happy person?

I'd say basically he was. He was an optimistic guy, a thumbs-up guy. He was looking for the silver lining—at the same time he didn't want to ignore the dark side of the cloud. He was not one who always looked for the dark side.

But Woody was a realistic guy and he wasn't going to ignore the sad side. The greatness of his lyrics, I believe, is that he was able to combine these in one song, often. "So Long, It's Been Good to Know You" has the tragedy of the Dust Bowl in it but it also has the humor of the situation. The sweetheart sings, "Oh honey, I'm not talking about marriage, I'm saying, 'So long, it's been good to know you.' " "They hugged and they kissed, they sighed and they cried . . ." and so on, but then, "So long, it's been good to know you." [*Laughs*]

Another song of Woody's that combines sadness and humor is "Tom Joad." As the story goes, you let him use a typewriter, he worked all night while finishing off a jug of wine, and in the morning the song was complete. Were you surprised that he could create a masterpiece in this way?

Well, not surprised. I'd seen him do that before. "Union Maid" was done that way. I saw him sit down early in the morning, tap-tap-tap on the typewriter and an hour or two later he had gotten five verses. Actually, only two of them were good enough to last.

I read once that you first discovered folk music at the age of sixteen.

Well, that's an oversimplification. After all, I sang Christmas carols when I was eight. Most of them are English folk songs or French folk songs. "King Wenceslas" is a Swedish folk song with new words put to it. I sang in school the folk songs which they had in the school songbook: [*sings*] "The keeper did a'hunting go . . ." And so on. This was what many people think of as the early attempt to popularize folk music. It failed, just as I think the second attempt failed in the sixties. It failed in the twenties.

My father put his head together with Alan Lomax in the thirties and said, "Why did it fail?" And the conclusion was that they hoped that people in school could learn a folk song off the page of a book. You can't do that. You've got to hear the style.

It wasn't enough just to read the skeleton of the melody on the page. You didn't get the delicate subtleties. And it was understandable that children weren't particularly attracted to it. So in the thirties, my father and Alan Lomax said, "Let's insist that young people hear the music first. Then they can decide for themselves how they want to sing it. And most of them will sensibly want to play it just like they hear it."

I was one of these young people. I was sixteen when they took me down to a festival in North Carolina. So I was one of the first of many Yankee college students who fell in love with Southern folk music. And I think Bob Dylan and a whole lot of others were doing the same thing. A very similar thing. They said, "Hey, this is great music. What am I listening to this crap on the radio for? This is the best thing I've ever heard."

Of course, then, we see what happened in the fifties and sixties. The commercial people seemed to have the Midas touch. Only not everything turns to gold; it often turns to garbage. And gold is a rather unsatisfactory thing to live by. People need food and love. They don't need gold.

Tin Pan Alley, by which I mean the entire commercial music business, has a tendency to say, "Hey, this sells. Promote it." And when they promote it they try to think, "What is it that really sells? Let's get rid of the stuff which doesn't sell." And they try to censor out the protest songs. In the twenties they censored out the sex. All these great folk songs that were full of sex got bowdlerized in the twenties in England and in this country.

When the ABC "Hootenanny" show got on the air in 1964, they were very careful to see that there were no Vietnam protest songs on it. This is like going up to a painter and saying, "Mr. Michelangelo, you're a fine painter. *Love* the way you treat rocks and trees and so on, and these flesh tones are great. But take this person off the cross. Put him in an armchair."

Well, I'm very glad that the so-called "folk-scare" of 1964 passed us and had its day. And when people say, "Do you think there's gonna be more folk music again?" Right away I say, "I hope not." I hope it comes back with a much deeper understanding of what folk music really is.

First of all it's a process. It's not any particular song, it's not any particular singer. It's a process by which ordinary people take over old songs and make them their own. They don't just listen to it. They sing it. They sing along with it. And they change it.

This is what black people have been doing ever since they've been on this continent. Because the folk process is very, very strong in Africa. When African people found themselves here, they just kept doing what they had been doing for centuries. And they got hold of trumpets and clarinets and created jazz. They got guitars and created the blues. And I'm fascinated to see that this process is still going on.

Many of your songs were written using that process. "Talking Union," for example, was based on the talking blues that you learned from Woody Guthrie, right?

First of all, I was a lesser member of three people who wrote that song. Lee Hays and Millard Lampell did most of that song. Until the last two verses. For some reason, we couldn't get beyond that point. We'd created problem after problem after problem. Looked like they wouldn't win their strike, that they wouldn't succeed.

Then one afternoon I suddenly realized that it was the old story that we do succeed when we insist upon sticking together, in spite of our disagreements, in spite of the danger, in spite of our inherited ways of doing things that cripple us—the sexism that is all around us, the language we use, the racism— all sorts of things we've inherited, even having to sit in a square room. Do you realize how the ninety-degree angle has inflicted itself upon the industrialized world? All these things cripple us as human beings. But in spite of these things, if we insist that we are going to find a way to work together, then, all of a sudden, we do succeed. So that's how I ended the song: If we stick together, we'll win.

[*In rhythm, fast, while clapping hands*] "If you want higher wages let me tell you what to do / Got to talk to the workers in the shop with you, got to build you a union, got to make it strong / And if you all stick together it won't be long, you'll get shorter hours . . ."

Back then you knew that music was one of the best forces for uniting people—

I knew it before then. I knew it was powerful with me. When I heard good music, I couldn't keep my mind on anything else. I just gravitate towards music. I would go out and get as close to it as I could. Stand close to the orchestra. Or if it was a loudspeaker, I'd practically stick my head in the loudspeaker.

As a child, if there was a piano in the room, I just forgot what I was supposed to do and just went over and started tinkling on it. And my parents were good enough to let me find my own way.

My father was approached by a friend who said, "Dr. Seeger, you must have your son study voice. He will ruin his voice, singing the way he does." And my father said, "If I catch him studying voice, I'll stop him immediately."

Well, of course, at age sixty-nine, my voice is half-ruined because I sang very incorrectly for fifty years. I stretched my neck. You should not stretch your neck. I'm not sure if I'll do much more singing. I can hold a short note, no problem: [*without sustain*] "John Henry . . ." No trouble—high or low. But to sing [*sings legato*] "Irene, good night . . ." The voice just starts to wobble. What I do now is play the accompaniment and let the audience—or teach the audience [to] sing it.

You sure do. And in that way, it's almost gospel, singing harmony over the audience, using call and response—

Yeah. I've learned from gospel singers. It's one of the greatest folk traditions in this country. And my big argument with most folk song societies is that they don't pay enough attention to it. They say, "Oh, this isn't folk music, this is gospel music." Well, that's a bunch of *crap*. Rather racist crap, usually.

You wrote "If I Had a Hammer" with Lee Hays, right?

In January of 1949, Lee sent me four verses. He said, "See if you can make up a tune." And I sat down at the piano and plunked it out. And it was not a bad tune but, probably, in most people's opinion, not as good of a tune as the one it was changed into. Peter, Paul and Mary rewrote my tune. And I'd say it's at least thirty or forty percent changed, though it's hard to quantify like that.

Is the version that you now perform the way it was changed or the way you wrote it?

The way I sing it is kind of more the way they do it but still something of the way I originally wrote it.

When you wrote it, did you have any understanding that it would become one of your most lasting and beloved songs?

Oh, you always hope. Songwriters usually think their most recent song is the best one they ever wrote. [*Laughs*] I didn't know.

I sang it around that year and it was well liked. The Weavers even recorded it, in this early version, for a microscopic recording company. We made a single 78-rpm record of it which probably sold all of one thousand copies and then the company went out of business.

I understand that the song was a bit dangerous for the Weavers to sing at that time.

Oh, yes. A year later, when we got a manager, he said, "Folks, I'm trying to get you jobs and those blacklisters are out to put you down. But please take my advice, and some songs don't sing." And this was one of the songs he didn't want us to sing.

It wasn't until some eight years later, when Peter, Paul and Mary latched onto the song and very creatively adapted it to their own voices, that it really spread around the world.

Curiously enough, when I sing it the way I sing it now, what I often do is joke with an audience. I point out that you can sing it the way I wrote it or the way Peter, Paul and Mary rewrote it, or half a dozen other ways, and they all harmonize with each other.

I say, "This is a good moral for the world." As a matter of fact, I'm convinced that musicians have got a more important role to play in putting a world together than they're usually given credit for. Because musicians can teach the politicians: Not everybody has to sing the melody.

One of the wonderful things about the African-American tradition, which we call jazz or whatever you want to call it, is that it's an ancient tradition not only of Africa, but India and other places. The melody which you sing the first time is just considered as the bare bones. And then you dress it up one way or another way or a jillion different ways. You improvise upon it.

Curiously enough, you know the way I sing it now? I just sing the first two lines and from there on I just let the audience sing it.

You've heard me do it. I just shout out the words: "I'd hammer out danger (hammer out danger). I'd hammer out warning (hammer out warning)."

Generations have learned it as kids. It's one of those songs we grew up singing.

Well, I'm delighted it has proven its lasting power. The melody isn't *bad* but what really makes it was Lee Hays's genius. You know, I used to think he was just cantankerous and hard to get along with, but now I'm convinced he was some kind of a genius. Because he distilled a great deal of wisdom into a few short lines. And like in an old spiritual, they're purposely very simple. They're not supposed to have any one meaning. They have many meanings. As life gives you more experiences, why, the song bounces back new meanings, just like a basketball backboard.

That song, as well as many of the songs you and Woody wrote, seem to be folk songs, like they've been around forever.

Well, even the most original song you can think of is liable to have a good deal of tradition in it. After all, the major scale and the minor scale were invented thousands of years ago. And the 2/4 time and the 3/4 time were invented [*laughs*] likewise, a long time ago. And the English language was invented a long time ago, and the phrases that we use. And we're just rearranging these ancient elements.

One of the most famous songs you created using this process is "Where Have All the Flowers Gone?" Where did all the elements of that song come from?

As I read the famous novel, *And Quiet Flows the Don*, a story about Czarist Russia. In one of the early chapters, it describes the Cossack soldiers galloping off to join the Czar's army. And they're singing, and they quoted three lines: "Where are the flowers? The girls have plucked them. Where are the girls? They've all taken husbands. Where are the men? They're all in the army. Gallop, gallop, gallop, wheeee!"

I said, "That's a good basic idea for a song and I must locate the original." I stuck the words in my pocket. A year or two or three went by and I never had time to look up the original.

Meanwhile, I'm sitting in a plane, kind of dozing. And you know, when you're dozing, that's when the creative ideas come. And all of a sudden came a line I had thought about *five* years earlier: "long time passing." I thought that those three words sang well: "long time passing." All of a sudden I fitted the two together, along with the intellectual's perennial complaint, "When will we ever learn?"

I thought I wrote the melody until about a year later when a friend wrote me and pointed out that it was similar to a lumberjack tune I had recorded from the Adirondacks: [*sings to same tune*] "Johnson says he'll unload more hay / Says he'll unload ten times a day . . ." There you got the basic idea.

Another one of your great songs that came from an interesting source is "Turn, Turn, Turn," which you adapted from the Book of Ecclesiastes.

I wrote that one down in my pocket notebook, too. I got a letter from my publisher, and he says, "Pete, I can't sell these protest songs you write. Can't you write me another song like 'Good Night Irene?' " And I was angry.

I sat down with a tape recorder and said, "I can't write the kind of songs you want. You gotta go to somebody else. This is the only kind of song I know how to write." I pulled out this slip of paper in my pocket and improvised a melody to it in fifteen minutes. And I sent it to him. And I got a letter from him the next week that said, "Wonderful! Just what I'm looking for."

Son of a gun, within two months he'd sold it to the Limelighters and then to the Byrds. I liked the Byrds' record very much, incidentally. All those clanging, steel guitars—they sound like bells.

And they added beautiful harmonies to it. Was that one of your favorite sections of the Bible?

I don't read the Bible that often. I leaf through it occasionally and I'm amazed by the foolishness at times and the wisdom at other times. I call it the greatest book of folklore ever given. Not that there isn't a lot of wisdom in it. You can trace the history of people poetically.

It's quite obvious that once upon a time the human race shared everything equally; it was like living in a garden. And then we got smart and invented farming. And all of a sudden we had class society and injustice and male supremacy and a whole lot of other cruddy things.

But the priests wanted to keep women in their place. So they invented the story about Eve and the apple. You can see that was invented by a bunch of male supremacists: "These women are misleading you. They are evil. They misled you before; don't let them do it again." Women threatened the power of the priest. They undermined the priests' power with their husbands: "Oh, don't listen to that priest. Listen to me, honey."

You wrote that time is the devil in your song, "Old Devil Time."

Well, the nice thing about poetry is that you're always stretching the definitions of words. Lawyers and scientists and scholars of one sort or another try to *restrict* the definitions, hoping that they can prevent people from fooling each other. But that doesn't stop people from lying.

Cezanne painted a red barn by painting it ten shades of color: purple to yellow. And he got a red barn. Similarly, a poet will describe things many different ways, circling around it, to get at the truth.

My father also had a nice simile. He said, "The truth is a rabbit in a bramble patch. And you can't lay your hand on it. All you do is circle around and point, and say, 'It's in there somewhere.' "

And while you're trying to bring out that truth in a song, your publisher is asking you to write another song like "Goodnight Irene" that will sell.

This is a dilemma that so many songwriters have to face, wanting to write songs that will sell while still trying to express the heart. You're certainly not someone who has gone the commercial route very often. How have you reconciled the two?

Well, bless my stars that I met people who had nothing but contempt for the commercial world. At times I felt grateful to people in the business world. I'm grateful to you and your gang for keeping *SongTalk* magazine going. And I'm sure if it wasn't for a firm control of the income and outflow, *SongTalk* wouldn't keep on going. You got to get the money from the advertisers and other places, and you've got to pay the printers and other people.

But, in general, I go along with Woody Guthrie. I write a song because I want to. I think the moment you start writing it to make money, *you're starting to kill yourself artistically.*

Now, at least with me, this is [the case]. I know the guy who wrote "Rudolph the Red-Nosed Reindeer" just kept on trying. He wanted to get a hit song out of Christmas somewhere. My publisher turned that song down. He said, "That's a silly song." And that song, my gosh, has made millions.

At one point, though, didn't you realize that you could reach more people working with a group like the Weavers, who were much more commercial than your previous group, the Almanac Singers?

We didn't really want to be a commercial group. Fred [Hellerman] was going to go back to college and become a writer, Ronny [Gilbert] was gonna raise a family, Lee [Hays] was going to write short stories, and I wanted to sing with a group. And as a last resort, a fate worse than death, we got a job in a nightclub.

They paid us all of $200 a week. I'd made $200 a week by myself singing in this little nightclub and the guy was willing to hire *me* but I wanted to sing with a group. He said, "No, I don't want a group." I said, "What if the group doesn't cost any more than me?" He said, "Well, I guess I can't complain."

So we sang, all four of us, for $200 a week plus free hamburg.

Then a month or two later he came in and saw the size hamburgs I was making—like a half a pound of hamburg three times a night—he says, "Change that to $250 a week. But no more free hamburg." Nice guy. Max Gordon. He just died last year.

Do you remember writing "Last Train to Nuremberg"?

[Pause] Well, you know crisis brings out some of the best art the world has ever known. Whether it's somebody being in love or a country at war or revolution. And in this particular case, it was being in agony over a country I loved very much doing a terrible thing. And I wrote one song after another.

I think of "Waist Deep in the Big Muddy," too, which you sang on the "Smothers Brothers" TV show after the blacklist was lifted only to have it imposed again immediately.

That's one song that could have been a big seller but it was *thoroughly* blacklisted. I don't really mind being blacklisted that much; I made a living. But I think that if that song had been given a chance to be distributed, it would have really gotten around.

I met a young fella working in a Columbia Records distribution office in Denver, Colorado. He said, "Pete, I was there when your record came in and my boss said, 'What are those people in New York thinking? They must be nuts to think that I can push a record like this.' " He said, "Pete, your record did not even leave the distributor's office." It didn't even go out to the stores.

A different department sent records to radio stations as promotional copies. Somebody who works in a radio station found one of my records and on it was scrawled, "Do not play this side." That was by order of the head of the radio station.

This still happens, you know. People who run TV and radio stations know pretty well which side of the bread is buttered.

You once said, "All songs are love songs." This certainly applies to your song "Rainbow Race," which is a love song for the earth. How was that one born?

Well, it was about six in the morning. I don't know how other people are, but a number of my ideas come early in the morning or late at night. When the brain is somehow released from the pressures of the day.

I was in a motel in Hollywood and I had been in Japan the month before, and I'm leafing through the *Hollywood Reporter*, and there's an advertisement from Yamaha for a songwriting contest. And in the middle of the page there's a batch of music staffs. It said, "Fill in these staffs. Send them to us. You may win a prize—a free trip to Japan."

Well, by gosh, I sat down and wrote the song. Took me an hour or two. I don't usually write songs that quick. Took me several weeks to write "Waist Deep in the Big Muddy."

Anyway, I wrote it out and mailed it in to Yamaha. I never heard from them. I know I didn't win a prize. But I thank them, because if it hadn't been for their advertisement, I never would have gotten that song written.

I only adjusted it in a few small ways. Usually when I start singing a song, then I iron out a few of the details of it. But I'm in favor of the folk process, I really am. It tends to improve songs over the years. Leadbelly, I could hear him changing songs over the years, though I only knew him for ten years. He would change it musically, rhythmically, as well as lyrically.

Woody Guthrie did the same thing. He first wrote "This Land Is Your Land" as "God Blessed America for Me." And ten years later he had finally, little by little, changed it and recorded it the way that most people know it.

Do you remember when you first heard that song?

Yeah, and I have to laugh, I thought it was one of Woody's lesser efforts. I said to myself, "That melody doesn't go anywhere." [*Sings full melody through twice very quickly*] "Da da da dee dah . . ." It repeats over and over. Well, I couldn't have been more wrong. That song hit the nail on the head for millions of people.

You mentioned Leadbelly—did you and he write "Kisses Sweeter than Wine" together?

No. Leadbelly had changed around an old Irish tune and given it rhythm. He learned it from an Irish artist named Sam Kennedy. And at a crowded

Greenwich Village party, he takes Sam aside and says, "Sam, I'd like to sing you a song but I changed the rhythm. Is that okay with you?" Sam was very generous. He says, "Leadbelly, you sing it your way. I'll keep singing it my way."

Well, about a year after Leadbelly died, the Weavers were sitting around, of all things, a swimming pool in a fancy hotel where we had a job. And we were thinking up ideas for songs. So I pulled out my little pocket notebook and leafed through it, and said, "Oh, here's this melody that Leadbelly used. But I never could dig those words, see, I thought they were kind of trivial. But I could just change the chorus to 'Oh, kisses sweeter than wine.'" Lee Hays says, "Pete, let me try to do something with it." And the next day he came back with about six or seven verses. And the other three Weavers pared them down to the four or five that we know now. And we *recorded* it.

It was a minor hit, nothing big. It was the singer Jimmie Rodgers, some four or five years later, who made it a much bigger hit. But I'm glad to say it's kind of a standard now with many people.

Your song "My Generation" seems to me like a Jacques Brel song. Do you recall writing that one?

I should get back to that one. I've almost forgotten it. Can't remember where I wrote it. I did come across the phrase in some little radical magazine: "Our generation wears sandals like the Vietnamese." And I took that line and built a song out of it.

That quite often happens to me. I'll read one phrase somewhere. A middle-aged woman in Ohio wrote a poem that said, "The month of April, when we pay for the burning of the children." Talking about the income tax, of course. That's where we *pay* for the burning of the children. So I built a whole song around that, called "The Calendar."

You mentioned that ideas come to you sometimes when you're dozing, or very early in the morning. Why do you think that is?

In solving a problem, you often have to make connections between two things that aren't usually connected. You know, E.M. Forster, the novelist, was asked, "What are your words of wisdom for future generations?" He said, "Only connect."

An inventor might search for the two substances to put together. In the case of the poet, it's the two words or three words. With a musician, it's the notes or the rhythms. Whatever it is, your brain often suppresses such idle connections because you're busy with the business of the day. You're doing whatever you're supposed to do. But there come times when you're no longer doing what you're supposed to do and you're just kind of rambling, making strange connections. Now some people can turn this on. They can just say, "Brain, ramble on. Let me see what happens."

It's been well known that many a poem or song has been written when someone was dreaming. Coleridge's famous "In Xanadu did Kubla Khan / A stately pleasure dome decree . . ." This is fantastic poetry. And he thought of it all in a dream. Then somebody interrupted it before he got it all written down, so he only got about fourteen lines and that was that.

Many songwriters devote most of their time to writing; that is the business of their day—

I confess I don't. If I get one good line, I'll put it down in my little pocket notebook and if I get time, I might complete it. It's a lazy man's way of working. It's not working at all. I'm trying to buckle down.

Do you think people are always in need of meaningful songs?

Well, I would say so. But what's meaningful at one time is not meaningful at another. Some songs are meant to calm you down, to relax you. Others are meant to stir you up, to get you to tighten your belt and say, "Okay, I'm going to lick this problem."

I confess that all my life I've either switched off the radio in disgust because I can't find anything worth listening to or else I've just laughed at them, because they're so stupid.

Are you optimistic about the future of music? Do you think good songs will continue to be written?

Yeah. I think Marc Antony was wrong when he said, "The good gets buried and the bad gets remembered." An architect's best buildings stand; the worst ones fall down. A songwriter's best songs are remembered and the worst ones are mercifully forgotten. And who knows? You can't prove a thing. But I'm glad to see *tens* of thousands of people writing songs these days. And sometimes an absolute gem will come out of a person no one has ever heard of before.

So many songwriters nowadays have been influenced by people like you and Woody.

Well, I hope so. I look upon myself and other songwriters as links in a long chain. All of us, we're links in a chain. And if we do our job right, there will be many, many links to come.

I don't write as many songs now as I used to, partly because I'm writing more prose. I'm convinced that if we can't persuade scientists to straighten up and fly right, they're going to destroy the world. Einstein, late in life, is supposed to have said, "Ach, mankind is not ready for it." But no one seems to have learned from it. Everyone wants fame and glory. And I think fame and glory are two of the most foolish things to yearn for. I mean, five hundred years from now, if there's a human race, none of us are going to be remembered. [*Pause*] Well, Woody Guthrie might be. But I really think five hundred years from now there'll be too many things to think about to memorize the names of all the people who went before.

I suspect your songs will be remembered along with Woody's.

If we do a good job. Many a parent has died and felt, "I die happy because I've got some good children who are carrying on."

And that's the way you feel?

Yeah. That is the way I feel.

* * *

Jay Livingston & Ray Evans
Beverly Hills, California 1987

"We didn't want to work" was Ray Evans's immediate reply when asked why he and Jay Livingston, with no experience, decided in 1938 to become songwriters. They had met earlier while attending the University of Pennsylvania, and they traveled around the world together, playing in a summer dance band. (Ray was adequate on alto sax; Jay was then, and is now, a marvelous pianist.) After that excitement, the prospect of taking a nine-to-five job seemed extremely dismal.

"Ray was a little bit more optimistic than I was," Jay Livingston recalled. So behind his back, Ray took what they now call a "crazy stab" that paid off: He answered an ad in a New York paper requesting new material for the vaudeville team of Olsen and Johnson, who had a huge hit running on Broadway called "Hellzapoppin'." Though the ad was a puff piece, involving no truth whatsoever, it happened that Ole Olsen had just hired a secretary who had no concept of the term "publicity." So when she read Ray's earnest letter, she made Livingston and Evans an appointment to meet her bosses.

It was during a matinee that Ray and Jay arrived at the theater, explaining to a disbelieving stage manager why they were there. After a lengthy wait, they were ushered backstage to the piano—one place where Jay always feels at home—and given an audience with Olsen and Johnson. Though Ray and Jay had a bunch of songs to play, only one was well received, a song called "Goodbye Now." One song was enough. "Goodbye Now" was on the Hit Parade for eight weeks in 1940 with four names on it: Olsen, Johnson, Livingston and Evans.

It was five years before they had any more success. Thanks to the help of Johnny Mercer, they got staff writing jobs at Paramount Pictures, first writing for shorts and eventually for full-length features. Within six months they had a miraculous five records in the Top Ten, all versions of the same song: "To Each His Own."

From that unprecedented beginning in the music business, Jay Livingston, working mainly on music, and Ray Evans, working mostly on the lyrics, went on to write songs that are now more than standards, they are an ingrained part of American culture: "Silver Bells," "Mona Lisa," "Que Sera Sera," "Buttons and Bows." They also wrote many of the most famous TV theme songs of all time, including "Bonanza," which has a full lyric that matches its famous melody, and "Mr. Ed," in which Jay sang Ed's part.

Talking with Livingston and Evans is not unlike talking to a couple married for many years; after fifty years of collaboration, each knows the other's opinions by heart, and squabbles surface from time to time. But like most couples who have stayed together this long, the overriding emotion one senses in their presence is that of great love—for each other, for a collection of astounding songs they have written together, and for a lifetime lucky enough to have been spent making music.

Do you remember writing "To Each His Own"?

LIVINGSTON: It was during our first six months at Paramount. A picture came along called *To Each His Own*. Victor Young did the score and he always wrote the title song. He was one of the few writers who had hit songs. But that phrase, "To each his own," had never been heard before. So Victor said, "I'm not going to write a song with a dumb title. I don't know what it means." And since nobody else wanted to write it, they asked us.

So we worked on it for three weeks, getting it better and better, and finally we played it for them and they liked it. An unknown named Eddie Howard made a record of it that was a hit.

EVANS: A little band out of Chicago. One week in August of 1947, out of the Top Ten records in *Billboard*, five of them were versions of "To Each His Own." The first time this ever happened and, so far, the last.

LIVINGSTON: Eddie Howard, Tony Martin, Freddie Howard, the Modernaires and the Inkspots. 1, 3, 5, 7 and 8. And you know what that did for us.

EVANS: Omigod, five records in the Top Ten!

LIVINGSTON: You're sitting in the studio and they didn't even know you existed and all of a sudden the phone starts ringing.

EVANS: It actually sold over a million copies of sheet music in one year. This was right after the war. People were coming from overseas and it was sentimental; it caught on a chord.

It's become part of our language now: "To each his own." And that's because of the song.

Another song that has become very much a part of our lives is "Silver Bells." It's one of those songs that seem to have always existed; it's surprising that someone wrote it.

LIVINGSTON: I've heard that many times.

EVANS: We didn't want to write it. We thought, "Who needs another Christmas song?" But we were wrong. Thank God we *did* do it.

The winter imagery is so important to the song. Do you think it would have been a hit with a different set of lyrics?

EVANS: I doubt it.

LIVINGSTON: It was the first time, that we knew of, that anybody wrote about Christmas in the city. And it had a folk song feel, in 3/4 time. None of the other Christmas songs were in 3/4 time. So it had a lot going for it.

We also constructed it so that the verse and the chorus could be sung together. Bing Crosby did the record with Carol Richards singing the alternate part. But nobody sings it that way anymore.

Originally, the title we were using was "Tinkle Bell." We didn't want it to be too close to "Jingle Bells." But my wife said to me, "You must be out of your mind. You can't use that title. It has a toilet meaning." So I went to Ray and explained it to him. We threw the whole song out and started something else. But we kept stealing from "Tinkle Bell." We ended up with "Tinkle Bell" exactly as it was written. Except we changed the title to "Silver Bells."

When you finished it, did you have any idea that it was a classic?

LIVINGSTON: No. No idea.

EVANS: Luckily, Bing Crosby recorded it. A Bing Crosby recording at Christmastime causes some attention.

LIVINGSTON: I had no idea that "Silver Bells" would be a hit.

The only song that we wrote that I ever thought would be a hit was "Que Sera Sera."

Where did the title to that one come from?

LIVINGSTON: It was from a picture called *The Barefoot Contessa*. And in it, Rosanno Brazzi got married and took his bride to his ancestral castle in Italy. And carved in the stone was "Que Sera Sera" spelled with a "Che," which is the Italian spelling. He said that it means "What will be, will be." I wrote it down in the dark. I knew it was a good title for a song. It was very rare that we would write a song without an assignment. But we wrote it because it sounded like a hit.

Two weeks went by. We got a call from Alfred Hitchcock. And he told us that he had Doris Day in his picture, whom he didn't want. But MCA, the agency, was so powerful that they said if he wanted Jimmy Stewart he would also have to take Doris Day and Livingston and Evans. It was the only time an agent got us a job that I can remember.

Hitchcock said that since Doris Day was a singer, they needed a song for her. He said, "I can tell you what it should be about. She sings it to a boy. It should have a foreign title because Jimmy Stewart is a roving ambassador and he goes all over the world."

EVANS: And he described "Que Sera" that was sitting in our office down the hall. It was perfect, the kind of song a mother could sing to a child.

LIVINGSTON: So I said to Ray, "We've got that song," and he said, "I know we do." But we didn't tell Hitchcock for two weeks. Then we walked in and said, "Mr. Hitchcock, we've been working on this song real hard." I sat down and played it for him and he said, "Gentlemen—I didn't know what kind of song I wanted. *That's* the kind of song I want!" And he walked out. We never saw him again for years.

Jay, when you think of melodies, do you do it in your head or at the piano?

LIVINGSTON: Often in my head. When you're at the piano, your hands follow old familiar patterns. If you're away from the piano, you're freer. Your mind goes anywhere you want. I've written better melodies that way.

One day I was sitting in the car at the intersection of Whitley and Hollywood Boulevard. And I was thinking of this great line that Ray had come up with: "Two lips must insist on two more to be kissed." That's pretty. So I thought of the melody in my head while sitting there in the car. And that turned into "To Each His Own." [*Gets up to play melody at piano.*]

Another time Ray had a title. "Prima Donna." And on the way to work I wrote [*sings, to the tune of "Mona Lisa"*] "Prima Donna, Prima Donna," the whole melody. I walked in and said to Ray, "Don't say a word, I've got a good melody." We started "Prima Donna" and it was awful. But Ray came in the next day with the new title and that was it. I would never have come up with the "Mona Lisa" melody if Ray hadn't first come up with "Prima Donna."

How did the song "Buttons and Bows" come into being?

EVANS: We wrote it for a picture called *Paleface* with Bob Hope. The producer told us, "Bob Hope's a tenderfoot out west; he hates everything about the West. Why don't you write a song about how he misses civilization and everything back east?" And thinking about Jane Russell, who was also in the movie, I came up with the idea of "Buttons and Bows" as a symbol of a girl all dressed up. The kind of a girl, pretty lady, that Bob Hope would have left back east.

I started with: "Frills and flowers and button and bows / Rings and things and buttons and bows."

LIVINGSTON: Which he told me, and I came up with the melody just walking along.

And the two of you performed that song yourselves in the classic movie *Sunset Boulevard.*

EVANS: Which is great. And you know, from now until the end of time, our name will be on screen because we got cast credit.

LIVINGSTON: Billy Wilder is one of the great directors so I wasn't worried; I figured he would tell us what to do. I'm at the piano and Ray is standing by my side.

He said, "You're songwriters. Act like songwriters." That's all he said. Then we started and he said, "Cut . . . You look like you're not having a good time." Which we weren't. It felt like an execution. So I said, "We're not." So he put girls all around us, sitting on the piano, legs dangling in front of me. . . .

EVANS: Beautiful girls.

LIVINGSTON: . . . And we're kind of smiling because of that. That's something a good director can do.

What do you think of the state of music today?

LIVINGSTON: I like a lot of country music; it's very honest. Sometimes it's funny, clever. Once in a while there's a good melody. I don't mind country as a category. But rock—

EVANS: Rock's nothing for us. My cliche is that if George Gershwin or Cole Porter were alive today, there would be nowhere for them to go.

LIVINGSTON: I think it's getting better. It's not as noisy and you can hear the lyrics. I think it's improving.

EVANS: But not by my tastes.

LIVINGSTON: But you can't turn the clock back.

EVANS: Of course you can't.

LIVINGSTON: So if it's improved, that's something.

EVANS: That's a subjective value. Have you heard anything you're going to go out whistling?

LIVINGSTON: Not in rock.

EVANS: But what else is there?

LIVINGSTON: Well, we're part of our generation. If we were young now and starting to write, we'd probably write rock. If you grow up into that, that's all you know.

EVANS: But by artistic terms, to me, it's like comparing Picasso to a comic strip. In art, the great things last through the ages. I don't think any of the rock stuff is going to last.

LIVINGSTON: I think that's the criterion. The songs that we have liked have all lived.

EVANS: The Beatles' songs will live.

LIVINGSTON: Yeah, some of their songs are *beautiful*. Especially the later ones. One advantage writers have now is that they can write about anything. We wrote a 32-bar stereotypical way.

EVANS: "Mona Lisa" wasn't that way.

LIVINGSTON: Not all of them but most of them.

Did you feel restricted when writing your songs?

EVANS: No, because that was the way you went. There wasn't any other way.

LIVINGSTON: We were considered pretty far-out because we'd have a 9-bar bridge cause I needed another bar. And they said, "You can't do that." And I said, "Why not?" You see, you got to the end of the bridge and you couldn't breathe, so I put an extra bar in. And this was considered breaking the rules. And as time went by we broke more rules.

When Johnny Mercer and Harold Arlen wrote "That Old Black Magic," the people at Paramount said, "You can't do that." It had a 64-bar melody.

And that was considered to be too long?

EVANS: Yeah, it was too long.

LIVINGSTON: But they [Mercer and Arlen] were big enough to say, "We're going to do it anyway."

EVANS: People did break rules. You see, there shouldn't be rules at all in songwriting. Nobody can predict a hit. Every hit we had was turned down all over the place.

Is that right?

LIVINGSTON: Yes. "Mona Lisa" was not even going to be released. Nat King Cole said, "Who wants this? Nobody will buy this." We went over to see Nat even though he didn't like songwriters to play for him. He was a very gentle man and didn't want to have to say no.

EVANS: "To Each His Own" was laughed at. They said, "Who wants a song with that title?"

And I remember that we played "Buttons and Bows" for the head of Famous Music, and he said, "We might be able to get a hillbilly record out of it. That's the best we can do."

What should we learn from these experiences?

EVANS: [*Emphatically*] Never give up. Nobody knows.

LIVINGSTON: When Doris Day did "Que Sera Sera," she only did one take. She didn't want to record it but the studio pressured her. She did it in one take and said, "That's the last you're going to hear of this song." That's nothing against her, it's just that nobody knows.

EVANS: Nobody knows—

LIVINGSTON: She thought it was a children's song. And that's our biggest record.

EVANS: They didn't even bother to record "Tammy." They said, "Who's ever going to want a Debbie Reynolds record?" So that could be evidence of how absolutely unpredictable the music business is.

And it shows that it never makes sense to trust any single opinion of a song.

EVANS: You can't!

Do you have a single favorite song that you've written?

LIVINGSTON: "Never Let Me Go" is my favorite. It's harmonically complex. It has tremendous changes. I'm proud of that as a composer. It has good lyrics, too.

EVANS: It's hard to say. It's like saying which child you like the best. But if I had to choose one, I would choose "Mona Lisa."

LIVINGSTON: It's not complicated but it's a pretty song. It has a good song lyric to it. And it's short.

EVANS: Just eighteen bars or so.

LIVINGSTON: Twenty-four. Jerome Kern wrote "Lovely to Look At" and it was sixteen bars. They said, "You need more." He said, "I've got nothing more to say." And I think that about sums it up.

* * *

Willie Dixon
Glendale, California 1988

"All blues is happy blues," Willie Dixon said, sitting on the sofa of his suburban home. The blues made him a happy man, not a bitter one as some may think. He happily suggested we take his photo wrapped up in the computer read-outs that BMI sends him; since he had more than six hundred songs registered with them (a mere fraction of his total output), they periodically sent him royalty statements as thick as a phone book.

"Take this end and walk with it out the door," he told me, handing me one end of the monstrous document. I walked backwards out into the glaring Glendale sunshine, trailing yards of Willie's lifework before me, thousands of titles, decades of the blues. I could have walked for miles and still had my arms full.

He was born in the deep south of Mississippi in July of 1915, when slavery was still a recent memory. He brought the southern blues with him to the North, moving to Chicago as a teenager. He became a boxer and even won some titles; had he not gotten into a fight with his own manager in the boxing commissioner's office, in which "furniture got rearranged," the history of American music would have been written differently. (Mentioning my shared love for the Windy City to him, Willie said, "I've got the key to the City of Chicago around here somewhere," and proceeded to fish it out from a bowl of the countless keys-to-cities he's received.)

He wrote so many songs that his catalog is like a closet filled with a thousand coats; if you go in, there's bound to be one that fits perfectly. Singers have tried on and worn Willie's songs comfortably for years, and have gained style and definition by doing so: Muddy Waters was the "Hoochie Coochie Man" as Jim Morrison was the "Back Door Man" and Mose Allison the "Seventh Son." Eric Clapton bent "Spoonful" into an anthem for Cream. The Rolling Stones recorded "Little Red Rooster" while others, such as Howlin' Wolf, Chuck Berry, and Bo Diddley, sought Willie out in Chicago to try on one of his songs.

Willie Dixon died in Los Angeles in January of 1990, but fortunately not before experiencing a blues resurgence in which many House of Blues clubs opened around the country. He recorded a new album in the year prior to his death produced by T Bone Burnett, and performed live in concert with Los Lobos as his back-up band. At his 75th birthday party, he smiled profusely as famous fans, such as David Hidalgo, Richard Thompson and Bernie Taupin, stepped up to pay their respects to him. "It's the blues that have brought me all this," he said happily, surveying the throng of admirers. "And that's a fact."

In fact, it's the facts—the real truth—that mattered more to Willie than anything else. It's something he reminded me many times in his deep resonant voice, happily booming like a big stand-up bass in his genuine house of blues.

You've been called the "Father of the Blues"—
Well, you know, when you get to a certain age they think you're old enough to know something about it. Especially if you've been involved with it. I don't consider myself the father of the blues. I've just been involved in it all my life. And I've started to do better things in it since I've found out more about it.

How old were you when you first started playing music?
Oh, when I first started *playing* music I was full grown, but when I was a youngster I used to sing with spiritual quartets. And learning the bass lines, naturally it was easy for me to pick up the bass after I got in. I knew most of the patterns of the bass and the harmony and all this kind of stuff.

So bass was your first instrument?
Yeah, bass was really my first instrument. I had several instruments but I never actually played any of them.

Legend has it that your first bass was one string attached to a tin can. True?
Oh yeah, that's right. That was the tin can that Baby Doo Caston made for me. He made my first musical instrument which was that one-string tin can bass.

How did you learn to play the blues?
Well, I'd been knowing the blues all my life because everyone in the South, just about, sung blues. Spirituals and blues. In fact they were the same thing. Only one was dedicated to a better situation on earth and the other dedicated to heavenly things.

Did the blues in America come from the slaves?
It came from work songs. They used to not let slaves sing, they wouldn't let them talk, they wouldn't let them beat on the drums or tap on wood or

nothing because it felt like they could pass messages to each other. They wouldn't let them use no kind of religious activities or nothing. But when they found out that the slaves could chant these certain songs and work in time, that it made them do better work and made them forget about a lot of the troubles, the bosses decided to let them go and chant these songs.

Eventually the slaves found out, "Why, hell, as long as he's letting us chant these songs, we can begin to pass messages with these same songs." They were singing about going home: "If I never see you no more, I'll meet you on the other shore." And they were singing about "Jerusalem, my happy home where I may find my God." And "Roll, Jordan, roll, I want to go to heaven when I die . . ."

In singing these songs they converted the idea that you ain't going to Africa, you're going to heaven when you die. And that's why so many songs were sung about women and mistreatment and going back home and work songs because they would have to sing these kind of songs to keep the big boss unbalanced. "If you don't leave my woman alone, I'm tired of picking cotton and pulling corn."

They didn't know that the black man was singing about the real facts of life. And that's what the blues are. And the blues themselves can educate you about the facts of life.

People ask me often, "What does this song or that song mean?" The blues consist of the past, the present and the hopeful future also.

When did guitars start being used to play the blues?

In Africa they had these string instruments with two strings and one string that they played on years and years ago before America was even born. So evidently they had to derive from that.

Just like the drums. Just like the patterns of music today—all of them are drum patterns that are used as rhythm for music. And they all started from where everybody knows. They used drums in Africa thousands of years ago to deliver messages. And they still use them today. That's how you got your chord systems. But all these things have been hid. So this is why it's necessary for these things to come out. Because things done in the dark have to come to the light. And today is the day to come to the light.

What kind of music were you listening to as a kid?

Well, I listened to everything. Most of the time I listened to the blues in the fields where the people would be singing. They made songs of *facts*. Boss going with somebody's old lady, he'd start singing about it: "You don't leave my woman alone / Death Valley gonna be your home."

These are the ways that blues was born. That's why when they sing songs today, guys ask me all the time, "Hey, you know so much about the blues, what does it mean when they say, 'Blues jumped a rabbit and run him for a solid mile.' That don't make sense." I say, "It makes sense to me. Because lot of times when I was a kid, if my old man didn't shoot a rabbit or kill a squirrel or something, hell, *we wouldn't eat. All day.*" So, hell, it meant hell of a heap to me. It don't mean nothing to nobody today because they never hardly seen a rabbit.

You were a boxing champion, weren't you?

I won Golden Gloves championship in Chicago in 1937.

Looking back, do you think it was a lucky move to get out of boxing at that time?

Well, I feel like it now but at that time I didn't. Because at that time I felt like I would be champion of the world.

But after getting out there a little bit with the boys and having a little fun and seeing the good time on the other side, why should I be out there suffering when I didn't have to? And the amount of money they were paying me wasn't enough for me to live on, no way. I could get more fooling around with the music. Because we'd pass the hat around and hell, sometimes I'd be making a whole lot more in the hat in one night than I was getting when I was fighting.

Do you remember writing your first song?

Oh, I'd been writing songs practically all my life. I used to write a lot of poems. My mother used to write poems, you know, spiritual poems. And show me and explain the sweetness in them and the goodness in them and all like that. That's why I always tried to write songs that were *positive*, that meant something, you know? Because the things she wrote about were positive things, cause they were about heaven and the future. And so I started writing about the *earth* and the future.

I made lots of poems from way back and I can't remember all of them because I had several books of these. But I never thought they would become popular, you know, and I left them in the south when I left. I guess if I'd have kept all the poems that I'd wrote, man, I'd have a stack of them as tall as I am right now.

At that particular time, I didn't know that people were trying to keep the blues as a down thing. And my old man used to explain: "Long as you write blues, they ain't gonna write about it, they won't give you no publicity about it. 'Cause blues is facts and the world don't want to know facts." And he'd say, "But if you can get the people to hear these blues, they can get a lot of wisdom out of it."

As you said, most people think the blues are down. But so many of your songs are happy blues, such as "I Love the Life I Live."

In fact, *all* blues are happy. All blues are the facts. The facts, whether they're good or bad, are the truth. Most people can't understand that. Of course, they've been brainwashed into believing that it's got to be down or it wouldn't be blues. But it's not so. It's got to be a *fact* or it wouldn't be blues.

See, they ain't gonna be singing about the nutty squirrel or three little pigs and all that kind of stuff. They're gonna say the facts: "I just wanna make love to you." How many times did you feel like that and not say it? Evil, ignorance and stupidity are a fact. All these are true facts of life.

The reason I put them into the type of songs I put them in, is so people *can remember* these facts. And when you remember a fact, whether it's good or bad, it gives you encouragement to live a decent life, one way or the other. To judge.

You've been putting the facts into songs now for more than fifty years. I understand you've got hundreds of them nobody's ever heard.

I got thousands of songs that people never heard about. I got a song about *anything* you can think about. I got them in my drawers, in books. Some completed, some never been completed. I got over six hundred with BMI that are registered.

How often do you write songs?

Well, whenever the various facts come to your mind that you think are interesting, it can do somebody some good.

Where do you get these facts?

From life. Life itself is a fact.

Do you remember writing "Hoochie Coochie Man"?

I wrote "Hoochie Coochie Man" years ago. Well, you see, it has always been a fact that people believe in mystic things. Like people today believe in astrology. That's been going on for generations, since biblical days.

People all over the world believe in it. Even before Jesus was born, according to the Bible. The wise men saw the stars in the East and were able to predict about things.

All of these things are mystic. They say, "Hoochie coochie people are telling fortunes." You know, like the wise men of the East. They call them "voodoo men" or "hoochie coochie men." They used to call them "hoodoo folk" and "two-head people." They got many names for everybody.

Is your song "Seventh Son" about the mystic?

Well, the seventh son is part of the scriptures of the Bible. "The seventh son of the seventh son born on the seventh hour of the seventh day of the seventh month . . ." And all of these things have been going on for generations.

You were born in the seventh month, right?

Oh yeah, I was born in the seventh month and I was the seventh child of my family.

"Hoochie Coochie Man" also has a verse about the seventh day, the seventh hour, the seven doctors saying you're a lucky man—

Well, yeah. You know if you go down to Louisiana and places, they got them people there supposedly wise enough to tell fortunes, the seven sisters and the seven brothers and all that kind of stuff. Whether you believe in it or not, there's somebody believing in it or they wouldn't be making a living off of it.

Mose Allison is famous for his jazzy version of "Seventh Son." Do you like the way he does it?

Oh yeah, yeah. I remember when I gave that to Mose Allison a long time ago. Oh yeah, Mose is a beautiful guy, you know. I used to work with him 'round New York occasionally. I gave him that song but he rearranged it to suit himself. A lot of times I'd give guys one arrangement, they'd change it to another.

How about Muddy Waters? Would he change your arrangements?

Well, Muddy, he'd probably go the way I'd tell him to do it. Because I always try to give guys the type of arrangement I think they could best use.

You worked with the Rolling Stones, when they came to Chicago in the early sixties, on their version of your song, "Little Red Rooster."

Oh yes, I remember that. I had known them before they came to Chicago. I left songs in Europe when I was over there with Memphis Slim when the Stones were just *kids*, you know? I didn't know they were going to be the Rolling Stones. But they liked the blues when we first went there and they liked the songs so I put a bunch of them on tape. In fact, there was no tape; it was wire recording then. I left them and different folks got to them one way or another.

Then way later, when I got back to Chicago, a few years later, here come a bunch of guys with hair on their face and I didn't know it was the same kids!

Did the Rolling Stones understand the blues?

Well, we talked about them a little bit, you know. A lot of people don't understand them but you see, when people start seeking information, it makes them wiser.

That's what I like about the youngsters today. You can't hand them a lot of baloney like you used to tell the old folks years ago. Kids ask me today, "Where does this song come from?" Well, if you don't give him a decent answer, he gonna seek it for himself. And when he goes to seek the roots of American music, he's gonna find the blues. These are the roots. And from these roots come the fruits. And these fruits are the music.

Besides the Rolling Stones, other rock groups recorded your songs; the Doors did "Back Door Man" and Cream did "Spoonful." Did you like how those sounded?

Well, yes. It proves that great variations can be done for a better understanding, one way or the other. Some people like the way Big Mama Thornton did "High Heel Sneakers" and "Blue Suede Shoes." Some people liked it but it didn't sell as big as when . . . who was that who did it?

Elvis? Elvis Presley?

Yeah. Elvis Presley. Naturally, when he made it different ways, it sold different. And then, on top of that, you see, hers was called "blues" and his was called "rock." And it's the same identical song, only one's faster than the other.

Do the blues have to be restricted to a twelve-bar form?

Well, you see, people always tried to do the blues like they did black people: They tried to put them in a condition where they couldn't move. The world tried to say the blues is only a twelve-bar music and can't go no further, but that's a lie. Today we can make the blues in any amount. You can make it an *opera*, if you want to. It could last all day, as long as it tells the truth. That's the way the blues are today. People tried to brand the blues as one thing like they tried to brand black people as one thing. The world is too wise for that today.

Is there one song of your own that is your favorite?

Well, as of today, my favorite is on the album we're working on. The one that says, "It don't make sense, you can't make peace." That's a fact of life too, you know. The world has made everything else and still it can't make peace. And the reason it can't make peace is because of the evil, ignorance and stupidity. I have songs that explain these facts. And that's the blues.

Do you still live the life you love and love the life you lead?
I sure do. That's everybody's intention, whether they make it or not.

* * *

Sammy Cahn
Beverly Hills, California 1991

When I walked into Sammy Cahn's Beverly Hills mansion, the first thing that struck me was the art. On the walls were enormous abstract expressionist canvasses, huge, dramatic splashes of color surrounding the living room, with the swimming pool outside through the windows blue and bright as a David Hockney vision of a typically radiant California afternoon.

But Sammy was not to be found here. Ushered into his office near the back of his house, I found myself in a room that might have come directly from Tin Pan Alley circa 1950. Behind a big old fashioned desk sat Sammy, surrounded by the memorabilia of a life in music: gold records, photos of stars and friends, four Oscars, an Emmy, and other trophies and awards. When I referred to the art in the other rooms, he said, "Oh, that's my wife's world. In here, this is my world."

Sammy's world was perhaps best illustrated by his famous joke, "Which comes first, the words or the music?" The punchline is: "The phone call." It's a world where songwriters didn't have time to wait around for inspiration. They wrote songs on assignment, when the phone call came, and often had to create on the spot, such as when Sinatra was waiting in the studio for a closing song. So Sammy didn't like to dwell on the roots of his creativity. "If they needed a ballad," he explained, "I wrote a ballad."

Sammy's world was a world of words. He called himself a lyrist (preferring this word to "lyricist" because Oscar Hammerstein did) who wrote words to the melodies of many of the world's greatest composers, such as Jule Stein, Saul Chaplin, and his most frequent collaborator, Jimmy Van Heusen.

Sammy's world was a world of classic songs cut by the world's greatest singers. Sinatra alone recorded 87 of them. "Some of them two or three times!" Sammy reminded me.

His songs are standards in the truest sense of the word in that they transcend generations and are cherished by all: "High Hopes," "My Kind of Town, (Chicago Is)," "It's Been a Long, Long Time," "Thoroughly Modern Millie," "Love and Marriage," "Call Me Irresponsible," "It's Magic," "Come Fly with Me" and countless other classics. Though Sammy passed away in 1992, all of these songs live on. And he had a story for every one of them.

Many of these stories were heard in Sammy's own stage show, "Words and Music," which had been playing to sold-out audiences around the country at the time of our interview. It was always a secret passion of his to perform, and in this show he proved that he was every bit a showman. He belted out his own greatest hits with phrasing he learned from Sinatra, danced up a surprising storm, and recounted the hilarious true stories behind his songs. He also poked a lot of fun at himself. One night, upon seeing a young couple in the audience, Sammy said, "Your parents made you come, didn't they?"

Some of these stories were also included in the introduction to the *Sammy Cahn Rhyming Dictionary*. Sammy admitted that there are other rhyming dictionaries with more words in them, and even showed me a monstrous one that he owns. But his is special, he said, because of the stories in it. "Everything you need to know about songwriting is there," he said.

He was born Samuel Cohen in 1913 on the lower East Side of New York. "So low," he said, "that one step backwards would have landed me in the East River." He played the violin in bands as a kid, and eventually began writing songs with his first collaborator, Saul Chaplin.

He quickly gained a reputation as not only a colorful wordsmith, but one who could come up with the perfect lyric in a matter of minutes. In his show, he illustrated this tendency by quickly typing out a lyric, ripping the sheet out of the typewriter and slapping it on the piano. "Many might have written these lyrics better, " he said. "But none *faster!*"

His immense joy writing lyrics is contained in all of his songs, and in the heartfelt way he spoke about his many collaborators, especially Van Heusen. In his later days he spent much of his time writing lyrics not to new melodies by young composers, but to the old melodies written by his friends. He adapted his old songs to various occasions, writing special lyrics to fit, and in doing so was able to collaborate again with Van Heusen and the others with whom he had his greatest successes.

Sammy spoke to me in his office from behind his big desk, but jumped up frequently to refer to files and books, and to go to the piano to play his songs. Many of his memories were musical, and his answers were sung almost as often as they were spoken. The combination of his age and his New York upbringing gave him a speaking voice and delivery almost exactly like that of Groucho Marx on *You Bet Your Life*. When he offered me rhymes for "Chicago," for example, "embargo" and "Wells Fargo," with his accent they were perfect rhymes.

Of course, being Sammy Cahn, he would settle for nothing less.

You once said that you don't write songs, but that songs write you.
Absolutely.

Can you explain that?
I will try. Music has a mesmerizing effect on me. For instance, while I'm riding in the car and I hear a recording, the first time I heard the recording of Ray Charles singing "Georgia," I had to stop the car, pull over to the side of the road. Otherwise I would float away. *Literally.* I'm not making any jokes. I just would be so mesmerized.

So music has special meaning to me. You might listen to a melody and hear what you hear but when I listen to a melody I hear words. In my show, I only tell stories about forty songs on the stage. I have a songbook that has a *hundred* songs in it and I could tell you a story about every song.

So, this is the best example of what I'm trying to say. I had just written "I've Heard That Song Before." Big hit. I come into the room with Axel Stordahl and Paul Weston. And they say, "Look at him. Takes him fifteen minutes to write a song and it takes us hours to make it sound good." They were making an arrangement for Tommy Dorsey.

I said, "Why don't you folks write a song?"
They said, "We've written a song."
I said, "Can I hear it?"
They said, "Wait until we finish this introduction. Do you want a long introduction or a short introduction?"
I said, "Who cares about the introduction? As far as I'm concerned it could be one note." And so the Tommy Dorsey arrangement to "I Heard That Song Before" was a one note introduction. It went like this, [*sings intro*] "Baaa . . ."

Now they go to the piano, two fellows, to play their song. [*Goes to piano and plays melody.*]

That melody is architecturally great for lyrics. It's written architecturally correct. I thought, "I should call it 'I Should Care.'" Now I wait for them to finish and then I say, "What do you call that?"

They say, "We don't call it anything."
I said, "Start at the top." They play and I sing, "I should care, I should go around weeping." I stop and they both nod. When they nod, it's written. Cause then I just follow the architecture of the music. I repeat, [*sings*] "I should care . . . I should go without sleeping." It can only be "I can go without sleeping." It can't be weeping, leaping, creeping. It can only be "sleeping."

"Strangely enough I sleep well, 'cept for a dream or two, but then I count my sheep well. Funny how sheep can lull you to sleep. So, I should care. I should let it upset me. But I swear that it just doesn't get me . . ."

And Paul Weston, who is a religious man, stops me and says, "Do you have to say 'swear'?"

I say, "I don't have to say 'swear.' " So I repeat it: "I should care, but it just doesn't get me. Maybe I won't find someone as lovely as you, but I should care, and I do."

Now, on my mother in heaven when I started, did I have the faintest notion that I would end it like that? No. I just go where the lyric leads. It leads me. That's how I mean a song writes me more than I write it. Do you follow?

Yes. You once said that anybody can be a lyricist. Does it take a certain genius, or special talent?

You call it genius. You've got to have a natural bent or natural feeling for it. If you don't know what music is about, the feel of music, or what singability is, nobody can teach you how to do it. But if you have the urge and the feeling, and above all, natural talent, then you can do it.

How do I explain? You know when people ask which comes first, the music or the words, I say the phone call? It's a joke, a joke. With Jule Stein, the music came first a great deal of the time. With Jimmy Van Heusen, the music and words came almost together. We'd sit around and talk and I'd say a line and he'd go to the piano. We'd incubate together.

When I hand a fellow a lyric, I know exactly what I'm supposed to get back. I can go to the typewriter and type you a march, I can type you a waltz, I can type you a wedding song.

You know the song "The Tender Trap"? Well, the title came first. Sinatra came to me and said he was doing a picture called *The Tender Trap*. It might sound like I'm kidding, but I promise you when I hear "trap," I hear "snap." Think about it.

"You see a pair of laughing eyes and suddenly you're sighing sighs." See? That's the architecture of the lyric. That's a professional lyric.

The song "Let It Snow" was written on Hollywood and Vine on the hottest day of the year. I said to Jule Stein, "Why don't we go down to the beach and cool off?" He said, "Why don't we stay here and write a winter song." I went to the typewriter. "Oh the weather outside is frightful,"—architecture—"But the fire is so delightful, and since we've got no place to go, let it snow, let it snow, let it snow." Now why three "let it snow"s? Why not two or four? Because three is *lyric*.

Writing songs for me is one of the most pleasurable things I do. And a day doesn't go by that I don't write lyrics. My main occupation now is special lyrics for special occasions. Lee Iacocca has a birthday, I'm hired. I take all my songs and change them for the occasion: [*Sings*] "He was born one wintry morn a lot of years ago, it's been a long, long time . . ." [*Then, to the tune of "Thoroughly Modern Millie"*] "Everything today is Lee Iacocca . . ."

Is it still fun for you?

Oh, it's beyond fun.

Do you like puzzles and word games?

No. I hate word games. My life's a word game. Who needs to play word games?

[*Gets up to show file of special lyrics, reading the names*] Joey Bishop . . . Nat King Cole . . . Bing Crosby . . . Cedars Sinai . . . CBS . . . Milton Berle. . . . The Variety Clubs . . . You can't believe. It's the history of this town. The Sinatra file, you can't even lift it. You know Ray Croc of McDonald's? I did his 75th birthday: "It's quite beyond belief all of this from buns and beef, it's magic, I might go on to say they sell a billion every day, it's magic. . . ."

Were you good with rhymes when you were a kid?

I think I had a natural bent. I've got an instinct for rhyming.

Saul Chaplin, his real name was Saul Kaplan. One of our first songs was "Love For Sale." On the original copy in 1935 my name was Sammy Kahn, K-a-h-n. And his name was Saul Kaplan. So I said to him, "Kahn and Kaplan, that's a dress firm. We have to change our names. I'll be Sammy Cahn, C-a-h-n." He said, "Okay, now I'm Saul Caplin, C-a-p—." I said, "No. Cahn and Caplin, C or K, is a dress firm. You've got to change your name." So he changed it to Chaplin.

Jimmy Van Heusen and I created the idea of opening and closing songs for albums. "Come Fly With Me." An opening. "It's Nice To Go Trav'ling." Closing. So now we come to *Come Dance With Me* [for Sinatra].

First song is easy: [*sings*] "Hey there, cutes, put on your dancing boots, and come dance with me! What an evening for some terpsichore! Pretty face, I know a swinging place, come on, dance with me! Romance with me on a crowded floor. And while the rhythm pings, oh, what lovely things I'll be saying, for what is dancing but making love set to music playing . . ."

Now we have to write a last song. And every dancing idea, Irving Berlin has used. There's nothing left. So now we're stuck. And I want your readers to know very carefully, and please enunciate it: I am very, very careful about repeating a title. You know why? If Cyndi Lauper had written "Time After Time" after me, I wouldn't have written "Time After Time." I would have called it "Time After Time After Time." Three times. Just to make it unique, your own title. Because when ASCAP listens, who are they crediting, her or me?

So every dance I did was done by Mr. Berlin. "Cheek to Cheek," "Change Partners." Every song about music and dance, name it, he did it.

So now Sinatra gets impatient. He keeps saying, "Where's that last song?"

I say, "Frank, I promise you the minute we finish it, you'll hear it." Because we spoiled him. If we finish a song in the morning, he gets it in the afternoon. Seriously. But this was a problem.

Finally, one day I turned to Van Heusen and said, "Has there ever been a last dance?" Now he knows a lot of songs and he says, "Hmmm . . . I don't know . . ." So we call ASCAP and no, there's never been a last dance. There's been a last *waltz* but no last dance.

I went to the typewriter. "It's the last dance, they're playing the last dance, they're dimming the lights down, they're hoping we'll go. It's obvious they're aware of us, the pair of us, alone on the floor, still I want to hold you like this forever and more. It's the last song, they're playing the last song. The orchestra's yawning, they're sleepy, I know. They're wondering just when will we leave, but 'til we leave . . ."

Sinatra's recording it and he sings, "They're wondering just when *we* will leave . . ."

I said, "Wait a minute, it's not 'when *we* will leave,' it's [*sings*] 'When *will* we leave but 'til we leave . . ."

He says, "Who talks like that? You'd say, 'When we will leave.' You don't say, 'When will we leave.' Who talks like that?"

I said, "Frank, you're not *talking*. You're *singing*."
And that's the story of lyrics.

Often your lyrics are conversational, but other times they are poetic. A line like "rainbows I'm inclined to pursue" from "Call Me Irresponsible" is not conversational at all but beautiful. Which is most important?
You see, again, it's [*sings*] "Call me irresponsible, call me unreliable, throw in undependable *too* . . ." So I have to come up with an 'oo' sound. Something that is hard to pur*sue* or to *view*. "Waterfalls I'm inclined to view . . . *Rainbows* I'm inclined to pursue."

The lyric to "The Second Time Around." Jimmy Van Heusen and I had to write a love song for a widower and a widow. Bing Crosby is a widower and he meets a widow. Now what kind of song do you write for a widower and a widow? So we made some jokes, like "I'm glad you're dead, you rascal, you."

Then I said, "How about 'The Second Time Around'?" He said, "How do you mean?"

I said, "Love is wonderful the second time around, just as beautiful with both feet on the ground."

He said, "Love is *lovelier* the second time around." That was his first line. And that's how songs get written.

One of my very favorite lines that I've ever written is in that song. "Love is more comfortable the second time you fall, like a friendly home the second time you call." I love that.

There are some lyrics I'm very *pleased* to have written. Like the lyrics to "The Christmas Waltz." That's a lovely lyric: "Frosted window panes, candles gleaming inside, painted candy canes on the tree; Santa's on his way, he's filled his sleigh with things, things for you and me. It's that time of year, when the world falls in love, every song you hear seems to say: 'Merry Christmas, may your New Year dreams come true.'" It's one of my favorite lyrics.

Another favorite lyric of mine was written for the show *Our Town*. *Our Town* was one of the great, great, *great*, experiences of my life, writing lyrics to Thornton Wilder's classic. People ask me, "Where do ideas for songs come from?" In this play the first act is called "The Daily Riots." The second act is called "Love and Marriage."

I said to Van Heusen, "Would you mind giving me a vamp please?" [*Sings*] "Love and marriage, love and marriage, go together like a horse and carriage." Of course, it's horse and carriage. What else could it be? Now, in my life, in daily conversation, I never use the word "disparage." But if I have to rhyme "marriage," "it's an institute you can't disparage . . ." Then, "Ask the local gentry and they will say it's element'ry . . ."

Then there's a song in there called "Look To Your Heart." "Look to your heart, when there are words to say, and never leave your love unspoken . . . Speak your love to those who seek your love. Look to your heart, your heart will know what to say—look to your heart each day."

You see, you're lucky to have a play like that to bounce off of. I don't dwell on where ideas come from; I know some people do. I write a ballad when they *ask* me to write a ballad.

One of my favorite stories about my so-called gift. The son of Gus Kahn comes to see me, Donald Kahn. Son of Gus Kahn, the great songwriter. One of the greatest of all.

So he goes to the piano and plays me this. [*Plays melody*]

I say, "I like when it rains." He says, "Yeah, I like when it rains."

[*Sings to same melody*] "Pit-pitter-pat, pit-pitter-pat, I like when it rains . . ." Now you could sit here and write a million other lyrics to that song. But that's what I heard. That's where I come from.

Do you feel the urge to do more of that, new lyrics to new melodies, than writing parodies of your own songs?

I don't write parodies. I write *special lyrics*. My lyrics that are written special are as special as any lyrics written.

I've won five Academy Awards. [*Motions to shelves of trophies and memorabilia*] See, that's the Emmy and four Oscars. Five Academy Awards. But one of my greatest, greatest honors came from Frank Loesser, one of the great lyric writers. I was at a party and I was singing special lyrics at the party. I finished and I got a lot of applause and all of a sudden Frank Loesser banged on a glass. "I'd like to say something to you people," he said. "A lot of you people may think you're just listening to some parodies. What you heard tonight is about the most special lyric writing you can write."

It gave me a great sense of pride because *that's* the way I write.

Let me tell you another thing. Tell your young writers: if they are music writers, if they are trying to be a composer, let them take the great lyrics, let them take "All The Things You Are" by Jerome Kern and write *his* melody to those lyrics.

On the other hand, if you're a lyric writer, take Jerome Kern's "All The Things You Are" and write your lyrics. So then you're writing with Jerome Kern, aren't you? So when I get special lyrics to do, it's beyond belief to write in the same *tracks* of the great writers.

At the Jimmy Van Heusen tribute, I closed the event with a special lyric to the song "But Beautiful." It was one of the great songs: [*sings*] "James Van Heusen was the best as this evening did attest, every song may I suggest, but beautiful. Beautiful in every note, in each and every bar, right from 'Rainy Day' to 'Swinging on a Star.'" Look, I'm sitting here telling you, you can't write better than that.

So, it's one of the great training grounds. I do this every single day of my life. Practicing my craft.

The rhyming book is valuable more than anything for the story in the front of it. The stories in this book tell you how to write songs. The words are all the same words. There's a book by Clement Wood, do you know that book? Let me show you. [*Gets down dictionary-sized book*] See? It's four times as large as mine. You can't believe what's in here. But for all practical reasons, mine is better. And I cannot tell you how many young people I've met who walked up to me and thanked me, thanked me for this book.

Do you use a rhyming dictionary when you work?

It's all in my head. [*Laughs*] People say to me, "Do you have a rhyming dictionary?" I say yes. It's for the composer.

But you see. Jimmy Van Heusen and I were trying to write a song for Frank Capra. Great director. We'd written "High Hopes" for that picture *Hole in the Head*. Now he has a picture called [*laughs*] *Pocketful of Miracles*. Phone rings. Jimmy Van Heusen and I are in New York. It's Frank Capra.

"Sammy? I need a favor."

"Hey, Frank, anything."

"We just finished a picture called *Pocketful of Miracles*." The minute he says it, I freeze. Cause one of the greatest popular songs is "Pocketful of Dreams": [*sings*] "I'm no millionaire but I'm not the type to care, 'cause I've got a pocketful of dreams . . ." Why would I want to write a song called "Pocketful of Miracles"? Again, trying to protect titles.

So I say, "You don't really want to—"

He says, "Please. The picture's finished."

"Can I see the picture?"

He says, "It's playing tonight. In New York at the little Sheraton down in the village."

Jimmy Van Heusen and I go down there and we see *Pocketful of Miracles* with Glenn Ford, Hope Lange, and Bette Davis playing Apple Annie. Now I'm fighting this. I don't want to write a song called "Pocketful of Miracles." Van Heusen says, "We must, we must. It's Frank Capra. We must."

So finally I go, "What's the opposite of a dream? Practicality." "Practicality doesn't interest me, Love the life that I lead. I've got a pocketful of miracles, and with a pocketful of miracles, one little miracle a day is all I need."

He writes a melody and the melody goes like this. [*Sings melody.*] He says, "What do you think of it?"

I say, "It's terrible."

He says, "Terrible? Why?"

"Because you need a choreographer for this song. [*Sings*] 'Practicality *umm* doesn't interest me *umm* . . .'"

He says, "Why don't we put a word there?"

"A word?"

He sings, "*Real* practicality *sure* doesn't interest me . . ."

I say, "Now it's more terrible. Are you crazy?" So we look at each other, staring kind of funny. I say, "How about 'Pee-racticality dee-uzn't interest me'?"

He says, "What the hell does that mean?"

I say, "I don't know but I know I can stand in front of a guy and go, 'Pee-racticality dee-uzn't interest me.' I can't go, 'Umm practicality *umm* doesn't interest me . . .'"

That again is instinct. That again is salesmanship. That is singability. Call it whatever you want.

Is singability something you always understood?

See, I wanted to be a performer myself. You've seen me on the stage. I'm unerring. Every move I make is unerring. And that's due to a man named James Barton. B-a-r-t-o-n. He was the world's single greatest entertainer.

One thing I noticed about your writing is that when you have a tough word to rhyme in a song, such as Chicago, you don't put it in the title.

Instead, you make the title "My Kind of Town" and "Chicago is" answers the title. It's a great way around a problem.

Same thing with "Thoroughly Modern Millie." I know by instinct, gift, whatever you want to call it, Millie is silly, Piccadilly, frilly, chilly . . . So you don't rhyme the word Millie. Chicago, Wells Fargo, embargo, I know all the rhymes. They don't make it.

The main thing was that I didn't want to write a song called "Chicago." See, if they came to me and said you've got to write "New York, New York," I'd say, "Wrong fella." I would have called it "My New York, New York." Or "My New York, My New York." Because there are *five songs* called "New York, New York," you know that, don't you? You can't copyright a title. I could write a song tomorrow called "Stardust." But I wouldn't. Why would I? So instead of "Chicago" I wrote "My kind of town, Chicago is."

How come you like the word "lyrist" better than "lyricist"?

[*Softly*] Because Oscar Hammerstein liked it. [*Laughs*]

But you know who the number one lyrist in the world was?

Who?

W.G. Gilbert. Of Gilbert and Sullivan. Number one. Of anybody. There are many giants, but reigning above all the other giants. Because he did it first before anybody. Every kind of funny rhyme scheme.

Did you like Ogden Nash's work?

Yes! He was very good. But, see, he wasn't actually a lyric writer. He was a humorist. He worked with a man named Vernon Duke and they wrote a great score. Like Harold Arlen took Truman Capote. Yes. Wrote a great score. Check it out. See, if you have a great composer, he can take a fellow who's not actually a lyric writer and form him.

Because poems are poems. They read to the eye, to the heart, to the mind. Lyrics you have to sing. They sing to the *ear*, to the mind, to the heart. There's a difference. You can read a poem but you can't sing some poems. Like my joke is that Shakespeare would have been a lousy lyric writer. "Love can laugh at locksmiths"? You can't sing "locksmiths." "Locksmiths"? Forget it.

Many writers, such as Bob Dylan, worked to incorporate poetry into their lyrics—

No, but you see, most of those writers have no sense of the architecture. Any one of my songs, you see a word under a note. You won't see three words under a note. In those songs, every section has a different twist. If I gave Van Heusen a lyric that wasn't architecturally correct, he wouldn't write it.

They don't really understand it. Those who write today rhyme sounds. You know what a pure rhyme is against a impure rhyme? "Mind" and "time" is impure. "Dime" and "time," pure. "Wine" and "fine," pure. "Wine" and "time," impure.

Many songwriters have said that you can only rhyme "time" and "dime" so many times, but that meaning is more important.

Let me talk to that point. Whatever the number one song in the world is at *this moment*, I wish my name were on it. The *number one* song. Because it's very special. Not two, three, four, five, ten. The number one song I wish my

name was on because it's *special*. I love the song "Wind Beneath my Wings."
It's a song beyond. The meaning and the thought of that song is so all encompassing, it doesn't matter what the words or notes are. I wish I'd written it. But
the point is, if I had that song, I'd probably neaten it up, maybe spoil it. But
it's a beyond incredible song. Beyond incredible song.

**That song is unusual in that it's old fashioned, and has a great melody.
But many songs that make it to number one don't necessarily meet your
melodic or lyrical standard. Do you hear many songs nowadays that you
would really want your name on?**

See, the point is, many of the songs nowadays are one-week wonders.

Disposable—

No, I don't like to use that word, but they go like this: [*Motions with hands
a plane going down.*] They hit the top and went down. See, the *Beatles* are lasting because they wrote music. *Noise diminishes; music lingers.* See how simple
that is? You must write something that you'll take away. A beat? A beat is
something else.

Some say that melodies are out of fashion.

A melody will never be out of fashion. Sinatra recorded eighty-seven of my
songs. *Eighty-seven* of my songs. Some three times. And the amazing popularity
of this man, how many people in the world living now do you think made love
to the sound of Sinatra? So when people go to see this man, he represents
something *beyond* words and music. It's a presence. There's a famous writer in
London for one of the big newspapers. His name is Mark Steyn. And he paid
me a high compliment. He said, "Sammy Cahn's songs have been the background score of our lives." Well, that's Sinatra.

Do you think he was the greatest singer to do your songs?

Look, let me tell you something. When he sings, [*sings*] ". . . It's such a
lovely day," he makes the word "lovely" sound lovely. 99 singers out of a hundred wouldn't sing it that way. [*Sings*] "When somebody loves you, it's no good
unless he loves you . . ." The word "love." He gives the words their full meaning. And that's why he's Sinatra.

There's a time and a place for everything. Life repeats itself and regener-
ates.

* * *

Mose Allison

Hollywood, California 1988

"The singer-songwriter Mose Allison might have been a lot better off if he fired the piano-player Mose Allison," Mose said about himself during a swing through Hollywood to perform at the Vine Street Bar & Grill. But he's not a guy content to be only one thing. He's a songwriter, a singer and a jazz pianist. He's also a jazz legend. And while this combination of attributes hasn't spelled huge commercial success, Mose is not unhappy with his lot in life. In the words of a song on his album, *Ever Since the World Ended,* "I'm not downhearted, I *am* not downhearted, but I'm getting there."

Similar to the subject of the "Seventh Son" who was born on the seventh day of the seventh month, Mose was born on the eleventh day of the eleventh month—November 11, 1927—in Tippo, Mississippi. He started playing piano at the age of five and wrote his first song, "The Fourteen Day Palmolive Plan," when he was ten. It griped about the difficulty of hearing music on the radio with constant commercial interruptions. Even then, Mose avoided writing the easy love song in favor of a little social commentary.

His dislike for the martial beat of rock music is easily understood when one hears the shifting, flexible rhythms he and his band get cooking. When I asked his drummer and bass player at Vine Street how they would categorize Mose's particular groove, they both laughed at the folly of attempting to articulate something so abstract, and eventually explained Mose's theory of "anti-time." "You know what time is, right? Anti-time is moving against that, in music and in life."

Mose doesn't try to define it. He simply does it and leaves it to others to analyze. And he does it with a singing style that has been called "the essence of cool," a voice that is bluesy, conversational and always understated, allowing him to use words like "dogma" and not sound pretentious. The best descriptions of his musical style can be found in the lyrics of his own songs, such as "mixing up the boogie with the do-si-do," which perfectly pinpoints the merger of country swing and pure jazz that's at the heart of his work. His southern accent comes across more clearly in his speaking voice, which is low, resonant, and punctuated by frequent outbursts of what can best be called "jazz laughter."

Your songs combine jazz, blues, folk and country. They are essentially jazz compositions but with a great emphasis on words, as in folk music.
Yeah. You know, I've always been asked which is more important, words or music. But it's all part of expression to me.

I've done all three, you know; I wrote songs and sang them and played piano when I was in grade school. In fact, I ran into a girl who I went to high school with in Phoenix a few years ago. And she said, "You know, you're doing the same thing you were doing [*laughs*] in grade school."

Even your vocal style was the same back then?
Well, I was imitating my heroes, who were Louis Jordan, the Timpani Five, the Nat King Cole Trio, Big Bill Broonzy, Roosevelt Sykes, those kinds of people. So it was a simplified version of what I'm doing now.

And even then you were mixing up the blues with jazz and folk?
Yeah. You know, all the great jazz players have played blues. Louis Armstrong, man, he played and sang blues all the time. So then when the country blues players were discovered later, then people started discriminating between that kind of blues and the kind of blues jazz players played.

At what age did you start playing the piano?
Took piano lessons as a child, five years old. There was a piano at home. My dad was a self-taught stride player; played semi-pro before he took over the farm.

Did you know at that age that you wanted to spend your life writing songs and being a musician?
Not really. I always wanted to be a musician. I always wanted to *play.*

I played weekends in one of the local honkytonks in Greenwood, Mississippi, when I was in high school. And I liked that atmosphere. That was the way I got my attention. I wasn't big enough to be a football star and I didn't particularly dig duck hunting. [*Laughs*] So, that's the way I got noticed.

I ended up with an English degree. I was considering the possibility of trying to write, or teach, if necessary. But after graduating from LSU, I got a job at a nightclub in Jackson, Mississippi, and I missed the graduation exercises to go play the job. I've been doing it ever since. [*Laughs*]

Ben Sidran has called you the "William Faulkner of Jazz."
Oh yeah. Well, I've gotten "The Mark Twain of Jazz," "The Will Rogers of Jazz." I consider those names complimentary. I suppose they all have a certain relevance. . . .

Why do you think you get that? Because you spin yarns in your songs?

Well, I don't think so. My things aren't yarns; they're more like commentaries.

I used to divide my songs into three categories: slapstick, social comment, and personal crisis. But in the last few years I realized I'm trying to put all three of those things into a lot of songs. Most of the songs on the new album have a slapstick line, to get your attention. And then they bring in a little social comment and a little personal crisis, too. So evidently I'm putting all three things into the same songs now.

That's a chief characteristic of your work, combining the optimistic with the cynical. The one song of yours that seems to be the epitome of that attitude is "Getting There," which has the great lines: "I'm not downhearted, but I'm getting there."

Yeah, that summarizes a lot of the things I've been working on. An old guy in Chicago told me one time, "Man, the thing I like about you is that you don't ever say, 'I'm dead.' [*Laughs*] You say, 'I'm down but I'm not out.'"

There is a reality . . . everything should point towards reality as far as I'm concerned. And reality as opposed to *appearance*. What I'm trying to do is to illuminate different types of realities.

You know, most love songs are really self-love songs. And at this point in time, if you get right down to it, we need a whole new set of morals in order to survive. Because anything that helps to increase the likelihood that the human race will survive is good, and the things that make it likely that it won't survive are bad, you know. So we have to find out what the bad things are and what the good things are and try to do something about it.

The average love song doesn't address that at all. The average love song says, "If I just had you, I wouldn't care if all the children starved." [*Laughs*] And also, I don't like any song that says, "You're mine, you're mine." Nobody belongs to anybody. I don't go for that at all. So my songs are sort of contrary to the actual average money songs, which are mostly love songs.

Your song "I Don't Worry About a Thing" is very much about reality. The main line of it is, "I don't worry about a thing because I know nothing's gonna be all right."

Well, I think that's the way we are. One of my formulas in life is "Ambivalence plus interdependence equals contrariety." [*Laughs*] Now you can look that over, think about it. What I mean is that nothing is cut and dried, nothing is completely black and white, you know; all day long we're being pulled in one way and pushed in another way, you know? It's all part of the interaction of opposing forces. Which is the real nitty-gritty. [*Laughs*] So if I can just suggest this in my songs, that is what I try to do.

You imply in that same song that you don't want those forces to shift. You say, "If you get too fat, someone else gets thinner."

We all have to consider our karma, you know? I think that people who are over-rewarded for their achievements accumulate some sort of psychic debt. [*Laughs*]

How about people who are under-rewarded?

Well, if you're under-rewarded, then you have a psychic surplus.

How do you collect on it?

Well, you have to assume that you *are* collecting. [*Laughs*] But I feel that I'm adequately rewarded for what I've done. I've seen a lot of talent disappear, you know, without ever getting anywhere.

Over the years, that's one of the things that's a real bring-down. We'd like to think, you know, "True talent will always rise to the occasion," and if somebody really has something, they'll make it. But unfortunately, I don't think that's the case. Not at all. I've seen too many people that obviously had great talent and were unable to keep it up. Either because of economic considerations or psychological or sociological or whatever . . . a lot of talent never gets realized. And of course, these days as long as you're warm, dry and well fed, you're better off than most people in the world, anyhow. [*Laughs*]

Success in the jazz world seems especially hard to come by. Why?

Because there was a jazz boom in the late fifties, when jazz was sort of accredited as being an American art form. But after that rock and roll came in and became commercial and all the young people went to that. So what was left for the jazz audience sort of got split up into different sections: the blues people, the jazz people, and so on.

It's just a matter of sales. There's no sales in jazz, you know. You know, a big-selling jazz album sells one one-hundredth of what a big seller is in the pop category. There's just not that much market for it. The bottom line is sales.

The chords you use in your songs are always so warm and interesting. How do you voice your chords to make them sound this way?

Well, you know, you get some dissonance in a chord, either in the middle of it or at the bottom of it. Some place in the chord you have a little half-step. For instance, the voicings I use in the right hand take on different colorations depending on what the bottom note is. So by using the same voicing on the right hand and varying the tonic, you give it different colorations. And the chords, you can suspend them and leave them unresolved. You can lead the chords toward a place where you will resolve them, now and then.

The voicing is this: if you have an F in the bass, and then a G, an A flat and a C in the right hand. That's one of the manifestations of the chord. Then you can put different tonics with it and get different effects. I'm giving away my secrets here!

I've also noticed that even when you play the blues in a major key, your solos never sound like they are in a major key.

No. I always tell guys the blues is neither major nor minor. [*Laughs*] Yeah, it's like you have to try to get between the major and the minor.

Because if you listen to the very pure country blues people, they don't play that minor sound that some of the jazz people started playing later. And also, they don't play strictly a major third thing, either. The tonality is more of a pentatonic tonality. So the way you get that is by using the major third and the minor third together; you don't ever use just one of them by itself. So you never fall completely into a major or completely into a minor mode.

Do you always write your songs on piano?

I start out with words, the idea, the line. Then after I get a line or two, I try to see what melodic line those words would better suit or be suited to. But as soon as I find out the form that I'm going to use, I can complete the song pretty much in my head and then go to the piano later and figure out the changes.

Sometimes, though, sitting at the piano and playing changes will change the direction of the tune to a certain extent.

When you go to the piano, do you find yourself playing in certain keys that feel the most comfortable?

Well, you know, the range of my voice designates a certain key, depending on the harmonic relationship of the melody line. So when I get the melody line, then I can tell pretty much what key it's gonna be in because if the melody line hangs on a fifth, the comfortable fifth for me would be B flat [*laughs*] or in the neighborhood of B flat. So that means that that tune would be in E flat or in F.

That's another thing. I'm writing for me. I'm writing for me to sing the song. So that is a consideration, too.

In fact, you know, a few years ago Murray Horowitz, the guy who brought *Ain't Misbehavin'* to Broadway, did a little off-Broadway show of twenty of my tunes. So I was sitting in the audience listening to these theatrically trained singers do my tunes. [*Laughs*] It was a real revelation! It was a good thing, because I could see that they could be done by people who have nothing in common with *my style* at all. They sang them in their style.

And did you like how it sounded?

I left the show whistling the tunes! [*Laughs*]

You're on the road almost nonstop, doing about two hundred nights a year. How do you manage to fit in the time for songwriting?

I write the songs when I can't sleep. If I wake up too early in the morning or if I'm waiting for an airplane. I can come up with ideas for a song any time, any place, and start working on them. But it's very seldom I'll just do a whole song in one place.

So many writers I talk to have to be completely alone with the telephones cut off and everything.

Oh yeah. No, that's not necessary for me. A lot of people keep notes and things and it's probably a good idea, especially at my age. But a writer once said, "The only things worth writing about are the things you can't forget." So I sort of took that for my rule.

I wait for the things to keep coming back. If something keeps coming back, if I keep thinking of that phrase, if I see manifestations of it at different times and different places, then I feel that it's worth trying to make a song out of.

Your songs reflect that. A song like "Your Mind is on Vacation" is so natural and economical. There's not a single wasted line in it.

I've always been a devotee of the economical approach. I've never tried to write songs with complex chord changes or anything like that, because as a jazz player, I went through the era where all these jazz players were learning all these show tunes, and everybody was trying to see what complicated chord progression they could find to play on. So when I got ready to do my vocals and my thing, I wasn't compelled to write complicated tunes.

My songs are meant to have that rhythmic impetus that would lay down a good foundation for jazz improvisation.

Do you remember where you were when you wrote "Your Mind is on Vacation"?

Only thing that I remember is the place where I was playing when I got the idea. It was called the Showboat Lounge in Washington, D.C., in 1957. [*Laughs*] That's when I first got that idea. Like I say, sometimes I get these phrases and sometimes I won't complete the song for ten years.

One song I wrote is called "The Fires of Spring." Of course, nobody ever heard of it. I spent about fifteen years on that one song. I think I wrote one verse in 1960 and one verse in 1970. Sometimes it's a very long time between the original idea and finishing a song.

"Your Mind is on Vacation" was on my first record for Atlantic. It must have been around the early sixties. So I probably toyed around with it for a few years before I recorded it.

You have so many lines in that song, and others, that are almost homilies. Like "If silence were golden, you couldn't earn a dime."

I believe in taking lines from our collective idiom, as long as they aren't too overused. That's another one of my guiding thoughts, to try to keep it in the language of normal people. [*Laughs*]

I will throw in an exotic word sometimes. In another song of mine that nobody ever heard [*laughs*] called "Perfect Moments," I spent a lot of time trying to track down the right line. And I ended up with the word "Miocene," which is a geological term. The line is "Miocene valentine." Which is supposed to imply that the mountains and the oceans were like a valentine from the universe. [*Laughter*] And so I have done that a few times. But mostly the stuff is in pretty plain language.

In your song "Ever Since the World Ended" there's the line, "Dogmas that we once defended . . ." But you can get away with using a word like "dogma" because in your style it doesn't sound forced, it sounds cool.

Yeah, I know. I spent a lot of time deciding whether that word would work. [*Laughs*] But it was the only thing to make the thought that I wanted perfectly clear. But I took a chance with it. [*Laughs*]

You were talking about getting the rhythmic feel right for your songs. Ben Sidran has discussed how explicit you are with drummers, telling them never to play the backbeat. He described your general groove as a "free-form zydeco feel."

Yeah, well, I liked that term. I thought that was pretty perceptive. I liked that because I am playing basic, sort of funky New Orleans rhythms. But I don't want those heavy backbeats because to me that's too much emphasis. To me, they're completely superfluous. The music doesn't need it.

I like a more free-floating type time. The sort of time hand-drummers get when they play with their hands. Because that's the basis of all this music, anyhow. It all came from hand-drumming: jazz and blues and rhythm and blues. And all the music which has been built on those forms, which is practically everything lately. [*Laughs*]

It all came from Afro-Cuban, Afro-Caribbean hand-drumming. So I'm interested in listening to ethnic music that has a lot of rhythm and percussive rhythmic effects and things. I've listened to a lot of it and I never heard a backbeat yet. [*Laughs*] So for me, the backbeat is an overemphasis that was probably put on for commercial reasons.

Why do you think this one rhythm is so prevalent? It's in every single song you hear on the radio.

Oh yeah, it's *the* pop beat. It's supposed to show people where to clap hands. [*Laughs*] But I'm a contrary type. I used to go to jazz concerts and clap on one on purpose. [*Laughter*]

But the backbeat, the heavy backbeat, became the commercial staple of most music. To me, it's completely restrictive because it completely limits you to what you can do rhythmically. I like the time flexible, where I can go off in different directions when I want to. If you're sitting there and the guy is playing two and four, banging away, you know, everything you *do* has to be completely restricted to that, to what he's doing. I call those kinds of drummers "slavedrivers." The new slavedrivers. [*Laughs*]

Of course, you know, the singer-songwriter Mose Allison would have been a lot better off if he had fired the piano player. [*Laughs*] Because that's the thing that has kept me from a lot of markets, the fact that I play jazz piano. But I'm happy with that because playing jazz piano is just as important to me as singing and writing songs.

Your solos always seem to comment on the songs themselves; they add another level to the songs.

That's what I try to do. I always say I think I'm at my best when I'm singing one of my songs and playing improvisations with that song.

When you are working on a song, is the solo a part of it?

No. I wait until the song is complete. Then I start playing the song and *then* I start getting into the improvisation part. And if the song doesn't lend itself to improvisation, then I probably won't do it much.

Do you try to play a brand new solo on each song each time?

You know, you can get an infinite variety out of playing the blues, actually, if you've got enough imagination to do it.

There are blues cliches, you know. There are some very revealing records around, if someone wants to dig them up, where you'll have an all-star lineup of jazz men playing the blues. I've heard a lot of them, and you know, a lot of the guys will just play blues cliches. Just the old standard blues cliches, just like reciting the Gettysburg Address over or something. [*Laughs*]

But then there'll always be one or two guys who will really try to invent something and use some imagination on the twelve-bar blues. And you know, *it's still there* to be done.

I always offer up, as a model for what can be done with a twelve-bar blues, Charlie Parker's "Parker's Mood." Now if you want to hear what someone with

imagination and energy, what a genius can do with a twelve-bar blues, listen to
that.

Many of your solos seem to have a very classical influence.
Yeah, I listen to a lot of classical music; still do.

Bartok?
Oh, Bartok, Hindemith, Ives . . . Scriabin. I went the whole route. I started
out with the contemporary people and went all the way back to Bach. And
now Bach is the one I like to listen to more than anybody. It's amazing, all the
things he did staying within the diatonic scale. His harmonic mode was limited
in relation to what people can use now, but he was able to get an awful lot of
variation within that one mode. I listen to all kinds of music. And anything I
really like usually ends up in my arsenal for things to use in improvising.

**Your version of "You are my Sunshine" is a classic. How did you alter
that song harmonically to make it sound the way it does?**
You know, I was just sitting at home one night by myself and it was back
when there were a lot of tunes about sunshine. In the sixties, I guess, when
everybody discovered sunshine all of a sudden. [*Laughs*] And I said, "Man,
there's *already* a great tune about sunshine but the only thing wrong with it is
the way it's played. And the harmony is so monotonous and dull, so simple,
that nobody would want to do it." And so I started singing it and I put it into
a minor mode and it just fell into place.

And that was the basic shift, making it minor?
Yeah. And I play it more like a dirge. And I think it's more effective that
way myself. I think it makes the words more effective.

**That song was written by Jimmy Davis, who was the Governor of Lou-
isiana?**
Yeah. I think he's still alive. Somebody told me he's still playing.

**Another song that you didn't write but that you are very famous for is
Willie Dixon's "Seventh Son." When did you first hear that song?**
When I first started recording and I hadn't written many songs, I was looking mainly at the country blues section to try to get some material. And I ran
across that down south in one of those blues record stores. And I thought that
that was a great song of that type. One of the common things is to feel that
you are supernatural sometimes. And most people have felt that at one time or
another in their life, I think. Felt that they were really the seventh son. So
right away I knew I wanted to do it.

When I first started doing it, it probably got me through some of the early
years. It was one of the tunes that everyone wanted to hear.

That's one of the essential attitudes. That's another thing I'm looking for:
basic essential attitudes. And so, you have to get both ends of the thing, de-
spair and elation. And that's on the elation end.

**Speaking of the supernatural, do you have any idea where your ideas
come from?**
You wonder yourself. A lot of things just pop into my head, you know?
[*Laughs*] I used to say jokingly that I was just another middle-class white boy

out trying to have some fun. And I never thought I'd make a song out of it. [*Laughs*] Nowadays I see how, usually, when I start saying something like that, it probably will end up as a song.

Do you ever go through periods when you get no new ideas?

Oh yeah. I'm in a period right now where I don't even want to bother with them. Because I just finished a record and recording for me is a real survival test. It takes so much out of you. But I have a lot of ideas. And I have one new song called "The Getting Paid Waltz." [*Laughs*] And I'm already doing that one.

Do you have any technique for keeping in shape creatively?

I think the best thing to keep you in shape creatively is to keep yourself in shape physically. I run, I swim, I do whatever I can to try to keep myself together. If I don't exercise, I feel miserable. But it's hard to tell. Feeling miserable, sometimes something comes out of it.

But there's no formula for it. That's one thing I've learned: There's no formula for it. That's something that jazz players always find out eventually, too: There's no formula for playing well. You don't know what's gonna make you play well. Some nights you feel like you are Superman or the seventh son and you can do anything. Other nights it's just hard labor, man. You wish you were somewhere else. And you're just trying to get something going and you can't.

And the irony is that sometimes when you felt terrible playing, you listen back to it three weeks later and it might sound better to you than one on the nights when you thought you were playing great. So it's very subtle. I've always said that it never sounded as good to me as it *felt*.

Do you like to wait for inspiration before you work on a song?

I like to let it become stronger and stronger. And then maybe some other song you hear might have a form that you hadn't thought of for that particular phrase. A lot of things might help you along.

I'm interested in the universal aspect that the blues has. And I think it is related to folk music from around the world. I have a record from Java, man, and certain elements of it sound like a blues picnic in Louisiana or something. [*Laughter*] I'm interested in those kinds of things, the really fundamental, essential, universal things.

I assume that, given your distaste for the backbeat, you don't listen to much pop or rock music.

If you want to run me out of a room, just play anything that has that heavy backbeat. [*Laughs*]

You must simply loathe all this drum-machine music we hear, which is even more mechanical sounding than a person playing a backbeat.

Well, you know, I think it just detracts from the music. I've heard some good bands that I thought were destroyed completely by the soundman's overemphasis on the bass and the drums. The musicality is completely wiped out by all this excess of low sound.

Of course, I've heard the theory that it's the heartbeat, it's the heartbeat. Young people want their hearts stimulated. [*More laughter*] The sonic massage.

I think that's a discredit to any music, when you completely obliterate it with excessive sound.

Whatever happened to old-time listening to music? Now you don't listen to music, you go out and sit in the highway and let yourself be run over by an eighteen-wheeler. [Laughs]

Some of the ideas in today's songs are okay, but what I don't like is that everything is turned into a march. Most of the songs these days, the pop songs, the money songs, are marches. You know, I was in the army. [Laughs] I marched a lot. And that's another thing that's so ironic to me, that young people would end up with a beat that sounds like a march. [Laughs] It's a march, man, it's regimentation. And that's not what I'm after at all.

I'm interested in blues and jazz. And if you listen to the early Muddy Waters or people like that, you won't hear that heavy backbeat in what they were doing. Because they didn't have drummers in the first place. And they played a rhythm that I still like to play myself, the shuffle, which I feel is one of the basic things.

Is it hard for you to find drummers who can play the way you want them to?

Not really. A lot of drummers are *relieved* when you tell them that. Drummers have a word for those kind of gigs. They're the "sawdust" gigs. The reason it's called that is because they knock so much wood off the sticks that a little pile of sawdust collects by the drum. You burn up a lot of wood doing that. [Laughs]

Stravinsky once said about jazz that it has beat but it doesn't have rhythm. If you emphasize one beat all night, then you remove the flexibility of the rhythm.

Do you have musicians stashed all over the country?

Oh yeah, sure. They know me now. When I get a new drummer now he'll say, "I heard about it. I heard you don't like backbeats."

And no high-hat on two and four?

Well, I don't mind that if they keep it down, you know, as part of the flow. I don't like it with the stick out. You know, boom-chick, boom-chick ... it's like a metronome.

And a lot of that is based on the old idea of the drummer as timekeeper, which is outmoded completely. The drummer isn't the timekeeper. Everybody is the timekeeper in jazz. Any jazz player who is a good jazz player is his own timekeeper. He can keep time or else he wouldn't be able to play jazz. Any jazz player who doesn't have his own time is in trouble.

So you don't have to have somebody ticking away back there like a metronome. The drummer is supposed to be back there to respond to what the soloist is playing and embellish it in ways. He should keep a rhythmic flow going, but he doesn't have to try to dominate it or get it into one groove. And also, it's a matter of laziness. It's very easy to play a rim shot on two and four. You don't even have to think.

Do you have a favorite song of your own?

Not really. I used to say that the one you're working on is your favorite. And that's true to a certain extent. But I do have favorites over the years, you know. Some of the better ones I think are "Hello Universe," "I Feel So Good It Must Be Wrong," "If You Only Knew," and "Everybody's Crying Mercy." I like ones that stand up. The ones that I do every night, those are among my favorites.

You always want to write the perfect song. I still want to write the perfect song. It would be nice if I had already written the perfect song. But that remains to be seen. But no one will ever write the perfect song, I don't guess. I'd just like to write one that has all the elements of what I'm trying to do. And I'm working on it. I'm always working on it.

* * *

Dave Brubeck
Santa Monica, California 1995

At this point in his life, sitting outside at a sunny Santa Monica hotel, Dave Brubeck is one of America's few living legends of jazz. Most famous for a song that he didn't write but did inspire, "Take Five," written by his cohort Paul Desmond on Brubeck's suggestion, this master of the keyboard is in town to perform with his quintet at the Hollywood Bowl, a venue he's not crazy about. "You can't hear anything at the Bowl," he said softly, while munching on almonds and drinking bottled water. "The distance between the audience and the musicians is much too great."

It's that distance that he's been trying to overcome over the years, convinced that the public, much more than the honchos of the record companies who often call the shots, can appreciate all the complexity and richness his music can hold. When it was time to put out his now classic *Time Out* album, featuring the famous "Take Five" in 5/4 time and other pieces in odd time signatures, the record company told him it would never fly, since it's impossible to dance to anything outside of a strict 4/4 meter. They were obviously entirely wrong—the album became the biggest success of Brubeck's career, and he gained the wisdom that has guided his career: follow the music first wherever it leads. All else is secondary.

His mother played the piano when he was in the womb and this prenatal exposure to real music might well have altered his consciousness. "My mother was a very fine pianist," he remembered with a warm smile that surfaced when talking of his mother and his brother, "and then she decided to teach instead of trying to concertize. She never stopped playing—she was either teaching or practicing, even when I was in the womb. I learned the best piano literature from her 24 hours a day. It certainly had a big influence on me."

He was born in Concord, California in 1920, a good 3000 miles from his current Connecticut home, and raised on a 45,000 acre cattle ranch in Ione. "I was actually thinking of being a cattle-man back then," he said. "But chemistry and zoology were too difficult and music seemed easier so I switched!"

He attended the College of the Pacific as a music major although vision problems (one eye is crossed) kept him from learning how to read music. "Strangely enough," he explained, "I could write music down, and that helped me to read gradually. It took me a long time to admit to this problem because I knew it would disgrace my mother, and my whole family." In 1942 he left music for the war, returning four years later to continue his studies with Milhaud at Mills College in Oakland. It's there that he formed his first group, an octet. As the years progressed, that group became a trio and eventually the famous quartet with which he earned his fame.

Many myths about Brubeck have sprung up over the years. One, no doubt deriving from the Satie and Debussy influences in his compositions, not to mention his studies with the composer Darius Milhaud, is that he began as a classical pianist before branching out into jazz. It's not true. In college he studied composition, theory, and ear-training. Piano was a compositional tool for him at first; his time was devoted to creating his own music, rather than playing that of others.

Brubeck became world-famous as the leader of the Dave Brubeck quartet, featuring Paul Desmond on alto sax, Eugene Wright on bass and Joe Morello (starting in 1956) on drums. Their music, as defined mostly by East Coast journalists, became the epitome of the "cool" West Coast jazz sound. Disbanding the group in 1967 so that he could focus on composition, these days he does everything from performing with his quintet, writing songs, suites and ballets, and performing with symphony orchestras.

With the rushing water of a nearby fountain lending some liquid percussion to our talk, the white-haired Brubeck spoke with great fondness of his family and fellow musicians. But his tone turned angry as he discussed the narrow-mindedness of most music business execs and the gaps in their thinking which prevail to this day.

Did you ever want to be a classical pianist like your mother?
Never. I was very much against it. I liked it but I didn't play it well. I didn't try very hard. I was interested in jazz.

Do you remember the first jazz that affected you?
Fats Waller, and Billie Kyle Trio, Teddy Wilson, Art Tatum, Duke Ellington. I'd listen to them on the radio. And then—do you remember the Del Horton band? They used to rehearse at our house in Stockton. He was also in the Gil Evans band. He was an arranger. So I heard a lot of good jazz. He was a jazz drummer. My other brother was a composer. Both of them have passed away.

When you started playing jazz, it was all by ear?

Oh yeah.

Did your mother want you to stay in the classical field?

Yes. But she finally gave up. Because it was something I wasn't too adept at and I wasn't interested in.

Is it true that you can write down music but that you have trouble reading it?

Yes. Very true. To this day I'm not a good reader but I can write quickly. I can't figure it out so don't ask me why. I didn't have any trouble playing jazz. I could play a piece I heard a few times usually.

When you embraced jazz, did you look at it as a pianist or as a composer?

Started as a pianist and then gradually I wanted to write more and more. I spent a lot of time arranging for dance bands and then my quartet, trio, octet, and now symphony orchestras I write for.

Do you enjoy writing for an orchestra as opposed to a small combo?

Oh yes. It's a lot more work. But when you hear the full orchestra it's a lot more satisfying I think. Although it doesn't make that much difference. If something is well played and it comes off, I don't care whether it's orchestra or solo piano, the quartet or what.

You studied composition with Darius Milhaud?

Yes. That was just before the war in 1942 and then I was gone for four years and then went back to study with him at Mills College in Oakland.

What kind of pieces were you writing with him?

I would write small piano pieces. Sometimes two-piano pieces. Sometimes for a small orchestra like a ballet.

Did you write for yourself as the performer?

Yes. Or sometimes the students would play my two-piano music. It was a very good girl's school with many wonderful young players, especially in the piano department. I would often write for two young ladies who would play my piano music. They played better than me.

At that time at Mills, the octet was there, which were G.I. students who could go to a girl's school after the war. Milhaud decided that we should write our fugues and counterpoint for the jazz musicians and out of that came the octet and then he asked us to play for the girls at assembly, and that was very successful. So my thoughts were largely with the octet and with composition for the octet or piano composition.

Did you write your music for the octet on the piano?

I usually, in those days, wrote everything at the piano. Today I write on airplanes and everywhere. Writing at the piano is where Stravinsky did all his writing, so I guess it wasn't a bad thing to do.

Do you write a melody first, or do you ever start with a rhythm or a set of chord changes?

I start all different ways. If I'm doing an oratorio, I look at the words and try to match a melody and an emotional response to the words. I just wrote a piece based on the speech of Chief Seattle, so I used Native American rhythms, to some extent, and melodies, and the orchestrations have a feel of Native American orchestration. It uses percussion—rattles and things—and cello, which is not Native American but which seems to work. And bassoon and string bass. And two flutes. And the two flutes really work well to set up a Native American sound. We recorded that with the Greg Smith singers. I hope to have it out someday soon. It's called "Earth Is Our Mother."

Is there piano in it?
There can be. I've left room for myself. I might mean to do it without piano. We'll see.

You're known in your solos for being more rhythmic than melodic—
There's a lot of melodic things that people don't know. I don't think you can get much more melodic than the "Over the Rainbow" I did in 1951. It's about as melodic as anyone got and as soft as anyone plays jazz piano. So these pigeonholes that people attempt to put me in, I can always tell you that they're not true.

So that's not an accurate representation of your style, that it's more rhythmic than melodic?
It's there, sure. But the other is there, too. You see, I believe you should approach playing through all the emotions and all the sensibilities. The piano was originally called pianoforte, which means loud and soft. And that's the way I approach it. If you look up in orchestration books, the piano is often found to be in the percussion section. So what's it doing there if you're not supposed to be percussive? [*Laughs*]

It seems that your use of rhythm is one of the most influential parts of your work. When you did "Take Five," it was pretty unheard of at the time to have a piece in 5/4 time, wasn't it?
Right. Yeah. And then we did things in seven, in six. Have you heard the boxed set on Sony? The first track, "1946," is in six. Which probably hadn't been used before. I mean in jazz. So I started early using odd meters that weren't odd in classical music. But most of jazz—I'd say 99 per cent—was in 4/4.
When I first used waltz time, I'd never heard any other jazz players use the waltz. And then I found Fats Waller's "Jitterbug Waltz," and so he beat me. But I didn't know it. So I thought I was the first. . . . Dangerous to think you're ever first. [*Laughs*] You'll find somebody long before you who did it.

"Take Five," though, is certainly the most famous jazz piece in five.
Oh, for sure. It's still the most played jazz tune, maybe in the world. Oftentimes I'll see a poll where a radio station has asked listeners to name their number one jazz favorite and "Take Five" usually wins. And "Take the A Train" is usually second. So if you can be above "Take the A Train" you know it's pretty well known.

Is it true that you suggested to Paul Desmond that he write some tunes in 5/4 time?
Not some tunes. That he write *a* tune. And use Joe Morello's beat. It was

Joe's rhythm that I told Paul to put a melody over. So Paul put a couple melodies. But he didn't have a tune. He just had two melodies. He said, "I can't write a tune in 5/4," and he had given up. I said, "You've got two good melodies here, let's work out a form." So I worked out an A-A-B-A form and Paul caught on immediately. And that's the way the tune came into being.

When you first heard it—that A section especially—did you know that was a great one?

Nobody knew that. Especially Joe Morello. [*Laughs*] If he knew how far that beat was going to go—you've heard people like Lalo Shifrin use it, and in TV shows, and it's used constantly, all day long. Right here in this city you hear people using the rhythm of "Take Five." That Delta commercial for their airline terminal. They had somebody write just a slightly different melody over that rhythm. When I listen to the TV I'll hear another way it is used. It's been used so much it's *incredible*. Just the ideas of something being in five was really revolutionary. And it's still being used all over the world. There are four different commercials right now in Europe using "Take Five." [*Laughs*] Yeah, right now.

That melody makes the five seem so natural. It's such a strong melody that I doubt most people even realize it's in five. Was Desmond brilliant in that regard or was that a fluke?

He could have come up with a lot more but he didn't. And he should have.

You knew that something in five would work?

I knew that Joe's beat would be great. After all, I was doing an album where I wanted the quartet to be in all different time signatures. And I heard Joe do this 5/4 so I asked Joe and Paul to do this 5/4. "Blue Rondo," which is in 9/8, "Three To Get Ready, Four To Go," and there was one in 6/4. But this album is still selling all over the world. It's one of the big jazz albums.

Was it at all tough for you to write or play in odd time signatures?

No. It came pretty naturally. At first it was tough. But I love to play in seven now, and five. And ten. The piece I wrote in thirteen, I was always glad when that one was over because you have to really think. Sometimes you get into a bind where you've got to be on your toes so much that you can't relax.

Because you're counting?

Aw! If you start counting, you're going to lose it. You know, you've got to do these things without counting.

You've got to feel it.

I think so.

I read that when you first started playing "Take Five" with the group that you, on piano, had to really pound out the rhythm for it to work.

Yeah. The whole first session where we did "Take Five," you can hear me, I never left that rhythm. Because Joe Morello said, "Keep that rhythm going for me." And, of course, Paul wanted it to keep going. Paul is great at playing in five.

You've written and played so many great melodies in your career. Do

you have any idea what makes a melody great?

[*Pause*] I don't know. You know, if you knew, you could just always go and write one. I know that all of a sudden I can say to myself, "Boy, this is great." Like the first time I heard Satie in 1946, I thought that was some of the most beautiful melodies I had ever heard. And Ravel, beautiful.

Chopin?

Chopin for sure. And then the Italian opera is full of great melodies: Verdi, Puccini. If you grow up in a country like Italy, you must be hearing great melodies all your life. It just becomes part of you to assimilate that. And there's great Broadway show melodies: Jerome Kern, Gershwin, Bernstein. Ellington wrote great melodies.

The secret of a great melody is a secret. [*Laughter*]

That's true. You mentioned Satie, and much of the beauty of his melodies have to do with the chords and the harmony. Is that part of the greatness of a melody, how it is harmonized?

A lot of times. But it can be unaccompanied and be great. What do you think makes a great melody?

I'm not sure, which is why I ask people like yourself. It seems that some of the melodies we hear nowadays have very little movement or range, where great melodies often have a large range and some big melodic leaps or skips.

That can be part of it.

In your version of "Yesterdays," you start off with a Chopin quote.

Yeah. I can get into that kind of feeling I love. I once wrote a piece on the day after I had been to Chopin's home. I had seen his piano. That night we played this piece in Poland that reminded me so much of Chopin. What a great composer and pianist he was. And Liszt.

You knew Chopin from hearing your mother's music?

Yeah. She played all of Chopin's piano music. Great way to grow up is to hear Liszt and Chopin and Mozart and Beethoven. And from my brother to hear the jazz pieces. [*Smiling and laughing softly*] He loved Cab Calloway . . . I heard so many different kinds of music. My dad loved cowboy music, so I heard that.

Is it surprising to you that after the huge success of "Take Five" that almost all of pop music has gone back to 4/4 time and a straight, regimented rhythm?

Well, there's probably a reason for the 4/4. But you know the music that you hear in Greece and the Balkan countries and in Turkey and the middle east is so much more complex rhythmically than our music that we hear so much here. And if you hear the more difficult folk music, I'll tell you that music is so difficult I can't believe that these untrained musicians are dancing and singing in these odd times that *scare me* they're so complicated. And it's too bad that we get locked into 4/4. And I think it's largely because the population doesn't hear music from other cultures. Like when we became more aware of the Indian culture, Ravi Shankar, people like that who came here, I think it influenced our music. Some jazz was influenced by that. Some movie scores. If we had wider radio exposure to more complicated things, I think we'd catch on right away as a culture.

What do you listen to for enjoyment these days?

I love Stravinsky and Bartok. Duke Ellington. I used to love Stan Kenton and Woody Herman and Count Basie. Benny Goodman, Tommy Dorsey. See, when I grew up, the popular music that you heard all day long would have wonderful people singing like Ella Fitzgerald, Sarah Vaughan, Carmen McRae. Tony Bennett, Frank Sinatra. The Andrews Sisters. You know, popular music was some of the best jazz. It's hard to believe but it was popular. People like Louie Armstrong and Red Nichols. And there were other groups that were more complicated than, say, Benny Goodman. I just think that we aren't challenging the public with good things. After all, the public loved "Take Five." And the record company didn't want to put it out.

Oh really?

Oh really? I'll say oh really. You don't know the fights that we had to put that out.

Why didn't they want to put it out?

It wasn't in 4/4 time, just what you were talking about. That's exactly where your problems start, with the sales force. The president of Columbia records was Goddard Leiberson. He wanted to put it out immediately when he first heard it. He wanted to put out "Blue Rondo" and "Take Five" as a single. I think it took him a year and a half. The album came out but the sales people, they have formulas that are unwritten laws about what's going to work, what's going to sell. And my album couldn't have worked because it's all originals. [They said] you should never put out all originals, you have to put in some standards and some show tunes. Well, they were wrong. It worked. [*Laughs*] And you have to be in tempos that the public can dance to. Well, they couldn't dance to most of *Time Out* unless you got into some dance halls where people *could* dance to five-four and they did dance to it. So it's exposure. And also they didn't want a painting on the cover. They didn't want that. So I was breaking a whole bunch of rules. And then the album turned out to be the strongest selling album to come along in years. So they were wrong.

What you have to have people do is to challenge the record companies and music publishing companies. And they will come up to the challenge. *Time Out* is proof of that. You don't have to be always doing what the sales force thinks is going to sell. Because they don't always know. They just have a clue because the last record sold, so let's all go make another one just like that. And individuality gets killed. And people should really go back and do what they love. Usually it will turn out. It might not be immediate. It took me maybe fifteen years to get *Time Out* into my quartet again. Those ideas started in the early forties and *Time Out* came in 1958. So you have to be patient and keep pushing, keep pushing against the power that controls a lot of what people do. And too often you give up before you wear them down. And beautiful things do finally get in and get recorded and get heard by the public and then the public loves them. You just have to fight all these rules and regulations and customs and just go for your best inner thoughts and what you're really driven to do and don't give up.

After Time Out did the record company give you more support for your ideas?

Sure. They know how to support anything that's successful. We did *Time Further Out, Time In Space* and *Time In*. Part of my contract was that they had to let me do what I wanted. It doesn't mean they were happy about it. When I say the president of the company, Goddard Leiberson, was very supportive, it was the sales force that wants things to go in a certain direction. And this is wrong. It should go in the direction of the individuals who want to create something new. They shouldn't have to follow a pattern.

That still happens so much today. And often what are the biggest successes nowadays are not always the best music.

That's true. Just hope that people won't give in and still go for their highest ideals. Because that's going to inevitably be the best thing they ever do. So they're cutting themselves short if they don't hold out for that.

How did it affect you when you suddenly got that enormous success? Did it change you?

No, it didn't change me at all. I still kept doing what I wanted to do. If it had been the failure that the sales people said it was going to be, that might have affected me. I thought it might be a failure too but it was still what I wanted to do.

You were surprised that it was the hit that it was?

Oh sure. All of us were. But disc jockeys started playing it and then people started wanting it. That's the way that it happens. But if we hadn't made it the disc jockeys wouldn't have had it there to play. That's the point. You have to go ahead and give it your best shot and keep doing it. Don't give in, don't give up. I was a tough guy when somebody would tell me how to write. In fact I look back at the answers I gave people and I'm shocked that I was that brave. Well, then I'll get out of here, that kind of thing. And that's tough to do when you're struggling.

Nowadays do you listen to radio at all?

Very rarely. I don't have time. Yesterday I listened to the classical station in New York, going to the airport from Connecticut. There's no good jazz stations anymore in the New York area. There were stations you could listen to. Again it's a shame that you can't have everything available. Let us all choose whether we want to listen to jazz or not. It's a shame that New York lost a great jazz station. And it's because it didn't seem like it was as popular as western. The next day all of the jazz records were gone—they took all the jazz records out and loaded them into a big truck and taken them out during the night, and the next day all western records were put in place. The end of a great station.

You can't find good jazz on the radio, yet it's the most important music that comes out of the United States. Jazz. You know people often get very disgusted with me because I'll say, "Just look what jazz has contributed." They'll say, "What do you mean by that?" I'll say, "Just look at country music. Do you think jazz hasn't influenced that? Just look at the bandstand. See that full drum set up there? [*Laughs*] Where did that come from?" You remember Homer & Jethro? I've played concerts with them and backstage they are wailing jazz musicians.

I know Jethro Burns was great on the mandolin.

Oh, great! So the influence got into western music by a lot of great guitar players that loved jazz, whether they played western or not, they loved jazz too and their influence came into western music, what you call country today. So it's been there for a long time.

Outside of the states it seems that American jazz is understood and appreciated much more than here.

Yeah. You see, jazz really is America. Whether you're listening to a movie score or a Broadway show, that jazz influence is there in some way. Whether it was in Gershwin or Bernstein or most of the other great Broadway show writers. I still think jazz is the foundation of most of the great music that has come out of the United States. Even classical music—Copland and Charles Ives, and again, Gershwin and Bernstein—you have to give a lot of credit to jazz. Jazz that is not being played on the radio should be represented as a part of America a lot more than it is.

Do you think that can change?

It changes. Maybe through the schools. They're studying jazz a lot more and they have stage bands in schools. So there is the importance there. But I'll talk to kids and they'll say that they don't know what jazz is. And I'll say, "You're hearing it all day long. And you still don't know what it is." At least half of the commercials are using a jazz bass beat, quick piano trio in and out, and they don't know it's jazz. It's a lack of education and exposure. And so many of the TV shows use jazz. The chase scene, cops and robbers shows, usually it's a jazz band playing. But the kids don't know it's jazz. To them it's just music. Appreciation for jazz, in a very subtle way, it could come back through. Both Branford and Wynton Marsalis are doing a good job of bringing jazz to the forefront again. That's a good thing. And Dave Letterman's got some guys there who I'm sure could play jazz and often do. So there's hope that these leaders on TV shows, they can help bring it back.

I know you love the music of Keith Jarrett. Are there any other current jazz pianists that you would put in his league?

Oh, the world is full of them. Maybe not as good as Keith or Herbie Hancock or Chick Corea or Jessica Williams—

That's one I don't know, Jessica Williams—

You'll know her. She's playing great. Denny Zeitlin, do you know him? He's fantastic. There's so many guys playing jazz piano that I respect who aren't well-known that should be.

Can you describe a signature Brubeck chord?

I use polytonality. That usually identifies me. Which means you use a chord in your left hand against a different tonality-chord in your right hand. Like C major in your left hand against F# major in your right hand. That would be one, there's a lot more.

That would be quite an advanced chord, C and F# together.
Stravinsky wouldn't find it advanced. He used it years ago.

When you approach something like that do you think of it as chords, technically, or just the sound of it?
When I first started it was just the sound. Then there were other reasons that I got into polytonality. Mostly from listening to classical music and studying with Darius Milhaud, who was probably the greatest master of polytonality that ever lived.

Besides the C and F# together are there any others you can tell us?
Oh! It's unlimited! Well, always up the full step, like C and D major. It's starting to sound like a 9th chord already. But if you're thinking polytonal like I do, then the old idea of a diminished chord going in contrary motion. So if you start on C, you go to E-flat in your left hand, A major in your right hand, then you go to G-flat major in both hands, then you're on A in your right hand and E-flat major in your left hand. All those combinations work very well.

When you sit down to write, do ideas usually come easily?
It comes in all ways. Sometimes melody first, sometimes a chord progression, sometimes a rhythmic pattern. Sometimes I'll dream it. And I have sense enough to jump right out of bed and jot it down, or I'd never remember it. That's great when that happens. And don't go back to sleep!

Does that make you feel that they are gifts, that they are given to you?
Yeah, a few times. It doesn't happen very often.

Certain songwriters have said that they feel songs are like gifts, coming from somewhere beyond them.
Yeah, I can see how they could say that. Because all of a sudden it's there in your mind and you might not be at the piano and you might not even have thought you were trying to compose. You're driving a car or something and *pow*, it's there.

* * *

Tom Lehrer
Santa Cruz, California 1990

"Tom Lehrer is an entirely mythical figure, a figment of his parents' warped imagination."

from the original liner notes
to *Songs By Tom Lehrer*
written by Tom Lehrer, 1952.

As a kid I read those liner notes on the back of one of my favorite albums in my parents' collection, *Songs By Tom Lehrer*. At the time I didn't really get the joke, and I seriously wondered whether Tom Lehrer really was real or not. After all, there were never any pictures of him on any of his albums to confirm his reality. I was led to conclude that perhaps the songs of Tom Lehrer were written by committee, not unlike the way some said those Shakespeare plays got written.

Whether or not he was real, I always found his songs to be the funniest I'd ever heard, the musical equivalent of those classic Charles Addams cartoons. His songs were always askew, sometimes hilariously morbid and perverse, possessing a darkness that was thrilling to discover, especially in sunny suburbia, circa 1965.

I loved these songs even before I understood that there was more to them than the great lines and jokes. It's been a bit of a revelation to look at these

songs today and realize that besides satirizing a subject, they all satirized a specific genre of song, and used that genre to contain the humor. Lehrer never
wrote parodies, that is to say, takeoffs of existing songs. What he did instead
were takeoffs of specific genres themselves, turning them on their heads just
slightly so that one is carried in his twisted world so gently one might not even
notice it.

His songs were hilarious when first released in the fifties and early sixties,
and they are still funny today, precisely because they are so well-crafted. His
mastery of all forms of the song craft enabled him to take the conventions of
the day, such as the love ballad that professes eternal romance, and invert it in
such a way that it is the convention of the song itself that enables the humor
to succeed. An ideal example is his song "When You are Old and Gray" which
takes the conceit of undying devotion and puts it in a new light, one that's not
only connected more closely to reality than a typical love song, but which is
also set up by a brilliant use of rhyme, meter and melody:

"Since I still appreciate you,
Let's find love while we may,
Because I know I'll hate you
When you are old and gray."

An even more extreme example of his artistry and ability to transpose lyrical and musical conventions is his song "I Hold Your Hand In Mine," which
also starts with a simple romantic song idea and takes it as far in the opposite
direction as it can go. Again, the idea of everlasting fidelity has gone terribly
wrong:

"I'm sorry now I killed you
For our love was something fine;
And till they come to get me
I will hold your hand in mine."

And as extreme as this lyric is, it's the deft use of music that crystallizes
the humor, such as the romantic, heroic melody that peaks dramatically on the
word "I" in the final line of the song. Lehrer's choice of genre to attack his
subject has always been dead-on: the jazzy shuffle that is the perfect counterpoint to "The Vatican Rag," the wistful nostalgia of "My Hometown," the in-
sincere anthemic quality of maybe his most famous song, "Pollution," the
tender romanticism of "The Old Dope Peddler."

It was Pete Seeger who encouraged me to seek out Lehrer, suggesting that
he might be found somewhere within the ivy-covered walls of Harvard University. Having heard the legend that Tom was a professor of mathematics at Harvard, as well as knowing the songs he's written about both Harvard and math,
I called the university's math department, and eventually contacted a woman
who led me to the artist himself. She informed me that Lehrer teaches both at
Harvard and in California, and it was at the University of Santa Cruz that Tom
Lehrer himself was found.

He was born in 1923 and raised in New York "back when it was still wonderful. Kids could walk in Central Park at night." Though many people assumed him to be a Roman Catholic because of the expertise displayed in "The Vatican Rag," he's Jewish, but he qualified that by saying, "More for the delicatessen than the synagogue." He also said that being Jewish was a union requirement for being a comic songwriter.

He never seriously thought of music as a profession, even when he was doing it, which might be the reason his songs all sound so effortlessly conceived: he wrote them purely for fun, and when the ideas stopped coming, he figured he was done and happily continued teaching. In a note accompanying a photo of himself he said, "My early retirement was in the tradition of J.D. Salinger, Deanna Durbin and Sandy Koufax."

His first album was recorded for fifteen dollars, and distributed initally among friends at Harvard. He understimated the tremendous appeal of the songs, as he still does to an extent today, and much to his own amazement he became a successful songwriter/performer/recording artist, as detailed in the following conversation.

The following biographical notes are excerpted from the original liner notes which Tom wrote himself for his first album:

"But enough of Lehrer the artist. What of Lehrer the bon vivant, man about town, and idol of three continents (and Madagascar, where half a million gibbering natives think he is God)? At last reports he had settled in Cambridge, Massachusetts, where he spends his declining years with his shrunken head collection, his Nobel Prizes, and his memories."

In the liner notes from his second album, *An Evening Wasted With Tom Lehrer*, he elaborated further on his own myth:

"Tom Lehrer stayed on at Harvard until June, 1953 as a graduate student and teaching fellow in the field of mathematics, living simply and hoping only, like Pinocchio, to become one day a real boy."

I'm glad that we could finally find you and that you're willing to talk.
Well, talk is cheap.

You've always been especially mysterious, and one reason for that is that there was never a photo of you on any of your albums.
That was in my contract, actually. I don't like to be recognized. That's why I hardly ever did TV.

When did you start writing songs?
I think I wrote songs when I was a kid. Popular type songs. And then in college and graduate school. But mostly just for special occasions or for fun or for exercises.

Did you ever consider making music your main profession?
Oh, no. No, I was never that good. Or interested in being a performer.

What happened to cause you to make the shift from writing for fun to doing it professionally?
I used to sing these songs at parties. When I was in graduate school, they had a quartet contest. A few friends of mine and I entered this. And we were

such a success we were hired for other little things like that. Then they all got their degrees, being much more sensible than I, and people began asking me to do things. There was a small nightclub in Boston I would play at and people actually paid me money for this. And that was fine. And that seemed to be the limit of it until I made a record of these songs. It was not with the idea of selling it. I thought they were funny but that the public wouldn't get it.

I did the mathematical calculations and, as I recall, I figured I could absolutely sell 300 records. I figured if I ordered 400 I could break even at 300 and have a little profit to make some more.

So I looked in the yellow pages for custom record places, and there were two in Boston, and one was rude to me and one was nice to me, so I went to the one that was nice, and that was it. A friend drew the cover and I wrote the liner notes. Young people said to me, "You made your own record. I'd like to make my own record. How did you do that?" And I'd point out to them that the studio cost for my first record was fifteen dollars.

I sold it around Harvard on Lehrer Records. It came out in spring of 1953 and a lot of the students brought it home with them for the summer. And that's when it started. I started getting these mail orders because I put my address on the back. Then some newspaper and magazine people wrote it up and put the address in, and I started getting orders from all over.

The LP had just come in and it was cheap to do. It was on a 10-inch LP first and then when the 12-inch LPs came on, I felt a little guilty putting it on that because it was only 22 minutes long, but nobody seemed to mind. It's one of the shortest LPs ever.

One of the merits of your work is that the songs are so complete and yet they're very short songs.

I have trouble with attention span. It seems most songs just go on and on. I think a minute and a half is the optimum for a comedy song, and more than enough to get the idea across.

When the album started selling, did you change your ideas about being a performer?

No, just the opposite. I felt, "Now, I don't need to be a performer because people can buy the record." It was a great relief. I thought a real performer was Danny Kaye and I couldn't do anything like that.

I went into the army then—there was no war going on, I waited carefully until they weren't shooting people—then in those two years, the record really got around and there was a demand for it.

In those days there weren't any humorists in music, except for Victor Borge, who was really more classical. And I was asked to do half a show with Odetta. I said okay and gradually it accumulated into a whole evening.

Then I decided to quit [doing concerts] in 1959. I had done it for a few years and I used to say, "If you've been to Detroit, there's no point in going to Cincinnati." I'd been everywhere I thought I could go, including England.

I put out my second album in the fall of 1959. And then I got a chance to go to Australia and New Zealand, so I did that in the spring of 1960 and that postponed my retirement for another six months. Then in '60 I went back to school. So it was only three years that I did this, and then not very often at that.

I can understand why you didn't want to be a performer, but you're such an excellent songwriter. Why didn't you want to continue writing songs?

It didn't seem anyone wanted that kind of song and I didn't feel like going around to people saying, "Will you please sing my song?" And people would ask me to write songs and I would say, "Yeah but what about? I can't just write a song." I was writing for a particular persona, which was me, really. And that character didn't require doing anything but sitting at the piano, facing to the right. And I didn't really have any more ideas, so that was it. I'd sort of done all the types of popular songs I could do. They were take-offs of popular songs.

So it sort of all was over in 1960.

Four years went by. I was teaching at Harvard and MIT part-time. Then came this TV program called *That Was the Week That Was.* They were using topical stuff and I wrote songs for them. They asked me to perform but I didn't want to be on television, so I would send the songs in. They'd use them and sometimes they didn't. I shouldn't speak ill of people who are still alive, but they had a singer named Nancy Ames sing most of my songs, and she obviously had no sense of humor. She was hired because of her diction and her body. I would write in and say, "Please have anyone but Nancy Ames sing these songs!" But they did not heed this. When that program finally died a well-deserved death, I found I had nine or ten songs, so I decided to do another album of all of those songs. So I called the Hungry i nightclub, where I had performed years before, and asked them if I could do a couple weeks to try out the material. They said sure, and I did that and then I stayed longer. Dick Gregory was picketing somewhere and didn't want to come in, so I did a few more weeks. Meanwhile, Reprise Records bid on the album and I went back and recorded the album live at the Hungry i. Reprise was pretty adventurous; they had Alan Sherman and others then. And I made a deal that they would re-release my other albums.

So they put out my last album, which was called *That Was the Week That Was,* and took over the first two.

That was the album that had the song "Pollution" on it, which, as I recall, was somewhat of a hit then.

It was the only one that didn't offend anybody. Everybody was against pollution. Or, I should say, nobody was for pollution. The various environmental groups used to use it, and Arthur Godfrey liked it a lot and he used to sing it on his program. It was just generic, so everyone could say, "Yes, isn't that terrible?"

We used to sing it in school, and I recall then being impressed by its wit, especially compared to everything else we sang in school.

Yes, it's in a number of children's reading books and songbooks. I even saw a book about teaching Japanese children to speak English and it's in there. So that was, in a sense, a hit. Warners did put out a single but nobody bought it.

Then, basically, I quit. I did one concert in L.A. And that was my last

American appearance, and then I did a few things in Germany, Australia, Denmark, Norway. The only other things I did were some benefit concerts for totally hopeless candidates. We did that for George McGovern. Like the line in "Beyond The Fringe": "We need a futile gesture at this point." So we were doing that.

But you never felt any desire past that point to write more songs?

I never really could. I needed some deadline or something, and all the ideas I could think of were just variations on the old ideas. So, no. Nothing came of it. I never finished anything or really even tried.

Do you remember much about your songwriting process, how you used to go about writing songs?

The ideas just came. That was the thing. I could never really sit down and say, "Okay, today is all clear, I'm going to sit down and write a song." It just didn't work that way. I'd jot down ideas and jot down lines, and sometimes there'd be a line that didn't fit in for ten years. Ideas for songs would just be there, and that stopped. I'd get a title, an idea, a line that could be used somewhere, a rhyme. Once I got the idea for what kind of a song it would be, is it a waltz, a march, and where the title went, it gradually developed. Sometimes I'd get a musical idea from some song that I just happened to like. I don't consider myself an original musician. I was mostly writing "in the style of . . ." They weren't deliberately stolen.

When you would work on your songs, did you spend a lot of time editing and rewriting?

The main idea was to get a whole song done, even if it involved a dummy lyric, to get the whole song worked out, and then go back and polish and perfect. A lot of time I would get half a song and that would be it. Like "In Old Mexico," that whole middle section about bullfighting was originally another song, but I couldn't finish either of them, so I put them together.

Generally, I would try to get the whole song formed first, the rhyme scheme and all, and then go back and see if I could do better.

You're a great rhymer. Did rhyming come naturally to you?

Yeah. That's kind of fun. Just finding the rhyme isn't enough. But to have it rhyme and have it fit and also say what you're trying to say.

I think of "I Want to Go Back to Dixie" and the line: "The Southland is my nominee/Just give me a hamhock and a grit of hominy."

Sometimes you just leap out of bed with them. Yes, it's relevant, it's not just a forced rhyme. So that's exciting. But it was always designed, as Sondheim would say, to shore up the lyric. Sometimes the whole song depends on the cleverness of the words, like Cole Porter's list songs. But really it's to make things more interesting, and I think most comic songs are not interesting enough to listen to many times because there's not enough in between there, apart from the joke. You can hear a joke and once you've heard it, it's not that funny the fourth time. But if it's done really well, like one of Bob Newhart's bits or Nichols & May, then you can hear it over and over and over again and it's still funny even though you know it by heart. That problem was to pack in as many rhymes, inner rhymes, variations, not just couplets.

I think that's the reason these songs hold up so well today, even know-ing the jokes. It's the set-ups, and the use of rhymes and certain words.

I just love, every now and then, hearing an amazing word. Noel Coward was very good at that. Using some word that you don't expect to use in a song. Or when there's a real rhyme. Allan Sherman had a few: "In the archipel-ago/As everywhere a fella goes . . ." That's from "Bye Bye Blumberg."

Was writing these songs a fun process for you?

Oh yes. That's why I couldn't really sit down and do it as a chore: "I've got to write a song today; I owe it to society to write a song." No. It was fun once I got the way the song was going to be formed. The topic isn't enough. People say, "Look at all the funny things that are going on." I can always pick up the paper and see a topic but how do you make that into a song? That was always the hardest part, not just having a one-liner. If I had a one-liner, I could use it in the spoken introduction. But you can't make a whole song, particu-larly, unless there's some larger form.

I could do it then and I don't seem to be able to do it now.

Is is surprising to you at all how extremely relevant most of these songs are today?

Yeah, it's surprising but it's sad. A friend of mine used to say, "Always pre-dict the worse and you will always be hailed as a prophet." It's true. Practically all the subjects that were dealt with, of any consequence, are still around. I don't think anything's gotten better. There's been some improvements in tech-nology but I think those only benefited the people who were already well-off. So it hasn't cut down on pollution. And maybe the nuclear threat is less from some quarters but it's greater in others.

Nothing has changed. Certainly, brotherhood has not advanced.

I think of "The Old Dope Peddler."

That has a different slant now than it did, which is kind of interesting. I wrote it in 1948 when the idea was to take some really reprehensible member of society and write a song about it in the style of "The Old Lamplighter" and "The Old Umbrella Maker." I thought of doing "The Abortionist" but at that time that was too touchy. So "The Old Dope Peddler" was fine because neither I nor anyone I knew actually has any experience with dope. That was some-thing that jazz musicians used. So it was okay. But then twenty years later, and forty years later, it has a whole different meaning and you've got to be more careful. Certainly today you can't make light of it the way I made light of it.

Another one of my favorites of your songs is "Lobachevsky."

That was based—stolen from, actually—a number that Danny Kaye used to do called "Stanislavsky." I had this idea, again just for academics, to take the basic form of the song. So I chose the name "Lobachevsky" only because I needed a name that would match Stanislavsky. He was a famous mathemati-cian, but I had no reason at all to suspect that he had anything to do with plagiarism. Turned out, many years later, he was accused of plagiarism. But he was cleared of that.

In the years since you've released your albums, other writers such as Randy Newman have come along using the untrustworthy narrator that you

have used. Your song "I Wanna Go Back to Dixie" can be seen as a pro-
totype of songs he's written, such as "Rednecks."

He's really fierce. His songs are much stronger than mine. I think he's
marvelous, and one of the few current songwriters I really admire a lot. But his
are much nastier than mine. He really gets into the character in a way that I
couldn't do. I think "I Wanna Go Back to Dixie" is a little literate for that
character. It's like preaching to the Northerners. I think I was in my own character more throughout these songs, the smart-aleck college student with a bow-
tie being clever, as opposed to really getting into it.

Are there other songwriters that you admire?

I don't like abstract poetic songs. I like comic writers, but there haven't
been many of them. Randy Newman, Paul Simon has written some songs that
are funny. Loudon Wainwright is good. Dave Frishberg is probably the leading
one that comes to mind. He's also a great respecter of rhyme, which neither
Randy Newman nor Paul Simon or Paul McCartney or anybody cares about as
much. I don't rhyme "home" with "alone." Frishberg is great: "I remember
Notre Dame where we got to meet the hunchback/and that dimly lit cafe
where we had to send the lunch back . . ." Things like that. There are very
few. I like some theater writers: Sondheim, of course.

**Your introduction to "Clementine" was very funny when you said that
the reason most folk songs were so atrocious is because they were written
by the people. If professional songwriters had written them, you said, they
would have been better.**

Yeah. That's very elitist. But that's the way I feel. In the '50s, and you
were spared this, I had to sit through these parties where people would bring
out their guitars and compete with who knew the most verses, all these illiterate songs. It was similar to college students in the '60s writing songs that would
say, "I ain't got no," which they never would dream of saying in ordinary conversation. But it made them feel more down-to-earth, so there was a kind of
inverse snobbery where you don't want to speak good English. And I've always
been in favor of good English wherever possible, unless there's a reason, such
as if you're playing a character.

Do you recall writing "The Vatican Rag"?

Originally I had some idea about doing a song about religious rituals in the
style of "Balling The Jack" or "Hokey Pokey." I had this title, "The Presbyterian
Rag" which I thought had a wonderful ring to it. But unfortunately, when I
looked into it, there wasn't enough Presbyteriana there to work with, and even
if there was, nobody else would understand it. Then I thought of "The Roman
Catholic Rag" but that seemed a little too clinical somehow. Then I thought of
"The Vatican Rag" which identifies what it is but without being too direct.
Then it was just a matter of digging up enough to fill it out with.

I learned the word "genuflect" from hearing that song.

Yeah, a lot of people said that. A number of people thought that I must be
Catholic because only Catholics know these words. "Liturgy" they think is
some arcane word that only people in the brotherhood know. I do think most
people don't know what "transubstantiate" means. I learned that in school and

I was quite amazed.

Your song "The Elements" lists the entire table of elements. Was that tough to write?

Danny Kaye, who was my idol, was my model for a lot of these. He did a song in *Lady In The Dark* called "Tchaikovsky" that was a list of fifty Russian composers that Ira Gershwin wrote the words to, and Kurt Weill wrote sort of a melody to. I was too young to see the show but the lyrics were printed in *Ripley's Believe It Or Not*. So I learned it and practiced doing it really fast. I used to do it at parties. And it used to go over so well, even though it had no meaning, it was just a tongue-twister. So I thought, "Well, if that goes over well, why don't I find another list?" So I tried the states of the union, but there weren't enough rhymes. And then I tried the United Nations, but again it didn't fit together. Finally I came up with the idea of the chemical elements, and tried writing an original tune. It was clearly a Gilbert & Sullivan type of tune, so I deliberately set it to "The Major General" song instead of trying to write a poor Gilbert & Sullivan tune. It wasn't tough to write once I had the idea. I rewrote it once when they discovered new elements, and there have been many discovered since then but I can't fit them in. As of 1959, it was correct.

"My Hometown" is another song that gets even better with the passing of time.

That was a reaction to a song called "Dear Hearts and Gentle People" and there were several songs around that time about that nostalgia for a small town. So I thought that I'd use a tune that was deceptive. It's kind of a pretty tune.

There are a couple of lines in that song that you leave out—

Yeah. People always ask me about that. I think there were some lines, but nothing that wasn't too crude. Again, it was too direct so I decided that I couldn't really think of anything that wasn't better than leaving it to the imagination. In my songbook I wrote that there will be a prize for anyone who comes up with some lines, and I did get a few entries. But none as good as leaving it out.

It's very funny, trying to figure out what you had in mind.

Yeah, I think that's what makes it more interesting than if I made it more explicit.

Another favorite—actually, they're all favorites—is "When You Are Old and Gray."

It was funny when I was twenty-one when I wrote it. [*Laughs*] But it's not that funny anymore. That was based on this romantic idea from all these songs that if you're in love, you're going to be in love forever. The divorce rate was soaring and people clearly don't go along with that anymore. I decided I would go all the way there.

It's got a great use of inner rhymes.

That's what I think makes it bearable. Just "you're gonna get fat and old" is not sufficient.

Did you ever write any songs that weren't humor songs? I ask because it's evident that you had a real mastery of the song form.

I could write in that form. I look back at the first record and I'm embarrassed by how many of the songs were AABA. It was just so obvious. But in that day most songs were that way, so it wasn't as obvious that the songs were alike. But now I wouldn't want to do that many in that form.

When I was much younger, I used to try and write pop songs. I was writing nice, pretty tunes and acceptable, generic love lyrics that people were writing then. I realized that they were perfectly good, but there was no reason anybody would buy them or want to sing them.

That's one of the bits of advice I can offer to young people who listen to the radio and say, "I can write a song as good as that." They really don't need anyone to write songs as good as that. They already have people to do that. And they're doing it. So you have to have something that's a little different. Not necessarily better, but different.

* * *

Bob Dylan
Beverly Hills, California 1991

"I've made shoes for everyone, even you, while I still go barefoot."

from "I and I" by Bob Dylan

"Songwriting? What do I know about songwriting?" Bob Dylan asked, and then broke into laughter. He was wearing blue jeans, a white tank-top T-shirt, and drinking coffee out of a glass. "It tastes better out of a glass," he said, grinning. His blonde acoustic guitar was leaning on a couch near where we sat. *Bob Dylan's guitar.* His influence is so vast that everything that surrounds him takes on enlarged significance: *Bob Dylan's moccassins. Bob Dylan's coat.*

Pete Seeger said, "All songwriters are links in a chain," yet there are few artists in this evolutionary arc whose influence is as profound as that of Bob Dylan. It's hard to imagine the art of songwriting as we know it without him. Though he insists in this interview that "somebody else would have done it," he was the instigator, the one who knew that songs could do *more*, that they could take on more. He knew that songs could contain a lyrical richness and meaning far beyond the scope of all previous pop songs, that they could possess as much beauty and power as the greatest poetry, and that by being written in rhythm and rhyme and merged with music, they could speak to our souls.

Starting with the models made by his predecessors, such as the talking blues he learned from the songs of Seeger and Woody Guthrie, Dylan quickly discarded old forms and began to fashion new ones. He broke all the rules of songwriting without abandoning the craft and care that holds songs together. He brought the linguistic beauty of Shakespeare, Byron, and Dylan Thomas, and the expansiveness and beat experimentation of Ginsberg, Kerouac, and Ferlinghetti, to the folk poetry of Woody Guthrie and Hank Williams. And when the world was still in the midst of accepting this new form, he brought music to a new place again, fusing it with the electricity of rock and roll.

"Basically, he showed that anything goes," Robbie Robertson said. John Lennon said that it was hearing Dylan that allowed him to make the leap from writing empty pop songs to expressing the actuality of his life and the depths of his own soul. "Help" was a real call for help, he said, and prior to hearing Dylan it didn't occur to him that songs could contain such direct meaning. When I asked Paul Simon how he made the leap in his writing from fifties rock & roll songs like "Hey Schoolgirl" to "The Sound of Silence" he said, "I really can't imagine it could have been anyone else besides Bob Dylan."

There's an unmistakable elegance in Dylan's words, an almost biblical beauty that he has sustained in his songs throughout the years. He refers to it as "gallantry" in the following interview, and pointed to it as the single thing that sets his songs apart from others. Though he's maybe more famous for the freedom and expansiveness of his lyrics, all of his songs possess this exquisite care and love for the language. As Shakespeare and Byron did in their times, Dylan has taken English, perhaps the world's plainest language, and instilled it with a timeless, mythic grace.

As much as he has stretched, expanded and redefined the rules of song-writing, he's a tremendously meticulous craftsman. A brutal critic of his own work, he works and reworks the words of his songs in the studio, and even continues to rewrite certain ones even after they've been recorded and re-leased. "They're not written in stone," he said. With such a wondrous wealth of language at his fingertips, he discards imagery and lines other songwriters would sell their souls to discover.

He was born Robert Allen Zimmerman on May 24, 1941 in Duluth, Min-nesota. Inspired by the writing and music of Woody Guthrie, he moved to New York in 1961 ostensibly to meet Woody, who was suffering in a New Jersey hos-pital from the illness that eventually took his life, Huntington's Disease. Mar-jorie Guthrie, Woody's wife, told me that Dylan was a nice enough kid, and quite respectful of Woody, but she didn't like his singing, and suggested he try to better enunciate the words to his songs.

More impressed than Mrs. Guthrie was the producer John Hammond, who heard Dylan sing at Gerde's in Greenwich Village, and signed him to a record deal with Columbia. Though his debut album contained only two original songs, including his tribute to Guthrie, "Song To Woody," by the second album he'd already written classics such as "Blowing In The Wind" and "Masters Of War," manifesting the new potential inherent in popular songs.

He went on to change the world and bend our minds with successive mas-terpieces, including such classics as *The Freewheelin' Bob Dylan, Blonde On Blonde, Nashville Skyline, The Basement Tapes* [made with The Band], *John Wesley Harding, Blood On The Tracks, Desire, Oh Mercy* and much more.

"It's too much and not enough," he said, in reference to the extended nature of many of his songs. The same could be said of any attempt to express the full impact of his greatness in words. Such an attempt would take volumes and still be lacking, as the countless books on the subject attest. Suffice it to say that, like the writing of Shakespeare, the full significance of Dylan's work may not be understood for centuries, at which time scholars might very well look back in wonder that one man could have produced such an immense and amazing body of work.

"Yes, well, what can you know about anybody?" Dylan asked, and it's a good question. He's been a mystery for years, "kind of impenetrable, really," said Paul Simon, and that mystery is not penetrated by this interview or any interview. Dylan's answers were often more enigmatic than my questions, and like his songs, they offer a lot to think about while not necessarily revealing much about the man.

In person, as others have noted, he is Chaplinesque. His body is smaller and his head bigger than one might expect, giving the effect of a kid wearing a Bob Dylan mask. He possesses one of the world's most striking faces; while certain stars might seem surprisingly normal and unimpressive in the flesh, Dylan is perhaps even more startling to confront than one might expect. Seeing those *eyes*, and that *nose*, it's clear it could be no one else than he, and to sit at a table with him and face those iconic features is no less impressive than suddenly finding yourself sitting face to face with William Shakespeare. It's a face we associate with an enormous, timeless body of work, work that has changed the world. But it's not really the kind of face one expects to encounter in everyday life.

Though Van Morrison called him the world's greatest poet, he doesn't think of himself as a poet. "Poets drown in lakes," he said. Yet he's written some of the most beautiful poetry the world has known, poetry of love and outrage, of abstraction and clarity, of timelessness and relativity. Though he is faced with the evidence of a catalogue of songs that could contain the whole careers of a dozen fine songwriters, Dylan told me that he doesn't consider himself to be a professional songwriter. "For me it's always been more *con*-fessional than *pro*-fessional," he said in distinctive Dylan cadence. "My songs aren't written on a schedule."

Well, how *are* they written, I asked? This is the question at the heart of this interview, the main one that comes to mind when looking over all the albums, or witnessing the amazing array of moods, masks, styles and forms he's presented over the years. How has he done it? It was the first question asked, and though he deflected it at first with his customary humor, it's a question I tried to return to a few times.

"Start me off somewhere," he said smiling, as if he might be left alone to divulge the secrets of his songwriting, and our talk began.

Arlo Guthrie recently said, "Songwriting is like fishing in a stream; you put in your line and hope you catch something. And I don't think anyone downstream from Bob Dylan ever caught anything."

[*Much laughter*]

Any idea how you've been able to catch so many?
[*Laughs*] It's probably the bait. [*More laughter*]

What kind of bait do you use?
[*Pause*] Bait. You've got to use some bait. Otherwise you sit around and expect songs to come to you. Forcing it is using bait.

Does that work for you?
Well, no. Throwing yourself into a situation that would demand a response is like using bait. People who write about stuff that hasn't really happened to them are inclined to do that.

When you write songs, do you try to consciously guide the meaning or do you try to follow subconscious directions?
Well, you know, motivation is something you never know behind any song, really. Anybody's song, you never know what the motivation was.

It's nice to be able to put yourself in an environment where you can completely accept all the unconscious *stuff* that comes to you from your inner workings of your mind. And block yourself off to where you can control it all, take it down . . .

Edgar Allen Poe must have done that. People who are dedicated writers, of which there are *some*, but mostly people get their information today over a television set or some kind of a way that's hitting them on *all* their senses. It's not just a great novel anymore.

You have to be able to get the thoughts out of your mind.

How do you do that?
Well, first of all, there's two kinds of thoughts in your mind: there's good thoughts and evil thoughts. Both come through your mind. Some people are more loaded down with one than another. Nevertheless, they come through. And you have to be able to sort them out, if you want to be a songwriter, if you want to be a song singer. You must get rid of all that baggage. You ought to be able to sort out those thoughts, because they don't mean anything, they're just pulling you around, too. It's important to get rid of all them thoughts.

Then you can do something from some kind of surveillance of the situation. You have some kind of place where you can see it but it can't affect you. Where you can bring something to the matter, besides just take, take, take, take, take. As so many situations in life are today. Take, take, take, that's all that it is. What's in it for me? That syndrome which started in the Me Decade, whenever that was. We're still in that. It's still happening.

Is songwriting for you more a sense of taking something from someplace else?
Well, someplace else is always a heartbeat away. There's no rhyme or reason to it. There's no rule. That's what makes it so *attractive*. There isn't any rule. You can still have your wits about you and do something that gets you off in a multitude of ways. As you very well know, or else you yourself wouldn't be doing it.

Your songs often bring us back to other times, and are filled with mythic, magical images. A song like "Changing of the Guard" seems to take

place centuries ago, with lines like "They shaved her head/she was torn between Jupiter and Apollo/ a messenger arrived with a black nightingale. . . ."
How do you connect with a song like that?

[*Pause*] A song like that, there's no way of knowing, after the fact, unless
somebody's there to take it down in chronological order, what the motivation
was behind it.

[*Pause*] But on one level, of course, it's no different from anything else of
mine. It's the same amount of metric verses like a poem. To me, like a poem.

The melodies in my mind are very simple, they're very simple, they're just
based on music we've all heard growing up. And that and music which went
beyond that, which went back further, Elizabethan ballads and whatnot . . .

To me, it's old. [*Laughs*] It's old. It's not something, with my *minimal*
amount of talent, if you could call it that, minimum amount . . . To me somebody coming along now would definitely read what's out there if they're seriously concerned with being an artist who's going to still be an artist when they
get to be *Picasso's* age. You're better off learning some music theory. You're just
better off, yeah, if you want to write songs. Rather than just take a hillbilly
twang, you know, and try to base it all on that. Even country music is more
orchestrated than it used to be. You're better off having some feel for music
that you don't have to carry in your head, that you can write down.

To me those are the people who . . . are serious about this craft. People
who go about it that way. Not people who just want to pour out their insides
and they got to get a big idea out and they want to tell the world about *this*,
sure, you can do it through a song, you always could. You can use a song for
anything, you know.

The world don't need any more songs.

You don't think so?
No. They've got enough. They've got way too many. As a matter of fact,
if nobody wrote any songs from this day on, the world ain't gonna suffer for it.
Nobody cares. There's enough songs for people to listen to, if they want to listen to songs. For every man, woman and child on earth, they could be sent,
probably, each of them, a hundred records, and never be repeated. There's
enough songs.

Unless someone's gonna come along with a pure heart and has something
to say. That's a different story.

But as far as songwriting, any idiot could do it. If you see me do it, any
idiot could do it. [*Laughs*] It's just not that difficult of a thing. Everybody writes
a song just like everybody's got that one great novel in them.

There aren't a lot of people like me. You just had your interview with Neil
[*Young*], John Mellencamp . . . Of course, most of my ilk that came along write
their own songs and play them. It wouldn't matter if anybody ever made another record. They've got enough songs.

To me, someone who writes really good songs is Randy Newman. There's
a lot of people who write good songs. As songs. Now Randy might not go out
on stage and knock you out, or knock your socks off. And he's not going to
get people thrilled in the front row. He ain't gonna do that. But he's gonna
write a better song than most people who can do it.

You know, he's got that down to an art. Now Randy knows music. He knows music. But it doesn't get any better than "Louisiana" or "Cross Charleston Bay" ["Sail Away"]. It doesn't get any better than that. That's like a classically heroic anthem theme. He did it. There's quite a few people who did it. Not that many people in *Randy's* class.

Brian Wilson. He can write melodies that will beat the band. Three people could combine on a song and make it a great song. If one person would have written the same song, maybe you would have never heard it. It might get buried on some . . . rap record. [*Laughs*]

Still, when you've come out with some of your new albums of songs, those songs fit that specific time better than any songs that had already been written. Your new songs have always shown us new possibilities.

It's not a good idea and it's bad luck to look for life's guidance to popular entertainers. It's bad luck to do that. No one should do that. Popular entertainers are fine, there's nothing the matter with that, but as long as you know where you're standing and what ground you're on, many of them, they don't know what they're doing either.

But your songs are more than pop entertainment—
Some people say so. Not to me.

No?
Pop entertainment means *nothing* to me. Nothing. You know, Madonna's good. Madonna's good, she's talented, she puts all kinds of stuff together, she's learned her thing . . . But it's the kind of thing which takes years and years out of your life to be able to do. You've got to sacrifice a whole lot to do that. Sacrifice. If you want to make it big, you've got to sacrifice a whole lot.

It's all the same, it's all the same. [*Laughs*]

Van Morrison said that you are our greatest living poet. Do you think of yourself in those terms?
[*Pause*] Sometimes. It's within me. It's within me to put myself up and be a poet. But it's a dedication. [*Softly*] It's a big dedication.

[*Pause*] Poets don't drive cars. [*Laughs*] Poets don't go to the supermarket. Poets don't empty the garbage. Poets aren't on the PTA. Poets, you know, they don't go picket the Better Housing Bureau, or whatever. Poets don't . . . poets don't even speak on the telephone. Poets don't even *talk* to anybody. Poets do a lot of listening and . . . and *usually they know why they're poets!* [*Laughs*]

Yeah, there are . . . what can you say? The world don't need any more poems, it's got Shakespeare. There's enough of every thing. You name it, there's enough of it. There was too much of it with *electricity*, maybe, some people said that. Some people said the *lightbulb* was going too far.

Poets live on the land. They behave in a gentlemanly way. And live by their own gentlemanly code.

[*Pause.*] And die broke. Or drown in lakes. Poets usually have very unhappy endings. Look at *Keats'* life. Look at *Jim Morrison*, if you want to call him a poet. Look at him. Although some people say that he really is in the Andes.

Do you think so?

Well, it never crossed my mind to think one way or the other about it, but you do hear that talk. Piggyback in the Andes. Riding a donkey.

People have a hard time believing that Shakespeare really wrote all of his work because there is so much of it. Do you have a hard time accepting that?

People have a hard time accepting anything that overwhelms them.

Might they think that of you, years from now, that no one man could have produced so much incredible work?

They could. They could look back and think nobody produced it.

[*Softly*] It's not to anybody's best interest to think about how they will be perceived tomorrow. It hurts you in the long run.

But aren't there songs of your own that you know will always be around?

Who's gonna sing them? My songs really aren't meant to be covered. No, not really. Can you think of . . . Well, they do get covered, but it's *covered*. They're not intentionally written to be covered, but okay, they do.

Your songs are much more enjoyable to sing and play than most songs—

Do you play them on piano or guitar?

Both.

Acoustic guitar?

Mostly.

Do you play jazz? It never hurts to learn as many chords as you can. All kinds. Sometime it will change the inflection of a whole song, a straight chord or, say, an augmented seventh chord.

Do you have favorite keys to work in?

On the piano, my favorite keys are the black keys. And they *sound* better on guitar, too.

Sometimes when a song's in a flat key, say B flat, bring it to the guitar, you might want to put it in A. But . . . that's an interesting thing you just said. It changes the reflection. Mainly in mine the songs sound different. They sound . . . when you take a black key song and put it on the guitar, which means you're playing in A flat, not too many people like to play in those keys. To me it doesn't matter. [*Laughs*] It doesn't matter because my fingering is the same anyway. So there are songs that, even without the piano, which is the dominant sound if you're playing in the black keys—why else would you play in that key except to have that dominant piano sound?—the songs that go into those keys right from the piano, they *sound* different. They sound deeper. Yeah. They sound deeper. Everything sounds deeper in those black keys.

They're not guitar keys, though. Guitar bands don't usually like to play in those keys, which kind of gives me an idea, actually, of a couple of songs that could actually sound *better* in black keys.

Do keys have different colors for you?

Sure. Sure. [*Softly*] Sure.

You've written some great A-minor songs. I think of "One More Cup of Coffee"—

Right. B minor might sound even better.

Why?

Well, it might sound better because you're playing a lot of open chords if you're playing in A minor. If you play in B minor, it will force you to play higher. And the chords . . . you're bound, someplace along the line, because there are so many chords in that song, or seem to be anyway, you're bound some place along the line to come down to an open chord on the bottom. From B. You would hit E someplace along the line.

Try it in B minor. [*Laughs*] Maybe it will be a hit for you.

A hit is a number one song, isn't it? Yeah.

When you sit down to write a song, do you pick a key first that will fit the song? Or do you change keys while you're writing?

Yeah. Yeah. Maybe like in the middle of the thing.

There are ways you can get out of whatever you've gotten into. You want to get out of it. It's bad enough getting into it. But the thing to do as soon as you get into it is realize you *must get out of it*. And unless you get out of it quickly and effortlessly, there's no use staying in it. It will just drag you down. You could be spending years writing the same song, telling the same story, doing the same thing.

So once you involve yourself in it, once you accidently have *slipped* into it, the thing is to get out. So your primary impulse is going to take you so far.

But *then* you might think, well, you know, is this one of these things where it's all just going to come? And then all of a sudden you start thinking. And when my mind starts thinking, What's happening now? Oh, there's a story here, and my mind starts to get into it, that's trouble right away. That's usually *big* trouble. And as far as never seeing this thing again.

There's a bunch of ways you can get out of that. You can *make* yourself get out of it by changing key. That's one way. Just take the whole thing and change key, keeping the same melody. And see if that brings you any place. More times than not, that will take you down the road. You don't want to be on a *collision course*. But that will take you down the road. Somewhere.

And then if that fails, and that will run out, too, then you can always go back to where you were to start. It won't work twice, it only works once. Then you go back to where you started. Yeah, because anything you do in A, it's going to be a different song in G. While you're writing it, anyway. There's too many wide passing notes in G [on the guitar] not to influence your writing, unless you're playing barre chords.

Do you ever switch instruments, like from guitar to piano, while writing?

Not so much that way. Although when it's time to record something, for me, sometimes a song that has been written on piano with just lyrics here in my hand, it'll be time to play it now on guitar. So it will come out differently. But it wouldn't have influenced the writing of the song at all.

Changing keys influences the writing of the song. Changing keys on the same instrument. For me, that works. I think for somebody else, the other thing works. Everything is different.

I interviewed Pete Seeger recently—
He's a great man, Pete Seeger.

I agree. He said, "All songwriters are links in a chain." Without your link in that chain, all of songwriting would have evolved much differently. You said how you brought folk music to rock music. Do you think that would have happened without you?
Somebody else would have done it in some other kind of way. But, hey, so what? So what? You can lead people astray awfully easy.

Would people have been better off? Sure. They would have found some-body else. Maybe different people would have found different people, and would have been influenced by different people.

You brought the song to a new place. Is there still a new place to bring songs? Will they continue to evolve?
[Pause] The evolution of song is like a snake with its tail in its mouth. That's evolution. That's what it is. As soon as you're there, you find your tail.

Would it be okay with you if I mentioned some lines from your songs out of context to see what response you might have to them?
Sure. You can name anything you want to name, man.

"I stand here looking at your yellow railroad / in the ruins of your bal-cony . . ." [from "Absolutely Sweet Marie"]
[Pause] Okay. That's an old song. No, let's say not even old. How old? Too old. It's matured well. It's like old wine.

Now, you know, look, that's as complete as you can be. Every single letter in that line. It's all true. On a literal and on an escapist level.

And is it that truth that adds so much resonance to it?
Oh yeah, exactly. See, you can pull it apart and it's like, "Yellow railroad?" Well, yeah. Yeah, yeah. All of it.

"I was lying down in the reeds without any oxygen / I saw you in the wilderness among the men / I saw you drift into infinity and come back again . . ." [from "True Love Tends to Forget"]
Those are probably lyrics left over from my songwriting days with Jacques Levy. To me, that's what they sound like.

Getting back to the yellow railroad, that could be from looking some place. Being a performer you travel the world.

You're not just looking out the same window everyday. You're not just walking down the same old street. So you must make yourself observe what-ever. But most of the time it hits you. You don't have to observe. It hits you. Like "yellow railroad" could have been a blinding day when the sun was so bright on a railroad someplace and it stayed on my mind.

These aren't *contrived* images. These are images which are just in there and have got to come out. You know, if it's in there it's got to come out.

"And the chains of the sea will be busted in the night . . ." [from "When the Ship Comes In"].
To me, that song says a whole lot. Patti LaBelle should do *that*. You know?

You know, there again, that comes from hanging out at a lot of poetry gatherings. Those kind of images are very romantic. They're very gothic and romantic at the same time. And they have a sweetness to it, also. So it's a combination of a lot of different elements at the time. That's not a contrived line. That's not sitting down and writing a song. Those kind of songs, they just come out. They're in you so they've got to come out.

"Standing on the water casting your bread / while the eyes of the idol with the iron head are glowing . . ."
[*Blows small Peruvian flute*] Which one is that again?

That's from "Jokerman."
That's a song that got away from me. Lots of songs on that album [*Infidels*] got away from me. They just did.

You mean in the writing?
Yeah. They hung around too long. They were better before they were tampered with. Of course, it was me tampering with them. [*Laughs.*] Yeah. That could have been a good song. It could've been.

I think it's tremendous.
Oh, you do? It probably didn't hold up for me because in my mind it had been written and rewritten and written again. One of those kind of things.

"But the enemy I see wears a cloak of decency . . ."
Now don't tell me . . . wait . . . is that "When You Gonna Wake Up"?

No, that's from "Slow Train."
Oh, wow. Oh, yeah. Wow. There again. That's a song that you could write a song to every line in the song. You could.

Many of your songs are like that.
Well, you know, that's not good either. Not really. In the long run, it could have stood up better by maybe doing just that, maybe taking every line and making a song out of it. If somebody had the willpower.

But that line, there again, is an intellectual line. It's a line, "Well, the enemy I see wears a cloak of decency," that could be a lie. It just could be. Whereas "Standing under your yellow railroad," that's not a lie.

To Woody Guthrie, see, the airwaves were sacred. And when he'd hear something false, it was on airwaves that were sacred to him. His songs weren't false. Now we know the airwaves aren't sacred but to him they were.

So that influenced a lot of people with me coming up. Like, you know, all those songs on the Hit Parade are just a bunch of shit, anyway. It influenced me in the beginning when nobody had heard that. Nobody had heard that. You know, "If I give my heart to you, will you handle it with care?" Or "I'm getting sentimental over you." Who gives a shit? It could be said in a grand way, and the performer could put the song across, but come on, that's because he's a great performer not because it's a great song. Woody was also a performer and songwriter. So a lot of us got caught up in that. There ain't anything good on the radio. It doesn't happen.

Then, of course, the Beatles came along and kind of grabbed everybody by the throat. You were for them or against them. You were for them or you *joined* them, or whatever. Then everybody said, "Oh, popular song ain't so bad," and then everyone *wanted* to get on the radio. [*Laughs*] Before that it didn't matter. My first records were never played on the radio. It was unheard of! Folk records weren't played on the radio. You never heard them on the radio and nobody cared if they were on the radio.

Going on into it farther, after the Beatles came out and everybody from England, rock and roll still is an American thing. Folk music is not. Rock and roll is an American thing, it's just all kind of twisted. But the English kind of threw it back, didn't they? And they made everybody respect it once more. So everybody wanted to get on the radio.

Now nobody even knows what radio is anymore. Nobody likes it that you talk to. Nobody listens to it. But, then again, it's bigger than it ever was. But nobody knows how to really respond to it. Nobody can shut it off. [*Laughs*] You know? And people really aren't sure whether they want to be on the radio or whether they don't want to be on the radio. They might want to sell a lot of records, but people always did that. But being a folk performer, having hits, it wasn't important. Whatever that has to do with anything . . . [*laughs*].

Your songs, like Woody's, always have defied being pop entertainment. In your songs, like his, we know a real person is talking, with lines like, "You've got a lot of nerve to say you are my friend."

That's another way of writing a song, of course. Just talking to somebody that ain't there. That's the best way. That's the truest way. Then it just becomes a question of how heroic your speech is. To me, it's something to strive after.

Until you record a song, no matter how heroic it is, it doesn't really exist. Do you ever feel that?

No. If it's there, it exists.

You once said that you only write about what's true, what's been proven to you, that you write about dreams but not fantasies.

My songs really aren't dreams. They're more of a responsive nature. Waking up from a dream is . . . when you write a dream, it's something you try to recollect and you're never quite sure if you're getting it right or not.

You said your songs are responsive. Does life have to be in turmoil for songs to come?

Well, to me, when you need them, they appear. Your life doesn't have to be in turmoil to write a song like that but you need to be outside of it. That's why a lot of people, me myself included, write songs when one form or another of society has rejected you. So that you can truly write about it from the outside. Someone who's never been out there can only imagine it as anything, really.

Outside of life itself?

No. Outside of the situation you find yourself in.

There are different types of songs and they're all called songs. But there are different types of songs just like there are different types of people, you know? There's an infinite amount of different kinds, stemming from a common folk ballad verse to people who have classical training. And with classical training, of course, then you can just apply lyrics to classical training and get things going on in positions where you've never been in before.

Modern twentieth century ears are the first ears to hear these kind of Broadway songs. There wasn't anything like this. These are musical songs. These are done by people who know music first. And then lyrics.

To me, Hank Williams is still the best songwriter.

Hank? Better than Woody Guthrie?

That's a good question. Hank Williams never wrote "This Land Is Your Land." But it's not that shocking for me to think of Hank Williams singing "Pastures of Plenty" or Woody Guthrie singing "Cheatin' Heart." So in a lot of ways those two writers are similar. As writers. But you mustn't forget that both of these people were performers, too. And that's another thing which separates a person who just writes a song . . .

People who don't perform but who are so locked into other people who do that, they can sort of feel what that other person would like to say in a song and be able to write those lyrics. Which is a different thing from a performer who needs a song to play on stage year after year.

And you always wrote your songs for yourself to sing—

My songs were written with me in mind. In those situations, several people might say, "Do you have a song laying around?" The best songs to me—my best songs—are songs which were written very quickly. Yeah, very, very quickly. Just about as much time as it takes to write it down is about as long as it takes to write it. Other than that, there have been a lot of ones that haven't made it. They haven't survived. They *could*. They need to be dragged out, you know, and looked at again, maybe.

You said once that the saddest thing about songwriting is trying to reconnect with an idea you started before, and how hard that is to do.

To me it can't be done. To me, unless I have another writer around who might want to finish it . . . outside of writing with the Traveling Wilburys, my shared experience writing a song with other songwriters is not that great. Of course, unless you find the right person to write with as a partner . . . [*laughs*] . . . you're awfully lucky if you do, but if you don't, it's really more trouble than it's worth, trying to write something with somebody.

Your collaborations with Jacques Levy came out pretty great.

We both were pretty much lyricists. Yeah, very panoramic songs because, you know, after one of my lines, one of his lines would come out. Writing with Jacques wasn't difficult. It was trying to just get it down. It just didn't stop. *Lyrically.* Of course, my melodies are very simple anyway so they're very easy to remember.

With a song like "Isis" that the two of you wrote together, did you plot that story out prior to writing the verses?

That was a story that [*laughs*] meant something to him. Yeah. It just seemed to take on a life of its own, [*laughs*] as another view of history [*laughs*]. Which there are so many views that don't get told. Of history, anyway. That wasn't one of them. Ancient history but history nonetheless.

Was that a story you had in mind before the song was written?

No. With this "Isis" thing, it was "Isis" . . . you know, the name sort of rang a bell but not in any kind of vigorous way. So therefore, it was name-that-tune time. It was anything. The name was familiar. Most people would think they knew it if from somewhere. But it seemed like just about any way it wanted to go would have been okay, just as long as it didn't get too close. [*Laughs*]

Too close to what?

[*Laughs*] Too close to me *or* him.

People have an idea of your songs freely flowing out from you, but that song and many others of yours are so well-crafted; it has an ABAB rhyme scheme which is like something Byron would do, interlocking every line—

Oh, yeah. Oh, yeah. Oh, sure. If you've heard a lot of free verse, if you've been raised on free verse, William Carlos Williams, e.e. cummings, those kind of people who wrote free verse, your ear is not going to be trained for things to sound that way. Of course, for me it's no secret that all my stuff is rhythmically orientated that way.

Like a Byron line would be something as simple as "What is it you buy so dear / with your pain and with your fear?" Now that's a Byron line, but that could have been one of my lines.

Up until a certain time, maybe in the twenties, that's the way poetry was. It was that way. It was . . . simple and easy to remember. And always in rhythm. It had a rhythm whether the music was there or not.

Is rhyming fun for you?

Well, it can be, but, you know, it's a game. You know, you sit around . . . you know, it's more like, it's mentally . . . mentally . . . it gives you a thrill. It gives you a thrill to rhyme something you might think, well, that's never been rhymed before.

But then again, people have taken rhyming now, it doesn't have to be exact anymore. Nobody's going to care if you rhyme "represent" with "ferment," you know. Nobody's gonna care.

That was a result of a lot of people of your generation for whom the craft elements of songwriting didn't seem to matter as much. But in your songs the craft is always there, along with the poetry and the energy—

My sense of rhyme used to be more involved in my songwriting than it is. . . . Still staying in the unconscious frame of mind, you can pull yourself out and throw up two rhymes first and work it back. You get the rhymes first and work it back and then see if you can make it make sense in another kind of way. You can still stay in the unconscious frame of mind to pull it off, which is the state of mind you have to be in anyway.

So sometimes you will work backwards, like that?

Oh, yeah. Yeah, a lot of times. That's the only way you're going to finish something. That's not uncommon, though.

Do you finish songs even when you feel that maybe they're not keepers?

Keepers or not keepers . . . you keep songs if you think they're any good, and if you don't . . . you can always give them to somebody else. If you've got songs that you're not going to do and you just don't like them . . . show them to other people, if you want.

Then again, it all gets back to the motivation. Why you're doing what you're doing. That's what it is. [*Laughs*] It's confrontation with that . . . goddess of the self.

God of the self or goddess of the self? Somebody told me it was goddess of the self. Somebody told me that the goddess rules over the self. Gods don't concern themselves with such earthly matters. Only goddesses . . . would stoop so low. Or bend down so low.

You mentioned that when you were writing "Every Grain of Sand" that you felt you were in an area where no one had ever been before—

Yeah. In that area where Keats is. Yeah. That's a good poem set to music.

A beautiful melody.

It's a beautiful melody, too, isn't it? It's a folk derivative melody. It's nothing you can put your finger on, but, you know, yeah, those melodies are great. There ain't enough of them, really.

Even a song like that, the simplicity of it can be . . . deceiving. As far as . . . a song like that just may have been written in great turmoil, although you would never sense that. Written but not delivered. Some songs are better written in peace and quiet and delivered in turmoil. Others are best written in turmoil and delivered in a peaceful, quiet way.

It's a magical thing, popular song. Trying to press it down into everyday numbers doesn't quite work. It's not a puzzle. There aren't pieces that fit. It doesn't make a complete picture that's ever been seen.

But, you know, as they say, thank God for songwriters.

Randy Newman said that he writes his songs by going to it every day, like a job—

Tom Paxton told me the same thing. He goes back with me, way back. He told me the same thing. *Every day* he gets up and he writes a song. Well, that's great, you know, you write the song and then take your kids to school? Come home, have some lunch with the wife, you know, maybe go write another song. Then Tom said for recreation, to get himself loose, he rode his horse. And then pick up his child from school, and then go to bed with the wife.

Now to me that sounds like the ideal way to write songs. To me, it couldn't be any better than that.

How do you do it?

Well, my songs aren't written on a schedule like that. In my mind it's never really been seriously a profession . . . It's been more confessional than professional. . . . Then again, everybody's in it for a different reason.

Do you ever sit down with the intention of writing a song, or do you wait for songs to come to you?

Either or. Both ways. It can come . . . some people are . . . It's possible now for a songwriter to have a recording studio in his house and record a song and make a demo and do a thing. It's like the roles have changed on all that stuff.

Now for me, the environment to write the song is extremely important. The environment has to bring something out in me that wants to be brought out. It's a contemplative, reflective thing. Feelings really aren't my thing. See, I don't write lies.

It's a proven fact: Most people who say I love you don't mean it. Doctors have proved that. So love generates a lot of songs. Probably more so than a lot. Now it's not my intention to have *love* influence my songs. Any more than it influenced Chuck Berry's songs or Woody Guthrie's or Hank Williams'. Hank Williams', they're not *love* songs. You're degrading them songs calling them *love* songs. Those are songs from the Tree of Life. There's no love on the Tree of Life. Love is on the Tree of Knowledge, the Tree of Good and Evil. So we have a lot of songs in popular music about *love*. Who needs them? Not you, not me.

You can use love in a lot of ways in which it will come back to hurt you. Love is a democratic principle. It's a Greek thing.

A college professor told me that if you read about Greece in the history books, you'll know all about America. Nothing that happens will puzzle you ever again. You read the history of Ancient Greece and when the Romans came in, and nothing will ever bother you about America again. You'll see what America is.

Now, maybe, but there are a lot of other countries in the world besides America . . . [*laughs*]. Two. You can't forget about them. [*Laughter*]

Have you found there are better places in the world than others to write songs?

It's not necessary to take a trip to write a song. What a long, strange trip it's *been*, however. But that part of it's true, too.

Environment is very important. People need peaceful, invigorating environments. Stimulating environments.

In America there's a lot of repression. A lot of people who are *repressed*. They'd like to get out of town, they just don't know how to do it. And so, it holds back creativity. It's like you go somewhere and you can't help but feel it. Or people even *tell* it to you, you know?

What got me into the whole thing in the beginning wasn't songwriting. That's not what got me into it. When "Hound Dog" came across the radio, there was nothing in my mind that said, "Wow, what a great song, I wonder who wrote that?" It didn't really concern me who wrote it. It didn't matter who wrote it. It was just . . . it was just there.

Same way with me now. You hear a good song. Now you think to yourself, maybe, Who wrote it? Why? Because the performer's not as good as the song, maybe. The performer's got to transcend that song. At least come up to it. A good performer can always make a bad song sound good. Record albums are *filled* with good performers singing filler stuff. Everybody can say they've done that. Whether you wrote it or whether somebody else wrote it, it doesn't matter.

What interested me was being a musician. The singer was important and so was the song. But being a musician was always first and foremost in the back of my mind. That's why, while other people were learning . . . whatever they were learning. What were they learning way back then?

"Ride, Sally, Ride"?

Something like that. Or "Run, Rudolph, Run." When the others were do-ing "Run, Rudolph, Run," my interests were going more to Leadbelly kind of stuff, when he was playing a Stella 12-string guitar. Like, how does the guy do that? Where can one of these be found, a 12-string guitar? They didn't have any in my town.

My intellect always fell that way. Of the music. Like Paul Whiteman. Paul Whiteman creates a mood. To me, that creates a mood. Bing Crosby's early re-cords. They created a mood, like that Cab Calloway, kind of spooky horn kind of stuff. Violins, when big bands had a sound to them, without the Broadway glitz. Once that Broadway trip got into it, it became all sparkly and Las Vegas, really. But it wasn't always so.

Music created an environment. It doesn't happen anymore. Why? Maybe technology has just booted it out and there's no need for it. Because we have a screen which supposedly is three-dimensional. Or comes across as three-di-mensional. It would like you to believe it's three-dimensional. Well, you know, like old movies and stuff like that that's influenced so many of us who grew up on that stuff.

[*Picks up Peruvian flute.*] Like this old thing, here, it's nothing, it's some kind of, what is it? . . . Listen: [*Plays a slow tune on the flute*]. Here, listen to this song. [*Plays more.*] Okay. That's a song. It don't have any words. Why do songs need words? They don't. Songs don't need words. They don't.

Do you feel satisfied with your body of work?
Most everything, yeah.

Do you spend a lot of time writing songs?
Well, did you hear that record that Columbia released last year, *Down In The Groove?* Those songs, they came in pretty easy.

I'd like to mention some of your songs, and see what response you have to them.
Okay.

"One More Cup of Coffee."
[*Pause*] Was that for a coffee commercial? No . . .
It's a gypsy song. That song was written during a gypsy festival in the south of France one summer. Somebody took me there to the gypsy high holy days which coincide with my own particular birthday. So somebody took me to a birthday party there once, and hanging out there for a week probably influ-enced the writing of that song.

But the "valley below" probably came from someplace else.
My feeling about the song was that the verses came from someplace else. It wasn't about anything, so this "valley below" thing became the fixture to hang it on. But "valley below" could mean anything.

"Precious Angel" [from *Slow Train Comin'*].
Yeah. That's another one, it could go on forever. There's too many verses and there's not enough. You know? When people ask me, "How come you don't sing that song anymore?" It's like it's another one of those songs: it's just too much and not enough. A lot of my songs strike me that way. That's the natural thing about them to me.

It's too hard to wonder why about them. To me, they're not worthy of wondering why about them. They're *songs*. They're not written in *stone*. They're on plastic.

To us, though, they are written in stone, because Bob Dylan wrote them. I've been amazed by the way you've changed some of your great songs—
Right. Somebody told me that *Tennyson* often wanted to rewrite his poems once he saw them in print.

"I and I" [from *Infidels*].
[*Pause*] That was one of them Caribbean songs. One year a bunch of songs just came to me hanging around down in the islands, and that was one of them.

"Joey" [from *Desire*].
To me, that's a great song. Yeah. And it never loses its appeal.

And it has one of the greatest visual endings of any song.
That's a tremendous song. And you'd only know that singing it night after night. You know who got me singing that song? [Jerry] Garcia. Yeah. He got me singing that song again. He said that's one of the best songs ever written. Coming from *him*, it was hard to know which way to take that. [*Laughs*] He got me singing that song again with them [The Grateful Dead].

It was amazing how it would, right from the get-go, it had a life of its own, it just ran out of the gate and it just kept on getting better and better and better and better and it keeps on getting better. It's in its infant stages, as a performance thing. Of course, it's a long song. But, to me, not to blow my own horn, but to me the song is like a Homer ballad. Much more so than "A Hard Rain," which is a long song, too. But, to me, "Joey" has a Homeric quality to it that you don't hear everyday. Especially in popular music.

"Ring Them Bells."
It stands up when you hear it played by me. But if another performer did it, you might find that it probably wouldn't have as much to do with bells as what the title proclaims.

Somebody once came and sang it in my dressing room. To me [*laughs*]. To try to influence me to sing it that night. [*Laughter*] It could have gone either way, you know.

Which way did it go?
It went right out the door. [*Laughter*] It went out the door and didn't come back. Listening to this song that was on my record, sung by someone who wanted me to sing it . . . There was no way he was going to get me to sing it like that. A great performer, too.

"Idiot Wind."
"Idiot Wind." Yeah, you know, obviously, if you've heard both versions, you realize, of course, that there could be a myriad of verses for the thing. It doesn't *stop*. It wouldn't stop. Where do you end? You could still be writing it, really. It's something that could be a work continually in progress.

Although, on saying that, let me say that my lyrics, to my way of thinking, are better for my songs than anybody else's. People have felt about my songs sometimes the same way as me. And they say to me, your songs are so *opaque* that, people tell me, they have feelings they'd like to express within the same framework. My response, always, is go ahead, do it, if you feel like it. But it never comes off. They're not as good as my lyrics.

There's just something about my lyrics that just have a *gallantry* to them. And that might be all they have going for them. [*Laughs*] However, it's no small thing.

* * *

Paul Simon

New York, New York, 1990
Bel Air, California, 1990
New York, New York, 1993

"There is a girl in New York City
Who calls herself the human trampoline
And sometimes when I'm falling, flying,
Or tumbling in turmoil I say,
Oh, so this is what she means:
She means we're bouncing into Graceland."

from "Graceland"
by Paul Simon

These lines from "Graceland" had been haunting me for weeks before and after I interviewed Paul Simon. And I didn't quite know why, but like most of his work, they are lines that resonate deeply; you find yourself thinking about them at unexpected times. They are funny and serious, simple and complex, big and small, clear and perplexing; they work on many levels at once, as do all of his songs, and speak to the heart and mind at the same time.

When I mentioned these lines to Simon, he said that he wasn't quite sure why he wrote them, but that they occurred to him one day while walking past the Natural History museum in Manhattan. It's these kinds of lines that he values the most, as he explains in the following interview: the lines that are discoveries instead of inventions; the ones that surprise him, and surprise us as well.

The most surprising thing about Paul Simon himself may be that he doesn't have all the answers about songwriting. For any student of songwriting, the assumption that he does would be an easy one to make—there are few other living songwriters who have individually contributed as much to the art of songwriting. In the sixties, along with Dylan and the Beatles, Paul Simon expanded the potential of the popular song, both in terms of music and content. And while other songwriters of his generation have recently approached the greatness of their past work, Paul Simon has surpassed his and moved on to new possibilities.

But he has done so by always looking for new answers about songwriting and new approaches to an art that has been transformed by the impact of his own work. His songs have done everything songs can do, yet he isn't satisfied. "The thought that life could be better is woven indelibly into our hearts and our brains," he wrote in his song "Train in the Distance," and it's a truth that not only explains that specific song, but also the miraculous wonder that is Simon's career. In a world where the quality of almost everything is in decline, the songs of Paul Simon continue to flourish and to amaze.

When you ask him how he does it, how he continues to grow artistically even after having been to the musical mountaintop so many times, he answers that it's because he's still basically *interested* in songwriting and record making. It's an interest that is demonstrated by the richly reflective and thoughtful answers he offers in the following discussion. They are answers that often hold both sides of a question at once, and that demonstrate a marriage of opposites that we see instilled both in his songs and his thoughts.

"And I may be obliged to defend
Every love, every ending;
Or maybe there's no obligations now;
Maybe I've a reason to believe
We all will be received
In Graceland."

At the time of my first two interviews with Simon in 1990, he was most interested by his current approach to songwriting, a method of making a musical track first and later writing the melody and the words to go with that track. It's the method he used to create the entire *Graceland* album, arguably the most inventive and influential album of the eighties, and an album that served as a catalyst for the evolution of "world music." Simon has been making world music for years: He wrote English words to the Peruvian melody of "El Condor Pasa" back in 1969, and in 1971 went to Jamaica with his friend and engineer Roy Halee to record the reggae rhythms that became "Mother and Child Reunion" long before reggae was well known in America.

Born in Newark, New Jersey, on October 13, 1941, he was raised in Queens, New York, only blocks away from that curly-haired kid named Arthur who could charm the girls with the sweetness of his singing voice. They met backstage in a school production of *Alice In Wonderland*—Simon was the White Rabbit and Garfunkel the Cheshire Cat—and started singing together at thirteen, forming an a capella group with two sisters, Angel and Ida Pelligrini.

This was a time of musical discovery for all of them; though his dad was a musician, Paul had yet to study music at all, and learned it by doing it: "I remember the day we discovered that if each person held a different note, you could sing a chord," he said. "I'd get confused and sing the other note." He wrote his first song at this time, a doo-wop number for the group called "The Girl For Me."

When they were fifteen, realizing they sounded best on their own without the Pelligrini sisters, Paul & Artie created a duo called Tom & Jerry. Inspired by other singing twosomes such as the Everly Brothers and Robert & Johnny, they rehearsed like seasoned professionals from the start, developing a miraculous precision and vocal blend. They entered the world of rock and roll with a song they wrote together and recorded called "Hey Schoolgirl." It became a hit, and Paul and Artie started living out their dreams while still in high school, appearing on Dick Clark's *American Bandstand*. But when their next three records failed to fly, they broke up for the first of many times.

Simon went on to study English at Queens College, where he met Carole King, and the two earned extra money by recording song demos. He peripherally haunted Greenwich Village folk happenings, then being sparked by Dylan and others. "I hung around that scene," he recalled, "without really penetrating it, coming from the disadvantage of Queens." In 1964, he and Artie came together for the first time as Simon and Garfunkel, to sing folk songs and some of the new poetic, Dylan-inspired songs Simon had started to write.

They auditioned for Columbia Records and got a deal, recording the folky *Wednesday Morning 3 A.M.*, which featured an acoustic version of "The Sound of Silence" and many traditional songs. The album went nowhere at first, and figuring it was a complete stiff, Simon & Garfunkel broke up again, and Paul moved to England. While there he wrote many great songs (almost all of which he later recorded with Garfunkel), launched a solo career and recorded an album called *The Paul Simon Songbook*. In a way he was distressed when he discovered that a producer back in America had added drums, bass and Byrds-like electric guitar to the acoustic "The Sound of Silence" and turned it into a major radio hit. Returning to America, Simon united again with Garfunkel, recorded their own folk-rock version of the song and others for a new album, and stayed together for the rest of the decade, creating one masterpiece after the next: *Sounds of Silence; Parsley, Sage, Rosemary & Thyme; Bookends;* and *Bridge Over Troubled Water.*

In 1970, after the enormous success of *Bridge*, Simon and Garfunkel broke up once again, and Paul returned to his solo career, continuing to define each decade with an expanding, amazing capacity for musical and lyrical invention and a flawless attention to his craft. In the seventies came his first solo albums—*Paul Simon, There Goes Rhymin' Simon* and *Still Crazy After All These Years*. In the eighties he created *One Trick Pony* (as well as writing and starring in the movie of the same name), *Hearts and Bones* (a masterpiece of songwrit-

ing woefully under-appreciated, both by the artist and his audience), and the
astounding *Graceland*.

He was working on a second album of world music when we first spoke,
The Rhythm of the Saints, a continuation and an expansion of his process of
making the record first, before writing the songs. This time, though, instead of
going to South Africa as they did for most of *Graceland*, Simon and Halee
turned first to Brazil, for a foundation of percussion and drums, and then to
West Africa for the exuberant guitar playing of West African musicians such as
Vince Nguini, from Cameroon, and others.

This combination of the music of Brazil and Africa broke new ground as
had Simon's marriage of African music with American thoughts on *Graceland*,
forging new musical connections in the world, like synapses in the brain, that
enlarge our understanding of what a song can do. "I believe that we're all connected on this very basic, emotional level by music, rhythm and harmony," Simon said. "But how can we begin to communicate if we don't appropriate a
wider vocabulary? If you don't speak in someone else's language, how are they
going to hear you? So I'm someone who speaks . . . broken music."

Our first talk took place in a New York recording studio where Simon and
Halee were working with Vince on the guitar parts for a song then called "the
shuffle tune" and later retitled "Thelma." (As the album's eleventh song, Simon
later excluded it from *Saints* because he felt "people got tired by the time they
got to it." It was completed and included for the boxed set *Paul Simon 1964–
1993*.)

Vince sat in the control room next to Halee, his electric guitar in his lap,
and repeated intricate finger-picking parts over and over, with the patience of
a saint, until both Paul and Ray were were satisfied. To demonstrate the precise
feel he wanted on one section, Simon asked for his black acoustic guitar and
used the instrument to translate his emotions into a language much more direct than English, and was instantly understood.

A few weeks later Simon came to California, and we continued our talk in
his bungalow at the Bel Air Hotel, beneath an enormous abstract painting, as
jacaranda leaves fell from the giant trees outside the windows. Thousands of
miles away from his native New York, he was especially reflective and expansive in his answers, delving deeply and generously into the mysteries of songwriting and the evolution of his own musical history.

In 1991, I was invited to contribute liner notes to his CD-set, allowing me
to interview him again, this time at his apartment in Manhattan. We met on a
crisp and sunny November day, just a few months after his wife, Edie Brickell,
had given birth to their first child, Adrian. Simon had completed the lyrics for
"Thelma" to be included in the boxed set, and they were scrawled in a notebook on his recording console. Next to it was a book on the religion of Sante-
ria, which he pointed to when I asked him about the source of some of the
deities mentioned on *Saints*.

He had just embarked on another new collaboration—writing a musical
with the poet Derek Walcott called *The Cape Man*.

At the time the writing was going well, and Simon was encouraged by
Walcott's inclination to work quickly. "Derek told me not to worry if it comes

fast," he said. "Just because it's fast doesn't mean it's not any good. Which is just thrilling to me. Because the idea of every project taking years and years is exhausting. In advance."

The following interview is constructed from all three of these talks, conversations continued on opposite coasts, connecting east and west as his music spans the globe. It's an account of explorations both internal and external, and of songs from the sounds of silence to the roots of rhythm.

Did you and Garfunkel start singing together before you played guitar?

Yeah, I didn't play anything. Wasn't interested. I didn't want to do anything but play ball. That's what I was interested in.

Hard ball?

Yeah. Hard ball, soft ball, football. Any ball. Hockey. Street hockey. Stick ball and all ball. That's all that I was interested in.

Why did you start playing guitar?

Elvis Presley.

Your father was a professional bass player?

Yes, he was. When I was growing up he was. In his mid-fifties he retired from music, got his Ph.D., became a professor at City College in linguistics. The music of his youth was the big band era, and when he played on the road, he played with big bands. Then when he settled down and had a family, he was playing on radio stations, occasionally television shows, some recordings, club dates. That's how he earned his living.

As a kid growing up, looking at him, did the career of a professional musician appeal to you?

No. I wasn't interested. Until rock and roll.

When you wrote your first song, did you play it for him?

Yes. He encouraged me. I'm sure he didn't think very much of that but he encouraged me. He's the one that taught me the rock and roll chords—the I-VI minor-II minor-V. He said, "These songs all have the same chord structure. I'll show them to you." And he got a guitar teacher for me.

Did your dad have any other musical influence on you, or was your music and his pretty separate?

The music was separate but there was a lot about being a professional musician that he taught me, that I absorbed from watching him. Though it had nothing to do with music, he certainly gave me my attitude towards musicians and my feeling of respect and affection for musicians. Feeling that I was a musician.

That was an enormous piece of information that was very helpful for me. Because by the time we were making records, Artie and I, a group of musicians would walk in. They were going to be the guys who were going to play on your record. So the fact that I related to these guys as a group of people that you would respect and like and feel at home with came from the fact that that was my father's world. A world where guys were older musicians and I liked his friends and I liked their sense of humor, I liked their joking around.

That's how I got to see the world. I'd go on a club date with him and all the musicians, and they would go in through the kitchen and eat their meal. It was not a group of people that was highly respected except among themselves. Among themselves they had a great sense of humor and I always felt comfortable with that. That helped me a lot, I think, in dealing with musicians and relating to musicians as people, and being part of that world. It was always the world that I wanted to be in. I didn't want to be a lead singer. I wanted to be a musician.

Was being a composer and a writer part of that?

Yeah. That was in there. Artie and I grew up at the same time and on the same music, and he approached it from a whole different point of view, as a singer and not as a musician. That was a big gift that my father gave to me. Because he didn't like doo-wop music.

Did he want you to become a musician?

No, he didn't want me to be a professional musician. He wanted me to be able to play good so that I could earn some money to get through college with it. Sort of the way that he grew up. He looked at his world and said, "Well, I can see as far as I could go as a musician. So I'm not going to tell my kid to be a musician."

It's ironic how extremely successful you then became as a musician.

Yeah. That was not something that was available to him. The fact that a teen culture burgeoned and rock and roll became a field where you could make a *fortune*, was something he would have no way of anticipating. He grew up in a world where what you aspired to was to be in a good band and make a living for your family. Stardom wasn't an option.

When you started writing a lot of songs, did he respond to them positively?

Yeah, but not as a musician. Just like as a father. I don't think he felt that much about them musically. He was proud that I was making a record. In later years when my music got better, he liked it.

And you said that you spoke to him once and asked him if he wasn't proud of all that you had accomplished.

That was recently. That's not uncommon. Children will look for their parent's approval long into their adult life. A lot of people have told me that they have that kind of relationship with a parent, usually a father.

You said that one of the first things to impress you about a song at an early age was in "Earth Angel," how great that title is.

An oxymoron to a twelve-year-old, that's a pretty big thing.

Who were your first musical influences?

Well, a lot of different influences. My first songs, they were just imitations of doo-wop. The early people that I liked in doo-wop were the Moonglows and the Penguins . . . Frankie Lymon, of course. Not as a writer but those records . . . I wasn't really aware of who the writer was then. Chuck Berry, I would say he was probably the first really major influence. But I didn't really know that until later.

But these early influences, they had more to do with *sound* than words. The reason that I single out Chuck Berry is because that was the first time that I heard words flowing in an absolutely effortless way. That were not just cliche words. He had a very powerful imagery at his disposal in a lot of songs. "Maybelline," particularly, was one of my favorite Chuck Berry songs and records.

So that was the fifties, and because Artie and I started recording when we were fifteen, we learned to sing as a duo imitating a duo called Robert and Johnny. They had an interesting sound. They sang with a below-harmony which we did quite a bit. They were superceded by the Everly Brothers as soon as we heard the Everlys. But they were first. They had a hit record called "You're Mine and We Belong Together."

Then the Everly Brothers influenced us. But I guess I'm drifting into what influenced us as singers, but it also influenced me as a writer because I was imitating all those different forms.

Was there a point in your writing when you consciously made a change from writing what were essentially pop songs, such as "Hey Schoolgirl" to more artistic songs such as "The Sound of Silence"?

[*Long pause*] Well . . . I'm trying to find out if there's anyone besides Bob Dylan who could have influenced me. But I really can't imagine . . . that there was. It might not have been Dylan directly but it was the folk scene of Bleeker and MacDougal [*in Manhattan's Greenwich Village*]. But [*Dylan*] was so dominant a force in it that in a way you can attribute it to him. Although, I'm sure that he was influenced by the street, too. That scene probably influenced that kind of writing.

And I think as a writer, since my writing was very much connected to record making, that one of the things that's characteristic of my work is that I have a very strong aural recall. I really remember sounds of a lot of things. Much stronger than visual. And so I remember how records went and I can remember obscure records and what part of the record that I liked; did I like the drum sound?

These were thoughts that I had when I was fourteen. And I've kept that and really, I'm always recapitulating those early sounds in records today. *All the time*. I mean, I *doubt* that anyone could hear it but me, but I know exactly what those sounds are connected to, and they go back to adolescence almost every time.

In terms of really major influences, I don't think there's anything of really major significance past the sixties. With a couple of notable exceptions.

Such as?

Antonio Carlos Jobim. He had a big influence on my thinking.

Did you study his music?

Yeah, I studied it.

Lyrically I've had a lot of influences since the sixties. Lyrically things are going on all the time but really not in terms of making records and writing music. Since the sixties.

Even the African music I heard as something akin to fifties music. The harmonies—they're different, but that's how I first heard it—but when I actually went to get the harmonies, they were a lot more difficult than when I first heard them. They're simple chords but where they came, that was very different. But the notes and the melodies are basically major scales. And major scales are like Christmas carols and Sam Cooke, though he used the sixth a lot, the sixth of the scale.

Gospel quartets . . . that came later, but really Gospel quartets was the completion of my education that doo-wop started. Doo-wop came from Gospel quartets which I didn't know when I was thirteen years old.

Who influenced you lyrically since the sixties?
Different poets that I read. [*Pause*]
Wallace Stevens.

Derek Walcott. I read a lot of his poetry. A poet from St. Lucia. Caribbean influences, a wonderful poet.

Seamus Heaney, an Irish poet whose work I like quite a bit.

Of the English poets, I like Philip Larkin. And various other people. John Ashberry's a good poet whose work I like.

I read quite a lot of poetry. But those people all, in some way, influenced my thinking. Or allowed me to go to some place that is really was my instinct to go to anyway. Once I saw that I had a model that I could . . . absorb.

In fact, I just met Derek Walcott which was very . . . very pleasant for me. His work had a lot to do with [*Saints*] because he writes a lot about that part of the world and the Caribbean. I usually carry his stuff with me. I don't think I brought it this time but I think I brought Seamus Heaney with me . . . and a book on Yeats.

Your songs have always been remarkable in that the music and the words are equally inventive and interesting. You've always devoted as much energy to both elements.
I still think that's the crucial balance. Yeah, that's the crucial balance. I think on most of the *Rhythm of the Saints* album that I might have gone further than I should have gone in terms of sound and lyric. Now I think maybe I should be *clearer* about things. . . .

Do you think *Saints* is too complex?
No. I opted for an abstract choice if it sounded good on *The Rhythm of the Saints*. But, see, now the main thing I'm working on is a play that I'm working on with Derek Walcott. We're writing the lyrics together. So we really try to get the information into the song. And that becomes more important than how perfectly the sound matches the track. So it's more songwriting than record-making. *The Rhythm of the Saints*, I think, is songwriting and record-making but when the two were in conflict, then the record-making was what dominated.

In this period of time, though, it's songwriting because these are all songs that were written before the record was made. I only started to write songs after the record was made starting with *Graceland*. But I did it once or twice more, as with "Cecilia."

My point is that the balance—where you put that balance—is crucial in defining what kind of song it's going to be. And, you know, for certain people who are very word-oriented, you can put much more emphasis on words and lyrics and they will follow you. And other people—*most* people I think—are not word-oriented and kind of just hear an overall soundscape. And that's really the way I was writing the last two albums. That way. That was a technique I had only really begun to develop towards the end of these recordings.

Looking at *Saints* in retrospect, do you feel those are a successful group of songs, in terms of the songwriting?

I think they are probably a successful group of songs but they have the characteristic of being asymmetrical and abstract. Yeah, I think it's interesting to hear that kind of song. Especially if you've been listening to something that is very clear and symmetrical. After you listen to the abstract, well, then, it becomes something very simple and clear. You're always making the correction from the last piece of writing.

Garfunkel said once that you have a natural instinct for popularity. And throughout your career, throughout all the different kinds of music you've made, you've managed to be immensely popular. Whereas most serious songwriters don't connect with the mass culture in the way that you have. Do you think it's a natural instinct that you have?

Yeah. Yeah, maybe. Because I don't think about how to make a hit. So if something turns out to be a hit, it's not because I understood the marketplace and fulfilled a need that was out there. It was something that I went to naturally. So I guess that's a gift. That's part of a gift.

You said that it was usually your easier songs that were hits until *Graceland,* which you felt managed to fulfill your objective of making something that is both sophisticated and simple. Is that still an objective?

Yes. Yeah, of course. The easier it is for people to understand, the better it is, I think. As long as you're not sacrificing intelligence or insight or feeling in order to make it easier. If you can capture something that you feel is real and express it in a way that a lot of people can understand, that's rare and there's something about that that makes a piece have a certain kind of life. And if it enters into popular culture and it's not just about popular culture, then from a writer's point of view, that's a satisfying achievement.

Does your best work come from active, conscious thinking about what a song should say?

About what the song should say? No, not any more. Not in my writing in recent years. I don't consciously think about what a song should say. In fact, I consciously try *not* to think about what a song should say.

Why is that?

Because I'm interested in what . . . I *find*, as opposed to . . . what I'm planting. I like to be the audience, too. I like to discover what it is that's interesting to me. I like to *discover* it rather than plot it out.

So I let the songs go this way and that way and this way and whatever way it is and basically what I do is be the *editor:* "Oh, that's interesting. Never mind *that,* that's not so interesting. That's good, *that's a good line.*"

And the *most* that I can do is say, "There's a good line, and the rhyming pattern, I don't know, let me see how I will set up that line." And that's the most I'll do. To construct the first half of a thought that's the set-up to the second half.

A lot of time the whole thought comes, not connected to the thought before it in any appreciable way. And then you say, "Well, what *will* this connection be?" And by the time you get your choice of the third thought, you're off in a direction. Because *three consecutive thoughts imply direction.* They don't necessarily imply *meaning.* But they imply direction.

And I think direction is sufficient. When you have a strong sense of direction, then meaning clings to it in some way. People bring meaning to it, which is more interesting to me than for me to *tell* meaning to somebody. I'd rather offer options to people. Options that have very pleasing sounds.

So the first impression is that the sound of something is nice. You don't have to think about what it means at all. And then when you do think about it on the first level, it could mean a lot of different things.

And that's really the way I write. Where there are a lot of different meanings that are available. And *valid.* I mean, there have been people who have interpreted some of my songs in ways that I hadn't really thought of, but were absolutely valid. All of the evidence was there and it was valid. And it was more interesting, sometimes, than some of the thoughts that I had, which just happened to be from *my* life. They had a more interesting thing happen in *their* life.

I'm sure you've had the opposite happen, too, in which people come up with perverse ways to read your songs?

Well, yeah, that's true, too. But to *sustain* those interpretations, you'll find that people just have to twist themselves into a pretzel to do it. I mean, there was a whole period of time where "Bridge Over Troubled Water" was supposed to be about heroin.

Yeah. "Silvergirl" was supposed to be a syringe.

That's a tough one. It's a tough one to *prove* 'cause, of course, it's absolutely not so, so how are you going to do it?

It was said that "The Boxer" was written about Dylan. And "lie la lie" had to do with the lie of his name. Did you ever hear that one?

No, I never heard that. [*Laughs*] But, of course, that's not so, either. In fact, for me, I thought that "lie la lie" was a failure of songwriting.

You did?

Yeah. I didn't have any words! Then people said it was "lie," but I didn't really mean that it was a lie.

But, it's not a failure of songwriting, because people like that and they put enough meaning into it, and the rest of the song has enough power and emotion, I guess, to make it go, so it's all right. For me, every time I sing that part . . . [*softly*] I'm a little embarrassed.

That's hard to believe, since the song is now so much of a classic. Do you remember writing it?

All I can remember is a time on a plane, I had taken a Bible from one of the hotels, and I was skimming through the Bible, and I think I saw the phrase "workman's wages." That's all I remember from that song.

Years ago you said that "Bridge Over Troubled Water" was your best melody to date. Do you still feel that?

Well, it's a very, very strong melody. It's hard to know now, now that the song has become a gospel standard. Maybe it's a standard in pop records, I don't know, but it's certainly a standard as far as the church is concerned. So I don't know; I don't have a perspective on it anymore.

Did the music and the words for "Bridge" emerge at the same time?

Yeah, they did. The whole phrase "like a bridge over troubled water, I will lay me down," the words and the melody, all of that came [*snaps fingers*] like that.

At the guitar?

Yeah.

Did you know at the time that it was great?

Oh, yeah. You can always tell when you've got a good line.

Is it surprising to you how often that title is used incorrectly as "Bridge Over Troubled Waters" instead of "Water"? And also "Sounds of Silence" instead of "Sound of Silence"?

I can't remember myself which way it goes.

It's "Water," right?

I don't know. [*Laughs*] Maybe. I don't remember. And I don't remember, is it "Sounds of Silence" or "The Sound of Silence"? I don't remember myself. I think it's "The Sound of Silence" and "Bridge Over Troubled Water." I *think* but I don't know.

Nothing surprises me. When they brought in the *arrangements* for "Bridge Over Troubled Water," the arranger was handing out the music to the string part, and it said, "Like a Pitcher of Water." That's what he heard off the demo. So nothing surprises me.

Is it at all weird to you that your titles have become such a part of our consciousness that people use them in bizarre ways? The other night there was a story on a tabloid TV show about Chappaquidick that was called "Teddy Kennedy's Bridge Over Troubled Waters."

Well, [*laughs*] that's like the way the *Enquirer* uses them. But no, it's not weird. I mean, several of those titles or lines have become established in popular culture. "Sound of Silence." "Bridge Over Troubled Water." "Still Crazy After All These Years." "Fifty Ways . . . to do anything." "Slip-Slidin' Away."

I just saw a review of Thomas Pynchon's novel [*Vineland*] that Salman Rushdie wrote that was quoting *Graceland* all over the place. "These are the days of miracle and wonder. . . ." So a lot of that has come in. And I feel good about that. That's nice.

You described yourself when working on the *Graceland* album, sitting in a room and tossing a ball against a wall while working. What effect, if any, does that physical activity have on your mental activity?

I think it's very calming. It's like a Zen exercise, really. It's a very pleasant feeling if you like playing ball. The act of throwing a ball and catching a ball is so natural . . . and *calming* that your mind kind of wanders. And that's really what you want to happen. You want your mind to wander, and to pick up words and phrases and fool around with them and drop them.

As soon as your mind knows that it's on and it's supposed to produce some lines, either it *doesn't* or it produces things that are very predictable. And that's why I say I'm not interested in writing something that I thought about. I'm interested in *discovering* where my mind wants to go, or what object it wants to pick up.

It *always* picks up on something true. You'll find out much more about what you're thinking that way than you will if you're determined to say something. What you're determined to say is filled with all your rationalizations and your defenses and all of that. *What you want to say to the world* as opposed to what you're thinking. And as a *lyricist*, my job is to find out what it is that I'm thinking. Even if it's something that I don't want to be thinking.

I think when I get blocked, when I have writer's block (though I never think of it as writer's block anymore), what it is is that you have something to say but you don't want to say it. So your mind says, "I have nothing to say. I've just nothing more to say. I can't write anything. I have no thoughts." Closer to the truth is that you have a thought that you really would prefer not to have. And you're not going to say that thought. Your mind is protected. Once you discover what that thought is, if you can find another way of approaching it that isn't negative to you, then you can deal with that subject matter.

It's funny to me that you've written two songs called "Think Too Much" and yet you are striving not to think too much in your songwriting.

Well, the fact that I had two songs called "Think Too Much" is just a joke. I write one song called "Think Too Much," and I think, "That isn't even the way I should write it. I should write it this way." [*Laughs*] It's just another example of never letting it go and thinking too much. That's why I did two songs.

But they are two entirely different songs. One was saying, "I think too much and ha, ha, ha, it's a joke. Look at that. Maybe I think too much." That's the fast song. ["Think Too Much, A."]

Then I finish and I say, "Well, maybe it isn't a joke. Maybe the point is that you think too much and you're not in touch with what you feel. And the *proof* of it is that you've written this *joke song* about a very serious subject." So now I wrote a song that is all about feeling on the same subject. So there were two ways of approaching that subject.

Was the entire *Graceland* project an attempt to not think too much in your writing and to feel more?

Yes . . . yes. That's so. Had *Hearts and Bones* been a hit, I would never have written *Graceland*. So for me, it was a tremendous flop.

But at the same time, I was using a different technique in writing, which in a way started with *One Trick Pony*, but really, you could see clear evidence of it in *Hearts and Bones*. The language starts to get more interesting in *Hearts and Bones*. The imagery started to get a little interesting. And that's what I was trying to learn to do, was to be able to write vernacular speech, and then intersperse it with enriched language, and then go back to vernacular. So the thing would go along smoothly, then some image would come out that was interesting, then it would go back to this very smooth, conversational thing. So that was a technique that I was learning.

There was a touch of it in *One Trick Pony*. There's a song called "Oh Marion" where I wrote a line, "The boy has a heart but it beats on his opposite side." That may have been one of the earlier times when some piece of imagery was striking.

It didn't have anything to do with logic or anything. I don't know where it came from. But on *Hearts and Bones* there's more of that: "Magritte" has more of that; "Hearts and Bones" has more of it; "Train in the Distance" is in itself that kind of speech: "Everybody loves the sound of a train in the distance / everybody thinks it's true . . ." That's imagery and that's the title.

So by the time I got to *Graceland*, I was trying to let that kind of enriched language flow naturally in the course of it, so that you wouldn't really notice it as much. I think in *Hearts and Bones* you could feel it, that it was coming. You could sort of see it.

Whereas in *Graceland* I tried to do it where you didn't notice it, where you sort of passed the line and then it was over. And let the words tumble this way and that way. And sometimes I'd increase the rhythm of the words so that they would come by you and then when a phrase was sort of different, it came by you so quickly that all you would get was a *feeling*. So I started to try and work with moving feelings around with words. Because the *sound* of the record was so good, you could move feelings.

"You Can Call Me Al" seems like the perfect example of that combination of the colloquial with enriched language. The chorus is extremely conversational, set against enriched lines like "angels in the architecture, spinning in infinity . . ."

Right. The song starts very ordinary, almost like a joke. Like the structure of a joke cliche: "There's a rabbi, a minister and a priest"; "Two Jews walk into a bar"; "A man walks down the street." That's what I was doing there.

Because how you begin a song is one of the hardest things. The first line of a song is *very* hard. I always have this image in my mind of a road that goes like this [*motions with hands to signify a road that gets wider as it opens out*] so that the implication is that the directions are pointing *outward*. It's like a baseball diamond; there's more and more space out here. As opposed to like this. [*Motions an inverted road getting thinner.*] Because if it's like this, at this point in the song, you're out of options.

So you want to have that first line that has a *lot* of options, to get you going. And the other thing that I try to remember, especially if a song is long, *you have plenty of time.* You don't have to kill them, you don't have to grab them by the throat with the first line.

In fact, you have to wait for the audience—they're going to sit down, get settled in their seat . . . their concentration is *not even there.* You have to be a good host to people's attention span. They're not going to come in there and work real hard right away. Too many things are coming: the music is coming, the rhythm is coming, all kinds of information that the brain is sorting out.

So give them easy words and easy thoughts, and let it move along, and let
the mind get into the groove of it. Especially if it's a rhythm tune. And at a
certain point, when the brain is loping along easily, then you come up with the
first kind of thought or image that's different. Because it's entertaining at that
point. Otherwise people haven't settled in yet.

So "You Can Call Me Al," which was an example of that kind of writing,
starts off very easily with sort of a joke: "Why am I soft in the middle when
the rest of my life is so hard?" It's a joke, with very easy words. Then it has a
chorus that you can't understand. What is he talking about, you can call me
Betty, and Betty, you can call me Al? You don't know what I'm talking about.
But I don't think it's bothersome. You don't know what I'm talking about, but
neither do I, at that point.

The second verse is really a recapitulation of the first: A man walks down
the street, he says . . . *another thing.* And by the time you get to the *third* verse,
and people have been into the song long enough, now you can start to throw
abstract images. Because there's been a structure, and those abstract images,
they will just come down and fall into one of the slots that the mind has already made up about the structure of the song.

So now you have this guy who's no longer thinking about the mundane
thoughts, about whether he's getting too fat, whether he needs a photo opportunity, or whether he's afraid of the dogs in the moonlight and the graveyard,
and he's off in, listen to the sound, look what's going on, there's cattle and . . .

Scatterlings.
Yeah, and these sounds are very fantastic, and look at the buildings, there's
angels in the architecture. . . . And that's the end of the song. It goes
"phooomp" and that's the end.

**You mentioned the difficulty of finding a song's opening line and it oc-
curred to me that so many of your songs have classic openings. If you don't
mind, I'd like to mention a few of these opening lines to see what response
you have to them.**
Okay.

**"One-and-one-half wandering Jews, free to wander wherever they
choose . . ." ["Hearts and Bones"]**
Well, Carrie Fisher is half-Jewish, so . . . and Wandering Jew is a flower,
isn't it?

**Was it a conscious move to get Jews and Christ into the beginning of
a love song? The next lines discuss wandering together in the Blood of
Christ mountains.**
No, it wasn't conscious. [*Pause*] In fact, I thought it was actually funny.
One and one-half *anything* is funny.

**It's your only song, with the exception of "Silent Eyes," that discusses
being Jewish. And once you said that you try to keep spirituality and religion out of your songs—**
Yeah, but it seems to come in all the time. Not so much religion but spirituality.

Do you think that your Jewish consciousness has anything to do with your abilities as a songwriter?

I don't know that there's a connection, no.

I ask because so many great songwriters are Jewish—

That's so. I guess it's not a coincidence, but I don't spend a lot of time connecting the two things. But maybe their words . . . *brain and heart*, you know? I think one would have to strain to make the connection. I don't think there's an *obvious* connection, but I think everything is explainable and connected. So there's a connection, but I don't know what it is.

"Couple in the next room bound to win a prize . . ." ["Duncan"].

That song was written before I had an opening verse. Then I put the opening verse in.

"Fat Charlie the Archangel slopes into the room . . ." ["Crazy Love, Vol. II"].

[*Laughs*] I remember I liked the image of sloping into a room. It had a very clear and amusing mental picture for me. But I don't know where Fat Charlie came from, or the Archangel. It doesn't represent anyone. It's a composite of different people but *only* for the purpose of creating a character. It doesn't represent anyone.

Why did you call that "Crazy Love, Vol. II"?

Well, it had two meanings. There are two other "Crazy Love"s that I know of and I'm sure there are more. There's the Van Morrison song, so I wanted to distinguish it from that. And the other [meaning] was that romance had started, stopped, had come back, and stopped again. So it was like *that*, volume two.

Your hit singles have gotten so much attention that many of your greatest songs get overlooked in comparison. I think of that song or "Overs" or "Jonah" or "Everything Put Together Falls Apart." Do you feel that the greatness of your huge songs sometimes overshadows the others?

[*Pause*] Yeah. The song that is a single or a hit is not necessarily the best song. In *my* opinion. But on another level, aside from people who are students of songwriting, the songs that are the hits are the easiest. And the ones that people have to work at, they're going to go away, probably, except for a much smaller audience of people who are very interested in the subject matter of songs.

I never know which songs are going to be the singles. In fact, I now feel that nothing I do is a single.

You never write a song to be a single?

No. Whereas there was a time when I didn't have a hard time writing songs that could be hits, I think now that it's very *unlikely* that I would write a song that would be a Top Forty hit. It *could* be a hit; "You Can Call Me Al," which was a big hit, was *barely* a Top Forty hit.

"Graceland," which was the Record of the Year, never got higher than eighty-one on the charts. It went on for three weeks and it went off; nobody played it. So I think those songs are hits in a certain sense, but they're not Top Forty hits.

"Why don't we stop fooling ourselves?" ["Overs"].

Well, I don't know about that one. That's a little cliche-sounding.

You don't like "Overs" anymore?

No, I don't like that song. It's not real. That voice is not real. It's too young. Too young to have those emotions. Too young to be that world-weary. It's a pose of a certain age.

Yet on that same album, Bookends, you have the song "Old Friends," which is an unusual song for a man in his twenties to write.

Yeah, that was unusual, too. But that's a good song. It's true that I really didn't know much about being old, but there's something about that that's true about us.

"When I was born, my mother died . . ." ["That's Why God Made the Movies"].

[*Laughs*] My favorite part of that one is "I said, 'Where you going?' " [*Laughs*] That's the part I like in that. "When I was born, my mother died, she said, 'Bye bye, baby, bye bye,' I said, 'Where you going?' "

"I'm just born"—

" 'I'm just born,' she said, 'I'll only be gone for awhile . . .' " Which is about how long life is, really. A little while and then [*laughs*] you'll be dead, too. All this bad news right when the kid just got born. And that's why I'm in fantasy, that's why God . . . that's why we have little escapes here, because this bad news is *overwhelming*, like for somebody who just got here.

That wasn't a good record. That was a much better song than a record. That was much too slow. It was too slow and soft and it doesn't get across; that's why nobody knows it. But that was a nice song. It wasn't a good record. That's how I feel. That's why I feel it didn't have any impact.

If you have a really good track, and you write a decent song, it's going to have a pretty good impact. But if you write a good song and you make a decent track, it's not going to have any impact.

[*Softly*] Except to songwriters.

"I met my old lover on the street last night . . ." [from "Still Crazy After All These Years"].

Yeah. I know who that is. It's good to start with some thing that's true. It's *very* helpful to start with something that's true. If you start with something that's false, you're always covering your tracks. Something simple and true, that has a lot of possibilities, is a nice way to begin.

Sometimes these are second verses, and I say, "Oh, that's really not a second verse; it's a first verse." In "Still Crazy After All These Years," that [title phrase] came to me first. And it didn't come with melody, either. It just came as a line. And then I had to create a story.

That song has beautiful chord changes, and a very cool and subtle key change in the last verse.

Yeah, I was studying with a bass player and composer named Chuck Israels at the time so I was doing more interesting changes. I was studying harmony with him so I was more concentrated on that kind of stuff.

Do you recall what kind of harmonic things he was showing you at the time?

Well, one of the things I know that was his suggestion was the modulation in the last verse, taking that minor chord and turning it into a major chord and therefore going up a whole step in key. That was a nice idea. The rest of the changes were things I was working on. I think probably the bridge—it seems that once I was working with Chuck Israels I began to write some songs where the bridge jumped a whole step up and went to the major-seventh a whole step up.

His suggestion?

I don't know if it was his suggesting or something I inferred from studying with him. But prior to studying with Chuck I didn't use that device. Either I learned it from him or I discovered it because I was studying with him and started to experiment harmonically with what he was showing me. I don't remember.

Because I wrote "Still Crazy" on guitar and then made the record on piano, I didn't play it. So I forgot.

You said once that on that song you took every note that hadn't been used in the twelve-tone scale and constructed the bridge using those notes. True?

Yeah, I used to do that. It was something that I noticed in Antonio Jobim's music. In fact, I once mentioned that to him and he said that he wasn't aware of it at all. [*Laughs*]

It was kind of an exercise that I did, which was to try and get every note from a twelve-tone scale into the song. So what would happen is that I would cover most of the notes in the song and there would be maybe three notes that you couldn't get into the scale of the key you were using. And those three notes were really the key to the bridge.

Usually it would be a tritone away from whatever key you were using. If you were in the key of C, the farthest away you can go is F sharp. That's the key that's the least related to C.

Do you recall why you decided to make it a keyboard-oriented song?

It probably didn't lay right on an acoustic guitar. I don't know, it was just some instinct. The same with "Bridge Over Troubled Water," I just knew immediately. So when I write the song on guitar and transfer it to piano, I lose touch with what I did. And also because I was working with really gifted pianists like Richard Tee, Barry Beckett, they might change the chord subtly. Change the bass of the chord. So the song might evolve harmonically because of some other musician's input after I took it off the guitar and gave it to them.

The original record of that is a very satisfying record. It's one of the best records I've made.

Steve Gadd's drumming on that record is so minimal and yet so perfect, it's really extraordinary.

He's the great drummer of his generation.

The line in that song, "I'm not the kind of man who tends to socialize

/ I seem to lean on old familiar ways . . ." is an intimate line, showing more of yourself than you often do in songs.

It sounds like I was talking about where I was then, yeah. I have the same instinct as all writers. If something from my life works, I use it. If I have to change it and exaggerate it because that works, I'll change it and exaggerate it. I'm not committed to telling the truth. I'm committed to finding what the truth is in the song. But that's not a commitment to telling everyone what's going on with me. That's very common.

You once said that you thought of that title before you wrote the song. Do you recall that?

Sure I do. I remember it very well. I was stepping into a shower when the thought came to me. And I wasn't very happy about it either. I didn't say, "Oh that's clever, that's a good one, I can use that." It was at the time an assessment of where I was at, in terms of my life. And I wasn't very happy that that was my assessment. But I soon turned it into a song. And that's what you do with those things and that makes it something else. In fact, now it has almost no relevance on a personal level to me. That was a long time ago. I've long since stopped feeling that way. I probably wouldn't describe myself that way. I probably wouldn't think that way at all. But as a rhythmic title—I mean, in a way it's amazing that it appears I originated that. It seems so idiomatic. But I don't think there was a "Still Crazy After All These" anything before that.

The song could have actually been more accessible. The song was kind of personal on a dark level. But it doesn't matter because it's just the title. And the melody of it. People know that melody in a way that they know "like a bridge over troubled water," that melody attached to those words, they know the melody of "Still Crazy."

Why do you think that title is so powerful? The word "crazy" does work well in songs.

Yeah. It has the kind of catchiness that country music titles have. You get the whole story in the title. People relate to their own lives immediately just from the title. There are very few other of my titles that are catchy in that way. "50 Ways" to do whatever. That also became a catch-phrase. If "Mrs. Robinson" had been called "Where Have You Gone, Joe DiMaggio," well, I guess it wouldn't have made any sense. But that also had the same kind of quality. It just applied to a lot of situations.

As does "Bridge Over Troubled Water."

Yes, "Bridge Over Troubled Water" is a metaphor that worked.

Earlier you described discovering a thought and then consciously trying to think of the beginning, or set-up, to that thought. Doing this are you creating an illusion that the song appeared in order when in a sense it was written backwards?

Well, backwards is still an order. That's not out of order. I think a piece surges forward and backward and forward and backward until finally it stops. And sometimes things will have that classic form where they seem to build to a certain peak and then conclude. I think people are very satisfied by hearing that form.

But I think that's just one of the forms, and it doesn't necessarily satisfy me.

Sometimes I'd rather hear a shape closer to life. Amorphous is a closer shape to life than symmetry.

It seems that much of the greatness of songs is that they are perfectly ordered—

When they're right, when they're really right, then they do something to us. They make us feel really good.

Your current work is so much more concerned with rhythm than melody. Is it your feeling that melody is no longer important?

We're long out of the age of melody. Long out of there and we probably won't be going back into it.

You don't think so?

I don't think so. Something literally earth-shattering would have to happen. For us to change *direction* away from rhythm. You can't have melody without more interesting changes. It's very hard to have melody over mechanized *drums*.

Don't you think we'll hunger for melody again?

It's possible. But I don't think so. I'd like that to happen, but I don't think it will.

I think the opposite will happen. People will forget about melody and they won't hunger for it. They won't know what it is.

That's a startling thought. It seems to me, though, that the desire to hear melodies is an inherent human need. It's something we can't do without.

Well, you don't see it much reflected in music. What you see reflected in music is rhythm.

But don't you feel that nowadays, with the emphasis on rhythm, people feel especially relieved and nourished when they hear a good melody?

Yeah, I *do*. I think people are nourished and relieved to hear interesting lyrics, too. *Any quality at all* that comes their way is really appreciated given the fact that it's a world where the quality of life is being eroded. The quality of *everything* is being eroded except technology.

And as the marketplace expands to a world-wide marketplace, it's not like the market is going to have any effect upon the writing, because the writing can get worse and the sales will go up. So there's no easy way to make a big movement. Certainly the corporations don't care to.

So who will be the melody writer? Where are they going to learn it from?

Maybe from old records? Or CDs?

Well, that's what would have to happen. But, you know, people don't read history, people don't listen. Some do. *Most don't.*

When we take this generation now and go a generation past this, they won't be listening *before* that. It took me a long time to listen to music that existed before rock and roll. A long time. And the people who were born years later, even they can't seem to go back beyond the sixties. They don't listen to the fifties rock and roll, which had its own melodies. Fifties music had its own melodies. I really liked that kind of melody.

Early fifties music also had a different kind of melody, more melodic. But then you're closer to the age of melody. Because the big band era and post-war, that was still all about melody.

The days of Irving Berlin and *those* great songwriters was about *melody*. Nobody's come close to writing melodies like *they did*. Nobody.

[*Pause*] Maybe Paul McCartney.

He's the one you would choose?
I think he is probably the most notable melody writer. Stevie Wonder, also, is a notable melody writer. I don't know anybody else that is really—

Jimmy Webb?
Yeah. Jimmy Webb is a good writer, you're right.

How about yourself?
Not in the same league with Paul McCartney. But I still have memory of melody, so I mean, I do write melody. But I think he has a really great gift. He didn't study, but he's *very, very* musical. He thinks clearly about it. He thinks about the shape of it. Yeah, I heard him describe music in terms where he understood the shape. He plays a few instruments. And his ear is really fine.

When I was working on *Graceland*, on the tracks, writing the songs, I saw Paul. He said, "What are you working on?" And I said, "This stuff." "Can I hear it?" I said, "Yeah, sure, yeah."

So we went into my *car*, and I was just playing him the tracks. And I'd finished quite a few of those songs and I had spent a lot of time writing them, and I played those tracks for him and he began to improvise melody, and *many of them were very good*. I mean, they weren't as good as the melodies that I had but I had *reworked* those melodies for a long time. His *first* impulse was very musical. He got it, sang easily, effortlessly, over the top of it. He's a very musical guy.

With your indulgence, I'd like to mention some of your songs we have not yet discussed, and get your response to them. "Save the Life of My Child."
That was a record that we used the Moog synthesizer on. That had some interesting sounds for when it was made because it was made in 1967 or so. And some of those sounds sound contemporary, with the distortion and all.

As a song, I didn't really pull it off. It was a nice idea but I didn't really understand the idea. I was dealing with surrealism and I didn't have my skill down yet.

It's a song about a kid who's standing on a roof and people are screaming and running and he flies away at the end. So something about its subject matter is limited. It's not a very inventive surrealistic sketch.

It had one of the first examples of sampling, the bit of "Sounds of Silence" that breaks through.
Yeah, that's right. It wasn't bad for record making. It was experimental in a way that was interesting. But even that wasn't fully realized. It wasn't bad.

"The Only Living Boy in New York."

I like that record, and I like that song, too. That was written about Artie's going off to make *Catch 22* in Mexico. I liked the "aaahhhs," the voices singing "aaah." That was the best I think that we ever did it. It was quite a lot of voices we put on, maybe twelve or fifteen voices. We sang it in the echo chamber, I remember that, too.

"The Only Living Boy in New York" and "So Long, Frank Lloyd Wright" have always seemed like companion songs to me.

Maybe. One's a twelve-string song, very much about the twelve-string, "The Only Living Boy in New York." And the other ["Frank Lloyd Wright"] is nylon-string, Brazilian influenced.

"Frank Lloyd Wright" has an astounding melody.

Yeah, I don't know how I wrote that because I didn't know those chords then. It was really before I was familiar with Brazilian music. I've heard some Brazilian covers of that song, too, which is nice.

"At the Zoo."

If it weren't for the fact that they used that song as a commercial for the zoo, which makes me happy, and children like it—there's a children's book based on it—I wouldn't like that song. But it seems to be sort of so happy in a kind of nursery school way that maybe I'm being too hard on it. It's very sixties. And it has a nice title.

Another nice title is "Punky's Dilemma."

Yeah, that came from someplace. This is a period of songs from back in the sixties. When you go back to the sixties, I really only think of a certain handful of songs that I like. The rest I never think about. "Punky's Dilemma"? That was fun at the time. These things don't stand the test of time, I don't think, in any way. But in the context of the sixties, if you think of *Donovan*, that was that. It sort of came out of the whimsical aspects of the English folk movement.

I think they do stand up. *Bookends* is a great album to this day, one of the best.

I like "America" on *Bookends* very much. I liked "Voices of Old People"; I liked those voices and I loved what Artie and Roy did with the stereo mix of those, the way one fades in and one fades out. I enjoy those voices quite a bit. And what was the last song on that side?

"Old Friends" and then the "Bookends Theme."

Yeah, *Bookends* in a way is like the quintessential Simon and Garfunkel album, I think.

"I Am a Rock."

Well, that's a very young song. I wrote that in England and that's an adolescent song, or really, a post-adolescent song.

Probably if I could, like, not have a song for a hit, I would pick "I Am a Rock." And "The Dangling Conversation." If they would go away, I would be happy. But to be kinder to myself, I would just say it's very young.

"Tenderness."

That's a nice song. Doesn't that have the Dixie Hummingbirds on it? That's a nice little love song. It's sad. But that wasn't a happy marriage. That song is nice. I never think about that but I don't have any objections to that one. *Liked* the Dixie Hummingbirds quite a lot on that.

I've felt it's a seminal love song, especially the line, "Don't give me your honesty, I just want your tenderness."

That was a fair thing to say. That was an honest thing to say. That was an okay thought.

"Flowers Never Bend in the Rainfall."

Too early. That's too early, that's too generic. It doesn't sound enough like me. It sounds like the folk movement of that period. It's a very early song. Everybody was writing the same thing: Tom Paxton, Eric Andersen . . . they were all like that, they were all . . . Bob Dylan.

"For Emily, Wherever I May Find Her."

It's funny you're picking songs that I don't really like. Artie likes that song an awful lot. He liked to sing it. It was a very romantic song but I don't really like it.

"Homeward Bound."

Again, these songs feel like they're before there was a me. [*Laughs*]

That was written in Liverpool when I was traveling. What I like about that is that it was a very clear memory of Liverpool station and the streets of Liverpool and the club I played at and me at age twenty-two. It's like a snapshot, a photograph of a long time ago.

I like that about it, but I don't like the song that much. First of all, it's not an original title. That's one of the main problems with it. It's been around forever.

No, the early songs, I can't say I really like them. But there's something naive and sweet-natured, and I must say I like that about it.

They're not angry. And that means that I wasn't angry or unhappy. That's my memory of that time; it was just about idyllic. It was just the best time of my life, I think, up until recently, these last five years or so, six years . . . This has been the best time of my life. But before that, I would say that that was.

"Scarborough Fair/Canticle."

Well, that was a gorgeous song. I learned that from Martin Carthy. "Scarborough Fair" is like three hundred years old. Martin Carthy had a beautiful arrangement of it, and my arrangement was like my memory of his arrangement. He was a wonderful guitarist and singer. Very popular and still playing. He's the guy who taught me "Angie."

"Gumboots."

If it wasn't that "Gumboots" led me into the whole [*Graceland*] project, I would have dropped "Gumboots" from the album, because I think it's the weakest of the South African cuts.

But it was that track of "Gumboots" that I heard on an album called *Gumboots: Accordion Jive Hits, Volume II*. That's what led me into the whole project. That's how I found out about Township Jive, and from Township Jive I learned about the other South African music. "Boy in the Bubble" is Sotho and "I Know What I Know" is Shangan. Black Mambazo is a kind of Zulu choral singing. "Gumboots" is what brought me in there. We extended the track and added a sax solo. Otherwise it was the same record as what I heard.

Was that the first song you finished writing for the album?
Yeah. I finished that before I went to Africa.

"Mother and Child Reunion."
Well, of course, everybody knows that's from a dish I had in a Chinese restaurant, chicken and eggs.

The title itself was on the menu?
Yeah.

And you knew right away it was a song?
No, I just liked it as a title. "Rene and Georgette Magritte With Their Dog After the War" comes from a photograph. The photograph was a photo of Rene and Georgette [*laughs*] with their dog.

Was that a hard song to write?
I don't think that song was particularly hard. I think it came relatively easy. Of all the songs and how hard some of them are, this one was towards the easier end of the spectrum.

"Mrs. Robinson."
"Mrs. Robinson," of course, was written during *The Graduate*. And at one point I considered calling it "Mrs. Roosevelt." I used to sing sometimes "Mrs. Roosevelt" and sometimes "Mrs. Robinson."

I was working on it; and it was Artie who said to Mike Nichols that I had this song called "Mrs. Robinson." And he [Nichols] said, "You've written a song called 'Mrs. Robinson' and you never told me?"

So I sang sort of just the chorus for him; I didn't have the verses. In the movie, it's only the chorus. It's only after we made the record that it became a big hit and that was after the movie came out.

The Joe DiMaggio line was written right away in the beginning. And I don't know why or where it came from. It seemed so strange, like it didn't belong in that song and then, I don't know, it was so interesting to us that we just kept it. So it's one of the most well-known lines that I've ever written.

In the song, is Mrs. Robinson in an institution?
I think so, yeah . . . Hippie paranoia.

"Hearts and Bones."
Oh, I think that was one of my best songs. It took a long time to write it and it was very true. It was about things that happened. And I like it, I like the record. It's probably the only track that I really like on that album. I should have put it as the first track; I should never have put "Allergies" as the first track.

"Hearts and Bones." I liked it. I was beginning to understand about writing on that album, about lyric writing.

What were you understanding?
How to do it, when to use ordinary language and when to use enriched language.

Of course, that's a story song and although I never tend to think of it in that way, my story songs tend to be a more natural form for me. Of course, "Graceland" is the continuation of the same story. "Hearts and Bones" and "Graceland" go together. But then, "Graceland" is also a story song, and in story songs ... I don't know ... I think I get very comfortable when I find myself in a story song.

I never set out to tell a story. I find the story coming along, characters emerging. But in "Hearts and Bones" the characters are very near to autobiographical.

In "Graceland" there's that haunting line: "There's a girl in New York City who calls herself the human trampoline."

Yeah. That line came to me when I was walking past the Museum of Natural History. *For no reason* I can think of. It's not related to anybody or anything. It just struck me as funny. Although that's an image that people remember; they talk about that line.

But *really*, what interested me was the next line, because I was using the word "Graceland" but it wasn't in the chorus. I was bringing "Graceland" back into a verse. Which is one of the things I learned from African music: The recapitulation of themes can come in different places.

You do that a lot on *Graceland*, the inner echoes.

Yeah, yeah. I do it probably more now. I think it's now a part of my writing style. It's a way of breaking things up so that the chorus isn't so much almost like a helmet on your head. It doesn't seem like it's so separated.

Was the title "Graceland" a title you had before writing those songs?
No.

Do you remember when it occurred to you that using the name "Graceland" would be the key to that album?

Very late. Very late in the thing. After everything was finished, I had no title for the album. In the chorus where it says "Graceland," I fought for a long time to get rid of it. I didn't like it.

Why?

Because I thought it was *distracting*. I figured people would think I'm writing about Elvis Presley, and this is a South African record and I'm now writing a song about Mississippi and Graceland ...

It took a long time before it settled and I got comfortable with it and said, "Oh, that's fine. You're not writing about Elvis Presley and it doesn't matter if they think you are. Those that get it will know that you're not, and those that don't get it won't care, they'll be just as happy that you're writing about Elvis Presley. It's not going to do any harm and in fact, it's kind of fun in a way."

And once I got comfortable with that, then it wasn't that hard to come and say that was what the album really should be about. The album *was* about that, but it takes a while before everything settles down and you can understand what it is that you've done.

On this album, I've had the title *The Rhythm of the Saints* for a long time, though. *Graceland* didn't have a title until very close to the end.

Gerry Goffin said that since his life has become so comfortable, it's not as easy for him to write. He felt he needed some turmoil in his life to stimulate him. Do you find you need turmoil or can you create when things are calm?

Well, that's a very good question, really. It's a very hard question to answer.

I'm not really sure. Turmoil does provoke or elicit emotions more. But I wouldn't purposely put my life into turmoil in order to write. There's plenty of turmoil that you contain with you for years and years and years that you can tap into. And not every song is about turmoil, anyway.

But, yes, that's true that when you have an active emotional life, there's more subject matter. I think that's so.

Randy Newman said that you are one of the few writers from your generation who has never let the quality of your writing diminish. Do you have any thoughts as to how you are able to do that?

I think that, for me—I really don't know about the other guys, what they are thinking about their writing—I'm as interested in the subject of writing and making records as I ever was. From when I started, which was at the age of fifteen, I've been very interested in this. So I'm blessed, really. I'm never bored. I'm always interested in problem solving in this area and I can always seem to go from one problem that I want to solve to another.

I mean, *Graceland* led me to West African drumming and West Africa led me into Brazil and the Caribbean. Because the Southern Africans are reputed to be the great singers of the continent, but the West Africans are the great drummers of the continent. So one piece of information is adjacent to another.

You sort of just follow whatever's interesting to you. And my interest level on writing and making records has never diminished. It's as strong as it ever was. I think that describes what happens with me in my work.

With the other guys, I don't know if they're as interested or not. I don't know. But I know it was very helpful for me to go and play with musicians from other cultures. That was *very* stimulating for me. If I had to sit and play songs that I wrote on guitar, I don't know if I'd be as interested. I'm stimulated by other musicians. But I've always been interested in music from other places. Since I was a little kid, really. That's just my natural inclination to be that way.

You, Dylan and the Beatles almost simultaneously brought the song to a new place. What influence, if any, did the Beatles' writing have on your writing?

I didn't think they influenced me a lot. I think it was inevitable; they were so powerful that you couldn't really escape the influence. But I tried as hard as I could not to be influenced by the Beatles or by Bob Dylan. Or the Rolling Stones. Which made it hard to stake out some territory that was your own, because between them, they [*laughs*] really had covered the map. And I thought that as Simon and Garfunkel, we just *barely* got a wedge in there, which I then tried to expand. But it was just impossible not to be influenced by that.

Did you ever recognize your influence on them? McCartney said re-

cently that when he first heard "Bridge Over Troubled Water" he attempted to write a song like it. The song he wrote was "Let It Be."

McCartney said that? But [the Beatles] listened to everything, too, much more than Bob [Dylan] did. Whatever it was that struck them . . . "Bridge Over Troubled Water" is influenced by gospel writing. So it's not really my influence, it's really gospel writing. But then maybe he heard it from me.

But you took it and put it in a new form. It sounds different than a gospel song.

Not very. Not very. I mean, I think the way that Artie sings it is different. But if you listen to Aretha Franklin, who recorded it a year later, she's singing it just the way it would be played.

And as for Bob [Dylan], I don't know. He's like the most mysterious of all the people of our generation. He's sort of impenetrable, really.

I read in a book about you that once you went to his house and looked through his garbage to see "how Dylan did it."

I did? [*Laughs*] I would *never* do that to anyone. *I heard that.* Yeah, I remember that. It's absolutely not so. Absolutely not so. I remember that being said. I don't know why anyone would think that they could find out anything by looking in his *trash*. No, I never did that.

On your first solo album you had two songs reconsidering the wisdom of the sixties and using drugs, "Run That Body Down" and "Everything Put Together Falls Apart." Was that a reconsideration you were going through at the time?

Yeah. It probably was. That's a long time ago. I don't remember what it was that *surrounded* the songs from that long ago. But that sounds right. That could have been.

Did you feel that smoking pot got in the way of your best work or did it ever help?

Well, you know, that's another question that's a tough one. [*Pause*] I would say that it probably doesn't make any difference.

There's a temptation, and a desire even, to be able to expand your imagination. I mean a lot of artists try that or do it. Something. Some chemical . . . alcohol, or whatever. And I think sometimes it produces some kind of creativity that wouldn't be there if the chemical wasn't there. And sometimes it produces nothing. Except the *feeling* of creativity, which is not the same as creativity.

So, I don't know how to answer that question. I've done it both ways with success and failure both ways. I don't think that altering your state with a chemical is going to give you anything that isn't in you already. It *may* help you get it out. And it may . . . not. It may just mess you up quite a bit.

In "Slip Slidin' Away" the theme is the inevitable movement towards death, as in "That's Why God Made the Movies." Yet in "Graceland" your attitude seems to have shifted. You say, "We all will be received in Graceland." Has your attitude changed?

Well, I don't have one attitude. I have many attitudes that incorporate opposites. Now I try to get all the opposites into the same song, if I can. I try to resolve it one way or the other, but opposites—having two very strong feelings about the same subject—we *all* have that. So that's a good thing to have in a song. Then you don't have to pick. You can just describe how you feel on both sides of the issue.

Do you think a technical knowledge of music theory is important for songwriters?

It can't hurt. It can help. Yeah, there are some problems that you solve by information that a teacher can give you. You'll have a much harder time solving those problems without that information. You might solve them, anyway. But why reinvent the wheel when the information is there?

Is it possible that the knowledge can get in the way of the spontaneity? I'm conscious when I'm going out of a key, for example, and maybe not as free because of it.

I guess it can go the other way. But certainly in popular music and rock and roll, that's not the problem. The problem is people don't know enough.

Has the use of guitar in pop music caused popular music to become less complex?

Yes, that's right. The early doo-wop records have a piano and a drum and a group singing. That's what it was. Maybe there was a stand-up bass. Maybe there was an electric guitar playing lightly in there. That's all the instrumentation there was. The sound was the group. Once you got into Chuck Berry and the rhythm and blues that came out of Chicago, the street-corner stuff went away. Doo-wop became like a cul-de-sac when rock became about the electric guitar as opposed to the voice. That was the end of people's interest in doo-wop. And, of course, when rock came back from England, they got very little doo-wop. It was not an English phenomenon at all. It's not part of their heritage of rock. So it sort of went away. It was considered unsophisticated music by musicians. But, as I was very young when I first heard it, it was music that really affected me.

In your songs you've expanded the vocabulary of chord changes used in pop songs. You made a comment in the past that you really aren't interested in two and three chord songs.

Well, that's probably a comment from a decade or so ago. *Graceland* is almost *all* three chord songs. It's just that the chords come in different places. [*Saints*] is not quite as three-chordy.

When you're dealing with rhythm, you're more naturally inclined to go to the simple chords because the rhythm . . . *dominates*. You can do some interesting changes, but it's a lot harder. And what I found with *Graceland* is that the African way of using the three chords was so different that it was fresh.

"Train in the Distance" is the only one of your songs I know of in which, after the main part of the song is over, you analyze it for us: "What is the point of this story / what information pertains? The thought that life could be better . . ."

Right. That's right. The title of the song and the line that keeps recurring is a metaphor. And although I liked the metaphor and I thought it was effective, by the time I got to the end of the song I said, well, look, I don't know if anyone will understand what I'm talking about here. So, in case you didn't get what this metaphor is about, let me just say this is what it is: everybody thinks things could be better.

And that seems to be a quality that the species has. It's probably how they got out of the caves. They just felt there was a better place to go.

And we *still do*. I mean, it may be that it'll destroy us. It certainly was our survival instinct for all these thousands and thousands of years, but it may be that if we don't recognize that there's danger in how things are going to be better, it may destroy us.

But in either case, it seems to be a human characteristic that people think—unless they're just *terribly* defeated by disease or by hunger, *terribly* depressed they'd have to be—most people will believe that *things could turn around*. I mean, look at what's happening in the world today. It's turned around for people who were characteristically oppressed. And that seems to be what people think. They think a break could come my way, or I could do this, or this . . .

And the answer is so beautifully phrased: "The thought that life could be better is woven indelibly into our hearts and our brains."

When I first wrote that line, I wrote, "The thought that life could be better is *programmed* indelibly." But a few of my friends really didn't like that. They really didn't like the thought that we were programmed. So I changed it because they really didn't like it. But really what I meant was it's programmed into us.

It does have a far different feeling.

Yeah. It's cold. "Woven" is nicer. "Woven" is a better choice. It's easier. Obviously the other word was upsetting. That's why I took it out. It was getting in the way of what I was saying.

People think of you as a perfectionist. Do you see yourself that way?

No. It isn't perfectionism. It was waiting for the thing to come alive. I would say, actually, I'm a little sloppy. The *perfectionists* are really Roy Halee and Art Garfunkel. Those guys are much more perfectionists. They would really stay on one detail. Whereas if I *see* what it's supposed to be, that's enough for me. I'm ready to move on. Whereas they want to get the fine shading right.

But in terms of the writing, I can see why people would think you are a perfectionist. So many of your songs seem so perfectly conceived.

I don't see it that way. I don't think I come *close* to perfect.

"Hearts and Bones" seems to me to be perfect.

"Hearts and Bones," I was just thinking, does have a high percentage of being true, telling a story, wrapping it up, capturing an emotion, all of that. "Graceland" also has a. . . .

I don't know. When I start thinking like this, I don't know what the percentages are. If I went through all the lines, line by line, I would say, "Well, that line, I just couldn't think of anything better to say. I tried and tried and couldn't think of a better way." That's the way it is with all of them.

The thing about it is, you don't even know if you're right. I tried for months to try to dislodge the idea that I was writing a song about Graceland.

I mean, really, I just spent months and months thinking, "When is this going to go away?" And I ended up calling the album that. So I don't think that I *know* either. I don't really know.

When *Graceland* was released to almost unanimous critical acclaim, the press often praised it by putting down your past work. Did you notice that?

Yeah, there was revisionism and *Graceland* in a way brought it out. But the style of music had changed a lot. And the generation of writers who were writing, they were coming from that same place.

But, like I say, fortunately it's *not my job* to describe how I am and where I stand. Whether one piece of work is good or not. And I know this: if they tend to dismiss a piece of work, it'll be rediscovered.

You do feel that?

Yeah. I think *Hearts and Bones* is a *great* flop. What I learned having had *Hearts and Bones* and *Graceland* come right next to each other, and it was a *hard* lesson: [*softly*] it didn't matter that much whether you had a flop and it didn't matter that much whether you had a hit. The only thing that mattered was the *power* to write the song. And that was after you were playing on your own field, you were making up your own game and your own rules and it was comfortable. It was more responsibility but it was more comfortable.

I'm very critical but at least I can stop short of being brutal. Whereas when it's in other people's hands, if you believe it, it can get brutal. People can be brutal.

I don't think it's very good for a serious songwriter to pay attention to what [*critics*] say. It's just too hard. And it's not informative. They don't know what they're talking about. And *can't* know what they're talking about, by definition. Unless you write songs and make records, you just really can't know what it's about.

A critic is not capable of distinguishing between a safe move that is executed, and an interesting mistake. An interesting mistake is by far the more valuable.

Do you ever feel restricted by the song form?

Yeah. Yeah, sometimes I think I'm *bored* now. I'm bored and it's not going to improve itself by adding another piece of information. A, B, C, it's not going to get better if I put D in there. A lot of the songs, there is C there. A lot of the songs. Some have more distinct sections. But usually there's three, there's the A, B and C sections. I found that having just two sections wasn't enough.

You've written some great C sections—bridges—in the past.

They set you up to come back to the other part. You're ready to hear it again and you feel good. You feel like it's the return of an old friend.

I sang a song last night at this benefit for the Rainforest. I sang "Slip Slidin' Away," a song I always thought didn't work. It starts out like it's going to be really good, and then it turns out it doesn't work. It's too long. It doesn't have another section. It's just verse-chorus. And that verse-chorus thing, it *numbs* me. I can't keep hearing verse-chorus-verse-chorus because I know what's going to happen.

Although "Slip Slidin' Away" is verse-chorus, I find that the final verse of "God only knows / God makes his plan" surpasses any repetition.

Yeah, the last verse is a powerful one. But the chorus, it keeps coming back to the chorus. You know what that chorus is going to say. I always felt it should be shorter but I didn't know which verses to take out. Either the last verse or the father/child verse. But they all seemed like they had to be in there, so I left it. But I always felt that the record and the song stayed on a plateau. It didn't build.

A final verse from another song of yours that has that culminating effect is from "Jonah": "Here's to all the boys who came along / carrying soft guitars in cardboard cases . . ." The music and the words both lift up at that point.

Those words are nice but you know, *generally speaking*, those words don't fit with that melody. That's a Brazilian type of melody and it's about this kind of folk singer. That melody, it should have been a love song of some kind. It was a too sophisticated way of describing that subject. I think the *music* is very interesting. I wish I'd written other words to it. I think that I might just take that melody and write other words to it. It's interesting harmonically. I was pleased with the melody. It wrapped itself up in a nice, tidy way. And the lyrics were okay, [*laughs*] they just shouldn't have been the lyrics to that melody.

"50 Ways to Leave Your Lover" is unusual in your work because the verse and the chorus are very different, and the title is in the verse. It could work well without the chorus. Did you conceive of the verse and the chorus separately?

No, it was always that way. The big discovery on that song was Steve Gadd's drum part. That was from the studio.

Was that rhythm your idea?

No, it was his. It's probably what made it a hit.

It's one of the most distinctive drum parts of any song.

Right. When Steve used to be in the studio he used to practice these little marching things. It was like a little exercise for him. I guess that's what it was. It's tricky. I've watched a lot of drummers try to play that. They never quite get it. It's really tricky.

When he played it, did it appeal to you right away?

Yeah, it appealed to me. I liked it. As I say, I didn't think of that song as any more important or commercial than any song. So it was, "Yeah, that's fine, Steve. Let's do it. That's fine." I didn't think any more of that, certainly, than I thought of "Still Crazy," which I'm sure I thought was a really good ballad.

"50 Ways" is unusual because it's both a ballad and a rhythm tune. The verse is in a minor key and has some complex changes, and the chorus is all major-chords and has a completely different feel.

Yeah. The chorus is "After Midnight." The changes—there are a lot of chords that are those changes. G, B flat, C, D.

Do you remember how you felt about it when you wrote it?

No. I don't remember thinking anything about it. It feels like I just knocked it off. That song came pretty easily. I always think of that song and "You're Kind" as similar songs. They're probably about the same person.

Did it surprise you that it was a hit?

Yeah, it surprised me. I seldom have known what was going to be a hit. Even with Simon & Garfunkel I didn't know what was a hit. I didn't know "Bridge Over Troubled Water" was a hit. Which was not to say I was surprised when it *was* a hit. I wouldn't have been surprised if it wasn't a hit.

There was a long period of time when I made an album that there was always two or three hits on it. So I began to feel relaxed and confident that there was going to be a hit or two or maybe three on any album that I made. And that was the case up until *Hearts & Bones*. That was the first time that there were no hits. And really, since then, the same thing is true, really. There are songs that are very famous. *Graceland* has songs that everybody knows. But they weren't hits. Everybody knows "Diamonds on the Soles of Her Shoes" but it wasn't a hit. Everybody knows "Boy in the Bubble" but it wasn't a hit. "Graceland" wasn't a hit. "You Can Call Me Al" was a kind of a hit. And there were no hits on *Rhythm Of The Saints*. The albums were big hits.

You've shown us in your work that there are a myriad of topics people can use in songs; ideas most people would never consider using.

The subject of popular songs has been the same forever. And if you put it in the right setting, that is the subject matter of popular songs. People need it. They never get tired of hearing . . . songs about love. It's one of the big things that we think about, and this is one of the areas where we can express it.

In today's writing, the songs are really about the rhythm. And the subject matter of songs, with the exception of rap, is usually not important. And nobody seems to object.

I feel like if you can satisfy people's rhythm-jones, then why not say something interesting? As long as that doesn't take away from the satisfaction you can get from the rhythm. If it does, then you're defeating the purpose. But if you say something that's interesting or provocative along with rhythm, it's going to be a much better song, obviously.

For the rappers, I mean, when they get onto an interesting subject or interesting set of imagery, that's key because they don't have the element of melody. You've only got words and rhythm. So you've got to make those words say something. But in terms of other popular songs, you've got rhythm, melody and words, and the words are the least important. *Unless* you can make those words so interesting that people really enjoy it.

Your fusion of African music with American ideas is powerful on *Graceland*. You mention Africa in "Under African Skies," but that is really more about music than Africa, about remembrances of where music comes from.

Yeah. But in "You Can Call Me Al," the guy is in . . . "Maybe it's the third world, maybe it's his first time around . . ."

I thought that it was interesting to combine what was on my mind with that music. I thought it would be interesting to an African audience, if they could get to the point of hearing it. And they did, once the album became a big hit. It was a *huge* hit in South Africa. It had all the biggest bands in South Africa on the record.

So here's all these songs with what must be relatively strange subject matter, and I guess on the frivolous subject matter, like "I Know What I Know," maybe it's meaningless. But "The Boy in the Bubble" with that imagery, that must be pretty interesting to somebody that's hearing it there. That's not the way songs are coming at them.

So I thought it was interesting. I always try to be interesting to everybody. I always talked about what I knew, and I was trying not to pretend to be an expert about something that I didn't know.

Usually when I'm finished, I don't go back. Usually once I'm finished I'm really happy to be finished. I know I felt that way with *Graceland*. I was happy to let it go. A little bit emotional and all that after the tour and all . . . but it has to be done. You're with it a long time.

It's enjoyable when you're doing it. I *love* to work. I really have a good time. Some of it more than other. Like going to Brazil to record. I mean, that's just pure fun. The hard thing is writing the song. But even that has its really good parts because when something comes, you're happy.

I saw Bruce Springsteen last night and he said he was really happy because he wrote a new song and he felt it was really good, and he really liked it and felt really happy. So that's great.

How long does that feeling last for you after you've written a good song?
Well, it can last for years, once it's a fact.

You and Springsteen both have been unusual in that you're extremely serious songwriters who have been popular on a massive level.
Most of [my songs] that were hits were the easier songs. And the more sophisticated stuff wasn't a hit. It really wasn't until *Graceland* where it was sophisticated and simple at the same time that it starts to spread across boundary lines.

And that—getting things sophisticated and simple at the same time— that's an objective. *Try and do that.* Try to simplify and simplify without losing what was really interesting.

When you are in the midst of writing, do you give any thought to who will hear the song, and how it will be received?
I think when people write, they have an imaginary audience in mind. A lot of times you hear a song on a record, and you know it's aimed at a certain audience, people communicating with their group. And when I started to combine groups that hadn't been combined before, the songs became richer. They were a little more exciting to a lot of people. And they were more antagonizing to a lot of people, too.

I think that's part of what this discussion is about: cross-cultural musical experiments. When you use elements of one culture to address elements of another culture and vice-versa. I take traditional African rhythms and sounds and address an American audience. I take what works for an American audience and address an African audience and that was upsetting for a lot of people. And stimulating to other people.

But I believe that there's a very basic feeling that music gives to all people and we're all connected on this very basic, emotional level by music, rhythm and harmony. And that many, many people can understand you when you're using that vocabulary. Or maybe they don't understand you but they still listen because the sounds are inviting and they're familiar, they don't threaten. And then whatever it is that you start to say with those sounds, that's where the fur starts to fly.

But how can people begin to communicate if we don't begin to appropriate a wider vocabulary? If you can't speak in someone else's language, how are they going to hear you? So I'm somebody who speaks . . . broken music.

Do you think that there is any limit to the imagination?

Yeah, I do think some people have shallower pools to draw the water from. It's true.

Do you ever find that your own pool has gone dry, that there's nothing left there to draw from?

Yeah, sure, all the time. On every album I say that. And one of these days that's really going to be true. At least that's my fear. But so far, it's been that if you have enough patience, it will come.

Patience is the key?

I think so. Patience, persistence . . . whichever. Sometimes you have to be very *tenacious*, and sometimes you have to give yourself a break and not beat yourself up and say, "Where is it? Where is it?" It's not here, you know. It'll be here when it gets here, and that's it. There's nothing more you can do.

Sometimes you say, "Try and work a little harder. Maybe you'll get a little more." And sometimes you will. [*Softly*] Sometimes you won't . . . Those are different strategies you can use to provoke yourself.

For the last few months I've been finding that the work comes at absolutely unexpected times. I had one period last summer where every day for four days I woke up *exactly* at 5:30 in the morning with lyrics—I didn't set an alarm. I woke up at 5:30 every day with some song in my head. It was like, "Wow . . . this is great—" Then I began to expect it. I woke up one day at 5:30 and there was nothing. [*Laughs*] That was the end. It didn't happen again.

Then big periods of time would go by when I would get nothing, then I'd get a bunch of lines on several different songs for a day or two or maybe three, and I'd think, "Okay, here we go," and then it stops. And that's been the pattern now for many months.

I have patches where I do sit and do it every day. But after a certain amount of time, you just get tired and you have to stop anyway and let whatever's happening beneath the surface bubble around and wait for it to break through. Then you can go back.

Once you reach a certain point of exhaustion there's really no point in pushing it. You just have to stop for a little while. Not long. Stop for a week.

So you feel now that it's more beneficial not to force yourself?

I haven't felt that it's done me any more good to do that. But I think this is because I have somehow come to believe that the only lyrics that I'm really interested in are the lyrics that I find, not the lyrics that I invent. If it doesn't come to me in that surprising way, I don't tend to believe it or get excited about it.

But then, I guess I'm really talking about certain types of lines and phrases or images that are really interesting. They're sprinkled throughout the song. Most of the song is not that. Most of the song is just meat and potatoes, lines that are either moving the narrative forward or setting up these other lines which are observations. And so I have pages of these lines that aren't in songs, that are just interesting lines or images or combinations of words. I keep playing the songs and looking at the lines to see if they will fit anywhere rhythmically; will they belong?

You said that you're more interested with what you find in songs than with what you invent. How do you draw the line between discovery and invention? Don't they overlap?

Yes, they do. [*Pause*] You just have no idea that that's a thought that you had. It surprises you. It can make me laugh or make me emotional. When it happens and I'm the audience and I react, I have faith in that because I'm already reacting. I don't have to question it. I've already been the audience.

But if I make it up, knowing where it's going, it's not as much fun. It *may* be just as good, but it's more *fun* to discover it.

I mean, it may be that that's what is slowing me down to such a slow pace, you know, that I keep waiting for this stuff instead of just writing. But just writing what? How do I know what I'm going to write if I don't discover it? If I make up what I'm going to write, all I'm going to write is what I saw on television or what I read in the paper or what I saw . . . it's not going to be from the underground river of your subconscious. Because that just comes to the surface occasionally and you have to capture it when it happens.

Do you ever feel that those thoughts that surprise you come from beyond you?

No. Beyond? No. I don't know what that means.

Many songwriters, including John Lennon, have expressed that they feel like channels, and that songs come through them from a source that is beyond.

Well, it's coming from their subconscious. Unless you believe that someone is sending you a signal from another planet or another sphere. But maybe that's an explanation for your subconscious. I don't think that way.

But doesn't it ever seem to you that the process is rather magical?

Yes, and that's why it's more fun to write that way.

But that magic is something you possess?

You don't really possess it. That's the feeling that it comes through, that you're a transmitter. It comes through you. But you don't possess it. You can't control it or dictate to it. You're just waiting. You're just waiting . . . Waiting for the show to begin.

You mentioned how "Bridge" came to you in a flash. Is that an unusual experience for you, or does that happen frequently?

No, it's neither unusual nor frequent. It does happen from time to time but it's not frequent.

When it does happen, does it usually produce the best work?
Not necessarily. There is a certain quality to things that come out effortlessly. They have that quality. It doesn't necessarily mean it's going to be really special. But it does have a certain ease that *could be* special if the rest of the song has a point or a strong melody or is about something real enough. Then it could.

You mentioned earlier that it was that effortless quality that first attracted you to Chuck Berry's work. And it's a quality that your songs certainly share, a sense of inevitablity, as if the song always existed. Is that a quality of the song emerging on its own or is it the product of a lot of work?
Mostly a lot of work. *Mostly*, it's a lot of work and patience waiting for the stuff to get simpler and simpler and simpler. More than ever now, my writing process has really slowed down and the rewriting goes on constantly.

Do you feel that a lot of your best work is yet to come?
I tend to think so.
A lot of work, I *don't know*. It's slowed down so much. And then again, you know, fortunately, I don't have to think about that. Because if I had to be the critic of my own work, it would be *very* hard. I'm just *very* critical. But I don't really have to.
I don't think, "Well, I'll go and do another if it could be my best work." All I think is that I love what I'm doing and they're going to let me do it again. They're not kicking me out of the business. And they're going to let me do it again and that's great. So I do whatever I'm interested in.
Whether it's my best work, I *don't really know*. I know so much more than when I wrote "Bridge Over Troubled Water" but I doubt that I'll ever write anything that has that ease and simplicity again. So I don't know what "best work" really means. I'm more in control of what I want to do.

You ended the introduction to your first songbook with the phrase, "My next songs will be better." And I think of the line in "Train in the Distance," "The thought that life could be better . . ." Have you ever gotten to the point where you have felt satisfied with what you have accomplished?
No, I'm not, personally. I think of Simon & Garfunkel's period as my early work. Young work. Most of it, not particularly good. Not good in the sense that it was young. But some of the good stuff was good in a sort of mature way, really, considering it was all stuff I wrote in my twenties. But I always thought of it as very early, very early stuff. The stuff in the seventies, that's a bit more sophisticated. The mistakes that I made in the seventies . . . I keep going to whatever it is that interests me and eliminate what it is that really becomes unimportant.
But the experiment, the *investigation*, is important. Even if you discover that, well, really, I'm *not* going to write another reggae song. But I'm not sorry that I went to Jamaica and recorded "Mother and Child Reunion." I'm *happy* I

did. It was good for me. But, in terms of reggae, I'm not taking anything from that because I'm not going to use that information. *The experience of going and recording there* was helpful to me when I went to record *Graceland.*

What you find is what it is you are always interested in. What sounds you like, what rhythms you like, what chord changes you like, and as you become more in command of your vocabulary, you're able to express yourself better.

Are you looking forward to the future songs to come?

Oh, yeah. If I can get them out. If I can write them, they will be better. When they come, they seem better.

But anyway, I don't have to think about that. I don't think it's something that I *want* to think about either.

I mean, writing songs is what I do and I enjoy it. I'm grateful that people are . . . *still interested* after all this time. That I can keep doing it. That they will keep letting me make records.

It's great. I've been interested in writing songs and making records since I was thirteen years old. And I'm still absolutely enthralled with it.

* * *

Brian Wilson
Los Angeles, California 1988

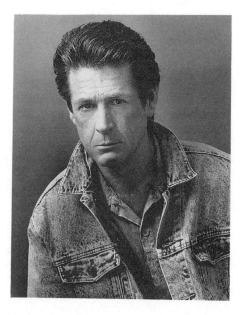

Sleighbells in the summer. Darkness in the sun. These dichotomies have been at the heart of Brian Wilson's music since the start of the sixties when he, his brothers, a cousin and a neighbor started a band that would become an American institution: the Beach Boys.

Born on June 20, 1942 in Inglewood, California, he was the Beach Boy who preferred to fill his living room with sand rather than go to the beach. Though he was the architect of the "California Sound" and introduced surfing into the vocabulary of the popular song, he never surfed himself. He was a musical innovator who could never hear stereo due to deafness in one ear. As a kid, he was so terrorized by his father that he retreated to the only haven of safety in their suburban home—the piano. He was the one member of the Beach Boys who elected not to perform with them during their heyday, preferring instead to be at home writing songs of sea and sun while staying in the darkness of his own room, away from the ocean.

Eventually the darkness in him overcame his ability to escape it. Music was his only light source, but it got tainted by the burden of the label "genius" and the pressure to produce sunny hit songs. He began spending months perfecting small masterpieces, such as "Heroes and Villains," written with Van Dyke Parks, fine-tuning them to a degree that only someone with a dog's ears could discern, according to a bandmember. "Good Vibrations" alone took six months and fifty thousand dollars to produce. In time the shadows completely obscured the sun and Brian was lost.

Brian's late brother Dennis Wilson admitted once that Brian *was* the Beach Boys. And this was true: During the making of the landmark *Pet Sounds* album (which Paul McCartney later admitted inspired *Sgt. Pepper*), Brian would wipe away the supporting vocals of the others and replace them with his own, creating closer and more perfectly balanced harmonies. He recorded the tracks to many of his most famous songs with studio musicians while the rest of the group was on tour. He was always able to make the Beach Boys sound best on his own, without the others around.

I met with Brian in the summer of 1988, soon after the release of his first solo album, *Brian Wilson*. Driven by sleighbells, the album is supported by those same signature barbershop/beach harmonies he's always created, with or without the boys. He credited Eugene Landy for his own reemergence into the world and for his reconnection with his creativity. (Landy was Brian's psychologist at that time, enlisted by family members. Months later Landy's license was revoked for entering into a business relationship with a patient, and today he remains Brian's "partner.") "He helped rejuvenate my soul," Brian said. "He reacquainted me with myself."

Having heard the strength of Brian's new songs, the power of his voice, and the beauty of his harmonies, it seemed to me before meeting him that he had fully recovered from his time in the heart of darkness. He hadn't. It was clear that he was still in turmoil, his expressions alternating between dread, depression and confusion. We met in the cluttered surroundings of Landy's West Los Angeles office and were monitored by one of Landy's young assistants. Brian spent most of the time talking while lying on the couch, facing the ceiling, as if he was in analysis.

At first he seemed quite far away and would only give the briefest responses to my questions. But then, as suddenly as a cloud passes from before the sun, something shifted and he relaxed, smiled, and began to open up. It was when he mentioned the spirit of the sixties and how naturally he connected with it. For a moment the sunshine of that spirit shone through him, and Brian Wilson seemed happy.

Do you mind talking about the past as well as the present?
No. The past's a good thing, too.

Do you remember writing your first song?
Yeah. "Surfer Girl." I was about nineteen when I wrote that.

Do you remember what it was that started you writing songs?
Yeah, my dad was a songwriter and I wanted to be like him.

You're famous for writing happy, sunny songs. Is that something that naturally happened?
No, it's just that I got jazzed on the renaissance of the sixties, you know. And I latched onto that spirit, and it's very contagious to creativity. It's like a bug that gets into you, like a flu bug.

For a long time, you haven't come out with any new music. Were you out of touch with that spirit?

Yes, I was. I got too into drugs and I got too out of touch with that spirit.

And you stopped writing songs altogether?

Yes, I did. The Beach Boys just sort of floundered for a while there. They weren't really happening; they weren't really that big of a group for a while.

How did you get that spirit flowing again?

It was from Dr. Landy. Dr. Landy has helped me a lot to get it back. Actually [*louder and faster*] to get that spirit back. I got some of it back on my own but Dr. Landy talked me into it.

In 1983 I went with Dr. Landy's program. And from there he helped rejuvenate my soul, the part of me that writes music. He got me reacquainted with myself; he turned me back onto myself and my songwriting ability. And I started writing songs.

So you had written a lot of songs during this time?

Yes.

Was it hard? Did you have to sit at the piano for hours to get it going?

No. It was rather spontaneous. It just came automatically. Because he got me so in tune with my feelings that, when I applied my feelings to songwriting, the songwriting just flowed.

What was the first song that you wrote for the album?

"Love and Mercy," I think. I wrote 173 songs in a four-year period. We handpicked the songs that we wanted.

Were those 173 songs completed or were they sketches?

They were finished, but Dr. Landy wanted to fine-tune my lyrics. Gene fine-tuned the lyrics.

Did that feel good? To have someone who is not known as a songwriter work on your songs?

It worked out well. We worked *together* on the lyrics, but he would fine-tune them on his own. He had a technique where he would take the lyrics, and then adjust them, and then send them back to my house. I would check them out to see if I liked them. And if I said I liked them, we would go with that set of lyrics. Then we made a decision to leave those as the final lyrics.

You've been regarded as a musical genius throughout your career. Has that put too much pressure on you?

No, it doesn't put pressure on me. The only thing that puts the pressure on me is having to live up to my name, you know. As who I think I might be or should be or am. According to people, what they think I should be. You know, *everybody* goes through it. I'm not the only one who goes through that. Everybody goes through it.

But not everybody is the driving force of the Beach Boys. You had the pressure to produce sunny, happy songs, even if you didn't feel that way. What was that like?

I was on the spot. You know what it was, though, that's when I was younger. Right? When I was in my twenties I was on the go all the time, producing, writing, you know, just *creating* all the time. It was such that it was a big burden on my shoulders. I took on a lot of karma and burdens on my shoulders. For some unknown reason, I just found myself involved in a name dilemma. After my twenties, when I was in my thirties and forties, I had age dilemma problems.

I say to myself, "I miss the feeling of being young." I say, "Okay, so I do. That's established." Then I go through that, I get back on the track, and I say, "Yeah, but I got a great brain. Maybe I don't feel like taking a *sprint* every ten seconds down the street, but I have a great brain." Know what I mean?

Yeah. And we see that being a songwriter is not like being an athlete. It's not something you can do well only when you're young.

Yeah. First of all, I want people to understand that I'm here to create for them. To create music for people so they'll know that I'm a source of love. And they can depend on my name.

When you say the name Burt Bacharach, right away, [*snaps fingers*] it triggers off love melodies, *harmonies, beautiful records, incredible songs* that he wrote with Hal David. Know what I mean? That's a source of love, right there, Burt Bacharach is. His *name* is. He might not be in that frame of mind today but his name is *always* in that frame of mind. Know what I mean?

That's why when you're sitting in a hotel room and somebody from another *city* around the world is getting-off on your music, you know, while you're bumming it somewhere, it's a well-taken thing. It's taken very well by me and I appreciate the very thought of being able to entertain and write songs for people; it *turns me on*, personally. I feel turned on by it, I can't help it. I can't help myself.

People have been wanting to feel that spirit again for a long time.

Yeah. There's love in it. Love is something that is not needed. There's no need for it. The only need for love is spiritual love. Spiritual love. A kiss and a hug every six months, if it's really felt and it really feels good, is a good thing. But *love* is different, you know.

The album begins with "Love and Mercy," in which the narrator is watching a "crummy movie." Was there a real movie?

No. There was no movie that I was referring to. You go to the theater and at least half the time you're going to end up in a bad movie. *But you take your chances.*

Do you find that's the same with music nowadays?

Yeah. I think music's the same way.

The harmonies on the new album all have the sound you achieved with the Beach Boys. Is there a way you can explain how you achieve that sound?

It's partly because my voice was the chief voice in the Beach Boys' background sound. Therefore it has to take on characteristics of my voice.

Yes, but what are the intervals you sing to create that kind of harmony?

Some of the harmonies are major-seventh chords. Some are minors. Some are just straight chords.

You did all the background vocals on this album by yourself. Did that feel natural to you?

Yeah, it was very natural for me to do that. I didn't have any trouble doing that. I took my time. I took hours and hours to do it. But I did it.

I understand that you did the harmonies on the song "There's So Many" in fifteen minutes. It seems pretty amazing that you could create that whole wall of sound in only fifteen minutes.
Yeah. You know, that's how the Beach Boys did it. They got stumbling along on this career as background singers. Not stumbling along but *moving along*. Like going faster than they could actually run. So everyone was so tuned into the sound we were making that there was no problem with it.

Your use of drums on the new album also has your old sound, where instead of a heavy backbeat you often use sleighbells to set the rhythm.
We wanted to try to establish *somewhat* of a sixties album combined with an eighties feeling. So we had to take liberties with the drums, to make the drums sound original again; having a little more originality in a drum beat. Other than just a 2/4 [*claps hands*] metronome beat. And it worked. The cuts turned out sensationally.

"Melt Away" is an especially gorgeous ballad.
It is a nice ballad. I wrote that in my house in Malibu. I just wrote it because I needed to write something mellow. Because all my other songs were like workhorse songs.

I took it in stages. I'd write a line and then think about it before writing more. I really thought that one through. "Melt Away" was very, very thought out.

That song has such a strong melody, like so many songs you've written over the years. Do you have any idea what it is that makes a melody strong and durable?
There's no way you can tell what makes a melody good. Every song is different. There are *thousands and thousands* of songs that have good melodies that have been written. The only way to know if a melody is good is to actually play it for somebody so that they can hear if the melody is good.

When you are working on a song, how do you generate melodic ideas? Do you play chords on the piano?
Yeah. What I'll do is I'll first get a key. Then after that I try to find a chord pattern, some kind of a chord pattern that I can write a melody to. Then I play the chord pattern and I play in rhythm in a certain key, and I start thinking of these great, outrageous melodies.

Do you have favorite keys to work in?
E and B.

Do you have any idea where your ideas come from?
They come from . . . let me think . . . from God, I guess.

How do you get in touch with that source? Does it take a while when you sit down at the piano to get it going?
It does, it does.

Any advice for songwriters on how to best do it?
Don't drink coffee. Because caffeine screws up your mind. Don't drink cof-

fee for inspiration to write a song. Do it out of your *own* inspiration, and the song will come more naturally.

Caffeine screws with your creativity. A lot of people who are creative—like writers, scriptwriters—use coffee and amphetamines to be more alert and to try to see the bigger picture while they're doing it. And I don't agree with that philosophy at all. I say it should all be done on the natch.

Yeah?
Yeah. Because you can get to that same place if you exercise. By running and swimming and working out with weights, you can get to the *same place* that coffee or any of those amphetamines takes you. And you don't get the jangles.

And that's how you got your spirit strong again, by exercising?
Yeah. And healthy foods. It was a daily regimen; I did that.

Did you also have a daily songwriting regimen?
No. Not every day.

You mentioned that your harmonies sometimes use minor chords. But I notice that you've rarely written a whole song in a minor key.
Yeah, I hardly write anything in a minor key. I just don't. I write major songs.

Why is that? Because you're going for a happier sound?
Sometimes.

Even though this album has a very happy sound, the lyrics contain a lot of darkness. Were you purposely trying to bring more darkness into your music?
No, I was just going with what I felt. Obviously I don't feel like being in a real sunshiney mood for a rock and roll song, right? So I'd write songs that were conducive to the times I was in.

Paul McCartney said that the Beach Boys' album *Pet Sounds* was a major influence on the Beatles and inspired him to come up with the concept for *Sgt. Pepper*. Were you aware of your influence on the Beatles?
[*Pause*] I thought what he said was very nice; I appreciated it and it made me feel very good.

But at the time were you aware that they were paying that much attention to you?
I thought of it as an intergroup rivalry. An intergroup inspiration. Both.

Were you paying much attention to what they were doing?
I was paying attention to what I was doing more than what they were doing. I was listening to their albums but I don't know . . . I liked the Beatles more than just about any group in the world. And I think the Beatles made very good music. They were very inspirational to me in my career.

Paul McCartney's spirit, his drive and his aliveness, turn me on.

Like him, you've created many songs that are masterpieces.
Here's my idea of a masterpiece: You write a song, you work every day at it for a couple of months. You see, every day I'd get up, and I'd water my

plants, and I'd nurture along my thoughts and my trip that I'm on, and that's my masterpiece. Just like a masterpiece that you work on, know what I mean?

What I'm saying is that a masterpiece is not something that comes in two days. No masterpiece ever came overnight. A person's masterpiece is something that you nurture along. You don't get the masterpiece over like shooting down a piece of candy. Eating candy's too easy. Know what I mean?

That it can't be rushed, that it takes work.

Absolutely. Like Gene has taught me, life is work. And when you're done working, you play. You don't take your mind off your work at all. Until you are done working.

Is music work or play?

Work. Definitely work, oh, yes. It's play because it's fun, it's music. But most of it comes out work. For some reason, it all comes out work.

Is writing songs a fun process for you?

It's a fun process. Producing is not as much fun as writing. Producing is recording, right? Recording has much more pressure than writing. It just has.

What's your songwriting routine like nowadays? Do you work often?

The songwriting has diminished a little bit. I'm slowing down, man. In favor of concentrating on and keeping an eye on my solo career to see just what's gonna happen.

Even a moderately successful record would constitute a solo career, though. You don't have to have a number one record to be a solo artist. Some people don't think the charts are the best measurement of a man's success. Know what I mean? I've always been psyched out by the Top Ten. Whenever I think "Top Ten," I think, "That's a way of measuring your success. By the Top Ten." You say, "Hey, I got a Top Ten record. How 'bout you, buddy?" I feel *good* that way. It's a competitive feeling, you know?

Yes. You're one of the few songwriters who has been able to write commercial songs that are also very artistic, creative songs. But often the artistic songwriters never get on the charts. Do you work at making songs commercial?

Oh, yes. You write in two ways. Here's the two things you do: One, you go where your heart tells you to go. If that heart says, "Hey, this kind of song today," you go, "Thumbs up! That's what I'll do today. I'll do a hot song." And you also consider, "What is it that people like? *What would somebody like?* What is that certain something that everybody is looking for?" *Commerciality*, they call it. There should be another word for it. What is that word? Commerciality might mean mass appeal. That's how I feel. I think it's a positive plus to go down that road. I mean, it's a good place. Know what I mean? It's creative.

You have room to work. You can go anywhere with it, really. It's a wide open field. Look at the sixties. Look how scary that was. Talk about a scary time period for music—the sixties were heavy. The sixties were very heavy.

How come?

Because of Phil Spector. Phil Spector's records, obviously, were the best records. Best *production* records. His style of production was so copied. [*Louder*]

Unbelievable influence in the recording industry. The whole industry was rocking right alongside Phil Spector. Everybody was saying, "Wow, did you hear 'Be My Baby,' man?" I heard that record somewhere in my head. It's always going to be a mystery to me how that sucker got that record together. All those records, castanets and all those sounds. I'll never know how he did it.

People listen to your albums and wonder the same thing.
Yeah, some. Some of our albums were pretty good. We had some good albums.

"Heroes and Villains" is an amazing piece of music.
Oh, *that* was a cool record. That was a cool record, that really was.

You wrote that with Van Dyke Parks?
Yeah, yeah, I did.

I was wondering if you know if he has heard your new album.
I don't think so. He might have, I don't know. I never sent him a copy. He might have gone out and bought one. Who knows? You never know. Sometimes he doesn't listen to anybody. And other times he does.

Did you ask him to work on this album with you?
Well, yeah. Some . . . some stuff I thought maybe we could do together and collaborate on. And on others I wouldn't. You know, I'm the fall guy, I'm the heavy. I go out there and take chances. That's okay, though. It pays off to be courageous. Courage pays off. Honesty pays.

What was it like putting "Good Vibrations" together?
The whole idea behind "Good Vibrations" was that we were setting out to create a record that everybody would spook out to. It would scare people and that would be a really heavy record. And what we did was, we got so into it that the more we created, the more we *wanted to create.* You know what I mean? So there was no real set direction we were going in. Know what I mean? And the whole deal just came together like gangbusters. That record came together like *nobody's business.* That really was a good record. It was one of the heaviest records that we ever made, if not *the* heaviest record we ever made. And we'll ever make.

Heavy in what sense?
Heavy in the sense that it sucks you in. It sucks you in to hear it and it gets your gut; it gets you to feel it in your gut. It gives you a response. That's what Phil Spector's did and that's what some of our records did. It hooked people in. It raked them in; we hooked them in and it got them right in the gut.

And it still does. What do you think it is about that song that makes it sound so good even years later?
It's what you call eternal. An eternal record. Something that will recur in eternity.
[*Then, in a slightly different voice at a faster tempo*] Well, yeah, if you look at it that way. It depends on *all* your attitudes. Like if you look at a record and say, "Yeah, it's a great record but man, it's like, passe." You know? Does that change the fact that the record sounds good? Does the record sound any worse because you call it passe? No, it sounds just as good if you call it passe or if you call it current. A record from 1959 you could listen to and you say, "Well,

that record's old hat." Yeah, but I like it.

How about if you listen to "Venus"? What if we played "Venus" by Frankie Avalon right now? It's gonna sound just as good as it did then. And you're gonna think, "Gee, that takes me back. All the way back to 1959 when I first heard that record." In that case, then you have what we call duplication of feeling. It duplicates the feeling you had when you first heard it.

So many of your songs have that timeless element to them. Do you feel they will remain beyond your lifetime?

Uh, yeah. I think "Surfer Girl," believe it or not, after I'm dead and gone, that one's gonna be just great.

Do you think that's your best song?

I think so. I believe it in my heart. It's our theme song. It may not be the best "record" we ever made, but if you consider the song, if you think of it as a song, it's so *simple*. And the bridge is so lilting. It tells a story about love, you know. And it just is something that will just be forever, you know?

Randy Newman told us that "Help Me, Rhonda" is one of his all-time favorite songs.

"Help Me, Rhonda"? Oh, I'll be darned. He thinks that's a good record? Really? [*Looks totally amazed*]

Do you have a favorite song that you didn't write? Somebody else's song?

Yeah, millions. Let me think . . . I like that record "Spooky" by the Classics Four. I always thought that record had a lot of class. The lyrics were great.

Who the hell knows? Who knows what's good or what's bad? Could be just a drop in the bucket . . . in eternity. Yet a little drop in the bucket's all we got; we better like that.

Do you still like your song "God Only Knows"?

If you take it as a song, not a record; "God Only Knows" wasn't the best record ever made. But if you take it as a *song*, you got something going. You got something going because then you can hear the melody and the chords. It's not a great Beach Boys record. But it's still a good song.

Does it make you happy to see how people are responding to your record?

Yes. The record is getting raves, man! People are saying, "Yeah, *yeah!* More! We like that!" I say, "Wow. Whoa. I got some more, folks." I don't know. I think maybe there could be genius [*pronounced ge-ni-us*] inside me. It could be the genius in me that makes me continue.

I think about a lot of music a lot of time. I think about music . . . and I think about girls . . . and I think about business, which is hard. Because it's all a bunch of calculated, hard cold facts, you know. It's hard. Believe me, it's hard. I know you know it and I know everybody knows how hard business can get.

You get upset sometimes; people let you down sometimes. You go through all those trips, you know. But it's worth it, my God, man, you get a little something and you *hang on to it*. You keep going with it. You kick it around, *kick it around*. Get off your ass! Do something! That's all I can say to you.

* * *

Gerry Goffin
Hollywood, California 1989

Though it was a cold day for Los Angeles, only five days before Christmas, meeting with Gerry Goffin at his home was a warm experience. With his four-year-old daughter dressed as a fairy princess with cat ears and a magic wand, playing with the kittens scampering about in the sparkling light of an enormous Christmas tree, Gerry tuned out all of these homey distractions and spoke at length about the early days of rock and roll and about writing with his former wife and collaborator Carole King.

It was the last days of Tin Pan Alley, when writers would go to their offices in the Brill Building (and nearby) in New York every day and churn out new songs like factory workers turning out cars. These were the days when a song could be written, recorded and released all within a month, as was Goffin and King's first hit, "Will You Love Me Tomorrow?" which was recorded by the Shirelles.

Then came the age of the singer-songwriter and Carole began performing her own songs, rather than writing them for others. And though many of the songs on her landmark *Tapestry* album were Goffin/King collaborations, Gerry didn't feel right "putting words in her mouth," and the two stopped writing together for years.

He was born in New York in 1941 and met Carole King at Queens College in 1958, where they found few things more engaging than writing songs. Though Gerry insists that they wrote an abundance of bad songs for years, they soon started writing hits, and generated many that have since become standards, including "The Loco-Motion," "Up on the Roof," "One Fine Day," "Chains," "Natural Woman" and many more.

Gerry has since written words to the tunes of other composers, most notably Michael Masser, with whom he wrote "Saving All My Love for You" for Whitney Houston and "Theme from Mahogany" for Diana Ross.

After our interview was over, I was happily surprised when he asked me to join him for a game of chess. Though the last time I played was around the time *Tapestry* was first released, I agreed, and Gerry brought out his ornate set. Using the same thrifty acumen he brings to lyric writing, he beat me quickly and easily with a minimum of moves, checkmating my king without even capturing many of my pieces. "I never win," he said afterward with a smile. "You can play me anytime."

One thing that you and Carole did was to bring traditional songwriting structures, such as the use of inner rhymes, to rock and roll.
Yeah, it was sort of a synthesis. We didn't really write what you would call a rock and roll song like Chuck Berry or Little Richard wrote a rock and roll song.

How, in your mind, were they different than those kind of songs?
Well, Carole had a great capacity to write great melodies. She was aware of chordal structures. She didn't use the typical I-IV-V chord progressions. It was a great experience for me. She was studying to be a schoolteacher and I was studying to be a chemist, and I think we made out pretty good [*laughs*] as far as an easier life.

Did you and Carole enjoy the same kind of songs back then?
Carole liked some music that rubbed me the wrong way. I'd rather not name the music, but it was the kind of music that just went so far lyrically. And the songs didn't seem to have the soul that I wanted to put into a song. And we ended up writing in an entirely different way than all of them.

We liked all the music that was out. It was a great time. It was like music coming from the streets. I know when I was growing up, most songs sounded great. We loved everybody's music just as much as our own. And now it seems like there's maybe fifteen to twenty good songs a year that really stick with you. The rest sort of get in this collage of the same electronic sounds. . . .

Do you remember when you knew you could make your living as songwriters?
Well, Carole's parents were very much against the idea of songwriting. My father encouraged me but my mother said I was crazy. My marks in school fell down a whole lot.

I remember telling my mother I could still do both. Carole ended up coaching me on all my subjects one day and failed all of hers. [*Laughs*]

The big change happened when we met Don Kirshner. He was a great publisher and he gave us confidence. He gave us money to live on—not too much [*laughs*] but he gave us money to live on.

I was working as an assistant chemist, I was in the Marine Corps Reserve,

I was going to night school. I wasn't putting my eggs in one basket. I came from a middle-class background, you know, where there are not too many successful songwriters.

Did you wait until you had your first hit before making a commitment to being a songwriter?

I had trouble making a commitment until I was thirty-two, even after I had maybe fifteen or twenty BMI awards. I still had doubts as to whether this was a fit occupation for somebody. I went back to school and got a job as a chemist for eleven thousand dollars a year. Then I said, "The hell with this," and went back to writing songs. I realized then that I didn't want to play with test tubes anymore.

You said that you and Carole wrote about 150 songs that weren't any good before you wrote "Will You Love Me Tomorrow?"

Oh yeah, they were terrible. The way "Will You Love Me Tomorrow?" was written was that I was out bowling. She went to play mah-jongg [*laughs*] with her mother. I came home and I found this melody on tape and I wrote it all down, except for the bridge.

We had this huge Norelco tape machine. The words just got written in about fifteen minutes. She came home from playing mah-jongg and we wrote the bridge together. About two days later the Shirelles recorded it. Carole did a great string arrangement on it.

It almost happened overnight. All of a sudden we were writing bad songs and then we keyed into what was happening and what was necessary for the market. We still wrote our share of bad songs, but the majority of them were good. We had, from about 1960 to 1965, almost eighty Top Thirty records.

So that's primarily how you learned to write songs, from doing it?

Yeah. It's something I can't do today because I don't get the opportunity to write as much. But we always kept the flow going. We always had this work ethic going where we learned by working. And we tried to write every day. You can't write a great song every day, but we kept the flow and our minds were in tune. Now I throw out the ideas that are bad. In those days, I didn't.

As for advice for young songwriters: Don't be afraid to write a bad song because the next one may be great. It's just like anything else; you've got to keep the synapses in your brain going. And you have to think about it every day. The main thing is keeping your head free just to think about songs, which is a hard thing to do when you're raising kids or you've got a job and you're hustling for money. It's a hard thing.

Is being married to your collaborator a good way to keep the creative flow going? Or does that closeness get in the way?

Being married . . . our daughters sort of suffered because as soon as we made some money, we got someone to take care of the kids so that we were free to write.

It's all part of the hunger of being young. The energy you have. I wish I had that energy right now.

Did you and Carole have any routine way of working together? Would you bring in a finished lyric or write a lyric to a finished melody?

Both ways. I'd write a lyric first, or else she'd play a chord progression on the piano and I'd write a melody over it. I can't do that now because melodies are more sophisticated and not as symmetrical. And I don't sing on key that well, but Carole was always able to change a melody enough to make it interesting.

She mentioned to us that you would often come up with melodic ideas.
On the better songs she wrote most of the music. Songs like "Take Good Care of My Baby"—I wrote most of the music to that. Very obvious melodies. Melodies that wouldn't hold water today, but for those days they were good enough.

Carole had this great songwriting piano feel that everybody loves. If I was doing a session, I don't know if I would hire her to play piano. But she had a way of playing where you could hear the record just by her piano feel.

Also, she would put arrangement ideas on demos. We would go to make demos, and Donny Kirshner was always trying to get us to save money on demos, so Carole would put down a basic piano feel; if we were lucky, we would have a drummer or a bass. We had no synthesizers, so Carole would just put string lines on the piano. So it was piano over piano over piano over piano.

Some people say that there's a new generation of music every three years. And I've been writing songs for thirty years, so I must have lived through ten generations of popular music. I've learned there's no one way to write a song.

You've written a number of songs that have been huge hits in today's market. "Saving All My Love for You," for example, which you wrote with Michael Masser, was a big hit for Whitney Houston. Do you consider that an old-fashioned song to have been a hit nowadays?
"Saving All My Love" could have been written in the thirties. I've got to give a lot of credit to Michael Masser. When he used to play me his melodies, I used to laugh because they sounded like traditional ballads. And I said, "I don't think a traditional ballad is going to make it in today's market." But I'd write to them anyways 'cause I liked his music. And I'm happy he proved me wrong.

Does Masser give you a finished melody to write to?
Oh, it's the most frustrating thing to write with Masser because he finishes a melody completely, and he writes very complicated meters. They don't seem complicated when they come out, but they are.

I'm not used to that because Carole would change a whole melodic line if I had a good line. But Michael won't do that. I have to write exactly to his melody.

So with "Saving All My Love," did you fit that title into his melody?
Well, that was one of the few songs we wrote together. We were both a little drunk [*laughs*] and we just decided to write anything. It's one of the simplest songs and it turned out to be a big hit.

Carole mentioned that one of your strengths was simplicity; saying a lot in a simple way.
Simplicity is necessary to some extent for the mainstream pop market. But if you want to do something artistic, simplicity is in some ways a drawback. I've

always been frustrated because I always wanted to write on a higher level. And all of those songs that I would submit never made it. I think that some of my better songs were never recorded.

Do you feel that your ideas for songs come from within you or from beyond you?

Well, Carole always says they come from God. But [*laughs*] I'm not that pretentious to think that God's gonna send me a lyric. [*Laughs*]

You don't feel that there's a source of ideas that you can tap into?

Well, John Lennon used to say that when you've written something good, you know you've been somewhere. Carole says they come from God.

I think it comes from the emotional experience of life's situations. I'm having a tough time writing lyrics now because my life situation's stable now for the first time in my life. We have a young daughter and we make the birthday party circuit on Sundays. Sometimes she lets me sleep through them. It's getting harder. I can't write off experience anymore.

Do you believe an artist needs turmoil in his life?

Yeah. I'm approaching fifty and it's getting kind of hard. But I want to keep going. I don't know, maybe a play or something. When I have a chance to write for a movie, I can write very well because I get into someone else's persona. And I don't have to think about my own life.

Carole said that one way her lyrics differed from yours is that hers were not born out of pain in the way that your lyrics were. It may be pain but it may be intelligent pain.

[*Laughs*] I always looked at myself as being very lucky to be a lyricist. I remember that before I wrote "Mahogany"—I was living in New York at the time—I was working on a song and it was coming very slow. They were building an apartment house right next to mine. And I said, "Dammit, they're gonna have that apartment house built before I finish this song." [*Laughs*] So I'm glad I wasn't a construction worker.

But you don't think a songwriter can write good songs while living a happy, settled life?

No. My productivity of late proves it to me. I think living in opulence is a drawback. There has to be a hunger. But a lot of people disagree with me about that.

You wrote many of your great songs in New York. Is it harder for you to tap into that creative energy on this coast?

It's a little harder. For me.

Do you have any method for staying in shape creatively?

When I wrote with Carole, it was an every day, nine-to-five thing. Here in L.A. you can call people and say you want to write today, and they'll say, "I gotta get my car washed today" or "I gotta make this meeting" or "I'm writing with someone else." I wish I just had one partner that I could try to write with every day.

You said that it's important to say old things in new ways. Is it hard to write new love songs after all the love songs that have come before?

Yeah, but I think there are still love songs to be written. It's kind of harder in a high-tech society. People are not as vulnerable to sentiment. It's harder but I still think it's possible.

Do you remember what working with Carole at the Brill Building was like? Was it similar to working a normal, everyday job?

Yeah, it was like going to a normal job. It wasn't really the Brill Building; we worked at 1650 Broadway, around the corner from the Brill Building. The Brill Building had even more of the same madness. Barry [Mann], Cynthia [Weil], Carole and I used to plagiarize each other's songs because we had cubicles directly next to each other. Carole could hear what Barry was playing and I could hear what Cynthia was writing. [*Laughs*] And we'd end up finishing each other's songs. Some of the ideas sort of drifted through.

Did you have any idea at the time of your contribution to music history?

No, we were just interested in putting food on the table and buying baby diapers.

I know that when Lennon and McCartney started writing songs, they wanted to be the next Goffin and King—

I think they did that twenty times over. In the late sixties, when all these groups came in, I thought it was a more honest thing because you had bands writing their own music and singing what they personally wanted to sing instead of singing what some other songwriter said. I thought it was good, and so did Carole. And that sort of led to our divorce, because she wanted to go out there and make a statement on her own, and I said, "I can't put words in your mouth." And she came up with some pretty good lyrics on her own.

But you did put a lot of great words into her mouth—many of the greatest songs that she did on her own had lyrics that you wrote, such as "Natural Woman."

It's sort of different when you're writing for an artist. My favorite writer is still Bob Dylan; it'll always be Bob Dylan. I always put him on a level way above the average. He sort of blew my mind. When I first started listening to his records, I went nuts. I said, "Nobody ever told me you had to write poetry." [*Laughs*]

Did you like the Beatles' version of your song "Chains"?

Oh, yeah. That's a great honor, to have a Beatles record.

Did you have any idea of what a big influence you were on Lennon and McCartney?

I was watching some daytime show that John Lennon was on. He said, "When we were growing up we wanted to be Goffin and King." And that blew me out of my seat. [*Laughs*] That was a great compliment.

After the Beatles came along, we wanted to be the Beatles. [*Laughs*]

Carole told us that "Natural Woman" was a title that Jerry Wexler suggested to you.

I was in New York and just coming out of the office. A limousine pulled up and it was Jerry Wexler; and he said, "I've got a great title for you: 'Natural

Woman.' " I went home and wrote it with Carole, and Jerry produced a great record. It's a classic record.

Do you remember coming up with the title for "Loco-Motion"?

I had that in my head for about two years and it seemed silly. Then Donny Kirshner said, "I got to Didi Sharpe"—this should show you the mentality of the time—"and she wanted a follow-up to 'Mashed Potatoes.'" So I said, "Why not?" We had a girl who took care of the kids called Eva Boyd, who became Little Eva. Donny said, "Hell, if I'm gonna give this to Didi Sharpe," and he put it out as a master. Sold a million-and-a-half copies. . . .

So it was never the plan for her to be the artist, she just sang the demo?

Yeah. And then she bad-mouthed us in *People* magazine saying Carole and I made all the money out of it. We didn't make all the money. [*Laughs*] Donny made all the money.

Did Little Eva continue recording after that?

We made three records afterwards. They all went Top Thirty. A terrible song called "Keep Your Hands Off My Baby" was a follow-up. That went Top Ten.

That's a funny song to write for the woman who was taking care of your kids. How did you know she could sing?

I heard her singing around the house. She had a good, pristine voice.

You said that you and Carole didn't write real rock and roll songs. Yet "Loco-Motion" seems like a rock and roll song, even though it does have minor chords in it. Do you think of it as a rock song?

Yeah, but it's still not coming out of Jerry Lee Lewis-type piano. That was what rock and roll was. Carl Perkins. Some of my favorite songs were written by Leiber and Stoller. All the old Coasters' hits, "Yackety Yak," "Poison Ivy." They put a certain intelligence into their writing and producing. All the Drifters' hits I really liked because they used strings but they didn't use them in the conventional ways as sweeteners. They would use cellos as rhythm instruments. They were great producers. That's why I wanted to have Carole do a string arrangement on "Will You Love Me Tomorrow?" I still think that's a great record.

Did you write "Will You Love Me Tomorrow?" to Carole?

No. That was a classic "will you still respect me in the morning" idea from the fifties. You know, "Will you love me tomorrow if I make love to you tonight?" I was a horny young teenager, just like everybody else, and I heard that line a million times.

Is your connection as collaborators as strong as it was when you were married?

Well, now we're like brother and sister. When we were man and wife it was different. She's on her fifth husband, I'm on my third wife. It's time to put all our past grievances behind.

There's less urgency now. And the urgency was what made us write so prolifically. Now she'll come over and if she doesn't have anything and I don't have anything, we'll say, "Let's go out and have some sushi." In the old days, we would just keep pounding away until we got something. We don't push ourselves as hard.

Is there one song that you and she have written together that is your favorite?
I think "Up on the Roof" is my favorite song that I wrote with her.

Do you remember writing it?
I was living in New York, where to get away I wouldn't climb up the stairs but I'd take the elevator [*laughs*] to the top of the roof and just get a little space away from the electricity of the city.

That was a great melody, a very lasting melody. Carole just came up with it one day when we were driving home in the car. She came up with the melody a capella.

The whole thing?
Well, not the bridge but the verses.

And how would that work then? Would she go home and tape it for you?
No, we had to carry around these big Norelco tape recorders so we didn't mess with tape recorders. [*Laughs*]

Maybe it's age or maybe it's too many drugs, but I just can't retain a melody like I used to. I have to listen to it over and over again on the tape recorder. Maybe it's just laziness, I don't know.

Would you take her melody and change it at all?
Not on that song. A lot of times when we would work I would bend phrases to fit in the lyrics. Which is sort of cheating according to Masser, [*laughs*] but . . . it's a lot harder for me nowadays. It's a lot harder, but you make a lot more money on the songs nowadays than you did then.

Nowadays you don't write for singles like you did in the old days. In the old days you could write a single and you'd be working on the follow-up while the single was out. But now you could die before your record comes out. [*Laughs*] It's a long process.

You used to be able to turn them out pretty quickly—
Yeah, there was a momentum you built up.

So you find that being a songwriter is a lot harder these days?
It is. It's definitely a lot harder.

Both you and Carole mentioned your use of inner rhymes. Was that something that came to you naturally?
That's where my father's influence came in. He showed me that when I was very young, playing me the songs of Cole Porter or Rodgers and Hart. He'd play "My Funny Valentine" or "I'm in the Mood for Love," and things like that.

I've heard so much great music. Even if I never wrote a song, it would have been rewarding enough to be tuned in to hear so much great music, so many diverse fields. You can go back to "Rock Around the Clock" or "Somewhere Over the Rainbow." Just to be a part of music history is something very important.

* * *

Carole King
New York, New York 1989

She is one of the most successful female songwriters of all time. Even before her two-sided hit of "It's Too Late" and "I Feel the Earth Move" went to number one in 1971, Carole King had already written eight other number one records. They were co-written with Gerry Goffin, whom she met in 1958 at Queens College in New York. Together, Goffin and King churned out an amazing flow of hit records, inspiring the likes of the Beatles with their success.

Born Carol Klein in Brooklyn on February 9, 1941, she took piano lessons from her mother when she was four and started writing her own music only a few years later. She met a young songwriter at Queens College named Paul Simon, and the two of them teamed up to make demos for others, with Carole covering piano, vocals and drums. She also met Gerry Goffin at Queens, and when they started dating, they found more excitement at the piano than anywhere else, "even the movies," Carole said. So they started to write songs together—Carole generating most of the melodies and Gerry most of the words—and wrote about 150 "bad songs" (according to Gerry) before coming up with their first hit, "Will You Love Me Tomorrow?"

It was when they began working for Don Kirshner's Aldon Music that their success blossomed, writing hit songs for a myriad of artists, including the Drifters, Bobby Vee, the Animals, Herman's Hermits, the Monkees, the Righteous Brothers, and Blood, Sweat and Tears. The Queen of Soul, Aretha Franklin, recorded the classic "Natural Woman," while the Beatles paid a tribute to their idols by recording "Chains" in 1963.

Carole has never been the type of songwriter who pays attention to trends, knowing after all these years that a great song transcends them all. Even at the inception of rock and roll, when most writers were using a variation on a blues progression, she brought a sophisticated harmonic sense to their songs that few other writers were using. And Gerry, brought up on writers like Cole Porter, and Rodgers and Hammerstein, brought traditional lyrical values to the songs, such as the use of inner rhymes. The combined results are deceptively simple songs like "Loco-Motion" (the only song in history to have gone to number one four times) and the eternally jubilant "Up on the Roof."

In 1968, Carole and Gerry ended their collaboration and their marriage, and Carole moved to Los Angeles, where she began to reluctantly perform her own songs. "I never wanted to be the performing artist," she recalled. "I was always the vehicle through which the songs could be communicated to a *real* singer. The switch occurred when I moved to California in 1968. I was encouraged by Danny Kortchmar and Charles Larkey to perform with them as a group, and we made an album called *City*. I didn't have any intention of going out and performing live. It was a way to make a record while hiding behind a group situation. Having done that, the next transition was to do a solo album. I still had no idea about performing live. I was just gonna do the same thing I always did, make demos, only instead of having them go to a real singer, we just figured we would put them out with me singing."

Although the idea of being a recording artist seemed like a natural progression to her from inside the studio, the thought of performing live was horrifying. But thanks to James Taylor, she was eased into it gradually. "Just around the time of *Tapestry* I met James and watched him perform, and he made it look so easy. And he invited me onto the stage to play piano. And then one night he said, 'Why don't we let you play one of your songs?' I think it was 'Up on the Roof,' which he always loved. And I did, and I was pre-loved because they already loved James. And then they knew the songs, so it was really a no-lose situation. I could have been terrible, and they probably would have dug it that I just did it anyway."

In 1971 *Tapestry* emerged an instant classic. Packed with hit after hit, many of them written while still with Gerry, it outsold *Sgt. Pepper*, became one of the best-selling albums of all time, and quickly erased any doubt as to the viability of Carole King as a recording artist.

Do you remember writing your first song?
Not really. Young. Nine?

You were playing piano at that age?
Yeah. I was classically trained but periods of lessons on and no lessons.

Do you remember what it was at the time that made you want to write songs?
I didn't think of them as songs. I thought of them as melodies, I guess. They weren't whole songs. I would just put melodies together and make music.

When I was about fifteen I started writing my own lyrics, and they were so bad that I didn't want to write songs again for a while. Until I met Gerry.

Did you and Gerry have any kind of regular songwriting routine? Would he give you a finished lyric?
It varied. All of the above. It varied then; it varies now.

Was your song "You've Got a Friend" written for anyone in particular?
No. That song was as close to pure inspiration as I've ever experienced. The song wrote itself. It was written by something outside of myself through me.

Is that an unusual feeling for you?
It happens from time to time in part. That song is one of the examples of that process where it was almost completely written by inspiration and very little if any perspiration.

Does that give you the feeling that these songs come from beyond you?
Absolutely.

Can you give us any advice about how to get in touch with that source?
Songwriters, both lyricists and melody writers, are often plagued with the thing most often known as writer's block. All writers are, writers of prose as well. I have found that the key to not being blocked is to not worry about it. Ever.

If you are sitting down and you feel that you want to write and nothing is coming, you get up and do something else. Then you come back again and try it again. But you do it in a relaxed manner. *Trust* that it will be there. If it ever was once and you've ever done it once, it will be back. It always comes back and the only thing that is a problem is when you get in your own way worrying about it.

I'd like to say that I almost never have worried about it. Because when it seemed to be a problem, when I seemed to be . . . I don't even want to say "blocked" because it seems like too strong a word. But when the channel wasn't open enough to let something through, I always went and did something else and never worried about it and it always opened up again. Whether it was an hour later, which is often the case, or a day later or a week later or sometimes a few *months* later, I just didn't worry about it.

So when you're at the piano and it's not flowing, you don't force it; you just get up and come back to it at a different time?
Right. Another thing that I do is I might play someone else's material that I really like and that sometimes unblocks a channel. The danger in that is that you're gonna write that person's song [*laughs*] for your next song. It's just sit down and, again, if you're a lyric writer, read something that you really like, enjoy something that you really like. Or sometimes I'll play something of my own that I really like, something that is already existing that is *fun*.

Do you find that your hands go to old familiar patterns at the piano? How do you avoid repeating yourself?
I *don't* think about it. If I'm writing something and it sounds too much like something I've already written, I might consciously try to change it but, again,

I don't worry about it; I'm not overly concerned with the mechanics of how it's going to work.

Once the inspiration comes, that directs where the perspiration goes, where the work goes. I don't mean to sound like it's some hippie philosophy of [*in a high, fairy-like voice*] you just sit down and it's *all* flowing through you. Because there's a lot of hard work involved in songwriting. The inspiration part is where it comes through you, but once it comes through you, the shaping of it, the *craft* of it, is something that I pride myself in knowing how to do.

I like to be unpredictable. For example, in the songs on my album, *City Streets*, the A&R man looked through them and said, "Each song has a different structure. And not one song has a structure that is recognizable." There isn't one song that's AABA or ABAB. They all turn left somewhere. [*Laughs*] And that's something that I work at.

I do not like to do the predictable thing. That's not to say that it's invalid to do that. Just for me, the challenge and the fun is when you start to write a song that might go AABA, and you might take your B section and go somewhere else before you come back to A. Or you go AA-B-C and then you go back to A. Because one of the things that I try to be conscious about in writing a song and crafting a song is the concept of bringing it home. That is, there's a beginning to a song, and there should be an end of a song, and of course there's a middle. And I like to take the middle any place it wants to go. But whenever I take it to the end, I like to bring it somewhere familiar, someplace that people feel it's resolved, it's settled; it comes back *home* at the end, whatever home means.

Do you ever feel limited by the song form?

No! The song form is limitless. You can do anything you want. Given the fact that a song is generally something that takes between three to five minutes on a record. But if you feel like going seven minutes, you can go seven minutes. If you want to write a really short song, you can do that. I think it's kind of nice because you're given a task to make a statement, musical and lyrical, and you do it and you don't have two hours to do it in. That's kind of nice; but I don't think it's limiting at all. I think it's liberating.

Is there any kind of musical signature you would consider your own, any set of chord changes that defines the Carole King sound?

[*Laughs*] Well, it's been widely quoted back to me that a four chord with a five bass has been one of my signatures. I guess I still use it. It's one of those things I guess I got known for doing. Musicians have called it the "Carole King chord" although I'm sure I didn't originate it. But I did use it a lot.

I try not to overuse it since it's sort of become a thing you expect. I try to be unpredictable, in my life and in my work. [*Laughs*]

Is there a single song of your own that is your favorite?

I can't say that there is because they're like children. There are some songs that I know are better than others. There are some that I still think about and I still like, and there are others that I've basically forgotten, although sometimes I'll listen to something and say, "You know, that wasn't bad." But, I don't know, the ones that are standards, the ones that hold up longest I don't want to say I'm proudest of, but they've stood the test of time. You know, "Natural Woman," "You've Got a Friend," "Will You Love Me Tomorrow?" The first and the last I mentioned were written with Gerry but ones I've written myself hold up, too. To my everlasting surprise.

I want to say something about my writing of lyrics. When you write with Gerry Goffin, you become intimidated, like why bother to write your own lyrics when you have a Gerry Goffin to write with.

But when our marriage ended and our relationship changed a little bit at the time, in terms of ability to work together easily—it was a temporary condition that we weren't able to work together for a little while, and it was only for a little while—that was when I sort of thought about doing it again [writing lyrics] and I really didn't like what I was doing that much, but suddenly it clicked into place for me at that time. It was just before *Tapestry* I guess. By the time we wrote *Tapestry* I was writing with Gerry again but it just didn't click into place, and that's what sort of what motivated me to try doing it myself.

I was always mindful of things that Gerry had taught me about writing lyrics. Above all, try not to be corny. [*Laughs*] Umm, internal rhymes—have fun with internal rhymes. My lyrics are vastly different than his but there's a simplicity about my lyrics that I strive to emulate Gerry in his utter simplicity.

I think that my lyrics are a little more—I want to say childlike—and not born out of so much pain. I think his lyrics reflect either his own pain or the pain of the persona that he's writing for. He has been able to be in touch with a gut level of emotion that I'm only beginning to approach in my lyric writing now. I still look up to him. He's just the best, and I really look up to him as a lyricist very much. He's been of enormous help in guiding my melodies, the direction my melodies take.

Often when we would write, he might actually sing a melody to me along with his lyrics, and I would probably have taken almost the exact melody he sang and just made it so it was more musical sounding. 'Cause he's a singer with guts but he's not a singer that you listen to for the melody of it. You listen to him probably, more for the soul of it. Nobody sang "Will You Love Me Tomorrow?" better, ever. But I was able to melodicize what he gave and maybe make it more accessible to people who wanted to hear it sounding like a singer was singing it.

That's interesting, because so many of the songs that you and he wrote together sound like they were written by one person; the words and music fit so perfectly together.

We always talked about marriage. It's not a new phrase; many songwriters talk about it. The marriage of the music to the lyrics is key. And our personal marriage was an outgrowth of that, and it was hard to tell which was which. But the marriage between our words and our music continues to this day.

When we're connected, which is most of the time when we write together, the magic is still there; the marriage of the music and the lyrics is an understood thing that requires very little discussion. It just happens. And there's just a little fine-tuning done between us. But when we write, we write like one person.

An example of that would have to be your classic song "Natural Woman," which doesn't seem like a lyric a man would write.

The title was Jerry Wexler's, which is why his name appears as writer on the song. But Gerry took the title and ran with it.

I know that when Lennon and McCartney started writing songs together for the Beatles that they wanted to be the next Goffin and King—

I was actually told that by them. They were very much aware of us as writers and I was extremely complimented.

I love that process as well because then the Beatles, who having been influenced by myself and Gerry, came back and made such an impact and, of course, left their mark on me as somebody to aspire to and emulate.

Did you like the Beatles' version of your song "Chains"?

Yeah!

They were listening to your songs when starting out; which songwriters were you listening to at the start of your career?

Jerry Leiber and Mark Stoller, primarily. They had a huge impact on us, a major influence in our early songs. The idea of taking street rhythm and blues and combining it with classical music, like "There Goes My Baby" with the timpani by Ben E. King; "Spanish Harlem" with the violins and the entire string section arrangement. That was amazing because my background and Gerry's was in classical; it was pretty strong. But we also loved rock and roll and street music. So to have them put together was like, yeah!

Tapestry became one of the biggest selling album of all time. Did you have any idea that it would be that huge?

No.

Do you have any idea what made it such a popular album?

Right time and the right place.

Is that all?

I think so. I mean, good tunes. But there's been lots of albums before and since with good tunes.

It seems to be one of the few albums in which every song is a potential single.

I like to believe that. [Laughs]

So many great singers, from James Taylor and the Beatles through Aretha Franklin, have performed your songs. Do you have a favorite?

Oh, not at all. I love singing my own songs, but I'm always the first one to sing my songs anyway. So it goes to someone like Aretha. One of my highest moments in time is to have heard what the consummate gospel singer did to one of my songs. To hear the Beatles do it, to hear Springsteen sing "Going Back" and James Taylor's versions of "You've Got a Friend" and "Up on the Roof." The Byrd's versions of stuff, the Monkees' versions of stuff which are kind of fun to go back and listen to. What joy to hear what someone else brings to something of mine. I mean, I throw it out there and they run with it.

In a couple of cases, and I will not ever mention a name, there has been a time or two where a singer has interpreted my song in such a way that I was really let down, that I said, "That is so wrong. I hate this." But it's only happened maybe once or twice in my career. And those times it's probably just a misunderstanding; the person just didn't get it, you know? [*Laughs*] For the most part, the joy of being a songwriter is to hear your song interpreted by somebody else.

The other joy is to hear what the musicians do with it. The band, you know? I come in to a session, and I play it down for the band, and the ideas they bring to it make it coalesce and come together. Because I hear in my head generally what I want it to sound like. But they bring in things that are either true to the vision or not true to the vision. Generally, it takes just a second and they know right where I'm going with it. And that's the magic for me, to have really excellent musicians play on my songs.

So songwriting is still a joy for you?
Yeah! Songwriting is always a joy.

* * *

Lamont Dozier
Los Angeles, California 1987–1988

Along with his partners Eddie and Brian Holland, Lamont Dozier was a main architect of the Motown sound, creating an amazing array of hits in the sixties for the Supremes, the Temptations, Marvin Gaye, and others while shaping a musical genre. Between 1963 and 1967, Holland-Dozier-Holland miraculously created forty-six Top Ten singles (including "Stop in the Name of Love," "Heat Wave," "Where Did Our Love Go," and "You Can't Hurry Love") and established Motown as the supreme source of soul in America.

He was born in Detroit in June, 1941, and made his first records at the age of fifteen as a member of the Romeos. He met Berry Gordy in 1958 and recorded for him under the name Lamont Anthony on Anna Records. He soon began collaborating with the Holland brothers, writing and producing a slew of hits, as well as playing keyboards and singing harmonies on the records.

In 1968 he left Motown to pursue a solo career, recording several albums and two hit singles, "Fish Ain't Bitin'" and "Trying to Hold On to My Woman," in the early seventies. He's also written countless hits for other artists and collaborated with songwriters from Eric Clapton to Phil Collins. Yet, even possessing such an astounding body of work and an unceasing talent, he's one of the most humble and spiritual songwriters around. "I can't take credit for it," he insists. "I'm only human and these things are the making of God."

In 1987, Lamont took the time to help his fellow songwriters by serving as the Chairman of the Board of the National Academy of Songwriters. As editor of *SongTalk*, the journal of the academy, I wisely took advantage of his gener-osity and invited him to contribute a column to each issue. He wasn't crazy about the idea of sitting down and writing one each time—he already had enough writing to do—but was persuaded to do it when I told him that he had only to answer questions, and I'd handle the writing. Editing out my questions, I constructed the columns from his copious and often inspirational responses. Though he's quite shy and soft-spoken in person, over the phone he felt com-fortable enough to speak freely and at length about all facets of songwriting, a subject about which he's clearly acquired a world of wisdom. What follows are those reconstructed conversations with one of the true fathers of soul.

You've written so many wonderful songs over so many years. How do you keep in shape creatively?

I've found over the years that the best way to fight off fatigue is just by doing. I've run into brick walls, so to speak, creative blocks. When that hap-pens, I step away from it, have a diversion or two, watch TV or something. But I don't stay away from it very long, only for about a half-hour or so then I'll go right back into it.

I find that's a form of creative rejuvenation. Then I dive right back into it. Sometimes you have to retreat to go forward. That's what I do. I don't wait and let it linger because then psychologically you form a mental block. Then you're really in trouble.

You're only human, you know. And the human body and mind will take the attitude, "I don't want to do this. I'm tired." And you have to keep that energy up. You are your own worst enemy. We all have the tendency to be lazy. So we give up and start making excuses for not being able to finish what we start.

Do you find that songwriting is something you have to do every day to keep the spirit flowing?

Yes. I have to do it every day. That's one thing I got out of Motown that was very productive for me. We got up early and worked late. We started by punching a clock. That sort of working regimen stayed with me over the years. I still get up quite early. That's what I do: write songs. It's a full day of work every day.

Writing songs is a twenty-four-hour job. You dream in it, you eat it, you sleep in it. You are having a conversation with people and you're working; you find yourself listening for a certain thing that might strike a chord for a song. It's a constant work thing for me. It's my relaxation, my fun, my everything. Outside of my kids, of course. It's therapeutic as well. When I'm down, I can work. That's what brings me out of it. And when I'm up, I even work better.

Music is a constant energy source for me for all occasions. It's a back-up for me in every walk of life.

Today I woke up writing because I went to bed writing, and I didn't quite feel what I was writing last night was up to par. So I went to bed with it on my mind, and then when I got up, I woke up fresh and I knew exactly where the problems were. Almost like I worked it out in my dreams.

Do you have any technique for tuning out the world and tuning into the source of ideas?

During those moments when I'm at the piano coming up with melodies and ideas, I'm somewhat in a trance. If you listen to my tapes, you hear all sorts of background noises, like children playing, and you wonder to yourself how a person can create under those circumstances. But you learn to just shut out everything around you.

I focus in on what I'm doing and nothing else can really penetrate my psyche at that particular time. It takes a while to work into the trance. It takes me about ten or fifteen minutes and I'm into it.

Do you have any idea where your ideas originate? Do you feel that they come from beyond you?

Yes. I can't take credit for this stuff. I've been too successful too long. I'm only human, and these things are the makings of God. I feel that I've been thoroughly blessed over the years with an abundance of songs and material. I'd be stupid to say that there is no force other than my own that is guiding me through all of this. There is definitely God behind this thing that I do. Everything I do—that's good, at least—is a reflection of His hand.

If ideas come from God, must a writer be a righteous person to be worthy of that source?

I believe so. It's possible to connect with the creative source by thinking right and being right. That's the secret to having a successful life, no matter what it is. Thinking right and being right. And you'll tap into all these positive forces.

If you walk around negative-thinking, nothing but negative things will come up. I think about the good things, in spite of all the bad things that are all around us, I'm always looking for that ray of sunshine. And it's always there for those who have eyes to see.

You've written some of the world's sweetest and most memorable melodies. How do you pursue them?

It's trial and error. You sit and play chords. Everybody has their own way of doing things. There's no law and there's no book. You can go to Juilliard and Oakland and all of these places. A lot of people come out of these schools and they never do anything; they never tap into these things. Because you have to find that yourself.

Is physical exercise a means of tapping into that energy?

Yes, but you have to be careful. Running tears down too much of the body. So I do a lot of walking now. You need to have a source that will put back that energy you use up. You use up so much energy creating; tapping into that force that gives you that creativity is mind-boggling and draining. When I get through a day of work, I am drained. Proper exercise is important to get your head together. It's good for putting back what you take out.

I exercise sometimes before and sometimes after songwriting. But I don't feel exercise wears you out for songwriting. Song writing is a whole different ballgame. It's strictly mental; you have to tap into another force that has nothing to do with the physical.

Do you feel that melody is as important as it once was?

Melodies in songs are not as prominent as I'd like them to be. But I think melodies are more on a surge now than they used to be. We've run the gamut. It comes and goes in cycles. I think it's coming back.

The nature of people is to walk down the street and whistle a tune. So with that in mind, I think we're going to have melody. People will buy a good melody if it's there.

When writing, if I get a gut reaction from a melody, if it moves me, then I know it's good. I never pick a melody unless I've slept on it, so to speak. I may write a melody today and then I'll let it sit by itself for two or three days. I'll put it down, ignore it, come back to it, in two or three days, and if it still hits me, I know it's good. It's like hearing it for the first time.

If a melody comes back to me, if I start humming it, if it's made a mark on my unconscious in some way, then I'll know it's melodic and I'll continue.

What makes a melody great? Does a tune need a large range to be powerful?

No, a melody doesn't necessarily need a big range to be strong. You can take a minor melody that has no really significant highlights to it—it can be a down kind of melody—but if it has a haunting refrain that is so infectious that it stirs the spirit, that's what makes a great melody.

When I listen to some of the old tunes, by Richard Rodgers or Cole Porter or Irving Berlin, their melodies stand up today. You can pick them up anytime, if you're a music lover; those melodies have been around for years. There's a reason why. They carry a certain mystique about them and a feeling that grabs you right away.

I've always had this philosophy that if I don't like it, nobody's going to like it. "Stop in the Name of Love" is a good example of a strong melody we wrote.

But the melody isn't the only important part of a song. There's a marriage between the melody and the harmony—the chords you use that the melody has to stand on—that must be strong. And you have to have the lyrics that work with that melody—there are those three elements, and if you have all three, you will have a song that can stand the test of time.

People still write great melodies but not as much. In these days of "Get-the-money-and-run-music," as I call it, we have a tendency to overlook some things. I think some writers might find a lush melody to be square. In this age of rap and disposable music, there's not a great emphasis on writing great melodies. But there are still serious writers who tend to take their craft seriously and put in the time to come up with a great melody.

Nowadays rhythm seems to be more important than melody when it comes to hit songs. How do you balance what is commercial with what moves you musically?

The executives at the record companies want something that is gonna sell. And it's hard to stick to a craft if nobody wants it. So you find yourself between a rock and a hard place. You want to write good melodies, but you want to survive and you want people to hear the stuff. You wind up joining the bandwagon.

But for the few that have the heart to stick with their own personal convictions as far as melodies go, who stick to their guns as far as writing good songs regardless of who likes them, I think in the long run, they're the ones who are going to contribute the most to keep the music flourishing.

Rhythm is very important as far as dance records go. America's in love with 4/4 time, especially when it comes to dance. When it comes to listening or ballads, it can be in 6/8 or any other type of beat.

When it comes to dance, throughout history, the 4/4 beat is easiest to follow. Rhythm always came first in the Motown songs. The rhythm carried the feeling of the song across. It's very important for the melody to sit on something rhythmically infectious that will carry the melody. If the melody doesn't have a good rhythm to sit on, it falls apart, and there's no continuity.

You've written countless hits through so many phases of popular music. Do you listen to the radio to see what is currently a hit, or do you follow your heart in that regard?

You have to write from your heart, but at the same time you have to keep abreast of the trends. You have to do both. I always have. I think every writer owes it to the public to at least know what it is they're responding to.

Every note has been played. Every backbeat has been beat, so to speak. You can only learn from your peers. You might come up with something different, but music is not something I invented. It was here long before any of us were here. So there's nothing wrong with listening to other work.

Listen to the great writers of the past, present and future. If you're serious about having a career, you have to listen to everything, all types of music—from opera through country-western. There are so many facets of music. If you're serious about a career in music, you have to have the adaptability to adjust to whatever it is you're called on to write. You go into your library of knowledge and dig down deep inside of yourself to come up with the right thing.

I don't think about commercial concerns when I first come up with something. When I sit down at the piano, I try to come up with something that moves me. Writing is a very personal thing. Then you invite the other people in—the influences of the marketplace. You adjust it to make it something that can be commercial and potentially a big hit. But it all starts with the heart, with writing what moves you.

* * *

Jimmy Webb

Los Angeles, 1988
New York, 1993

"Jimmy and me are stonecutters,
building a structure to God."

—Art Garfunkel
from *Still Water* poem #59,
discussing the making of *The Animals' Christmas*
with Jimmy Webb

"When I was a kid, I was a science fiction freak," Jimmy Webb recalls. "I re-member one Sunday that I was sitting in my dad's church. He was a Baptist preacher. I was sitting about halfway back and I had a science fiction novel snugged up under my Baptist hymnal and I was reading away. My dad was preaching a mighty sermon. He looked back and I guess the sight of me in this pious pose must have struck him as altogether unlikely.

"He said, 'Jimmy, what are you doing back there? Come down here right now.' So I took that long walk down the aisle of the church to the front. He said, 'Stand up right here.' I turned around and faced the congregation. He said, 'Tell this congregation what you're reading.' So I had to say, '*Martian Chronicles*, sir.'"

With a gentle Oklahoma drawl, Jimmy Webb is transported when telling stories like this one. The pictures he carries with him hold such power that they don't simply remind him of the past, they take him there. In the same way, his songs transport the listener with an immediacy unmatched in most music. (Listen today to Glen Campbell's version of "Wichita Lineman" and see if it doesn't sound as good, or even better, than it did in 1968.)

His songs reflect a genuine America, from the dam builders who lost their lives constructing the Hoover Dam ("The Highwayman") to the lineman working the wires high over Wichita ("Wichita Lineman"). His use of vivid place-oriented imagery, combined with a sophisticated, piano-based, gospel-inspired genius for melody, make him one of the few real masters of the American song.

In Hollywood to perform at the historic Cinegrill in the Roosevelt Hotel, Jimmy Webb sat with me in the hotel's formal dining room, sipping Earl Grey tea. When I brought up his wistfully nostalgic song, "Wooden Planes" (beautifully rendered on Garfunkel's *Watermark* album), he smiled, pleased and surprised that I opened this door to his childhood, and was back in the "west Texas wind," playing with the wooden planes his father used to fashion. Later, at the piano in the Cinegrill, he quietly played the chord sequence from that song, smiling, and said, "Hey, thanks for bringing that one up. I almost forgot about that one."

He was born on August 15, 1946 in Elk City, Oklahoma, a part of the country that has always strongly colored his writing and his thoughts. When I asked him about the source of "Wichita Lineman," for example, he said, "Really where I got the idea was in the Oklahoma panhandle. It is very close to Kansas, very flat territory. Very lonely highways and telephone poles sort of disappearing into infinity." He stayed there his entire childhood, moving at the age of 18 with his family to Los Angeles. Starting out as a music transcriber in 1964, by the age of 21 Webb was already one of Hollywood's most notable hit songwriters, having written a succession of songs that would be impressive for any songwriter, and especially one so young: Johnny Rivers recorded "By the Time I Get to Phoenix," The Fifth Dimension covered "Up, Up and Away," and Webb was more than on his way, he was already there. Glen Campbell was never so beloved as when he sang a Jimmy Webb song, and so recorded many, including "Wichita Lineman," "Galveston," "Where's the Playground, Susie," "By the Time I Get to Phoenix" and "Honey Come Back." And Richard Harris had the biggest hit of his career when he recorded Webb's momentous L.A.-inspired suite, "MacArthur Park."

Like P.F. Sloan, who Webb immortalized in his song of the same name, Webb has never achieved the kind of success as a singer as he has as a songwriter. Yet he's made many great albums, from *Words & Music* in 1970 to 1993's *Suspending Disbelief.* And in 1996, he recorded *Ten Easy Pieces,* a beautifully intimate album of his most famous songs that no lover of great songwriting should allow to go unheard.

In this age of fabrication, Webb's work is remarkable simply because it's real; it comes from the heart. When I told him that I was astounded by the beauty of one of the new songs he was playing in his show, "Just Like Marilyn," he smiled warmly, and I could tell that this measure of affirmation for one of his still unrecorded, untested songs mattered to him. Days later I was thrilled when a piano-demo version of the song appeared in my mail. "There's something familiar in that style," he sings in the song, "If you listen for a while, can't you hear a heart that is genuine?" Listening to the songs of Jimmy Webb, it's inspiring to remember how moving the expressions of a genuine heart can be.

Were you ever a Wichita lineman yourself?
No, not at all. It's an image; it's a picture.

How do you construct a melody to be as sturdy and lasting as that one? It has a big range with a lot of melodic skips. Is that one way to make it work so well?
I think so. I think it gives you more possibilities. I'm not universally acclaimed [*laughs*] for the range I put singers through. Something like "Up, Up and Away" is pretty hard for a single person to sing; it almost needs boys and girls.

I started writing a lot of skips probably because I was under the influence of Burt Bacharach so much when I started writing. His melodies are very unpredictable, and skip in not odd but unusual directions. And I like that. I think that's the way you get a kind of a new melody, a catchy melody, by playing with intervals like that.

How do you pursue melodies?
All different ways. I write a lot to lyric. In the old days I can remember writing a song in the car with no piano. Just singing melodies and lyrics and driving down the road. Probably the only time *that* ever happened. And I've had words come first, music come first, words and music happen at the same time.

What I like to do is to write down my ideas and my lyrics. I use legal pads and I like to start with at least a sketch of a verse or something. And then I'll probably go to the piano and start working on music and start trying to get a mood. Because I usually know what kind of song I'm after. I know what I'm trying to do when I start. I don't always *get there*. But I try to visualize the way the song's gonna *be*. What it's actually gonna be.

Lyrically and musically?
Yeah. And then, again, I might be led in a totally different direction. But at least when I start out I like to think I know where I'm going.

What leads you in these different directions?
To accomplish the communication behind the lyric.

And usually you have that lyric first?
It's happening that way more and more, yeah. I like titles. I like to have a good title to work with or at least to organize my work around. And the song may end up with another title. And the title may be a fragment or a phrase from the lyric or what have you. But if you start out with a go, if you start out with a *tangible*, then the whole song stays more focused for me. I almost *have* to do it that way.

Speaking of titles, one of your most evocative titles—and beautiful songs—is "The Moon's a Harsh Mistress." Is that a title you came up with before writing the song?

The title is from a short story written by Robert A. Heinlein from an anthology called *A Man Who Sold the Moon*. And I liked the title and it stayed with me for years and years and years and years. It *haunted* me. And I finally wrote the song.

I've hardly ever *done* that. That's a special case. Taking a title from someone else's work. But I'm very straightforward about it; that's what I did. But it was because it was so hauntingly beautiful.

That song has an absolutely soaring melody, but it's based on a fairly simple chord structure.

Well, simple but grainy. Even though chords are simple, they should rub. They should have dissonances in them. They should be interesting even if they are simple. I've always used lots of alternate bass lines, suspensions, widely spaced voicings . . . different textures, really, to get very warm chords.

I've been amazed by your ability in songs to consistently create new chord patterns and progressions, and new melodies. Do you consciously strive to avoid old patterns and invent new ones?

There's no inspiration in it for me otherwise. I just don't enjoy it. It's not any fun and I'd rather be chopping down trees or something. It just has to be interesting from the get-go.

So before I start writing a song, I'd have to know that I had some chordal material that was going to stay under me like my legs. That I've got some good structure underneath me before I ever launch into this highly terrifying process of trying to write a song, which I never believe I'm going to be able to do anyway. Every time I sit down and do it I know I'm not going to be able to do it. It's awful. So before I ever commit myself to try to write some idea, I'd have to have some chord structure under me that was inspiring and I felt was reasonably original—and I know this isn't always possible—but if it fell too far below par in terms of just being interesting to me, there's no way I could write the song. I'd run out of gas very, very quickly.

So you spend a lot of time working only with chord patterns and no melody or words?

Yes.

How do you go about that? Do you actively reverse or alter old patterns?

I'm doing substitutions, I'm taking bass notes that are not in the tonic and putting them with another chord. I'm taking the third out of the right hand and playing it in the left hand, and adding a suspended second to the right hand. I'm playing around with voices. I'm moving things, on one chord I have the seventh in the bass. Which sounds very strange all by itself—if you went over to the piano and hit that chord you'd say that's not a very nice chord. But sometimes it depends on the chord that comes before and the chord that comes after. Sometimes you're setting up what might be deemed strange chords by placing a chord in front of it that's going to set it off the way you might set off a diamond in a gold band. An interesting setting. All of a sudden something that sounds quite particular all by itself will sound quite interesting when it's set up with the proper two bookends of chords. And so a lot of it is not just sitting around and pecking around until you find an interesting chord. But it's sequencing chords. It's stringing them together like pearls on a string. So I do a lot of that.

Once I have a chord that I like and that is different and that buzzes me, I start thinking about where it would go. And then maybe working backwards to figure out how I would set that up. Where would I come from to get to that place? And just a lot of trial and error and mathematic free-association.

Sometimes I work graphically and look at the keyboard as if it had nothing to do with music and it's a mathematical grid. And going, "What if I move that there and move that there?" And not even listen to the sound of it very much at the outset and just trying to gain another mathematical insight into how to move voices around and not be afraid to move them around. And not to be shy about something having a peculiar sound at the outset. And if I start with original material, even if I end up simplifying it, I'm going to be further along the road to originality than I would if I just sat down and played some Gs and some Cs and some A minors.

When working with those chords, are you giving any thought to melody or does that come later?

I really just start out with the structure of the chords. And what I've found is that interesting chords will compel interesting melodies. It's very hard to write a boring melody to a really interesting chord sequence. The chord sequence will push the melody around in really unexpected, interesting ways. And then I think the trick is to make sure they're not too unexpected so you don't end up with some unsingable melody. Or even if it's not unsingable you don't want something that's not memorable or visceral or emotional. I don't want ever to end up with some dry, mathematical exercise for the sake of originality. I want originality—but not at any price.

In your music there's a sense that you have an unlimited, expanding musical expression, as opposed to many writers who seem to have fully expressed the limits of their musical language. Do you feel that there is always new musical ground to be broken?

I'd address that in two ways. First of all, I definitely go into slumps where I feel that I'm recharging and I don't know where I'm going. And like I said before, I never feel like I'm going to be able to write a song anyway. It's usually just something that finds me in terms of inspiration and when it happens, it just happens, and I know there's going to be another song. It just grabs me that way.

I don't think about it much. I'm so superstitious about it and so terrified of the possibility that someday I might sit down at the piano and not be able to write something that I think is good that I just don't think about it. It's like death. I just don't think about it.

What I think in another sense—and if you relate this back to the original question I'm sure you'll find out that I'm talking about the same thing—is that the more complex the music, and the more I try to push the envelope of song-writing, the more frightened I am of a lack of public acceptance.

We live in a country here that is about 50% illiterate. Nobody argues with that figure. I could go an incredible distance into the realm of the art song. I would like to do it. As an intellectual exercise I can see where a lot of things could be done with songs that haven't been done with them. We haven't seen a lot of songs written in free verse. We haven't seen a lot of songs written in a chain of consciousness form with no particular verses, chorus or bridges. Aside from the thing that Van Dyke Parks wrote a few years ago [*Song Cycle*] and a few others, there have been very few legitimate song cycles written in the pop field.

I can see a lot of things that could be done. I just don't think that anybody would be interested in them except me. I wrote a cantata called *The Animal's Christmas* with Amy Grant and Art Garfunkel, the London Symphony orchestra, a 40-voice boy's choir, the organ from St. John's Divine on 110th street. Maybe we sold a hundred records, I don't know. It was not something that could be defined as one thing. You wouldn't say it was rock, you couldn't say it was rap. So there are constraints there because people have to eat, you know. But could a lot of things be done with pop songs that haven't been done? Definitely.

Using existing structures or different ones?

Absolutely. Using different structures. Because you have to break down the structures to get out into another realm. And verse-chorus-bridge-verse-chorus structure has been done so many millions of times that we don't even have to think about it anymore. We already know what to expect. We already know what is going to happen. We take that for granted like that's okay. But that's not necessarily okay.

Does working in the existing song structures seem limiting?

It feels boring because I know exactly what's going to happen next. And I think that what we've done as an industry is to ingrain these ideas into the public over a certain number of generations now where they're completely shocked when anything happens except for a verse or a chorus. Completely shocked! They don't know what to think!

It's a very limiting thing. It's sort of stupid in a way, because it's taken for granted that that's what a song is. I'm not going to go out on my next album and write a lot of free-form tunes. I'm not necessarily going to try to break that ground all on my own. I've had enough problems selling my solo albums over the years. But the original question was: Could other things be done? Are there other worlds to conquer? Are there other things to discover? Are there other things to explore? That's the way I took your question. I think there's a whole universe of possibilities out there.

Do you have a favorite version of "The Moon's a Harsh Mistress"? It's been recorded by Linda Ronstadt, Judy Collins, Joe Cocker, Glen Campbell, and Joan Baez.

Well, you know, it puts me on the spot to say which one. [*Laughs*]

I was wondering if anything can compare with the Joe Cocker version.

You know, I don't know. They're all so good. I know that sounds like a cop-out. Judy's has one of the most beautiful little string arrangements, it's just gorgeous. Linda probably sings it the best. You know, her pipes are just so beautiful. Each version has its own attributes. Not the least of which is Joe Cocker's. It's a totally different message from him; it's more of an angry cry.

Do you have any notion what it is about that one song that allows it to be recorded by so many different people and still retain its power?

Well, I don't know. For one thing, it's simple.

It changes key in a real neat way.

It goes from G to B flat. Yeah, it goes up a minor third. And it's that cycle of chords, that kind of windmilling effect coming down . . . It's a very distinctive intro. I think that's been really important, too. I know when I start it, people already know what it's going to be. It sort of made me realize how important intros can be. You can really use an intro as an integral part of the song, not just as some little piece that you tack on to the front. So I wish all my songs had strong, identifying intros like "The Moon's a Harsh Mistress."

Some of your songs, such as that one and "All I Know" have a very churchy quality, revolving around that I-IV-V pattern but with a melody that keeps building and ascending.

It's interesting that you should mention that because that definitely is straight out of the Baptist hymnal. [*Laughs*] It reminds me of probably what I think is like the most beautiful hymn tune; we sang it as "Come Now, Fount of Every Blessing." It's very Appalachian. It's very simple and haunting. I'm swayed by it. So I definitely borrowed on that and used that energy in "All I Know" and "The Moon's a Harsh Mistress," definitely.

My Dad was a Baptist preacher for twenty-two years. And I got all my training, basically, in the Baptist church.

Where were you raised?

I was born in Elk City, Oklahoma, and spent seventeen years living in southwestern Oklahoma, Oklahoma City, the panhandle of Oklahoma . . . west Texas . . . the flat country, which is the country that I like best, really.

Many of your songs, such as "Galveston," "Wichita Lineman," "By the Time I Get to Phoenix," and others, have a very intense sense of place. When you mentioned west Texas, I instantly thought of your beautiful song "Wooden Planes" and the line: "Wooden planes, propellers spinning in the west Texas wind . . ."

When I think about those days, the only way I can imagine them is sort of with a picture. I can see a house by a road. That's the only way I can *recall* it really, because I was so young. I was six years old in that particular place, where "Wooden Planes" is, where I remember that.

I just have this picture of my brother and I. My father made these airplanes by hand. He made them out of orange crates. And he whittled propellers for them. And when you held them up, the wind would turn them. They were fabulous. They were *magical*. The wind blew all the time [*laughs*] so they were virtually . . . perpetual motion machines. Those were the kinds of toys we had. They were things that my Dad made.

And so to communicate that, I almost have to go back to that photo-graph. That painting in my mind of my brother and me holding those planes. So, I don't know how else to communicate about something like that. As we grow older, our paths become so divergent. And the song is sort of about that. It's about the divergency of siblings, really.

You said that you wouldn't know how else to translate those feelings into a song without showing those pictures. But many songs contain only abstract emotions without any imagery. Songs that give us pictures let us feel our own emotions.

I learned that way of expressing myself really from other writers. I'd be the first to say that Lennon and McCartney had a tremendous effect on me when they came on the scene. And songs like "Penny Lane" had such a cinematic impact on me that that was something I wanted to do.

Paul Simon as well. He is a very evocative writer. He conjures up all kinds of beautiful and surreal images. I would like to think that sometimes I do that.

Is it tough to pull off?

[*Pause*] I think it's a tricky business. [*Laughs*] Sometimes I don't make it, either. I'm in there swinging. I *really want to believe* that I communicate with people who are listening to it, I really do.

Another one of your songs that has very unusual imagery as well as a strong sense of place is "MacArthur Park." Do you remember how that song was born?

[*Laughs*] Oh, yeah! Oh sure. That song was born in Bone Howe's brain. Because he was producing a group called The Association and he wanted a long, structured, rock-like piece for them. And he wasn't afraid of the word "classical." And he was in a completely inventive mood and just invited me to go for broke on something. And I thought, "Great."

I was living on Kirkwood Drive up on Laurel Canyon and I had just bought my first piano. I bought it with the royalties from "Up, Up and Away." It was my only possession. I had cushions under it so I ate under it and slept under it. [*Laughs*] Every once in a while I crawled out from under it and wrote something on it. So it's really my friend; it's really my good old friend.

So I sat up for a couple of days and I experimented. I knew it needed movements. I knew that I wanted something very soaring that I could come back to at the end, and I put the basic thing together. As it turned out, The Association passed on it. They didn't want to do it. And I had it in my trunk for a long time. In fact, it would have stayed in the trunk except that Richard Harris wanted to do it.

How did he hear it?

I was working for Johnny Rivers and Johnny was engaged to write the mu-sic for a theater performance that Richard Harris was directing. We met on the job. And we really liked each other.

At rehearsals backstage there was an old piano and we would play and we would sing. . . . He was my best friend. We went everywhere together. He took me to Dublin and said [*with brogue*], "Jimmy Webb, you must sleep in the bed where I was conceived." So he made me do that. [*Laughs*] He was just a tre-

mendously energetic individual. Almost overpowering; extremely charming, seductive, volatile, *amazingly funny*, and we just got to be good mates.

He sent me a telegram once and it said, "Come to London and let's make
a record. Love, Richard." [*Hearty laughter*] That's all there was to it!

I went over, I took the songs over; he said, "I'll take that one, that one
and that one." I came back here and cut the tracks at Sound Recorders up on
Yucca and Argyle [in Hollywood], took the tracks back there under my arm.
We got a little studio in London, and we overdubbed the vocals. We had a
mighty pitcher of cold Pimms standing by, in case of emergency, and we cut
the vocals in a couple of weeks.

**When you wrote "MacArthur Park," did you originally write it with
that big instrumental section in it?**
Oh, yeah. That's the way I played it the first time I ever played it, really.

How about the cake line—do you remember where that came from?
No.

Did you spend much time in MacArthur Park?
Oh, much. Much. I lived in the Silverlake district at the time and so did
my girlfriend. She worked in the building on Wilshire Boulevard, right on the
park. I'd go over there and we'd have lunch and walk around the lake . . . you
know, do what boys and girls do.

**People go there now and say, "So this is MacArthur Park." How does
it feel to have taken a local spot and made it world-famous?**
[*Laughs*] I don't know. It was beautiful . . . [*softly*] it was beautiful. I will always remember it that way. It really doesn't *matter* how strange that might
sound to someone else because it's another one of those pictures that we were
talking about a while ago. And that's just the way I see that. That's the way I
remember that person, and I remember it through that place.

Do you have favorite keys to work in?
Well, I got used to working in flat keys in the Baptist church; because
quite often they would say to play it in flats because maybe the organist would
rather play it in flats. So maybe it's hard for them to read in sharps. And many
times I was asked to play things in flats. And I sort of got used to it. It's sort
of a common church thing on a local level. I like being forced into sharp keys
but I'm probably most comfortable in E flat or A flat . . . B flat. I like B flat.
And I like F.

**That's interesting because those are keys the guitar is not best suited
for. Your songs have a unique flavor because they are very pianistic.**
I wish I could play the guitar. I wish I had some guitar songs. [*Laughs*]

Your song "The Highwayman" is kind of a guitar song.
Yeah, it is, kind of. I play an acoustic picking style on the piano which I
sort of learned to do years ago. Which is why "Highwayman" sounds like a guitar song, I think.

**It's an amazing song. It's been called a song about reincarnation. Is that
how you look at it?**
You know, I think reincarnation is irresistible. [*Laughs*]

As a theme to write about?

Yeah. I also think that there might be something to it.

What really suggested the song is a very vivid dream I had in London. And it was the only one I ever had like that. And in essence, it's the first verse of the song. It was a wild pursuit of me by guys with . . . It was just terrifying and I woke up and I had sweat pouring off of me. I had a piano in my suite and I went right to the piano.

The last three verses are kind of suggested by the first. I just put another layer on and then another layer on and worked on the original idea. It is not meant to be a personal account of *channeling* or anything like that. It has, for me, a lot of symbolism. It's about the kind of people who built this country up.

The first verse is the rogue, the outlaw nation, the highwayman nation. The second verse is the seafaring nation; the trading and the growth of a nation, and its subsequent generations adding to that. And then the dam builder is a generation of construction and science and technology. And then the last verse is a spacefarer; he's gonna fly a starship. And so, it's an *American* allegory. It's Everyman, in a way.

It's interesting that the first verse came from a dream. But the next verses, especially about the dam builder, seem so real.

Oh, well . . . You know, I like that song *so much* that on the inner sleeve of my album, *El Mirage*, is a photo of Hoover Dam. That picture just terrifies me for some reason. It's so solemn, it's so . . . magnificent. It has such power, that image. The *mass* of that dam. And the truth is that guys were trapped in it.

The final verse of the song contains the lines: "I may become a highwayman again / Or I may simply be a single drop of rain / But something will remain . . . " And that goes beyond reincarnation; it gives a sense of timelessness, of man's energy going on.

Well, that I believe in. I mean that, I just believe it. One of the things that Einstein speculated on when he was working on his Unified Field Theory at the end of his life was the nature of human consciousness, and he believed that if he could prove the Unified Field Theory that it might prove that human consciousness is an electrical phenomenon that can exist independent of human tissue.

I think that even the most callous of us must feel that there is something timeless about this experience. That it might be true that we live it over and over again. That might be equally true. But we are a part of eternity. And we sometimes seem to remember things that we shouldn't remember. And sometimes we see things coming that we shouldn't see coming. Someone knows that a plane's gonna crash. For three days he dreams about it, and it crashes.

There is a hidden agenda of some kind. I believe in God very strongly, but I don't presume to speculate on how He chooses to run His universe.

Do you believe that your songs will remain?

I don't think much about history in terms of my own music. It's just something that I'd rather not speculate on. I sometimes definitely hear the timeless in other people's music.

Not in your own?

Well, I don't criticize my own music. I write it and I forget it. I mean, I pretty much leave it behind me. Because . . . [*softly*] because I'm trying to do more. I'm always trying to do something else. As soon as possible, I'm trying to get on with it.

I think you have to leave it behind. I try to get on to the next song, get on to the next project and try to put the failures, such as they may be, behind me.

And the successes, too?

Why not?

You mentioned having the title, "The Moon's a Harsh Mistress" for years before writing the song. Do you ever have the sense of a song being complete before you wrote it? That one, especially, seems to have always existed.

Oh, I don't know, I don't know. You're even now, see, you're out-speculating *me*, now. [*Laughs*]

That's okay. I appreciate that notion. If we've all lived this life before a thousand times, maybe I've written them a thousand times.

[*Pause*] To *me*, though, it feels like I have to do it every time. [*Laughs*] It always feels like it's the first time to me—I have to get it going. It's sort of like warming up for tennis or vocalizing before you sing. I just have to get that thing going. Sometimes at the beginning it just seems like an impossible task . . . sometimes, until you plant yourself, put your hands on the keys, and actually push one of them down. *Make yourself push one of them down!* Sometimes that's really hard for me to do. I sit there and I go, "I don't want to play a G. And I don't want to play a B flat." It *all* looks unpromising. And I just sit there, and I have to make myself play. I say, "Play. Play one note." And that way I get myself going, very slowly sometimes. And then momentum builds and I really get into the joy of it. And I'm going, "Oh, look—there's the piece I need right there!" You know, I'm like a kid with a jigsaw puzzle. A glittering magical *jigsaw puzzle*.

It becomes very rewarding for me as I approach the end of it and I keep fitting things in, and it continues to feel *good* to me. It's just the best feeling I've ever had.

Sometimes it goes off the rails and I can feel that I'm losing it. I'm like a kid with my skateboard skidding out in front of me, and there's nothing much I can do about it. I will put something like that away, and maybe I'll come back to it sometime. [*Pause*] They don't always gel for me. They really don't.

How do you keep in shape creatively? Do you have to have a daily writing routine?

Randy [Newman] was one of the first guys that I ever heard talking about getting into a routine and going down to the office every day, that that really helped him get organized and get some work done. When I moved back to the East Coast, I started doing that. I thought, "I'm willing to risk whatever this inspiration thing is, this intangible. I'm willing to risk that it's not at the beach or in Hawaii or in the Big Sur or in some other country, on some trip, some *external* influence. And I'm willing to bet that I can find it at my office if I go there every day."

And I started going to my office every day as an experiment just to see, could I work there, would ideas come? I found that it's just been a totally enjoyable experience. A really enriching thing to be centered like that and work every day and really have so much time, so much time to do it. Because I give myself the time. And I do it. And so, just to have that luxury of all that *time to work on songs.*

Do you have any idea where your ideas come from?

Well, yes, I do. I believe. As I said, I believe in God. And I believe that He's the author of all of this stuff, anyway.

One of the gems I discovered while listening to your solo albums is your song "P. F. Sloan," which I noticed you recorded twice.

P. F. Sloan is the heroic figure of the songwriter who goes on and keeps writing no matter what. You know, he's a great songwriter. "Eve of Destruction" is one of the best political statements, or any other kind of statements, ever made in a song. And you can go home and play it right now. And everything that he was talking about is still going on right now.

He just played the Bottom Line in New York last year and played a lot of his great songs that he wrote with Steve Barri: "Secret Agent Man," and "Go Where You Wanna Go," which he wrote for the Mamas and the Papas. Lots and lots of great songs.

The guy was hot. He was one of the first songwriters to want to be a singer and to really try to do that. And it was tough then to do that. There was definitely pressure for me just to stay a songwriter. Just to behave myself and be a songwriter and everything would be fine. He was one of the first guys to go up against all that and I look up to him, I admire him. I wish he'd write some more great songs. He probably *is* writing some great songs right now.

Art Garfunkel's *Watermark* album contains ten of your songs. Did you write those songs for the album or did he choose them himself?

Oh, yeah, he made his selections. Yeah. But very well. The songs, the way he organized them, almost sound as though they all were written for that album, in a way. They're very nicely fused together.

The first we heard of Garfunkel after the breakup of Simon and Garfunkel was your song "All I Know." And your song, "Another Lullaby," one of my favorites, ends the album. He has such a special voice; were you happy with how it worked on your songs?

Oh, yeah. You know, he's just got the cleanest, most elegant *line.* He's a real artist in the true sense of the word. He's very particular about the way he records and what he does.

I went up to San Francisco to see Artie. I came down to the studio and Artie says, "Hi." We didn't even know each other very well. And I said, "What do you want me to do?" And he said, "Well, just do everything." They turned the tape machine on, and I played and sang for two days. [*Laughs*] I played and sang everything I knew. And he still has those tapes. I mean, when I ran out of songs I started playing Baptist hymns. I started playing "Come Now,

Fount of Every Blessing." And he said, "That's great. Have you got some more of those?" And we started doing Baptist hymns. We did Baptist hymns for an afternoon. "I Will Arise and Go to Jesus." That's a good one.

And in all of that material was "All I Know" tucked in there somewhere. [*Laughs*]

Do you have a single song of your own that is your favorite?

No. It's always the last thing I'm working on. I'm doing a song in my show right now called "Just Like Marilyn." Right now it's my favorite song. I would play it anytime, anywhere, at the drop of a . . . dime.

It's a beautiful song. You mentioned being superstitious. Do you have any superstitions about songwriting—things you do that help it flow?

No, except I try not to think about it until it's time to actually do it. Try not to think about it too much. Really get involved completely in other things.

I'm doing a lot of watercolors, and I'm thinking in a different matrix. I'm not thinking frequency and meter and words. I'm thinking about colors and it's a different flowing state of mind. It's a completely different state of mind. And I like to totally submerge myself in something like that. Or I like to go fly. I like to fly airplanes. I do anything, really—build a model ship, play tennis, which I do every day—and get submerged in those things. Because it's like a brain scrub. And it just washes out all the old notes that are hanging around. And all the old prejudices that are hanging around. Any old chord pattern that is lurking back there wanting to be copied. I never want to be ambushed by something I've retained, suddenly finding myself rewriting something I've already written. That's my worst nightmare. So the idea of a scrub, just blowing out the brain, and starting with a fresh brush, if you will, is important.

Do you ever come up with melodies away from the piano?

I remember writing the song "Didn't We" in a car on the way out to Newport Beach to see some friends of mine.

Words and music?

Yeah. But not very often. I'm usually playing a vamping kind of chord structure on the piano and singing over it. I don't think I've ever sat down and picked a melody out on the piano. I leave that to the voice, to my voice to find its way through the chord structure. And I think that's probably a good idea because I think you can pick melodies out on an instrument that aren't necessarily that sonorous when you put it with voice. So, in a way, when I write, I'm always accompanying myself. It's the accompanist as a singer. Here's the chord pattern, here's the rhythm, here's the shape of the verse. Now let me see: Let me sing along with this thing here and let me see where this chord structure leads me melodically.

Do you tape this process?

Yeah, sometimes. I have a tape machine that sits on top of my piano. And what I do when I start is I put it in record and I tape everything that I do. Most of the time I don't refer to it at all but sometimes, forty-five minutes into a writing session, I'll play a chord pattern completely by accident and I'll know instantly that I'll never be able to do it again. And immediately I go to the tape recorder and go back. And maybe, if I really like it, jot it down. It's just a memory saver.

Then let's say I'm in a first draft of a song and I've written a verse and a chorus, and it stands up pretty well—I like it. I'll put the tape on rewind, take it all the way back to the top of the tape, put it on record and I'll do as much as I've done up to that point. I'll do that verse and chorus as well as I can. Now I let the tape run again. And I'll keep working. But I know at the top of the tape I have a check-point, I have a place where I can go back and be fairly confident about what I have done up until that point. And it's mostly just an aid to memory for me because sometimes when I'm really striking out and trying to drastically change chords around, I get completely lost, and I forget what key center I'm in sometimes. So you hit rewind, go back to the top of the tape. So I know where I was, what I was doing. I just lose track of it sometimes.

When you start out, do you choose a key to work in?

No. I just choose a chord. A lot of times I don't even know what key I'm in for a long time because the key center moves around in my tunes. Quite a bit sometimes. I don't think key until it's time to write something down for somebody else to play. Sometimes it's really embarrassing because somebody will say, "What key is this in?" [*Laughs*] I can generally figure it out if I sit there and look at the chords a little bit. I'll say, "Well, we're starting in E flat even though we're not starting on the tonic. Then we're modulating to G major." But I just don't think about it very much while I'm doing it.

After writing songs all these years, you certainly know which chords go with which chords, and countless chord progressions. When working do you actively go to chord progressions in which you don't know how they will sound?

I certainly hope so. That's why it's real important to have a tape machine running. Because if you're playing along and all of a sudden you make a mistake, and it turns out to be one of those glorious God-given mistakes, chances are you're not going to remember how you did it. If more than five or six seconds elapse before you find it again, you may not find it. It was a mistake, you see.

I'm happy you recorded "Adios," which was also beautifully recorded by Linda Ronstadt with Brian Wilson doing harmonies. The old cantina you refer to is Lucy's, here in Hollywood?

Yes. I think I wrote it right after I moved out here to the east coast. It was kind of like my goodbye song to Los Angeles.

I love the line "Our dreams of endless summer were just too grandiose . . ."

I have a lot of mixed feelings about California. It was a great place to be a senior in high school, and it was a great place to be young and successful. It's not so great when you're older and less successful. And I think a lot of people find that. There's a lot of emphasis there on youth and success. I just had to have a change.

When you write a song, do you generally have to remove yourself from other people?

I find it very difficult to write with anyone else in the room with me. Including other songwriters, which is why I'm not particularly known for my collaborating skills. I can be very easily distracted. One noise—something dropping on the floor, or the door slamming or something, and I can definitely lose my train of thought.

I have this office here in New York where I pretty much come in and close off the doors and sit and work. Just the way real people work.

Are you optimistic about the future of—
Of me? Or of you? [*Laughs*] Or just the whole damn planet?

The whole thing.
Yes. I'm optimistic. I'm really optimistic. I think we're gonna get it together. And I have to, because I have five sons.

* * *

Joan Baez
Universal City, California 1987

When I mentioned to a couple of my friends that I was about to embark on an interview with Joan Baez, they grew suddenly solemn, and began a long process of begging and pleading to be allowed to go along, "if only to bask in her presence." Two of them did eventually convince me to let them go; this was unprecedented, but they were so unrelentless in their quest that I gave in, and they adopted roles, that of photographer and note-taker. Though I was worried that one or both could lose control, start hugging her and refuse to let go, they sat perfectly still and silent at her feet, mesmerized. For them and many other children of the sixties, she's still the goddess, the mythical "Johanna" Dylan sang about decades earlier.

This reverence for her didn't faze her in the least. After all these years, she's accustomed to being worshipped by those who have been touched by the beauty of her voice. Since 1959, when she was invited by Bob Gibson to be part of the Newport Folk Festival, her career has soared on wings of glory. Vanguard Records released her first album only months after that first performance, and her "achingly pure soprano voice" was exuberantly praised by the press.

In 1962 she embarked on a concert tour that broke racial barriers by only stopping off at black colleges, causing a controversy carried on the cover of *Time* magazine. It was clear from this moment on that Joan Baez was more than a great singer; she was the voice of her generation.

She used that voice to introduce a generation to the songs of a "scruffy" young writer she heard in New York named Bob Dylan. Not only did she officially sanction his songs by performing them, she also introduced the young, bashful writer directly to her audience by letting him join her on stage. Doing so, she progressed from the "archaic and ethereal songs of yore" to the new, expansive songs of the sixties, and brought pop music along with her, expanding its potential for power and meaning.

The first songs that she sang when she was growing up were not folk songs but the pop songs of the day that she heard on the radio, such as "Earth Angel." But when she heard the songs of Odetta and Pete Seeger, she became aware of the fact that music had the potential to say more. Within a year she switched from "Earth Angel" to "We Shall Overcome."

Today many people turn to Joan Baez for nostalgic reasons. She was, after all, the embodiment of the sixties. But she's got no time for nostalgia. Mostly, she is concerned about the issues of today, even going to the length of holding up what could be her most commercial album ever to include "China," her elegy for the students of the failed revolution, a move that her record company wasn't thrilled about but allowed nonetheless.

Barefoot and wearing a black gypsy dress and bracelets of silver and turquoise when we met, she projected an air of graceful and relaxed elegance, bringing much warmth and laughter to a cold hotel room.

Often we have an idea of the artist in seclusion, writing songs away from the world. So many songs in your career, such as "China," have to do with being in the world and the actual occurrences going on.

On the other hand, I've written too much all by myself. At this juncture in my life, which is another right angle, I'm putting the emphasis on music.

Do you think a musician can accomplish more with music than with other forms of activism?

I think that I wouldn't want to have anything to do with social activism that didn't have music in it. On the other hand, let us not kid ourselves about the fact that at some point people need to be serious about something.

I mean, I came from a whole background of doing for other people. So for me it isn't a big deal. It's what I've done with my life. But I think that people are suddenly realizing here they are with the talent, the exposure to all these kids, so they should do something.

There's lots of songwriting about important subjects. And 99 percent of it is no good. That's the problem. I have certainly received in the mail hundreds and hundreds of well-meaning, good-hearted songs, but the talent factor isn't always what it could be. And that's why great songs are rare.

It is easier to preach a message in a song than to be understated and use a metaphor, as you did in "China" when you say, "There was no summer at all in Tianenmen Square."

And that took me a long time to learn. When I wrote a song like "Cambodia," it came from an article in *Newsweek*. And every grim fact I found, I repeated in the song. So it was really grisly, but melodically and because of my voice, there is a pretty sound to it. But really grim. I don't think I want to be that grim anymore, either for myself or for other people. Practically speaking, the times have changed in such a way that people have such an enormous intolerance. And they don't want to hear anything that they don't want to hear. It's an interesting process of trying to get *anything* through. The seventies and eighties have really been a greedy time. People look after themselves and they don't really want to hear about it. You have to package it in a certain way so that it can break through the wall people put up.

Did folk music speak to you differently than other kinds of music, and when you first heard it, did you see a career for yourself?
I never saw a career in my life until this year. [*Laughs*] It just didn't compute. There was no computer on the left side of the brain. I'm an instinctive person; I act on instinct and I think in a way that served me well. I don't know the deeper reasons for my shying away from the commercial world sort of neurotically. I was turned off when I saw gold records on the wall. It threatened me.

Folk music spoke to me. It was just *perfect* for my voice. People would say, "Gosh, Miss Baez, you sing all these sad ballads; was there any reason?" Yeah, I was as screwed up as any other teenager and they spoke to my condition. I was not a bebopper. I had a lot of sadness in there, and I would sing these ballads until five in the morning, making myself more miserable, I suppose, but it comforted me. It absolutely spoke to my heart. Beauty and death.

Is it true that when you met Odetta you did your imitation of her for her?
I was *so nervous*, I was just shaking from head to foot. I knew I had to tackle this somehow, so I just went right smack up to her and sang, [*sings, in Odetta's huge voice*] "Oh, my mama is gone . . ." [*Laughs*] And she looked at me like I was some kind of a lunatic, which I was, and then she put her head back and *roared with laughter* and embraced me. She just folded me into this great chocolate human being.

You're a good mimic. Besides Odetta, you did a good impersonation of Dylan on your version of "Simple Twist of Fate." And you also dressed up like him on the Rolling Thunder Tour.
[*Sighs*] To everyone's delight. [*Laughs*] A couple of times I fooled his wife and kids. I thought that was pretty good. I also fooled his kids doing *her*. Then it was getting a little bizarre so I quit.

During Rolling Thunder, there was a lot of strange role playing—
Yes, indeed. [*Laughs*] That's putting it very mildly.

Was it fun?
The first one was loads of fun. The second one wasn't. I felt I should be upgraded, and it was getting competitive and stupid. But in the first one, I knew just where I stood and accepted it happily and enjoyed the whole show. Every night. I watched the whole show. It was pretty, for one thing. Bob was into wearing hats with flowers and bright scarves and it was just beautiful. It was a *complete circus*, but it was fun. There was a lot of good music.

You explained in your book the way Dylan's songs brought you from the "archaic and ethereal songs of yore" to the music of the sixties. Without Dylan, would you have made that transition?

Well, people say to me, if I hadn't discovered Bob, people wouldn't have heard of him. People would have heard of him.

You did sanction him for people.

In those days, since he was such a grubby little thing, they needed to have him sanctioned before they would listen. So, yeah, I'm happy that I did that.

What was it about his songs that struck you?

His were just the best. I was already comfortable with protest songs. But with Dylan's songs it was, "Aha!" Because they're so good. After he wrote those images, *thousands* of young kids scribbling on their pads have tried to duplicate that and nobody's been able to.

He's influenced every songwriter in rock and roll and folk. And whether or not he was involved in social action or not, he wrote this artillery for us.

Was "Diamonds and Rust" a song that emerged all at once?

It started off as a song about Vietnam veterans. Then I threw that all out and wrote it as a love song. I think the tune was around for a while in my head.

In your book you wrote that you told Dylan that your song "Diamonds and Rust" was written for your ex-husband David.

I had to get a little chuckle, so I did say that.

But that was Bob's song, right?

No, I wrote it. [*Laughter*] Let's move on.

Your song "Speaking of Dreams" has a gorgeous, chromatic melody. Did you write that on piano?

Yeah, I did. I made just enough mistakes on piano for it to be an interesting song. [*Laughs*] In some of the changes, my hand went to the wrong place, and it sounded so good I kept it.

A beautiful Frenchman. It was one of those ethereal falling-in-love processes and really and truly not being able to tell which is reality and which is fantasy. It's all true. The only image that's not absolute reality is "I'm the Queen of Hearts and the daughter of the moon." [*Laughs*] And I challenge anyone to tell me otherwise.

When you work on songs, is it an everyday thing or do you wait for inspiration?

It depends on the song. With "Speaking of Dreams" I had the luxury of having written the melody about a year-and-a-half before, and I bumbled around with it on the piano whenever I was in a piano-playing mood. So I knew it was there, and I knew some day the words would come to claim it.

Do they come to you from beyond?

The good ones do. Like "the spring in Beijing" [from "China"], I had nothing to do with it. That was not work or research or anything. They just come.

We've talked about the hunger for substance in songs. There are many songwriters writing meaningful songs, yet they are not easy to succeed with

in today's times. Do you have advice for songwriters wanting to follow in your path?

Get a day job. Get a day job. You have to be willing to roll with the punches. If you want to love your music, and not feel that you have to sell your ass down the river to get something going, you're probably going to want to keep your day job.

But don't be discouraged. I was discouraged for a while. I had to get over blaming everybody for my own predicament. Because it was really my own fault. I was saying, "They don't understand how wonderful my music is. The record company doesn't understand; they're all morons," and so on. I didn't understand that I needed management and publicity and all those things that were anathema to the old me in order to be efficient and have people hear the stuff that I create.

Guess what? It's the nineties. Yoo-hoo, Baez! I'm still in the Stone Age, but I'm toddling along.

* * *

P. F. Sloan
Los Angeles, California 1990

When they told me that P. F. Sloan was on the phone for me, I assumed it was a joke. After all, P. F. Sloan is famous not only for the classic songs he's written ("You Baby," "Where Were You When I Needed You," "Eve of Destruction," "Secret Agent Man" and so many more) but also for being notoriously absent for years, a genius missing in action since the conclusion of the sixties.

He's a figure so shrouded in mystery that Jimmy Webb was inspired to write a song called "P. F. Sloan" depicting both Sloan's disappearance and the simultaneous shift of American consciousness as the spirit of the sixties subsided. It's a song about idealism coming to an end and a world turned topsy-turvy: London Bridge has been moved to Arizona; Roy Roger's horse, Trigger, is not only dead but stuffed; and Richard Nixon is elected and reelected. And through it all, P. F. Sloan, the man who urged us with his music and poetry to recognize that we were perched inexorably on an "eve of destruction," is nowhere to be found:

"I have been seeking P. F. Sloan / But no one knows where he has gone . . ."

from "P. F. Sloan" by Jimmy Webb, 1970

I confess that when I interviewed Jimmy Webb back in '88 and asked him about this song, I had no idea at all that Sloan was an actual person. I simply loved the song and erroneously assumed Sloan was a fictional character invented by Webb as a symbol of the great songwriters of the sixties, abandoned as the hunger for heartfelt music began to wane. Webb, surprised by my admission of ignorance, said, "No, no, no! See, that's what I mean. The guy was hot. And he was one of the first songwriters to want to be a singer and try to do that. There definitely was pressure for me just to behave myself and be a songwriter. And he was one of the first guys to go up against that and I look up to him, I admire him."

When we printed Webb's interview in *SongTalk*, I didn't edit out my confession, and within weeks started receiving mail and packages sent by Sloan devotees from around the world. These people were shocked, quite appropriately, to discover that the editor of a songwriting journal should know nothing about P. F. Sloan, one of the most significant songwriters ever to match music with words. They sent me long lists of his achievements, the songs he wrote, produced and sang, as well as other tidbits of Sloan trivia—it was he who sang the falsetto part on "Little Old Lady from Pasadena," and he who played the famous guitar riff on the Mamas and the Papas' "California Dreaming." They sent me albums: Sloan's solo records (true treasures), records by Jan & Dean, The Grassroots, The Turtles and others, all packed with the songs of P. F. Sloan. And almost all of these letters implored me to seek out Sloan, wherever he might be, and interview him. Many of them believed that he was still writing songs, and that he could be found in Los Angeles.

Weeks later a young woman arrived in my office, introduced herself, and asked me if I had ever heard of P. F. Sloan. I showed her the Webb interview, the rash of letters that followed, and my cherished collection of Sloan records. Her eyes lit up and she told me she was a close friend of his, and that she felt "Philip was ready to talk."

So I was humored days later when I was told that P. F. Sloan was on the line. I suspected that it was maybe my brother, or a friend, knowing of my search for Sloan and using a creative psuedonym. It wasn't.

"I think the cosmos wants us to get together," was the first thing he said, in a low and gentle voice. P. F. Sloan. He gave no further explanation for his call, and none was needed. I informed him of my immense joy at finally reaching him, and told him about the profusion of Sloan disciples around the world urging me to interview him. He seemed genuinely surprised at the intensity of emotions that still existed after all these decades. It was the first of many times he would encounter it. We set up a time to talk and said goodbye.

He was born Phillip Gary Schlein in 1945 and raised "a wild, corruptible child" in Queens, New York. His sister gave him the name "Flip," hence the initials P. F. He came with his family to California (one of the reasons they moved west was to get Phil off the streets) when he was young, and he was already singing and playing violin upon arrival. For a long time, though, he kept his music hidden, a tendency he would return to over the years.

"The other kids were out playing ball," he recalled, "and I was up in my room playing violin, and there was a conflict between the two all the time. Then I found a one-string broken plastic ukelele in the garbage and I played that for about three years. Mastered it. I could play virtually every Everly

Brothers song on it. It was my great passion. It was mostly a secret passion; I didn't want anyone to know."

His dad bought him a guitar when he was thirteen, which he taught himself to play by listening to records. "Every time there was a new record, it sent shock waves through my system," he remembered. It's an energy that has been with him ever since.

"The juice of the original rock and roll is forever. It was an electrical charge that will go on as long as anybody will go on. The charge is still there. It's not over."

We met in a complex of apartments on the west side of Los Angeles, where Grace Jones was lounging in purple at the pool. As we walked past her, I wondered if she, or any of these poolside people, had any idea that there was a legend living in their midst. As always, when meeting great songwriters, there's the weird contrast of knowing the infinite effect their songs have on people and facing the finite form of the person who wrote them. Somewhere in the back of my head there's a voice that says, "This is the guy who wrote 'Secret Agent Man' and 'Eve of Destruction!'" And it's a little hard to fathom, sometimes, because songs are everywhere at once. And here is the songwriter himself, right here in the same room, no bigger than any of us. Sloan is a serious guy, and the fire in him that enabled him not only to write "Eve of Destruction," "Sins of a Family" and two other songs all in the same night also made life pretty awful for him when he found himself on the outside looking in. His struggle to be an artist when he had already proved himself to be such a capable and cunning craftsman took its toll on him, and even the faith of Dylan and Webb and others in the same boat could not keep him from succumbing to the shadows of his own soul.

When Webb's song about him was recorded by The Association and started getting radio play, Sloan said he felt like the phantom star of a circus that had already left town. "I was forced to play the tragic role," he said, "instead of the comedic role, which is more to my nature." For a long time, those shadows obscured his vision, and a division got drawn between P. F. Sloan, the artist, and Philip Schlein, the Jewish kid from Queens. This conflict was frequently reflected in our conversation, as Sloan would open wide his dark, sad eyes, like a fortune teller at a crystal ball, gazing into his own past.

But at other times, especially when talking about the joy of songwriting and the juice of rock and roll that has fueled his entire life, he smiled openly, and seemed happy with the knowledge that Schlein and Sloan are one and the same.

"It's living art captured for all time," he said of his songs. "And all the writers of the sixties, we were all flowing on that juice; all of us who were subjected to that cosmic rock and roll current that came through, we were all juiced from it. We literally changed the world. We modeled it in the image of rock and roll. Next to the ancient practice of religion, the juice from rock and roll of the fifties and the sixties seemed to be the only things in this world that were worth having of any consequence."

You said that music for you was a secret passion at first. When did it stop being secret?

I was selling papers on Sunset Boulevard every day after school, in front of Schwabs. I was doing that for a couple of years. My dad bought me this guitar to keep me company. And one day I saw a leaflet that said "Open Auditions at Alladin Records."

So I packed up my guitar in a pillowcase, got on a bus, went down to Pico Boulevard, and there's this line of about fifty or sixty black artists all around the block, and I went into the office and said I wanted to audition for a position. I was fourteen and the only white person there. I went in and sang a couple of songs: "Good Golly, Miss Molly," I think, and "I Don't Care if the Sun Don't Shine." And they said, "Here's a recording contract. Go home and have your parents sign it; report here Monday and we'll start a recording session."

[The people at Alladin] said, "Can you write songs? Go home and write some songs." So I went home and wrote about six songs in the next week or so. Those songs were absolutely geared to what I had been listening to, but there was a little mix of Judaism in there. It wasn't rock and roll per se because there's a lot of minors in it.

Was it tough for you when you went home the first time and tried to write songs?

No, it was easy. Because there was a really good inspiration, and that was love, wanting to be noticed. And inspiration is unstoppable.

Listening to the formats of songs became a school lesson; it sounded correct. The inspiration took care of itself: it filled it in like a printing shop; you put in the borders and the inspiration filled in all the words. So that was real easy.

Did it affect your life when that single was released?

Yeah, I was a has-been at thirteen. I was the only thirteen-year-old has-been in our school.

You and Steve Barri, who was older than you, became collaborators. What was it like, at that age, to collaborate with someone for the first time?

I was in electricity. I was electricity itself. When we would sit down to work, it was magic, it was electric. I would throw thirty lines out to him at a time, just *zip, zip, zip,* and if he blinked his eyes at one, I would write it down. Because it was happening so quick, he didn't have time to react. So whatever he would react to emotionally and mentally, I knew that was the one.

I looked up to him as a brother and I wanted to please him. It became very quickly a method of blending the two of us into one writing personality.

Did the two of you settle on a regular approach to writing?

Yes. Steve always said, "I can't play an instrument but I can play the ukelele," and he knew two chords. So all of his songs would have two chords in them. I would take the two chords and say, "How about if we throw three chords in between your G and D. How about if we put in a B minor and an E minor and an A minor and a C7?"

It was very difficult at that time because I was so overloaded with inspiration. And if one line didn't work, I would find one line that did. I would work

18, 20 hours, if that's what it took to bring off some electrical charge in him. So he would go, "That's it! That's the formula minus the formula plus creativity plus inspiration plus magic. That's it!" It was like watching the Master Poet play with us and see how in tune we were with the Master Poet.

We spent two years straight writing together. We wrote hundreds of songs. We were the Goffin & King of the west-coast follow-ups. We'd be given a list on Monday morning by Lou Adler with thirty names on it of the groups who needed follow-ups to their hits. So we would write follow-ups for the Drifters, and for all the black artists that were up for stuff. We did nothing for two years but write and record daily.

The record company wanted the follow-up to sound exactly like the hit. It had to be virtually the same song but set in a different way. The same changes, even. Because they were looking for a follow-up, not a new direction. So we were limited in that direction. So we wrote hundreds and hundreds of songs. And none of them were recorded. Not a one.

You were able to come in seven days a week and connect with your inspiration?

Oh, yeah. The juice from the fifties was so intense that I had already built up a backlog of maybe 1000 favorite records by then. That's not unusual. Don't we have in our mind now maybe 10,000 or 15,000 songs? There's a lot of songs that are giving juice. And it's really incredible to find out what it is that's the juice giver. It's a chord, sometimes. It's the offbeat chord change.

There are three principles to a song: there's the fantastic inspirational lyric that can take you over even if the music is nothing; then there's something that is so musically divine that that takes you over, and then there's something with either the vocalist or the instrumental artist that is so divinely inspired that that takes you over. Then if you put all those three together, you have something that has juice that is going to last for a hundred years. I guess the blues did that, and the juice is still going.

Would you and Steve work on words and music at the same time?

Once we had our first hit, we were able to hold writing sessions at my mother's house in the kitchen because that had the best echo of any place we knew.

Steve would say that he came up with a line last night. We'd write a song around the line; if it wasn't good, we'd write another song around the line. By the end of the day we'd have four or five songs based on that line. I'd say, "You go home and see if any of these songs start coming into your head and I'll do the same." If any one song starts coming into your head, we'd work on that one. If not, maybe we'd combine all five songs into one.

Being in the heart and mind of P. F. Sloan was a tremendous experience, probably the greatest experience of my life. Later came some of the worst.

What was your first breakthrough song?

A song I had written, "Kick That Little Foot, Sally Ann," for Harry Belafonte when I was fifteen. Screen Gems refused to publish it. They didn't think it was a quality song. And the record company next door was begging Screen Gems for a song. That's why they moved in right next door to them, so that they could get a hit. And they would come in every day and be told, "Get outta here. You're nobodys. You have to go through channels to get a Goffin & King song. You can't just come in here and be given a Barry Mann song."

So they cornered me one day in the elevator with a hooker. This 300-pound lady. And she lifted up her dress in the elevator and the owner of the record company said, "You like? Come in and it's yours if you give us a song." I said, "I'll give you a song but forget the lady."

So I went there and played them "Kick That Little Foot, Sally Ann." And they had an artist from Watts that they called Round Robin. He had just put out a Slauson record that was making news in L.A. They liked my song so they hired Jack Nitzche and they went in and recorded it. And it hit the charts. It went up in the charts and all of a sudden, Steve and I are hit songwriters.

And did your status change?
Yeah. We were looked at differently. The pay was still the same. It was still eight hours a day, seven days a week. $25 a week. Finally, Steve demanded more money because he was married, so he got $50 a week but they didn't see fit to give me more than a $10 raise.

Was there a point at which you decided you wanted to be a solo artist and not a songwriter for other artists? Jimmy Webb spoke to me about the difficulty you both had making that transition.
Yes. When the Grass Roots record came out, which I sang lead on, it hit the Top 40. When Jay Lasker heard that it was a hit and that performing offers were coming in, he made it clear that he wanted my voice removed and a new group brought in. And I was not allowed, under any circumstances, to go out and sing. So a new group was brought in [The Thirteenth Floor] and they overdubbed vocals on it and did all of the performances.

When "Eve of Destruction" was a hit and the first P. F. Sloan album escaped on its own, and performing offers started to come in for P. F. Sloan, that was quickly stopped. He made a deal with me that I could make another album but only under the auspices that it was an audition album for other artists. "You are not an artist," he said. "You are a songwriter for hire that I own."

When I met Jimmy Webb, he also had the aspirations to be a recording artist of a caliber that would set up its own domain. It would be a songwriter singing his own material. A songwriter who really can't sing but what he would add is a soul coloration of emotional personality, rather than vocalization that someone else was gifted with. So I think that he saw that was what I was trying to break through.

Do you think of P. F. Sloan as a different person than yourself?
[*Pause*] Yes. I think sometimes that I can reach into the personal philosophy and loneliness and talent of P. F. Sloan at times. But I don't live inside of P.F. Sloan. It was very difficult to be around when he was learning about life. The talent was so immense that there wasn't room for a social life. I needed to divine who I was before I became P. F. Sloan. I needed to have a life on my own.

There was no lovelife for P. F. Sloan. It was an all working life. And there wasn't any real reward in it, either financially or anything else. The reward was the songs. And they were divinely inspired for that 22-year old mind and heart.

In a way I was divining P. F. Sloan. I was divining him through me. But I couldn't be P. F. Sloan. Because his insights were too much for me, and I was too young and unprotected to fend for myself.

What about today?

These days what I'm doing is trying to be more in touch with the Master Poet who worked through P. F. Sloan. I'll see what kinds of songs come up in the future.

Do you remember writing "Eve of Destruction"?

Vividly. Totally vividly. I wrote five songs that night. I wrote "Eve of Destruction," "Sins of a Family," "Take Me for What I'm Worth," "This Morning," and "Ain't No Way I'm Gonna Change My Mind." I wrote those five songs in one night.

I was up most of that night battling. I don't know who I was battling or what, but I vividly recall saying to some higher music power, "Please let me be released from this. Please let me get it out. Let me be released." And I kept hearing this voice saying, "No, no, sorry, you've got to live with it. Can't let you go on this one." I would fight for hours. "Please let me get it out of my system. I can't live with this." Finally, words would start to come and I would see them and I would be filled with tears of joy, and I would be so happy that they were being given.

It was a fantastic feeling of being in another place. Pure witnessing. I was allowed to be present at times. The excitement was so great that I wouldn't even bear to witness it. Other times, as this greater power was beginning to love me a little bit more, it would say, "Watch this come out." I would watch it and say, "But that's what I always wanted to say. That's what I thought you would say." Sometimes I'd see a whole chorus that was written. It was mostly pure witnessing.

Were you sitting with your guitar when this happened?

No. I was in bed. My parents were asleep. I woke my mom up at three in the morning and said, "You'll never believe what just came through me." And I showed her the lyrics to "Eve of Destruction." She said, "Be quiet, you'll wake your father up."

Do you have any ideas as to how a songwriter can get to the place to experience that pure witnessing that you've described?

For me during that particular period, there was an immense need for attention, for identity, and a tremendous love of people. And knowing that I could probably, at my best, only come up to matching the standard of other great songwriters who have inspired me. It wasn't as if I could ever be the first songwriter who came with a stone tablet and showed it to the other cave-people and said, "Hey, I wrote a song" and they'd say, "Hey, let's do it."

But now when you see all the spiritual implications of this journey of being a songwriter and what it actually entails, it entails witnessing, it entails detachment. For a certain kind of songwriter who is socially conscious and aware of some inequities and wants to voice those inequities for himself and say, "This is where I stand. This is where I draw the line."

One of the reasons that I felt that P. F. Sloan, while he was evolving, was ostracized, was because of his immense scan of song. They would say, "How can you take anyone seriously who writes 'Tell 'Em I'm Surfin' one day and 'Eve of Destruction' next? What's he going to write tomorrow?"

So I wasn't taken seriously as a talent. Except by Dylan. Dylan recognized that I was a budding talent. He gave me some strong encouragement. But my career at Dunhill was destroyed, which he had predicted would happen. He told me that the word was out, that they were out to destroy me. And then he went his own way and P. F. Sloan was left, at that point, to face his karma by himself.

Do you think you did something to deserve this kind of karma?

I'm not sure. If my personal ego, my need for fame or glory, was too great, and if I wasn't aware of the meaning of fame and if I thought this was just personal glorification, I would think that that would have to be eradicated from a person as a human being. Perhaps that's what I needed to go through, I don't know. It gets you at a young age. When you're looking for attention and then you're given this attention, you feel, "They're glorifying me. I'm not a bad kid anymore. Mom, you shouldn't have yelled at me. I'm a genius here. You should have taken better care of me." And that leads to a very poor spiritual attitude.

Do you feel that songwriters can't take credit for their songs?

Oh, no. You have to take credit. I'm just saying that the songwriter is going to remain growing if he realizes that he is just the vehicle for that thing. The lessons that I've learned is that the Master Poet writes the songs and I'm just the vehicle that is used for that. So I need to keep myself in good health and in good shape and be around healthy people and do good things and work in the community and be of service, so that this Master Poet will choose me to be his vehicle. Because it's a wonderful, engaging process.

You use the name "Master Poet" for the source of inspiration that you've described. How do you envision the Master Poet?

My theory is that we are all one being all in the same consciousness, and that the Master Poet, who is writing our lives, is able to change our lives through that grace, is the source of all inspiration and the source of all joy and happiness. And knows all our grief and sorrow.

And through the Master Poet, that information is given so other people can give insights so that they don't need to stay in suffering, or on whatever level we're ignorant on. That's the job of the Master Poet, to be in touch with that divine inspiration and give it to your mind from that source and then deliver it to other minds, so that we can be happy no matter what comes to us, or what doesn't.

Back then your songs were covered by so many different groups. Did you have any favorites?

My personal favorites were the Searchers. "Take Me for What I'm Worth." "Where Were You When I Needed You" by the Grass Roots. The Turtles' version of "Let Me Be" I thought was real good.

Is it true that The Turtles turned down "Eve of Destruction" when they first heard it?

Yeah, so they say. I was threatened by the record company that if I played that song for anybody, I would have my royalties suspended. That was not a song that was to be recorded. But I didn't write it to be recorded. It was just a lyrical prayer that I wrote when I was digesting the Cuban missile crisis. This was a prayer, and I read it to Steve and told him that I had put music to it but that it wasn't for anybody. Who would sing it? This was my personal statement in a song.

Steve said, "I don't like it. It's got nothing to do with anything. It sounds like that Dylan shit."

I played it for the head of the record company and they said that under no condition would they publish that song. It was everything that they couldn't stand. It was making a personal statement. Music is not supposed to make a personal statement. Music is just good time feeling. The record company was looking for a hit and this was not what they considered to be a hit until Barry McGuire proved that to the contrary.

I did go down to the Turtles where they were rehearsing and played them a number of songs. I played them "Eve of Destruction" and they also felt that it was too incredibly different from any song that they had ever heard, and they couldn't conceive of themselves being able to make such a statement. So they passed on it. They did take "Let Me Be."

It's surprising to hear that people had a hard time with you writing pop songs and then writing protest songs. To me it seemed like a natural progression, not unlike the Beatles moving from "Love Me Do" to "Revolution."

I had to separate P. F. Sloan from Phil Sloan, who was writing "You, Baby" and on his nights off was writing folk songs.

The press and the community was very threatened by the Beatles and by Dylan and by "Eve of Destruction." They were extremely threatened. More so by the Beatles than by anything else. When I started coming out with tales about the society at large, it was a major threat. And we were to be done away with. At any cost. We were a threat to the society.

What was it like to hear Dylan for the first time?

It was almost too exciting to listen to. I felt the electricity go up my spine. His first two or three albums were stiffs—radio stations would throw them away. So I got them and I would listen to them, and I would hear Woody Guthrie and hear him, and how he put the two together. It was so exciting.

Listening to the first Dylan albums to me was almost like being in a church. A very enlightening church service that opened up my consciousness. It was an endless consciousness; infinity's consciousness of love towards mankind. I think he opened the consciousness up to 90% of the people who listened to him.

Jimmy Webb used you as a symbol for all songwriters struggling with similar issues in his song "P. F. Sloan." Do you remember first hearing that song?

Yes. I saw that look in his eye when he started writing it. He knew that I was being kicked out. We were at a party, as I recall, and he had these people around him. And they were his people, his support group. And I came in and he wanted them to bow down before me. He said, "Here's another songwriter, guys, who happens to be very good." But they didn't want to bow down to me. They said, "Who's he? Forget him. We're here for you."

And he looked at them and saw what it's like to be the king of a court with a bunch of morons around. He said, "My God, you can't even say hello to this person who has been a big inspiration for me." And they said they were there to worship him. So he looked at them and said, "But you don't even know who I am."

Sometime earlier he played for me lots of his songs that had been turned down by everyone: "Up, Up and Away," "Wichita Linesman," "MacArthur Park." The tears flowed out of my eyes. The tears were unstoppable and kept flowing. His heart was breaking. He was being rejected and no one understood his songs. He was asking me if this was good stuff. And the tears were flowing out.

I said, "Take a tear. Any tear. They're all yours." Later he was vindicated and all the ones that turned him down later learned better. And he was very angry at the way they destroyed my career and later started to rally around him. He could see that these people come and go very quickly. They demolish you one day and love you the next. So he wrote this song, "P. F. Sloan." The first time I ever heard the song on the air was a divine moment for me. I had had all my royalties suspended. I had absolutely no money. I had no place to live. I was at this hotdog stand on Vine Street and trying to scrape up 50 cents for a hotdog. And out of the speakers from the hot dog place was that song. And I was thinking, "Is this a divine play or what?" I went to make a phone call and tried to contact Jimmy Webb and he was gone. It was like the show had left town. And P. F. Sloan was its invisible star. [*Laughs*]

And it was like, "Hey, I'm here. I'm okay. I need help." But the traveling show had rolled out of town and I was left with this wonderful gift. Other people would say, "Oh, you're P. F. Sloan! I just heard a song about you."

It was an interesting role to play, the tragic figure. I was forced to play the tragic role rather than the comedic role that I feel is more to my nature.

Many people, even artists who recorded that song, didn't know it was about a real person.

But people know your songs. Everyone knows "Eve of Destruction" or "Secret Agent Man."

Yes. There are a lot of songwriters who are reckless and who are living on the reckless side of life and wanting to write songs from that perspective, and are willing to give it all up to get that message across, willing to give up all the money, the comfort. Sleep on a bed of rocks, if that's what it takes.

After you left L.A., where did you go?

I went back to New York, back to my roots, the west village, circa 1968. I went into a level of degradation that was vile. I put myself into jeopardy with vile, animalistic people on a very low level of being.

Then a stroke of luck happened in 1970 when Japan released my first album and the single from it, "From a Distance" began to sell. It went Top Ten, the singles began to sell hugely. Dunhill Records called me and said, "Gee, my goodness, we never figured that such a thing could happen. Come home. Everything's fine." So I returned to L.A. and they told me then that they had stopped the records in Japan, pulled them out, broke the deal; I wouldn't get any money from it and I'd better get out of town again. Instead I went to get psychiatric help.

I never got any money from the record company but they did ask me to do an album. P. F. Sloan had been given this psychedelic room for a madman. A rehearsal room with tie-dyed padded walls, an old broken piano. And I was asked—forced—to play in that room eight hours a day or I wouldn't receive $100 a week.

I made up my mind that P. F. Sloan is not to be used or abused anymore. And let the spirit go elsewhere.

And that was it. That was the last time P. F. Sloan was ever heard of. Until now.

How is P. F. Sloan doing these days?
I'm really feeling very good and happy. I love to make music. I love the process. I love the engaging nature of it. But I don't know how to make music for people in this day and age. I myself, apart from my spirit, feel disappointed in the music that's being presented today. So I see where my work is cut out for me. When you write a song, it's a trip. It's a spiritual trip and a growing trip for all of us.

* * *

Donovan

Marina Del Rey, California 1988

Mostly he lives in the California desert when he's not bouncing around between Europe and the Caribbean. He also keeps a small apartment in the marina of Los Angeles, and it's there that Donovan took the time to sit down and speak, above the sounds of cats clashing and the waves crashing, about many of the classic songs he has written: "Mellow Yellow," "Sunshine Superman," and "Atlantis" among them. While talking he kept some soft harmonica jazz playing in the background, sipped on a wine cooler, smoked many cigarettes, and gazed out of his window far off into the distance.

He was born Donovan Leitch in Glasgow, Scotland on May 10, 1946. In the early sixties, influenced by Woody Guthrie and other American folksingers, he started playing the acoustic guitar and writing imitation Bob Dylan songs. By 1966, spurred on by psychedelia, flower power and the Beatles, Donovan combined that folk music with rock and roll.

Although his songs are forever linked with a time gone by, they've lost none of the power they possessed when first we heard them. His records not only don't sound dated, they sound surprisingly modern. "His records hold up tremendously well," Randy Newman said. "Have you noticed that when you hear them on the radio they sound better than everything around them?" Many of his songs, such as "Hurdy Gurdy Man," sound even more appropriate in the turbulent present, a time when the tranquility contained in his work is needed more than ever.

Fortunately, he's making music again, invited by producer Rick Rubin, who has produced albums by Tom Petty, Johnny Cash and Mick Jagger, to record the new album *Sutras*. Gloriously, the magical music of Donovan continues to bloom, and the world is better for it.

Do you remember writing your first song?
I think maybe it was a train song. And it had the most unusual opening: " 'Twas a dark and stormy night / Not a cloud was in sight." Of course, that's a contradiction in itself. [*Laughs*] But as a young man I believed fully in those two lines and I sang them out.

Like the Beatles, who also never learned musical notation, you have a great freedom in your melodies and your phrasing that seems very natural, rather than learned.
Yeah, I would say so. I would harp back—harp being the key word—to the tradition of Irish and Scottish music where the lyrical poetry is natural. I played with classical musicians on my early albums and found that they couldn't improvise. Songwriting to me, as far as I know now, is this: You love a song and you play it, and you love it and you keep playing it. Then absentmindedly you discover a new little note that you want to add to it. Or you have a line of your own that you try in the same tempo or in the same meter. And out of the song that you know grows a new song of your own.
Music seems to be something I wasn't taught but that I knew.

You've discussed drawing on folk influences as well as the influence of visual art. Your song "Colours" combines both of these; it's a visual work which is in the form of a folk song.
Yeah, I would say that. It is a folk song in the sense that it has a folk melody. But it also has country flavors, yet it is in a modal tuning. And the way I sing it, it comes across in that early recording as country-folk. It was really just playing off of the D tuning, which is more like a banjo tuning. And I put a banjo in it for that reason. It has that lovely drone: the D drone.
One important way that my songwriting differs from others is that I will fit a phrase in a song how I want, no matter how many syllables it has.

Such as "A young monk meditating rhododendron forest" from "Epistle to Dippy"?
Yeah, right, the phrasing is very unusual and you fit in the syllables where you want to. And at first you might not understand the line that is being said. And therefore, rather than go for understanding, I would go for rhythm. Which actually goes back to what is the origin of words? Does it matter what they mean or are we charmed by songwriters who phrase well and use wonderful words?
In fact, lots of people buy millions of records that go straight up the charts and go out again, and years later you'll read the lyric and see you never really knew what the song was about. Like my uncle thought that I was singing, "I like a tree called banana," when I was singing "electrical banana" [From "Mellow Yellow"]. To his dying day he said, "Everybody *thinks* you're singing 'electrical banana,' but I *know* what you're singing."

I was just happily fitting in these syllables because I liked the way they sounded. The syllables are very important, and the *sound* of the words.

Since we are discussing the sound of words and you have mentioned a love for the work of Lewis Carroll, that brings to mind your song, "Barabajagal." Is that a word that you created on your own, in the tradition of Carroll?

Yeah, like "Jabberwocky." He would make up words. Also it was influenced by "Goo goo ga joob," from "I Am the Walrus." From those sounds that John [Lennon] made.

He was another big reader of Carroll.

Of course. We're very similar in that sense. "Strawberry Fields" is incredibly magical like Carroll's *Wonderland* stories. *Looking Glass* is just a very *strange, strange* theater of the mind book. "Looking glass people" and all those kinds of things. With "Barabajagal," I got this funky riff going. The rhythms were coming from the "Hurdy Gurdy Man" chunky rhythms playing away there. Usually cross-legged on the floor, probably in the cottage in England, probably reading Culpepper's *Herbal*, interested in herbal medicine, then seeing the story of the herbalist. And "Barabajagal" was an herbalist.

I didn't know that.

[*Laughs*] Once again you can love a song without ever looking into what the story is about. Lyrically it was about a young girl who goes to an herbalist for a cure.

It's interesting that you remember where you were when you wrote it and how you were sitting. Does finding the right environment have a lot to do with getting the ideas flowing?

I think it is important to have your space, but the way we were traveling then and the way life was, you just did it where you were. A lot of hotel songwriting went on then. I know George Harrison did what I did—he was basically on his own when he wrote a lot of his songs. Mainly reading.

It's a pressure thing that has to break through. You're explaining something to yourself. John Lennon would open a newspaper and see a line. We all do that.

I did write a lot of the songs on *Gift from a Flower to a Garden* in that little cottage. That was a great influence, to come from the city to the country. There was absolutely no street noise outside. It was all birds and animals.

With songwriting, it all comes out in one flash. Then you work it, then you craft it. Some songwriters tell me that it takes *forever* for them to write a song. Whether they're good or whether they're bad, mine come out quickly and I finish them quickly and very rarely go back to them. There's a timeless element to songwriting.

For me, perhaps your most timeless song is "Hurdy Gurdy Man," in which you tell the story of the bard, singing songs of love in spite of the darkness that humanity is going through.

Yes, it's from another tradition. I'm not sure if I wrote that song in India or on the beach in Jamaica. I'm pretty sure it was in Jamaica, where we had very good ganga that year and somebody gave me 110-proof rum. I fell asleep

on the beach and went into a dream in which I saw a cross-legged figure coming over the ocean: "Thrown like a star in my vast sleep / I opened my eyes
to take a peep / To find that I was by the sea / Gazing with tranquility. . . ."

Now you have to mix that up with the Indian trip because a cross-legged
figure is really a yogi, and I was always interested in yoga. And we did go to
India; and maybe Maharishi comes into it a little bit.

You went to India with the Beatles?
Yeah.

Do you consider the Hurdy Gurdy Man to be you?
Yeah. Oh yeah, I *am* the Hurdy Gurdy Man. But also the Hurdy Gurdy
Man is all singers who sing songs of love. The hurdy gurdy is an instrument
from the sixteenth century. The Hurdy Gurdy Man is a chronicler, the Hurdy
Gurdy Man is like a bard, and the Hurdy Gurdy Man is any singer-songwriter
in any age, whether they were in Ireland or whether they were in the streets of
New York during the sixties.

Songwriters tend to look for a world that will improve. The singing of
songs for a better world can be seen in any age. Especially in the twentieth
century. So any singer for peace is a Hurdy Gurdy Man.

There is a missing verse that George [Harrison] wrote: "When truth gets
buried deep / Beneath a thousand years of sleep / Time demands a turn
around / And once again the truth is found." And I didn't record it. George
was a bit upset there for a while. But singles in those days were only three minutes long.

Jimi Hendrix was going to do the solo but he was not around. As soon as
I wrote the song I wanted to give it to Jimi. But he wasn't available. Allan
Holdsworth did the solo in the end, and he did a great job.

But George wrote that verse and the verse describes well what the song is
about. That the Hurdy Gurdy Man is anyone who speaks this timeless truth.
There may be a dark age, but out of that dark age will come light and the answer to all men's problems.

**You mentioned Jimi Hendrix. While he was lighting his guitar on fire,
and Pete Townshend was destroying his, you were singing "Wear Your Love
Like Heaven." And that song is almost a prayer to God: "Lord, kiss me
once more, fill me with love, Allah. . . ."**
Yes. It is a prayer. "Wear Your Love Like Heaven," once again, had to do
with the use of colors. Obscure colors to describe a sunset. And it was a
painter who I got the first line from: "Wear your love like heaven." I expanded
it from there.

Can songs contain the spiritual?
Yes. They're transcendental.

**In the book *Seth Speaks*, in which Jane Roberts channeled the spirit
entity Seth, Seth was asked about the existence of Atlantis and answered
that it does exist, but in our future.**
When I wrote "Atlantis," I was reading one of those channel books. Not
Seth, but one that was presumably channeled a hundred years ago. I believe
Atlantis is a state of mind, yes. We're talking about different levels of reality

now. Was Atlantis an actual place? Do myths actually tell stories of real events? Or do stories fit into the archetypes that Jung talked about, in which *Romeo and Juliet* is not Shakespeare's story, it's the continuing story, the perennial story, of man and woman.

Atlantis is actually a state of mind, maybe a perfect society. Inside, humanity is the same. There are different colors, different locations. But *inside* there is a constant knowledge that everybody has in every age. And thus the myths are similar in all ages.

"Atlantis" is certainly one of the most mythical and magical songs ever to become a hit.

It is unusual to be a hit because the spoken word doesn't usually get heard on the radio.

The record of it is so powerful and yet delicate. Was it a difficult song to record?

It was recorded in the valley in Los Angeles. Gabriel Mekler was producing it, and he held the chords open on the piano and I strummed the strings in the piano and we got this *fssssshoooouuu* . . . sort of magic sound going.

Now I had the basic reading down and the drum track was made. And we had it worked out, how many verses would be spoken before the drums kicked in. But it was very difficult to figure out when to start so as to get that last phrase—"Hail Atlantis"—to come right before the drums kicked in. We didn't work it out, technically. I just took two shots at it and it worked. It was improvised, the reading, onto the track and it worked very well. As a reading, it came off right on time, and the drums kicked in, and I was more surprised than anybody.

There's something so comforting about the sound of your voice on "Atlantis." When we hear it we become children again and become absorbed by the story.

It is the sound of the voice, the comforting sound of the voice. Dylan may be the very opposite in the sense that he isn't comforting, but [his voice] is arresting and it is totally absorbing. Billie Holiday, too, has this amazingly powerful voice that absorbs you into its sound.

When I speak, people listen to what I say. And when it's sung, there is that double power. The word "comforting" is a good one to describe my impact on the listener.

Was there a woman named Jennifer Juniper, as in your song of that title?

Yes, Jennifer was Patti Boyd's sister. [Patti Boyd was married to both George Harrison and Eric Clapton.] A love song for a woman is for all women. It's for womanhood. Like "Lalena" is not about a particular woman but about all women, one aspect of them.

"Lalena" is a made-up word again. It was from Lotte Lenya, Kurt Weill's wife, from "Three-Penny Opera" in which she played the street girl. So it's about a woman who hasn't found love, who hasn't become a mother, who has become this sensual woman. So it was about all women who have dealt with the male world in that sense of using her sensuality.

It has a beautifully sad melody.
Yes. It starts in B minor. A minor ballad, with a touch of jazz, but it's very much like a Spanish melody. I think the melodies I write just serve the lyric. And the finding of the open chords in the song—B minor with the open B— shows my love of Spanish music. But with a jazz-classical arrangement.

While writing songs for women, are you also addressing these songs to a feminine aspect of yourself?
It's interesting to see that I was the first songwriter to speak about the feminine side of the male. And it has nothing to do with homosexuality. The gentle side of the male was coming out. I remember the headlines in the pop page in England: "Donovan thinks the world is *beautiful*." And it was kind of a put-down. They'd never heard a male sing about the sensitive side before. And, of course, this is part of what was going to happen anyway: the sensitizing of the male in relation to the female. And that would lead to the masculine side of the female coming out as a theme.

Do you remember writing "Mellow Yellow"?
I do believe I wrote it in Sweden while on tour. Similar to "Colours," it was in D tuning but again with a love of jazz. Jazz was more my influence than out-and-out rhythm and blues.

As far as the lyrics are concerned, it was interpreted by many people as many different things. But essentially, over it all, was the sense of being mellow and laid-back, which had something to do with smoking the pot or being cool.

We were in the studio with [producer] Mickey Most and the horns that we were using were coming off like a stripper song. They asked me what I thought, and I said, "I don't like it."

And they said, "What do you mean you don't like it?" I said, "It's not quite right." It wasn't mellow. So all the musicians went out, and they put the little hats on the ends of their horns, and it went, "Wah wah wah. . . ." And there it was. Once they put the mutes on, it worked perfectly.

That song came out of jazz, out of a love of jazz.

It begins with the line, "I'm just mad about Saffron."
Incense. And saffron is a yellow color.

Has smoking marijuana or doing other drugs been a positive influence on your songwriting?
I don't believe that any drugs influenced anybody to write anything. If you didn't have it in you, you wouldn't have written it anyway. But it took the edge off. Smoking grass or hashish is an actual key and a door into the inner world in the nicest possible way. Most other drugs are very hard-edged and extreme, even mushrooms. Whereas with marijuana you can still be alive, aware, and certainly the music was cooler.

You talk about it opening the door to the inside—
Yes. Time disappears.

Do you know of other ways of opening that door?
Well, meditation opens it but in the instant world that we live in, meditation takes a long while to open it. The world that you were contacting quickly

through the herbs is a world that is there anyway. And breathing, actually, is a way in. And marijuana slows down the respiratory rate. So if you do that on your own, you can enter the state without.

Do you consider these songs as having come from within you or from beyond you?

Nobody else was writing them. They come from within. The I-Ching describes music as the invisible sound that moves all hearts. It has this power over all the other arts. Wherever it comes from—and it's hard to talk about your own music—there are these tones, and when these tones are sounded, they presumably touch different parts of us. And when we're sad and we hear a sad song, are we elevated? Generally, we are. When we hear a basic rhythm, the body tends to move.

I have a bootleg recording of Paul McCartney and you singing his song "Blackbird." Did you have anything to do with writing that song?

No, not in the writing. Though I do recall that bootleg; it's one of my favorites. I believe Paul was writing that for the girl in the Supremes. Yes. Diana Ross. She was the blackbird.

One of your brightest and happiest songs is "Sunshine Superman."

Yes. "Sunshine Superman" was about Linda and I. A very positive love song. And although I was going through pain because I wasn't with her, it actually stated that I would be with her. And prophetically enough, I was with her. Linda was with Brian Jones very early and had a boy. I fell in love with her when she was still hurt by Brian. So I wrote this song as a letter to her though the airwaves. As "Epistle to Dippy" was a letter to an old friend through the airwaves.

Who was Dippy?

He was a school friend. He was actually one of three school friends, and we all had nicknames and he liked a Zen monk named Diplodocus or something like that, and we called him Dippy for short. And then I went my way in the late fifties. He went his and signed up for nine years with the British army and went to Malaysia. And I started writing to him, a letter, or an epistle, to Dippy. The song was about him and me and friends in school; it was a memory of school days.

"Catch the Wind" is one of the most beautiful songs ever written.

As a first song, and it was my first single, it is very well crafted. It is about a relationship that one can't have. Lost love, love unrequited. And it actually is about Linda, who I didn't meet until a year later. So once again it was prophetic. And even though I say so myself, as a first song it is quite amazing. It is not naive in any way; it is very knowing.

The melody is very similar to an early Dylan melody [sings portion of "Gates of Eden"]. Roger McGuinn pointed that out to me. But the lyric was about Linda, who I hadn't met. Because there was nobody around at the time who I was writing about. It was about all womanhood or the relationship that one wanted that one couldn't have: "Ah, but I may as well try and catch the wind."

* * *

Burt Bacharach & Hal David

Beverly Hills, California 1997

After ten years of polite but persistent pestering, I was thrilled to be granted an interview with Burt Bacharach on Valentine's Day, 1997, just in time to be included in this book. Though it had been a long wait, it seemed to be the perfect time. After all, what better day than Valentine's Day to talk to this man who has written the love songs that have graced our lives for so long? And 1997, so far, had been a great year for Bacharach, who was happily jazzed about several new projects—most notably his recent collaborations and performances with Elvis Costello—as well as by the renewed esteem he'd been receiving from everyone from Paul McCartney to Noel Gallagher of Oasis, both of whom have publically professed undying love for his work.

Of course, any time to interview Burt Bacharach would be fine with me. Along with his partner, lyricist Hal David, Bacharach has profoundly altered the art of songwriting as we know it, forever expanding both the harmonic and melodic potential of the popular song. Their songs shaped the sound of the sixties, and the perfect fusion of Bacharach's uniquely sophisticated, romantic melodies with David's elegantly economic use of lyrics are every bit as powerful today, if not more. Their influence on other songwriters has been extremely vast and continues to increase, as evidenced by the wealth of songwriters in this book who point to Bacharach & David as a major source of their songwriting inspiration.

"When you say the name Burt Bacharach," Brian Wilson told me with an almost religious reverence, "right away, it triggers off love melodies, harmonies, *beautiful* records, *incredible* songs that he wrote with Hal David. That's a source of love right there." Jimmy Webb admitted to "being under the influence of Burt Bacharach," and went on to say, "His melodies are very unpredictable, and skip in not odd but unusual directions." Even Frank Zappa, who was a harsh critic of most popular music, singled out their songs for uncharacteristic praise. "I really enjoyed the compositions of Bacharach & David," Zappa said. "I thought they were so good because prior to that time there had been little of bitonal or polytonal harmonic implication in American pop music, and we are to thank them for providing that through those early Dionne Warwick recordings."

The name Hal David is surely not as famous as that of his partner, except to students of songwriting and those within the music industry who know him to be one of the most accomplished lyricist of our time. Destined always to play the part of the less-celebrated wordsmith who exists in the shadow of the composer star, much like Ira with George Gershwin, Hal has always been happy to have written songs that are world-famous without having to be a star himself. Like the famous words he's written over the years, he's not the type to draw attention to himself, preferring simply to get the job done in the best possible way. His lyrics are distinguished for the graceful, uncomplicated ways in which they fit the often complex meanderings of Bacharach's melodies. As others have noted, David's lyrics make Bacharach's melodies seem easy, which they are not.

Take "Alfie," for example. It's a miracle of a song, really, and one made more miraculous by the knowledge that it was written by two men. It's a great lesson in songwriting, an ideal marriage of words and music. If one studies the chords and the way they relate to the flow of the tune, there's no easily discernible logic that dictates why they work so well, and yet they do. Like the shapes of snowflakes or autumn leaves, they possess an intrinsic beauty that is uniquely mysterious and undeniable. Bacharach's melody perfectly suits the meter and mood of the lyric, leaving the listener suspended by the use of unresolved melodic cadences that accentuate the beautiful yearning quality of the lyrics.

"What's it all about when you sort it out, Alfie?
Are we meant to take more than we give?"

Bacharach has rarely discussed the source of his style, preferring to allow his music to speak for itself. He was willing, however, to shed some light on his compositional technique by discussing what he calls his "horizontal" view of a melody, in which the tune is allowed to stretch and breath naturally, unhindered by the strictures of chords and rhythms. Even when writing a song to an existing lyric, as he did with "Alfie," Bacharach's allegiance to melody might produce extra measures within a tune, requiring David to fill in the added bars with connecting lyrics. It's the reason the songs remain so innately powerful today: their structures were generated by the emotional arc of the melody itself, and all other components became secondary to securing that natural flow. As Bacharach states in the following, the strongest source of creativity for him was the songs themselves: "Music breeds its own inspiration," he said.

Burt Bacharach was born in Kansas City, Missouri on May 12, 1928, and grew up in Forest Hills, New York, the son of Bert Bacharach, a former football player turned newspaper columnist and author. Burt's mother, Irma Bacharach, was a trained artist and self-taught pianist who played show tunes throughout his childhood. "I don't remember if I liked the songs she played," he recalled, during an interview at his Beverly Hills home, "but I used to marvel at the fact that she could sound things out by ear." Despite her example and his later pianistic proclivities, his first instrument of choice was not piano but drums, selected more for visual than musical reasons. "I found the drums to be very appealing when I'd see them at a restaurant," he said in characteristically hushed tones. "I loved the colors."

Playing football was more appealing to him than playing piano during his childhood, and he dreamed of following his father's footsteps by joining a professional team. His parents, recognizing his immense musical talent and wanting to preserve his gifted fingers, insisted instead that he devote himself to music. But the isolation from friends and football that music required caused him to hate the piano, and this hatred soon spread to encompass all forms of music. Jazz, however, quickly changed everything.

"No kind of music appealed to me, " he remembered. "I found music to be real drudgery when I was young. It wasn't until I was in my teens that I got really into some music. That was the Big Bands—Harry James, the Dorseys, things like that. And then the real eye-opener was hearing the music of the Bop era. It sounded, amazingly, twenty years in front of anything that I'd been hearing. Dizzy Gillespie. Thelonious Monk. Charlie Parker. I loved them all."

These pioneers of jazz shifted his feelings about playing music to the extent that when his parents relented and allowed him to quit piano, he declined and dove headlong into his studies, mastering theory, harmony, and counterpoint. Though frustated by his inability to sound out songs by ear the way his mother did, he could sight-read anything put in front of him, and was soon entertaining his fellow classmates at high school dances by playing anything and everything they cared to hear.

In time he branched out beyond classical and pop into realms of boogie-woogie and blues, styles that served him well during the years right after World War II. He'd play solo for the soldiers at the army hospitals during the day, and at night with a jazz combo at a small hotel. This exposure to many forms of new music only magnfied his awareness of how much he had yet to learn, leading him to study first with Bohuslav Martinu and Henry Cowell at New York's David Mannes School of Music, then later at Montreal's McGill University, and in California with the composer Darius Milhaud, with whom Dave Brubeck also studied. Bacharach also spent a series of happy summers, as have many great composers before him, absorbing musical wisdom and natural beauty at the Tanglewood Center in the Berkshire Mountains of Massachusetts.

It was in Milhaud's composition class that Bacharach's propensity for melodicism first surfaced. While his fellow students proudly displayed all forms of abstract atonal and polytonal music, Bacharach grew embarrassed by the sweetness of the melodies he was writing. Milhaud, however, recognized Burt's unique gift and celebrated his tonal tendencies, telling him that the ability to create a memorable melody is a rare and essential talent. It set Bacharach on the singular melodic path that he's followed for the entirety of his career, creating many of the most haunting and heartfelt tunes of our times.

He entered the army after the war was over in 1950, and spent the next two years with the special service at Fort Dix in New Jersey. Recognizing the specific abilities of each enlisted man, the Army regularly stationed Bacharach at the piano in the Officer's Club, where he'd perform medleys of popular hits, occasionally slipping in one of his own instrumental compositions, and claiming it was a recently discovered Debussy tune.

After his army years, Bacharach landed jobs as music arranger for both Vic Damone and The Ames Brothers. Sorting through songs submitted to the Ames, he was so unimpressed by their value that he decided to become a songwriter. "I didn't really have my *goals* set on anything," he said. "I never thought of writing popular music. I'd listen to these songs sent to the Ames Brothers and say, 'Jesus, I could easily do better than that. I could write two, three of those in a day.'"

He quit his job, moved back to New York, took an office in the famed Brill Building on Broadway, and got to work writing songs. He soon discovered, though, that his style was too sophisticated for the hit parade, and yet he couldn't tolerate any attempt at being imitative of others, a generally accepted songwriting practice of the day. "It looked simple. But writing something simple that sounded maybe a little derivative, or accessible, was not so easy or acceptable to me. I went a long time without getting *any* degree of success."

Needing to augment his income, he accepted his friend Peter Matz's invitation to take over as musical director for Marlene Deitrich. He toured with Deitrich around the world, and she became dependent on him. "He's my teacher," she said, "and also my critic, my accompanist, my arranger, and my conductor."

Success as a songwriter was soon to be his, but not before he met someone to write the right words for his often elusive melodies. That person was Hal David. Born in Brooklyn on May 25, 1921, Hal was the younger brother of Mack David, a well-known country songwriter. He studied violin as a kid, played in neighborhood bands, and revered all the great swing bands of the era. But words, more than music, were his true passion, and his first job out of school was as a copywriter for the New York Post.

The U.S. Army is to thank for turning Hal David into a songwriter. Stationed by the special service in Hawaii, he started writing songs and sketches for USO shows and discovered he had a natural inclination for lyricizing. After the war, with the help of his brother Mack, he hooked up with Famous Music and started writing hits there before anyone ever heard the name Bacharach. His first was written with Don Rodman in the days when songs were recorded by not one but many artists, resulting in four hit versions of "The Four Winds and The Seven Seas," first by Guy Lombardo, and followed by Sammy Kaye, Vic Damone and Bing Crosby. Hal also wrote "Bell Bottom Blues" with Leon

Carr, which became a #1 hit as recorded by Theresa Brewer, and "American Beauty Rose," made famous by Frank Sinatra in 1950.

In 1958 Bacharach and David united as a team at Famous Music, and though they spent months writing songs so forgettable neither will attempt to remember them, they both clearly remember their first two hits: "The Story of My Life," recorded by Marty Robbins, and "Magic Moments," by Perry Como. Bacharach today considers both songs to be musically unadventurous, and they are relatively tame when compared to what was to come. But in the context of 1958, these songs bore the distinctive stamp of a new presence in popular music—songwriters unafraid to stretch and redefine the rules that dictate the structures of pop songs.

While it appears in today's music that the writing of a pop song bears no conditions, the traditions of Tin Pan Alley were strict. A specific song structure was required, and even the length of a song was specified. In the forties, Harold Arlen's "That Old Black Magic," was a source of controversy because of its outrageously long 64-bar melody. So when Bacharach and David emerged right in the heart of Tin Pan Alley with "The Story of My Life," which defied the accepted form by having no verse and a 52-bar chorus, people paid attention.

By the start of the sixties, Bacharach and David were writing hit songs for an enormous variety of artists, all before hooking up with the one singer who was to record their most famous songs, Dionne Warwick. They first heard her sing in 1962, when she was still in pigtails and sneakers, yet her vocal abilities were astounding even then. She recorded their 1962 song "Don't Make Me Over," and her natural stylistic connection with their work cemented the relationship. "She's a beautiful lady," Burt said, "and the best exponent for me and for Hal that there's been. It's a wonderful kind of progressive, up-the-ladder sort of success story for the three of us."

"There was a certain chemistry that the three of us had," Hal said. "She's a wonderful singer and musician. I believe it was meant to be, frankly, because it clicked from the very first record we did with Dionne and it went on for a long time."

It's a success that was unprecedented, to have a songwriting team link up with one singer to produce so many outstanding hits, songs that have all since become standards. While Sammy Cahn wrote scores of hits all for Sinatra, it's more common for songwriters to have their work recorded by a wide range of singers to cover all stylistic extremes, from slow melodic ballads to uptempo rhythm songs. But Dionne Warwick could do it all, and whether the song was "Alfie," "Do You Know the Way to San Jose?" "What the World Needs Now Is Love, Sweet Love," "Walk on By," "I'll Never Fall in Love Again," or "Say a Little Prayer," she made it very much her own. Bacharach would tailor the arrangements to show off her spectacular voice, smoothly cushioning the sound with his signature use of muted trumpets and strings, and the records they made together were magic.

At the same time, Burt and Hal continued crafting hits for others singers, such as "One Less Bell to Answer" for The Carpenters and "Raindrops Keep Falling on My Head," from the film *Butch Cassidy and The Sundance Kid*, for B. J.

Thomas. Throughout the sixties, simultaneous to the reign of The Beatles, the songs of Bacharach and David powerfully shaped the sound and spirit of the time.

Their songs were often famously linked with the movies for which they were written: "Alfie" is from the movie of the same name, and they wrote title songs for *What's New, Pussycat?* and *Send Me No Flowers*. "The Look of Love" was written as a "sexual theme," according to Burt, for Ursula Andress in *Casino Royale*. Their first and only musical was *Promises Promises*, based on the book by Neil Simon.

For reasons never completely explained, Bacharach and David parted company after some of the greatest success two songwriters have ever seen, and began writing with others. Bacharach collaborated with many other lyricists, most notably Carole Bayer Sager, whom he also married. Together they wrote "That's What Friends Are For," an extraordinary record which was performed by four of the finest singers of our time: Dionne Warwick, Stevie Wonder, Gladys Knight and Elton John. More recently Bacharach collaborated, mostly long-distance via phone and fax machines, with Elvis Costello on the breathtaking "God Give Me Strength," from the film *Grace of My Heart*, and the two were about to embark on writing songs for an entire album when we spoke in February of 1997.

Hal David wrote the musical *Times Square* with Charles Strauss, and has been busy working on behalf of his fellow songwriters as a board member and former Chairman of ASCAP, and as a board member of the National Academy of Songwriters. Though I interviewed both songwriters separately, the two interviews are united here in the lasting spirit of their miraculous songs, in which their names will be linked for all time.

Part I: Burt Bacharach.

In listening to your songs, your use of melody is truly extraordinary. Do you think a melody is the most important factor to creating a good song?

I used to feel that way. Nowadays I pay much more attention to the lyrics than I used to. I used to think that nobody really whistled a lyric. I thought the thing people remembered was the melody. And I think that that's still true, but I think a bad lyric is going to down a song. I've heard some bad lyrics on some really strong melodies, and there's a lot of inferior material we hear, a lot of cheap lyrics, but there's something really hooky in the melodic content that grabs you and makes it survive. For a while, anyway.

Hal David certainly had a knack for finding a lyric that fit your melodies perfectly.

Oh, yeah. He always knew how to put the words in the right place. It's great when you have a lyric writer like that.

Would Hal generally give you a finished lyric to write to?

It'd go both ways. With *Promises Promises* there were a lot of lyrics that came first, as there was with "Alfie" and with "A House is Not a Home." Because they all were stemming from another source, like a book, as in *Promises*. Neil Simon asked us recently to write another song for a new Broadway production of *Promises*, which we did. It was kind of interesting; we did it the same way we originally wrote the show: Hal brought in a lyric, and I got a general kind of first floor of the house built, you might say, and then started designating where I wanted to change musically from what's just been written. I had a chorus, maybe, where there was no chorus before. And that's the way we wrote a lot of that stuff. Like in *Promises*, the language from the songs had to really come off the book, too.

And are there other songs in which you wrote a complete melody first, without any words?

Or if not the complete melody, certainly I got four, six bars, or eight bars and played those for Hal.

When writing music, do you work with pure melody, or do you generate melodies by playing chord changes at the piano?

I've got to get away from the keyboard to hear what I've really got. It's a pretty full situation for me, and it can get a little hypnotic with the chords you are playing, and it goes sort of by the bar rather than the long passage. I've always done that—you've got to get off the piano to the chair and just listen, in my head, to what's going on.

And what you're hearing is a single melody line?

Oh, I'll hear the harmonization, too. But I've got to back off from the keyboard because I don't get the long horizontal view at it. You've got to get the horizontal look and see what's going on horizontally. And then go back to the keyboard, straighten things out, write it out, look at it.

Does this process begin at the keyboard, before you move away from it?

Sometimes. Sometimes not.

The reason I ask is that with many songs, one can see how the melody derived directly from the chords. But with your songs—"Alfie" for example—the melody is supported by the chords in such a remarkable way, where often the melody note is extending the chord—as when a melodic cadence ends on the ninth of the chord. Can you recall how writing that kind of melody came about?

I don't know how that came about. The length of the bars, I think is probably a little bit irregular. But when I'm working with a lyric, and I'm working with the lyric first, I know that I am going to start hearing what that melody is in my head. It complicates it a little bit when I'm at the piano. So many great, great writers have written that way, at a guitar or keyboard, and written very successfully vertically. But for me I know it works better horizontally.

It's the same way with orchestrating: I've just got to get away from anything that my hands fall on. Particularly with what we've got as tools now, with these keyboards, it's all kind of seductive sounding. When you've got three MIDI sounds on the keyboard all going at once. And you've got the gloss, and the drum machine is playing. You play a pad on one keyboard, and on the other hand you play the bass, and you can make some extraordinary stuff. It's very inventive. But for me, I've got to peel it back and see what I've got as far as melody in that framework. I can put my four-year old on a MIDI keyboard, have him play two notes, turn on the drum machine, and it sounds *great*. With everything grooving along. But you've got to be careful. *I do.* Not everybody has to be careful.

I think there are some songs that I hear that sound so great. I don't want to mention them by name. But it's so appealing. I'll drive around in the car and listen. It's so well produced. The production is so extraordinary. The background is so special. Everything is coming at you—such a great groove. But I think when I get back and hear that song in my head, how memorable is that melody to me really when all the side-effects are taken away? It fooled me. It can *fool* me, because I'm driving in my car and listening to what I think are very, very strong records. And then maybe I'll find out, out of ten or eleven on that album, maybe there are two that really have got some value and can last.

Your songs are the antithesis of that, built on the strength of the melody itself. With "Alfie," it's amazing how the cadences of the song don't resolve; but end on the ninth of the chord, which propels you back to the next verse. Was that a conscious choice?

You know, I was working with a lyric. And when you're working with a lyric, it can take you to different places than you might have gone to left on your own. The lyric dictated that the melody needed to go there.

Your melodies often have big ranges. Is that one thing that makes a melody great, do you think?

I hope not. I never recognized, when I was writing the song ["God Give Me Strength"] with Elvis [Costello] how rangy it was. I thought it was pretty rangy but I never counted the notes, or let that be a potential problem, or did I ever know how long the song was until we got in the studio in New York and made it. It's over six minutes. And it's almost two octaves: just one note short of two octaves.

But, no, I think if you can make it easy, you're always doing it better. Easy for a singer, easy for somebody singing along. Because people can't *handle* two octaves. They're listening to a song and they want to sing along, or wanting to remember it in their head, and you're taking them out of the picture.

Yet a song like "Alfie" isn't easy to sing. That bridge, especially, is pretty tough.

No, it's not easy to sing at all.

Yet it's so beautiful and memorable.

Well, I'm grateful it existed. I'm grateful I had a chance to write it.

Can you recall, with "Alfie," how you wrote the bridge section? That melody is so amazing, yet the chords are unusual there—it's hard to imagine how it could have been written.

Can't remember that. I think it's very possible that melodically it went there because of where it was coming out of musically, and I was looking for the lift. [*Sings it softly to himself.*] Yeah, it's climbing. And there's only one chord that's probably going to work under that on the downbeat of the first bar of the bridge.

After all these years of writing, is it easy for you to connect with the source of creativity and get it going?

No. I think it's a very hard process. You're in a room by yourself. For me to say if it's good or acceptable, it's hard to say. I do like the collaborative process, because at a certain point, you're bouncing off of somebody. I always liked the thing when Carole and I would write with another writer. With Neil Diamond or Bruce Roberts. It was her idea and it was a *good* idea. You get to say, "Do you like it this way? How about this? Do you like this chord like this?" When you're in a room by yourself, you're asking the wall.

Do you have any kind of routine for songwriting? For example, do you do it at the same time everyday?

No. I think it's a discipline. And I don't necessarily go by this, but it's a rule I think I should go by, and when I'm right, I'll do it, which is: music breeds its own inspiration. You can only do it by doing it. You just sit down and you may not feel like it, but you push yourself. It's a work process. Or just improvise. Something will come. Or turn on the drum machine. Or turn on another stop on a keyboard. Or get away from the piano. But don't sit around and wait for something magical to happen in your head or heart.

You've got to push it and work at it to get it going—

I think there is something to be said—if you've got some talent, and I've known some people who have had some talent, and they've got discipline and a fierce desire to work—to *be there*. On a daily basis. And you'll get better.

Is it doing it everyday that makes it happen?

I think so.

Some songwriters have said that it felt as if their songs came from a source beyond them, like receiving a gift. Does it feel that way to you?

[*Laughs*] No, I think you have to have some special talent, you really do. I would say, loosely, it is a God-given gift. And when it is all said and done, you can doubt yourself, and have doubted yourself, and say it's not very good. But you've been blessed.

I just find that there's too many people who have liked my songs where I can validate myself. When you have somebody like Miles Davis telling you you're good, Quincy [Jones] telling you you're good, you may pay attention. Musicians on a date—your key rhythm players—get excited to work with you. So you start to maybe believe them more than you believe yourself.

You said that "God Give Me Strength" was something that Elvis Costello started writing in your old style—

I don't know whether it's an old style or not. I think maybe Elvis started it that way with me in mind. I think that because of the period piece movie that it's in, I think that it's just as okay now as it was then.

I agree, it is gorgeous. Did he actually begin writing the melody of that?

Sure. He definitely made a melodic contribution to that song. Elvis is very used to doing them both. It was an interesting process working with him, because, you know, we never were together in the writing—we did it by fax and answering machines. But we just spent a week together here in L.A. starting almost four or five songs. We're talking about doing an album together. So that was very interesting. I don't touch the lyric, but he touches music. And we're both coming from different musical sources, different musical *foundations*, I think, harmonically. But it was *fun*. We got used to each other. He'd sit at one keyboard, I'd sit at the other keyboard, and we'd work. He's a great writer, a great lyric writer.

In the sixties, parallel with the Beatles, your work expanded the musical potential of the popular song. Were you paying attention to what they were doing?

No way. I was just really going with blinders on. I was completed focused only on what I was doing. It was: next record, here we go, *boom*.

Was it conscious on your part to stretch the form of pop songs?

I think once I got Dionne in the studio and saw what she could do and the ease that she could do it, I felt I could stretch. And then when I heard that she could stretch, on the next record out I would stretch a little bit more. Or when you get somebody like Bobby Vinton singing "Blue on Blue," it changes gear for you. Or [Gene] Pitney doing "Liberty Valance" or "Only Love," you try to tailor make it to him.

Is there any way that you can explain what the Bacharach sound is, and what gives a song your distinctive flavor?

I remember thinking that what in England they used to call the Bacharach sound for songs like "Walk on By" and "What's New, Pussycat," that those songs were as far apart as songs can be. That's what I thought then. But maybe not. But maybe there's a sophistication that is the common thing there. But I thought that if they're looking to link a sound up with the Bacharach sound, then maybe say it comes from the orchestration. That was, maybe, the glue.

Do you have favorite keys to work in?

I don't like some keys, but other keys are fine [*laughs*]. I never write in B major. Or in C flat. I'm comfortable in E flat, F, G, C. Not so much in D, but I can write in D. It always helps me in writing, if I get stuck, to switch keys. Because maybe then you will hear something else. Maybe your hands will go somewhere else. It's the hands again. It's a problem that I find working at the keyboard, it's where your hands go, where they're comfortable going.

Do you have favorite chords or kinds of chords that you like the best?

I never feel comfortable with, like, a straight triad. A straight C major chord or F major. I'm always looking to make it something more. To expand it. Though I have found that [a straight triad] does work in D major. [*Laughs*] When you get in D major, a pure chord works a little bit better. But the bottom line is, whatever chord I choose, it's still governed by what I hear in my head and what that melody is dictating. Sometimes you add a major second to a chord, and it doesn't work. Maybe it doesn't work because the melody is crying out to be in a pure chord or triad.

When you are working on melodies, do words ever come to you?

Yes. When I'm working on something, I'm making up words. And the words might make no sense. With "Raindrops," as an example, I just kept hearing that phrase, "raindrops keep falling on my head." Hal tried to change it, and go to another lyric idea, but that was very good one. I will sing whatever phrase it is that I'm hearing with the music, and I've found a lot of lyric writers, recently, who will try to maybe use that. That will maybe be the title. Because it fits. It marries so well with the melody.

So when working you are singing the melody as well as playing the chords?

I sing the melody and play the chords, and maybe I'm just making up a dummy lyric.

Do you tape yourself while working?

Yeah, I do that, or write it down quickly on paper. But I used to write words or syllables on flugelhorn parts for a record date. So that it was more than a note. Because if musicians play those notes the way they might have sung them, with those words, then you're dealing with a little more expressive content.

Growing up, did you ever consider going into jazz?

No. I didn't know what I wanted to do. I just knew that music was appealing. And suddenly I had some interest instead of just having to do it because my mother said I had to practice everyday after school a half an hour. I didn't know that I was going to do this as a career, or do *anything* as a career. Didn't have an idea what I was going to do. It wasn't like I had aspirations to be a composer or play jazz. Nothing like that.

And yet all through your teens, you studied music seriously?

Well, I studied seriously, sure. I got interested in it and I got interested in serious composition, serious classical music.

You studied with Darius Milhaud. Was your intention then to be a classical composer?

I had thought that that might be something I wanted to do, and at that point in my life, I was interested enough to study it. Going in the army, then, caused an interruption and things just took a different course. When I was out of the army after a couple years, I was able to maybe think that maybe that's what I really wanted to do. But that's a very hard life, being a serious classical composer. Not much money. Maybe teaching at a university or teaching some students. I guess I was thinking about the comforts of life that I might not have.

I didn't want to do it enough, that's the main thing. I didn't want to pursue that. I wasn't serious enough.

Were your first songs good ones?

Probably not. But maybe a couple certainly must have been worthwhile. I had to think I had *some* ability.

You're well-known for introducing sophisticated harmonies to popular music. Was that something you had done from the start?

No, I don't think I was doing that. As I say, I think I was probably writing to what I felt was a common denominator. What I thought I'd seen or heard or was familiar with playing for the Ames Brothers. I thought, you know, maybe that's what you do—you write commercial that way. So I don't think I was doing anything particularly innovative at that time.

Do you remember what brought you to that place where you realized you could be successful doing your own style of music?

I think I finally had some songs published, and I had some hits with Hal [David]—"Magic Moments" and "Story of My Life"—it was a long time coming, but the thing was that they weren't particularly innovative songs. They were just, I guess, what you might think of as commercial songs. Or I thought of as commercial. I was so happy to have *had* them. To finally have had something. And then I guess from there, maybe it got my courage up a little bit more. I had some degree of success. And knowing Leiber & Stoller, and just being in the general environment, I think you grow. Maybe you start experimenting. I think that's pretty substantial: when you have a couple of hits after having a very disappointing first year—and maybe it was more than a year before those two songs happened—then you get a little more courage, a little more confidence to say, hey, I can do this again.

I think it really started to open up for me when I started to protect the material I had written, by going in to make the record. If I wasn't the record producer, I was the orchestrator or the arranger, I would go in and make the record. I didn't care whether somebody else got producing credit or not. I just was interested in producing the song and protecting the material.

What was the first time you had that control over a record?

I think where the first time somebody let me go in and make a record with strings was "Make It Easy on Yourself" with Jerry Butler. They let me go in and make the record the way I heard it. And write the orchestration, and go in and conduct. And I'm sure I got a lot of input coming from the booth. I don't think it was total carte blanche. But I did have a good feeling of control over the material, and it seemed to be appreciated by Jerry Butler and the record company. That was the starting point.

If it's okay with you, I'd like to randomly name some of your songs to see whatever response you might have to them.

Sure.

"The Look of Love."

"Look of Love" is a song from *Casino Royale*. It was written as a love theme, or a sexual theme, for Ursula Andress. It wasn't really a love theme as much as a kind of very understated sexual theme written for her body and her face.

"I Say a Little Prayer."

"Say a Little Prayer"—I never wanted that record of Dionne's to come out. I thought I had blown it on the record, that I took it too fast. I was very happy that I was very wrong. I loved Aretha's record. It's great. It makes me smile when I hear it.

"Walk on By."

"Walk on By"—I didn't know that it was innovative when we did it. Till people started telling me it was really innovative. But I knew it was special. It was a great recording date. I think I came in with 101 temperature and did "Walk on By" and "Anyone Had a Heart" and walked out with some heavy-duty gold.

"If Anyone Had a Heart."

That was an adventure right there—putting two grand pianos on the date with two piano players. Putting "Anyone Had a Heart" with the multiple time changes—not intentional—I didn't know they were there until I went to write it out. Sometimes when you get a 7/8 bar, it's hard to notice.

"What the World Needs Now is Love, Sweet Love."

"What the World Needs Now"—you know, I went cold on that song. I wrote it with Hal, and thought it was good. Played it for Dionne, she didn't love it. That to me was an invalidation for me. I would have just as soon put the song away in a drawer. Hal—and I give him all the credit in the world for this—suggested we play it for Jackie DeShannon—who we were about to do a record with—and she loved it. We went and cut it.

Did you then grow to like it again?

Oh, I loved it. Once I heard Jackie sing it. You know, you get a negative feeling—I play a melody for a lyric writer, and they say, "I don't like that—what else you got?" And then, you know, for me anyway, that kind of says, well, maybe it's not so good. Put it away.

"Close to You."

"Close to You"—I'm very grateful to Richard Carpenter making that record the way that they heard it. Because the way that I heard it was very different and not very good. I made the first few records of it with the wrong groove, wrong feel. Richard came in and nailed it.

"Always Something There to Remind Me."

I always liked that song. I did it with Lou Johnson first. And then Dionne, and Sandy Shaw. Liked the song. I don't write a lot of up-tempo songs [*laughs*] so when they happen, they're good.

"Message to Michael."

The first person who ever recorded "Message To Michael" was Marlene Deitrich when I made a record with her. It was in German. Pretty interesting. And then Dionne came in, and nailed it, was great. I like the song.

"Baby, It's You."

Written a long time ago. I was very happy the way that it turned out. The Beatles recorded it. And then Luther [Vandross] got his hands in there and made some substantial changes in it.

"That's What Friends are For."

Oh, I love that song. It's just very special. We wrote it first for *Nightshift*, didn't really happen. I mean, Rod [Stewart] made a very nice record. But he made it his way and when we did it with Dionne, that was a wonderful record, wonderful. Those four voices [Dionne, Gladys Knight, Elton John and Stevie Wonder] like that together, *Jesus*. Proud of that record, proud of that song. Proud of what it did at that time to the consciousness of the country.

"One Less Bell to Answer."

That was kind of a freak that it happened. I remember there was a program manager in New Orleans who started playing that record at a time when a key station.could influence the whole South. That title was born from working on

What's New, Pussycat? and Angie [Dickinson] was living with me in London. And a doorbell rang, and I think she made the comment, "One less bell to answer, when I get out of here." It was pretty intense, and it bothered her. We weren't married yet but we were living together. I think Hal heard her say, "One less bell to answer." He thought, that's a good song title and we wrote it.

"A House is Not a Home."
"House is Not a Home," I like that song. Lyric first, written for a picture, and again Hal provided a framework for me to write the music to.

"On My Own."
"On My Own," I love. I love the record. It's probably a way better record emotionally than it is actually a song. Great performances—*chilling* performances.

Michael [McDonald] comes in and blows you away, and Patti [LaBelle] is *great*. And it's a very special record. It could be the best record that I've ever been connected to. It's just wonderful. Great mix, great engineering. I must say, Carole mixed that final vocal perspective to the track. She sat there and had both levers—Michael and Patti—and she controlled it. And that makes all the difference in the world to me. Sometimes the voice is out there too far and you lose a lot. It's just got to be right. And if the voice is tucked in too much, you've lost the voice. So she got a great vocal mix.

"Do You Know the Way to San Jose?"
That's okay. Never was Dionne's favorite song. Again, it's an uptempo song. And I think a *brilliant* lyric by Hal. *Brilliant.*

"I'll Never Fall in Love Again."
Written very quick. Probably the quickest song I ever wrote with Hal. I got out of the hospital in Boston, tried to get it in the show the next night. That's where that line came from: "What do you get when you kiss a girl? You get enough germs to catch pneumonia." 'Cause I had pneumonia in the hospital.

Of all of your songs, do you have favorites?
"Alfie" is my favorite, of course. Also "That's What Friends are For." I'd put "Anyone Who Has a Heart" in there, and I think "What the World Needs Now is Love" should also be included, sure.

Part II: Hal David.

Did working with Bacharach click the first time you tried it?
In the beginning, for the first couple of years, we didn't write with each other exclusively. But early on we wrote two hits with each other, and then when we started having hits with Dionne Warwick, we decided we should stay together because it was going so well.

When you wrote with Burt, did he generally give you a finished melody to write to?
Very often. He would give me melodies from time to time—I would give him lyrics. Very often we sat in a room and banged out a song together, back and forth, back and forth. [*Laughs.*] Sometimes we'd work on perhaps three

songs at a time. We'd be working together on one song at Famous Music, and then I'd be working at home on some melody he gave me, and he'd work separately on a lyric I may have given him.

Would he put melodies on tape for you?
Back then, no. He would play it for me a few times and I would retain it. I retain a melody pretty well. Now we put everything on cassette.

His melodies are quite complex, and would seem hard to retain like that—
Yes, very complex and yet very natural. I never found Burt's music difficult. It was always very natural. That may be part of the chemistry.

It seems that your lyrics can make a melody seem even more natural. The melody to "Alfie"—
He wrote that almost entirely to the lyric. And that may be the reason that it works so well. I remember the lyrics that I gave him: "What's it all about, Alfie, is it just for the moment we live? / What's it all about, are we meant to take more than we give?"
And he added that music so I had to add: "What's it all about *when you sort it out, Alfie.*" It was written mostly to the lyric, but I would have to change it then to fit with his music.

Can you recall what inspired that lyric to be written in that way?
We wrote that for the film *Alfie*. It's a song that's very dear to me. It's a philosophy that is a nice one to have as an anthem for your life. I can't tell you what inspired it, except that it came out of me.
The way I write and the way Burt writes is to try and find something that is a little original, and not follow the pack. There's no fun in following the pack. And still you want to write songs that people like and you like.
I tended not to be concerned about whether a song was going to be a hit when I wrote it. Because it became evident that none of us knew what was a hit and what wasn't. There are songs that I loved that weren't hits and songs that I didn't think would be hits that were hits. So I tended to think that if I just write what I liked, why shouldn't people like what I like?

Which of your songs surprised you when they became hits?
"Wives and Lovers." We wrote it for Paramount and it was a very sophisticated song in many respects. It was a jazz waltz and I think it's sophisticated lyrically. I thought it was a little too hip to be a hit. And it was a big hit by Jack Jones. So that's one.
Though I love the song, I remember hearing the record of "Close to You" by The Carpenters. Jerry Moss sent it over for us to listen to. And I thought it didn't work. I thought Karen Carpenter was great, it wasn't that. It just didn't have what I thought it needed. In retrospect I can see I was a thousand percent wrong. It shows you, again, that there is nobody that smart.

Was "Close to You" written to a melody?
Yes, I wrote it to the music.

Would Burt ever suggest a title to you?
No.

Where do you think the ideas for songs come from?

Songs come from a million different places. Somebody says something. And suddenly it rings a bell. You're watching a movie or a show or a television program and you hear a line. You're in the audience and you hear a phrase, and suddenly there's an idea for a song.

I think most times they just come. I guess it comes to you because that's what you do. As opposed to doing something else. That's a specific talent you have, and the more you do it, the more it comes.

Early in my career, there were periods of times when ideas wouldn't come. And it used to worry me. I'm sure it worries any writer. Is it all over? [*Laughs*] Is this it? What do I do? Start learning how to make shoes, or cut salami? But I got beyond that at a certain point. And at this point in my life, when I work, I work. And the ideas come.

Any thoughts about where they come from?

Where they come from, generally speaking, I don't know. I don't think it comes from beyond me. I would say it's somewhere in me. Because I have to think of it. What makes me trigger it, I don't know. A thousand years from now, some medical science will figure out where creative ideas come from. It's in the subconscious somewhere. It's in the mind somewhere.

And you have found that the more you do it, the easier it is?

Yes. They flow easier. It's almost like the old-fashioned record player that you used to wind up, and you wind it up and it's slower and slower until it's up to speed. And starting a new project if you haven't been working for a while, it's a little slow until you get up to speed. But once I get up to speed, I can stay there.

Do you recall writing "What the World Needs Now is Love, Sweet Love?"

I gave Burt the lyric for that one. Almost all the lyric. We might have made a change here or there. And he wrote a great tune. I think it's one of our best songs.

Do you have a favorite song that you've written?

Of my own, I think I like "Alfie" the best. I like what it says, and I like the way it says it.

The whole trick of a song, in my opinion, is that it should seem that it wasn't written. It should seem not that two people wrote it or three people but that it came out of one mind. That's the ideal song.

A lot of times I hear songs in which the lyrics are good, but the music is just complementing the lyrics; it really has no character of its own. And when it's over, as much as I liked the lyrics, I'll find myself thinking that it's just *all wrong*. A song should be of a piece. The music and the lyrics should both be great, and it should be like one.

So many of your songs have become standards. How does it feel to be a songwriter who has written not one but many standards?

It feels thrilling. To turn on the radio as I do and to hear my songs, or for my wife to go to the hairdresser and tell me they were playing my songs, or to hear them in Europe or in other places in the United States—it's still thrilling. I love it and I'm very grateful for it.

* * *

Laura Nyro

Santa Monica, California 1994

"There's no doubt that music is a link with the divine," she said, and her songs stand as evidence of this connection with divinity. Though Laura Nyro departed from this earth on April 8, 1997, she left our world a world of her own creation, a world of music that sprung directly from the heart, so pure and intimately genuine that those who have gone there not only fell in love with her songs, they fell in love with her.

Laura loved writing songs. Unlike other songwriters who deplore the entire process, she embraced it with a reverential sense of joy that's instilled in all her songs. "In music there's a oneness and a sweetness," she said softly. "There can be delight there. There can be self-discovery there. You can dance there."

Without her music, the sound of the sixties would have been vastly different. "And When I Die" was popularized by Peter, Paul & Mary before it was a huge hit for Blood, Sweat & Tears. The Fifth Dimension had many hits with her songs, all of which are now standards: "Wedding Bell Blues," "Stoned Soul Picnic," "Blowing Away," "Save the Country," and "Sweet Blindness." With Three Dog Night's version of "Eli's Coming" and Barbra Streisand singing "Stoney End," Laura's songs both reflected and defined the free spirit of the times.

It usually takes great songwriters at least a few years of writing before they create a masterpiece. Randy Newman didn't write "Sail Away" until he'd been writing for years, nor did Simon write "The Sound of Silence" or Dylan "Blowing in the Wind" without years of work. Not so with Laura Nyro, whose very first song, written at the age of seventeen, was "And When I Die." While most songs—especially a songwriter's very first—celebrate the greatness of the self, her first one set the span of life itself in perspective, reflecting on a world that keeps going even after she's gone.

> "And when I die,
> And when I'm gone,
> There'll be one child born,
> And a world to carry on,
> Carry on."

Even if "And When I Die" was the only song she ever wrote, it's such an inspirational classic that she would still deserve an entire chapter in the annals of songwriting. But there's so much more: since her remarkable debut in 1966, she crafted a lyrical language entirely her own in songs, a kind of streetwise shorthand of the heart, wed to melodies of deep and joyous soul. Her songs, as recorded by herself and the bevy of artists who had hits with them, resounded with the authenticity of new American spirituals, sounding simultaneously modern and traditional.

On her first albums, she showed an uncanny affinity for songs of great emotional extremes. There are songs of pure ecstatic joy, a sense of boundless happiness that few songwriters, with the exception of Stevie Wonder, have ever been able to express. As songwriters know, writing a truly happy song that's not trite is tough; it's easier to write an effective sad one. But Laura Nyro has done it countless times, expressing both in her words and music the rare epiphanies of life.

She also wrote many brilliant songs that started at the other end of the emotional spectrum, as sad and deeply blue as songs can get. "New York Tendaberry" is a good example, paving the way for the emotional landscapes Rickie Lee Jones and others would concoct years later, a blending of jazz and blues with the intimacy of folk, structured on shifting rhythms and delicately beautiful imagery.

She was born Laura Nigro on October 18, 1947 in the Bronx, surrounded by all things artistic. She attended high school at Manhattan's Music & Art and by the age of seventeen, when she wrote "And When I Die," she was "already deep inside of music," absorbing the compositional genius of jazz greats such as John Coltrane and Miles Davis. Unlike most young musicians who are introduced to the language of music by learning its limitations, the first lesson she learned was that music has no limits, and this sense of freedom has shaped all her songs ever since. "I'm not interested in conventional limitations when it comes to my songwriting," she said. "I'm interested in art, poetry and music. As that kind of artist I can do anything. I can say anything. It's about self-expression. It knows no package—there's no such thing. That's what being an artist is."

> "Give me my freedom for as long as I be.
> All I ask of living is to have no chains on me."

from "And When I Die"

In addition to Coltrane and Miles, she was also inspired by a rainbow of different musical artists, starting with doo-wop and girl groups from the fifties, through Nina Simone, Smokey Robinson, Curtis Mayfield, Mary Wells, and Dusty Springfield. The sophisticated songs of Bacharach and David were also a primary influence, as was the music of classical composers her mother would play, such as Ravel, Debussy and Persicetti. At the same time she was drawn to folk music for its social consciousness—she loved Pete Seeger, Joan Baez, and Bob Dylan—and she read all the poetry she could find. It all came together naturally in her songs, which she first performed at the age of 18 at San Francisco's Hungry i coffeehouse. Though she was a New York native, writers referred to her music as representing "the San Francisco sound."

In 1965, she auditioned for Clive Davis, who recalled in his autobiography that because she was so young and shy, Laura kept the lights off, playing piano for him in a hotel room by the blue glow of a television. (She laughed heartily when I mentioned this, neither denying or confirming its authenticity.) Despite the lighting, Davis was overwhelmed by her talent, and signed her to Columbia Records. Her debut album, released in 1966, was called *More Than a New Discovery*. From 1968 through 1970 she released three albums, creating an amazing trilogy that established her as one of the truly great voices and souls of popular music: *Eli and The Thirteenth Confession*, *New York Tendaberry*, and *Christmas and the Beads of Sweat*. In 1971 she recorded *Gonna Take a Miracle*, an album of soul standards backed by the band Labelle and produced by R&B legends Gamble & Huff.

Then came years when she withdrew. We didn't hear any new songs from her until 1976 when she returned with a masterpiece called *Smile*. Combining all the ingredients that shaped her art—blues, jazz, soul, folk, Japanese music, beat poetry, haiku and more—*Smile* is maybe her greatest album, and certainly the most underrated.

Since then her work reflected "her time among the trees" and the "green spirituality" she found living in rural Connecticut. This and her transition into motherhood inspired another trilogy of great albums : *Nested*, *A Mother's Spiritual*, and *Walk the Dog*, all of which possess a quiet serenity and sense of oneness that connects issues such as ecology with the innate rights of children, animals, women, and Native Americans. Though these songs never earned the esteem of her early albums, there are many classics here, as great as her greatest work, such as "Broken Rainbow," her tribute to Native Americans. There are also two of the most moving songs ever written about motherhood, "Mother's Spiritual" and "To a Child," of which she was so proud she told me, "I can die now. I'm finished hassling with this world. I'm finished having children. This is my final statement."

Her songs have been recorded by a diverse array of singers and groups that includes Chet Atkins, Cass Elliot, Aretha Franklin, Julie London, Carmen McRae, Linda Ronstadt, Diana Ross, The Four Tops, Frank Sinatra, Sweet Honey In The Rock, The Roches, Mongo Santamaria, Junior Walker and the All-Stars, and many others. But it's her own recordings of her songs more than anything that explains why so many people—songwriters and non-songwriters alike—point to her as an idol, an artist who has profoundly changed their lives.

And when people love Laura Nyro, it's a love not taken lightly. Standing in a ticket line at a 1994 concert she gave in Santa Monica, I heard scores of her fans testify to their personal bond with her: "Laura saved my life." "When I was a kid, she was my only friend; her records are like touchstones for me." Even journalists, usually jaded by repeated exposure to stars, were in awe of her: "You mean you actually talked to her? I don't know if I could—I'd be too scared."

Seeing her in concert was a revelation. She would take the stage slowly with a sly smile as the crowd went wild. She sat at her keyboards with the countenance of a Zen master, at once completely relaxed and completely attentive. There was no conventional sense at all of a performance facade; she simply would get out of the way to allow the songs to take her over, and she would coast easily on the richness of the chords and the soulful shapes of the melodies. Sliding effortlessly from a low, smoky alto to high falsetto, she could hold down intricate piano parts while playing standards she didn't write, such as Goffin & King's "Up on the Roof," and standards she did write, including "Save the Country" and "And When I Die." Unlike the usual division in concerts between the audience and performer, her performances were celebrations. But rather than glorify her own greatness, which was certainly justified, they were celebrations of the sweetness of her songs, inviting all lucky listeners into that place where she was the happiest and most at home, deep within the oneness of music.

Your songs all seem so remarkably natural and unforced. Did they emerge at times from your life, or were they the result of sitting down and writing?

I think that it's important, sooner or later, to get on a disciplined schedule with writing. I'm finding that very important. Once I'm on that schedule and working everyday, or whenever I sit down and write, there are just those times when something, this song, comes together, that just feels kind of natural. And a little bit made in heaven.

It's just a feeling you get about the song. And, really, those are the songs that I kind of wait for. To happen in the writing. And those are the songs that I get more serious about and I would record that kind of song.

Do you always work at the piano?

I go to the piano. But once in a while I will get an idea when I'm not at the piano. And then I'm looking for a piano. [*Laughs*]

A musical idea will come to you?

Yes.

A melody might occur to you?

A melody or an image. A certain image.

Your songs are quite harmonically complex. What kind of music did you listen to growing up?

My background in music—I come from the arts in a certain way. I was not, let's say, raised on mainstream songwriting. For instance, when I was a teenager I listened a lot to John Coltrane. To Miles Davis. This was along with soul music and rock and roll that I was into. But I listened a lot to those incredible jazz minds. So interesting chord structures and chord progressions that were off the beaten track just are natural to me. Because I listened to so much of that music.

I was wondering if you listened to jazz, because your music is so jazzy, yet so soulful at the same time.
Yeah. I would say those two I listened to a lot. As a teenager.

Were you playing piano at that time, while you were absorbing that music?
Yeah, a little bit. And guitar. But mostly keyboard.

At that time were you considering being a songwriter?
Well, I just knew that, in life, music was the language that I wanted to speak. I was very drawn to the arts because I perceived something divine happening there. As opposed to your more mundane kind of perceptions. So I really felt that. I felt heart and soul energy in music.

I guess I was a natural singer, you know? And I used to sing, actually, with street groups on street corners when I was a teenager. That was a wonderful thing that was happening then.

You'd sing doo-wop?
Yes. Starting from when I was fourteen or fifteen. It was an every evening occurrence. That's what was happening. Out on the street. Right on the street. If it was winter, then it was happening in hallways or down in the train station. Which put a lot of echo on the sound.

That is a wonderful thing to grow up with. Because the whole day could go by, the whole week could go by. That was the delightful energy, going out singing. I used to sing with this Spanish guy's group. I kind of invited myself into the group. [*Laughs*] Because I was sitting at the top of the steps and they were down in the train station singing. I mean, it was *beautiful*. And then I just—listening to them—I started hearing this other harmony that I wanted to sing with them. And I just started singing. And they didn't ask me to leave. [*Laughs*] So I started to sing with them. But you could sing with different people—people knew the songs and the harmonies.

Did you start writing songs at that age?
Yes. I was starting to write.

Do you remember the name of your first one?
No. I know two songs I could tell you for sure, because I recorded them. "Wedding Bell Blues" and "And When I Die." Those were songs I wrote as a teenager. In my late teens.

Really? That's amazing. I would have thought you would have had to work up to something like "And When I Die." Those are pretty advanced songs to have written as your first ones. Were you surprised when you started coming up with songs at that level?
I think that, you see, I was reading poetry from the time I was really young. And I really liked poetry. So by the time I started writing songs, I was in a poetic frame of mind.

And musically, I guess I have just been passionately listening to music since I was so young. Like I remember a cousin of mine played me "The Wind." I must have been twelve years old. "The Wind" was one of the most beautiful early doo-wop songs. I listened to that and it just went right to my heart. So that's what I was interested in.

So by my late teens, when I wrote "And When I Die" and "Wedding Bell Blues," I was deep inside of music already. Because I was listening to John Coltrane and Miles Davis when I was fourteen, fifteen, sixteen, seventeen.

Do you recall if "And When I Die" came to you easily, or was it something you labored over?

I don't think I labored over it. And I think, also, that that song has a certain folk wisdom that teenagers have. They have that certain folk wisdom, under it all. So I think it just came through the song.

You said that you were attracted to the arts because in them you could sense the divine. Do you think in coming up with songs like those that you were tapping into the divine?

Yes, I think so. I really do. I think that in music there's a oneness, there's a sweetness. Or there can be. What I call music, anyway, the music I like. I go to it for that oneness and that sweetness. For instance, when I was young.

If you look at the world, there's so much separation. It's all polarities, wars. Not all of it, but there's a good deal of it. But to sense a oneness and a sweetness, I mean, that was it. That was the ultimate. The best thing in life. And I did sense that in music and I think there are moments. So that's what is divine to me. That's a form of the divine.

Is there any way you can explain how to tap into that source?

All I know is that when I start getting serious about songwriting, okay, and I start sitting down and spending time with it and spending time at the piano, it's like a playground. I find it to be like that, that all these other responsibilities kind of drift away and you really are with your essence. And you are really with delight. There can be delight there. There can be self-discovery. You can dance there. And there are swings, there are monkey bars, you can play. I think of it as a serious playground. In fact, I'm writing a song called "Serious Playground."

That's a very, very special world and I really honor that world and I must be crazy for not writing everyday. But it's like I get side-tracked, as most of us do, by other responsibilities, or your *list*, you know. And your time for writing starts to fall lower on the list until you stop writing. And you are taking care of other kinds of business but *you're not writing*. So you're keeping it together but there's something missing.

And also, well, it's wonderful, but also I'm in a stage now where I don't sweat it; I don't worry about blocks, because I don't answer to anybody.

When a song starts coming together, do you feel in the writing that you are guiding the process, or is it more a sense of following it?

If it's possible, I think both. As I'm thinking about it it seems as if both things are happening. It's a give and take.

While it's happening, do you stay conscious of where the meaning of a lyric is moving?

Sometimes the meaning of the lyric is in the sound of the lyric. Just the way that it feels and sounds. And sometimes there's a more straight-forward lyric. Like when I wrote "Light a Flame," which is on *Walk the Dog & Light the Light*, in order to say what I wanted to say, I had to tell a certain story. I had to make a certain story clear. But somehow the rhythm that I fell into with the song was almost a rhythm that an elephant might walk in.

The song has to do with elephants and animal rights, which I have been thinking about for many years. And when I got to the chorus: "Prejudice for the color of your skin, prejudice for a woman, prejudice for an animal, like the elephants of the plain," I knew that I was writing the song that I wanted to write because that chorus said what I had been thinking and what I wanted to say. A certain pattern got created with three short lines and basically the lines create empathy. And that says something to me about how I had been thinking about the animal rights movement and seeing all of these things connected, those three lines connected, through empathy. Through understanding.

I see racism and sexism as a lack of empathy.

Did those lines come from the music itself, or did you have them before the music?

They happened together. They just happened together.

Does that often happen, that the music and words will come at the same time?

Usually. I think usually. But I wouldn't rule anything out. If you have a very strong lyric idea, sometimes it can be dominant. If it means a lot to you, you can shadow it with the music. But maybe it's important enough to you to be dominant. But usually the song works with both things harmoniously.

Normally, do you start writing without a theme in mind?

Sometimes. I work both ways. Because I think that writing brings in self-discovery. So how that worked with "Light a Flame" is that I did want to write a song about animals because their spirits were with me at the keyboard. I wanted to do that. But I only knew that I had a solid song when I got those three lines. Those three lines were the foundation. And the music and the words came together. And actually the music has a simple repetitive feeling to it that just seemed to go with the animal. So there was that element of self-discovery there because what emerged was the idea of empathy. And how things are interrelated.

But sometimes I can just sit down at the keyboard and I have nothing in mind particularly and something occurs, something just comes to me.

Throughout your career has that been the more prevalent approach, coming to it without a preconceived idea?

[*Pause*] I think a song has a certain content. It always has a certain content. Sooner or later what you're interested in writing about has to be present in the song. Whether you want to keep it light or get heavy with it. So I think sooner or later you have to deal with that element. Sometimes a song is just like a sensual, beautiful feeling. But to even finish lyrics, you have to look at what are you saying.

You have to step back from it while working on it?
Yes.

Do you generally finish the music before the lyric?
[*Pause*] It just can work in different ways to get the complete song. Sometimes the structure of the music feels like it's there and you know that you have to still be working on the lyric. And sometimes it's the other way around.

Do you usually work on a song for a long time, or do you try to finish them quickly?
Sometimes I might go back to an idea. Like a lyric or a musical line or a rhythm. And just go back to an idea. And then one day it just starts to flow and be holistic and actually be a song. So I find you deal with both things.

Dylan said the hardest thing for him was to reconnect with an unfinished idea. Do you find it's tough for you to do that?
It only works if it's meant to be. If it's really a natural thing for you to do. I think if it's just coming from your mind, that's not good. You have to go back to it because you're drawn to the feeling of it.

Do you tape yourself while working to preserve ideas?
I write down the lyrics and I find that usually if it's a strong melodic thing, that I will remember it. Sometimes I will write down notes, actual notes and chords, and occasionally I might record it. But I'm kind of used to doing it my whole life the other way, just writing it out while I'm working. If it's easy and handy, I'll record it.

You said that chords and chord progressions outside of the beaten track always came naturally to you. While working, are you conscious of what chords you are using, or do you experiment with chords and progressions you've never used?
I do know what I'm doing even if I don't know the names of the chords. I work according to *some* kind of musical intelligence. [*Laughs*] And it's fun for me. I enjoy it. I enjoy following the journey of the chords to different places. But it's not random, the chords that I settle on. It just feels right that way.

Do you usually work with chord progressions before thinking of melody, or do you ever work on pure melody without chords?
Usually it works together. Because from the time I was very young I would sit down and sing. Because I feel as strongly about singing as I do about writing. So it's natural for me to sit down and sing just songs that are forever eternal that I just eternally love, and I'll just sit down and sing that song. So I'm used to that, because there you have your singing and there's the melody and lyrics and chord progressions and phrasing. So that's what sometimes happens with the writing. It's that kind of dance.

You've talked about the delight you get in writing, which not all songwriters seem to share. And that joy comes through. You've written some of the most genuinely joyful songs ever—
Thank you. Like which ones?

There's so many. "Stoned Soul Picnic," "Brown Earth," "Blowing Away," "The Cat Song," "The Brighter Song," "Sweet Blindness," "Save the Country." There's many. And not many songwriters can get real joy into songs, and write a happy song that isn't trite.

I feel very free to express whatever it is that I want in a song. Because my background, like I said before, is in the arts. And also there's that element of working things through, whether it's a sad thought, any kind of complicated feeling or bluesy feeling or joyful feeling; I really feel that music is a great way to work that through.

Yes. And your sad songs are as deeply sad as your happy ones are joyful. You've expressed the real extremes of emotion.

And it used to be more so than now. When I was a teenager I used to read Chinese heartbreak poetry. This ancient Chinese poetry from China about weeping into your jade sleeve. [*Laughs*] I used to, like, *really* get into that. [*Laughs*] And because my earlier work was more commercial, and got around more than some of my later work, when you're very young, you're just more emotional in certain ways. And over the years you kind of work things through a little bit more. I still feel that my music is emotional but some of that stuff, some of that stuff I was concerned about when I was nineteen, I just would not be concerned about now.

And also, as you grow, and with the years, I started to get more of a broader sense of experience. I started to just see a broader landscape. I wouldn't have written "To A Child" when I was really young. Because that has a certain maternal romanticism that came later on. And a song like "Light A Flame" also came later on.

"Trees of the Ages"?

Yes. That came from getting in touch with green spirituality. Those were things that came from going onto different parts of the world that you can write songs about.

Is songwriting still as much of a delight for you?

Yes, definitely. I'm not saying I haven't gone through my frustrations with writing because I definitely have. At this point I know the frustrations will pass and at this point it's not up to me to focus on frustrations, but to keep putting writing at the top of my list, and it's often falling way down and I stop writing, and I'm busy with everything else. So it's for me to keep putting it at the top of my list and being there present for the music. If I have to sit there every day for three *years*, then that's what I have to do. Until the song that I want to write comes to me. Because who is to say?

And also, the mentality of coming from the arts, that's my mentality, as opposed to the mentality of being a songwriter in the music business today. Because coming from the arts you might identify with someone like Gauguin or any of the painters who really got going with their prime vision when they were in their forties and fifties. And Picasso—what was he—seventies, eighties?

This is an ongoing thing. And I don't see any limitations in writing a song. That's the beauty of it. To record, that's when everything needs to be in place. It's highly expensive, you need a record company, so forth and so on. But to me, in writing I'm a free woman. I can do whatever the hell I want to do. And it's just so appealing, that side of it. But, like I say, I have gone through stages where I have felt frustrated or where I have stopped writing. But that passes.

I think someone who really wants to write shouldn't really take that stuff too seriously. They just need to get more disciplined. It really just needs to be their playground and they need to identify voices in their head telling them they're not good enough because that has no place. At all. In the realm of their creativity.

That sense of freedom is apparent in your songs, which have always stretched the form. Often they are more like suites with many sections than simple verse-chorus constructions.

Yeah, because I'm from the school that there are no limitations with a song. To me a song is a little piece of art. It can be whatever you like it to be. Structure of a song is a very interesting thing. And I've written some very simple songs and then some other songs with a more challenging structure. Because it felt interesting to try to do. And it's kind of exciting when you're at that point.

I know that you can write the simplest song, and that's lovely, or you can just write a song that is abstract art.

When images come to you during writing, is it necessary for you to completely grasp their meaning?

[Pause] It's almost like, when you're writing, you're catching sparks. You don't have a lot of space to go on forever in the literal way. You're creating some imagery and some pattern that says it. But in a different kind of space.

In some of your songs, you choose only one or two very strong images, such as the red watermelon and white doves in "Brown Earth," rather than piling tons of imagery into a single song.

Did you ever hear "The Japanese Restaurant Song"? That kind of has everything but the kitchen sink in it. [Laughs] That's an example of using tons of imagery. But the thing is that it creates a slight craziness in the song, which is important to the song. There's so much going on.

You've mentioned that Coltrane and Miles Davis were influences for you. Were there ever any songwriters who had a big influence on your work?

I loved Carole King's songs. I think first I was kind of listening to and singing some of the doo-wop songs. And then got into writing. So I think some of the songwriters of that time started to influence me. Of my favorite song-writers—I like Carole King, Van Morrison . . . I mean, there's many. Of course, I can't think of the rest now. [Laughs] And then poets, too.

Are there any specific poets you can name?

There are many. Over the years, a lot of the feminist poets I've read.

I asked because you've created such a complete language of your own in songs. Not only musically, but lyrically you've achieved a style that is entirely unique to you.

It seems that is so with different painters, sculptors . . . Many of the artists who are very soul-searching with the music, as opposed to following a formula when you're writing. All those artists tend to have a particular style. And also, over time, if you're looking over many, many years, they go through a blue phase, a green phase, a rose phase. Things change.

Do you feel that songs will continue to evolve? Are there still new places to go with songs?

Oh, definitely. Definitely. You know, it's kind of disgusting that I'm not just spending *every* single morning writing, come rain or come shine. Other life little urgencies come up. And you get busy with it and the writing falls to the bottom of the list. But I really have to not let that happen. Because I know that this is something I can take to the grave. I think that I'm excited about the world of writing.

I'd like to mention some of your songs to see what response you might have to them. Do you recall writing "Children of the Junks"?

I don't remember writing it. I remember the song, though.

Is that usually the case, that you don't remember what surrounds the writing of a song?

I think that with certain songs I do remember. I do remember.

That song is very haunting. I've always wondered what that emerged from.

When I was younger I traveled through Asia. I spent some time in Hong Kong. So I think that's one of the reasons that song got written.

"Upstairs by a Chinese Lamp."

[*Pause*] Spring. Sensual. That's what I remember of the song.

That's a good example of your very specific, detailed imagery, the merchant selling milk, tobacco, soap and matches.

Right. Only now we have to leave out the tobacco. [*Laughs*] So we can continue singing. We have to stop smoking. Actually, I did stop smoking. Oh, yeah. Five years ago.

"Stoney End."

I don't. I don't remember writing it.

When Barbra Streisand recorded it, she pretty much used your phrasing almost entirely, rather than really making it her own the way she usually does.

Yes. [*Pause*]

Of the songs I've recorded, the newer songs, I could hear someone singing, "A Woman of the World." More so than "Light a Flame." But it's really nice when somebody records your song. It's great.

Is it?

Yeah. I mean, it's a very nice feeling. Somebody gave me a little handmade cassette of a woman with a really nice voice—kind of like a street singer—she sings at Grand Central Station—and she makes her own cassettes and she sings "Broken Rainbow." And somebody gave me her cassette with "Broken Rainbow" on it and I thought it was so sweet.

How did that song come to be?

That was an unusual writing situation for me because I was asked to write that song for a Native American documentary that was being made. That was different.

That was their title originally?

Yes, it was. I didn't have to write to the title but my heart said that the song was called "Broken Rainbow." They didn't care what the title would be. That was interesting because once I said yes, that I would write it, I mean, that was a big responsibility. That was a heavy documentary and a really fine one. Once I took it on, I just knew that I had to approach it a certain way and just go to the keyboard every day and just be there. It wasn't my place to worry about it. It was only my place to be there. And then, thank the Triple Goddess, the song came. [*Laughs*]

Was it a long wait?

It seemed like a reasonable amount of time. I think a couple of weeks. Maybe a few weeks of just being with the piano. Being with the feeling of the song. And also I needed to write a song that wasn't like clashing styles. That didn't sound like a misplaced, European piano thing. Somehow it had to be sympatico with the documentary. Thank the Triple Goddess it was. [*Laughs*]

In recent concerts you've performed on a synthesizer. Do you always write on an acoustic piano?

I have an acoustic. Nothing feels like an acoustic. But whatever keyboard is available to me is what I'll write on. But I do have an acoustic at home, so I'll write on that.

Do you ever write on guitar?

I wrote "My Innocence" on guitar. I think I wrote "Mr. Blue" on guitar and "Springblown" I wrote on guitar. They translate well onto keyboard. You can make them happen on keyboard. But originally it started on guitar. I think I needed to write and I couldn't find a keyboard but I had a guitar. [*Laughs*]

"The Brighter Song."

Could you sing it for me? [*Laughs*]

You don't remember that one?

I don't remember the first verse.

"You are a free woman, you understand the earth, you say you want an end to violence, feel safe in the universe." It's a great song about the way women are in touch with the earth, and with nature, and how men are often disconnected from that.

I'll drink to that. [*Laughter*]

That's a subject that has come up in a lot of your later work, as in "Trees of the Ages" and "Talk to a Green Tree."

It's like further colors of feminism. I personally feel that feminism is women's roots. I also think that feminism's world view is one of peace. I'm a mother. I have a son. So I hold that umbrella over him. That's what I want. My children, as Mother Earth, I want them born into a peaceful world whether I have male or female. That's why feminism is not apart from men. If feminism is a powerful, peaceful vision of a mother, she is the one who brings the children into the world. So it's for her children, male or female. So I don't see feminism as this isolated thing that just a few women are into. I think it's a world vision, or a life vision. It's many things. So that definitely is in the music.

And other recent songs you're written are connected to that, such as "To a Child" and "Mother's Spiritual."
Right.

Do you remember writing "To a Child"?
Yes. Actually, when I finished that song I thought, "Now I can die!" [*Laughter*] No, actually, I said, "Okay, now I'm retiring! [*Laughter*] I'm finished. I'm finished hassling with this world. I'm finished having children. This is my final statement. That's it. I see no reason to be hassled for the rest of my life." [*Laughter*] But I didn't keep that commitment. [*Laughter*]

Fortunately. How about "New York Tendaberry"?
That was my very wild time of exploration. And a lot of the music was related to abstract art. Sometimes with music you're looking for different things. I don't think I was looking for simplicity that much there. And just very willing to experiment at the time. With everything.

The key line of that one seems to be, "You look like a city but you feel like religion to me."
Yeah. Well, you know, for most of my life now, at this point, I've really spent almost more time with the trees. I've spent a lot of time, okay. I live outside of New York with the trees. But, you know, I *love* to go into the city. I have soulful friendships there. There's another kind of beautiful thing happening with cities. There's something else that you just have at your fingertips there. And I also feel, like culturally, I'm a bit of a melting pot, and in the summertime if I sit in the sidewalk cafes in New York, people are speaking in different languages at the different tables all around me. And I relate to that. That feels like home to me. So that's where you get that international flavor, and I really like that.

Some songwriters who have moved away from the turmoil of the city to establish a peaceful life have lost some of the tension that inspired their best songs. Did you find that writing was as easy away from the craziness of urban life?
Well, I think in the overall picture, now that I'm 46 and I'm looking at the whole landscape, I think there's a reason, and I have an understanding, of the reaching for both. Or the coming from both places. One does need peace in their life. And then, also, one has their passions. So it's like you express both. And sometime at a particular time, yes, that's what you're into, a more peaceful mode of expression. And sometimes you just want to get super wild and crazy.

"The Confession."
I kind of remember that time. I remember, I guess I was about twenty, I'm not sure. And I remember singing it for a couple of friends. And it's funny because there are a few songs that I will still sing today when I go out to sing.

And I will still sing "The Confession." I don't necessarily at every show, but I can still stand by the song.

You don't feel you could stand by most of the other songs from that period?
Well, I would not feel inspired enough. I still enjoy singing the music and some of the messages in the song I feel are still connected to messages of songs I am writing now. Messages of freedom. That's a feminist message.

"Money."
That song I only remember writing about all the hassles of the ego world converging. As opposed to "Trees of the Ages." I think "Money" was about that other stuff.

Yet in the song itself you contrast that with the great image of mothers pulling "the nighttime in / calling their children with spoons in the wind."
I haven't thought about that line for many years. [*Laughs*]

It's one of those lines you can really see and feel.
Yeah, I think we can all feel that from our childhoods. Something about suppertime as light was turning to darkness.

Yes. And the other line from that which is so strong, "Children laugh like meteors rolling down the grass." Such a powerful, natural image. Do images come to you separate from a song, or are they usually generated by the music?
Those sound like there might have been a couple of images there where the music was there to support that lyric. I don't remember exactly but it sounds like that. Sometimes you're going for a groove thing. And then other times it's like you're seeing day turn to night and you want to capture that. And those are two different aspects of music. One is almost a poetic image and the other is almost a visceral, musical, physical feeling.

In your songs, the music and the words always seem ideally matched, as if they arrived together. It's rare that one of the two elements seems dominant in your work.
Maybe if I was the kind of poet like the poets that I read, they make their words sing just with words. That's all they use, words on the page. But really my poetry is in the marriage with the music. So that's why most of the time they're working together. But, you know, anything goes.

"Stoned Soul Picnic."
Well, the only thing that I can remember is being very, very young and . . . [*Pause*] Okay, "Stoned Soul Picnic," the way that I sing it now . . .
It's like this: I never thought that I would sing "Save the Country." I wasn't really interested in it. I haven't sung it for many, many years. Anyway, a friend of mine asked me like twenty times to sing it. I kept thinking, "Go away and stop bothering me." [*Laughter*] And then finally I sat down to sing it and I sang it in a completely different way and I just was at one with the song. I sing it with my voice lower and edgier. I used the essence of the song, I don't use every word and I don't sing it like how I used to.

I found renewal with the song, totally to my surprise, because I had no interest in singing it again. And then—by the way, since then that dear friend of mine has died. Actually died of AIDS—Anyway, now when I sing it—you'll have to hear it sometime. I go through the song and then the way it ends is: "In my mind I can't study war no more, save the people, save the children, save the country . . ." And then I go into this chant: "In my mind I can't study war, there'll be trains of blossoms, there'll be trains of music, there'll be music, in my mind I can't study war . . ." To me, that's my philosophy. In my mind I can't study war because there will be trains of blossoms, there will be trains of music. So that, I can stand by that. Because I didn't think I could enjoy singing it again. It was too fast and bouncy and young.

That song is very much like an American spiritual, as are many of your songs, with lines like "glory river" and "study war no more," "I've got fury in my soul."

There's gospel colors in my songs, and then there's the green spirituality in that recording I did, *Mother's Spiritual*. My spirituality is a very strong part of my essence, and I think it's the same with you or anybody else. I don't mean just myself. I think many people are aware of that within themselves.

"Louise's Church."

Yes. I remember writing the first line: "Sappho was a poet / Billy was a real musician." And then I knew that I had "Louise's Church." It's not a complicated song. It's kind of simple. But all I wanted was to have that feeling. Like a space. A space. I wanted the song to be a space for the heavenly muse and for inspiring artists.

Did you listen much to Billie Holiday growing up?

Yeah, I did and I still do. And I think that she is the great mother-musician-teacher of the art of phrasing.

I could always hear her sing "And When I Die."

Really?

Yeah. I think it would have been perfect for her.

My mother turned me on to Billie Holiday. She was talking to me about "Strange Fruit" at a young age. Explaining that to me and playing me her music. My mother was mostly into opera, like Leontyne Price, great opera singers. But I remember her telling me about "Strange Fruit" and telling me of the lyrics when I was very young. And it's funny, because I read a couple of things in some album jackets or something that that's when she started getting into singing "Strange Fruit," that's when the music ended. And I just thought, "Gee. I feel so opposite about it." That was her art and her consciousness just traveling deeper.

I agree. It's one of the first times the lyric became as deep and dark as the music.

Yes. But I think some people have a very conservative approach.

It was a conservative reaction. Like, why doesn't she just stick with just having a lovely voice and that's it? It was that kind of mentality.

Has that kind of thing ever been directed at you?

I think in general people want to control you and define you. And tell you what to do, tell you what to sing, tell you how to walk, tell you how to look. In general in the world and in general in the music business. That's always there. People who are independent, they just stay focused on their own vision and they keep the focus there. And they're saying, "Thank you but I don't think so," like *every day.*

From the start of your career you've had many singers and groups record your songs, and even then you were playing with the form, and never writing formula songs.

Also, if you think back to music then it was very very open. There was great variety in music. There was great abundance in the universe as far as music was going. I remember a time when pouring through my little radio was John Coltrane's "My Favorite Things," and wonderful harmony groups, soul music, R&B, folk music, *great* singers, all at the same time. It was all happening. There was just more freedom and abundance in music.

Today, the capitalist business thing is just way too present.

Has that had a detrimental effect on songwriting?

Yes, absolutely. There's no doubt about it. Well, to the arts. I think they should just support the arts and give lots of room. That's how I see it.

Has it been strange over the years for you to write songs, which are so full of heart and soul energy, and have them exist in a financial, commercial business?

Yes. I think that if you have a vision of peace, it's very strange living in a world that has so much war. I think if you are a woman who honors some of your feminist roots, I think that it's a little bit strange to be in a male-dominated business. I think that if you're aware or sensitive to animal rights, it's strange living in a world that generally doesn't acknowledge animals at all. And on and on. And with the music too.

How do you reconcile yourself to these conflicts?

I think that if it feels right to you, I think that you have to feel okay about having an independent point of view and realizing that you do. I think you have to feel fine about that. I think you get beyond the suffering. And you focus on the joie de vivre of your vision, the sweetness of your vision. And that's how you get through.

Any memory of writing "Captain St. Lucifer"?

That's a wild kind of song, huh?

Yes. It's got cool maritime imagery: shingles and cockleshells, coke and tuna and boots from Russia.

Yeah. "Meet me, Captain St. Lucifer." Well, I guess that was my idea of romance. [*Laughs*] That was my idea back then.

It was a fictional story?

It was just a feeling. "Meet me, Captain St. Lucifer. . . ."

When I've seen you in concert, you've always seemed so peaceful and happy.

Really?

Yes. Do you feel that?

When I go out to sing now, I just thank the Triple Goddess that I still have the fire. And for the gift of music and love and communication. And soul.

Do you have a favorite song of your own?

My mother died many years ago. But her favorite song was "Emmie."

Was there a real Emily that you wrote that for?

It's kind of the eternal feminine.

Is that one of your favorites as well?

Probably, because I still sing that. Yeah. And people always ask me to sing that.

Any others that are favorites?

Let's see. I still sing "And When I Die." I sing "A Woman of the World." Kind of a variety.

Are there many or any songs you've written that you didn't record?

You'll never know. [*Laughs*]

Do you get any happiness knowing how deeply your songs have affected so many lives, and that the songs continue to do that over the years?

There's a certain feeling, when I go out to sing, there's a certain feeling that happens with everyone. And it's almost like a healing thing. And I think that some of the old songs remind them of some sweet kid inside themselves. From many years ago. Some sweet innocent inside themselves. I think that really does happen. And you're dealing with the language of love. So it's like coming from that place.

Do they touch you in that way as well?

There are certain songs. The first time I first heard "The Wind" by the Diablos, this doo-wop song when I was about twelve, when I heard it I could just about drift away. I could feel the wind. I mean, I remember the feeling of hearing that song. If I hear it now, oh, that feeling comes back so strong.

Songs are magical that way, that they don't age or wear out.

Yeah, they're timeless.

Does it make you happy to know your own songs can touch so many lives?

Do you mean they've touched so many lives in a positive way? [*Laughs*]

Definitely positive.

Well, yes. That definitely makes me happy. Oh, yeah.

* * *

Felix Cavaliere
Los Angeles, California 1989

For many months when he was a kid, Felix Cavaliere didn't have enough money to buy the Hammond organ he fell in love with at Macy's department store in New York. So he'd visit it regularly, and was eventually allowed to play it each day, thanks to a kind-spirited salesman who was no doubt impressed by the chops this classically trained kid brought to the instrument.

Many years later that same kid is fully grown and is staying at a Los Angeles hotel, marveling at the abundant winter sunshine pouring in through the windows. He's in town to perform with the band he formed in the early sixties, the Rascals, with whom he created one hit after the next, all sporting the soulful, joyful sound of that Hammond organ. They are songs that contained so much pure happiness that their joy level hasn't diminished at all in the last twenty years, songs like "Groovin' (On a Sunday Afternoon)," "It's a Beautiful Morning," and "I've Been Lonely Too Long."

Maybe the reason that these songs still sound so great is because Felix didn't fabricate them to be hits, he simply instilled in them the genuine happiness he was feeling at the time. As he explains in the following interview, these songs were true; they were written about relationships he was having at the time with the actual details in place, such as only having Sunday afternoons to spend together with his girlfriend. And when a song contains something genuine, be it blues, folk, or pop, its power doesn't fade.

"If you write songs," he said, between bites of a room service lunch, "you don't have to go out there and jump around like a maniac. It's a nice way to make a living. It's clean. Let somebody else worry about whether it's gonna be a hit or not."

"Good Lovin' " was on the first Rascals album. How long did it take for it to become a hit?
It was like out of the box. Three weeks. It was like a rocket ship. It was too fast, too soon. I imagine it's like what the astronauts must feel. All of a sudden this thing took off. I thought, "It's a good idea, we'll orbit . . ." And all of a sudden, it *went*. Now there was no way you could stop it or control it. All of a sudden this thing happened. And it was a little scary. Everything changes. Your whole life changes. That was a phenomenon. It was a number one record.

And after that point, you started writing songs more seriously?
Yeah. Because now there was a beacon out there for us. It opened all kinds of doors that no one had even known existed. The Beatles wrote their own songs. Well, why the hell not? There certainly didn't seem to be anything in their songs that I thought we couldn't handle. So I went to my to-be partner and said, "We're gonna write." Just like that.
Eddie [Brigati] didn't really take to the idea poorly, but he said, "Do I have to do that, too?" He was a singer in the band at the time. I don't think he had written anything before, maybe some poetry. But I had never really felt comfortable with the lyrical points of view. Musically, I felt like *that* was my identity.
Basically, what I would do would be to come back to him with a theme, such as "Groovin' on a Sunday afternoon." I would ask him to overwrite. I must say I taught him about meter and rhyme and about the balances between the verses and the choruses. I oversaw him. Although he would *hate* me to say this, we are dealing with facts. And I took out the ones I didn't think were good. And we came up with hit after hit after hit. To this day, I couldn't tell you how. I have no idea.

Did you give Eddie the whole line, "Groovin' on a Sunday Afternoon," or did you just suggest the theme to him?
I wrote most of that whole chorus. He would do the verbal accouterments. I didn't feel comfortable doing it. And then when he started getting real good at it, then why not? Here's our key.

Is it true that title was born because you guys were so busy that you could only see your girlfriends on Sunday afternoons?
Well, think about it. I was seeing somebody at the time who was a student. And the only time that she could really go out is on Friday and Saturday night. Now we're working then, so there was none of that. That left one day, you see. And that was really what was behind it.

That song has been around a long time and it still sounds fresh. Other people have recorded great versions of it. Do you have any idea what it is about that song that makes it so sturdy and lasting?

No. I really don't. The chord changes in that song are not unique by any means. They're like chord changes that come from a Latin type of feel. Like Hall and Oates, their "One on One" is *exactly* the same changes.

What changes are those?

It's like a I to a II minor. And the I could maybe be a seventh. It's a very typical Latin change. It's in *thousands* of songs. I like to do that. It's a riff that's been around for a long time. The melody, obviously, is unique.

We had parts in there that we took right from the Beatles. We had a vocal line in there for the background that was exactly like them. There was no thought of stealing. It was just, "Hey, I like that. Let's do it."

So I don't know why "Groovin' " is still around, but I think if I had to make an opinion, an educated guess, I would say that we captured a *feeling* in that song. A real spirit that will never die because people will always be in love. And they really know what it feels like to groove, for want of a better word. It feels like *that*. And that's maybe why it lasts, who knows?

There is something about the tempo of that song, and the feel of it, that is very happy.

Oh, yeah, that's for sure. Oh, God. It was a very happy time.

I heard that it wasn't until you fell in love that you wrote "I've Been Lonely Too Long."

Well, that whole period of songs was from this one girl.

You sure got some good songs from her.

Oh, yeah, let me tell you. She calls me up and says, "You want some more songs? Give me a call, pal." It's true. Absolutely true.

In those days I think people were even more honest in their songs than they are today. I think John Lennon would be a great example. He really spilled his guts out in a song. But, yeah, most of the people were telling true stories when they wrote songs. Don't you think so? You know, maybe cover it up a little bit, use the third person.

I think the great songs, the ones that last, have some truth in them.

Maybe. I don't know. But I really knew that the songs that were around then were really happening in people's lives.

Another happy song that you wrote is "It's a Beautiful Morning." Is that also from that same time?

The only thing I can tell you about that is that things were going so well, both business-wise and personal-wise at that time. You know that old song, "Oh, What a Beautiful Morning"? That person must have been thinking the same thing. See, when I come out here I get the feeling. [*Moves curtain to let in the brilliant sunlight.*]

See, you guys are used to seeing this. We don't see this. When I walk out and I see a sky like that, I just want to go, "Whoa!" That's how we were at that time. I definitely was just totally freaked out. So happy I couldn't believe it. Had a beautiful girl, had a beautiful career. It was wonderful. That's what "A Beautiful Morning" comes from. It was just like "Thank you, everyone. Dig this!"

Do you have a single favorite Rascals song?

No. I'm very proud of them. I'm proud that they're still here.

Songs like "Groovin' " and "Beautiful Morning" seem like they'll be around forever, don't you think?

Well, I'll tell you. I'm really happy to hear that. When I started I came in from a classical point of view. So if a guy made it, he was here a hundred years. Not a hit on the charts, gone the next year. So I got a ways to go, know what I mean?

Do you have any idea where your ideas come from?

Well, I think that what I really believe is that we are sort of like beacons from another source. It's the same thing as the radio stations that are going through this room at this point. Yet until we turn on a tuner, we're not aware that KXJ or whatever station is going through. But they're still going through.

I feel some of us as human beings are tuners to this vibration that comes through us. What we have to do is train the basic fundamentals of music so that it has a way to come out and speak. Sometimes the channel is not clear. It's like I'm riding through the mountains of my life, you know?

I try to listen to a lot of classical music. Especially if I really have a lot of thinking to do. And I think that maybe some of those melodic lines will stick in my subconscious. Then I go through periods of time when I'll listen to different types of music.

I don't think you can always have that channel as open as you want it to be. And I really try to keep it as open as possible. You have to be stimulated, sometimes.

So you keep that channel open primarily by listening to other music?

Yeah. If you don't really love music, then this is not an easy thing to do. Let's face it. You've got to be a little nuts to join this business, right?

* * *

Harry Nilsson
Beverly Glen, California 1988

"Remember life is just a memory. Remember. . . ."

from "Remember"
by Harry Nilsson

We sat in Harry's big black car overlooking the canyons of west L.A. listening to "Save the Last Dance for Me," the old Doc Pomus song that John Lennon produced for Harry's 1974 *Pussycats* album. "We slowed it down to make it sexy," he said wistfully, his silky vocals sounding with a crystal clarity from the car's speakers. We'd been talking about Lennon a lot throughout the day, and with the sun shining brightly over lunch, the remembrances were happy ones. Now with the sun slowly beginning to set, Harry's sorrow for his absent friend came to the surface. "I still can't understand why that was never a hit," he said with tears in his eyes. "But it does sound great, doesn't it?" And I had to agree.

When John asked Harry to come up with "something American" to match a new melody, Nilsson suggested, "Trying to shovel smoke with a pitchfork in the wind," which Lennon loved, and together they wrote the great "Old Dirt Road." Harry had a way with words his whole life, and American words came to him naturally since he was American (born June 15, 1941 in New York and raised in Los Angeles) and not British as was believed by many. That misunderstanding might have sprung from his link with the Beatles: in 1968 they declared that Nilsson was their "favorite group." He also had longstanding and infamous friendships with both Ringo and John, and was often pictured in London, where he lived and worked for years.

It's not hard to explain why the Beatles would have chosen Harry, who was only one guy, after all, as their favorite group. There were hardly any other artists at the time who could create records with the same expansive range of expression as the Beatles, moving from sweet tenderness to raucous rock to surrealistic humor. Harry could do it all; he could croon beautiful ballads, such as "Without You" and "Me and My Arrow" as soothingly as McCartney, while rocking out in "Jump Into the Fire" and his primal version of Dylan's "Subterranean Homesick Blues," and brilliantly stretching concepts of reality in songs like "Think About Your Troubles" and others from his musical, *The Point*. He also shared the Beatles' rare talent for merging beauty and humor, as in his beautifully ironic ballad "Don't Forget Me," which Joe Cocker recorded on his *Performance* album.

Nilsson died in Los Angeles on January 15, 1994, the weekend of the big earthquake. His heart stopped, and before long the entire city began to erupt. At the time he was working on an autobiography, and was eager to get a record deal to record some of the new songs he'd been writing.

"I just hope Harry knew how great he was," said his good friend Randy Newman. In the seventies Nilsson recorded a wonderful tribute album to Randy called *Nilsson Sings Newman*, but used to minimize the significance of his own songs. "He was always putting himself down, making fun of himself," Randy said. "But then again, he used to make fun of me, too, the way I always play the same shuffles on the piano. But Harry was a great, great songwriter."

Randy was just one of Harry's famous friends who recorded a Nilsson song for a tribute album to him called *For The Love Of Harry: Everyone Sings Nilsson*. Also featuring Ringo Starr, Brian Wilson and Jimmy Webb, the album serves as solid evidence of the brilliance and versatility of Nilsson's songs, qualities that are sometimes overlooked when people concentrate on the notoriety of his friendships. Stories about Harry and John getting looped on Brandy Alexanders at the Troubadour in Hollywood, heckling the Smothers Brothers, and getting physically ejected, are still in constant circulation.

Nilsson's love for living was no exaggeration, though; no day passed by for him that wasn't worthy of festivities. He even managed to make this interview a celebration—we went to a fine Italian restaurant up at the top of Beverly Glen where the entire staff greeted him as if he was the Pope, ignoring the other diners to ensure Harry's happiness. And a week later, when I requested that our mutual friend, Henry Diltz, come over to shoot some photos, Harry invited him instead to the Bel Air Hotel, where they not only shared lunch, but revived much of the spirit of the sixties, an expansion of consciousness preserved forever in the proof sheets from this session. Starting with traditional portraits, the final shots are all near-microscopic examinations of flora and fauna found at the hotel.

Harry lived high in the hills of Los Angeles in an architectural wonder of a house, replete with a life-size wooden giraffe, wooden cows, real chickens, and a big family which he told me could best be remembered with an anagram: HUBBA-OK—for Harry, his wife Una, and their kids: Beau, Ben, Annie, Olivia and Kief.

His career was remarkable for many reasons, not the least of which was that he never performed live. Although he was a great singer who could croon and rock with the best of them, he got his start as a songwriter making up hits for others. In the sixties he worked at a bank during the day while writing songs at night. After getting a few recordings of his songs, he gave up his day job. The Ronettes had a hit with his song "Paradise," produced by Phil Spector, and soon many others groups followed their lead, including The Monkees, The Modern Folk Quartet [featuring the forementioned Henry Diltz], the Yardbirds, and Blood, Sweat & Tears.

In 1967 Harry made his own debut as a recording artist with the wonderful *Pandemonium Shadow Show*, followed quickly by *Aerial Ballet*, which featured his song "One," that became a hit for Three Dog Night. Other albums included his musical, *The Point* as well as an album of standards called *A Little Schmilsson In The Night* and 1971's *Nilsson Schmilsson*, his best selling album.

After our lunch together, we took a ride through the hills, during which Harry popped in some cassettes of new songs he'd been working on as well as some touching old ones: a recently discovered tape of he and Lennon working on their song "Mucho Mongo" together (also from *Pussycats*), strumming guitars and making up words between bittersweet bursts of laughter: ". . . must have been a sweet dream brought you here, brought you through the sorrow and the tears . . ."

Do you remember writing your first song?
Yeah. My first song was called "No Work Blues." It wasn't actually a blues. It was stolen from an Everly Brothers' riff. [*Sings*] "I got the no work blues . . ."

How old were you then?
Fourteen. "I got no money, honey, sure seems funny, everybody's working but me . . ."

At that age did you already want to be a songwriter?
Well, I wanted to do something. Maybe be an actor or a movie star, or . . . music . . . Little Richard, Ray Charles, the Everlys, Chuck Berry, the same groups that influenced everyone influenced me. I remember thinking, "If I could get my name on just one record, in any capacity . . ." I thought that that meant that you were rich and handsome and successful and wise and healthy.

It doesn't?
No.

You mentioned that "Think About Your Troubles" and other songs came to you in a flash. Is that how it usually works?
Yeah. Usually it's in a car, or on an airplane. Usually the expression or the thought will suggest a melody. [*Sings* "Think About Your Troubles"]
Usually the first line comes first and you take it and put it in the middle. The chorus will come out as the first line and you turn it into the chorus. Un-

like Johnny Mercer, who wrote a lot of songs with the first line as the title. A lot of my songs build to the punch-line or title.

Do you consider Johnny Mercer to be one of the best lyricists ever?
Yeah. Anyone who would rhyme "aurora borealis" with "red and ruby chalice" is not bad.

Where do you think your ideas come from?
I don't know. It's like whistling [*Whistles*] Why did I whistle that? Did it just pop into my head or was it a combination of preconceived programs or ideas? I don't know about the higher power.

I think, if you really want to get down to it, you have a file, in your mind, for every sound you ever heard. It happens so quickly it happens without you being aware of it, that's why it seems like it's coming from a different place. It's actually coming from the same place every time. It's just a bunch of electricity and chemicals up there. But somehow, creative people's mindset is somewhere in *creating* something . . . [*Whistles again*]

It happens so quickly it *seems* like it's coming from somewhere else. It's not; it just means that you're in sync with yourself. And whatever your goal is, in terms of hearing a melody or a lyric, the closer you get to it, the faster it comes out and the easier it is to *spit it out*, as it were.

It's just that you're not that conscious of it all the time.

You start studying it or analyzing it, it goes away. So I don't spend much time doing that.

"Everybody's Talking," which was written by Fred Neil, was one of your biggest hits. How did you first hear it?
It was earmarked for the group Stone Country. I was hanging around Rick Jerrard's office listening to demos together. I heard that one and I said, "That sounds like a hit. I could do that one." So he let me try it and when we finished the vocal, we were crossing the street, and Rick said, "Be very careful crossing the street. We haven't finished the overdubs yet." [*Laughs*] That's how much he liked it.

Your song "I Guess the Lord Must Be in New York City" is musically similar to "Everybody's Talking." Was that on purpose?
Yeah, actually I was asked to steal that for it. The producers [of the movie *Midnight Cowboy*] asked if I could write a song like "Everybody's Talking." They also asked Bob Dylan and Joni Mitchell to write songs for the movie as well. Dylan wrote "Lay Lady Lay," and I forget the one that Joni wrote, but it was also on the charts. And they didn't use any of them.

I tried to get as close to "Everybody's Talking" without pinching it, you know. Tried to get as close to the feel as I could. It was about a guy in Texas looking for a better life in New York who meets a guy who is looking for a better life in *Florida*. It's always over the next fence, or around the next corner. To me, that's what it was about.

You do a beautiful version of Randy Newman's song "Cowboy" on your *Nilsson Sings Newman* album. At the end of that song you go into the theme from *Midnight Cowboy*.

Oh, yeah, you caught that. Good. You're one of the few people who has ever mentioned that.

That's a wonderful album.

I heard it the other day for the first time in years. And I was surprised by how young you can sound. [*Laughs*] Yeah, it was a good album. It was one of the first albums where an artist recognized another artist. I think they used to do that in the forties a lot and in the thirties.

At the time he was writing a lot of songs, and I thought they were better songs than what I was writing. So why not do his, you know? His remark was "I hope I don't hurt your career." [*Laughs*]

Do you remember how you chose those specific songs of his to do?

As he put it, I chose all his "nice guy" songs. I just picked the best of the pack and waxed and shellacked from what I heard. The newest song was "Yellow Man." Nobody had recorded that yet.

And there was one that never got on there—I don't know what happened to it. It was called "Snow." One of Randy's first songs, a great song. "It fills the fields we used to know . . ."

You're one of the few singers, with the exception of Joe Cocker, to do his songs without leaving out both the humor and the pathos. People sometimes leave out that extra layer of irony.

Yeah. Just like mine. [*Laughs*]

Joe Cocker has done a good job with your songs as well. His version of your song "Don't Forget Me" is beautiful.

Yeah. Except for the bridge. I think that was Jim Price's fault. He decided to make it a jazzier bridge and he put in a strange chord which I never liked. Like a minor seventh or something.

Do you have any recollection of writing "Don't Forget Me"?

[*Laughs*] Let me think . . . it was written before we did the *Pussycats* album. It was one of the songs that John [Lennon] picked out. I remember he thought it was quite good.

I remember liking the opening: [*sings*] "In the summertime by the poolside / While the fireflies are all around you . . . " And "make it easy on me just for a little while" seemed okay.

It has the mixture of humor and sadness, too, with lines like "When we're older, full of cancer."

"It doesn't matter now, come on, get happy . . . " Don't worry, be happy . . . I remember people reacting to the cancer line but to me it seemed like the right thing to do at the time.

It adds another level to the song.

Yeah, without it, it's just another everyday love song.

The alimony line also adds that level. It's kind of a wistful humor.

"I'll miss you when I'm lonely / I'll miss the alimony, too." Yeah. That's probably the best line.

Do you remember coming up with the concept for *The Point*?

Yeah. As a matter of fact, I think I was on acid at the time. It was a long time ago and we experimented with those things.

Were you here in L.A.?

Yeah. I remember being fascinated by all the leaves and all the trees coming to a point. Everything seemed to come to a point. And I thought, "Everything seems to have one. Therefore I must have one too!" [*Laughs*]

And it occurred to you to write a whole song cycle on that theme?

Yeah. At first I was going to write a whole song on that. But instead I wrote "Think About Your Troubles."

A great song. It's circular, like an old folk song.

Yeah, the whale and the tea cup. I had a hard time with a word for a desalinization plant, to get the salt from the teardrop. But then I thought to just run it through a filter.

It seems like that could have been a hard song to write, though it sounds effortless.

Most of them I find you can write in less time than it takes to sing them. The concept, if there is a concept, or the hook, is all you're concerned with. Because you know you can go back and fill in the pieces. If you get a front line and a punch line, it's a question of just filling in the missing bits.

I remember trying to write it down when I was trying to write it. "And so, and so, and so, you run into a desalinization plant . . ." I'll work on that later. "And it comes out of a faucet," that's not bad, "and it goes into a teapot," should have been a kettle, "which is just about to bubble now. Think about your troubles."

Was "Me and My Arrow" written with a dog in mind?

Yeah. A dog, your alter ego, whatever it is. "Straighter than narrow." That meant narrow-minded, because the people in the story are prejudiced. Patricia Hearst named her dog Arrow. I got a kick out of that when I first heard it. Since then a lot of people have named their dogs Arrow.

"Without You" was a major hit for you. When did you first hear it?

I was at a friend's house in Beachwood canyon. It was one of those sixties sit-on-the-floor parties. And I heard that song. The next day I said, "What was that song?" It stayed in my mind. I thought it might be an obscure Beatles track. [*Sings in a Lennon-like voice*] "Living is without you-oo-oo . . ." Sounded Lennon-ish. But then I found out it wasn't the Beatles; it was Badfinger.

So we went in and recorded it. And we were right. Everyone was right about that one.

Do you remember hearing the Beatles the first time?

At first I was a little jealous and I thought, "How good are they?" And in my mind I was thinking, "I could do that, I could do that." I forget when I decided it's better to join them than be the enemy. It didn't take long.

Is it true that Lennon, at one point, said that you were his favorite band in America?

I think that came from Paul. During the Apple press conference they were asked who their favorite writer was and John said "Nilsson." A few minutes

later they were asked who their favorite group was and Paul said "Nilsson."
That was a day in my life, I'll tell you. I got phone calls all of a sudden from
New York in my little office at RCA. The phone started ringing off the hook.
The first phone call came and said, "Did you hear the Beatles just say you were
their favorite?" And I said, "Come on." And they said, "No, it just happened.
It was the largest press conference since the end of World War II. And you're
it." I said, "You've got to be joking."

What kind of influence did the Beatles have on your music?
There was lots of stuff: the way certain words were pronounced, affecta-
tions. . . . I think everyone was influenced by them. It was just like long hair.
All of a sudden everyone started combing their hair forward.

**Derek Taylor wrote in the liner notes to *Pussycats* that you and John
Lennon were shy with each other when you met—**
He wasn't shy, no. When we first met he was very open and friendly as
though we'd known each other for a long time. He was very gracious and
genuinely enthused about hearing the new album I was making, *Aerial Ballet*.
He was full of praise and was charming.

If anything, I guess I would have appeared shy because I was intimidated a
bit. Not that John was that intimidating to me, he was always open. There
were moments when he could turn it on and be whichever John Lennon he
wanted to be that day.

We got along great. I felt closer to him than to the others. It's odd that
Ringo and I have ended up being great pals for so long because he was a tough
guy to get to know. Much tougher to get to know than John.

I was invited by Derek Taylor to come to England during the making of
the Beatles' *White Album*. Everything was happening at the same time for me.
The phone wouldn't stop ringing with offers of movies and stage. I was overwhelmed.

It was during that period when I got a call from John in the middle of the
night. [*In a near-perfect Liverpudlian Lennon voice*] "You're fantastic, man, we
think you're fantastic." I said, "Who is this?" And he said, "It's John. John Lennon." I said, "Well, you're not so bad yourself. Is this really John?" And he said,
"Yeah, I just called to tell you you're frigging great. Let's get together and do
something."

I couldn't believe it, and the next week Paul called in the middle of the
night. [*In McCartney's voice*] "Hello, this is Paul. I just wanted to say you're
great, man. John played me your album."

So the next day at 4:30 in the morning I got dressed and ready, waiting
for Ringo and George to call. [*Laughs*]

Those two phone calls were a turning point. Finally I got a call from
Derek Taylor, instead of Ringo, and he said, "Would you like to come over?
They'd like to see you." Just like that.

So I went over and stayed at John's house in London and hung out. It was
a great night. We spent the whole night talking about music and divorce and
marriage and life and what does it all mean and fame and fortune. The next
thing you know it's morning, the sun is coming up, and a guy comes in with a

camera crew doing the movie *Smile*, Yoko's movie. It was also the day that Yoko moved in and Cynthia moved out.

We were in the kitchen making tea in the morning; we were just standing around, and I realized the impact of what was going on now that that night was over. And as I was studying the impact of it I happened to notice this jacket on a coat hanger. It was the woolly one John wore for "I Am the Walrus." It was inside-out, and I said, "That's wild," and he said, "Here, try it," and he gave it to me. I said, "No, I can't take that," but he insisted and said, "I want you to have it."

After that we wrote each other notes and letters and cards and started some projects together like "You Are Here."

What was it like watching the Beatles make the White Album?

I went for two sessions. It was sort of boring when I was there because it was during the period when George was doing overdubs on "Piggies." The exciting part was when John came in the room one day with a blow-up of the cover photo of *Two Virgins* [a naked portrait of John and Yoko]. He said, "What do you think?" I mean, what do you say?

Was there a sense that they were drifting apart then? Did he talk about leaving the band that night you spent together?

No. He talked about "The Beatles," you know? In fact, when I went to Abbey Road, there was no one there. There was an engineer in the studio, and the Fab Four were sitting at a table in this dining area by themselves. Nobody else. There were some kids outside and some cops at the door but no one else. There was just the four of them sitting there having tea. It was very normal, everyday. . . .

But in the studio you could see that they had been living there for a while. The guitars, the wires everywhere, things that people don't touch, you know?

Did Lennon have a different technique for writing songs than you do?

I don't think there's any technique involved. You sit down. There was a little electric piano there and a guitar, and you just sit there and do it.

When we were working on "Old Dirt Road" he said, "What's a good thing to say in American? I want something really American to say." So I came up with "Trying to shovel smoke with a pitch fork in the wind." Just then some lawyers came in and started talking to John, so he said to me, "Keep going, keep working on it. You're burning." So I kept at it.

That's a great line, the pitchfork line.

Yeah, I don't know where I heard it. It sounds like a Tennessee Ernie Ford line.

People have called that time in Lennon's life a "lost weekend" yet he produced Pussycats and Walls and Bridges.

We were always talking music. We were always thinking of titles or album covers or photos. I bought everyone in the band a Polaroid camera and told them, "When you're not playing, take pictures of those who are."

One time John had the funniest title. I loved it. We were sitting at the Pierre Hotel [in New York] and there was silence in the room. We were both thinking about something else. All of a sudden he said, [*in Lennon's voice*] "The Adventures of Bill and Wally." [*Laughs*]

* * *

Yoko Ono
New York, New York 1992

It was sad and a little spooky to walk into the Dakota on this dark and rainy winter night, an evening not unlike the one on which John Lennon was killed here twelve years earlier. It seemed like no time had passed since I stood here in shocked silence with hundreds of others on the terrible day after, the old iron gate woven with flowers. And now I was back at that same gate, but this time with an appointment to go inside and talk to Yoko. To enter the old building, one passes through the bleak guard's station, a gloomy room made more mournful by the recognition that this was where John staggered and fell, before being taken to the hospital.

But none of this gloom pervades the warm, elegant interior of Yoko's apartment, with its enormous windows overlooking Central Park, the rainy streets below sparkling like glass. As you enter the apartment, you're asked to take off your shoes in traditional Japanese style (having known this in advance, I wore my best socks), and ushered by one of her assistants into the famous "white room," with its giant white couch and tuxedo-white grand piano. It was at that keyboard that John was filmed performing "Imagine" as Yoko slowly opened up the blinds, letting in light.

Suddenly she arrived—she didn't seem to walk in the room, but somehow simply appeared—and her gentle demeanor and warm smile instantly caused all nervousness to dissolve. As soon as I met Yoko, I understood why John loved her. She's charming and beautiful, with a gentle smile in her eyes that photos never seem to reveal. Though she was a few months shy of 60 when we met, she looked younger and prettier than ever, especially without the dark aviator shades she wore like a veil through much of the last decade. In their place, she wore clear, round spectacles, the kind still commonly referred to as "John Lennon glasses." She was barefoot and in blue jeans, and nestled comfortably on the white couch.

Yoko's speaking voice is soft and melodious, her accent bending English into musical, Japanese cadences. Contrary to the usual depictions in the press, she's quite humorous, joking frequently and punctuating her comments with little bursts of laughter. She's also quite humble about her work and her influence on John and other artists. "People can listen to the music," she suggested softly, "and make their own judgment."

> "spring passes
> and one remembers one's innocence
> summer passes
> and one remembers one's exuberance
> autumn passes
> and one remembers one's reverence
> winter passes and one remembers one's perseverance
> there is a season that never passes
> and that is the season of glass"

—Yoko Ono, 1981

She wrote this poem more than a decade ago now, a time she said "passed in high speed." And like so many of the songs she wrote by herself and with John, the truth in them remains constant, undiminished by passing time. In this verse she miraculously conveyed what millions around the world were feeling during those dark days following that darkest day in December of 1980 when John died. That this was a season that wouldn't pass, a tragedy that wouldn't be trivialized by time, a wound that wouldn't heal. And in a way, we didn't want it to.

But perhaps one thing that has shifted since then is that the work of Yoko Ono can begin to be seen in a new light. Rykodisk Records released a six-CD set of Yoko's recorded works called *Onobox* in 1992, and for the still uninitiated this collection serves well as a revelation about one of the world's most famous yet still misunderstood songwriters.

Known for the high-pitched, passionate kind of "Cold Turkey" wailing she has employed through the years—what she refers to as "voice modulations"—in truth she sings the majority of her songs in clear and gentle tones, usually wrapped in rich layers of vocal harmonies. When her father discovered that Yoko as a teen wanted to be a composer, he objected and suggested instead that she become a professional singer. "I knew the whole world would laugh," she said, cognizant of the common misconceptions about her music, "but I had a good voice." She studied piano and music theory while growing up in Japan, and can both read and transcribe music—something none of the Beatles ever learned.

She's a musician who worked in experimental music for years before she inspired and aided in the creation of "Revolution # 9," the most avant-garde track ever included on a Beatles' album. In New York circa 1965, along with the composer John Cage and others, Yoko delved into areas of "imaginary music" and "invisible sounds," concentrating on the creation of an unwritten music, a music that transcended our need to notate. "You can't translate the more complex sounds into traditional notation," she said. "I wanted to capture the sounds of birds singing in the woods..."

She put on concerts with great jazz musicians like Ornette Coleman and Charlie Haden in the years before John insisted she record her songs with some of his "friends," an above-average assemblage of musicians that included George Harrison, Eric Clapton, Klaus Voorman and Ringo Starr. Most of her work with this group were jams at first, musical improvisations based on her poems. But gradually she started crafting songs, composing melodies as eloquent as her poetry. And contrary to the idea that John arranged and produced her songs, Yoko always had a firm grasp on the translation of her inner visions into recorded music. "Though, of course, you do make little mistakes," she admitted, laughing.

She's known both dire poverty and great wealth in her life, and has boomeranged between the two. She was born in Tokyo into a wealthy banking family in March of 1933, the Year of the Bird. The descendant of a ninth century emperor, she was raised mostly by servants as her father was often away on business in America, and her mother tended to social obligations. When she was 11 in wartime 1945, much of Tokyo was being destroyed by American bombers, and her family was forced, in her father's absence, to flee from their home. Yoko was sent by her mother with her brother and sister to a small farming village called Karuizawa. Until the end of the war they lived there in a little house on a cornfield, raising money by selling off kimonos and other possessions until they simply had to beg for food from door to door. Yoko and the other children were almost always hungry. After the war the family was able to gradually return to their wealthy lifestyle.

Yoko's father decided to pursue business in America, and the family moved to suburban New York. Yoko attended Sarah Lawrence College in Scarsdale and began spending a lot of time in Manhattan. It was there that she met a young Japanese composer named Toshi Ichiyanagi who was studying at Juilliard. In time she moved into a loft with Toshi and married him, much to her parent's dismay, and the two experienced a repeat of the poverty Yoko knew as a child.

In New York Yoko began to gradually establish a reputation for herself as an avant-garde performance artist. She put on a series of shows at the Carnegie Hall Recital Hall, performances such as the infamous "Cut Piece" in which she sat onstage in a black shroud holding scissors and invited the audience to step up and cut away portions of her gown, which they did, until she was nearly naked. She also wrote and published a book of instructions on how to see the world in new ways called *Grapefruit*, and launched a movement known as "Bagism," in which people would be invited to come onstage and get into large black bags with other people, their mysterious shapes creating an ever-moving art piece. She divorced Toshi around this time and married New York artist Tony Cox, with whom she had a daughter, Kyoko.

Yoko met John Lennon in London in 1966 at the Indica Gallery. It was the ninth of November, the number nine always prominent in their lives. When they eventually came together, many months after that evening, they made art before they ever made love, collaborating on the experimental recording *Two Virgins* until sunrise.

For days before John died, he and Yoko had been busy in New York's Hit Factory working on a song that surprised both of them for its fire and passion, Yoko's amazing "Walking On Thin Ice." Though they had released their dialogue of the heart, *Double Fantasy*, only weeks earlier and it was racing up the Top Ten, nothing on it matched the pure electric fury of this record. "It was as if we were both haunted by the song," Yoko wrote in the liner notes for the single. "I remember I woke up in the morning and found John watching the sunrise and still listening to the song. He said I had to put it out right away as a single."

The next music of Yoko's we heard was the album she started working on just months after John's death, *Season of Glass*. It's a phenomenal work, expressing the sequence of emotions she experienced, passing through shock, denial, outrage, madness, horror, pure sadness, and ultimately unconditional, undying love. It's an undeniable masterpiece of songwriting straight from the soul, and even critics who routinely attacked her music for years recognized in print the pure, naked power of this album.

Some of Yoko's sweetest love songs are here, such as the Spanish-tinged "Mindweaver," "Even When You're Far Away," and the irrepressible "Nobody Sees Me Like You Do." It also contains recordings of found sounds that expressed this time in her life: gunshots, screams, and her son Sean's voice. As always, she left no barriers between her life and her art, which is immediately apparent on the album's cover. It's a photograph she took in early morning with the skyline of Manhattan across Central Park looking purple and blurry in the background. In the forefront there's a table top on which sits the clear-rimmed spectacles John was wearing the night he was shot, one half splattered with blood, reflected in the transparent surface of the table. Beside the spectacles is a glass halfway full of water.

As Yoko expected, many people were outraged by this image. But they missed the fact that she was simply revealing the actuality of her life in her art as she always has, refusing to hide the real horror she had to endure. "It was like I was underwater," she confirmed. "Like I was covered in blood."

People also missed the fact that on the back of the album Yoko included a sign of hope. She's sitting beside this same table by this same window, and in the same spot where John's glasses were now sits a potted geranium, happily reaching towards the trees and blue Manhattan sky. Next to that geranium is a glass of water. And the glass is full.

From the beginning of her career, Yoko Ono's message has been a positive one. Though dark and negative motivations have consistently been attributed to her, any analysis of her songs reveals a dedicated optimist at work more than anything. A quick survey of titles makes this clear: "Give Peace A Chance" (written with John, of course), "It's Alright," "I See Rainbows," "Hard Times Are Over," "Goodbye Sadness," and so on. When John first met Yoko at her art exhibit at London's Indica Gallery on that legendary day in 1966, it was the fact that her message was positive, that there was a magnified "Yes" at the top of the ladder he climbed, that brought them together. And when I asked her about her hardships as a child during the war, she remembered the light in that darkness, "I fell in love with the sky during that period," she said, "The sky was just beautiful in the countryside. The most beautiful thing about it."

Through the eighties after John was gone, again and again her mission has been to give hope, and the exuberance of her music reflected this affirmation. *Its Alright*, which followed *Season of Glass*, is one of the most hopeful and inspiring albums ever made.

Despite all of it, though, Yoko Ono has been subject to some of the most extreme and bitter criticism any songwriter has ever had to endure. For years, hordes have held on to the notorious notion that she "broke up the Beatles," still refusing to give John Lennon credit for making his own choices. That John's life, both personal and professional, was entirely transformed when he fell in love with this woman, was never Yoko's fault. If anything, she deserves praise for her profound influence on his art. He felt reborn when he and Yoko came together, and his enthusiasm for artistic expression was renewed. "I was awake again," he said. "[Yoko] inspired *all* this creation in me. It wasn't that she inspired the songs. She inspired *me.*"

When the criticism came, though it wasn't ever easy to abide, it was never anything new for Yoko Ono. When she was a kid growing up in Japan, her writing was roundly rejected by schoolteachers who objected to the fact that it didn't fit into existing forms and that she had no desire to make it fit. "It's not that I *consciously* tried not to conform," she explained, smiling, "I was just *naturally* out of the system." Since that time she's bravely made her art regardless of whether it was embraced or rejected by the critics of the world. "It cost me my dignity sometimes," she recalled. "But who needs dignity?"

When did you first start writing songs?

I was sort of a closet writer [*laughs*]. I was writing in the style of atonal songs but with poetry on top of it. I liked to write poetry and I liked to make it into music, into songs. It was something I liked very much to do anyway.

And then in London I think I was writing a couple of songs before getting together with John. The songs were in quite an interesting style, really. I don't know how to put it. Maybe there's some tape that's left.

It was some interesting stuff I was doing. It was mostly a capella, because I didn't have any musicians with me in London. And doing a kind of mixture of Oriental rhythm & blues, I suppose [*laughs*].

I think "Remember Love" was the first so-called pop song that I wrote but before that, before I met John, I wrote a few songs and one of them was "Listen, The Snow Is Falling." I made that into a pop song later. "Remember Love" was probably the first one I wrote as a pop song from the beginning.

Do you generally have the same approach to writing songs?

I can't stand being in a rut, so I sort of always jump around. That's me. [*Laughs*]

Do you write on piano?

Yes. I use the piano because I don't know any other instrument, really. I tried the guitar once and it hurt my fingers so much and I didn't like it. John said, "Try it" so I tried it in L.A., when we stayed in L.A. But I didn't like it at all. So, I just naturally go to the piano.

If I'm not at a piano, I can write riding in the car. And I just write down the notes and bring it in to the piano later.

Do you find your songs come in a flash, or do they come from the result of a lot of work?

No, it's always a flash. And if I don't catch it [*laughs*] and write it down, or put in a tape [*softly*], it just goes. Never comes back. Isn't that funny?

Can you control when that flash comes? Do you ever sit down to write a song?

No, I never did that. But I mean, the point is that sometimes words do come back. The words are a different thing. Sometimes I will forget to write the music down and I'll have only the words. And then I'll put it to music at the piano, and it becomes a totally different song, you know.

When you first met John, did you have much enthusiasm for rock music?

Well, I started to have an incredible enthusiasm. In the beginning when I was sitting in the Beatles' sessions, I thought that it was so simplistic. Like a kind of classical musician, avant-garde snobbery. And then I suddenly thought, "This is great!" I just woke up. And then I really felt good about it.

There's an *incredible* energy there. Like primitivism. And no wonder. It's a very healthy thing and no wonder it's like the heartbeat. It's almost like the other music appealed to a head plane, like brain music, and then they forgot about the body.

[*Softly*] It's very difficult to go back to your body. You know that bit about without the body, we don't exist. You forget that! It's almost like we can just live in our heads. And a lot of intellectual, academic people, they tend to be that.

So I thought, "This is great!" It's a total music.

Then I realized what was wrong with the other music. It was removed from the body. It lost that kind of energy. And I thought, "No wonder I was just sort of wandering around. Okay, well, this is great." I went back to my body. It's true.

It seemed that you had a big effect on their music by being there. Even McCartney said that he felt that he had to be more avant-garde when you were around.

I don't know. It might have affected them that way on a peripheral level, the fact that I was there. But I was just living my own world inside. Dream world. [*Laughs*] I was sitting there just thinking about all the stuff I'm doing in my head. So I was there and in a way I wasn't there.

Some of your die-hard fans felt that being with John Lennon was detrimental to your art, while others have said that your work blossomed in a new way.

Probably it would have been easier for me, career-wise, if I didn't get together with him. In a way, I lost respectability or dignity as an artist. But then, what is dignity and what is respectability? It's a kind of thing that was a good lesson for me to lose it. What am I supposed to be doing, carrying respectability and dignity like a Grande Dame of the avant-garde for twenty years? That would have been . . . boring. [*Laughs*]

That was a kind of an option that was open to me, you know, and [*softly*] I didn't take it. It was quite more fun to go forward into a new world.

John's famous song "Imagine" originated from an idea in one of your poems from *Grapefruit* about imagining a different world. Do you feel people ever understood the source?

No. A song like that, it's a political statement in a way, and it's about changing people's heads. And I think that people don't have to understand anything except the message of the song, and hopefully that will get to them.

With John, people have named his songs to get his response, but no one has done that with you. May I?

Oh, sure. Do you mind if I just get my cigarettes? I still can't shake it, you know?

"Dogtown."

I was in an apartment on Bank Street with John. It was early in the morning and John was still asleep in the other room. I was at the window and the window was in such a way that the front room was very dark. The room was a few steps down from the pavement so from the window you would kind of look up at people walking. It was like that feeling. Early morning. It was just that. I lit my cigarette and listened to early morning sounds. The song was almost like a diary, describing what I was doing.

I didn't want to wake up John. I had an electric piano that you can tone down very very quiet, and you're the only one who can hear it, you know? That's how I made "Dogtown." [*Laughs*]

So it started as a quiet song.

Well, I wasn't thinking quiet, I was just making sure that he couldn't hear.

"Death of Samantha."

Oh, yeah, I know that one. There was a certain instant and I felt like I was really sad, so that's when it happened. Something terribly upsetting happened to me and then the next time we were at the studio, while the engineers were sort of putting the board in order, it flashed into me. So I just wrote it down.

This is funny because with "Death of Samantha," while I was writing I sort of saw this graveyard. It's not a graveyard, because when you think of a graveyard, you think of many, many gravestones. It's just a kind of gray kind of day, gray scene, and gray people standing around like somebody has died. And after John's death people said, "You were writing about his vigil, did you know that?" And I read the lyrics that they sent me from "Death Of Samantha" and I just reread it and realized, oh, that's true. Of course, I didn't realize it then. So it's *very strange*. You know, images come to me.

Many of your songs told of future things.
It's scary in a way.

Why do you think that is?
I don't know what it is. So I'm very careful about what I say or what I think or do. Cause it could mean something later.

"Yang Yang."
Oh, "Yang Yang" was based on a chord change I liked to use, kind of an ascending harmonic change. I showed it to John that instead of ascending by half-notes, you can ascend by whole notes, and that gives a kind of a vital power that is interesting. And "Yang Yang" is the first thing that came to me with those chords.

That song is in E minor and a lot of songs from this period are also in that key. Do keys have different significances for you?
Yeah. Each chord has a difference significance astrologically. I use F# a lot, and E minor too. And I'm thinking why, and it seems like it's agreeable to my astrology.

I was also thinking why sometimes I use the key of C [major] because C is so simplistic, most composers probably avoid it. But I don't avoid it. Why not? Why do I do that? C is a key of communication, I understand. So I used it in a song I had to communicate. The kind of songs that I wrote in the key of C or rewrote in the key of C, like "Give Peace A Chance" or that sort of thing, it's all to do with communication, of course. The widest communication you want, so you go back to the simplest key, which is C.

That's interesting. I've noticed that TV commercials are often in C, probably for the same reason.
Oh, yeah. It's *fascinating.* And I think that most writers instinctively go for something simple to communicate.

Your song "Silver Horse" is in C major.
Yeah. [*Laughs*] You know what it was? "Silver Horse" is like a fairy-tale. It's like a story that you tell your child. It just happened, you know. It's that kind of nursery rhyme feeling I was trying to give.

I love the spoken part on that song, when you say, "I came to realize the horse had no wings," and then you ask yourself, "No wings?"
[*Laughter*] Oh, by the way, John loved this song. Yeah. He kept saying, "Oh, that's a great song" because he liked the fact that I say, "It wasn't so bad, you know." [*Laughs*]

I know John also loved your song "Nobody Sees Me Like You Do," which has a wonderful chord progression.
Yeah, he liked the chord sequence. It's a chord sequence that is probably pretty prevalent in country music but you don't use that much in rock.

That's one of your happiest songs, and yet you bring in the sadness in the line, "The feeling of loneliness hangs over like a curse . . ."

We're all complex people, you know. You can't just sort of be happy all the time, you know, like zombies. [*Laughs*]

Another one of your happiest songs, which was also on the *It's Alright* album, is "My Man."
You like that?

Very much.
I just wanted to make a real pop one, you know? A lot of people think that wasn't artistic, like it's sort of silly or something. Which is true: "Bab-a-lou, bab-a-lou." I liked that. [*Laughs*] Dumb but nice, you know?

On "Woman of Salem," you used the year 1692 without knowing that was the actual year of the witch trials?
Isn't it amazing that I didn't know that year? After I visited Salem, you know, I just thought of it. It's *incredible*. It's *uncanny*, isn't it?

Yes. Any explanation?
No. [*Laughs*] I went to see her house and I was nearly crying. I mean, you talk about witches and it's not a witch at all. It's a sensible doctor's house, you know? Very intellectual, artistic kind of person living there, you just know it.

It makes me think of your song "Yes, I'm A Witch" in which you say "I don't care what you say, my voice is real and speaking truth."
Yeah, I know. That's me.

"A Story."
Okay, "Story." That, again, is like a nursery rhyme. It's a simple story, you know? I think it was in C, wasn't it?

One of the songs I've been especially loving on *Onobox* is "Yume O Moto" which you sing in Japanese.
That's nice, isn't it?

Very. What does it mean?
Let's have a dream. Yume o moto.

Do you find that it's more natural or pleasing to sing in Japanese than in English?
I don't think so. I don't feel that way.

The author Vladimir Nabokov said that English is like a blank canvas, that it doesn't have an inherent beauty the way other languages do. Do you find that?
I don't find that. I think English is a very beautiful language. *All* languages are beautiful, really.

Do you think in English?
Sometimes I think in Japanese, sometimes I think in English. But mainly in English at this point, you know. I mean, when I'm talking in English, of course I think in English.

Do you dream in English?
Yeah!

"Yume O Moto" was from an album called *A Story* which you recorded in 1973 during your separation from John, what you both called your "lost weekend." You decided not to release it at the time, and have included it here as the final disk of the *Onobox*. There are so many great songs on it, hearing it now it's surprising that you didn't want to put it out.

Well, you know, there are many things that I just chucked, you know, or shelved, you know. Like from my early days, like the stories that I wrote, that it was just in the course of going from one country to another or one relationship to another. Something I lost or whatever. It was one of those things. I didn't think that much about it.

John recorded *Walls and Bridges* during that time and he released it.

I know, John can do it, I can't, right? There's a difference.

Many of your best songs, such as "Loneliness" and "Dogtown" came from that album. Had you released it, do you think people might have recognized you as a songwriter earlier in your career?

Well, I couldn't put it out then, anyway. Let's put it that way.

Why not?

Well, I don't know, it's just . . . Look. Listen to *Feeling The Space*. That's a pretty good album. There's some good songs in there too, you know that, right? So? That was out there but nobody cared. *It's the same thing.* Now you say that people might have known I was a songwriter. At the *time*, putting out *Feel The Space*, people should have known, or putting out *Approximately Infinite Universe*, people should have known that I'm a songwriter, and they didn't, so *what are we talking about?* You know, one more album is not going to help, you know?

In a way, it's good that it came out now. You get it? Then if people hear it, without kind of the Yoko-bashing . . . I didn't think so. I thought it was going to be bashed again. But obviously they're taking it differently now. I don't know why. Let's put it that way. I'm very lucky because I could have died without hearing about it.

I think there's a small group of hardcore fans who had to *literally* go through the same bashing that I went through just because they like my music. So I'm doing it for them, too, this box. I felt I really had to make sure that every note was right. For them.

I've been surprised by some of the resistance to your work, especially when *Season of Glass* came out, because it was such a meaningful album.

I wasn't too aware of what was going on then, but it seems that it's easy to concentrate on the kind of things that I was doing, it was easier to concentrate on that than to go into the outside world.

"It's Alright."

Oh, that was so difficult. It was a very difficult one to make, really. But I loved it. That was after John's death and everything and I was really trying to get into music. So it was like getting into harmony, and putting in all the harmonies. There were many things that I wanted to get in, so I intentionally made it so that there were holes in it. And I filled those in with different kinds of little choruses. It was like a collage, and it was a big production. A big production with not many *people*, not many musicians. In other words, all those sort of overdub things that I did.

"Mindweaver."

Oh, "Mindweaver," oh . . . [*Pause*] I wanted to make it like a duet with the guitar and my voice. And I was thinking of basically making it like a Spanish mourning song. It has that kind of dignity.

"It Happened."

Oh. "It Happened" was actually composed in 1973 and at the time it had to do with moving away from each other. But then, when John died, I thought, "Oh, that's what it was about" [*laughs*] and I put it on the back of "Walking On Thin Ice."

I look at that period of separation like a rehearsal.

A rehearsal for what?

For the big separation that I didn't know would happen. It was very good that I had that rehearsal in terms of moving along. That helped me later.

"Cape Clear."

"Cape Clear" was first called "Teddy Bear." [*Laughs*] I was writing at the piano. I was writing at this piano in The Dakota and in Cold Spring Harbor. In those days I still had Cold Spring Harbor. And it was just one of those songs. Central Park gave me that inspiration, you get it? Like the girls are sitting in the park and the clouds passing by, you know? I was looking over Central Park and I was thinking, "Oh. I could be sitting there." It sort of flashed in my mind.

How about "Walking on Thin Ice"?

Oh. [*Laughs*] "Walking on Thin Ice." What about it?

It's such a powerful song, both musically and lyrically. Do you recall where it came from, or how you wrote it?

I was thinking of Lake Michigan. I went to Chicago. And Lake Michigan is so big that you don't know the end of it when you look at it. I was visualizing Lake Michigan. I was just thinking of this woman that is walking Lake Michigan when it is totally frozen, and is walking and walking but not knowing that it's that huge. [*A siren sound starts from outside, getting louder.*] I'm like one of those people. "Oh it's ice but I can walk on it." I walk like that in life.

That song is about yourself?

Yes, I think so. The spoken part, "I knew a girl . . . " and all that, that feeling came to me after we recorded it. But I wasn't sure about it. I just knew it had something to do with a girl who is walking. Then I sang the song, and I was still sitting in the chair by the mike, waiting for them to change the tape. That's when it just came. So I just wrote it down quickly. I said, "I got it!" And I told them I was just going to do something after the singing, and I just did it.

Where do you think those kinds of thoughts come from?

No idea. It's very interesting because it could be something that came totally from somewhere else. But, of course, it's about me, and that's how I was looking at it. But then, I don't know. I didn't think it was about me, really. I was just looking at this girl who is walking, you know.

It seems like a visual message. You see, in my mind, sound and visual is all very closely connected. It's mixed almost. So when I hear sound, I almost hear it in color as well.

When you listen to something like "What a Bastard the World Is," or something, you probably *see* something, some filmic image.

Many of your songs are very visual.

Yes. Because that's how I see it and I hear it. Seeing and hearing is very closely connected.

When I said, "I knew a *girrrl* . . . ," that I thought was to accentuate certain syllables that it's odd to accentuate. And that was like Alban Berg. Let's do like Alban Berg.

That's some of John's most passionate guitar playing.

Oh, *incredible*. He did great guitar playing on "Woman Power" and "She Hits Back." Very good. But also, not talking about those normal ones, what did you think about "Why"? He's *so* good, isn't he?

Yes. On something like that or on "Walking On Thin Ice" did you give him the kind of sound or direction that you heard in your head?

Kind of, yeah. I mean, we'd talk about it. Like I would say, "I'm going to go like this, you go like this." I don't mean "go like this" in terms of notes, but just the mood of it.

It depends. On "Cambridge" he wanted to know how to do it, so I kind of explained it to him before we went to Cambridge. With "Why" I was talking about the kind of dialogue we could do in terms of my voice and his guitar. But it's not like telling him what note to play.

Speaking of a dialogue, you also wrote songs in dialogue on *Double Fantasy*.

Yes. We sort of vaguely had this idea about doing a dialogue album. But some of the songs, like "I'm Moving On," were written before. In putting together the album, I'd bring out a song and say, "What about this then? When you do 'I'm Losing You' I'll do this." That part of the dialogue was a conscious sequence.

"Sisters O Sisters."

"Sisters O Sisters" was written for a rally in Michigan for John Sinclair in 1971. When we were in Ann Arbor, Michigan at the concert, John said, "She's got something, Yoko's got something." I said, "This is for the sisters of Ann Arbor, Michigan." And we sung it, and that was the premiere. [*Laughs*] And afterwards I didn't think much of it until we were making *Sometime In New York City*, which probably was in '72. At the time we did that, we did it in the recording studio for the first time with Phil Spector. And the way I'm singing in Ann Arbor, Michigan is very different from the way I sung in the Phil Spector version. And I think the Phil Spector version is a good one.

Season of Glass **was such a powerful record, and so meaningful at that time for many people.**

When I made *Season of Glass*, I felt like I was still like walking underwater or something, so I didn't really know people's reaction.

I understand that your record company was upset about you using that cover photograph showing John's glasses splattered with blood.
Oh, yes, very.

I read recently that in Nazi Germany, as an act of cruelty, they would send the blood-stained spectacles of a man that was killed to his wife.
Really? That's *terrible.* But isn't that symbolic of this? See, that's what I'm talking about. When I have an inspiration about doing something like that, I really stand by it. Because I think that there's something that I don't know about.

I also had anger in me. I was telling you this is what happened, and it's not a beautiful thing that happened.

The poem called "Season of Glass" on the back of the album is very beautiful and sad. Did you think of making it into a song?
I thought about it but I don't think I can. I don't know.

In that poem you wrote, "There is a season that never passes, and that is the season of glass." Which echoed the way so many felt after John's death, that this is a time that won't pass. Do you feel that we're still in the season of glass?
I don't know, because I may have been talking about something more than John's death in a way. At the time, of course, I was talking about my private experience. But I'm doing a piece right now for a gallery show which is about a family that is sitting in the park at meltdown time, and I was thinking in terms of the meltdown of the human race and the endangered species. And somebody said that it looked like genocide as well.

So it's like the season of glass is still here in terms of the whole world. We're still not reaching a point of not having . . . bloody glasses.

A very positive message you put out that I think people missed is that on *Season of Glass*, on the back cover, the glass of water that was half-full on the front is now full.
Yeah. Oh, you mean you noticed it? Very few people noticed that.

Do you think your positive messages often were overlooked?
Well, some people got them and some didn't. It depends on the person, too. I mean, you noticed something, you know? [*Laughs*] But most people didn't notice it.

So many of your songs are very positive. Does an artist have an obligation to have a positive message?
No. Some artists are writing depressive songs and killing themselves, you know? [*Laughs*] It depends on the artist. There are some depressive moments in my work, but, yeah, generally I try to fight back.

John was attracted to the word "Yes" in your art show when you first met.

Yeah. Well, we just have to, you know? It's not like I don't know that the world has various negative aspects. But writing about that is not going to help anybody.

Would it be okay if I asked you your response to some of John's songs?
Sure.

"Strawberry Fields."
I love it. You know what it is? That was the first John Lennon song that I encountered. And there was a party at the editor of Art Magazine's house in London. And I went to that, and I think I was a bit earlier than the others and I was in the house and the editor said, "Oh, listen to this, Yoko. When a pop song comes to this point, what do you think?"

And he played "Strawberry Fields." In London. And I thought, "Hmm-mmm. . . . " Because there were some dissonant sounds and I thought it was pretty good. For a pop song. [*Laughs*]

I thought it was cute. I thought it was some cute stuff. Because I was making songs with all dissonant sounds. It impressed me. I was surprised a pop song could be that way.

I *like* the song. Musically, it was very terrific. And there's a lot of connections about it. I mean, I think of John as an artist, a songwriter, a fellow artist. But also, he was my husband, you know. And I remember all his pain as a child, sort of looking at Strawberry Fields, which was an orphanage, you know. He always told me about his Aunt Mimi saying, whenever he was out of hand, Mimi would say, "You can go there. You're lucky you're not there, John." So, Strawberry Fields to him was connected with this strange kind of fear and love, love for the kind of children that were very close to his condition. John was in a bit of a better position. So there's that love and that strange fear for it.

It's a very strong thing for him. That sort of painful memory that he had of Strawberry Fields, he transferred that into a song. And made it positive. And that song was transferred into a park. [*Laughs*] It's a very strong thing that I witnessed. So it means a *lot* to me.

"Come Together."
Oh. Oh, that's a beautiful song. Well, that's very John. That's a very John song. And a lot of people came together to his music. It's like a symbol of that, you know?

"A Day in the Life."
Oh, another *beauty*. But "Come Together" is more political and "Strawberry Fields" has to do with his childhood. "A Day in the Life" is more like the sixties. You know, swinging London, hippies . . . .

"Starting Over."
Well . . . That's a nice song, isn't it? [*Laughs*]

Yeah. It's very happy.
Like me and him, right? [*Laughs*]

"Across the Universe."

Oh, "Across the Universe." That's beautiful poetry. And also, "Across the Universe," the kind of melody and rhythm and all that, reminds me of the beginning of the so-called New Music.

"Bless You."
Oh, "Bless You," of course. I have a special emotional thing about it, don't I? I remember when he first came and played it to me.

"Julia."
Well, that's very beautiful. I was there when he wrote it. I think it's such a strong melody.

He wrote so many beautiful melodies, yet McCartney has the reputation for being the melody writer.
No, no, no, no. It's not true at all. John was a great melody writer.

Is it true that "Because" was based on "The Moonlight Sonata" which he asked you to play backwards?
When you really listen to it, you see that he did play the chords backwards at one point but I think eventually it was cleaned up a bit into a pop format. So he didn't use all the chords. But that was the initial inspiration.

There were many songs he wrote with your name in it, such as "Dear Yoko," "Oh Yoko," "The Ballad of John & Yoko" in which you became almost a folk hero . . .
Well, I don't know about that. I think that from where I come from, in the art world, Picasso's always painting the wife, or Modigliani only had one model, who was his wife, so that kind of thing is normal. So it didn't strike me as anything unusual.

Did you and John ever discuss songwriting?
For me, it's so natural to use so many different chords. Because in classical music, you just do this. The kind of thing he would show me was that instead of using so many chords, just use two chords. It's funkier. That's a great trick. That's the kind of thing that classical musicians or composers lost, of course.

Do you have a favorite song that John wrote?
"In My Life" is a pretty good one, isn't it?

McCartney's song "Get Back" seemed to be directed at you.
We thought that.

How did you respond to that?
We didn't respond. [*Laughs*]

Did you have any inner response to that?
No. I don't know. That's another thing that is the strength of an artist, probably. Artists always think, "Oh, maybe they're trying to hurt me," or whatever. You think that but in the next minute you're thinking about your own songs, your own art or sculpture or films or whatever. So by doing that, you shake it off. So it doesn't stick so much.

You've had a lot of tragedy in your life. Do you feel that tragedy helps an artist to open up in any way?

I think that tragedy comes in all forms. No one should encourage artists to pursue tragedy so that they might become a good artist. I wouldn't encourage that. You don't have to have tragedy to create, really.

Was there ever a feeling on your part that you would want to leave the Dakota, and live elsewhere?

Not really. It was the spot that my husband *died*, you know? It was . . . like you don't want to leave there, you know?

These days this place represents teenagers, Sean and Sean's friends. It's quite a different scene, and it's very nice.

Early in your career you worked with John Cage and what you called "imaginary music" and music that can't be notated. Later you said you felt that the pop song was more powerful because it could reach more people. What do you think now?

I still feel that there's kind of an extra-sensory perception kind of area where you can pursue that sort of communication and sound vibration on that level, et cetera. But, yes, I really think the pop song, or rock, is a very good means of communication.

Do you think that the songform is restrictive?

Yes.

You once said that you felt songs were like haikus.

Yes, definitely. But also it's either way. Even if it's twenty minutes or an hour, in the context of the big world, it's very small [*laughs*], you know what I mean? It's all very relative, you know.

Was it difficult for you to continually create in the face of people's negative energy? Even when you were a little girl, your teachers were harsh with your writing, yet you always had the bravery to do your art regardless.

In a sense because of that I lost many writings. Because they would discourage me so I would keep on writing, but I wouldn't hold on to them. And the same with the tapes. A lot of the tapes I did, like "London Jam" kind of things with John, it's a pity that they're lost. And the reason why they were lost was because there was so much *antagonism* about it.

I would insist on going on and doing something, but I wouldn't keep them. It's not like I would intentionally destroy them. But it's like easy to let it slip out of your hands. That's how it's manifest.

In looking back at all this work, do you have a favorite song?

That's a difficult question, isn't it? I wouldn't know. The other day I was listening and I thought "What Did I Do" was one I liked very much. But that's just in passing. I did like "No, No, No" a lot but now I don't feel like listening to it. It's like different times, you know, something fixes in your head. Of course, I did like "Walking on Thin Ice" but [*laughs*] how long can you like "Walking on Thin Ice"? I got over it.

The number nine has been significant in your life, and now we're in the nineties. Are you optimistic about these times, and times to come?

Yeah, I think that we're going back to a good age. The 1980s were hard because it was a material age and people were just into materialism, I think.

But I always liked it that I didn't go into that expansion thing. I think that this decade people are going to start to sober up a bit, and start to really understand or appreciate the value of real things. So you can't just con them with a bit of commercial music. People are going to be more interested in real music. Genuine emotion.

Do you think songwriters can still write real songs?

We have to strive to be real, that's all. Being real is not something that just happens to you. You have to sort of keep at it.

In "Dogtown" you write about "the true song I never finished writing all my life." Do you feel that you have finished yet or are you still working on it?

I'm still working [*laughs*].

Do you feel that songs are timeless, and that they can last?

Oh, sure. I think that if you're really communicating on a basic level, you're going to be communicating all the time. Once it's there. Once a song becomes a song, it has its own fate.

* * *

Randy Newman
Los Angeles, 1988
Los Angeles, 1996

I burn down your cities;
How blind you must be.
I take from you your children
and you say how blessed are we.
You all must be crazy to put your faith in me—
That's why I love mankind.

from "God's Song (That's Why I Love Mankind)"

He's written a lot about God. Even before he wrote his famous "God's Song (That's Why I Love Mankind)," he'd written other God songs, such as "He Gives Us All His Love" and "I Think He's Hiding," the latter of which suggests that God isn't dead, He's just avoiding us. So it was a natural stretch for Randy Newman to carry through with a project he'd been talking about doing for decades, a musical version of one of mankind's most venerable tales of God and man, Goethe's *Faust*. In the works for years while writing other songs and a myriad of film scores, Randy's *Faust* resets the myth in modern-day America. It was the completion of his first-ever full-blown musical that was the ostensible occasion for my most recent interview with him.

Of course, any excuse to talk with Randy is good enough for me. Of all the songwriters I've spoken to, there isn't one who is at once as serious and hilarious as Randy Newman. It's the same mix he brings to his songs, fusing humor and darkness to reveal the often harsh realities of human existence. And he does so in the first-person, speaking from the source itself. In "God's Song," he explores religious faith by taking on the voice of God Himself. He delves into the mind of prejudice in "Rednecks" and other songs by looking through the eyes of racists and bigots.

And it is this trait, removing all distance from his subject by *becoming* that subject, that separates his work from that of his peers. There is no other songwriter who has shown us bigotry, ignorance, and human weakness as convincingly as Randy Newman. And he has done so in our own words, with a pianistic style closer to ragtime than rock and roll, evoking an America both of the past and present with all of the rough edges revealed.

The central issue of his life, however, seems to be to live up to the potential of his own talent; to keep on receiving the "gifts" that he refers to in the following interviews. He seems afraid of being overshadowed by the enduring brilliance of his past work. "Not that I think it's so good," he's quick to add. "I just don't want to get worse."

To explore this conflict, he played me three of the songs that he had written for his *Land of Dreams* album. The songs—"Dixie Flyer," "I Want You to Hurt Like I Do," and "Four Eyes"—were stunning to hear at such close range. "Four Eyes," especially, was incredible; his playing on this one, thundering from his grand piano, was astounding.

"As far as songwriters go," Bob Dylan told me, "there aren't many people in Randy's league." He's right, of course, as any student of songwriting knows. Everyone, that is, except Randy himself, who has elevated self-deprecation to new heights. But it's because songwriters in this day and age necessarily measure their own value in terms of hit songs and album sales that he often denigrates his own accomplishments, and underestimates his range of influence on other writers. Although his songs have consistently surpassed almost all others in terms of sheer brilliance over the years, they rarely rocket up the charts, with the odd exception of ones like "Short People" and "I Love L.A." that are closer to novelty material than his best work.

So to make a living and to support his recently expanded family (he's now got five children), he's followed the path of his famous uncles into the world of film composition, and in a few short years has become one of the world's most successful and accomplished film scorers. He'd just completed work on Disney's *Toy Story* at the time of our second interview, and has also written full orchestral scores for *Ragtime, Maverick, The Natural, The Paper, Parenthood, Avalon, James And The Giant Peach*, and more. For these movies he often writes songs as well as scores, such as "I Love to See You Smile" from *Parenthood*. But these movie songs are invariably what he calls "normal" songs, because, as he explains, "you've got to be normal when somebody's spending a million dollars."

He was born in L.A. on November 28, 1943 into a well-known musical family—besides his uncle Alfred Newman, one of Hollywood's most distinguished film composers, his uncles Emil and Lionel were also famous scorers.

And his father, Irving, a doctor, also wrote songs, and collaborated on a few with his son. As a kid, Randy spent hours at the movie studios, absorbing Alfred's music and methods of arranging, conducting, scoring and recording. And in the summers, during the war years when his father was overseas with the army, Randy and his mother would spend summers with her family in New Orleans, a geographical serendipity that's forever flavored his music.

He majored in composition at UCLA, where he had been known to turn around and go home when he couldn't find an easy parking place. He wrote his first song at the age of 16, and kept at it, pitching them to his best friend, Lenny Waronker, whose father Simon started Liberty Records. When asked why he chose to write songs rather than some other kind of music, Randy answered, "Lenny Waronker did. I was always being pushed and pulled. Probably I belong in another field, which is why I'm so conflicted and reluctant about what I do. I went and played for Lou Adler, and I played the melody along with the song when I sang, and he said, 'You know, Carole King plays an accompaniment when she plays.' I said, 'Oh' and learned about it. This publisher signed me up [at Metric Music] and I started. Trying to write follow-ups for people."

He wrote his first single, "Golden Gridiron Boy," for Pat Boone, which was recorded in 1961. Though he went on to write songs while there for singers including The Fleetwoods, Gene McDaniel, Cilla Black, Jackie DeShannon, and Gene Pitney, he never felt he had the commercial knowhow to churn out hits like his idol, Carole King. Gradually, a skewed perspective began to emerge, evidently borne out of his conviction that he couldn't write convincing and traditional love songs. Continuing to write in the first-person, he began to use a literary device he terms "the untrustworthy narrator" in his songs. It was something other songwriters didn't consider doing, bending maybe the most basic principle of songwriting, that the singer is sincere. Doing so, he turned the tradition of pop songwriting inside out.

"You know, it may be a psychological defect," he said, explaining why he chose this primary approach to writing songs. "I don't want to stand up there and say, 'I love you.' I don't want to do it. It doesn't interest me. Or I'm *afraid* of it. But it seems much more interesting to get into somebody else's head." By 1968, when with Lenny's help he got signed to Reprise Records and released his debut album as an artist, he was on a songwriting path very much his own, where he's remained ever since.

Today he's at a baby grand, doing a soundcheck on the afternoon prior to his performance at the annual "Salute to the American Songwriter" concert in Los Angeles. Technicians are struggling and failing to balance the sound, but he is calm. "If there's one thing I've learned after all my years in the business," he shares, "it's to lower your standards."

Your debut album, *Randy Newman*, was entirely orchestral. And it was subheaded "Creates something new under the sun."

That was by the liner-note writer. I intended it to be called *Randy Newman*. Naturally, I would never say "creates something new under the sun."

Was there an intention to create something as new in the arrangements as in the lyrics?

There was. I figured an orchestra could move things along rather than a rock and roll beat. I made some mistakes, some conducting errors because I had never conducted before. I took some things so slow; doing the track for "Davy the Fat Boy" was like building a mountain you can't climb. When I had to sing the thing, it was like, "Ah . . ." I couldn't really do it.

But I wanted to get the places right. I took songs *apart*. "So Long Dad," "Davy the Fat Boy." I made them different. I changed them completely—you can hear them on the demo—just to get the place right, you know. And no piano on "Cowboy" because it was outdoors. I never like hearing a piano outdoors; I never get used to it. And it mattered to me a great deal.

But then you have to look at if that's the best vehicle for your voice. And probably what I sing best is some sort of blues-oriented stuff or rock and roll. But I'm sort of proud of the temerity and the ambition of it, trying to do something like that. It's as though I didn't know the Rolling Stones existed, and they very much did.

I haven't heard it for a very long time. I think the singing's real bad. But I thought the singing was good at the time.

It's very emotional singing. Maybe not technically perfect but very human and moving.

That's the thing you get fooled by. Sometimes I'll think that I'm singing really fine, and I won't be. I don't get fooled by other stuff.

Does the first album still hold up for you?

I don't know. I haven't heard any of it for a long time. But I like myself for working so hard on the arrangements. Caring about whether an oboe should be on the double line, if it's too heartbroken, maybe it should be a sax . . . Maybe it's loss of energy—why I've done less of that lately. But I think the records are sounding better and better.

Was there a conscious shift not to make your second album, *Twelve Songs*, an orchestral album?

Yeah. I think we did think that at the time. It's so long ago, it's hard to remember. But it was more singable to me. And I like the way those guys played—Clarence, Ry Cooder . . .

I remember doing "Suzanne." I was going to do "Suzanne" with Hendrix and I talked to him on the phone. I kind of wrote it with him in mind, playing the guitar part. He said, "I'm not a real musician. I can't read music." And he said, "You know, we're both Sagittarius." I said, "Yeah, I know." I mean, I didn't know but I said that. But then he went to Hawaii, and he was going to come back to do it, but it never happened.

With a song like that, did you come up with the idea first? Do you approach songs from different ways?

Usually I approach them with nothing in my mind, and then a musical figure will hopefully spark something. Never a preconceived lyric. I have some ideas now and have had *occasionally*. I'd like to write something about Japan.

That's always been a vague idea. I like the idea of someone wanting to defect to Japan. I don't know how to do that, but I like the idea.

I knew I wanted to write something about South Africa last time. And I *sort of* knew how I was going to handle it. I wanted to get South Africa and California mixed up, you know, the surfing and all that stuff. And the weather—they're in the same latitude, sort of. But otherwise I usually have nothing.

So you're not a writer who scribbles down lines when they occur to you?

No. I never think about it when I'm not trying to work. I've never had an idea just *pop* into my head. [*Pause*]

"Rednecks" did. It popped into my head. I saw Lester Maddox on the Dick Cavett show. And Dick Cavett isn't a Jew, but the guy from Georgia is getting it wrong. I like untrustworthy narrators and things where the audience knows stuff that the narrator doesn't know. I *love* that kind of stuff. You don't see much of it in *songs*. You see it in literature a little bit.

That's one of the chief characteristics of your songs, the use of the "untrustworthy narrator."

Very unusual. You know it surprises me. You see it sometimes but not much. Maybe Springsteen does it. It's hard to tell with him; they've puffed him up so much. But with him, it's always the same guy.

But Springsteen started doing it long after you were doing it.

Oh, yeah. Dylan may do it. Maybe very old songs do it often, I don't know.

If someone said to me, "What makes your songs different?" that is sort of it. They are in first person, but they're not me. If they are about me, I'll dodge it. I'm doing this kind of autobiographical album now, but I won't admit to any of it precisely.

You called your song "Yellow Man" a "pinhead's view of China." How do you think you got to know pinheads' views so well?

I don't know! I think the people in my songs are generally exaggerations. They're worse and stupider than people *actually* are. For the most part. Though the more you listen to those talk shows, you actually hear people that are that stupid.

Specifically, I read the first Will Durant book about the history of civilization. The book is called *Our Oriental Heritage*. It's consigning, you know, six thousand years of Chinese history into *our* oriental heritage. It's a great book anyway . . . That's where I sort of got the idea. It was a little Jimmy Cagney, Shanghai Lil production number where they do this offensive, coolie kind of stuff.

It's interesting that you mentioned reading Durant's book to get that idea. I know that you read Nadine Gordimer's books on South Africa before writing "Christmas in Capetown." Do you think reading is important for songwriters?

It probably has been for me. There aren't really that many songwriters that I know well. And they're really a good bunch of people, usually. Maybe not as good a bunch of people as musicians, 'cause there's less pressure on musicians.

Reading has helped me. It's enabled me not to have to live, because I can read. [*Laughs*] No, not really. But it's helped me tremendously.

About that song, "Christmas in Capetown," I read that you said you weren't sure if the workers really had *Star Wars* painted on their lunch pails, as in your song. Do facts matter?

Sometimes they're *very* important. Like street names and places. Sometimes I don't care, 'cause when I *don't* care, I want people to know I'm getting it wrong. Like I have a song now about New Orleans ["Dixie Flyer"], and I say I lived on a street—Willow—in the Garden District, and Willow's not in the Garden District. But I would hope—at least down there—that they knew I was getting it wrong.

It was supposed to be a childhood memory. The song's kind of about how your childhood gets told to you. You know, your mom says, "Oh, remember when you were a little . . ." and you say, "Yeah, I remember." *You don't remember.* But your mother's told you, your father's told you. It's kind of about that. So sometimes I like getting it wrong.

You spent your childhood summers in New Orleans?

Summers and when I was about seven or eight days old. I'm from here, though [Los Angeles].

Did New Orleans have a big influence on your musical style?

Not consciously. Not in the slightest degree. But when I hear those old records, so often the ones that I like are the New Orleans records. Fats Domino . . . Dr. John . . . It's just a style of stuff that I like. I don't think I *heard* it down there. The white kids and the black kids—they weren't into music that much. But I may have. I've always liked it, even when I didn't know it was New Orleans.

That's why I've written so many shuffles now. It's a drag: I don't like writing them. I'll bring in a shuffle, and the drummer will be pissed off; it won't do me any good, it won't get on the radio. But I can't help writing them. I like them.

So getting on the radio is not a major motivation?

If it was, I'd be one of the worst writers of all time [*laughs*]. I admire people who do it, and I think it's a nice way to work, but I try to do the best that I can and write what I like. I don't worry about it.

You wrote "One More Hour" for the movie *Ragtime,* which, in terms of your work, is kind of a normal song.

That's right. You've got to be normal when they're spending millions of dollars, you know. I'll do it, if it's right for the movie.

Do you ever feel the urge to write a normal song for yourself?

No. I feel the urge to not get worse. Like *Rolling Stone* voted a couple of my albums in the Top One Hundred over the last twenty years, but they were like ten, twelve years old. What I'm doing right now I want to be the best. If I get worse, I'm going to have to do something else.

Did you feel that being a songwriter rather than a film composer was entering a lesser field?

No. I never felt that way.

Was being a songwriter as well respected within the Newman family?

Probably not, I would have to say. I may be wrong, but I think a good song is to be respected as much as any other piece of music. I might have some sort of bias about people not being musicians. Not being able to put stuff down or not being able to write a . . . string quartet, or something.

What gave you the idea to start writing songs from a character's point of view?

I don't know. You know, it may be a psychological defect. I don't want to stand up there and say, "I love you . . ." I don't feel like it. I don't want to do it. It doesn't interest me. Or I'm *afraid* of it. But it seems much more interesting for me to get inside of . . . someone else's head.

"Rednecks" seems to me to be one of the only songs you have written in which you step out of character. The redneck is speaking and then he gets into that whole section about the black man being "free to be put in a cage in Harlem," etc.

It's just a mistake. The guy wouldn't know that. It's an error, on my part, as a writer. But I did it anyway. I knew it. You see, with that guy, everything's fine, he's insulted, he's a bigot, right? He's insulted by the fact that they humiliate his governor—the governor of a state of ten million people—on this TV show, which they did. Not that Maddox wasn't a bad guy, but Dick Cavett didn't even give him a chance to be a bad guy. So the guy does this song, and the one thing wrong with it is he wouldn't know the names of all the ghettos, he wouldn't know Hough in Cleveland and all that stuff. So it is out of character, you're right, but it isn't *me* stepping in. It *is* me stepping in, but I knew it. Anyway, I knew I did wrong. [*Laughs*]

But is it wrong? It opens the song up in a way that your songs are not usually opened up.

No, not wrong. It's not wrong. It makes the guy's point, that all of those places are in the North—that's all. It's just that he probably wouldn't have known that. He *might* have, if he were real interested.

Is it surprising to you that even with that section in the song, people were still offended by it?

Well, people weren't really that offended. There was a black kid in Louisiana who was offended because he was sitting in an audience of fifteen-hundred white people who were *roaring* at the fact that they were rednecks. But I explained it to him and talked to him a few times; I saw him when I was out there again.

It got banned in Boston during the bussing thing. I don't blame them in the slightest for doing that. You hear a white guy say that word ["nigger"], and it's bound to offend.

It's dangerous stuff. As far as Tipper Gore and all the stuff that they're going to ban, I always thought I was a lot more out there than any of that stuff
that they're upset about. You know, I've done some songs that *really scared me*
to do.

Such as?
"Pretty Boy"—the language in there—"Rednecks," "Yellow Man," "Half a
Man." That one was such a delicate thing to get done. And it was a song that
I *really* liked. Now people tell me—gay people, you know—"We used to like
you, why would you do that?" And I said that I meant to make fun of the *idea*
that homosexuality is contagious. That's what the song is about, that you can
catch it from somebody, which is what maybe these idiots are afraid of and why
they're so *angry* at gay people. And maybe hopefully some people got it, but it
was scary. I love the transformation music in that one. I like that song very
much.

Are you surprised when people don't get your songs?
No. They get them much better now. But I am a little surprised, after all
these years, when people ask me about "Political Science," or something.
People's response to "Mr. Sheep" bothered me. I must have done it badly,
'cause the real intelligent people thought I was making fun of the guy with the
briefcase, the Mr. Sheep guy himself. But I was making fun of that rock and
roll voice. This sort of big, whiny, heavy-metal kind of bullying voice.

**In a song like "Political Science," is your purpose primarily to be funny
or to make a point?**
[*Pause*] To be funny . . . to make fun of that kind of chauvinism. I probably
partly believe in it . . . now. I don't think I did then at all. But I kind of think,
"Ooooh—I wish we didn't have to worry about any of these people . . ."

**To write about characters effectively as you do, is it necessary to spend
a lot of time observing people?**
Well, I'm interested. I always was a good listener. Less so now. I talk more
about myself now. I'm always waiting for someone to finish talking so that I
can go, "Oh, yeah, me, I did this and this . . ." Which is a typical showbiz mal-
ady. But I never was afflicted with it too badly.
I'm interested in *regular* stuff. Like what a guy who threads pipe does, what
a carpenter does, and all the stuff they know. I like shows on television that are
about things I know *nothing* about, like gardening. Or the guy who paints . . . I
like hearing them talk, their accents. Like "This Old House" with Bob Vila. It's
arcane to me. It's like the world, because I don't know how to do anything.
I like to know what makes people tick, what their mothers and fathers
were. Why they talk the way they do; using this sort of word or that sort of
word. What it all means. I've always had to listen very closely. I always have
listened very closely.

Do you have a daily songwriting routine?
Yes. For the most part I have to impose a discipline on myself and do that
every day, and not talk to anybody on the phone and set aside some time.
I just saw Don Henley last night, who I hadn't seen for a while. And he's
always suffering when he's writing, too. He said, "You know, I've got to work

somewhere else: the phone's always ringing." And I said, "Don, you know, you've got to cut the phones off." But you don't want to cut the phones off. It's terrible being in a room by yourself.

That's *one* thing I resent about the hit people, in a way, because maybe they don't have . . . [*Pause*] No, there's just as much bleeding going on, you know? Just as much blood on the floor. When you're thinking, "What's the hook going to be? What's this going to be?" It's a very professional, admirable thing. I sometimes think that what I do is more admirable. I don't have an artist that I have to write a hit for. Like, "Holy shit, I have to write a hit for the Pointer Sisters!"

You can look down at it and say, "What a contrived piece of horseshit. What are you doing, you're just making it like everything else." But it's not. There's as much blood, or more, that goes into it, as Henley, who is trying to write "Dirty Laundry" or "Johnny Can't Read." And I'm trying to write "Christmas in Capetown" or whatever the hell I'm trying to do. Or Prince, who is trying to do something that is both.

So you wouldn't say songwriting is something that is fun for you?

No. It's fun *when* I write something. I want more than *anything* in life to enjoy it all, to enjoy that process. And I think I actually do. I'll be glad when I'm done, but when I'm done then I'll think that that was actually the best part of it, you know: the process.

Because it's pretty awful when nothing's going on. Lots of bad thoughts go into your mind, like, "I'll never do this anymore. This is really terrible. I'm working and it's bad. I'm getting worse. Something's gone wrong with me. Maybe I've gone bad as a person and I can't write well anymore."

You'd think you'd get over it, and you'd think you'd stop complaining about it. I mean, why should I be whining about it? I get tapes from people who are just dying to get a break. So why whine? It's better than having a regular job or something like that.

Do you still have an office where you work?

Yes. I had to get a place where no one knew where I was. I needed a place where I couldn't . . . go outside and graze, or whatever I would do. I mean, it's very hard to sit there for four hours.

You know, I'm worried about this batch of songs I wrote [*Land of Dreams*]. I had this flu—the Epstein-Barr flu—there for a while. It used to be I would write a song and I'd be invulnerable to anything. Anything could happen and it wouldn't bother me, if I'd written a good song. It would, like, validate me. But it wasn't lasting me *fifteen minutes* before I'd be feeling bad again. I think it was because I was sick. I'd keep writing and I'd say, "Christ, there's nothing happening here." Then I got sort of feeling better and I looked back and the stuff wasn't so bad. People liked it.

How long did that validation used to last?

A week. More than that. And I'd be eager to play it for people: "Here, listen to this one." Now I go in to record and they say to me, "You want a demo of this? I'll make you a two-track," and I'll say, "No . . ."

Your first album came out in 1968. Do you think that after all these years you have a better understanding of how to get in touch with that source of ideas?

No. I wish I could give you something. My first advice would be to be tough enough to hang in there. It's like the theory of relativity. When you're sitting there, trying, trying, trying . . . You look at your watch . . . it's like school, you say, "I'm gonna guess that it's 9:40." But I know that it's actually 10:20. It will make me feel better to know I've been working for an hour and twenty minutes. And I look at my watch and it's 9:15.

But when you get something going, that's what I love. When I don't know what time it is. When I know that time is going. When you got something, it's a great feeling.

You've got to hang in there, first off. And fight it. You know, Paul Simon's a *tough, tough* fella. You can hear how hard he's worked on stuff. You can't really; if you could hear the work, it would be wrong. You know, he won't be satisfied with the same sort of change. "Still Crazy," you know, going different places and stuff. A lot of it's stamina and toughness. A *lot* of it.

Sometimes you just put anything down. The other day I was talking to Lenny Waronker, and he was talking about Prince. He said, "That's all he ever does, you know: he works." And I'm thinking, "Jesus Christ, I get out so little, I wonder if I could write a song a day." So I did it, and I never listened to it again. But I just went through it and didn't think, or let myself exercise my critical faculties. And it probably isn't too bad. I did it again the next day, just to see if I could work that way.

That isn't a bad idea for people, if this is like advice for songwriters. Don't let the critic become bigger than the creator. Don't let it strangle you. Go ahead and say, "I saw this girl / She was the best girl in the world." Let it go. Put a string of stuff together. Go ahead.

And then—I can't always follow this advice myself—and then futz with it. But make something happen. Write something down. Do something. Go ahead. *And* stay there. Stay there four hours. Three hours, four hours. And good things will happen.

Do you go back and polish your songs a good deal after the first draft is done?

More so lately. Some days you get things that are gifts. A song will happen and it will go all the way through to the end. You can see to the end of it right at the beginning. I think it happens more when you're younger. I hate to say that but I've gotten fewer gifts on this one.

Where do those gifts come from?

I don't know. But you'll just have it. You'll hear Elton John say, "I wrote that in a minute and a half," and that happens to people.

Do you hear your influence on the work of other writers, such as Paul Simon?

No. Other people told me that's possible, but I don't really hear it. His lyrics are more abstract than mine.

Do you hear your influence in other places? A song like "Money for Nothing," for example, by Mark Knopfler, is a character song very much in your vein.

That's a character. That's pretty good. They like me, both of them do like me very much, I know, Knopfler and Simon. But he's in character in that song, which surprised me. A big giant hit, too. And he's kind of nasty but you get your sympathy with him because he *is* carrying those big appliances. He's bitter but somehow likeable.

One characteristic that you and Simon share in your writing is suc-cinctness. Is that something that you strive for?

Not consciously, but I say what I have to say. A lot of it is use of small words: but, for, and . . . you get the right one and it takes you to a good place.

Some of your songs, such as "A Wedding in Cherokee County," seem as if they were written based on a plot idea.

With that one, I was real interested in Albania at the time. Four thousand people and eight thousand goats, real vitriolic. I wanted to write them an anthem: "Albania, Albania," but it didn't work out, so I wrote this Albanian wedding song. But I didn't have any idea of plot in mind at all. Then I moved it to Cherokee County, to fit in with the theme of "Good Old Boys." I didn't have to change it much.

Many of your songs, such as "Same Girl" and "In Germany Before the War," share the characteristic of wedding a very dark, very sad lyric to an absolutely gorgeous melody.

I think they fit together. I wouldn't know how to do it any other way. "In Germany Before the War." It's sort of vaguely German and classical in some ways.

"Same Girl" is a sad tune. About two junkies in love. Nice music in that tune. A lot of time I don't care about prettiness too much in what I write. And I didn't consciously in that one, but it's got lots of nice things, passing notes and stuff. And the record came out very well. I don't think it's as good of a *song* as "Real Emotional Girl," but it's a better record.

Do you have favorite keys to work in?

No, but there's a range where my voice sounds sort of good to me. And it causes me to write my "tessitura" [*goes to piano, plays beginning of "Jolly Coppers on Parade" and sings the opening line: "They're coming down the street . . ."*] It almost sounds like it could be . . . pop. [*Laughs*] But it's only three notes.

I didn't use to know that. I've done things in keys that are too low. I've made mistakes. Where on a piano you can sing it, and then with a band you can't get over. Now there are computers that can change keys without changing tempos—I've used those twice.

For good musicians it might sound bad in A and better in A flat, but I don't know whether I have that strong of a key sense.

Sometimes it won't feel right. There's keys I haven't used. . . .

Your use of dissonance to show a character's unbalanced state of mind, as in "In Germany Before the War," is very effective. How, technically, did you create that dissonance?

I changed the B-flat to a B. It's the sound of that B against the B flat [in the key of G minor]. I can show you. [*Goes to piano and plays progression*] It's sort of like bad voice leading. Then I had to think about doing all of them that way, but I didn't.

The use of dissonance is rather sophisticated for pop music, wouldn't you say?

Listen to Prince! That stuff's pretty dissonant. That whole album is the most dissonant album in rock and roll, that paisley purple whatjamajigger.

Do you like the work of writers such as Dylan and Joni Mitchell, who write longer, more extended songs than yours?

I'm not that familiar with their current work. Joni's album *Blue* is a great, great record. Her next album was too much about rich people for my taste. Dylan, at his best, is great.

Your songs are very clear compared to many of Dylan's songs.

That's a pretty brave thing. I think it's easier to be the other way. I mean, if I want to talk about crystal explosions in the eventide, I could *do* it . . . but actually *this* is what I mean, and I'm going to try to do it and you see if you laugh at it. Or, this is what it is, see what you think of it. That's kind of hard, I would think. If it weren't hard, maybe more people would do it. Country people do it.

Is it harder to be clear than to be abstract?

I would *think* so. I've often wondered about Paul Simon in some ways and his African record. As good as he is, I don't *understand* all of it. I don't understand, in "Hearts and Bones," for instance, what he's talking about. I mean, I know what he means because I've been told. You have to be one of his friends to know what he is talking about: that it's the wedding of one of his friends.

I've never wanted to do that. And I don't like it when people do it. It may be a depth that if you look at it long enough, you get what it means.

Do you ever have the urge to write an abstract song that people won't necessarily understand?

You know, talking to you's made me think of it. It may be that it's a step in another direction, you know. The best book I've ever read is *Ulysses*, and I don't understand 30 percent of it. But the good parts are so great. You know, you get to read it with this little "*Ulysses* helper," and it's just like being in another world.

You know, you see all these writers doing stream of consciousness, and I think, "What are they doing? Do they think this works?"

But if you listen to Simon closely, or Van Dyke [Parks] closely, you know what it is, sort of, maybe. It's not for *me*.

I like a song like "Vincent" by Don McLean. I mean, there it is, it's talking about the guy, a *beautiful* goddamn song. (Bad arrangement. Strings are bad. I'd like to fix them.) And there it is—it's great.

"Dock of the Bay." The Joni Mitchell stuff, actually talking about people. And Dylan, the story about that murder on that farm. And even "Stuck Inside of Mobile With Those Memphis Blues Again" which comes and goes.

Neil Young is a great writer, a great writer. He's very good about nature writing. He's like a little baby: he'll rhyme the first thing he thinks of, but it'll all work out. I don't know if Simon likes Neil Young, I wonder . . .

I mean, Simon did do it right on *Graceland*. It's such a great sounding record. I haven't heard three better sounding records in the history of rock.

So musically you enjoyed it?

Oh, man, I loved it. I mean, I like it all, anyway. He's got such energy. He *goes* to Africa. I think maybe if I were a novelist, I would be happy about doing research, going to the library. But I just don't want to listen to, you know, Brazilo-Gibo rhythms, and go to the new synthesizer convention. I want it all to go away.

I was talking to one of my cousins about another one of my cousins, David, who does movie scores. And he just finished *Throw Momma From the Train*, which is an orchestra score. So I said, "David probably doesn't work with synthesizers, does he?" And he said, "No, he has a whole synthesizer *bay* at his house." My heart just sank. This little kid, he's so into it he has a whole *bay*, whatever the hell that is. And I have this little Casio, a forty-nine dollar one.

I sometimes worry that I was given somehow a lot of talent and I didn't really jump on it. Like Prince, who has a lot of talent, jumps on it. I often feel I haven't lived up to my potential, as they used to tell me in high school.

Listen—it's a dangerous time now for songwriters in that a *monkey* can make a thing sound good now. I can take a drum machine and it sounds fine. But it's just hard putting content into it. You know what I mean? It's like, things sound better than they ever have. But I don't know whether there's more content in stuff. [*Pause*] Maybe . . .

Since we are talking about the use of drums, I listened to all of your albums from the first one to the last one. And one thing I noticed was that you didn't use drums as a primary instrument. You use them very sparingly, like another color.

I never liked them. I never liked them being in the way. I'm such a pain in the ass to drummers. And they're such a pain in the ass to me. I didn't like that banging away, like that. I do more of it now, but with Porcaro, because I like his playing.

I just went down an evolutionary path that didn't lead to the . . . Australopithecus. It led more to some other ape who didn't make it. You know, like, "Keep the drums down, no backbeat. We'll use the orchestra to move it." It just didn't go that way, you know what I mean? It went *exactly* the opposite way every time, you know? Now it's like segmented; everything quantized. Which should be irritating.

Often your beat would be one and three; not the backbeat but the reverse.

Yes. I tell you, I didn't even notice it at the time. It's just what felt better to me. From not listening to records enough and so forth. And playing with drummers who wanted to do different stuff.

I'd be interested to ask you what my things sounded like going all the way through. I *think* my last one's the best [*Land of Dreams*]. It's got the best set of songs. The best set of songs are on that one and on *Sail Away*, I believe.

You wouldn't consider the songs on *Good Old Boys* to be in that league?
Not song for song. I don't think it's as good. Though a surprising song is that old song "Back on My Feet Again." I *heard* that fairly recently. It's a very strange, insane kind of song.
What did you think when you heard all the albums?

The first album overwhelmed me. I'd never listened to it on a good stereo before.
I don't think I have either.

It's a very powerful record—"Bet No One Ever Hurt This Bad," "Cowboy," . . . Also the *Little Criminals* album is very moving.
Lenny Waronker always thought that it was my best album.

It's an incredible record, with "Old Man on the Farm," "Texas Girl at the Funeral of Her Father," "In Germany . . ."
Is "William Brown" on that album?

No. That's on *Born Again*.
Weird song. I tried to do nothing and I did.

Also, on the *Little Criminals* album, you have a series of songs with titles that are more like paintings or photographs than songs: "Old Man on a Farm," "Texas Girl at the Funeral of Her Father," "In Germany Before the War."
I think that came from a style of writing where I didn't hit an obvious title. "Old Man on a Farm" is nice. The chords are nice "In Germany," too. It works like a son of a bitch. There's nothing wrong with it. And "Old Man on a Farm" [*mutters through lyrics to himself*]. Those are all borrowed dominants. Hard song for me to sing. Perfect for a girl. Particularly someone with a Southern accent should do it. I could hear k.d. lang or somebody do it. Linda did it fine when we did it together.

"Baltimore" is also on that album, which is one of my favorites.
I had trouble with the lyric. The seagull.

What was wrong with it?
It was a "beat-up little seagull." I didn't like it. I wanted to get rid of it. I just never liked the lyric. And people *really* like that song.

Did you go to Baltimore to write that song?
No, I just drove through once on a train before I had written it, so it's a little unfair. I saw all those marble stairways and row houses, and I saw a story about it in the *National Geographic*. It looked like it was in trouble. Now they say it's gotten better, but they were really mad at me. It *was* a dying town.

You're great at taking dying towns and glorifying them. Like you did with Cleveland in "Burn On, Big River."
Yeah, and Cleveland has been all revivified, too. They have this new center there. They liked that song.

"I Love L.A." really captures the feeling of this city.
Yeah? I just feel people don't know the streets I named in it. And the reason I named them is because there's nothing on them.

Do you drive on the Imperial Highway often?
[*Laughs*] Oh, sure. All the time.

You allowed that song to be used in commercials—
Yeah, but I don't think it hurt it at all. I used that one, "Short People" . . .
I think it didn't affect them.

How about "Dayton, Ohio, 1903," the melody of which is used in the NutraSweet commercial? Isn't that one affected?
I wasn't crazy about that song. It's got kind of a false nostalgia that I don't
like. I don't *believe*, necessarily, that 1903 in Dayton, Ohio, is much better than
now.

That's interesting, because many of your songs bring us back to another time.
I'm interested in it musically. It's too bad that kids now don't know Irving
Berlin's songs. That I may be in the last generation that is really familiar with
the body of American songwriting.

Previous generations of songwriters put much more emphasis on craft aspects of songwriting, such as the use of rhymes. Do you think rhyming is important?
Yeah. I think I take liberties with it that most traditional songwriters would
not. You know, if I've got to rhyme "rain" and "game," I'll sort of do it.
There're things I won't do, but I can't tell you what they are until I get to
them. You know, whereas Lorenz Hart wouldn't have done them. And he was
a great artist.
Sometimes you don't have to rhyme at all.

Some of your songs are very conversational, like "Mikey."
Yeah, that one's good. I did a good job of getting that guy. Sometimes
that's difficult, sometimes you can get into it. I'm not sure if I got the guy completely right. Let's see . . . "North Beach . . ." [*Mutters through the lyrics of the
songs to himself*] He's like the guy in "Capetown." The guy in "Capetown" is
like a thirty-eight-year-old surfer, a little bastard who doesn't like the way
things are now. And this guy's the same kind of guy.
I like the joke about the music: "Where are we, on the moon?" [*Laughs*]
He comments on how ugly the music is on the record.

And then that great horn line comes in.
Yeah. [*Sings horn line like a bleating trumpet*] That's my favorite thing on the
record.

I read once that you didn't know you were Jewish until you were a teenager.
Not true. I did. And I ran into prejudice really early. But I never went to
temple.

Did your parents try to instill any sense of spirituality in you?
No.

I ask because you deal with the subject of God in many songs.
I'm *very* interested in it. In what a big deal it is. But I don't believe in it,
no.

Do you look at it like the narrator in your song "Old Man," who says to his father on his deathbed: "Won't be no God to comfort you / You taught me not to believe that lie"?

I'm not that cold. I'm not that cold to a parent. [*Pause*] But, yeah, that's how I feel about it. I don't think there's anything. It's not a popular view. [*Pause*] But I would hope my kids . . . wouldn't read this. There's no point in going around waving the atheistic banner. What good's it gonna do? I mean, I think to have that faith is pretty damn nice. I wouldn't begrudge anybody their faith. I wouldn't argue the point.

In "God's Song," you actually take on God's point of view. And you portray Him as a god who finds mankind pretty amusing.

Yeah. He's a kind of California god, too. I mentioned Yucca, and that's the only place it grows. Yeah. He says, "How can you believe in me—look at what I'm doing." [*Laughs*]

There are many subjects that people have never attempted to deal with in songs. "Dixie Flyer" touches on being Jewish, which is such a rare subject, even though so many songwriters are Jewish.

Really. Irving Berlin never did it. It really may have been the first time. That was what that song was about, trying to be like Gentiles, and making fun of the Jewish idea that Gentiles drink. But, yeah, I have a recently evolved theory that sometimes Jewish songwriters and Jewish writers get into American harder. They want to be part. Less so in literature, where writers write about their Jewishness. But Irving Berlin, you know—"Alabammy Bound."

"White Christmas."

Yeah. There's a great thing in one of Philip Roth's recent books where he says that after Moses, the next real Jewish genius was Irving Berlin. He took the blood out of Easter and made it about fashion. And he took Christ out of Christmas and made it about snow. [*Laughter*]

There's this wanting to be part, wanting to be accepted in America. I think sometimes it's why I glom onto whatever Southern background I have so hard.

I don't know if Simon's an example. I think Simon just examines what he examines. I don't think it's necessarily history that interests him. His songs are about relationships, and that's the same for everybody. But I sometimes wonder about Jewish songwriters and Jewish writers in general getting into America harder, or trying to.

It's interesting how many of the great American songwriters have been Jewish, from Gershwin to Dylan.

Dylan, yeah. And the same thing would apply to him, of running away from that.

Do you think there are other big subjects that could be dealt with in songs that aren't?

It's just that love has been the traditional component of songs for fourteen hundred years. Rap has covered a lot more ground than we have ever dealt with before. They're talking about life. There's more interest to those lyrics, all in all, than the bulk of pop music has produced, ever. When the very best people are writing love songs: Lorenz Hart, Dylan. But there's a little more to [rap]. It's a limited experience. There's a lot of straight aggression. But there's less bragging in it than there used to be. It's changed from that. It's also changed from having no tune to making damn sure they have a hook, just like we have for hundreds of years. I knew that would happen.

Even if it's lifted completely from another song.

Yeah. But they knew they had to get one. It's very practical. It's like evolution. Amos, my son, he really knew it early. He said that this is not going to go on this way, because people are going to want a tune. And so they get somebody to sing on there.

Do you have faith that your songs have meaning, that they will live on?

Will people be listening to them forty years from now? No. They'll be listening to hits.

But hits are the first songs we get tired of hearing.

There's already evidence. They're listening to Beatles. They're not listening to Jimmy Driscoll.

I have the feeling that over the years your work will be appreciated more and more.

You know, that happened to Schubert. But I don't know if it could happen nowadays. I *naturally* hope that they'll just say, "Wow, what an amazing body of work. He was really trying there." But I have a feeling that there aren't enough people like you, or like people I've met in radio. If the world were made up of people in the business, then I'd be remembered forty-five years from now.

But often, I find myself . . . you know, I'll listen to Irving Berlin . . . I sent away to an 800 number and I got Irving Berlin's four-record set. And that's what I like to hear. You know you like to hear a melody, and you like to hear . . . It's a strange thing . . . it's not a thing you'd want to turn your head on much for in the car. I mean, I'll like it when there's a song by Joni Mitchell or that girl's song about child abuse ["Luka" by Suzanne Vega]. But there's *so little* of it. There is so little of it. It's a wasteland for that sort of stuff.

It is. I like a strong melody, but it can only last so long if the words aren't interesting.

I agree as a writer. You know, if you're going to sit there and put words down, why put down something that has no content? I've done it, like "Bet No One Ever Hurt This Bad," which is a pretty pedestrian lyric: "Sit by my window, watch the rain . . ."

"I'll Be Home" is nothing. It means nothing to me at all. I wrote it for Mary Hopkin. And I didn't want to record it. People like it. And I've made more money off of it than off of "Davy the Fat Boy" by about a hundred times, and it doesn't even interest me except for the arrangement.

But I'm not sure. This is sort of a bleak view. Maybe it will all change and lyrics will get important. Listen, even when lyrics are important and you read in a paper, "This is the most meaningful lyric of the year," it will be something by the Clash, you know, or U2. And I'm telling you, man, "We're inside the wall, the walls are outside . . ." That's not hard. I don't want to judge U2 or the

Clash because I don't know their work completely. But I mean, *the things they'll pick out* and they'll write down.

It's a desperate business. It's a desperate business; they're not musicians, rock critics, for the most part. So they have to write about words. [*Softly*] And there's nothing to write about.

Whereas you will write a song like "Song for the Dead" in which there is a beautiful melody and also a place, Vietnam, and a character and a whole sense of American tragedy. It's a short song and yet it contains so much.

And it's in the character of some sort of dead guy, some sort of mythical leadership guy.

Is that guy dead? I thought he was just left behind to say a prayer for the dead.

[*Sings through song's lyric softly to himself*] I never saw him as quite real. It's sort of a ghost. [*Sings more*] I don't think people liked that song much.

Again, it has that trait of putting a beautiful melody up against this ugly situation, especially when the guy sings, "by these very gooks who lie here beside you . . ." The music peaks at the same point as the lyric.

Yeah—what is that, a cymbal crash? It goes real high there. So it isn't all black and white. I like people who have more inflections in them. So that they're not *predictable*. I like movies where you don't know what the people are going to do, necessarily. *Atlantic City* is a movie like that, where I didn't know what Burt Lancaster was up to, necessarily. He's more complex than a movie person. I like that kind of stuff though you don't often hear it.

You know, I might not notice some of these things that I did in a song, I might not be listening hard enough.

You've sent up certain American heroes in your songs. In "My Life Is Good" you satirize Springsteen for his heroics.

Sort of. I picked him because he's so famous. If I didn't sort of like him, I wouldn't have used him. I was kind of making fun of myself.

I find myself minding to some extent inflated artistic reputations. I think his reputation artistically probably is inflated a bit. But everyone who sees him changes his mind. A lot of musicians don't like his music. But when they see him, it's like they become a pod person. [*Laughs*] It's like [*softly*] "No, he's *great*, man." I say, "What do you mean he's great? Yesterday you said it sounded like it all came out of a well." And they say, "No, man, he's great, he's great." I don't know what it is. It's like hypnotism.

I may be missing stuff. Like "Born in the U.S.A." is not just "Hurray, we're in the U.S.A." But I'm not sure I even noticed that myself. I'm not listening that hard. We're not giving him a break, you know? But the *Nebraska* album's a great album. Well . . . not *great*, but pretty damn good.

But I never understood the Clash, U2. They're not great like Joni Mitchell is great or Dylan was great. Or Townsend. "My Generation," all that stuttering, that's *really* smart. You know, trying to be articulate to talk about "my g-g-g-g-generation" . . . you know, and the guy can't even talk. He's *really* a good writer.

Any people doing it right now who you think are of that standard?
Prince. Lyrically he does all this baby-sex stuff, but he'll get over that. But he also does funny stuff, like that song where he's talking about wanting this girl so bad he'd give up everything for her; he said, "I'd give up my pad for you, I'd give up my ride . . . Well, maybe not my ride." Which is great; I *love* that kind of stuff.

One of the most beautiful love songs ever written is your song "Marie." It seems to me to be a little unusual among your work because it is such a sincere song.
It is, but I was writing it like a character. It's the character of the guy in "Rednecks." So I was able to *do* it.

It's probably a deficiency, that I require a character, like an actor does, to write something like that. Otherwise I wouldn't have written it. It is atypical, but it's in character with the Southern guy.

Was there an actual Marie?
No.

You've written about sex in a number of songs: "Tickle Me," "Maybe I'm Doing It Wrong," "You Can Leave Your Hat On."
God! [*Laughs*] How odd.

That I would group your songs together like that?
No, that they're so . . . aberrant.

Is that a hard subject to tackle?
[*Pause*] Yeah, any sort of direct thing is a little tougher.

It's probably a flaw, when you really think of it. In fact, I'll probably do something about it now that you've brought it home to me *so* much. But it isn't my style to do.

You know, I'm doing it now. I'm directly saying things in my life, but I'm *lying* about them a little bit just for fun.

You know that new song, "I Just Want You to Hurt Like I Do," I'd never do that to my kid. [Walk out on him.] I may want everyone *else* to hurt like I do. But it takes the onus off of me, in my own mind, that I did it to my little boy, who I would *die* for. I hope I don't subscribe to that philosophy, but you know, *I* don't want Paul Simon to sell six million records every time out. I can't root for anyone *too* much. It's like a flaw. I think it's a human trait, but I don't know whether people will admit to it. But I did.

You mentioned "I Just Want You to Hurt Like I Do," which is one of your new songs. It's another one of those songs that has a funny lyric set against a beautiful melody. And the lyrics are so striking that on first listening, the beauty of the melody can go unnoticed, such as the use of the F-diminished chord in the chorus. But it gives the song a strength that holds it up over countless listenings.
It's a real good song. It's got a bad, sort of archaic background but there's *nothing* I can do about it.

That chord in the chorus is sort of a B diminished with F in the bass. I thought about that chord . . . That's a good song. When I have something like that, I'm happy, 'cause I think I am as good as I was. 'Cause a lot of people aren't. Face it, think about it.

Do you maintain that quality by not rushing the process? You certainly don't put out many albums.
I don't know. It's the only way I can. I don't know how else to do it. It seems like a terrible thing, doesn't it?

That you don't put out more?
No. It seems like a terrible thing not to be as good as you were. If you know it . . . It'd be a good thing to write about, wouldn't it?

Yes. Do you think that is your toughest challenge, to match the quality of your past work?
It's not that I think that highly of it. I mean, I still like what I did. [*Laughs*] I just want to like getting up and going to it.

Is there a single song of your own that you consider your favorite?
[*Long pause*] I guess it would be "God's Song." I don't know. I like "Old Man" though I never play it much. It's depressing. I like a song like "Mikey," actually. I like the arrangement of the orchestra on "Yellow Man." "Davy" is a good song. "I Want You to Hurt Like I Do" is a good song. I have this thing called "Roll With the Punches" that's a very good song. And "Dixie Flyer," that is a good song. "Girls in My Life" I've always liked.

I'm very proud of a thing I did for Van Dyke Parks. It's pure craftsmanship: "Vine Street." The very first record that he ever did was an instrumental version of Beethoven's Ninth. Naturally ahead of his time. And I worked that into the arrangement of "Vine Street" somehow, without even thinking.

There are things in songs that will surprise me. Like I don't know how I *thought* of them. Like: "*Boom* goes London / *Boom* Paree / More *room* for you / More *room* for me" [from "Political Science"].

It's neat. It's like a gift. Not that I have a gift, but it was like a gift from . . . Voton.

Do you think these gifts come from beyond you or from within you?
From within. But there's things I'll think about later and I'll say, "Look at that—I didn't even know I did that." Maybe it's just habit from doing it so long.

Many of your songs have inner rhymes and inner structures that I don't even notice at first. Like "Girls in My Life" seems at first to have no formal structure. But then after looking at it, I see how the verses link up on key words: "conversation," "disposition," "education."
Yeah, why should they rhyme? They're so far apart and yet I had them rhyme. It felt like they had to. I don't know if I notice it at first, but I will know it has to have it and without it will sound wrong. It's hard to say why.

You were quoted as saying, "Rock has the power of the beat. Rock is only five percent literature. That's why I've been so unsuccessful."
Well, maybe a little more than five percent. But it is *not* a medium where literacy and content of lyric is of equal importance as the music.

It is a strange thing. I don't want to work toward "Help Me, Rhonda." But I *love* "Help Me, Rhonda." You know what I'm saying? There's that dichotomy.

Yet you are consistently combining literature and music, the most extreme example of which would certainly be *Faust*. Did you write it over a long period of time?
I had a couple of the songs. I had "How Great Our Lord" very early. Maybe fourteen years ago. And "Gainesville" I wrote an appreciable time ago, maybe ten, twelve years. And the rest I wrote within the last couple years.

Hearing James Taylor's voice on "Glory Train," which is so much a typical Randy Newman shuffle groove, is great to hear. It's a great match.
Oh, that's good. Because he can sing anything. And a strange thing happens—it almost makes you religious—he's singing a song which lyrically is kind of nonsense: "Get on the glory train." It's before trains were invented, when he's singing it. And then the devil comes in in 7/8 in D minor and it's all this information he's pouring out, it's *reason*, and it goes from that "Get on the glory train" and then I come in with "If I might intrude . . ."
It really sort of sums up the effect that I've had on the public. [*Laughs*] I've got these songs with no real vocal tune with lots of information in it. And it's like that with the Lord and the Devil. The Devil is pouring out all this information in a horrible time signature in a strange key, no kind of tune, old-timey stuff, but word after word. And the Lord is saying nothing, but the music is rock and roll. It's so big. It's so powerful. Just like religion. And that's how it is.
If you were going to figure out who made the most effective case, even though He didn't make a case, it's the Lord. You can't compete with it, the power of gospel music. It almost makes you wonder. Not quite, but almost. You can combat it with reason, which is dry. It's not musical. Music's not reasonable.

Yet it feels good, so people are going to go with that—
Right, it feels good. *I* go with it. I love gospel. I don't like any kind of American music more than I like gospel music.

Really?
Oh, absolutely. Never had liked anything better.

***Faust* shows you have a real mastery of it.**
Well, I know it. I hear it whenever I get a chance.

***Faust* is extraordinary in all the musical shifts it has. It shows your ability to write in so many styles: rock, gospel, blues, country, heavy-metal.**
Stuff I never would have written, as you know. That's what was nice about it. I'd never have written "Gainesville." I can't sing it in a million years. I mean, I can, in a kind of stylistic, broken way. The range itself is impossible for me.
Yeah, there's a lot of different kinds of songs [in *Faust*] and I didn't make fun of anything, really. I like heavy-metal. I sort of did an old-fart version of it. But it was sort of the best I could do. If I were going to do rock and roll, it wouldn't be so different from some of those things that Henley does.

Faust **sounds like you had fun writing it. Was it fun—did it come easily to you—or was it hard work to put all those parts together?**

It came easily. Putting it in the orchestra is never easy. It's always very serious, and I lose my sense of humor and think about it hard.

I don't remember the writing. You know how sometimes they just come. The writing in general was a good deal easier than pulling [songs] out of the air. It had definite parameters, like writing a song for a movie, or an assignment. If you were going to give me an assignment, I'm confident that I could do it, no matter what it was. But just sitting down the way I always used to do, with nothing in my head, no idea, is much more difficult. In fact, I don't think I'll do it again. I'll make up an assignment. Which I've done occasionally.

You mean like a single theme for an album?

No. I'll just say, "I want to write a song about a white car." And then just set out and see where it goes. Just so I have something to start with. It's a little terrifying, the way I've done things in the past. You know, just sit there with absolutely nothing in my head. Really nothing. Until something is engendered on the piano. That's what I've done since I was sixteen.

So you never come up with lyric ideas apart from writing, and jot them down to use later?

No. Never. I've done that twice in my life, maybe. I never have had an idea when I wasn't trying to have one. I've had *big* ideas, like I had the idea for *Faust* when I wasn't trying to have an idea. But I never think of anything in the car, like it would be good to write about this, that or the other.

I don't think I like to think about it unless I have to. It's an old bad habit. I remember that I got the idea for "Rednecks" when I wasn't near a piano or anything.

It's funny: it's been a long time since I've looked at the world in that way that I don't even know what I would write about now. You know, I keep writing these race things, as you know. I've written so many times about it. It doesn't seem to have done any good. [*Laughter*] I mean, I think I'm done, and then I write another one. But I think it is a big thing. I don't think I've written too much about it. I think there's more to say.

So even a song like "Roll with the Punches" began with the music, and the words came out of the music?

Yes. Everything came out of the music. I got the first lines, and then I could see my way. It's not completely clear, but sometimes I can see all the way to the end right at the beginning. And sometimes, nothing happens at all, and it's something that I don't finish. The Bonnie [Raitt] song that I wrote ["Feels Like Home"] is not the kind of lyric that interests me. People love the song. In an outsized way. We do a version of it in [*Faust*] that is fast and is not as thoughtful as the version of the record. And they still love it. There's something about it that is like songs by people that they love, like Billy Joel. It doesn't interest me a great deal except musically. I don't know. Maybe I've got a hard heart as far as love songs. I don't care much about "I'll Be Home" or "Dayton, Ohio."

Do you ever finish the melody first and then work on the words, or are you always working on the both together?

Usually together. Sometimes I'll have a verse and then I'll need another verse with the same tune, yeah. Definitely. That almost always happens. But never a whole melody.

You know, some people record without lyrics. They'll do a whole track that sounds good, and have the melody and go "ba da da" at the hook, and then write them under great pressure.

But generally you're at an acoustic piano.

Always, yeah. One hundred percent.

When you're working on lyrics, after a verse melody is complete, do you work at the piano?

I sit in a room next to it. But I don't necessarily refer to it.

Do you notate songs while working?

No. I don't usually. Unless I have to. It's funny: I've never done it. I'm just like a guy who doesn't know how to write music when I write songs. I'll accept take-downs. And sometimes they're bad take-downs. I just never wanted to deal with all those 12/8 measures and the anticipated rhythms, whether I'm on the downbeat or whether it's the last eighth of the fourth beat. Like [*sings*] "Short people got . . . *boom* . . ." It's a pain in the ass. But I've done it when I have to.

Do you tape yourself while writing?

Yeah. On an old tape machine. It's what I've always done.

You keep it running?

No. Just when I've got something, I'll put it on.

Does your movie work enrich your songwriting in any way, or does it drain you for writing songs?

The songs I write for movies are less characteristic, because they have to serve the picture. They still sound like me in every case. But I wouldn't have written them without the movie. I wouldn't have written "I was born to make you happy / I think you're just my style." ["I Love to See You Smile" from *Parenthood*.] I'm glad I did, though. I put myself in a box, but all this first person stuff, which is the way I've chosen to go exclusively, it can be a bit of a corner to box yourself into. I think you can do anything with it. With that stroke. I can do anything I want to with the first person. But it is all indirection. These things [for movies] have to be a little more direct. I don't have to worry about who I am.

I don't know whether I started doing that out of shyness or wanting to be like fiction writers.

Using the untrustworthy narrator?

Yeah. It's very rare, as you know. It's really, really rare in music. It's a lot to ask people to get it. When you're driving your car down the freeway, you're not listening for irony out there. Ice-T said that's what he did with "Cop Killer." I try to make it plenty clear. But some of the things that interest me the most are things that are closest to the line—"William Brown," "Follow the

Flag." Like in "Follow the Flag," is he kidding? Yeah. I don't mean a word of it. I think for the flag to be that important to someone is a little bit outsized. It's a small life. There aren't many clues except little hints, not much. It interests me to do that.

It has that line about believing in something bigger than yourself.
[*Laughs*] Yeah. That's difficult for Hollywood to believe. But people do believe in things bigger than themselves. The family. So that one and "William Brown" are the closest to the edge.

"William Brown" is a character sketch in the third person. But most of your songs, like "Follow the Flag," are in first person, and you are singing as the character.
Yeah, that's right. So "William Brown" is a little different. So "Follow the Flag" is the closest. "Rednecks" is very close. The guy makes good sense.

But it's so extreme—
It has ugly stuff in it, yeah.

That if you weren't joking it would be objectionable.
It's got to be someone else. But at least what he's saying has some validity. Some of my people, what they really lack is self-knowledge. We know them better than they know themselves, I think.

On Land of Dreams, instead of using the untrustworthy narrator, for the first time you used yourself as the main character and wrote many autobiographical songs.
But I was untrustworthy. [*Laughs*] That's not all true. All the stuff about my father and exaggerating what is the New Orleans attitude of *bon temps*, letting the good times roll, but not knowing the war was over, and building a statue of my father, and all that. So even I am not completely trustworthy.

But, yes, I did the best I could. I wanted to do that purposely, because I hadn't done it. It is being in a bit of a box, the way I work. I think you can do anything with it. I can't be more intelligent than I am, so generally my characters aren't so bright. But once I notice something like that, I try and do something that is different. It's how I get ideas, trying to do something different than I did.

"Four Eyes," which is an amazing song, seems very autobiographical.
No. I did have crossed-eyes and worried about that. But I don't remember my first day of school, or whether my dad took me. He certainly didn't say any of that stuff.

He didn't dress you in your cowboy suit for your first day of school?
No. I don't think I had a Roy Rogers lunch pail. But there's a fair amount of truth in it emotionally. The big idea in it is that it's the first step away from home. You're starting on the road to work. And it's, "Work? You're not going to leave me here, are you?" That kind of attitude towards it.

One of the songs on Land of Dreams that is especially dark and mysterious is "Bad News from Home," which seems different from many of your songs.

Yeah. It's an angry guy. It's, again, one of those things that's a little bit like a made-for-TV drama in which he follows the wife to Mexico. It touches on the sort of Jim Harrison areas that I don't like: the tough ex-patriots. But it doesn't quite get there. But it feels good, and it works. It's dark, scary. I can see it very well. But it's unusual, yeah. It has a real anger in it, that's unmitigated by any other emotion. "Red Bandana" is also about someone who is dangerously ignorant—mad, bad and dangerous to know.

That line in "Bad News from Home" that always resonates, both musically and lyrically, is "Sat all night behind a big iron desk / the oil on the water made a rainbow."

Gas station. That's what I thought. It isn't clear. But I see him at a gas station in the rain, sitting behind one of those big iron desks that they have there.

That song, especially as it's on the same album as "I Want You to Hurt Like I Do" and "Four Eyes," also seemed autobiographical.

No. Maybe. For the first time in my life, I had difficulty with a divorce and getting married again. I had a hard love time. I had a hard time with matters of the heart, where I was getting pushed and pulled and getting hurt. "I Want You to Hurt Like I Do," I meant to be comedic, believe it or not. As you know. It is funny. That kind of callousness is funny, taken to that extent. I'm not sure that it isn't true about human beings: that when we're in a hole, we want someone in there with us. But if I did feel that way, I would never admit it, and I would never say it to a little boy, to my son. So that's what makes it okay. But I think people are surprised that it's comedic. But it's not surprising to me.

Simon is someone who hasn't allowed his work to diminish. He said it's because he's still interested, and that maybe people lose interest in it after a while.

Certainly you're less connected to what's going on. Or you get tired with what you're doing. Jimmy Webb was attacked for writing great tunes, and he wanted to rock. He was a young man living that rock life. And he was writing these great tunes, like "Wichita Lineman" and "Galveston." Sometimes people don't know the gift they have. He wanted to rock. So sometimes people drift away from it on that account.

With Paul or with me, interest is too moderate of a word. It's life or death, in a lot of respects. I can't speak for him, but to a large degree, wrongly, it's how we measure ourselves. How we judge ourselves as existing. It's how I do.

You know, movie songs and stuff like that are slightly less rigorous. It serves its purpose.

This guy Bloom wrote this book called *The Western Canon* in which he lists what he thinks are the great works of man. And this is a controversial list. There's tons of stuff in there: Homer. All the great poets. All of Shakespeare. But there were guys who tried consciously for the pennant. They tried to be best. Dante did, obviously. Maybe Cervantes did. Joyce did.

There was an idea that isn't talked about much in the arts now about being the best. We sort of know it's kind of foolish. There is no best. But that's what I've wanted to be most of the time. The best. *The* best songwriter that was. And you never get it, or you don't know if you get it. But sometimes you feel like you've got it. It's a tradition that has sort of gone away. I don't know if writers have that kind of ambition now. And when they do have it, it's a big sprawling thing that we sort of laugh at. But I know Paul's got it in him, the feeling. Like Sting does. Like Prince does. Of reaching for the banner.

In our field, I guess it's the Beatles. I never thought they were better than I was. I didn't have the same feeling about them that everybody else did. I'd get worried when I heard something like "Strawberry Fields" or a shocking thing like "A Day in the Life." Or what Brian Wilson would do. "Good Vibrations," the record. But it's that narrow of a focus. My mind did and does sort of work that way.

I'm not embarrassed to admit that I still think sometimes—not consciously while I'm working—that I want the laurel wreath. I should never say it, I guess. But I don't know how unusual it is anymore. I think Billy Joel feels that way too. There's some kind of burn in some people. I think a lot of people have it and they don't know. There are writers through history, in several cases, like Goethe, in Part Two of *Faust*, is trying for Shakespeare. And certainly Dante made it. And in music, I think the Beatles were thinking that way and made it. And Paul, in *Graceland*, he could feel that he made one of the best records of all time.

Dylan?

Dylan, yeah. Definitely. Yeah. He would never admit to it. But I believe he wanted the laurel, won the laurel, and wore the laurel. [*Laughs*] It's a smaller field. It isn't like novels. Mailer would do brawling attempts at it. Because usually the attempt doesn't work. You can't try to do art. You can't try to do Dante. But you try real hard. [*Laughs*]

Even Dylan wrote "When I Paint My Masterpiece." There does seem to be an urge among artists to create something that will be a masterpiece and outlive them.

Yeah, but it's an embarrassing thought in these times. I don't know if people would want to admit it. When I hear something great by Sting, I'm not unreservedly happy for him. And I used to hear stuff by Carole King, and I loved it, but I knew I couldn't do it, so I had to do better.

In this artform, great songwriting doesn't always equal hit songwriting.

But I'll tell you something: it's better than any other artform. In terms of sometimes good stuff being rewarded. Think of it. Broadway is absolutely dreadful. Movies are, for the most part, dreadful, and some really bad stuff gets rewarded. When we listen to hits of the past—listen to Hitsville, one of those Motown records—man, that's pretty good.

There's more good stuff done in this field that's been successful. Where merit has been rewarded. Than in other fields. The fiction Top Ten lists are absolutely the worst; the best guys are never in that. I mean never. Every once in a while, Updike will sneak up there or that good book by Cormac McCarthy. That's the biggest disparity of all. Pop music, what's being remembered, isn't some old guy squirreled away in an attic writing songs. It's "Stop, in the Name of Love."

You once said to me that one of your greatest fears was living up to the burden of your own talent—

No, I don't know whether that's it. I think it's a fear of not exploring it. I don't know how much talent I have. I've probably talked to you at times when I was worried that I wasn't working enough. That I wasn't trying enough. And as hard as I've been working—and I couldn't have been working any harder than I have been for the last year and a half—I still haven't been writing songs you've been talking about, a regular Randy Newman-type song, where I sit down and write a song for no reason. And still, the idea of having to do that kind of is daunting.

Just like when Henley sits down to write. It isn't like you're happy about it. I'm not. I envy people who are. But when I'm sitting down to an assignment, I don't feel that. I'm confident I can do it. I've done it so many times. I get scared if there's a scene sometimes and I don't know what to do, and I get stuck for a day. But assignment songs, I've only rarely had trouble. They come really, really fast. So fast that I don't want to say because I don't want people to know.

Because you think it diminishes their value that they came easily?

No. No, I never thought that. I remember "Political Science" came fast. And it's pretty solid. And "God's Song" was quick, with all those names that I didn't even know who they were, they are sort of right chronologically. I knew Cain and Abel but I didn't know who Seth was. But Seth was right in there, too. I was right sort of vaguely. I must have passed by a bible once. [*Laughter*]

Considering how enormous your output has been these last years—all the songs and movie scores, plus a complete musical—does it ease your feeling that you haven't used your talent enough?

No. I don't know what kind of song I'd write if I sat down to write today. I'm not so sure that I haven't been afraid always to compete . . . in the big arena, trying to have hits and stuff. Apparently, I can't write hits myself. Let's face it.

There are really good people in pop music. I don't always know who they are. But it seems to me—and this pisses off the Broadway people, because they've heard me say this—that writing the best score to a Broadway show in the past twenty years ain't like making the best album of the year. Do you know what I'm saying? I mean the best one by our standards. A bunch of great songs. That's tough company. It's sort of the major leagues, the way things are.

I mean, Broadway people are snobbish about it; Sondheim is enormously snobbish about it. I said to him, about *Faust*, I hope you don't mind a few "girl" and "world" rhymes. I do that. And he said, "I do mind." And I said, "I know you do." And he said, "You don't come from that tradition, either." And I said, "Oh, yes I do." Because I do. But I don't care about that.

More people will probably hear this Disney album I just did [*James and The Giant Peach*] than anything that I've done. And the songs are fine, they're not inferior to me. Yet it doesn't feel like being in the arena. What you're covering and what you're talking about, is what is. It's where it's at. It's interesting to talk about the craftsman and the Broadway stuff. But it's making a great record that makes me nervous. You're talking about songs in the big leagues. Broadway isn't the big leagues.

You will continue to try to make Randy Newman albums?

I don't know. Because I don't have a healthy attitude towards it. The other stuff I do. At this age, it's important to be confident. I think there will be. It depends on what kind of call there is. I mean, it's a bit of a fringe operation. I sold 200,000 records here and abroad last record. This one I don't know what will do. We'll see. If someone is interested in paying me to do it, I'll do it.

And I'll always write, I guess. I should have to try, at least, till I think I'm getting worse.

Right now, though, you feel you're still getting better?

I hope so. You don't know. I remember one time I was going to a psychologist, and she said, "I have never met anyone who was so ignorant about the fact that you have a subconscious." I always think I know all my motivations. But you don't know. There is a subconscious. I believe it. [*Laughs*] I think I'm aware of what's behind what I'm doing. But I really don't. I really don't know.

* * *

Van Dyke Parks
Hollywood, California 1989
Los Angeles, California 1996

You take Western, one of the busiest thoroughfares in Hollywood, a street replete with darkness and dereliction and all that is crass and cold about modern times, and you turn off it into a little paradise: a quaint and quiet lane that seems somehow saved over from a previous century.

It's an appropriate place for Van Dyke Parks to live, a man who both in his art and his life hearkens back to times gone by. Since the start of his career, he has followed his especially distinctive muse into musical worlds few writers ever venture near, courageously staying true to the music that moves him, regardless of current trends. He writes fully developed song cycles backed not by drums, guitars or synthesizers but by full orchestras. He steers clear of the modern and mechanical to build songs that are sturdy and that will last: "I don't think a song should fall apart," he says, "like a cheap watch on the street."

His songs haven't fallen apart over the years, neither the ones he wrote with Brian Wilson for the Beach Boys, nor the ones from his own albums. These include his now legendary debut, *Song Cycle*, (released in 1968 with an opening cut, "Vine Street," written and arranged by his friend, Randy Newman), the delightful musical Americana of *Jump* (released in 1985), based on the tales of Brer Rabbit, a magical world unto itself of authentic dialect set to soaring melodies accompanied by banjos, fiddles and full orchestra, and the magical Californian dreamscape of *Orange Crate Art*, with glorious vocals by Brian Wilson, in 1995.

"Van Dyke is ahead of his time," Randy Newman told me, and it's true: Parks is a songwriter able to ponder the future without forgetting or obscuring the past. When I first spoke to him in 1989, he had just put the finishing touches on *Tokyo Rose*, an orchestral scrutiny of America's evolving relationship with Japan. Setting the stage without words like the great cinematographers of the silent era, he allows the orchestra to tell the whole story in the opening song. It's an arrangement of "My Country, 'Tis of Thee" gradually infiltrated by an Oriental influence as Japanese drums, a koto, and the pentatonic scale overtake the patriotic melody.

Parks was born in 1943 in Hattiesburg, Mississippi, raised in Lake Charles, Louisiana and attended the Columbus Boychoir School in Princeton, New Jersey. As a child actor he appeared in many New York TV shows and played Andrew Bonino on the 1953 series "Bonino." After graduating from Carnegie Tech, he moved to Los Angeles and met producer Terry Melcher, who not only hired him to play piano for many recording sessions, but also introduced him to another young genius, Brian Wilson.

Brian was at work on the landmark *Pet Sounds* when he met Van Dyke, and they started writing songs together for the doomed *Smile* album, which never saw the light of day. Parks' penchant for lyrical abstraction troubled the other Beach Boys, who apparently felt their songs should focus only on sand, surf, and California girls. Even with their resistance, Brian and Van Dyke wrote great songs together, most notably "Heroes and Villains" and "Surf's Up."

In 1995 Parks reunited with his old friend Brian Wilson to make a new masterpiece ideal for the conclusion of this century, *Orange Crate Art*. Unlike their previous collaborations, however, Van Dyke did all the writing here, words and music, and Brian was enlisted as lead vocalist. *Orange Crate Art* is pure, undiluted Parks music—bringing us to a musical world mostly forgotten and unexplored by today's songwriters. It's a world of sweet, lush melodies, of lyrics with real rhymes, of orchestral glory and the timeless beauty of human voices in real harmony.

Evoking romantic visions of the California of the past which is preserved forever in the pastoral imagery of actual orange crate art, in these songs one can almost breathe in the fragrance of the citrus groves and orchards that once flourished in the valley before giving way to endless freeways and what Parks accurately refers to as "the suburban nightmare." It's an album that translates the original dream into songs as sweet as those oranges of the past must have tasted. We met at Van Dyke's home for our second interview in 1996 to discuss this extraordinary album.

With his Scottish terrier at our feet and a stubborn crow singing from above, we sat in the shade of ancient trees and talked about the worlds one can make out of words and music: "You're creating a world that you are subject to," he said softly. "It's transcendental, and beyond possession."

His priorities are perhaps most clearly revealed by a tale he told concerning his daughter, Elizabeth, who was nine at the time. When she confessed to him, in tears, that she wanted to love all of his songs but didn't like a song on

Tokyo Rose, he obliged her and removed it from the record. It was the album's solitary rock-tinged song, the one the record company had designated to be both the single and the video.

"Do what you do and do it well, and don't be doing what somebody else is doing," he said, collecting his half-smoked cigarettes in his hand as if to mark the time. "It is not natural to me to be successful doing what somebody else is doing."

Do you remember writing your first song?
My first song was called "Brown Dog." And it went, "Brown dog, brown dog, amen, amen."

Sounds religious.
Yes, I was on a very religious trip then. I can't calculate how old I was. It's not a remarkable effort. But it's from, I think, a four-year-old boy.
I did write it down. But it discouraged me, "Brown Dog" did.

Why?
Because there wasn't enough exposition and a whole bunch of stuff that makes a song interesting. And I must say, I didn't have the knack and I *still* don't. I work for everything I do. Very hard. I can only refer to my own private process because I don't know anybody else's private process. And I *wouldn't dare* to ask, simply because I'm in a more vulnerable position on this issue than you are [*laughs*] 'cause I haven't been asking what you did unto others. [*Laughs*]
Songs have a tremendous closeness to the soul. The psalms was my first all-time favorite in the Bible. David's psalms. I've always venerated a timeless, higher power. I always had the idea that I was under God, and that's the way I try to live, so I pay attention to things like the psalms.
I have no idea what's going on with this heavy metal stuff. I can't *understand* the theater of alienation. I don't think it should be done in song or reinforced musically. I think that it's called obscenity where I come from. I don't get it. I don't get the conveyance of hostility.
When I write a song, I do it for a purpose. Usually. Many melodies spring from a shower. And it's easy to hum them, but then something must be done. You must get out of the shower and get to the table. You have to get your clothes on and maybe make a bed. Then you must get to the piano with your cup of coffee or whatever *you do*, and you have to start. You have to write it down and capture the melody. That's how I work. I capture a melody.

And melodies generally come to you when you're not thinking about them?
Yes. When you're thinking of other things, when you're thinking of cabbages and kings and anything else but application or certainly, to me, commerce.
I love nineteenth century songs so much. Because I love the melodies of the pre-industry. I do want to be part of this century though. And I feel there should be in songwriting—if it's on a record, and it has been funded—it should

convey things. And what it should convey, in my case, is what is on the universal mind. So that's what I try to do. I try to make them understandable.

Do your songs always spring from an initial melody?

Yes. I always hang the words on a melody. You know the old joke, which comes first, the music or the words? The answer is the phone call. [*Laughs*] That's an old Brill Building saying. But for me, the music and the words usually come before the phone call.   —

The melody is always developed without any other purpose. To realize a good melody . . . *that* is what is happening in REM, in rapid eye movement. That is what happens in the dreamscape. That is the treasured moment when you don't *have* to think of anything. And every man would want to find the grace and the wisdom and the luck to have those moments every day.

For years you have written amazing, interesting melodies. What do you look for in a melody?

Music has to appear before me. Once it does, I try to find something in the melody that suggests a very specific place. An attitude, a feeling. No matter how ugly that feeling might seem. I do what's at hand.

I met William Saroyan once, the author, in New York after a play that I was in. And I said to him, "How do you get it done?" And he said, "I sit down every morning; I write 'The dog runs.' If it takes me ten days doing that, I write, 'Perhaps the dog runs fast.' " I stay on the clock. I don't get my knickers twisted if I don't get a certain amount of songwriting done. Because composure is what it's all about. But you must go there. You must make a habit of the luxury and the sanctuary that songwriting provides. You're creating a world that you're subject to. Or at least you're responding to a world that you're subject to. It's transcendental. It's beyond possession, it really is.

What do you feel makes a melody great?

A melody is first an exposition. It goes somewhere from somewhere. A melody takes us through time. A good melody indicates its harmonic development. The melodies that I work on are highly derivative. This is the way I work. I realize that I have heard something before. But *I never know* exactly where. But I think a good melody can be evocative. It can remind you of someplace that you've been. And if a melody jars memory, I think it serves a great purpose.

I use melodies as evocative tools. Tools which jar memory, so that a feeling of familiarity and safety is created. So that, perhaps objectionable or revolutionary thoughts, or unsettling thoughts, can be accommodated. The melody, to me, should be comforting. Or easily digested. Invitational. So that the thought may be accommodated. That's what I try to do.

Do you invent a melody note by note, or do you have the sense of a whole tune popping into your head?

It pops.

Does that happen a lot, or only when you're working?

That is when I'm not working. I do all of the grunt work when I'm working. Work is the grunt stuff. I do everything but what is important when I'm working. I work on the first violin. I've been working on setting a poem by

Lord Kirchener. And I've been working on only one phrase for a long time. It's a matter of eight syllables.

To me, songwriting is like a hydra. You slay one beast and you end up with two more. And it's a defiance, and you have to stay on it until you get yourself out of the problem. You're not satisfied until you've tied off the last suture. So I'm working on it now.

What do you think the source of those melodies that come to you is?

All of the melodies I lay some proprietary claim to have come from the Church. They come from plainsong, or from low or high hymns. They just come out of that experience. And I think of that the way I think about folk music. I think they come from your earliest recollections. I think you get them on the edge of your experience. That's where I get mine. Songwriting is all about memory. I think that that's what melody is all about. To me, it's the aesthetic equivalent of the Big Bang. This is where you find out where your origins are, and you find out why you want to go where it is that you are going. I think it's the greatest process of discovery. And those melodies come from a place that is beyond conscious ability. They expand and lengthen your experience, and take you beyond your time and place.

Recently the New York Times ran an article about what they called "the death of the standard." And their definition of what makes a standard is a great melody.

I think that melodies are what distinguish standards. But I think that there's a general confusion about what lyrics should do in a standard. I think people expect more from a song emotionally than they used to. Songs have to have a higher emotional impact, I think.

I agree. Yet when people discuss standards, many contend that those lyrics were superior to lyrics that came later.

But you listen to the old songs of a generation or more ago preceding us, and it seems to me—I'm not sure if this is my own take on it or if this is a fact—the lyrics are almost soporific, almost sleep-inducing. Compared to the lyrics that I hear today. Which are more along the lines of "Switchblades of Love," things of that sort. They have more of a bite to them. More violence. Relationships are more violent. And songs from the golden age of standards, the evergreens that came out during the '30s and '40s and even the '50s were more of a retreat, a comfort zone. Escapist by nature. Music I hear today is not so escapist.

Is this an improvement?

I don't know. I don't know what songs are supposed to do. [*Laughs*] I have fewer and fewer opinions. As I grow, I have fewer opinions. I have heightened sensibilities about it. I will say that to me, what's missing musically is that popular songs of our age are bereft, musically. They have very diminished musical accomplishment. In comparison to the songs of the craftsmen who were milling this stuff out in the lattice days of the Brill Building. I think that the New York Times article is correct in its assumptions about that. That the singer-songwriter, the personalities who have brought their own songs to the marketplace, have inundated the market with some inferior goods. That's the way I feel about it. Personality has much more to do with the selling of the song and musicality much less. Presentation is everything and substance is wanting. That's the way I feel about it.

You're speaking only about the music?

Yes. I don't have any opinion about lyrics. Because, to me, lyrics are no-man's land. Lyrics, to me, are sacrosanct. I have no complaints with anyone's lyrics.

One of the changes in songwriting is that so many of today's songwriters write on guitar instead of piano, thus greatly changing the harmonic and melodic structures of songs.

I've often wished I could still play guitar. The guitar produces special results. You know that. If it's used as a reference in songwriting, it produces much different results than songs conjured at a piano. You can just feel it. And I like them both. But I do miss the participation of the piano in today's music. You can feel that there is an absence of pianists as singer-songwriters. So in that way I step into the arena in a field of forfeit. As a pianist, a songwriter who writes at the piano.

I feel that on [*Orange Crate Art*] the songs are pianistic in nature. They are more or less piano exercises that happen to have words as an afterthought. Most of them.

Do you conceive of the melodies apart from the piano, as pure melody?

Absolutely. Then I go through an elaborate intermediary period where I'm working at the piano to bring the melody forth. Sometimes I'll spend a couple of months ruminating about it. In a certain key, or at a certain tempo. Then I'll lose that entire effort. I wrote "Orange Crate Art" in E flat and sing it in G. I like it there.

Do you feel each key has its own individual character?

Certainly on piano, keys have a personality and an atmosphere of their own. Away from the ephemera that all these great composers have felt about keys. The attitudes of keys, the synesthetic relationships of keys that composers like Beethoven or Mozart or Tchaikovsky, all have somehow without talking about it, have all agreed on the synesthetic relationships of these keys.

When you are thinking of a melody, do you choose a particular key for its nature?

Yes. Something does feel very romantic to me and introspective in a way about keys that have a lot of black notes. There's something tremendously exotic about G flat or F sharp. It's not bright. I get a visual impression of those keys. I think everybody does, whether they know it or not.

It seems to me that the majority of your songs are in major keys as opposed to minor.

Yes. That's true.

Why do you think that is?

I don't know. I was reading in the New York Times about the "Jewish song." Cole Porter wanted to write the Jewish song in a minor key. What was it, "I Love Paris"? He always wanted to write the Jewish song. Turns out the

American song was being written by a lot of recent immigrants to the United States, defining the American culture. A lot of them happened to be Jewish, and Cole Porter looked at the gifts of people like George Gershwin and Irving Berlin with an obvious envy. He didn't understand how it came so easily to all these people, to define America with their songs. A lot of them were in minor keys.

It's a funny thing, isn't it? How people think minor [key] songs are somehow more contemplative than major [key] songs.

Sting said he felt it's easier to write a pretty melody in a minor key.

Well, it is, yeah. Been a long time since I wrote one in a minor key. I wrote "San Francisco" in a minor key. That was written in E minor.

That one has a great rhythm.

That was a fun rhythm. It went from a shuffle feel to straight eighths. The song is very complex, actually.

Songwriting isn't something I do to express myself. I don't express myself. I express a point of view. But to me, songwriting is a discipline. It's no more familiar to me than the crossword puzzle, which I also do. It's an exercise. Sometimes I think it's an exercise in futility, considering the small popularity of the work that I've done. It's a subsistence. An avocation. But I love songwriting. It's also the most personal thing I do.

Isn't that contradiction? How can it be like a crossword puzzle and the most personal thing you do?

But it is, because crossword puzzles are very highly personal.

But the difference is that there's only one right way to complete a crossword puzzle, as opposed to writing a song.

Yes, that's right. But in any song, there is a central truth. And you either find it, or you allude to it. At best. But a successful song, there is something clairvoyant about it, and I had tried to find that. So it is a highly personal thing. But it also has a great deal of figuring to it. The point of inspiration is always a faint memory by the time the song is completed. There's so much to do. Just to rope it in. To get it into a form of memory, either paper—in my case I write them down—or tape.

I guess the highest praise for the form is that there is no one correct answer. I guess that's a high form of praise. That's probably why I like it. I have never learned a repeatable approach pattern to songwriting. There's no right way of writing songs. Isn't that funny?

Yes. And not one songwriter I've spoken to in all these years can offer a singular approach.

You've been with so many people in interviews, and I've read them and enjoyed the ones I've read. So much. And yet, nothing is revealed. Everything is revealed, yet nothing is revealed. What is transferable in the interviews with songwriters, what I get from them, is this sense of courage, of derring-do. This is transferable. This is infectious. I love that. That's highly contagious. And confirmational. It's as helpful as belonging to some religious sect, to me. Hearing someone say, "Amen."

But beyond that, I don't know what the hell any of these people are doing, or how they're doing it. I don't understand it. I don't know how Elton John can get these lyrics from Bernie Taupin and write a song in fifteen minutes. I don't understand it.

But he might say the same thing about you, that he doesn't understand how Van Dyke could write a whole lyric to a finished melody, which many people think is much more difficult than writing a melody to a lyric. And a lyric with inner rhymes and a perfect structure.

Lyrics are hard. I get the impression, when I'm working on a lyric, for example, because I love internal rhymes and a highly crafted lyric, what some people think of as highly pretentious or overly managed words. At one point, in our songwriting history, this was a prerequisite for a good song. A highly crafted, a heavy internal rhyme scheme. Those things are thought of as elaborate and somehow out of step.

And yet, I think, people do respond to that kind of structure when they get to hear it.

They should be aware of it. I'm comforted by such craft. I love it. But there is a time when instinct is the higher teacher. There's a time when internal rhymes—enough of them. There's enough of it. It's like you get to a point of what they say in New Orleans is "obzakee"—one too many spices in a dish. There gets to be a point when you don't want to have so many internal rhymes.

I remember watching Robert Altman when he was doing *Popeye*. With a camera on a boat. And a fast moving sky filled with clouds. Shooting an object on another boat. There were no fixed points, you see. I feel very much like I'm at sea when I'm working on lyrics. Melodies are easy to me. But lyrics are not. Lyrics are very difficult. There are no knowns to me. The lyric is a total leap of faith. And a highly abstract process. Melodies are easy in comparison.

Though your process might be abstract, the lyrics themselves are far from abstract, especially as compared to earlier work such as *Song Cycle*.

Yes, those days of free association in lyrics are over for me.

Was there a reason you made that shift?

Yeah. When I looked at the sales report from the songs I wrote, I decided I would not do that again. So I retired from that, but I still think it's a valid idiom. Certainly one for James Joyce, who influenced my decision to enter that in a poetical attempt. But, you know, I'm basically where I was then. I was too young to be a beatnik and too old to be a flower child. And basically, I still have this iconoclastic and highly individual approach to songwriting. And I enjoy it very much. It's an honor, and I'm happy to do it. Even without my abstractionist ideals of my youth. I enjoy songwriting and I think it's so dynamic a field that I hope to continue it till I die. I like the songs I last did the best. I think my work improved. The songs are, I think, more accessible than ever before, which is important.

I agree that these songs on *Orange Crate Art* are wonderful, as are the orchestrations, and the sound of Brian Wilson singing them. It's a nourishing thing to hear in this day and age.

Well, I hope so. It was important on personal terms. To be able to work on songs for Brian Wilson, with the power of his reputation and his body of work behind him. Those were all impressive precedents. As I worked on the record, I thought about his reputation and trying to protect it and nurture it, as I was trying to, of course, build my own by doing it. But it started out to be impossible to do the record, and I'm surprised we got it done.

I brought a lot of precious articles of thought to bear in this project, so I hope it reveals something of the timeless pleasures this sense of place has brought me. That's what the record was built for. It was highly responsive to the art that depicted California.

Was this an idea you had for a while?

I had no idea, before I began the record, what the record was about. And I never do. I never have an idea. Somebody came up with the expression, "concept record." And I thought that was an amusing description. I had no concept of any record that I've ever done. I just do the record. I just go from one song to the next, and follow the hope that I will complete the requirements of the job, which is now ten songs. And I just hope that I get it finished. That becomes the obsession. Then there does come a certain point when you realize you are finished. And at that point, if you have your act together, you claim territory for some concept. And I've never had that faculty for leadership. I don't know what I'm doing. I never do when I'm recording. And if you can find an executive producer or a finance department somewhere who will trust that process, I think sometimes you come up with something tremendously individual and valuable. If you're fortunate enough to find that degree of trust, I think you can find areas of exploration that matter.

How do you make the leap from not being able to escape a subject, to being able to effectively translate it into song? How, for example, did you create "White Chrysanthemum" from Tokyo Rose?

It starts with plainsong. Plainsong, that most ancient of Druid musical forces. The nice thing about plainsong is that you can put any number of notes onto it. It stays on one chord. I stayed on one chord and said, "Somewhat overwhelmed by the dimension of her lovely breast" and on the word "breast" I changed the chord. And I had to make that make sense so I said, "The rector turns his face from Mother Nature back to God." I wanted to make the priest human, so he's paying attention to Mother Nature's breast, [*laughs*] and then I reminded myself that I wanted to do something serious so I used the word "God." And then I decided he would say something, and that was, "Therefore in the valley of the shadow we are truly truly blessed," that rhymed—"now we return our brother to the sod."

Okay, so that all rhymed. I took that as a successful effort, probably taking me five days of rigorous work to repeat that on the next couplet where it gets harder. So I did the funeral scene. I got the man in the ground. That's why I say it's my most favorite song; it's the most successful song on this album. Because it took effort.

When working on songs, what tools do you use?

I've got music paper which has eleven lines at the top. I write the melody, the chords, and I write the words on the third line. After I do a great deal of writing, I go to the computer and refine what it is I'm trying to do. But the pen is mightiest. Actually I work with a mechanical pencil at all times. Not satisfied with the eraser situation in that kind of thing, but it's the best. I keep a gum eraser next to me. These are survival mechanisms. I have an easel. I have my computer to the right of the piano.

You've described detailed approaches to crafting a song, using a great deal of design and conscious thought. Are the best songs written this way?

Absolutely. Song is craftsmanship. You look at Randy Newman and you see what a craftsman is. The key is a great craftsman.

Randy told me that he sits at the piano every day and works. Is this what you do?

Oh, absolutely. I didn't know that. As a matter of fact, I think he's lying. But I'm telling the truth. I work hard for what I do. And I don't think anyone holds a candle to me in terms of effort.

So songwriting for you is a daily activity?

There are months that go by that I don't write songs. I go out and take care of the garden; I take care of the realities. I get the house reroofed and painted and stuff. Pick the kid up from school—both kids, if I'm lucky. And in the meantime I stay *plastered* to the news.

So to connect with those realities beyond everyday life you stay aware of this reality.

Yes. I find something that moves me. Kinky Friedman said, "Find what you like and let it kill you." [*Laughs*]

I have a small output of music. My best work, and least conspicuous, has been in the service of other records. But I'm inescapably interested in songwriting and about every five years I get interested in doing that. And I work very hard at it.

I can't afford to write songs all year. I have to do jobs. If the birds go up in the air for PBS, there are some flutes going up with them. Those projects are not temblors, as they say in the earthquake business. They won't shake the world. But those projects teach me something, and it influences the way I think when I write tunes. So I stay in a musical environment at all times.

What was it like the first time you and Brian Wilson tried working together back in the sixties?

He was very fair. He gave me a five thousand dollar check so that I could buy a car. He gave me half of the writer's royalties. He got me off of a motorcycle and into a Volvo without a contract. I call that pretty decent. I'm sure it was a pleasure working for him, but that's less important.

But what the two of you came up with was incredible. A song like "Heroes and Villains"—

Well, it was a start. It was stopped in its tracks. Not by sibling rivalry, but there was a very difficult time. The Beach Boys were in court for about eighteen million dollars at the time and an open admission that Capitol Records had been completely dishonest with them. It was a great scandal, and the pressure from that produced some good music [*laughs, and then softly*] but some not so good. . . .

Would Brian give you a finished melody to write words to?

He did the melodies. The melody to "Heroes and Villains"—every note has a sound syllable to it. It sounded like a Marty Robbins tune, like a ballad, so I thought it would be a good idea to have it: "I've been in this town so long that back in the city I've been taken for gone and unknown for a long time / Fell in love years ago with an innocent girl from the Spanish and Indian home of the heroes and villains." All those words. I was working like a son of a bitch. And then he would say, "That's good." And then he would say, "Let's call it 'Heroes and Villains,' " and I would say, "That's grand. Let's do." [*Laughs*]

Songwriting is a racket and we know that and we wish it weren't. I think you know that.

It seems it can be a racket or not, depending on how you play it.

The songs that come to the public attention are subject to the same processes that bring songs that shouldn't come to the public attention. But, hey—bright lights, big city. This is nice here. I have enough room to write.

But if you wanted to play the game, you could. Yet you do your own work, completely different from what is making it in the marketplace, and let the world deal with it.

I'm not trying to do anything novel. I'm trying to do what good songs have forever done. Songs should outlive their writers. They should stand the test of time. Some songs you hear the first time, and you know they haven't stood that test.

I like to come back to songwriting because it is, relatively speaking, an unobstructed window into the soul. It's a *very nice* escape, too.

Now that I'm getting older, I want to be known for having written good songs. That really matters to me. I want my children, if they find a trunk somewhere that isn't too mildewed, to think I was a real swell guy. On top of it in a way. [*Softly*] I want to look good to my family.

Did you begin writing the songs for *Orange Crate Art* with the thought of Brian Wilson doing the singing, or did that idea come later?

It was between jobs. I wanted to do a record because I had nothing else to do. So I went to Lenny [Waronker] and played him the song "Orange Crate Art" and he liked it. And then I went out to Brian and asked him to do it, and we went into the studio and got that one done, and I had no idea what I wanted to do next.

Did he like the song when he heard it?

He liked it okay. This is a guy who wrote . . . [*Pause*] "God Only Knows" what he wrote. [*Laughter*] Everything.

I didn't expect to get any flattery from him. And I worked in the studio for two and a half hours, and he was very nervous, and so was I, and we got it done in two and a half hours. And then Lenny liked the result, so we went on. But in each case it was very difficult to tell what Brian's real take on it was. I think it was more or less of a consolation for him to do the album. It was a labor of love for him. He didn't commit the songs to memory. We went sentence by sentence, and doubled each sentence. You miss a lot of proprietary values in a vocal performance when you do it that way.

Did you consider doing the singing yourself originally?
Yes, I did. When I wrote it. But then I thought of this word "orange." You know, it's just a fascinating word, for obvious reasons. And I thought Brian should sing that word.

Because of the California implications?
Yeah. I thought he would really put the right stamp on it.

So after the first song, you decided to have Brian sing all the rest?
No, I didn't think so. I think Lenny Waronker thought that I should do that. We went on to "Sail Away." We did the songs in the order that you hear them.

You had mentioned that Brian insisted on bringing in two bowls filled with ice water to dunk your heads into, which you did. And you said, "One can't deny the invigorating effects of your head in a bowl of ice water." [*Laughter*]
Brian did one thing during the album that totally astounded me. He loves Diet Coke, and when I tossed him one, he caught it behind his back and popped the top. It was incredible. If I was the president of Coca-Cola, I would want that on film. [*Laughter*] Harry Nilsson could do things like that. Harry once sunk a basket at the Forum from half-court. Just to remind you who was in charge. [*Laughter*] It was beyond belief. My God.
So I'm happy with the record. And I think it's the most distinct work I've managed in a thirty year career in avocational record production. But, it to me was important for one reason: it renewed my relationship with Brian Wilson. It helped bring new events to the relationship and the promise of working again. And that's why I did it. So I achieved my objective. Everything but sales.

Do you ever feel limited by the songform?
Limitation creates form. That's something that Krishnamurti said. It's always nice to think about when you're feeling limited.

In your work, you take traditional forms and use them in new, unlimited ways.
I do believe in gilding the lily. This is an industry in which you have to provide every move for demonstration of a song. You're not allowed to be poor and write songs. You must be wealthy. If you have a synthesizer, you're a composer. I mean, give me a break.

In light of that, is composing fun for you? Is creating and solving these puzzles enjoyable?
Yeah. It's a great privilege. I fight for it. I haven't been successful commercially. Every record is produced on a wing and a prayer. That doesn't change my sense of abandonment in trusting that it will develop well. If I just use my known gifts and work as hard as I can, something's gonna end up on a record that will be an entertainment.

I won't ask the question of you, but the question begs: Can anybody really be happy with work? If your work is in progress, in a way, I think you can be satisfied with the results, because they suggest a development.

I think too much attention is placed on what is seen. A song is a suggestion of the reality that lies beyond. The reality that makes these songs, to me, important is that they refer to a great issue. I think I've thrown some pretty good stuff up against the wall, and I think it should stick. I mean, I *believe* that.

Few people stretch the boundaries of what songs can do. Your work shows us that there is a world of content that hasn't even been touched yet in songs. Do you feel that?

Yes, I believe that. That songs could take on more. But I'm not trying to develop the songform. I'm trying to suggest in the geometry of the song the ideas that must be expressed. I give that room. This is not a commercial consideration, I'm sorry to say. And for that reason, these songs have a tendency to last.

Songwriting is a matter of self-discovery. I just don't want to have to wade through that dirt to get to that flower.

I don't think a song should fall apart like a cheap watch on the street. I think it's important to make a song a renewable resource. Something that can be listened to again.

When pouring the coffee, you said you didn't want to get too awake when writing songs. What do you mean by that?

A cup of coffee, to me, comes when I'm working on everything from the first violin down. Lyrics and melody—those things come in a non-narcotic state. They must be carved out stoically.

There's a German word for that moment between inspiration and execution. I get that, not with a paintbrush under the Sistine Chapel. I get that with this rather menial songwriting thing with the tools.

I want that moment of contemplation or meditation when you're moving with this thing, you're not in a lotus position, you're working like a hornet out of hell; all of that work is supportive of the original revelation. Something is revealed to you. Perhaps it's something that you've experienced many times but never on this level.

So you work within that emotional frame. And it's essential that a song convey emotionality. It doesn't have to be a first degree burn. It's an embarrassing pursuit because of its vulnerability.

You said songwriting is a revelation. What is the source of that revelation?

It is always the truth that matters. It's the truth that everyone wants.

An absolute truth?

Yes, the truth is absolute. Many people write for many different reasons. I know why I write. It's always nice when it goes well and every song is to me like offspring. It matters that much.

Songwriting should represent its central value, that it is a triumph. That it is born at all is a triumph of the human spirit.

* * *

Janis Ian
Hollywood, California 1988
Nashville, Tennessee 1992

Janis Ian is onstage alone, performing a version of her now classic "At Seventeen" that seems more heart-rending than ever on this rainwashed day. Off-stage, one of her first mentors, the great folksinger Odetta, turns her back on the throng of press folks tossing questions her way to rush stage-side and listen. Later, when asked if it was the song "At Seventeen" that was special to her, Odetta answered explicitly: "It's Janis Ian who is special."

Odetta is not alone in this estimation. Since Janis Ian was sixteen and stunned the world with the urgency and beauty of her song, "Society's Child," she's been on a special path in this world: a path of words and music, of gracefully honest poetry and stunning melodies, of rich albums filled with timeless songs.

I first spoke to Janis, along with her then-partner Kye Fleming, when they came to my Hollywood office for an interview in 1988. The occasion for our second interview in 1992 was the release of *Breaking Silence*, her first solo album in many years.

She was born Janis Eddy Fink on May 7, 1951, and wrote her first song, "Hair of Spun Gold" at the age of twelve, under the influence of many male folksingers, such as Pete Seeger, Phil Ochs and Bob Dylan. "I was real male role model identified at the time," she explained. "I thought, well, Dylan and Ochs were writing their own songs so why shouldn't I?" Gender, of course, wasn't the only difference between Janis and the others. They also happened to be adults and she was still a kid, one of many limitations she refused to let get in her way. While Dylan—as an adult—had trouble facing the fans who felt betrayed by his electric conversion, Janis—at sixteen—had to face similar hostility from folk purists about putting drums on "Society's Child." She also had to deal with the sad fact of racism in America—the integrational message she was delivering in her song was something many people actively tried to silence. "There were a lot of threats," she remembered. "There were whole areas of the country I couldn't tour in. A lot of bomb threats. A lot of envelopes with razor blades. That was scary because I didn't understand it. I didn't understand people wanting to *hurt* me."

She also had to deal with an enormous amount of notoriety and fame at such a fragile age that she never had time to adjust to it, and it was over before she understood what had happened. "It was pretty bizarre at the age of sixteen to be the hope of your generation," she said. "A lot of people expected me to burn out and die young or save the world somehow. And that's very scary. It's scary when you're thirty. But it's *real* scary when you're sixteen."

At seventeen, Janis Ian called it quits. She played her last concert, walked offstage and told her manager it was over. She turned away from her career, but she couldn't turn away from songwriting. "I always knew I had something to say but I felt like I had no clue how to go about it," she said. She didn't write another song for a long time. It wasn't until she heard Don McLean's "Vincent" on the radio that she regained the will and spirit to write. And the song she wrote was so close to the bone for her that she couldn't sing it in public for two years. It was called "Stars."

When she was ready to sing again in public, she essentially had to start over from scratch. "Stars" was rejected by seventeen different record companies. In a single week, one company said she was a great singer but should stop writing, while a manager was pushing her to stop singing and only write songs. "If you look at my career," she said, "which has been so up and down and so weird, I don't think anyone should ever be discouraged." Janis refused then, as she had many times before and since, to be discouraged, and eventually got a new deal, and made a number of great albums: *Stars*, which also includes maybe her most beautiful ballad, "Jesse," *Aftertones*, which features "Hymn," an absolutely breathtaking vocal collaboration between Janis, Phoebe Snow and Odetta, and *Between the Lines*, with "At Seventeen" as well as the beautiful "In The Winter."

"It's vital to give kids the knowledge that songs *begin* somewhere," she said, "and that there's something bigger than lasers and Nintendo. Otherwise, where will the next generation of songwriters come from?"

When working on a song, do you think out what it is you are trying to express, or do you let the words flow and then piece it together?

I think it's a combination. I write a lot from instinct. I'll go out on the terrace and come back with something, and I won't quite be sure where I'm going.

But as you're writing out of instinct, once you reach a certain level as a songwriter, the craft is always there talking to you in the back of your head. So you may be moving forward on instinct, but there's a little Geiger counter in the back of your head that tells you when it's time to go to the chorus, when it's time to rhyme. Real basic craft. And the nice thing about having enough craft is that you can go on instinct then, because it's second nature.

I love strange chords. But sometimes you've got to throw it out. You want to jar people when they need to be jarred. You don't want to jar them for the sake of jarring them. I think that's something that you do when you're real young.

Does having knowledge of music theory ever get in the way of the instinctual process?

I think it gets in the way just in terms of a mind-set. But I think that happens to anybody who writes or plays a lot, whether you've got theory or not. And I don't have formal theory training. I think what gets in my way more is just that I've written so many songs, I don't want to repeat myself, and there's a finite amount of chords.

Do you find, on both piano and guitar, that you go to the old familiar patterns you've played before?

That's a main advantage of co-writing. 'Cause when I played alone I was in a rut from about 1980 or so until 1986 when I started co-writing. And I think a lot of the reason was that when you first start writing, you have no preconceived ideas, you just have whoever you are trying to copy. And because you have so many different influences, you're going to try and fit them all into every song. But after about fifteen years or so, you develop your own style and sound and your own boring routines.

I'll automatically go from a Csus2 to a G/B to a Gm/B flat to an Asus4 and then resolving back to the G.

Yeah, you have a lot of those descending bass lines.

A *lot*. Because I like bass. I try to stay away from the same old chords, because I find them boring.

Do you feel that writing abstract songs is easier than clear, concrete songs?

It depends. When you write a verse that is abstract, and I think this is a lesson from country music, the chorus better make it clear. And when the chorus is abstract, you need a very basic verse.

It depends on your goal, too. I mean, my goal is to write great songs. Not basic songs or hit songs but great songs that reach the maximum amount of people, because I think we're touching on some real important subject matters that people tend not to write songs about, and that are hard to get an audience to hear. There is so much sloganeering about AIDS and about the homeless that people are fed up with slogans, and it is very hard to reach them on an emotional level with anything that sounds sociological.

How old were you when you wrote "Society's Child"?

Fourteen when I wrote it, fifteen when we cut it, sixteen when it was a hit.

Was it based on true facts?

Naw . . . I was living in an all-black neighborhood; I was one of three white people in the school. In New Jersey. East Orange. And I saw it happening a lot in reverse: Black parents would get very upset if their kids were dating whites. Because it's a harder life, and it was much harder then.

My own people, the folkies, had to wear work shirts and blue jeans, and I took a lot of flak for using drums on "Society's Child." And the other people were so caught up in what they looked like and what did the neighbors think. Which I thought was stupid.

At that age I saw it a lot less gently than I see it now. I think being a little older has made me a little more forgiving. But at the time of that song, I just thought they should change or they should all be shot. [*Laughs*] Real basic.

That was quite an advanced song for a teenager to write. Did it surprise you when that song came out of you?

I think there's too much made of age. Most people at that age were busy with other things. They're busy worrying about whether they're going to get into college, whether they have good grades. Stuff like that. I was busy worrying about music. I mean, most of the songwriters I know started writing songs or poetry way young.

I think the only disadvantage to starting at that age and having a hit is that you lose the slack people will give you. Because my first hit was well written musically, at least (lyrically I would do it much different now), it was well written for the time—not for my age, but for the time—I never had the slack that a normal beginning artist at that age might have. I was expected to be absolutely brilliant all the time. And that's a big burden.

Then again, Dylan was expected to be brilliant after that second album all the time. And he was only four or five years older.

Did that pressure get in the way of your songwriting?

Sure it did. I stopped when I was eighteen. I was fried completely for three years. That's when I learned how to orchestrate and how to do what everybody else had already learned, like take drugs for a year, *not* take drugs, date and fall in love . . . not date so much, fall in love . . . and have crushes and open a bank account and drive a car. That was all the stuff I had never dealt with at all.

A lot of people expected me either to burn out and die young or to save the world somehow. And that's very scary. It's scary when you're thirty. But it's real scary when you're sixteen and you're singing to people in their thirties who are coming backstage afterwards and telling you that you have changed their lives. Very scary.

There were a lot of threats from "Society's Child"; there were whole areas of the country that I couldn't tour in. A lot of bomb threats. A lot of envelopes with razor blades in them and things like that. That was scary because I didn't understand it like I can at this age. I didn't understand people wanting to hurt *me*. Pretty frightening.

And you stopped writing songs?

No, I didn't stop. I knew I had something to say, but I had no clue how to go about it, so I walked off stage when I was seventeen and a half and told my manager I was quitting. Very dramatic.

It wasn't until I wrote "Stars" which I wrote after hearing Don McClean's "Vincent" that I knew I could write a song that could make me happy, that would touch people. And I didn't sing "Stars" live for two years because I was too embarrassed.

Was it hard to get another record contract after that period?

"Society's Child" got turned down by twenty-two companies. "Stars" got turned down by seventeen.

That's actually encouraging for songwriters to hear, knowing that great work got rejected.

If you look at my career, which has been so up and so down and so weird, I don't think anybody should ever get discouraged. I mean in one week I had Elektra Records say I was a great singer and I should stop writing, and Harold Leventhal [manager of Pete Seeger, Arlo Guthrie and others] tell me I was a great writer and I should stop singing. So it's real hard to tell. The best you can do is go by your instincts, I think. Pray for rain. So that's the drama of my life.

What made you want to come back?

I thought I had something to say. At the end of the day, when you throw away the economics, and you throw away the age, and you throw away whoever you're with at the time and other assorted pressures, for me it always comes down to "Do I have anything to say or not?" If I don't have anything to say, it's stupid to make a record.

Do you remember writing "Jesse"?

Yeah. "Jesse" took two years. Because I had a first verse and I had no chorus for the longest time. Then I had the second verse and no chorus. And then I had half the chorus and the third verse. It was one of the few times when I was smart enough to not push it. I just let it ride.

One of the things that makes "Jesse" such a strong song, besides its gorgeous melody, is your use of details. Especially that great line about the spread on the bed.

I really write lyric out of instinct. And sometimes, out of the 120 songs or so I've released on albums, there's maybe fifteen or twenty songs that do that. Which is not a real good percentage. There's an attention to detail in "Jesse" that I had hoped to recapture. And just rarely did. I mean, I know the color of the wood on the floor in "Jesse." I know that room, I know that person.

Do you think including actual facts from your own life gives a song more resonance?

It can be a plus or a minus. Because if you get into being real factual, it can get real dead. There's journalistic songwriting, which is a whole different thing from what I do. That's more the Phil Ochs school or the early Bob Dylan school. "Ballad of Hattie Carroll."

How about "At Seventeen"?

Oh, that's me. That's one of the few. That's absolutely me. I don't think you can write a song like that—if it's not your personal experience.

Does it ever get too close to the bone? "Seventeen" is such a personal song. Do you ever feel you're giving away too much?

Yeah, I think that's what makes "Stars" such a hard song to sing. It's not comfortable to be onstage and expose yourself like that because you are so vulnerable at that moment.

How do you generate melodic ideas?
Frantically! [Laughs]

Do ideas ever just pop into your head?
Yeah, they pop in, literally. I mean, I'm not thinking about it, but if I think about it, there's always music going on in the background somewhere. It used to be very confusing when I was a kid, because there would always be something playing in my head. I mean, right now "Jesse" is playing.

Do you work on songwriting every day?
I do on and off. I try to. I talk about it all the time. I do go through periods when I sit down every day and work for four or five hours. And some of my best songs have come that way. But that's usually after a long period of not doing it.

You have to keep your motor oiled, as Stella Adler used to shout at me.

And how do you do that?
God, I wish I knew! [*Laughs*] A good portion of being available to be a writer is that emotionally you keep yourself open as a human being, you keep yourself healthy, you get enough rest, you get enough good food. Because without that you won't have enough energy, and writing takes an enormous amount of energy.

You have to keep yourself optimistic. Because if you're writing from darkness and the black hole of Calcutta, you are not going to be able to write as often as if you are coming from light and airiness and openness.

"Jesse" has a gorgeous melody. Any idea what makes that one, or any melody, so strong?
I don't know. That's something that those people who don't write songs and who write books think about.

That's why I like to talk to songwriters, to people who do it.
I don't think most of us have a clue. Most of us are just blowing air. Because at the end of the day, either you're talented or you're not. And all the craft in the world is not going to make up for that lack.

Do you feel that songs are a more powerful art form than others?
I do. I think music, and song, is the most powerful art form. Because music, with or without words, crosses all boundaries. You don't need education. You will be moved viscerally by music. And some songs are magic, like "Jesse."

Pythagoras felt that specific notes affected people to very minute gradations of feeling. And every songwriter, I think, knows that D is a great key for a love song. It just happens to work. And B flat is always a great jump key for jazz.

In lyrics, there is the hypnosis of the rhyme scheme. And when you combine that with music . . . Look at a song like "We Shall Overcome." How many more people were affected by that song together than by all the speeches in the world? The Woody Guthrie sign on the guitar saying, "This machine kills fascists" is not a lie.

I think you have an enormous responsibility as a songwriter in this world today. Because you have such an effect. I mean, it really scared me, after "Seventeen," when I saw how seriously fifteen year olds were taking the song and the effect it had on them. What is it that made them all feel like killing themselves?

It's a very serious business in that I feel an obligation, if we're going to open up sociological areas like incest or rape or wife-beating, to open them up and not leave them sitting there with your intestines sprawled all over the table.

People identified with "Seventeen" so closely because it's so real; there's comfort in knowing someone else has gone through a situation, even if it's not a hopeful ending.

But the trick in "Seventeen" is that, at the end of the song, the last line is "Ugly duckling girls like me." Because we all know, on an unconscious level, that the ugly duckling turned into a swan.

I think without that ending, the song might have been dismal and might have been a failure. Because it's a song that makes people sad but it makes them relieved.

Do you have any idea where your ideas come from?

[*Laughs*] I think so. Paul Simon said that he thought that the ideas were out there, and it was just whether you managed to grab them or not.

How do you manage to grab them, though?

[*Laughs*] If I knew, I'd have written so many more songs! Again, I think it's being in touch with yourself and being in touch with the world. I think part of being a good writer is that you have to be literate. I don't mean you have to read a lot, but you have to absorb a lot. And be in touch with yourself.

Do you write songs differently when you are writing them for someone else to sing?

Yes. When they're mine I might tend to go a lot more left than I would otherwise. Although, that's hard to say because a song starts to dictate itself after a certain point. You kind of hit that point of no return when you go, "Okay, that's the song." I think the hardest thing to learn as a young writer is to just go ahead and finish the damn thing. Say to yourself, "Okay, this might not be the greatest work of art in the world but I need to get the damn thing done."

So you shouldn't take the Leonard Cohen approach and wait many years if necessary?

It depends. I had the first half of the first verse of "Ride Me Like a Wave" back in '83. "Through The Years," I had the chorus five years ago. So, no, I appreciated a lot what Leonard said about the bits and pieces that will hang around for a lifetime until one day the time is right. It's really hard to know when you're pushing your own river and when to let go of it. I wreck a lot of songs that way by not getting to them fast enough.

It becomes too hard to reconnect with?

Yeah. Or whatever the heart of the original song was has changed. With "His Hands" I had had the idea and kind of the first verse laying there for about three years. And it was just pulling teeth to write that verse. I just couldn't figure out where to go with the chorus or where to go with the other verses.

Do you actively preserve those little pieces, or do you simply remember them?
No, I don't trust my mind to do that. [*Laughs*] No, I scribble a lot and then they all go into a file. I keep specific song notebooks. I've got a set-up where I have staff paper on one side and regular paper on the other, so I can write down melodies.

Most people don't write down music.
It's true, most people don't notate anymore. And if they do notate, they think of it as arranging. I never want to count on my batteries to be alive. All I need is something to write with and something to write on. I keep a lot of scraps. And lately I've been trying once a month to get the discipline to put them all in a book. But it's funny, going through these scraps. It's like going through your past.
Don't most writers write things down?

Mose Allison said that the real great ideas never go away, and the ones you forget aren't worth having anyway. But I do think most do write down their ideas.
I have so many melodies that just pop into my head in a day that if I didn't write them down and then look at them a month later, I'd get inundated. Or I forget that I had that idea. I think we talked about that in our last interview. I think I'm pretty prolific. Melodies pop into my head. There's kind of this running chatter.

And you generally write songs to the melody?
It depends. Sometimes the melody will come with a few lines.
You've been writing strong songs since you were a child. After all these years, do you feel you can trust that your talent will always be there for you?
Yes, I think so. Which is nice. Stella Adler used to always say, "Trust your talent." I think it's a real hard thing to come to grips with your talent in the first place and to not be afraid of it. Or to be afraid of it turning on you, or deserting you. I can pretty much trust it to be there. And that is a real luxury.

It's lack of fear that allows you to trust it?
It frees you up. Anything you can do to free yourself up as a writer, as opposed to indulging yourself, is good. When we're younger we tend to look on freedom as indulgence. And when we get older it becomes more of a responsibility.
Going back to our previous discussion, five years ago, I think therapy helps writers and artists a lot. Good relationships help a lot. Being aware helps a lot. To be aware of your own dark side as well as your light side. And to keep them

in balance. It's all a balance by the end of the day. Everything we do is a balance.

* * *

Frank Zappa
Los Angeles, California 1987

When he was thirteen years old and living in San Diego, Frank Zappa read an article about record seller Sam Goody in *Look* magazine. It claimed that Goody was such a genius that he could sell any album no matter how ugly it was musically. And the album they chose as an example of this ultimate ugliness was *The Complete Works of Edgar Varèse, Volume I*, which featured a percussion piece called "Ionizations." The writer described the piece as "a banging and clanging with sirens and stuff." The young Zappa was entranced, and knew he had to own this album. He made the trek to what was then referred to as the local "Hi-Fi shop," where records were played on the new equipment to demonstrate the magic of "High Fidelity sound."

"I walked into the store and saw this album with a black and white cover and a guy on the front who looked like a mad scientist," remembered Zappa. "I knew it had to be the one. I didn't have enough money to afford it, so I negotiated with him. And he was so happy that anybody would buy it that he sold it for six dollars. Just to get it off his hands. I took it home and listened to it day and night for years."

From that day on, Frank Zappa's life was injected with music both wild and weird, music few of his childhood friends had ever heard of, let alone elected to play in their own homes. As he grew up, Zappa continued in the tradition of his idol, Varèse, in creating sounds and melodies and rhythms and textures entirely his own—music the world had never heard before.

Zappa died on December 4, 1993 in Los Angeles. He was 52 years old. Though his life ended at such a tragically young age, he left behind a body of work much greater than most men ever achieve in a single lifetime. Besides the universe of songs he wrote, Zappa wrote chamber music, orchestral suites, ballets, jazz compositions, concertos, symphonies and more, experimenting with and pushing the boundaries of pretty much every musical form there is. In his songwriting alone there is such a vast range of expression that it shares a quality with Scott Fitzgerald's famous quote about Hollywood, that it's impossible for one person to hold all of its equations in his head at once. Zappa's lyrics were often so barbed and ironic, or so deceptively simple and direct, that people sometimes neglected the compositional complexity and beauty of the music that accompanied them. Even his hit "Dancing Fool" shifted into measures of 10/16 time, a rather complex rhythm for Top Forty radio.

Zappa's soul was perhaps most completely expressed in his instrumental music, in which he was able to explore every rhythmic, tonal, harmonic, sonic and melodic relationship available to human ears. Albums such as *Sleep Dirt* and *Jazz from Hell* are entirely instrumental works that feature music both breathtakingly beautiful and mind-boggling. As he learned at an early age from Varèse, there are no real rules restricting music. It can be anything and everything that a composer can imagine. And the imagination of Frank Zappa was limitless.

When I interviewed him in 1987, he was entranced with the potential of his recently attained Synclavier, which gave him a liberty that Varese never shared, to not only compose and experiment with new musical sounds and shapes, but to be able to hear the fruit of these labors instantly. He had just completed the wondrously instrumental *Jazz from Hell* when we met, and was in the midst of extending those discoveries into further realms of compositional exploration which he was happy to generously share with me in the warm inner sanctum of his home studio.

Zappa was one of the very first interviews I conducted for *SongTalk* soon after I became editor in 1987. I requested an interview, received a "yes" almost immediately, and was told to head over to the Zappa home. It led me to believe that all interviews could be set up as easily, and that all interview subjects would be as gracious, humorous and brilliant. Sadly, I was wrong. There is nobody else like Zappa.

He meant different things to different people. To some, he was the outspoken, political activist who went to Washington to speak out against the PMRC and all forms of censorship. To others, he was the long-haired Zappa of the 60s, fronting the Mothers of Invention, who, in 1966 released both the first double album and the first concept album in rock history (*Freak Out*). To others, he was a real guitar god, filling up full hockey stadiums with the sound of his extended guitar solos. To many he was the cynical, bizarrely humorous creator of such satirical gems as "Dancing Fool" and "Valley Girl." To many, especially those outside the realm of American influence, he was a compositional genius, writing his own distinctive brand of harmonically complex, rhythmically jangled music for everything from a rock band to the London Symphony Orchestra. He was one of the twentieth century's most innovative and creative musical forces.

At home, his demeanor was closer to an Einstein than a Hendrix. Prior to this interview, he caught a quick four-hour nap after leaving instructions with his engineer to make mixes of pieces he had been working on in his home studio. When we arrived, he was summoned from his bed—his face unshaven, hair all over the place—looking pretty weary. He had been literally working around the clock, always aware that there was the potential for new music to be made; maybe also aware that his time, on this plane anyway, was limited.

After the interview was completed, I had the great privilege of being ushered into Zappa's home studio and hearing Synclavier pieces in progress. Though he didn't smile much, his pleasure at being the first person ever to create this particular music was obvious, and great to share. (For example, he'd say, "Let's see what 22 notes in the space of one eighth note might sound like on a bassoon.") He put out a cigarette in the standing ashtray beside his chair, lit another (smoking was his only vice), leaned back and pushed the start button on the Synclavier. The music that filled the studio with all the force of a concert hall, was, like all the music he created in an especially prolific career, colorful, powerful and truly wondrous.

Do you approach a composition from a rhythmic viewpoint rather than a melodic one?

It depends on what kind of song it is. If it's a song where the text is important, the first job is to make sure that the setting is doing something for the lyric.

Sometimes it's like a difference tone. That's where you have a note and a note and the combination of these two notes gives you a third note, which is a difference tone. You get a theoretical difference tone from lyrics which are set ironically. The sum total of the package is more than just these words, this chord. You get the third concept, which is that these two things don't belong together but somebody put them there. And so you get the extra message there.

The other thing that you have to keep in mind, when writing a song, is who is going to perform it. When I write for myself, since I can't really sing at all—I have a very difficult time holding a pitch, can't hold long notes, can't do any ornamentation—the melody lines tend to be simpler in terms of how wide the leaps are, how long the notes have to be, and the orchestrational texture tends to be more complicated to compensate for the lack of interest that is in the vocal line.

When you're thinking of melodies, do you work on a keyboard or do you come up with melodies in your head?

I can do it any way. I can think of them in my head, I can do it on a keyboard, I can do it on a guitar, I can do it on a marimba.

And there's no one way that makes you feel the most comfortable?

It depends on what the end result is going to be. A song like "Strictly Genteel," for example, which has not only a fairly dense orchestral texture, but it's got complicated words, there's no way that I could have done that without the help of a piano, because the piano part is so integral to the thing. I don't play piano—I can plunk things out slowly and write down exactly what the thing is supposed to be.

Oftentimes, though, unless you have really skilled musicians in the band, you can't have the piece rendered properly because it takes a certain amount of skill to be able to do those things, and people with that kind of skill generally don't gravitate towards rock and roll. But I've been really lucky in having people available for auditions that want to go into the band and play hard music and actually turn out to be roadable people that can do it. And so I write for them.

When you are working on a composition, do you write everything down? For example, the pieces on *Jazz from Hell?*

Everything on that album was typed on the Synclavier except for "St. Ettiene" which was a live guitar solo.

By "typed on the Synclavier" do you mean that you play it on a keyboard or that you are typing it onto the computer screen?

You can do it either way: on the keyboard or by typing note names on sheet music. You look at a stave and say, "I want a G, one eighth note long, right there," and you type it in and presto, there's a G there.

And then it plays it for you?

Yeah, as any instrument that you'd like to have it be.

And do you enjoy this method of composing?

Well, since they have software updates every year, and since there's new hardware available every year, every album that I've done on Synclavier has gotten more and more sophisticated. Compared to what I can do now, it sounds technically crude. The second one I did was the *Mothers of Prevention* album where I used the voices of people in Congress.

Your new album, *Jazz from Hell*, contains all instrumentals. Is this because you feel restricted by the songform and feel freer to express yourself without words?

It's two different mediums for me. When you're writing a song with words you have one kind of job to do. I look at that challenge as to how do you take something that is basically in my case prose data and try to make the prose data rhyme with itself and not compete with the notes that are connected to it. So that's the game I involve myself with when I have to write a song with words. When writing an instrumental song, you don't have to make those two things fit together, so it's a different challenge.

So by talking about prose data, do you mean that you work on the words first before the music?

Not always. Sometimes I start with a complicated instrumental line and just for the hell of it see whether I can write words to it. "Inca Rose" is one of the songs that came out that way. It was originally done as a kind of fusion instrumental. I said, "If somebody has to sing this, and it is fiendishly hard to sing, what would be the words that fit on it as it came out?" "Montana" was done the other way. It was like an old story song. The chord changes and notes were fitted in later.

Another example of long prose data that had a musical setting put to it is a song called "Dumb All Over." I wrote it on a Lufthansa flight from Frankfurt to L.A., and it was pages and pages about the fundamentalist right and weird things that they do. And it took awhile to organize a setting that worked on that thing.

You talk about the words and music opposing each other—
Sometimes they're supposed to.

—but usually we talk about a marriage of words and music. Should they oppose each other?
Sometimes, yeah. I think the irony of the setting is one of the things that can enhance the words or, if the words are used phonetically to assist the music, then you design your entire piece so that the words will definitely take a back seat. They'll just function as texture to the music.

An example of that type of writing would be 1950s doo-wop music. The "Da-Doo-Ron-Ron." Now what does that mean? But that's your song.

And you have a great love for those fifties songs.
Well, it was the first rock and roll that I heard. It was like a brand new invention when I was going to high school. So I've got a pretty thorough grounding in that musical tradition.

Is that all you were listening to at that time or did you get into classical music too?
No, I was buying rhythm and blues records and avant-garde 20th century classical music at the same time and loving both.

I know Varèse was a major influence.
Well, see, in those days, albums were very expensive, and there were no albums of rock and roll music. The rock and roll album was something that came along long after the rock and roll single was invented, and the original first rock and roll albums were just compilations of hits. If the label had a bunch of hits they would just stick them onto an album. The first one that I ever saw was called *Teenage Dance Party* that had a bunch of songs from a New York label—I can see it now, it's orange—that was the first one I got. I think the wisdom in the marketplace was that the teenagers wouldn't spend money on albums, they'd spend it on a single but it was a major investment to spend more money on a big record to play it on a slower machine. Remember—most teenagers in those days had 45-rpm record players with a big nozzle in the middle of it that you can't play a LP on. So only a few of the consumers in the rock and roll marketplace actually had a machine that could play an album.

Anyway, I was not really financially in good condition in those days, but I managed to buy two contemporary classical LPs that I listened to day and night, because it was the only two albums I had. I had a cheap recording of "The Rite of Spring" on Camden budget line. It was the "Worldwide Symphony plays the Rite of Spring." And the other one I had was "The Complete Works of Edgar Varèse, Volume 1," which is on some obscure label called EMS.

Did you like the Varèse when you first heard it?
Yeah, sure, right away. My kind of music.

Did you have any friends at the time who shared your enthusiasm for Varèse?
No, but I would play it for them anyway. I mean, usually if they'd come over to the house. Everybody does this same thing: if you have records, you tend to play your favorite items for whoever comes in. And that gives them the test to find out what kind of person that individual is. What I used to do was play them parts of the Varèse album and then play them Lightning Slim things like "My Starter Won't Start" or "Have Your Way" or I'd play them some Howling Wolf. That would clear them out really fast.

They didn't like that stuff either?
Well, usually that would get rid of the girls and the ignorant boys and what was left over was somebody you could have a conversation with.

It's interesting that you mention these two separate currents because I was introduced to your work by a classical cello player who mostly listens to avant-garde 20th-century music and you.
Well, he's missing a good bet by not checking out those old records by guys like Lonesome Sundown and Lightning Slim. That's good stuff because it's real direct, it's not a matter of pretense there. It's right to the point.

Did you start writing music at this time?
I was writing chamber music. I didn't write a rock and roll song until I was about twenty or twenty-one. But I've been writing chamber music since I was fourteen.

Did you study keyboard?
No. I started writing music because I liked the way it looked and I had art talent when I was a kid, so I used to draw music. I figured that's what everybody else did, you know, just draw it till you liked the way it looked and then handed it to a musician. Theoretically a person who could read dots on paper and then translate your engraving into some kind of audio masterpiece. And I did, since I didn't know any musicians, labor under this delusion for quite some time and just draw music.

Without being able to read it?
Right, I couldn't read it. I could write it. I could make it look terrific.

Were you basing these drawings on any sheet music that you looked at?
No. I'd seen pictures of music before and I knew how to draw the clefs. That might sound ignorant and impractical but I would say there are many contemporary scores that probably don't sound as good as what I was doodling on paper.
In fact there was a reference—I guess in the early fifties—to a certain type of music common in the contemporary European tradition called "Eye Music." You couldn't play it and you didn't want to listen to it but it looked great on paper. I didn't find out about this concept until I managed to get these things played by musicians and I got the shock of my life when I realized that it didn't

sound like what I wanted it to sound like. So at that point I had to find out how the system really worked.

And that's when you learned music theory?

The standard theory that I know is really quite limited because I always found it quite boring. I got a hold of the Walter Piston harmony book when I was in high school and I went through some of the exercises in there. And I was wondering why a person would really want to devote a lifetime to doing this, because after you complete it you'll sound like everybody else who used the same rules. So I learned enough of the basic stuff so I got the concept of what harmony was supposed to do, what voice leading was supposed to do, how melody was supposed to function in a harmonic climate, what rhythm was supposed to do. I learned all of that and then chucked the rest of it.

I started writing my own music in which the thirds were omitted from the chords. That seemed to give me more latitude with the melody because if there's no third in the chord then you're not locked into an exact statement that your harmonic climate is major or minor. If you have a root, a fourth and a fifth, or a root, a second and a fifth, your ability to create atmosphere and imply harmony by having a variety of bass notes that will argue with the suspended chord gives you, for my taste, more opportunities. Then the melody line can go back and forth between major or minor and lydian or whatever else you want with ease. You have more flexibility.

But even to take that approach you'd have to have the understanding of how a triad is structured and the effect of a third.

Yeah, but that's really basic beginner mongoloid stuff.

Yes, but at the same time there are many writers who are at that stage and don't know what a third is.

They don't want to know. I think that when you have award shows that glorify the most ignorant among us for doing things that are called excellent merely because they've achieved large numerical sales, it is not much of an incentive for a young songwriter to come along and say, "I want to learn how music works." Because there's just no reason to participate in the construction of music on an intellectual level when all you have to do is just get lucky one time and then have the record company do the payola. Then you will be the next guy to be standing in line to get a major award. So that's the message that is sent to the marketplace for all the new guys coming in. And there's no glamour to doing the laborious job of developing a personal theory of harmony or a personal feel for how you want rhythm to function in your work.

See, I make a distinction between a songwriter and a composer. They're not always the same kind of a guy because the goals of the two types of disciplines are not always the same. Composers may write songs, but it is very seldom that a songwriter will do a composition.

And what makes something a composition rather than a song?

A composition is when you're dealing just in a theoretical and abstract way with the raw elements of music, and trying to do things with those basic elements which have not been done before. Instead of sitting down to write a hit, you're going to the raw material to go in a new direction.

Songwriters tend not to do that. They tend to write in a songform. And if you compare it to architecture, it's the difference between building a cathedral and building a Taco Bell. And fast food is important when you're hungry. Fast music is important when you need something to drive to.

So is it your opinion that the state of songwriting is bad and getting worse?

No, the only thing that saves it is the fact that the American's memory span is so short that they actually believe that when they hear the latest regurgitated version of a style that was prevalent five years ago, they believe it's new. I mean, I'm amazed that some of the stuff that is passing for New Wave music today is 1960s semi-folk-rock chord changes that have been reorchestrated to use 1980s technology. It really is the same.

Have you heard any songs recently that you thought were worthwhile?

I like "Living in a Box" by Living in a Box, and I like "Daddy's Home" by Walk the Moon.

So it is possible to use that very restrictive songform and still create something good?

Sure, it is always possible. But when a guy sits down to write a song, he's not sitting down to make history, he's sitting down to make money.

Do you really believe that is always the case? Don't you think there are some songwriters who want to write some timeless songs?

I don't think the urge to be timeless necessarily permeates the pop tune marketplace. The urge to be rich permeates the pop tune marketplace.

That's true, though I know the urge to be timeless does exist among songwriters, although they have to face the reality of the music business.

Any songwriter who had to choose between being rich and being timeless, if he chose timeless, he's probably out of a job. There are just too many commercial pressures on the guy at the end of the food chain, the guy who writes the song, because before he thinks about anything else, he's already looking at airplay or looking at MTV. I think there's got to be an inkling in the back of every songwriter's mind like, "How will this shoot? What will they do when they make a video of this one?" So what's that got to do with writing a song?

Not much. But isn't it possible for something new and great to be heard—even if it doesn't fit the pat hit-making formula?

Not unless there's a massive change of attitude at the distribution level, which includes the places where music is dispersed: radio, TV, jukeboxes, whatever, until current values disappear. Until then, there is little hope that a person who is doing anything other than formula swill will have an opportunity to have his music recorded, let alone transmitted.

But don't you feel that there's an inherent need among people to have serious, expressive music as a part of their lives?

The problem with that concept is: would they know it if they heard it? Would they like it or would they prefer it to other stuff? See, an audience gets trained. They're trained by their environment. And what they hear on the radio has nothing to do with life: it's all freeze-dried and dead. It's like dead ar-

tifacts that are repeated over and over again. The repetition helps to sell records, but the repetition reduces the composition to the level of wallpaper.

Does it?

Sure. Especially in the radio sense, you don't hear it anymore. It's a rock
and roll atmosphere that you play in your car, that you hear in an elevator, that
you experience in a boutique. It has reduced wallpaper to a lifestyle.

**But a great song, even if I hear it a billion times, can still move me. It
can't ever become wallpaper, no matter how many times it gets played.**

When's the last time you heard a song that fit into that category? Anything written in the '80s?

Yes.

Name one.

O.K. "Hearts and Bones" by Paul Simon.

I don't know that song.

**Well, you see, there are many great songs that have been written in the
'80s. They might not get any radio play or be seen on MTV but they are
still very good.**

Well, okay, I'll grant you that. But let's take a look at the broad spectrum
of what everybody knows as common American coinage, the musical experience of being an American. The boundary of your musical experience has been
determined by accountants. Unless you are going to seek out the newest and
the finest of whatever is available in any field, what you are presented with as
your set of alternatives that you will choose to inhabit your lifestyle is tiny.

**Because of the way that the business is structured? If a record sells
50,000 copies, it's a commercial failure. But you're still reaching 50,000
people. Would you consider that a failure, even if you're reaching that many
people and affecting that many lives?**

If you were a classical composer and you sold 50,000 albums, you'd be a
hero. I mean, the regular pop industry spits at 50,000 records. I regularly do
50,000 records. The only album I ever had that was in the million plus category was *Sheik Yerbouti* and the only reason that it sold that much is because
the song "Bobby Brown Goes Down" which could never be played in the U.S.,
was a hit all over Europe. The bulk of those sales were outside the U.S. so it
was an unpredictable fluke. Usually my record sales are in the 50,000 to
300,000 range depending on what the content of the album is.

Do you consider sales of 50,000 records to be a failure?

I think that that's about the bottom margin for feeling okay given what it
costs to make an album. You know, the success, if you're going to look at it in
financial terms, you have to look at the difference between what you spend to
make it and what it nets you after it's gone into the marketplace. And because
I have my own studio and do my own stuff, I can actually make a profit at
50,000 records, where another guy probably could not.

**So what would be your advice to the young songwriter when he sits
down to write a song—should he concern himself with writing a good hook
or should he simply try to write a great song?**

It depends on what he wants to do. If he just wants to make money, he should copy everybody else's stuff, which is what everybody else is doing.

But you can only do that for so long.
That depends on how good a copier you are.

How about if you want a career in songwriting?
Basically, it's a career in being a fraud. It's just like when someone says, "What would you advise a young composer?" I always say, "Get a Real Estate license." You can't earn a living being a composer in the United States. But as far as being a songwriter goes, you can make a lot of money if you will listen for what everybody else has done that has been successful, and tweak it around to the point where you can convince an accountant at a record company that you're fresh, new and original. This is usually accomplished by changing your hairdo periodically and having a good wardrobe. That's basically the business you're entering. The idea of writing a nice tune is the farthest thing from the minds of the people you will be doing business with, and that is the reality of the business.

I interviewed the songwriting team of Livingston & Evans who told me that they didn't think that a good melody had been written in about thirty years.
I'd say that's probably true, because the basic thrust of today's music is dance music, especially for Americans, who have an incredibly limited concept of what rhythm is. If you look at the typical dance rhythms that motivate an American dancer, you're very close to march music. It's boom-bap-boom-bap, and if there's anything more than that, an American's feet get tangled up.

So you start with a basic sort of fascist marching beat, and then you add a few parallel fifths to it (if you want it to be heavy metal) and make sure that your melodies don't have anything shorter than an eighth note. Make sure that there is an incredible amount of repetition in the composition, because you're presuming that when people are out there semi-marching and pumping their buttocks up and down that they couldn't really comprehend any more than a five note melody.

If you were to do a statistical analysis of some of the most popular, big-selling tunes that have been on the market in recent days, you'd see not too many notes, the chords don't give you too many surprises, and the beat is boom-bap. So if you want to do that and make a lot of money, it's not too hard to learn. But if you want to write the great American tune, I would say to get a Real Estate license.

Is it true that you had given up the guitar?
I did. I stopped playing it for the last four years. I only picked it up again in the last month. I keep it sitting next to my chair in the studio and I occasionally pluck around on it, but I'm only barely getting some callouses back. I literally hadn't touched it since December 23, 1984.

Why did you give it up?
I didn't think that there was any great demand in the marketplace for what I do on the guitar. I mean, why should I bust my chops, so to speak? There's plenty of people who play faster than I do, there's plenty of people who

dance around more than I do, and there was nobody doing what I was doing on Synclavier. Rather than stand in line and be just another redundant guitar player plying his trade in the music business, I thought I'd better come up with something new.

But isn't there always going to be an audience for what you do? Does Frank Zappa really have to worry about the marketplace?

Sure. Certainly. Remember—I'm self-financed. The money doesn't fly down from heaven or from a recording company. It's all what I can afford to spend to do what I do.

There is a practical side to making records. And then there is the amount of what you can refer to as assumable risk: How weird can you get and still make a living? I think I've experimented well with the fringes of that concept. I'll take it to the max. I will stick my neck out. I'll make albums of stuff that if I had a normal record contract with a normal record company, I would have been dropped from their roster centuries ago.

Some of the things that I've recorded that I happen to like the best are the things that people in the marketplace find the most repulsive about what I do. Songs like "The Dangerous Kitchen" or "The Jazz Discharge Party Hats" are unique in American popular music. There are no two other songs that are in that same style.

If you ask anybody what their favorite song is that I've done, most people would say "Peaches in Regalia" or "Mudshark." They have little or no concept of what some of the other more adventurous things would have been.

Could you name one album of your own that is your favorite?

By the time I finish working on an album, I never want to hear it again in my life.

And you don't?

No, I do, sometimes. For example, we're releasing the old masters collections and the old things have to be remixed or remastered again and you do get to hear them again. But usually what I hear is everything that went wrong during a session. It's very seldom that I'll listen to a song and say, "Yeah, that's a good song," cause by the time I'm finished doing the grunt work of putting an album together, the initial thrill of writing the song has vanished.

If you are the artist and the producer and the record company president and the art director, after doing all those jobs it becomes a blurr; the original songwriting idea is just something that happened in ancient history.

And when you're in the studio you don't reconnect with that original inspiration at all?

No. That's a one shot deal.

Do you find any satisfaction in your enormous body of work and the knowledge that it will remain?

Not in a way that you can identify with. You know, I think that what you have in mind is probably something more romantic than the way I look at it.

How do you look at it?

Well, all the songs that were dealing with sociological topics were things that needed to be said at the time. The comments made then still remain true today and will probably remain true as long as we have bad government and ignorant religion working in America. And on that basis I think they serve a sociological function as an encouragement to other people who have a similar point of view.

If you had to name a few songs, written by other people, that you consider to be great, what would they be?

I liked "Subterranean Homesick Blues" by Bob Dylan. I liked "Paperback Writer" by the Beatles and "I am the Walrus." And one may not underestimate the impact of "Louie Louie," the original Richard Berry version.

Were those the only songs by Dylan and the Beatles that you like or do you like them in general?

No, those are the only ones I liked. I generally liked the Rolling Stones better than the Beatles during that era; they were a little bit more to my taste because they were more involved in the blues.

I like the group Them, with Van Morrison. And the other thing that I really enjoyed were the early compositions of David and Bacharach. I thought that they were so good because prior to that time there had been little of bitonal or polytonal harmonic implication in American pop music, and we are to thank them for providing that through those early Dionne Warwick recordings.

What do you think of the New York school of composers, such as Phillip Glass?

Well, I'm not familiar with his music but the whole realm of the New York school of repetition music, it's like stuff to be played in the background of an art gallery. It's an atmosphere that people might enjoy participating in, but it's not my style; it's not my idea of a good time.

Should we expect in the future that most of your work will be on the Synclavier as opposed to working with a band?

I don't think it will be exclusively that because there's still certain things human beings do better than machines.

One thing about human beings, though, is that they really enjoy being paid. And one thing about doing records that are not selling 30 million units is you have to be very conscious of what you're spending to make the record so one day you have made a profit that allows you to make another record. That's another reason why that machine (the synclavier) is sitting there.

* * *

Leonard Cohen
Los Angeles, California 1992

We are sitting indian-style on the second floor of Leonard Cohen's home in Los Angeles. On his bookshelf are many books that's he's written himself, including two novels and several volumes of poetry. An unearthly rain is exploding outside as he scans countless notebooks of song, endless revisions that span decades and which fill thousands of pages within hundreds of notebooks. For every verse that he keeps, there are untold dozens that he discards. When I mention that a lesser writer would have been happy with simply two of the six verses he wrote for the stunning "Democracy" from his album, *The Future*, he answers, "I've got about sixty."

His tower of song isn't really that tall, only two floors that I can see anyway, but to him it's both a fortress of solitude and a factory, a place where he says, "I summon every version of myself that I can to join this workforce, this team, this legion." It's here that he gives songs the kind of respect bottles of fine wine receive, the knowledge that years—decades even—are needed for them to ripen to full maturity. Quoting from the Talmud he says, "There's good wine in every generation," referring to the new songwriters who crop up every few years. But his own work has extended across generations and decades, packing as much brilliance into 1992's *The Future* as he instilled into his first album in 1967. "I always knew I was in this for the long haul," he says, "but somewhere along the line the work just got harder."

Like Dylan, Simon, and few others, Leonard Cohen has expanded the vocabulary of the popular song into the domain of poetry. And like both Simon
and Dylan, Cohen will work and rework his songs until he achieves a kind of
impossible perfection. He didn't need Dylan's influence, however, to inspire his
poetic approach to songwriting. He'd already written much poetry and two
highly acclaimed novels by the time Dylan emerged, leading the poet Alan
Ginsberg to comment, "Dylan blew everybody's mind, except Leonard's."

In the beginning, Cohen was both a member of a Canadian country group
called the Buckskins and a member of what is now known as the Montreal
School of Poetry. When he wasn't playing folk songs on his guitar, he was lyrically chanting his poetry. It was only a matter of time until the words and the
music came together and Cohen became a songwriter.

Songwriting was for him then, as it remains today, a labor of love. Few
thoughts of making it a career entered his thoughts for many years. "We used
to play music for fun. Much more than now. Now nobody picks up a guitar
unless they're paid for it. Now every kid who picks up a guitar is invited to
dream."

The first song he ever wrote was aptly called "Chant," a poem he loosely
set to music: "Hold me heartlight, soft light hold me, moonlight in your mouth
. . ." When John Hammond, the same guy who discovered Dylan, Springsteen
and Billie Holiday, heard some of Leonard's early songs, he told him, "You've
got it," and signed him to Columbia records.

His first album, *The Songs of Leonard Cohen*, was an extraordinary debut
for any songwriter and recording artist. Like later debuts by artists such as John
Prine and Rickie Lee Jones, the level of writing on his first record achieved a
resounding maturity and musical grace seldom found on a first album. In songs
such as "Suzanne" and "Sisters of Mercy" Cohen moved beyond the realm of
the popular song to reach into places previously untouched with words and
music.

His following albums continued to resound with beautiful, intimate poetry
while stretching the boundaries of songwriting, as in such classic songs as
"Chelsea Hotel No. 2," "Joan of Arc," and "Famous Blue Raincoat." So
moved was Kris Kristofferson by the simple valor of Cohen's "Bird on the
Wire" that he requested its opening to be inscribed on his tombstone: "Like a
bird on a wire, like a drunk in a midnight choir, I have tried in my way to be
free." Bob Dylan made the accurate comment that Cohen's songs had become
almost like prayers. It's true: a certain sancity connects all of Cohen's work, a
timeless, devotional beauty that runs entirely opposite to almost everything
that is modern.

He was born on September 21, 1934 in Montreal. His father died when he
was nine. At seventeen he went to McGill University where he formed the
Buckskin Boys and wrote his first book of poetry, *Let Us Compare Mythologies*.
His second volume, published in 1961 and entitled *The Spice Box Of Earth*, was
acclaimed around the world. But as it's always been with his careers, the extreme acclaim that his work received never equalled extreme amounts of
money. "I couldn't make a living," he said.

For seven years he lived on the island of Hydra in Greece with Marianne Kenson and her son Axel. While there he wrote another book of poems, *Flowers for Hitler*, and two novels, *The Favorite Game* and *Beautiful Losers*. Again the praise was vast and forthcoming but the financial rewards were scarce. The Boston Globe wrote "James Joyce is not dead. He is living in Montreal under the name of Cohen." But he was frustrated by the inequality between the praise and the money, and rejected the novelist's life to move to America and become a songwriter.

Contradicting the old adage that the devil is in the details, Cohen has shown many times that the divine can be discovered there. As he once said to Jennifer Warnes, "Your most particular answer will be your most universal one." It is the unique specificity of his songs that enable one not only to envision them but to enter them. The miraculous "Suzanne" for example, is a song towards which many songwriters have aspired, and it is Cohen's descriptive use of details, along with one of his most haunting melodies, that distinguishes this astonishing song.

When I mentioned to him that to this day it seems miraculous to me that someone could have written it, he agreed, not egotistically but with a kind of hushed reverence. "It is miraculous," he said softly.

In conversation, he is often Whitmanesque, speaking in evocative and inspired lists of specific human activity similar to the touching human details found in all of his songs. For example, when asked if he felt that many meaningful songs were still being written, he beautifully expounded on the meaning of meaningful songs:

"There are always meaningful songs for somebody. People are doing their courting, people are finding their wives, people are making babies, people are washing their dishes, people are getting through the day, with songs that we may find insignificant. But their significance is affirmed by others. There's always someone affirming the significance of a song by taking a woman into his arms or by getting through the night. That's what dignifies the song. Songs don't dignify human activity. Human activity dignifies the song."

Are you always working on songs or do you write only for specific projects?

No, I'm writing all the time. And as the songs begin to coalesce, I'm not doing anything else but writing. I wish I were one of those people who wrote songs quickly. But I'm not. So it takes me a great deal of time to find out what the song is. So I am working most of the time.

When you say "what the song is," do you mean that in terms of meaning, where the meaning is leading you?

Yes. I find that easy versions of the song arrive first. Although they might be able to stand as songs, they can't stand as songs that I can sing. So to find a song that I can sing, to engage my interest, to penetrate my boredom with myself and my disinterest in my own opinions, to penetrate those barriers, the song has to speak to me with a certain urgency.

To be able to find that song that I can be interested in takes many versions and it takes a lot of uncovering.

Do you mean that you're trying to reach something that is outside of your immediate realm of thought?

My immediate realm of thought is bureaucratic and like a traffic jam. My ordinary state of mind is very much like the waiting room at the DMV. Or, as I put it in a quatrain, "The voices in my head, they don't care what I do, they just want to argue the matter through and through."

So to penetrate this chattering and this meaningless debate that is occupying most of my attention, I have to come up with something that really speaks to my deepest interest. Otherwise I nod off in one way or another. So to find that song, that urgent song, takes a lot of versions and a lot of work and a lot of sweat.

But why shouldn't my work be hard? Almost everybody's work is hard. One is distracted by this notion that there is such a thing as inspiration, that it comes fast and easy. And some people are graced by that style. I'm not. So I have to work as hard as any stiff, to come up with the payload.

So you're not a writer for whom ideas simply appear?

I haven't had an idea in a long long time. And I'm not sure I ever had one. Now my friend Irving Leighton, the great Canadian writer, said, "Leonard's mind is unpolluted by a single idea." And he meant it as a kind of compliment. He's a close friend and he knows me, and it's true. I don't have ideas. I don't really speculate on things. I get opinions but I'm not really attached to them. Most of them are tiresome. I have to trot them out in conversations from time to time just to cooperate in the social adventure. But I have a kind of amnesia and my ideas just kind of float above this profound disinterest in myself and other people. So to find something that really touches and addresses my attention, I have to do a lot of hard, manual work.

What does that work consist of?

Just versions. I will drag you upstairs after the vacuuming stops and I will show you version after version after version of some of the tunes on this new album.

You do have whole notebooks of songs?

Whole notebooks. I'm very happy to be able to speak this way to fellow craftsmen. Some people may find it encouraging to see how slow and dismal and painstaking is the process.

For instance, a song like "Closing Time" began as a song in 3/4 time with a really strong, nostalgic, melancholy country feel. Entirely different words. It began:

The parking lot is empty;
They switch off the Budweiser sign.
It's dark from here to San Jobete,
It's dark all down the line.
They ought to hand the night a ticket
For speeding, it's a crime.
I had so much to tell you,
Yeah, but now it's closing time.

And I recorded the song and I sang it. And I choked over it. Even though another singer could have done it perfectly well. It's a perfectly reasonable song. And a good one, I might say. A respectable song. But I choked over it. There wasn't anything that really addressed my attention. The finishing of it was agreeable because it's always an agreeable feeling. But when I tried to sing it I realized it came from my bordeom and not from my attention. It came from my desire to finish the song and not from the *urgency* to locate a construction that would engross me.

So I went to work again. Then I filled *another notebook* from beginning to end with the lyric, or the attempts at the lyric, which eventually made it onto the album. So most of [my songs] have a dismal history, like the one I've just accounted.

Generally do you finish the melody and then work on the lyrics for a long time?
They're born together, they struggle together, and they influence one another. When the lyric begins to be revised, of course, the line can't carry it with its new nuance or its new meaning. And generally the musical line has to change, which involves changing the *next* musical line, which involves changing the next lyrical line, so the process is mutual and painstaking and slow.

Do you generally begin a song with a lyrical idea?
It begins with an appetite to discover my self-respect. To redeem the day. So the day does not go down in debt. It begins with that kind of appetite.

Do you work on guitar?
It usually was guitar but now I have been working with keyboards.

Does the instrument affect the song you are writing?
They have certainly affected my songs. I only have one chop. All guitar players have chops. Especially professional ones. But I have only one chop. It's a chop that very few guitarists can emulate, hence I have a certain kind of backhanded respect from guitar players because they know that I have a *chop* that they can't master. And that chop was the basis of a lot of my good songs. But on the keyboard, because you can set up patterns and rhythms, I can mock up songs in a way that I couldn't do with my guitar. There were these rhythms that I heard but I couldn't really duplicate with my own instrument. So it's changed the writing quite a bit.

Writing in that way could be either more freeing or more restrictive. You have a rhythm that is set but you are free from playing the guitar.
Well, freedom and restriction are just luxurious terms to one who is locked in a dungeon in the tower of song. These are just . . . ideas. I don't have the sense of restriction or freedom. I just have the sense of work. I have the sense of hard labor.

Is this hard labor ever enjoyable for you?
It has a certain nourishment. The mental physique is muscular. That gives you a certain stride as you walk along the dismal landscape of your inner thoughts. You have a certain kind of *tone* to your activity. But most of the time it doesn't help. It's just hard work.

But I think unemployment is the great affliction of man. Even people with jobs are unemployed. In fact, most people with jobs are unemployed. I can say, happily and gratefully, that I am fully employed. Maybe all hard work means is fully employed. We have a sense here that it's smart not to work. The hustle, the con, these have been elevated to a very high position in our morality. And probably if I could mount a con or a hustle in terms of my own work I would probably embrace the same philosophy. But I am a working stiff. It takes me months and months of full employment to break the code of the song. To find out if there can be a song there.

When you're working to break that code, is it a process of actively thinking about what the song should say?

Anything that I can bring to it. Thought, meditation, drinking, disillusion, insomnia, vacations . . .

Because once the song enters the mill, it's worked on by everything that I can summon. And I need everything. I try everything. I try to ignore it, try to repress it, try to get high, try to get intoxicated, try to get sober, all the versions of myself that I can summon are summoned to participate in this project, this work force.

I try everything. I'll do *anything*. By any means possible.

In your experience, do any of these things work better than others?

Nothing works. Nothing works. After a while, if you stick with a song long enough it will yield. But long enough is way beyond any reasonable estimation of what you think long enough may be. In fact, long enough is way beyond. It's *abandoning*, it's abandoning that idea of what you think long enough may be.

Because if you think it's a week, that's not long enough. If you think it's a month, it's not long enough. If you think it's a *year*, it's not long enough. If you think it's a decade, it's not long enough.

Some songs take a decade to write. "Anthem" took a decade to write. And I've recorded it three times. More. I had a version prepared for my last album with strings and voices and overdubs. The whole thing completely finished. I listened to it, there was something wrong with the lyric, there was something wrong with the tune, there was something wrong with the tempo, there was a lie somewhere in there, there was a disclosure that I was refusing to make. There was a solemnity that I hadn't acheived. There was something wrong with the damn thing. All I knew is that I couldn't sing it. You could hear it in the vocal, that the guy was putting you on.

Is "Anthem" in any way an answer to Dylan's song "Everything is Broken"?

I had a line in "Democracy" that referred specifically to that Dylan song "Everything is Broken" which was "The singer says it's broken and the painter says it's gray. . . ." But, no, "Anthem" was written a long time before that Dylan song. I'd say '82 but it was actually earlier than that that that song began to form.

Including the part about the crack in everything?

That's old, that's very old. That has been the background of much of my work. I had those lines in the works for a long time. I've been recycling them in many songs. I must not be able to nail it.

You said earlier that you had no ideas, but that certainly is an idea.

Yeah. When I say that I don't have any ideas, it doesn't come to me in the form of an idea. It comes in the form of an image. I didn't start with a philosophical position that human activity is not perfectable. And that all human activity is flawed. And it is by intimacy with the flaw that we discern our real humanity and our real connection with divine inspiration. I didn't come up with it that way. I *saw* something broken. It's a different form of cognition.

Do images usually come to you in that way?

Well, things come so damn slow. Things come and they come and it's a tollgate, and they're particularly asking for something that you can't manage. They say, "We got the goods here. What do you got to pay?" Well, I've got my intelligence, I've got a mind. "No, we don't want that." I've got my whole training as a poet. "No, we don't want that." I've got some licks, I've got some skills with my fingers on the guitar. "No, we don't want that either." Well, I've got a broken heart. "No, we don't want that." I've got a pretty girlfriend. "No, we don't want that." I've got sexual desire. "No, we don't want that." I've got a whole lot of things and the tollgate keeper says, "That's not going to get it. We want you in a condition that you are not accustomed to. And that you yourself cannot name. We want you in a condition of receptivity that you cannot produce by yourself." How are you going to come up with that?

What's the answer?

[*Laughs*] I don't know. But, you know, I've been lucky over the years. I've been willing to pay the price.

How much does it cost?

[*Pause*] It's hard to name. It's hard to name because it keeps changing.

Is it a sense that you are reaching outside of yourself to write these songs?

If I knew whère the good songs came from, I'd go there more often. It's a mysterious condition. It's much like the life of a Catholic nun. You're married to a mystery.

Do you consider the tower of song to be a place of exile or of retreat?

I think you can use it a retreat but it doesn't work. It's best thought of as a factory. It's some combination between a factory and a bordello. But it's just the tower of song.

You've spoken about the hard labor that goes into your songs, and part of that must be due to the fact that your verses are so rich, and that you write long songs with many verses. I think other songwriters might have come up with two of the verses in "Democracy" and stopped.

I've got about sixty. There are about three or four parallel songs in the material that I've got. I saw that the song could develop in about three or four different ways and there actually exist about three or four versions of "Democracy." The one I chose seemed to be the one that I could sing at that moment. I addressed almost everything that was going on in America.

This was when the Berlin Wall came down and everyone was saying democracy is coming to the east. And I was like that gloomy fellow who always turns up at a party to ruin the orgy or something. And I said, "I don't think it's going to happen that way. I don't think this is such a good idea. I think a lot of suffering will be the consequence of this wall coming down." But then I asked myself, "Where is democracy really coming?" And it was the U.S.A. But I had verses:

> It ain't coming to us European style:
> Concentration camp behind a smile.
> It ain't coming from the east,
> With its temporary feast,
> As Count Dracula comes
> Strolling down the aisle . . .

So while everyone was rejoicing, I thought it wasn't going to be like that, euphoric, the honeymoon.

So it was these world events that occasioned the song. And also the love of America. Because I think the irony of America is transcendent in the song. It's not an ironic song. It's a song of deep intimacy and affirmation of the experiment of democracy in this country. That this is really where the experiment is unfolding. This is *really* where the races confront one another, where the classes, where the genders, where even the sexual orientations confront one another. This is the real laboratory of democracy. So I wanted to have that feeling in the song too. But I treated the relationship between the blacks and the Jews. For instance, I had:

> First we killed the Lord and then we stole the blues.
> This gutter people always in the news,
> But who really gets to laugh behind the black man's back
> When he makes his little crack about the Jews?
> Who really gets to profit and who really gets to pay?
> Who really rides the slavery ship right into Charleston Bay?
> Democracy is coming to the U.S.A.

Verses like that.

Why did you take that out?

I didn't want to compromise the anthemic, hymn-like quality. I didn't want it to get too punchy. I didn't want to start a fight in the song. I wanted a revelation in the heart rather than a confrontation or a call-to-arms or a defense.

There were a lot of verses like that, and this was long before the riots. There was:

> From the church where the outcasts can hide
> Or the mosque where the blood is dignified.
> Like the fingers on your hand,
> Like the hourglass of sand,
> We can separate but not divide

From the eye above the pyramid.
And the dollar's cruel display
From the law behind the law,
Behind the law we still obey
Democracy is coming to the U.S.A.

There were a lot of verses like that. Good ones.

It's hard to believe you'd write a verse like that and discard it.
The thing is that before I can discard the verse, I have to write it. Even if
it's bad—those two happen to be good, I'm presenting the best of my discarded
work—but even the bad ones took as long to write as the good ones. As someone once observed, it's just as hard to write a bad novel as a good novel. It's
just as hard to write a bad verse as a good verse. I can't discard a verse before
it is written because it is the writing of the verse that produces whatever delights or interests or facets that are going to catch the light. The cutting of the
gem has to be finished before you can see whether it shines. You can't discover
that in the raw.

**I love the verse that has "I'm stubborn as the garbage bags that refuse
to decay / I'm junk but I'm still holding up this little wild bouquet."**
Most of us from the middle-class, we have a kind of old, 19th century idea
of what democracy is, which is, more or less, to over-simplify it, that the masses
are going to love Shakespeare and Beethoven. That's more or less our idea of
what democracy is. But that ain't it. It's going to come up in unexpected ways
from the stuff that we think are junk: the people we think are junk, the ideas
we think are junk, the television we think is junk.

**You also have the line "The maestro says it's Mozart, but it sounds like
bubble-gum." That junk is sometimes promoted as great art.**
Some stuff is being promoted as junk and it is great art. Remember the
way that a lot of rock and roll was greeted by the authorities and the musicolo-
gists and even the hip people. And when people were putting me down as being one thing or another, it wasn't the guy in the subway. He didn't know
about me. It was the hip people, writing the columns in the hip newspapers,
college papers, music papers.

So it's very difficult to see what the verdict is going to be about a piece of
work. And the thing that really makes it an interesting game is that each generation revises the game, and decides on what is poetry and song for itself.
Often rejecting the very carefully considered verdicts of the previous generations. I mean, did the hippies ever think that they would be the objects of ridi-
cule by a generation? Self-righteous and prideful for the really bold and
courageous steps they had taken to find themselves imbued in the face of an
unmovable society; the risks, the chances, the dope they smoked, the acid they
dropped? Did they ever think they would be held up as figures of derision, like
cartoon characters? No.

And so it is, with every generation. There's that remark: "He who marries
the spirit of his own generation is a widower in the next."

You've written novels and books of poetry. And you once made a comment about having a calm, domestic life as a novelist before becoming a songwriter. Is the life of a songwriter entirely different than that of the poet or novelist?

It used to be. Because I used to be able to write songs on the run. I used to work hard but I really didn't begin slaving over them till 1983. I always used to work hard. But I had no idea what hard work was until something changed in my mind.

Do you know what that was?

I don't really know what it was. Maybe some sense that this whole enterprise is limited, that there was an end in sight.

An end to your songwriting?

No, an end to your life. That you were really truly mortal. I don't know what it was, exactly, I'm just speculating. But at a certain moment I found myself engaged in songwriting in the same way that I had been engaged in novel writing when I was very young. In other words, it's something you do every day and you can't get too far from it, otherwise you *forget what it's about.*

It wasn't that way for you prior to that time?

It was, but I'm speaking of degree. I always thought that I sweated over the stuff. But I had no idea what sweating over the stuff meant until I found myself in my underwear crawling along the carpet in a shabby room at the Royalton Hotel unable to nail a verse. And knowing that I had a recording session and knowing that I could get by with what I had but that I'm not going to be able to do it.

That kind of change I knew gradually was there and I *knew* that I had to work in a certain way that was nothing I had ever known anything about.

In the early days, did a song such as "Suzanne" come easy to you?

No, no, I worked months and months on "Suzanne." It's just a matter of intensity. I was still able to juggle stuff: a life, a woman, a dream, other ambitions, other tangents. At a certain point I realized I only had one ball in my hand, and that was The Song. Everything else had been wrecked or compromised and I couldn't go back, and I was a one-ball juggler. I'd do incredible things with that ball to justify the absurdity of the presentation.

Because what are you going to do with that ball? You don't have three anymore. You've just got one. And maybe only one arm. What are you going to do? You can flip it off your wrist, or bounce it off your head. You have to come up with some pretty good moves. You have to learn them from scratch. And that's what I learned, that you have to learn them from scratch.

There is some continuity between "Suzanne" and "Waiting for A Miracle." Of course there is; it's the same guy. Maybe it's like you lose your arm, you're a shoemaker. You're a pretty good shoemaker, maybe not the best but one of the top ten. You lose your arm and nobody knows. All they know is that your shoes keep on being pretty good. But in your workshop, you're holding onto the edge of the shoe with your teeth, you're holding it down and hammering with your other hand. It's quite an acrobatic presentation to get that shoe together. It may be the same shoe, it's just a lot harder to come by and you don't want to complain about it.

So maybe that's all that happened, is that I got wiped out in some kind of way and that just meant that I had to work harder to get the same results. I don't have any estimation or evaluation. I just know that the work got really hard.

Why did you move from writing novels and poems to songwriting?

I never saw the difference. There was a certain point that I saw that I couldn't make a living (as a poet or novelist). But to become a songwriter or a singer, to address an economic problem, is the height of folly, especially in your early thirties. So I don't know why I did it or why I do anything. I never had a strategy. I just play it by ear.

I just know that I had written what I thought was a pretty good novel, *Beautiful Losers*. It had been hailed by all the authorities as being a work of significance. Whether it is or not, who knows. But I had the credentials. But I couldn't pay my bills. It had only sold a couple thousand copies. So it was folly to begin another novel. I didn't want to teach, it just wasn't my cup of tea. I didn't have the personal style for that. I was too dissolute. I had to stay up too late, I had to move too fast, it wasn't a good place for me.

Have you ever had the desire to write another novel?

You toy with it but it's the regime that I like very much, writing a novel. I like that you really can't do anything else. You've got to be in one place. That's the way it is now with songwriting. I've got to have my synthesizer and my Mac. I can't really entertain a lot of distractions. [Otherwise] you forget what it's about very easily.

Is it more satisfying for you to write a song, something that you can enter again after writing and perform?

The performance of songs is a wonderful opportunity. It is a great privilege. It is a great way to test your courage. And to test the song. And even to test the audience.

Earlier you said that you could only write something that you would be able to sing, that—

I'm not trying to suggest that this has any dimension or hierarchy of better, worse. It's just a shape that it's got to have, otherwise I can't wrap my voice around it.

There are songs like "Dress Rehearsal Rag" that I recorded once and I will never sing. Judy Collins did a very beautiful version of it, better than mine. I would never do that song in concert; I can't get behind it.

But it's not a matter of excellence or anything but just the appropriate *shape* of my voice and my psyche.

Earlier you said that you couldn't sing an early version of "Anthem" because it had a lie in it. Does this mean that the songs have to resonate in truth for you to be able to sing them?

They have to resonate with the kind of truth that I can recognize. They have to have the kind of balance of truth and lies, light and dark.

Jennifer Warnes said that you once told her that the most particular answer is the most universal one.

I think so. I think that's advice that a lot of good writers have given me and the world. You don't really want to say "the tree", you want to say "the sycamore."

Why is that?

I don't know. And it's not even true. But there is a certain truth to it. We seem to be able to relate to detail. We seem to have an appetite for it. It seems that our days are made of details, and if you can't get the sense of another person's day of details, your own day of details is summoned in your mind in some way rather than just a general line like "the days went by." It's better to say, "watching Captain Kangaroo." Not "watching TV." Sitting in my room "with that hopeless little screen." Not just TV, but the *hopeless, little* screen.

I think those are the details that delight us. They delight us because we can share a life then. It's our sense of insignificance and isolation that produces a great deal of suffering.

It's one of the great things about your work, your rich use of details. So many songs we hear are empty, and have no details at all.

I love to hear the details. I was just working on a line this morning for a song called "I Was Never Any Good at Loving You." And the line was—I don't think I've nailed it yet—"I was running from the law, I thought you knew, forgiveness was the way it felt with you" or "forgiven was the way I felt with you." Then I got a metaphysical line, about the old law and the new law, the Old Testament and the New Testament: "I was running from the law, the old and the new, forgiven was the way I felt with you." No, I thought, it's too intellectual. Then I thought I got it: "I was running from the cops and the robbers too, forgiven was the way I felt with you." You got cops and robbers, it dignifies the line by making it available, by making it commonplace.

Each of those three versions work well. And so many of your lines, though I understand how hard you work on them and revise them, have the feeling of being inevitable. They don't feel forced; they just feel like the perfect line.

I appreciate that. Somebody said that art is the concealment of art.

Is there much concealing?

Unless you want to present the piece with the axe-marks on it, which is legitimate, [to show] where the construction or the carving is. I like the polished stuff too.

At a certain point, when the Jews were first commanded to raise an altar, the commandment was on unhewn stone. Apparently the god that wanted that particular altar didn't want slick, didn't want smooth. He wanted an unhewn stone placed on another unhewn stone. Maybe then you go looking for stones that fit. Maybe that was the process that God wanted the makers of this altar to undergo.

Now I think Dylan has lines, hundreds of great lines that have the feel of unhewn stone. But they really fit in there. But they're not smoothed out. It's inspired but not polished.

That is not to say that he doesn't have lyrics of great polish. That kind of genius can manifest all the forms and all the styles.

When you're working on lines such as those that you mentioned, is that a process of working just with words, separate from music?
No. I don't remember the chicken or the egg, I know the song began. But I keep moving them back and forth between the notebook and the keyboard. Trying to find where the song is. I had it as a shuffle. I had it as a kind of 6/8 song like "Blueberry Hill."

So when working on a lyric, there's always a melody in your mind that accompanies the lyric?
Usually, yes, the line will have a kind of rhythm that will indicate, at the very least, where the voice will go up and where the voice will go down. I guess that's the rudimentary beginnings of what they call melody.

I asked that because your songs, unlike most, are always in perfect meter and perfect rhyme schemes. It seems it would be possible to work on them just as lyrics, without music.
It doesn't seem to work that way. Because the line of music is very influential in determining the length of a line or the density, the syllabic density.

You mentioned working on a Mac. Is that musical work as well as lyrical work?
I like to set them up. They usually go from the napkin to the notebook to the Mac. And back and forth. And there's a certain moment when there's enough. I like to see it.
They say that the Torah was written with black fire on white fire. So I get that feeling from the computer, the bright black against the bright background. It gives it a certain theatrical dignity to see it on the screen. And also word processing enables you to cut and paste. But I generally have to go back to the napkin and the notebook. But at certain periods during the making of the song, I'll mock it up as a song just to be able to study it in a certain way.

You mentioned that whole verse about the Jews in "Democracy" that you took out, and in "The Future" there is that line, "I'm the little Jew who wrote the bible." There are so many great Jewish songwriters, yet it's so rare that any of them mention being Jewish in a song—
[Laughs] I smiled to myself when that line came. A friend of mine said, "I dare you to leave that line in."

You were tempted to remove it?
I'm tempted to remove everything. At any time. I guess I've got a kind of alcoholic courage. Most people are reluctant to remove things. My sin is on the other side. I'm ready to discard the whole song at any time and start over. And I think it's just as grave a defect because probably, at some point down the line, I've thrown away some songs that were pretty good. And they're buried out there somewhere.

Do you ever construct songs from things you've discarded?
I continually recycle.

Do you think being Jewish affects your writing?

I have no idea. I've never been anything else. So I don't know what it would be like not to have this reference. This reference that you can reject or embrace. You can have a million attitudes to this reference but you can't change the reference.

You've studied the Torah and the Talmud?
Yeah, yeah. In a modest way.

When you're writing a song like "The Future," for example, which is in A minor, do you choose a key that will match the tone of the song?
Yeah. I choose a key not so much as Garth Hudson [of the Band] would, who has a whole philosophy of music based on keys and colors and what moods different keys produce. I think that's quite valuable, I just don't have the chops to be able to do that because I can't play in all the keys. So I can't really examine the effects of all the keys. With the synthesizer I could play in all of them but I don't try that.

Do you think that there are colors that coincide with each key?
I think there are but mostly for me it's range. Some keys will place the voice a little deeper than others. My voice has gotten very very deep over the years and seems even to be deepening. I thought it was because of 50,000 cigarettes and several swimming pools of whiskey that my voice has gotten low. But I gave up smoking a couple of years ago and it's still getting deeper.

You actually do sound like a different person on the earlier records.
Sounds like a different person. Something happened to me too. I know what it was. My voice really started to change around '82. It started to deepen and I started to cop to the fact that it was deepening.

That very low voice is such a resonant sound. Are you happy with how it has evolved?
I'm surprised that I can even, with fear and trembling, describe myself to myself as a singer. I'm beginning to be able to do that. I never thought I would but there is something in the voice that is quite acceptable. I never thought I would be able to develop a voice that had any kind of character.

In terms of keys again, do you ever change keys while writing?
Oh, yeah. It's funny, today I was thinking about modulating in a tune which I have never done. I've never modulated a song in midstream.

Key changes can be quite corny. I can't think of a song of yours where you would want one.
No, I don't know. I think it could be nice. I've never tried it. I might find a way to do it—maybe in the middle of a line except in the beginning of a verse. There might be some sneaky ways to do it.

I did it in a certain kind of way in "Anthem." When I went up to the B-flat from the F. It threw it into another key. So in a sense, that chorus is in another key and then it comes back through suspended chords into the original key. So I have looked into them.

Do you feel that minor keys are more expressive than major keys?
I think the juxtaposition of a major chord with no seventh going into a minor chord is a nice feel. I like that feel.

In "Famous Blue Raincoat" which is A minor, the chorus shifts into C major which is very beautiful.

Yeah. That's nice. I guess I got that from Spanish music, which has that.

You mentioned how much you discard of what you write. Is your critical voice at play while writing, or do you try to write something first and then bring in the critic?

I bring all the people in to the team, the work force, the legion. There's a lot of voices that these things run through.

Do they ever get in the way?

Get in the way hardly begins to describe it. [*Laughter*] It's mayhem. It's mayhem and people are walking over each other's hands. It's panic. It's fire in the theater. People are being trampled and they're bullies and cowards. All the versions of yourself that you can summon are there. And some you didn't even know were around.

When you finally finish a song, is there a sense of triumph?

Oh, yes. There's a wonderful sense of done-ness. That's the thing I like best. That sense of finish-ness.

How long does that last?

A long time. It lasts a long time. I'm still invigorated by having finished this last record and I finished it six months ago and I still feel, "God, I finished this record. Isn't it great?" You have to keep it to yourself after awhile. Your friends are ready to rejoice with you for a day or a week. But they're not ready to rejoice after six months of "Hey, lets go get a drink, I finished my record six months ago!" It's an invitation people find easy to resist.

Does drinking ever help you write?

No. Nothing helps. But drinking helps performing. Sometimes. Of course you've got to be judicious.

Would it be okay with you if I named some of your songs to see what response you have to them?

Sure.

"Sisters of Mercy."

That's the only song I wrote in one sitting. The melody I had worked on for some time. I didn't really know what the song was. I remember that my mother had liked it.

Then I was in Edmonton, which is one of our largest northern cities, and there was a snowstorm and I found myself in a vestibule with two young hitch-hiking women who didn't have a place to stay. I invited them back to my little hotel room and there was a big double bed and they went to sleep in it immediately. They were exhausted by the storm and the cold. And I sat in this stuffed chair inside the window beside the Saskatchewan River. And while they were sleeping I wrote the lyrics. And that never happened to me before. And I think it must be wonderful to be that kind of writer. It must be *wonderful*. Because I just wrote the lines with a few revisions and when they awakened I sang it to them. And it has never happened to me like that before. Or since.

"Hey, That's No Way to Say Goodbye."

The first band I sang that for was a group called the Stormy Colvers, a Canadian group out of Toronto. I wrote it in two hotels. One was the Chelsea and the other was the Penn Terminal Hotel. I remember Marianne looking at my notebook, seeing this song and asking, "Who'd you write this for?"

"Chelsea Hotel No. 2."

[*Pause*] I came to New York and I was living at other hotels and I had heard about the Chelsea Hotel as being a place where I might meet people of my own kind. And I did. [*Laughs*] It was a grand, mad place. Much has been written about it.

That song was written for Janis Joplin?

It was very indiscrete of me to let that news out. I don't know when I did. Looking back I'm sorry I did because there are some lines in it that are extremely intimate. And since I let the cat out of the bag, yes, it was written for her.

"Hallelujah."

That was a song that took me a long time to write. Dylan and I were having coffee the day after his concert in Paris a few years ago and he was doing that song in concert. And he asked me how long it took to write it. And I told him a couple of years. I lied actually. It was more than a couple of years. Then I praised a song of his, "I and I," and asked him how long it had taken and he said, "Fifteen minutes." [*Laughter*]

Dylan said, around the time that "Hallelujah" came out, that your songs were almost like prayers.

I didn't hear that but I know that he does take some interest in my songs. We have a mutual interest. Everybody's interested in Dylan but it's pleasant to have Dylan interested in me.

It seems that his comment is true. Songs like "Hallelujah" or "If It Be Your Will" have a sanctity to them.

"If It Be Your Will" really is a prayer. And "Hallelujah" has that feeling. A lot of them do. "Dance Me to the End of Love." "Suzanne." I love church music and synagogue music. Mosque music.

It's especially resonant in this time because so few songs that we hear have any sense of holiness.

Well, there's a line in "The Future": "When they said repent, I wonder what they meant." I understand that they forgot how to build the arch for several hundred years. Masons forgot how to do certain kinds of arches, it was lost. So it is in our time that certain spiritual mechanisms that were very useful have been abandoned and forgot. Redemption, repentance, resurrection. All those ideas are thrown out with the bathwater. People became suspicious of religion plus all these redemptive mechanisms that are very useful.

"Famous Blue Raincoat."

That was one I thought was never finished. And I thought that Jennifer Warnes' version in a sense was better because I worked on a different version for her, and I thought it was somewhat more coherent. But I always thought that that was a song you could see the carpentry in a bit. Although there are some images in it that I am very pleased with. And the tune is real good. But I'm willing to defend it, saying it was impressionistic. It's stylistically coherent. And I can defend it if I have to. But secretly I always felt that there was a certain incoherence that prevented it from being a great song.

I'd have to disagree.
Well, I'm glad to hear it. Please disagree with any of this.

I think the greatness of that song lies in the fact that you're alluding to a story without coming out and giving all the facts, yet the story is more powerful because of what you don't say, or can't say.
Yes. It may be. When I was at school there was a book that was very popular called *Seven Types of Ambiguity*. One of the things it criticized was something called "The Author's Intention." You've got to discard the author's intention. It doesn't matter what the author's intention in the piece is, or what his interpretation of the piece is, or what his evaluation or estimation of the piece. It exists independently of his opinions about it. So maybe it is a good song, after all. I'm ready to buy your version.

This is all part of this make-believe mind that one has to present socially and professionally if you care about these matters. It's like asking somebody in a burning building if they care about architecture. [*Laughs*] Where's the fire-escape? That's all I care about in terms of architecture. Can I open the window?

"First We Take Manhattan."
I felt for sometime that the motivating energy, or the captivating energy, or the engrossing energy available to us today is the energy coming from the extremes. That's why we have Malcolm X. And somehow it's only these extremist positions that can compel our attention. And I find in my own mind that I have to resist these extremist positions when I find myself drifting into a mystical fascism in regards to myself. [*Laughs*]

So this song, "First We Take Manhattan," what is it? Is he serious? And who is we? And what is this constituency that he's addressing? Well, it's that constituency that shares this sense of titillation with extremist positions.

I'd rather do that with an appetite for extremism than blow up a bus full of schoolchildren.

When I first started playing guitar and writing songs, one of the first songs I ever learned was "Suzanne." And I remember thinking, "How does anyone write a song this beautiful?" And to this day, it's a miracle.
It is a miracle. I don't know where the good songs come from or else I'd go there more often. I knew that I was on top of something.

I developed the picking pattern first. I was spending a lot of time on the waterfront and the harbor area of Montreal. It hadn't been reconstructed yet. It's now called Old Montreal and a lot of the buildings have been restored. It wasn't at that time. And there was that sailor's church that has the statue of the Virgin. Gilded so that the sun comes down on her. And I knew there was a song there.

Then I met Suzanne, who was the wife of Armand Villancour, a friend of mine. She was a dancer and she took me down to a place near the river. She was one of the first people to have a loft on the St. Lawrence. I knew that it was about that church and I knew that it was about the river. I didn't know I had anything to crystallize the song. And then her name entered into the song, and then it was a matter of reportage, of really just being as accurate as I could about what she did.

It took you a long time to finish?
Yes, I had many work sheets. Nothing compared to the work sheets I have now. But it took me several months.

Did she feed you tea and oranges, as in the song?
She fed me a tea called Constant Comment, which has small pieces of orange rind in it, which gave birth to the image.

I always loved the line, "And she shows you where to look among the garbage and the flowers, there are heroes in the seaweed." They're hopeful lines.
Yes. It is hopeful. I'm very grateful for those lines and for that song.

"Bird on a Wire."
It was begun in Greece because there were no wires on the island where I was living to a certain moment. There were no telephone wires. There were no telephones. There was no electricity. So at a certain point they put in these telephone poles, and you wouldn't notice them now, but when they first went up, it was about all I did—stare out the window at these telephone wires and think how civilization had caught up with me and I wasn't going to be able to escape after all. I wasn't going to be able to live this 11th-century life that I thought I had found for myself. So that was the beginning.

Then, of course, I noticed that birds came to the wires and that was how that song began. "Like a drunk in a midnight choir," that's also set on the island. Where drinkers, me included, would come up the stairs. There was great tolerance among the people for that because it could be in the middle of the night. You'd see three guys with their arms around each other, stumbling up the stairs and singing these impeccable thirds. So that image came from the island: "Like a drunk in a midnight choir."

You wrote that you "finished it in Hollywood in a motel in 1969 along with everything else." What did you mean?
Everything was being finished. The sixties were being finished. Maybe that's what I meant. But I felt the sixties were finished a long time before that. I don't think the sixties ever began. I think the whole sixties lasted maybe fifteen or twenty minutes in somebody's mind. I saw it move very, very quickly into the marketplace. I don't think there were any sixties.

"I'm Your Man."
I sweated over that one. I really sweated over it. I can show you the notebook for that. It started off as a song called "I Cried Enough for You." It was related to a version of "Waiting for a Miracle" that I recorded. The rhyme scheme was developed by toeing the line with that musical version that I put down. But it didn't work.

You quoted Dylan once when you said, "I know my song well before I start singing." Do you always have the song completely finished before you begin recording?

Yeah. Sometimes there's a rude awakening. As there have been several times in the past. As with "Anthem." Several times I thought I had sung that song well and then when I heard it I realized I hadn't.

What do you think of songwriters who write in the studio?

I think they're amazing. I have tremendous admiration for that kind of courage and that kind of belief in one's own inspiration. That the gods are going to be favorable to you. That you're going to go in there with nothing but the will and the skill, and the thing is going to emerge. And great stuff has been done that way. It's not like this never works. There are masters of that style. Dylan is one of them. I think he's gone in with nothing and come up with great things. That is to say that my impression about Dylan is that he's used all the approaches: the spontaneous, the polished, the unhewn, the deliberate. He masters all those forms.

There aren't many songwriters of your generation who have been able to maintain the quality of their past work the way you have been able to.

First of all, you get tired. There aren't that many bull fighters in their forties. You do your great work as a bullfighter in your twenties and your thirties. There is a certain age that is appropriate to this tremendous expenditure of energy and the tremendous bravery and courage that you need to go into the fray. It often is a young man's game, or as Browning said, "The first fine careless frenzy." That is what the lyric poem is based on, the song is based on. But there are some old guys who hang in there and come up with some very interesting work.

In your work you've shown that a songwriter can go beyond that early frenzy and come to a new place and do new things that haven't been done.

I certainly felt the need to find that place. I always thought I was in it for the long haul, touch wood.

Does it have to do with interest, that you're still interested with the process?

It was to do with two things. One is economic urgency. I just never made enough money to say, "Oh, man, I think I'm gonna get a yacht now and scuba-dive." I never had those kind of funds available to me to make radical decisions about what I might do in life. Besides that, I was trained in what later became known as the Montreal School of Poetry. Before there were prizes, before there were grants, before there were even girls who cared about what I did. We would meet, a loosely defined group of people. There were no prizes, as I said, no rewards other than the work itself. We would read each other poems. We were *passionately* involved with poems and our *lives* were involved with this occupation. And we'd have to defend every line. We'd read poems to each other and you were attacked! With a kind of savagery that defangs rock criticism completely. There ain't anybody that I've ever read who can come up with anything like the savagery, and I might say the accuracy that we laid on each other.

We had in our minds the examples of poets who continued to work their whole lives. There was never any sense of a *raid* on the marketplace, that you should come up with a hit and get out. That kind of sensibility simply did not take root in my mind until very recently. [*Laughs*] I think maybe it's a nice idea but it's not going to happen when you write seven minute songs.

So I always had the sense of being in this for *keeps*, if your health lasts you. And you're fortunate enough to have the days at your disposal so you can keep on doing this. I never had the sense that there was an end. That there was a retirement or that there was a *jackpot*.

You mentioned the early frenzy of youth. Do you find you need frenzy or conflict in your life to write great songs or can you create from a place of calm?

I certainly think so and I'm looking forward to achieving that interior condition so that I can write from it. But I haven't yet. I've come a long way compared to the kind of trouble I was in when I was younger. Compared to that kind of trouble, this kind of trouble sounds like peace to me. But of course one is still involved in this struggle and while you're involved in this struggle you know peace is just a momentary thing, but you can't claim it. I'm a lot more comfortable with myself than I was a while ago. I'm still writing out of the conflicts and I don't know if they'll ever resolve.

Do you find the song to be a more powerful artform than others?

I love it. As a mode of employment. I don't even think about artforms. I'm very grateful to have stumbled into this line of work. It's tough but I like it.

Do you have the sense that some of your songs are lasting and timeless?

Sometimes I have a feeling that, as I'm fond of saying, a lot of my songs have lasted as long as the Volvo.

They're sturdy.

They seem to be sturdy. This last album [*The Future*] I think is very very sturdy. If it has any faults it's that it's a little too well armored. It seems to have a kind of resilence like a little Sherman Tank, that it can go over any landscape. I don't know whether that's something you want parking in your garage, but it seems to have a kind of armored energy.

I've tried to make the songs sturdy over the years.

Is it your feeling that songs will continue to evolve, that there are new places to go with them?

I think they will. It's a very good question and it summons the whole aesthetic. I think it's not important that they change or that anybody has a strategy for changing them. Or anyone has to monkey with them experimentally. Because I think that songs primarily are for courting, for finding your mate. For deep things. For summoning love, for healing broken nights, and for the central accompaniment to life's tasks. Which is no mean or small thing.

I think it's important that they address those needs rather than they look into themselves in terms of experimenting with form or with matter. But I think that they will, of course, change. I think that, although there's got to be songs about making love and losing and finding love, the fact that you're on the edge of a burning city, this definitely is going to affect the thing. But it affects it in surprising ways that you don't have to worry about.

Like "Lily Marlene" came out of the war. It's a very conventional song. A very beautiful song. It touched the troops on both sides. People who had undergone the baptism of fire sang "Lily Marlene" though they thought it was the corniest song in the world. So I don't think it's necessary to tinker with the form. It's just necessary to let the world speak to you.

Do you have a discipline for writing? Do you write at the same time every day?

I get up very early. I like to fill those early hours with that effort.

Most of your writing is done in the morning?

Yes. I find it clearer. The mind is very clear in those early hours.

Is that a daily thing?

Usually. I blow it and fall into disillusion and disrepair. Where the mind and the body and the writing and the relationships and everything else goes to hell. I start drinking too much or eating too much or talking too much or vacationing too much. And then I start recovering the boundaries and putting back the fences and trimming the hedges. But when the thing is working, I find early in the morning best.

I get up at 4:30. My alarm is set for 4:30. Sometimes I sleep through it. But when I'm being good to myself, I get up at 4:30, get dressed, go down to a zendo not far from here. And while the others, I suppose, are moving towards enlightenment, I'm working on a song while I'm sitting there. At a certain moment I can bring what I've learned at the zendo, the capacity to concentrate, I can bring it to bear on the lines that are elluding me.

Then I come back to the house after two hours, it's about 6:30 now, quarter to seven. I brew an enormous pot of coffee and sit down in a very deliberate way, at the kitchen table or at the computer, and begin, first of all, to put down the lines that have come to me so that I don't forget them. And then play the song over and over again, try to find some form.

Those are wonderful hours. Before the phone starts ringing, before your civilian life returns to you with all its bewildering complexities. It's a simple time in the morning. A *wonderful*, invigorating time.

Do you find that your mind is always working on songs, even when you're not actively working?

Yes. But I'm actively working on songs most of the time. Which is why my personal life has collapsed. Mostly I'm working on songs.

* * *

Neil Young
Redwood, California, 1990

He writes a lot of songs in his car, in motion, going forward, rarely looking back. It's the way he lives his life, moving from one intersection to the next, flowing with the traffic of time. And on the freeway, as in life, Neil Young doesn't spend a lot of time worrying about the other cars. Instead, he's in the backseat of his old Cadillac, playing an acoustic guitar, writing another song. "That's my only rule," he says. "No matter where I am, or what's going on, if I have an idea for a song, I write it. Right then and there."

He's been alternately praised and panned throughout his career for continually moving on, and refusing to repeat himself. After periodic enormous successes over the years, such as *Harvest*, and *Rust Never Sleeps*, Neil has gone swimming in eclectic and experimental waters, constantly reversing and extending himself, from acoustic to electric and back again, from folk to blues to country to R&B to computer generated music to garage band rock and beyond.

At the time of our interview, the press was in the process of lavishing vast praise onto Young's album, *Ragged Glory*. And it is a truly great Neil Young album, but one of the likely reasons its glory has been so unanimous is that it's a music that critics can easily understand: rock and roll, plain and simple, two guitars, bass and drums. Many writers utilized a not uncommon form of rock revisionism, extolling the greatness of this album by denouncing past work. One critic went so far as to wax poetic, describing Young as moving through the eighties "flitting from style to style like a moth banging on a chain of lightbulbs." The implication here, apparently, is that songwriters would be better off banging on only one lightbulb.

In truth, Young created a lot of great work in the eighties, and it's a greatness that is not diminished by his dabbling in a variety of styles. Few albums better suited the greediness of the late eighties than *This Note's for You*, and he did it in the guise of an old bluesman, fronting a killer ten-piece band. It was followed by the album *Freedom*, with its anthemic "Rockin' in the Free World," mirroring the miracle of Eastern Europe's liberation and the fall of the Berlin Wall.

It's true there were times when Young's writing in the eighties wasn't always as eloquent and descriptive as his greatest work. But through times of hardship, such as the heartbreak of discovering that his newborn son, Ben, was afflicted with cerebral palsy, Young kept his car moving down the freeway, and he never stopped writing. When the words were hard to find, simple ones sufficed, and he sometimes expressed his emotions in the most elemental of ways: "Got mashed potatoes. Got mashed potatoes. Ain't got no T-Bone."

But this is nothing new. Neil has always made some statement in song, even at the times when life was so painful that saying anything at all was an effort. When Danny Whitten of Crazy Horse died of a drug overdose, Young responded with *Tonight's the Night*, an album that stripped away all veneer to reveal the anguish of living with a friend's absence. It was an album, Neil said, that was hard to play for the record executives, especially when they responded to it by saying, "Maybe instead of putting this out, Neil, you should take some time off and come back when you're ready." But put it out he did, and it stands to this day as one of the most emphatic examples ever of songwriting straight from the soul, of translating into art elemental emotions usually kept concealed.

And after taking us with him to the depths of his anguish in that album, he brought us completely to the opposite end of the spectrum a few years later with *Comes a Time*, an acoustic anthology of inner peace and joy, the happiest album he or just about anybody has ever made. And miracles of miracles: he's actually smiling on the cover! Preceding his undisputed masterpiece, *Rust Never Sleeps*, by a full year, *Comes a Time* seems like one of the only moments in his career when he veered off the freeway for a little while, and simply enjoyed the beauty of the countryside all around him.

What critics don't always grasp is that, regardless of the instrumental attire of his records, at their heart is always solid, imaginative, joyful writing; songs which accurately reflect Young's state of mind at that moment in time. Maybe because he's produced simply so much material in his career (thirty-plus solo albums since 1968), the sheer brilliance of his songwriting gets underestimated. But his use of natural imagery (such as those famous "blue blue windows behind the stars" from "Helpless"), and his uncommon mastery of the narrative song, has set him apart from other songwriters since he began.

As an example, check out "Powderfinger," a song so vivid that it resounds like a chilling dream, a dream that ends none too soon. It's a tremendous lesson in the art of narrative songwriting, set to a passionate, folk-rock feel. A graphic picture is painted in the opening line, establishing the setting: "Look out, Mama, there's a white boat comin' up the river / With a big red beacon and a flag and a man on the rail. . . ." The narrator leads us through a conflagration, describes his own death, and then speaks to us from beyond the world of the living.

In "Pocahantas," Young again transcends linear time to show us an America of the past and present simultaneously. The first two verses of the song describe ancient Indian activities, canoes cutting through cold waters under still starry skies. But the ways of the white men soon spoil this splendor, and by the third verse, native memories have become little more than trinkets and souvenirs.

All of these songs have a particularly American slant, but an America that encompasses both our origins and the sad slapstick of contemporary life. In the final verse of "Pocahantas," Marlon Brando and the Indian princess sit together at a fire, talking about Hollywood, reflecting the merging of movies and memory in the American mind. It's a perspective colored by Young's Canadian roots, allowing him to view America from the outside.

He was born in Toronto, Ontario, on November 12, 1945. His father, a well-known Canadian sports writer, gave him a ukelele for his thirteenth Christmas. It started off that forward momentum which has never ceased since: from the uke he moved to the banjo, and from there eventually to the acoustic guitar and then to the electric.

His first band was called the Jades and his second the Squires, which he formed in 1963. Being in a band inspired him to start writing songs, and his first emerged about a year later. For a little while he shared an apartment in Canada with a black singer then named Rick Matthews, who later changed his name to Rick James, had a huge hit with "Super Freak," and became the king of new wave-punk funk. James, who was only 15 then, was in Canada hiding out, having gone AWOL from the U.S. Navy.

Young moved to New York and worked as a folksinger on the coffeehouse circuit for a while, until he met Bruce Palmer and formed a band with him called the Mynah Birds. At Neil's urging, Rick James came down from Canada to join the band, and the Mynahs recorded an album for Motown. It never got released, however, because James was soon arrested for desertion from the Navy.

Dismayed but driven, Young and Palmer moved to L.A. It was when they were on the freeway, appropriately, in the midst of a traffic jam, that they nearly collided with two old friends from New York, Stephen Stills and Richie Furay. The four decided to form a band, and along with drummer Dewey Martin, they called themselves The Herd. When Young discovered that there was a steamroller named after a buffalo, that was deemed an even more fitting analogy for their music, and they renamed the band Buffalo Springfield.

The band's first self-titled album contained their one and only Top Ten single, Stephen Stills' "For What It's Worth" ("Stop, hey, what's that sound?"). But as with all of the bands with which he's ever played, Young doesn't stay in one place very long; if he gets caught in traffic, chances are he'll get off the freeway at the nearest exit and take a side road. In 1968, when Buffalo Springfield was scheduled to appear at the Monterey Pop Festival, Neil didn't show up. The band went on without him that night, but broke up soon thereafter, releasing the posthumous *Last Time Around* in 1969, long after Young had gone.

He returned then, as he would many more times throughout his career, to the role of a solo performer, and landed a record deal with Reprise in 1969. It was his second solo album, though, *Everybody Knows This is Nowhere*, that put him on the map, with classic originals such as the title song, "Cinnamon Girl," and "Cowgirl in the Sand." It was also the first of many albums he recorded with Crazy Horse as his backing group, providing him with a raw and visceral energy that would empower him many times over the next decades.

Following the release of his third album, *After The Goldrush*, he was invited to join Crosby, Stills and Nash, reuniting with his Buffalo Springfield bandmember Stills, as well as David Crosby from the Byrds and Graham Nash of the Hollies. He added his name to theirs in a law firm style which was then still uncommon, creating an unearthly vocal blend and an overabundance of songwriting talent that inspired all four artists, then at the peak of their collective power, to create a true masterpiece of folk-rock music, *Deja Vu*. Their live album, *Four Way Street*, released in 1971, offered up a tasty mixture of acoustic and electric material, and signaled, with its title, the separate paths the four artists were about to take. When they parted later that year, "clashes of personality" was the reason given for the break-up.

Thus was Young launched into a constantly shifting cavalcade of albums, both solo and group efforts: folk, rock, country and blues, always with compelling songwriting at their center.

When we spoke, he was in the studio of his ranch in Redwood, California, rehearsing with Crazy Horse. It's a kingdom of music—Neil is known to send music from his studio in stereo: the left channel goes to the giant speakers in the barn, the right channel to the speakers in the house, and they're played simultaneously at stadium-sized volume. Neil then goes out on a rowboat on his lake with the music playing and shouts, "*MORE BARN! MORE HOUSE!*" until he achieves the mix he desires.

Though he's recently completed compiling a new collection of unreleased and rare recordings from his personal archives, he doesn't like to spend a lot of time looking back. The way he has maintained an active interest in his music over the years is by always moving forward, in music and in life. "It's what I'm doing now, man, right now, that matters," he said emphatically. "Not yesterday, or the day before that, but now. Right now."

When you get a song going, do you always stay there and try to finish it then or do you come back to it?
Usually I sit down and I go until I'm trying to think. As soon as I start thinking, I quit.

What do you mean by that?
I mean that I start consciously trying to think of what I'm going to do next. Then I quit. Then when I have an idea out of nowhere, I start up again. When that idea stops, I stop. I don't force it. If it's not there, it's not there and there's nothing you can do about it.

Do you ever feel that these songs come from a source that is beyond you?

Well, that's all theory. I don't know if there's a hard and fast rule about that. Some of them I know must be coming directly through me, because they're more personal. And other ones . . . it's a subconscious thing.

I think the spirit is all around us and we all have minds, you know, and it's a chemical thing going on. There's the conscious mind and the subconscious mind and the spirit. And I can just only guess as to what is really going on there, I can't tell you. [*Laughs*] So whatever I would say, there's no rule. I can't say. Someone may say but they don't know. So I'm not even going to bother to say because I have no idea.

Do you have any advice at all for songwriters as to how to get in touch with that spirit?

Stop trying. Let the force be with you. [*Laughs*] May the force be with you! I loved that movie when it came out and they said that. I said, "Yeah, right on. That's exactly right."

You begin to recognize it after you've written a few songs. You start to recognize that when you have an idea for a song and you start hearing a melody over and over again with words in your head, that's when you should write the song. If you don't have an idea and you don't hear anything going over and over in your head, don't sit down and try to write a song. You know, go and mow the lawn.

There are a lot of songwriters who don't hear those ideas—

Well, there's a lot of songs that sound like they don't hear them.

It reminds me of your song "Crime in the City" with that great verse about the producer who comes up with a perfect track before writing the song.

[*Laughs*] Yeah. And there's a lot of that going on.

How are you able to stay artistically inventive and fresh?

Because I don't really care about what people think about it. I mean, I do care if people like it or not. But that doesn't affect what I'm doing. So I can go ahead and do something like *Everybody's Rockin'* and get completely into it knowing that a lot of people are going to think, "Hey, this is bullshit. Neil shouldn't be doing this. This doesn't *mean* anything; the songs are meaningless. I mean, 'I'm Kind of Fond of Wanda,' I mean, what the hell is going on here?" But that doesn't bother me at all. As far as I'm concerned, that song is just as important as any other song that I ever wrote. And it stands up just as well. It's just written in an attitude and a genre that nobody understands. That they don't want to understand! They don't want to see me like that. So I'll write a song like that and then I'll write a song like "Will to Love," you know. It's two different things. But they both happen the same way.

It's a character thing. You get into a character. Subconsciously you could be a whole different person than you are consciously.

You've been able to do that in ways that hardly any other artists have done. It seems that the industry tries to keep artists in very narrow areas—

Imaging. You need imaging here. They all want it.

Do you think the industry is detrimental to songwriters being able to express themselves?

No. Songwriters are detrimental to expressing themselves if they *don't*. If they're waiting for somebody to tell them what to write, then they're the cause of the problem. It's certainly not the fault of the music business. If all the songwriters were tuned into what was going on, then it would be cool.

Who knows? I'm just me. There are other songwriters who do it a different way. Some other guys might lock themselves up with a bunch of amphetamine pills in a hotel room and get out the thesaurus and try to find words that rhyme and just go *completely nuts!* And write a great album.

Do you think that approach can produce anything worthwhile?

I don't know. I don't advise that. [*Laughs*]

Can drugs ever help a songwriter or do they get in the way?

Well, you know, I think an aspirin now and again is not too bad. [*Laughs*]

I don't know about drugs and songwriting. I mean, I've taken drugs and written songs but I don't advise it.

Do you remember writing your first song?

I think I was about 14 or 15.

Do you remember what music you were listening to then?

I listened to music all the time from when I can first remember. So I don't really know where it started. It's like it always was there.

I liked Jimmy Reed. And I guess the Beatles were just about to happen.

When did you begin playing guitar?

Well, I started playing ukelele when I was eight or nine. I had a little plastic one, which I taught myself to play. It just went on from there.

And when you started writing songs, you kept at it?

Yeah. It's just one of those things. Once I started, I never wanted to stop and I've been doing it ever since.

Do you remember how you taught yourself to write songs?

It just happened. You sit down and start playing and all of a sudden I'm writing down some words or thinking of some words or singing some words. Once you get started, then you stop when you're done.

You've written such an amazing amount of songs. Is songwriting an enjoyable process for you?

Oh, yeah! That's all I do. It's my main thing. Writing and playing music. There's really nothing else that I care about as much. Songwriting is my life.

Some songwriters approach their writing like a job, on an every day basis. Is that how you do it?

No. I just write when I feel like it. Day or night, no matter where I am, that takes precedent. That's the only rule I have. If I have an idea, I work on it. [*Pause*] It's not even like working on it. If I have an idea and I want to work on a song, I find space to do it.

Do you always write on guitar?

No. Anything. It doesn't matter, really. Don't even need an instrument. Sometimes I write them in my head.

You were talking earlier about adopting a character when writing, and I thought of your Bluenotes album, in which you became a blues artist with a blues band—

I love that record. There's another record of the Bluenotes that's really good. No one's ever heard that. It's a double live album. And it's really great. I love it. It's music that no one wants to hear. [*Laughs*] Except for a few people.

Your song "Powderfinger" [from *Rust Never Sleeps*] is one of the most amazing that you've written; it's a great example of narrative songwriting, telling a very vivid story that even goes through the narrator's death. Do you remember writing it?

Yes, I do. I started writing that song in 1965 at David Briggs' house in Topanga Canyon. But I didn't finish it until 1974.

I had "Look out, Mama, there's a white boat coming up the river / with a big red beacon and a flag and a man on the rail. . . ." That was the beginning. I got that before my first solo album. But the rest of the song didn't happen until 1974.

But that's an interesting song because, as you said, the guy singing it dies in the middle of the song, so maybe that's why it took so long to finish it.

The same thing happened with my song "Cortez the Killer." It's the same kind of song and the person in that one kind of dies during it. That song all happened in one sitting.

Do you remember what inspired either of those songs?

No. What inspires the lyric is a subconscious thing, so I don't remember it.

Do you remember writing the song "Southern Pacific" [from *re-ac-tor*]?

Yeah. I like that one. I wrote it on a dobro. I was thinking about the sound of a train.

Your song "Wrecking Ball" [from *Freedom*] is beautiful.

That's an interesting song, too. In that there are two complete versions of that song with different sets of lyrics. Completely different songs with the same melody, and the same chorus.

That song has such a strong melody. And many writers nowadays feel that melodies are unimportant and in time will be forgotten. Do you feel that?

Hey, a melody is a melody. It catches your ear. And just when things get to the point where people say melodies are on their way out and they won't be coming back, that's when they come back. As soon as everybody is sure that they're gone. You can't come back until that's happened. I think there's plenty of room for melodies.

Do you remember writing "Pocahantas" [from *Rust Never Sleeps*]?

I wrote that in a car, I think. I might have written it at a friend's house and in a car. I probably started it in the car on the way over and finished it at the house. Late 1974.

How about your song "Comes a Time"?
Fort Lauderdale, 1976–77.

That album, *Comes a Time*, is such a bright and happy album and you're actually smiling on the cover—
That's because it was so much fun to make! I had a good time making it. I did most of the original tracks by myself, playing guitar and all; I did them by myself and then went down to Nashville and added a few things. I enjoyed that one.

Where were you when you wrote "Mr. Soul"?
I was on the floor. In my bathroom. In a little cabin in Laurel Canyon. I stayed up late writing that one. I recorded that one twice.

Where were you when you wrote "Fountainebleau"?
Coconut Grove. That's where I wrote that. And the place you write a song has a big effect on the way the song turns out. Yeah, it's geographic. That's what affects it more than the subconscious: the geographic situation. The place you are when you write the song has a huge effect on the way the song is going to turn out. That's why it's important for songwriters to be in a good place.

Your song "Sunny Inside" is one of your happiest songs. It's a blues, but a happy blues.
Oh, yeah. Thanks for bringing that one up. That's a good song. I like that one. It was the first one that I wrote for the Bluenotes album.

Do you have a memory of writing "Sugar Mountain"?
Yeah. I wrote it in Canada in a little rented house. I think it was late at night that I wrote it. I put it on a B-side of a single and there just never seemed to be any reason to record it again. And we put it on the *Decade* album.

The song "Ohio"?
I wrote that in Atascadero, California. I wrote it, [David] Crosby was there, he picked up the phone and booked studio time and we went in and recorded it the next day. The song was written, recorded and released in about two weeks, something that would be completely impossible to do today.

So many of your songs have such striking imagery. I think of "After The Gold Rush" and "Helpless." Is using pictures in songs something that came naturally to you?
It's always been the way it's been with me. Big pictures. Wide open spaces. That's why the guitar solos are so good. That's why it's good to have a guitar solo along with a song, because you can play a long, extended solo that kind of fills in the open space. It's hard to get open space in lyrics.

Bob Dylan said that when he first heard "Heart of Gold" on the radio that he felt, for the first time, that here was somebody doing his thing. Was Dylan an influence on your writing?
Oh, yeah. A great influence. I admire his work very much. Especially his newest work. I think it's great.

Do you remember writing "Heart of Gold"?

I think I wrote it on a tour. Wrote it on piano. It was originally part of "A Man Needs a Maid." It was like a suite and then I decided to make them into two separate songs, and one of them became "Heart of Gold."

Do you have favorite keys to play in?
I've written a lot of minor songs. E minor, A minor.

There are also a lot of them in D major.
Yeah. D modal, really. D with no thirds. It's not really major or minor but somewhere in between.

Does a key have a strong effect on a song, or can you interchange keys?
The original key is usually the best.

"Married Man" is an unusual blues. You sing, "I'm a married man, respect my happy home."
Oh, I like that song. I think I wrote that song in my car. I have a '54 Caddy limo. I was on my way down from Northern California to play with the Bluenotes. I was on Highway 5. Ben Keith and I were sitting in the backseat. Our driver, Wog, was driving and listening to tapes, and I was playing my guitar. And I wrote that song and a song called "Downhill Slide." I wrote those on that trip. "Twilight" I also wrote on that trip.

Do you have a favorite song?
There's a song by the Troggs that I always loved. Not "Wild Thing," though that's a great song. I can't remember the name of it but it's a ballad.

You've got such a huge body of work. Do you have a sense as a songwriter that your work will live on beyond you?
No, not really. I try not to think of those things.

Why?
Because it doesn't have anything to do with today. It doesn't help me with what I'm doing now.

Are you looking forward to the songs you haven't written yet, the ones still to come?
Oh, yeah. I hope I get to do this for a long time to go. I don't see any reason to stop now.

* * *

Graham Nash
Encino, California 1993

Graham Nash was amazed. After performing on the same bill as the legendary songwriting duo Leiber & Stoller at the 1993 "Salute to the American Song-writer" in Los Angeles, he humbly asked for their autographs. Their inscription surprised him greatly: "To Graham Nash—with envy—Leiber & Stoller."

"It was actually kind of a shock," he said a few months later, sitting at a colossal wooden table in the spacious sunny kitchen of his L.A. home. "To realize that Leiber and Stoller would even know who I was, and secondly that they would envy me."

But as Nash's wife, Susan, pointed out to him, all songwriters want to be performers, and Leiber & Stoller never had that chance, writing their songs for other artists to record.

It's that distinction that has set Graham and his cohorts apart from previous generations of songwriters: Songs necessarily become more deeply genuine and heartfelt when a songwriter writes them for himself to sing. Along with good friends like Joni Mitchell, David Crosby, Jackson Browne and others, Graham Nash wrote songs from the heart, songs about his own life and visions.

It wasn't always that way. He started his career in the British pop-rock band The Hollies, and along with Allan Clarke crafted songs that were designed to be hits, and to race to the top of that Top 40. And he was great at it: Nash has always had a great gift for concocting sweet, simple, memorable melodies. But when he started to match those melodies with words that re-

flected the free spirit of the times, inspired by the experimentation of the sixties, The Hollies grew uneasy. His first really experimental song, "King Midas
in Reverse," was recorded by the group against their wishes, and when it failed
to be a hit they felt justified in attacking his expansive inclinations, and refused
to record his new songs.

When he brought in "The Sleep Song," with the lines, "I will kiss your
eyes open, take off my clothes and lie by your side," the reference to nudity
was considered objectionable, and it was rejected. Rather than fight forces he
knew were detrimental to his artistic soul (although economically beneficial),
he left The Hollies to pursue a more unrestricted, individual form of musical
expression. Inspired by the open-ended possibilities he found in the lives and
songs of Californian friends, he moved to Los Angeles.

Soon after his move, Nash added a third harmony part to a song being
sung by Stephen Stills and David Crosby. His harmony was so effortlessly perfect, and such a sweetly smooth complement to the earthier voices of Crosby
& Stills, that all three singers had to stop and laugh; they knew they were in
the presence of something important, something bigger than the three of them.
And musical history was made.

Maybe his greatest gift as a songwriter is his capacity for graceful simplicity. While Crosby would write asymmetrically abstract melodies based on open-
tunings such as "Deja Vu," and Stills would write extended suites such as
"Suite: Judy Blue Eyes," Nash contributed gems of sweet melodic and lyrical
simplicity such as "Our House" and "Teach Your Children," providing the same
complementary balance in his songwriting as he did in his harmony vocals. On
later Crosby–Nash albums he continued to brilliantly balance Crosby's abstract
musings with his own solidly symmetrical songs. A perfect example is the progression from Crosby's ambitious "Critical Mass," which is a four-part vocal
cantata, into "Wind on the Water," Nash's glorious elegy for the whales.

These days he's a very busy man. We met very early on consecutive morn-
ings so that he could get to other activities. Besides rehearsing and recording
with Crosby and Stills for an upcoming album and tour, Nash is also busy writing new songs (lyrics for a tribute to departed friends Harry Nilsson and Frank
Zappa were in the works on the piano); taking photos; sculpting; and running
Nash Editions, a fine art press. Outside his home in buildings behind an enormous turquoise swimming pool, he has two studios going simultaneously—one
for music and one for photography—both filled with happy active people working on a myriad of projects. In the backyard is an immense chunk of white
marble which sits unsculpted, perhaps a conscious metaphor for work left to be
done.

Despite the whirlwind of action around him, Graham Nash is a thoroughly
peaceful, happy, humble and generous man. "I'm not into being a star," he says,
distinguishing himself from others with whom his name is famously linked. "I
like to be a regular person."

He was born on February 2, 1942 in Blackpool, England, where two major
events shaped his musical life. The first was when his mother gave him the
choice of a bicycle or a guitar for his thirteenth birthday, explaining that the
family could only afford one. He chose the guitar. Allan Clarke, a friend since

they both were five, also got a guitar, and the two began to perform skiffle songs together. They already knew how to harmonize, a skill they had perfected by singing "The Lord's Prayer" and other songs in glee clubs and minstrel shows. When skiffle music became the latest craze, the two jumped on the bandwagon.

"Skiffle came along and we realized, hey, it's a cheap guitar, it's a tea-chest bass, it's a washboard with thimbles, this is not high-tech here. Every kid in the city, including us, wanted to do that. And we did."

His first song, written at the age of seventeen, was a collaboration with Clarke called "Hey, What's Wrong with Me?" It was inspired by hearing the tremendous energy of the Everly Brothers at a high school dance, the second main event to shape his life. "Halfway across the dance floor, the opening bars to 'Bye Bye Love' came on," he said. "My life has changed in very specific moments, and this was one of them. It stopped me and Allan dead. We'd been doing skiffle, but this was something different. And I have always, all my life, wanted to make people feel what I felt then when I first heard those first bars of 'Bye Bye Love.' That incredible internal pressure of being overwhelmed by chord structure and sound and melody and voice timbre. It floored me! And I've always wanted to do that for the rest of my life."

What was the main thing that inspired you to move from writing pop songs with The Hollies to writing "The Sleep Song" and more artistically ambitious songs?
It was only until I started to smoke enormous amounts of dope with Crosby that I began to realize there was a lot more I could do. And so, because I was experimenting with mind-expansion drugs, and The Hollies to a certain extent were continuing their drink mode of the north of England, that I began to think differently and think more about the responsibility of someone who had this to reflect what's going on around them, reflect what's going on in their personal lives; and in an attempt to talk to myself about my problems, about things I'd see, and externalize them as songs, I began to write better songs.

And "The Sleep Song" was the first?
No, probably "King Midas in Reverse" was the first one of those songs. We wrote that in what was Yugoslavia. We were in this hotel and I was looking at my life and realizing that on the surface I had everything: I had a successful band (The Hollies), I had a successful life, I was creating—yes, maybe shallow stuff—but I was creating, I was feeling good about myself. But at the same time there was this sadness in me about not really "doing it." You know, there was something missing in my life, that on the surface everything was golden, but underneath it was all crumbling to dust. And that was what "King Midas" was about.

It was one of the first songs where I really attempted to bring The Hollies into a new kind of relationship with their music. And they trusted me, they followed me; we made the record, we added the orchestra, et cetera. It was a pretty far-out record for the time. And it failed miserably. So that gave them ammunition to say, "We're not going that way. We're gonna go back and stay in what we do best." Which, in hindsight, was probably a good decision for them. But it wasn't a good decision for me. And at that same time, I'm hanging out with Crosby. He started sending me tapes with strange songs, with titles like "Guinevere" and "Deja Vu."

I left The Hollies on December 8, 1968. I was in Los Angeles, in David's house, on December 10, 1968, two days later. Gave it all up, took a deep breath.

David and Stephen [Stills] took me for a ride, we were smoking joints in the back of Stephen's Bentley; and I'm sitting in the back, and he's talking with David, and David leans over and says, "Okay, which one of us is gonna steal him?" 'Cause they checked me out; they knew they wanted to make music with me. They instinctively knew—as Cass Elliot, I believe, had set this whole thing up—for the three of us to make music together.

It was either in Joni's living room, or in Cass' kitchen. The reason that we can't remember, of course, is that: Who can remember anything from the sixties? But what happened is that they had made a demo that sounded pretty good, and it was very much David and Stephen's demos: "Wooden Ships," "Long Time Gone," "49 Bye-Byes," stuff like that. They said that they just worked out a two-part harmony to the song, "You Don't Have to Cry."

They sang it, and it was pretty good, two-part. And I said, "That's really great. Sing it again once." So they said, "Okay," and they sang it again. And I said, "Just indulge me; sing it a third time." I'd always been a quick study of stuff that I like, as most people are—when you really like something, you can get into it immediately. By the third time they sang it, I had my third part down, completely cold—phrasing, melody, everything. And it was so staggering to us, that we stopped in the middle of the song and burst out laughing. Because we had always had a sad history with bands—David would be thrown out of The Byrds, Buffalo Springfield had broken up, I'd left The Hollies; and here was this sound. I'd heard that glimpse from heaven. I'd heard it, and I wanted it, and I knew that it was fabulous. Because it thrilled me to no end.

So when people used to say, "You're leaving the bloody Hollies and all that fame and money, are you daft, lad?" They didn't know what I had heard. They didn't know that I was placing my life in my own intuition of something that I'd heard that I wanted desperately. They had heard my songs; they'd heard "The Sleep Song," I played them "Marrakesh Express," which The Hollies didn't want to record.

Do you recall what inspired "Marrakesh Express"?

It was just me on the train, with my guitar, you know, jamming with the experiences of what was happening around me. I mean, every line in that song is true. We were sharing a cabin with American ladies five foot tall in blue. We were in the first-class cabin. But I, as always, would go and wander. And I wandered back, to the back of the train, where there were people in djellebas lighting fires, and had pigs and ducks and chickens and goats and straw. So I spent most of my time back there, just observing. Then I went back to my cabin to write about it. I was open enough to react to the circumstances, and lucky enough to be in the right place for this melody to come through.

In all the years you've been writing songs, has your approach to writing songs changed in any way?

It's still the same process. I see something, I react, I internalize it, and I externalize it as music. I have probably saved myself several million dollars in psychiatry bills because I talk to myself a lot. I think most songwriters do. I think most people do, have internal dialogues. I just happen to have trained my internal muscles and the internal spirit to create music. You've always had a great gift for melody.

It's a craft. You know, if I can't get you in the first 30 seconds, you're gone. You're onto the next channel. You're channel-surfing through music. And I learned that with The Hollies. And I'm very grateful for the instruction or background that I went through by being in The Hollies for eight years. When you have to write a song that has to grab them immediately or else they're gone, that wears off.

You were talking about how music just comes to you. Do your songs generally start with a musical idea and then a lyrical idea, or do words and music come to you at the same time?

I've done it every way. I have a conveyer belt in my mind, and I see this conveyer belt. And I'll take a little melody that I'll hear, and I'll just mull over it, and keep thinking about it during the day, and keep thinking about it. They formulate themselves, so that when I get to the physical act of, "Okay, now it's time for either the piano or guitar," I'm halfway there. I do a lot of pre-thinking about it.

Lyrically and musically?

Lyrically and musically. And sometimes it's a melody that hangs me up, and sometimes it's lyrics. And sometimes I get pissed that whatever it is won't leave me alone. At the same time, I'm completely thankful that it still happens. I mean, I get pissed in a good way. It's more, "God, this is great, I'm hung up on this one phrase again," and that's what happens. I get hung up on something and it won't leave me alone. It's like a melody that you can't forget, and it won't leave me alone until it finishes itself. I don't know whether I've trained my body to do that, or whether it's something way beyond.

Does it feel as if song ideas come from somewhere beyond you?

I think they're coming from somewhere beyond me but they're very much based in the physical world. I'll hear a bird go whistle and it will start me off. I take influence from everywhere, from taking my first breath in the morning to laying it down last thing at night, I'm always creating something.

Have you found in all your years of writing that anything affects those times when songs come to you?

Time is our only currency. The only important thing in my life is time. Time to deal with me, time to deal with my wife and my kids, and then everything else. It's like this Eskimo sculptor who did a beautiful walrus, and a critic came to him and said, "How did you make this beautiful walrus?" And the Eskimo kind of looked at him quizzically and he said, "Well, it's easy; you just get a stone and you cut away everything that doesn't look like a walrus." So I try and keep myself suspended in creation.

So songwriting is not something you do like a job—
[*Laughs*] No! It's constant. It's constant with me. Constant.

Neil Young said that when he gets an idea for a song he has to sit down right there and do it or he'll lose touch with that original inspiration.
It's not that way with me.

You can work on something over a period of time?
Oh, absolutely. It took me four years to write "Cathedral."

It wouldn't finish itself. It was such an important topic for me, this realization that most of the world's wars to that point had been, in part, in most part, created from religious differences. "My god's better than yours, so I'll kill you."

"Cathedral" is about a real experience of me being on LSD and going to Stonehenge, lying in the middle of Stonehenge. Trying to figure out what was happening with my life, going to Winchester Cathedral, opening the door, feeling this strange presence at my feet, looking down at my legs which are now wavering, and seeing that I was standing on the grave of somebody who had died on my birthday. I mean, it's all completely true.

So you came to that song with the intention of writing about religion?
Yeah. But it was such an important idea to me that I had to make sure that I got it right. And I'm still not sure that I got it right.

Is it unusual that you'll approach a song with such a specific idea of what you want it to say?
Absolutely.

Generally is it more a feeling of following than leading?
Yeah, I follow it but I do guide it the way I want, you know, the way this melody is making me feel. I will guide it because by the time I've been intoxicated with the melody and the opening verses, I know what it is that I want to say with the song, so I will guide it that way.

A song like "Immigration Man," for example—
That came out of pure anger. I was in Vancouver with CSNY. Coming back across the border, Neil got in, David got in, Stephen got in, but I didn't, because I was on an H-1 visa at the time from England, I was not an American citizen, and they weren't going to let me in. In the meantime, there are people asking me for my autographs, you know? When I finally got back, I got off the plane in San Francisco, I took a cab to my house, and sat down immediately to the piano. And I wrote "Immigration Man" on the back of a book called *The Silver Locust* by Ray Bradbury. It was the first thing that I could find.

You wrote the words and music at the same time?
Yeah. Yeah. It came to me completely out of anger.

Your songs have always had a message of hope in them, even when you're talking about the whales, in "Wind on the Water," or about what happened to the Chicago Eight in "Chicago." The message is that change is possible.
Well, it's what I explained to you before. I'll always take the positive path, because the negative ends up in darkness, and I won't go there.

"Wind on the Water," for example, is very musically beautiful. It gives us hope that if something this beautiful can come from this, that there is hope.

Yes. I have great hope. I have to. I look in the faces of my kids and I've gotta hope. I have to.

Was "Wind on the Water" a song where the words and the music came together?

Yes. You know the famous story about "Scrambled Eggs"? [In which Paul McCartney used "Scrambled Eggs" as a working lyric for "Yesterday."] Well, we all have our "Scrambled Egg" versions, and mine was that there was *Time* and *Newsweek* in the back of my car, so it started out as "*Newsweek* on the backseat, and there's *Time*. . . ." It started out as something completely different. And then it went to my feelings for Crosby. I don't know why the two were related, but they were, about people throwing harpoons at him, in England—you know, the press that hated The Byrds and all that stuff. And people have always been throwing harpoons at Crosby. Always. Some of them stick, some of them don't. So, as a matter of fact, even though it is a song that evolved into a statement about how we treat the great whales, and that great statement of Gandhi's that the signpost of every civilization is how it treats its pets and its animals, it really started with two magazines in the back of my car, and my thoughts about David.

And then he came up with "Critical Mass" after you had "Wind on the Water" to go with it? That one came afterwards?

No, I believe he had "Critical Mass" before. I've always loved that piece of music, I always will. I can never separate the two pieces of music now.

Did "Chicago" come quickly?

Yes. From complete anger. I got a call from a man called Wavy Gravy. A dear friend of ours, one of my heroes, in 1969, saying that the people who had been on trial for the Chicago Eight needed funds for their defense, and would CSNY be interested in doing a benefit concert for them. David and I wanted to go, and Neil and Stephen didn't. So "Chicago" was my song to Stephen and Neil, to say, "Won't you just come to Chicago just to sing?"

Because I wanted to raise money for that defense fund, because you cannot, to me, bind and chain a man to a seat, and call it a fair trial. What happened in Chicago was shocking. And Mayor Daley's attitude was shocking.

Another of your most hopeful songs, of course, is "Teach Your Children."

That was written at the Olten Motel in Leeds, England. It was one of the very last shows I ever did with The Hollies. I wrote three songs that night: "Sleep Song," "Lady of the Island" and "Teach Your Children."

Quite a night!

I was feeling good about where I knew I was going, meaning that I'd heard me and David and Stephen sing. I knew that my time with The Hollies was coming to an end. I knew that I was going to America, because I wanted to go there. I mean, this is an incredibly beautiful, life-sustaining country.

I have my original demo for "Teach Your Children" that I recorded in England in 1968. It's a completely different record. And the way it's completely different is that when I played the song for Stephen, it was this kind of English folk song delivery. And Stephen said, "Hey, man, you gotta make it swing. You gotta put a groove to this. Show me the chords." I showed him the chords. He said, "Well, go away for ten minutes." And I went away for ten minutes and came back and he said, "Let's try it like this." And he played it the way that "Teach Your Children" is known to millions of people. To let go and trust your partner, to follow his instinct with it. If Stephen Stills wants to take a piece of my music and do something to it, I'm gonna let him. You know? Because he is Stephen Stills.

"Our House" is another example of a sweet and simple lyric with a beautiful melody that's just timeless. Was it written for Joni Mitchell?
Yes. One day we went to breakfast, and on Ventura Boulevard there was a small antique store. And Joni was, at that point, just coming into money, and was buying special things for herself. She's never been extravagant. She's always been very careful, because I think people who were born without money are that way, because they never had any. We were in this antique store, and she found this beautiful vase, and bargained with the people, got it for the price that she wanted, and we took it home. And it was chilly, and I said, "You know, I'll light a fire, you go put flowers in the vase." [*Laughs*]
It was stupidly simple. But it really happened. And to this day, at her house in Beverly Hills, there is a shelf in the kitchen, about nine feet in the air, small niche in the wall, and in that niche is the vase. And I wrote it on Joni's piano.

Do you remember writing "Girl to Be on My Mind"?
New Year's Eve. New Year's Eve, San Francisco, in my house where the back window overlooks Haight-Ashbury. It was the first time that I played on my Wurlitzer piano. And I'd just gotten it, and was just testing it out, and it was New Year's Eve, hence, the coming of the year. This was like 11:00 at night, and in an hour another year was coming. New Year's Eve, 1969, coming into 1970. The end of the decade.

Also, "Frozen Smiles," also from that album, is a great song.
My song to Stephen [Stills].

Really? I always thought it was written to a woman.
I love Stephen. But I have the courage to tell him when I think he's screwing up. As my friends have the courage to tell me.

Do you remember writing "Just a Song Before I Go?"
Very quick song. I was in Hawaii. I had a 2:00 flight, and this was like 12:30, and this guy who we were visiting in Maui said, "Hey, you've got a half-hour before you have to catch your flight. You're supposed to be some big hot-shot writer. Why don't you write a song before you go." I said, "Well, yeah, I will write a song." And sat down and wrote to this guy that I hardly knew, his name is Spider.

There's that great line in there: "traveling twice the speed of sound, it's easy to get burned."

I'd just been on the Concord. And traveled twice the speed of sound. And its easy to get burned, 'cause I kept thinking all the time, "Here we are in this aluminum tube, going twice the speed of sound, which is, what, 1200 miles an hour? And if anything goes wrong, you're dead." Like that! You know what I'm saying? You could really get burned. And then I kind of made the inference about cocaine, if you're living your life twice the speed of sound, it's easy to get burned.

In your song "Black Notes," you give permission to a songwriter to write: "Write a song, sing along, and understand that you can play."

Yeah, that was an interesting song. I was performing at Carnegie Hall with Crosby. And there's Stephen sitting in the wings. So me, ever the showman, says to David, "Okay, you go get Stephen—and bring him on. No announcement. It'll drive people crazy. We'll do some CSN stuff and have a great time. I'll just bullshit with the folks; I'll just talk to the audience while you go get him."

He goes off, and I'm talking to the audience, and there's no David or Stephen. So I keep talking, I'm looking around, and there's no David or Stephen. I'm running out of things to say. So I think, well, you know, use it, go with it. I sit down at the piano, and I just start to bang on the black keys. And I'm bangin' and this melody's comin' to me, and I'm goin', "Sit yourself down at the piano / Just about in the middle / Put all your fingers on the black notes any way you want to." I'm hitting them with my elbows, and I write this, and we were recording that night, and that was the song. And that was the song that appeared on the album.

Many of your songs are about America and reflect American ideas. "Military Madness," though, starts off in your birthplace, Blackpool, England.

Because in Blackpool I was born three houses down from the Fun Fair, on the beach, during the end of World War II. And I had to write that song because military madness was killing my country literally. I had relatives who would go to work in the morning, and come back and find the entire block gone when they came home from work. Entire families, entire lives, entire existences snuffed out.

Do you remember writing "Cold Rain"?

I sure do. Making the 1977 CSN album in Miami, we rented this house in West Palm Beach where we all lived together. Big house. I brought my electric piano and my sculpting of David that I was doing. And my unicorn bedspread. And I was living in this room and I had to take a break from the album and go to do some family business in England. And it was wintertime. And I was standing on the steps of the Midland Hotel. I was standing in the snowstorm, and I was watching the people go by. I'm an avid people-watcher. I love people. I love faces. I love lives. And I began to realize that, one, for the grace of God I could still be trundling around Manchester in the freezing miserable weather, and two, that half my friends who had never made that leap were still in Manchester, still digging, still working at the mill, still doing what their fathers and their fathers before them were then, waiting to get that gold watch and lie down and die.

Half my friends are still there doing that. I didn't want that for me. I was the first one in my generation of my family to say, I don't want that as my life. I don't want to work in the engineering factory where my dad worked, where his dad worked. I don't want that. There's something better for me. And I made the leap to come to America. But when I went back to Manchester on this family business, and stood on those steps in the snowstorm, looking at these faces, I wrote "Cold Rain." And I came back.

And whilst Walter Cronkite was reading the news, I finished the song. I started it when he opened the news, and by the time he finished the news a half-hour later, it was done. We went into the studio that night and cut it.

* * *

David Crosby
Encino, California 1993

"Hey, I'm the happy guy!" he says joyfully as he enters his big kitchen in this big house in this big valley of Los Angeles. Though it's barely ten in the morning, David Crosby has been up for hours, having just returned from the offices of Castle Rock Films, where he's been pitching a movie idea. He bursts into the kitchen, and first embraces his mother-in-law and then photographer Henry Diltz, who has joined me today to capture some new pictures of his old friend. The house is bathed in bright, crystalline sunlight, a good match for his sunny demeanor. Though it's been a couple of years now since he kicked drugs and did time in jail, David Crosby is still absolutely delighted at being alive.

The immense joy in this big man, though, is nothing new. Years ago, when he and Joni Mitchell first met in Florida, before her debut album or the debut of Crosby, Stills & Nash, she remembered Crosby's contagious sunniness. "When it comes to expressing infectious enthusiasm," she said, "he is probably the most capable person I know. His eyes were like star sapphires to me. When he laughed they seemed to twinkle like no one else's and so I fell into his merry company . . ."

This joy is aptly expressed in *Thousand Roads*, a solo album released just weeks before our interview, which contains some collaborations, including a song that Crosby wrote with Joni, "Yvette In English," as well as many cover versions of songs by his favorite writers, including Jimmy Webb.

The fact that Crosby has only got a few new songs is not unusual for him. He's never been a prolific songwriter, and when he was in group situations—as in CSN—he was required to write only a third of the songs. But those songs would invariably be, as he called them, "stunners," timeless songs like "Wooden Ships," "Deja Vu," and "Guinevere." Unlike the songs of his close friend Neil Young, Crosby's songs came few and far between. But when they did come, maybe precisely because of his patience in allowing them to emerge naturally, they came like a force of nature, like a storm at sea.

> "We have a lot of trouble because we write our songs just
> right out of what's going on. . . . So sometimes it's really
> hard to sing them, too. . . ."
>
> —Crosby's spoken introduction to his song "Triad"
> recorded in concert for the live Crosby, Stills, Nash &
> Young *Four Way Street* LP

More than anything, his songs are intimate. Rather than write stories or symbols around a subject, he directly approaches the heart of his song, like a guy at a party who blurts out the very thing no one else has the guts to say. In his songs you know a human is speaking right to you: his voice always jumps through the veneer of the record production to go straight for the soul, making statements both blunt and beautiful. "Why can't we go on as three?" from his song "Triad" not only questions the entire foundation of monogamy on which our societies are built, it's also beautiful poetry, as sweet and succinct as a line can get.

His songs have always been about genuine feelings of love: for women, for the sea and for humanity. He's never contrived a song to be a hit and finds beauty in concoctions of the heart that result in organic non-formulaic structures, melodies that flow naturally, wrapped in rich, open-tunings on his guitar. His songs, which are usually asymmetrical, might first appear to be chaotic, like a Jackson Pollack painting or the veins of a leaf, but ultimately fall together with a natural inevitability that instills in them a lasting, haunting power.

There are two things Crosby says he knew how to do long before he was old enough to learn them: sailing and singing harmony. He could sail as easily at the age of six as he could sing close harmony, two talents that have merged in countless songs of the sea, such as "Wooden Ships," "The Lee Shore," "Delta" and "Shadow Captain." All of this maritime imagery might lead astrologically-minded folks to believe he's a Pisces or some other water sign. In fact his chart is full of fire: Born on August 14, 1941, he's a Leo with Aries rising, one of the most combustible combinations that can exist within a single person. With his stars thus stacked, his brother Ethan said, "He just can't not have a big ego trip going."

But Crosby, although bursting with genuine joy, isn't arrogant. In fact he often bounced the praise to his cohorts, saying that it's Graham Nash who is the truly great harmony singer, and it's Neil Young who is the truly amazing songwriter. In fact, in CSN, Crosby almost always sang the middle part, the part that his friend and collaborator Craig Doerge called the "glue that holds the other parts together." Not only is it the most integral part, it's also the toughest and most elusive to sing.

Art Garfunkel, an obvious expert on harmony, said this about Crosby's singing: "You have David, the velvety sort of cement in their sound. It's what used to be in the Hi-Los or in those old Four Freshmen groups—the middle man does the stuff that makes the chord work, but you never notice it. David can be right in front of your eyes in a sort of velvety way and you'll never notice him. There's a Zen-smooth kind of exhale in David's delivery."

Your songs all seem so unforced. Have they generally emerged naturally from the flow of your life, or do you ever sit down with the intention of writing something?

I *can't* do it that way. My songs emerge from my life or wherever they do unbidden and unplanned and completely on a schedule of their own. [*Laughs*] I can't legislate a song into being, it just will not happen for me. I can make a *space* for it to happen, and sometimes it will come and fill the space. Sometimes I'll just pick up the guitar the way I just did just now and fool around. Or go to the piano and just fool around. [*In a cartoonish voice*] "Hello muse? Are you out there? Hellllooooo? Yooooo-hooooo?" But whether they'll come or not. . . .

Lately a thing has happened to me that I had to notice because it keeps happening. Lately, over the last few years, this has happened many times. I'll be going to sleep and the busy mind—the verbal-crystallization-level mind that's talking to you—will be starting to nod off. And the intuitive, imaginative levels of the mind, the part that makes the longer leaps and wider synthesis, gets a shot at the steering wheel for a second, before you actually go unconscious. And in that little window something will leap up, and I will wind up grabbing for the lamp and *frantically* writing pages of lyrics. And it's happened again and again and again.

The first time I remember it happening was "Shadow Captain" several years ago. I was about two hundred miles offshore from here on my boat, and it was three in the morning and I woke up and wrote that *entire* set of lyrics, word for word, and then went back to sleep. You've got to understand, I had *never* thought any image in that song or anything about that entire concept ever before *ever*. And when I got down the bottom: "Shadow captain of a charcoal ship . . ." I went, "*Oooh, Cros, you bad, you BAD!!!*" [*Laughter*] Like I know I love this and I know I never thought it before. So I know it isn't this busy mind, the tap-A, slot-B kind of mind.

And that's a very dreamlike lyric, "Shadow Captain."

Yeah. You know, I don't construct them. *Somebody* in here does. But it is not the verbal, crystallization, currently awake, busy mind that does it.

Do you think it comes from your unconscious mind or from a source beyond that?

I think human minds have as many levels as the Empire State Building or probably a thousand times that many. And I'm sure we don't really know how the creative process works. I know that I *can* work consciously on a song with another person. But there's another kind of chemistry that takes place. And it works best if I come into it with some scraps from the other place. And say, "What do you think it is?" And that nudges something in the other person. And they say, "What if we did this?" And I get a flash myself.

You know, it comes every which way, man. Sometimes you write the music first and sometimes the lyrics come a lot later. Sometimes you write the lyrics and the music comes a lot later. Sometimes you have scraps that *years* later will come to fruition.

Neil Young told us that when he gets an idea he has to write the song immediately or he will lose it, and Dylan said the same thing, that the hardest thing to do is to reconnect with an idea or an inspiration. Do you find that?

When I get an idea I want to pursue it immediately because there is a certain surge of muse juice right at that point. [*Laughter*]

Getting that surge is exactly what leads a lot of people to use different substances while writing—

Yeah, well, you always think—all of us thought—I'm sure every writer thought, not just songwriters but every writer thought, "Oh, man, I'll take some of this whatever the hell it is, and now I'll really write some far-out shit." And it's hogwash. It's bullshit. It actually gets in the way.

The reason I believe that is that—and there were two plottable curves—as the increase of drugs curve went up the amount of songs and creativity curve went down at the same rate. Until it got to the point where I wasn't writing at all. For the last three or four years that I was a junkie and a free-baser and a drunk, I didn't write *anything*. Nothing. I wrote "Delta" and then nothing. *Nothing.* And Jackson [*Browne*] had to pry "Delta" out of me with a goddamn crowbar. Sitting at Warren Zevon's piano in Santa Barbara. And saying, "No, David, you can't get up and take any more drugs until you finish this." [*Laughs*] "No, no, NO! *Finish!*"

Because he knew I was on the track. And he's a great friend, a wonderful guy. But after that I didn't write *shit*. So so much for the drugs enhance creativity theory.

And then, conversely, when I went to prison, I started writing letters. Then I would write a scrap in a letter that I liked. Then I would write a line that I liked. Then I would write three lines that I liked. Then I would write a whole lyric that I thought was okay. And then I wrote "Compass." And I said, "Wait a minute. These are good images, man. This is me again. I'm writing stuff that I believe again. I *love* this." And the only conclusion I can draw is that the drugs smothered it [*hitting the table with hand for emphasis*], and that when the drugs stopped it came back. So there you have it.

In the early days, though, do you think it helped you get out songs you might not have written?

I don't think so, man, I think I would have done three times as much work. Because I spent so much time just sitting there being a vegetable. Being

zonked. I would have had more energy, more focus, more ability to communicate, and I think I would have written better stuff.

The only drug experience I don't regret is the psychedelics, and I did them
almost like a sacrament. I did them seldom and carefully, out on a beach or
some beautiful place and with specifically gentle people. [*Laughs*]

Everybody's got to draw their own conclusion, man. I'm not proselytizing
for or against them. I can tell you *exactly* what happened to me. What happened to me leaves me no doubt whatsoever. Any person who asks me,
"Should I take drugs, will it be good for my art?" I will tell them *absolutely* not.
You know, but you've got to ask me to get that.

**It's quite a different message. I remember years ago you made the state-
ment that every single song you wrote and every record you made were created stoned—**

That's true.

**And I remember thinking that there must be something positive about
that because, after all, you came up with all these beautiful songs and these
great records.**

Well, you know I did say that and I believed it. Not only did I write it all
stoned but I performed it all stoned. The first time I played straight was in a
prison band. And it was also the first time since I was a teenager that I made
love straight. I had to relearn all of that. You know . . . I didn't mean I made
love in prison. When I got back out. [*Laughter*]

HENRY DILTZ: I was hoping you'd say that.

CROSBY: No, I was too old and ugly in prison, you don't got to worry . . .

But the thing was, you know, that when we started getting loaded, we
were not doing coke and heroin. We were doing psychedelics and pot. And we
thought, "Wow, this is going to blow us loose from the fifties." You know, Pat
Boone, white bucks, remember? We kind of needed to get away from there, you
know? And we believed in it. And I said it in all sincerity. But where I wound
up, you know, I think there's no question but that it destroys creativity.

Has it been a hard transition to start writing songs straight?

No. I've been writing more and more as I go along. And I'm liking it. I've
got a song called "Somehow She Knew" that's one of the best that I've ever
written. I just wrote it. I've got another that's called "Until It Shines On You"
that I absolutely love. I just wrote another set of lyrics out on the boat two
weekends ago that I am just entranced with. Not only do I love the stuff I'm
writing now, I *love* "Thousand Roads." I *love* it. Not only do I like the stuff that
I'm writing, but I'm writing easier and more.

**"Yvette In English," which you wrote with Joni Mitchell, is such an
intriguing and haunting song. How did that one start?**

I had a lyric. I wrote the lyric in a rent-a-car—it's *so* weird—driving from
Tokyo out to Narita Airport. And I have no idea why. They come when they
come, you know. And I'm sitting there in Japanese traffic and I wrote this lyric.

The entire lyric?

The entire lyric. Then, later on, when I was putting this album together I
go to all of my favorite writers. Of whom one is, obviously, Joni. And I said,

"Joni, I don't have enough songs from women on this record. I need some really great songs from women, and there you are! [*Laughs*] You're as good as it gets. And I would just be so stoked if I could record a song of yours." And she said, "Well . . . I don't have anything except this one thing and it's very personal . . ." She sang it for me and it was something only she could do.

Then she said, "Let's write one." And I went [*gestures with empty hands*], "Uhhhh. . . . " And I went back home. And I had this lyric so I just thought, "Just show it to her. It ain't gonna happen but what do I have to lose?" So I showed them to her and she said, "These are great!" And I went, "Think so?" And she liked them and kept them. And she called me back and read me off her first rewrite of them onto my answering machine, which I should have saved. Because I was just blown out of the water. She had taken them and gone for the horizon. She was [*whistles*] . . . gone. Then she rewrote them more. She's a great craftsman as well as a great artist. And she came back to me with it and I was just full of excitement—it was so good I couldn't believe it. She had melody and changes. And I changed the melody some when I recorded it. And the changes a little bit. It just was a very happy circumstance.

And this is part of the best part: She liked it well enough that she recorded it too. It's going on her record too.

I was wondering what it would sound like with Joni singing—
Great. I'm sure. And she also said something which really stoked me, which was that she'd like to do it again, which would make me happy. I think it's a genius.

Musically it's really cool.
You know what happened musically, I wanted to take it away from Joni's place, the open-tuning, slap-guitar kind of feel. And there's a guitarist I love, Dean Parks, who is a certifiable genius. And I said, "Dean, you know what I would love to do is to take this thing to Brazil. Because this internal shift chord here sounds like Brazilian music to me. I'd like to take it in that direction, and I'd like you to co-produce it with me." And he did. And we just had the *most fun*. We had a ball.

Did you write the lyric originally with that title?
I'm not sure if that was the title. I don't think I had a title. I think Joni was the one who said that we ought to call it "Yvette in English."

Did you have the story?
Yeah, I had the story.

Is it based on a true story?
No. Pure fantasy. No, it couldn't be true. I would never date a girl who smoked. [*Laughs*]

There is a lot of a cigarette imagery in it. Also that great line: "Walking, talking, touched and scared / uninsulated wires bared . . ."
Mine.

It's probably the least immediately accessible song on the new album, and like much of your work and Joni's, for that reason it lasts the longest and is the most haunting.

We both were actually very stoked by it. Both of my writing collaborations on this record were like that. I had the same experience writing "Hero" with Phil Collins. When we got into it we were both *really* stoked. Really happy about it. We felt, "This is good."

I've been trying more and more to write with other people. Because I love my own stuff. I love "Thousand Roads." It got me off totally. But if this is the width of your palette [*gestures with his hands together and his fingers spread out*], your palette of colors that you're painting from, when you're working with someone else, it's about twice as wide. Because there's a synergy, synthesis, whatever you want to call it, there's a multiplication of effort that takes place there where the whole is greater than the sum of the parts. I absolutely love it. I love the sparks back and forth, the communication, the going somewhere I would have gone. That to me is essence stuff. So I'm currently trying to write songs with all kinds of people. I'm trying to write one with Paul Brady, with Shawn Colvin.

How did "Thousand Roads" emerge?

"Thousand Roads" just jumped right out whole. I wrote the words out—same thing, falling asleep: [*mimes scribbling down the song*] "Oh, yeah! Oh, YEAH! Jan—WAKE UP!" [*Laughter*]

Many songwriters feel that they are given songs, that the songs are gifts. Do you feel that ever?

I feel that what they're feeling is it coming from a level that they don't consciously monitor to a level that they consciously do. I don't feel that it's coming from outside of them but from a level in them that they're not consciously monitoring.

Any other advice as to how to get to that place besides when falling asleep?

Get the busy mind out of the way. I asked a science fiction writer that I admire greatly, William Gibson, who wrote *Neuromancer*, about coming up with lyrics right before I go to sleep. He's an absolutely brilliant guy. I turned him onto the fax machine so that I can abuse him [*laughs*] over the fax machine all the time. We have ongoing fax warfare. I said, "What about this?" And he said, "Yes, it's a known phenomenon. I call it 'The elves take over the workshop.' That's why all authors keep a pad and pencil or a typewriter or word processor right where they go to sleep. Happens to everybody. It's no surprise." I said, "Okay."

But they happen every which way. There's no predicting.

Does music come to you in the same way that lyrics will?

Yeah. I have whole developed melodies and chord changes. I have changes without melodies. I have stuff waiting for words.

Your music is not as verse-chorus oriented and symmetrical as most songs. Like Joni's music, your melodies flow naturally and organically.

Well, if you don't know the rule book, then you don't stick to it. And I'm a completely untutored musician. I can't read or write music, I don't know what the rules are at all. I haven't a clue. And I do what feels good.

Do you play [guitar] in open-tunings mostly?

Constantly. And a lot of people influenced me in that. I absolutely love it. I was very knocked out by [the jazz pianist] McCoy Tyner. When I first heard Coltrane's "My Favorite Things," the chords [on the piano], I thought, "I want those chords. That's the shit I want." And I can't play that shit. I'm not good enough. To play it in a normal tuning [on guitar] you have to be a jazz level, position player, closed chord, thumb curled over the top—I can't do it. So I started fooling with tunings. And I started getting stuff like "Guinevere," "Deja Vu" out of tunings.

There's a natural progression. Every guitar player, somebody shows him right away that if you take the low E down to a D, then you're in D. And the minute you do that, you're lost. It's over for you. And everybody around me likes to do that. Neil loves to do it. Graham has farther out ones than I do. Man, you should hear the tuning for "House of Broken Dreams." Ah! It's a sick thing. [*Laughter*]

Or Joni. Totally *spectacular* musician. Works constantly in tunings. Joni is an instinctive genius.

When you would be discovering a song with one of these tunings, would you have a tape recorder going to preserve it?

No.

Because they seem so elusive, it must have been easy to lose stuff—

I did. I can play you a song right there that I've got a tape of that has a *totally characteristic* set of Crosby changes right from the period of time of "The Wall Song," when I was doing a lot of parallel lines of vocal and guitar. *I'd forgotten it completely.* Somebody found it on a tape and played it back to me, man. I didn't remember *ever* thinking that up. And it *is* me. There's no question.

"The Wall Song" and that whole first Crosby–Nash album, often called "The Black Album," is wonderful.

Yeah. The one that sticks out to me now is "Where Will I Be?" leading into "Page 43."

I wanted to ask you about "Page 43."

I wrote it in the main cabin of my boat in Sausalito. And it was under the influence, musically, of James Taylor. I had been listening to how many passing chords he used and it was like saying, "Jesus, man, where does he *get* that shit?" Because he's *so good,* you know. And so the next song that I started writing I was fooling around with a set of changes that was like that, and that's what came.

It's a song about diving right into life.

Yeah. Don't wait for it. Taste it. Go with it.

Was "Page 43" a page from a specific book?

No. As a matter of fact, some very peculiar things happened with people saying [*in a low whisper*], "Page 43. Yeah. I read that too. I know that nobody else knows but that was really far out." [*Laughter*] And I'm thinking, "Yeah? What book are you thinking about?" "The *Kaballah!*" [*Laughter*] You have no idea which page 43 they're absolutely sure that I'm talking about. But they're sure.

One guy told me he was absolutely sure it was page 43 of the New Testament.

The New Testament. See, that's the one I didn't read. I read the Old Testament. [*Laughs*] You know, Zap Comix, Issue 28. It could be *anything*. And they're *sure*. And they come up to you in a very conspiratorial way and say, "Page 43, yeah, I got it, man."

Do you remember writing "Deja Vu?"

It came out of a very distinct feeling that the reincarnation thing had felt like it was real. I can't prove anything, nobody else can either. But it feels like it to me. There's things in my life that I can't explain any other way. I knew how to sail a boat the first time I saw one. I was eleven and I got in a sailboat and I knew how to do it. And it's not an obvious thing how [sailing] works and *nobody* gets it the first time. And I didn't have to get it, I already knew.

Same thing for singing harmony, man. I started singing harmony when I was *six*. You're not supposed to know how to do that. And I've always instinctively known where to go with music and songs and stuff. And I don't have a clue. I have no schooling *at all*. Zero, period, none. So both of those things make me feel as if I've done them before. That's what I believe.

Did "Deja Vu" pretty much come out in one piece?

Pretty much.

It's quite musically complex.

Yeah, and non-repetitive, non-cyclical.

Like many of your songs. Which is unusual. Most songs are much more symmetrical.

[*In a mock-Liverpudlian accent*] I'm an unusual sort of guy. I've an asymmetrical mind, is what I've got.

One of the most magical, asymmetrical songs ever is "Wooden Ships." You wrote it with Stephen Stills?

Stephen and I and Paul Kantner. Paul Kantner contributed some of the best stuff.

I didn't know that. He wasn't credited. Do you recall how that one came together, or who started it?

Again in the main cabin of my boat. I had that music, I had those changes. And we were sitting around. Paul has always had this science-fiction approach to writing songs anyway. He's steeped in that very heavily and he has written a lot of post-apocalyptic stuff. That's where the idea of Starship came from. He read a lot of Robert Heinlein books, same as I did, and the idea of wrapping ourselves in our tie-dye and stealing the starship and going away was real close to our stoned little minds.

And he was the one who tilted the song in that direction in the first place. And I saw it immediately too. I saw it as a post-apocalyptic survivors metaphor thing. And it rang my bell completely. And Stills, you know, fortunately, was able to get there too on that one.

You all wrote it together, tossing out lines?
Yeah.

It's got one of the great instances of dialogue in songs, the "Say, can I have some of your purple berries?" part.
Yeah, that was mine.

Also the ending always seemed to have come from you, the part starting with "And it's a fair wind . . . better set a course and go. . . ."
Yeah.

Do you recall recording the vocals on that? Would you all sing together?
Yeah. We sang a lot of air blend together. It works sometimes. It doesn't always work.

Do you remember writing "Games"?
Yeah. I like that song. In fact the other day I was listening to it and thought, "Jesus, I should start doing that one."

It's got some great lines—"the ego game of power, the ugly game of war kills love. . . ."
Yeah. I particularly like those lines because they are uneven lines. It doesn't scan. The line just comes to an end and keeps on going.

On your first solo album there's that great piece called "Song With No Words."
Yes. Yeah. That and "Tamalpais High." I would love to think that at times I had pushed back the envelope of what was currently possible in pop music. And at that point I'm sure I did. Because nobody had done that. And I love both of those songs. I think they came out *great*. They make you feel something and they do it without words. And people to this day still come up to me and say, "Man, that first record *killed* me. That stuff killed me!" And I love that. I'm particularly happy about that. Also, it was a good sounding record too, he said modestly. [*Laughs*] But I was very pleased with that record.

Did you ever try to write words to either of those songs?
Yeah, I think I did try. But it's like I said, you can't legislate them into being. If they jump onto my page sometime, I'll put them there.

I also think of "Critical Mass," which is another incredible song without words.
I think "Critical Mass" might be the best thing I ever wrote. That or "I'd Swear There Was Somebody Here." But "Critical Mass," I'm pretty sure, that comes from having listened to a lot of classical music as a kid.

Did you write that to be connected to "Wind on the Water?"
No. It came out of tape improvisations that we slowly sorted out voice by voice until we found the ones that worked. Graham sang a couple of them and I sang a couple of them.

You wrote it without any instruments?
On a tape machine.

When you wrote "Shadow Captain," you gave the lyric to Craig Doerge to write the music?

Yeah, because I didn't have the music. I gave it to him and he came back with that. Which is why I've written a lot of stuff with Craig.

Yeah, he's great. "Out of the Darkness" is a powerful song.

That's he and I and Nash. And one we are going to do with a symphony orchestra this summer.

Do you remember how that one came together?

I think Craig had the changes and Nash and I wrote the words to fit the changes.

Another classic from your first solo album is "Music is Love" which you wrote with Nash and Young.

That was an improvisation. That was a couple bits I had fooled around with once or twice, and I was sitting there with Neil and Graham. And at that point we were very experimental, man. We would go in with no pre-plan and just record stuff. And get stuff. Unthinkable in this day and age. We just did that—that's a one-take, improvisational thing that came out. I said, "Well, that's fun, now let's get on to some serious stuff." And Neil looked at Graham and Graham looked at Neil and they said, "Uh huh, sure." And they took the tape. They stole the tape and added Neil on bass and Graham on conga drums and gave it back to me and said, [*in a high-pitched voice*] "It's going on your record, man. It's really cool. You ought to start with it." And I said, "You're out of your minds!" And they said, "It's going on your record, man. Seriously, man."

You didn't like it?

I didn't know. I had no idea, are you kidding me? Do you know how long this relationship [*gesturing to Henry Diltz, who is snapping his photo*] has been going on? Thank God he didn't catch me with my clothes off. Or maybe he did . . .

HENRY: Once, just disappearing into the pool.

DAVID: That's right. Christine and Reine had their clothes off which meant you weren't shooting me. [*Laughter*] We know that.

Do you remember writing "Almost Cut My Hair?"

Not really. I might have written that at in my house in Beverly Glen or partly there and partly at a house that Stephen and Graham and I rented out in Sag Harbor. When we were fooling around with trying to put the group together.

You would play your new songs for each other?

Yeah. It's called the reality rule. If you can't sing it, it doesn't exist.

Can you talk about writing "Guinevere?"

I don't know exactly how specific I want to get about it. There's some mystery about it that I sort of like preserving.

There are at least two different women in there. And one of them is Joni. And it will probably be the one that everyone remembers: "Oh, yeah, Crosby's the one who wrote 'Guinevere.'" Down the line. It's probably the best . . . I love it. I still do it. All the time. I haven't gotten tired of it.

The thing that surprised me was that I wrote it without having any plan as to how it should happen, and somebody showed me afterwards that it goes 4/4, 6/8, 7/4 each verse. And I went, "It does?" I didn't know.

You spoke about reincarnational feelings and that one certainly feels as if it taps into another time.

Yeah. Somebody said that they thought that came from me going to the Renaissance Fair on acid. [*Laughter*] Not true.

I also wanted to ask you about "Triad."

"Triad" came out of real stuff. And also out of that era in our lives when we thought that the old rules really didn't apply and anything was possible, and multiple relationships *should* be possible, and if you were evolved enough, could be. Turns out it's pretty hard for human beings to pull that off. They tend to get jealous and not be able to be even-handed with each other. And someone feels they're getting slighted in the relationship. For short periods of time in my life there were things that happened like that. And I saw others happen around me. And it wasn't always one guy with two girls. Sometimes it was one girl and two guys. Sometimes it was four people. Sometimes it was more. There were extended families. There were a lot of kinds of relationships that did not fit the old mold and that's basically what that's about.

You introduced that song on the *Four Way Street* album by saying that these songs come straight from your life and for that reason they are some-times hard to sing. Was there ever any song you couldn't sing, or any sub-ject you couldn't put into a song?

If there were, I certainly wouldn't put them in an interview. [*Laughs*] There are things that I have written in songs that are very close to me and that *are* difficult to sing. The song that I told you about, "Somehow She Knew," the new one, is very difficult for me to get through. It's *very* close to the bone. But that's what makes it good. And there have been other times when different songs were hard. One of the other people that "Guinnevere" is about is this girl Christine Hinton, who Henry knew too, and I was in love with her and she got killed. And I had no way to deal with that. I'm still trying to clean that one up. They don't give you an instruction book on how to deal with that. I was never really given a good role-model on how to deal with my emotions, anyway.

So, yeah, there were times when I cried in the middle of that.

You've always been very intimate in your songs. The lyrics always jump out of the record and it's very clear a real person is talking.

Hopefully. That's the idea.

I can't think of a song you've ever done of your own in which that's not the case. You've never actively contrived a pop record.

I can't think of one either but I'm sure it's probably happened! [*Laughs*] I certainly don't write *"PARTY DOWN, DUDE!"*

You know you write what trips your trigger. What trips mine is making you feel songs strong. That's what I love about the writers I love. That's what I love about Joni and James. And everybody else that I really admire. That's what I love about Marc Cohn and Shawn Colvin: they write stuff that makes your heart trip.

One of the most intimate moments in your work is in the great song "Anything at All" and the line, "Just below the surface of the mud, there's more mud here. . . ."

[*Laughs*] Yeah, I was real happy about that line. If you listen closely, I giggle right after I deliver that line. There's a little laugh in there. Because I loved it.

I think I wrote that one on piano. I should be doing that one, too. There's so many, man.

It's also got one of your greatest openings: "If there's anything you want to know, just ask me . . . I'm the world's most opinionated man."

Yeah. That's also true. [*Laughs*]

Do you remember writing "Lee Shore"?

"Lee Shore" I wrote on my boat. Again. At anchor in a lagoon between two islands in the Barry Islands which is in the Bahamas chain. And it was just, you know, there it was all around me and I just wrote it.

Do you have any vision of your musical future?

Grow. I'd like to write with more people. I'd like to learn a *lot* more. I'd like to get better and better at focusing my energy and be able to do it more. I don't expect to be able to control it. I don't expect to be able to get it like turning on the tap. I'm not even asking for that. I just want to do it a *lot* more. Any way that I can get that to happen, I will.

* * *

Robbie Robertson
Los Angeles, California 1991

The story starts in a small town. "It's one of those places that's only there because the railroad came through a long time ago," Robbie Robertson relates in
smoky tones. All of the songs on his album, *Storyville*, grew out of seeds planted
in this story, a cinematic and spiritual tale that he carried around in his head,
not wanting to confine its magic to the written page. "It has about as much to
do with Storyville as *Chinatown* had to do with Chinatown," he said of this tale
which starts in that small town and snakes through New York, New Orleans,
and the sacred Indian lands of Hopi, before ending where it began, in the same
small town. "Sometimes you have to go all the way around the circle to get to
the beginning," he said.

 Robbie Robertson's trip around the circle is mythic. It started when he was
only sixteen and got the job of playing guitar for the Hawks, Ronnie Hawkins'
backup band. That band metamorphosed into Bob Dylan's backup band for his
first-ever electric tour, with Robbie providing burning electric guitar as the
crowds booed and Dylan was castigated for "going electric." When that carnival left the road and the dust settled, the band became The Band (the name
The Crackers was rejected by the record company), and settled down in a big
pink house they named Big Pink in West Saugerties, New York.

 It's there that Dylan and The Band congregated to write and record songs
in an unhurried, unpressured environment. It was a peaceful, rural respite from
the madness and confusion of the electric tour, and the songs that resulted

from this time in the country have a humorous, happy charm, and a soulfulness that Robbie felt was lacking from some of Dylan's earlier songs, as he discusses in the following conversation. Classic songs like "Tears of Rage," "This Wheel's on Fire" and "I Shall Be Released" all emerged from these sessions, which were eventually released as *The Basement Tapes*. Many of the songs were also included on The Band's first album, the legendary *Music from Big Pink*, and Dylan's *John Wesley Harding*.

As the name The Band was used in rebellion to the long, psychedelic names many bands chose, the songs that Robbie wrote for The Band were also rebellious. Rather than reflect the impatient tempest of youth, Robbie's songs resonated with the timbre of time, as if they had been passed down through generations. His lyrics often depict the past, and possess a historicity few songs possess. A song such as "The Night They Drove Old Dixie Down," for example, written from the perspective of a Southerner in the Civil War, is so authentically and emotionally rendered that it's not hard to believe it was written in the nineteenth century. It's a quality many of his songs share, that they belong to the ages, and it's expressed in the music as much as in the words: a distinctively American amalgam of ragtime, rock, blues and Dixieland. "We tried to do things that had a musical sensitivity," he said. "As everybody else was getting louder and louder, we were getting softer and softer."

Robbie rarely sang his own songs while in The Band, preferring to cast them like a director casts a movie. And The Band provided him with a glorious cast of characters to choose from: Could anyone have rendered "Stage Fright" as convincingly as Rick Danko, warbling in his trembling scarecrow voice? Or could anyone hold a candle to the soulful southern intensity that Levon Helm brought to songs like "The Night They Drove Old Dixie Down"? And could it be possible to match the pure, uncompromising spirituality of Richard Manuel on absolutely everything he sang?

At the start of the seventies, The Band released a number of albums, including *Big Pink*, *Stage Fright* and *Cahoots*, and a live recording of a concert they shared with Dylan called *Rock of Ages*. They also backed up Dylan on one of his own albums, *Planet Waves*, recorded in a manic three day session in Los Angeles, and toured with him again in 1974, recording an album of those concerts called *Before the Flood*. The next year, much to the relief of The Band's followers around the world, brought a new collection of superb songs called *Northern Lights—Southern Cross*. Though it featured some of Robbie's most moving writing ever, such as the heartrending "It Makes No Difference," and the unbridled genius of Garth Hudson branching out from his signature organ licks to work in the world of synthesizers, it was to be the last album ever of original material from The Band.

On Thanksgiving night of 1976, Robbie Robertson and The Band gave their farewell performance in a concert preserved forever in Martin Scorcese's film *The Last Waltz*. Presented at the Winterland Theater in San Francisco, not only is *The Last Waltz* the most elegantly filmed rock concert ever, it's also a historic document that features many of the most dynamic forces in modern songwriting: Bob Dylan, Joni Mitchell, Neil Young, Van Morrison, Eric Clapton, Muddy Waters and more.

Robbie and Scorcese continued to work and play together after *The Last Waltz*. Besides spending endless days and nights together in a Hollywood mansion absorbing the history of cinema and other amusements, their collaboration was also professional: Robbie contributed music to *The Color of Money* and compiled an outstanding score for *The King of Comedy*, which, besides wonderful songs by Van Morrison, Rickie Lee Jones and Talking Heads, featured Robbie's first solo performance, the majestic "Between Trains."

It was the first and the last that we heard of Robbie as a solo artist until 1987, when he released his first full solo album, *Robbie Robertson*. It was well worth waiting for—few songs to this day can equal the beauty and passion of "Broken Arrow," a song which Robbie says is so close to him that he couldn't imagine anyone else singing it, or "Fallen Angel," a true masterpiece of song-writing. Written in memory of Richard Manuel, who was found dead in a Florida motel room of an apparent suicide in 1986, it's one of the most forceful statements of faith ever contained in words and music: "Sometimes I thought you felt too much / And you crossed into the shadowland . . ."

We met in the midst of an unforgivingly feverish L.A. day, yet the frantic swarm of traffic was a distant memory in Robbie's inner sanctum—a cool, dark studio with walls of guitars both electric and acoustic. He sat back into a deep couch, wearing jeans and a dark jacket, holding a cigarette in his fingers for a long time before lighting it, and looking a lot like he did in scenes from *The Last Waltz* in which he knowingly and humorously fielded Scorcese's questions. He's a born storyteller, and this inclination surfaced immediately when he answered the first question by relating, in long and dreamy detail, the entire story on which he based *Storyville*. By the end of this spectral tale, in which two lovers meet on an old wooden bridge, we were both transported into the realm in which Robbie resides, a mystical place peopled by the ghosts of jazz and blues, far from the streets of L.A.

Since the start of your career, the art of songwriting has gone through many transformations. Do you see it now continuing to be transformed?

About the only thing that we've done in songs in the last years that is new is really eliminate turn-arounds, and fool with structures a little bit. In modern songwriting, that's all it is.

We end the chorus and instead of there being a turn-around, you go into the next verse. This isn't a huge revelation in music. That's one of the things, and structure: is this the bridge or is *this* the bridge? This is the chorus, then what is this? Oh, that's the *refrain*. Oh, I see. Chorus, *refrain*. Okay. This is Adventures in Songwriting.

Do you think that songs will continue to evolve?

Yeah. It's just mathematical. It would be nice to abandon the verse-chorus-bridge structure completely, and make it so none of these things are definable. You could just call those sections whatever you would call them. Make up new names for them. Instead of a bridge, you can call it a highway. Or an *overpass*. [*Laughter*] We're at the overpass now.

When you write, do you start with a musical idea?

Just anything. Sometimes it's a musical idea. I like very much when the idea for the lyric is a direct link out of the music. Sometimes when you write a song idea, and put music to that, you *stick* the music to it a little bit. And the other way, you say, "I recognize this place. I recognize the textures of this song." And it kind of *dictates* to you what the song is about.

So it's pretty *organic*. It kind of *grows* out of the ground. And when you're running around with an idea that you're trying to accompany, it can sound pretty stuck on. But anything works.

Your songs have a timeless quality about them, as if they've been around for generations. So many of them take place in the past and are about a different time. Does this come instinctively or is it the result of a lot of work?

It's the result of a lot of work. Nowadays. There's a lot of ideas that you find yourself recycling. And you find yourself writing sequels without knowing it. And somebody else already did that, or I did it, so let's move on. So I think there's a little more searching to be done, even for the most simple idea.

You said once that it's much better to have a line in a song that's rooted in the past, like 'the congregation gathered at the riverside' than using modern images. Why do you think that it is that modern images are not as effective in songs?

Well, I think that they can be. Except it seems to be more *moving* when you use things from the past. There's something about that that's kind of touching. When you say, "I just went down to the Burger King," there's something about that that seems not so touching. But it could certainly be done. It's finding the right atmosphere, the right place.

This album is not a period piece. It takes place from then until now.

Do you think there's just less beauty in modern life?

I think there's less beauty in modern language.

Do you always write music on guitar?

No. Piano. Just because of the way the instrument is laid out in front of you. And on guitar, to make some chords, your fingers have to go into acrobatics. On piano, you just move one note over. It's laid out in a way that it's a little easier to deal with. And changing a note on the bottom is easy, whereas on guitar it would be tricky if not even possible.

You discussed writing a story that your new album is based on. Did you finish this story before writing all the songs for the album?

I didn't finish the story because I only wrote it in my head. I never wrote it down on paper. I thought there was a *jinx* in that. Because I had this fear of looking for an idea on page thirteen and this whole technique becoming very mechanical. That I was no longer taking these ideas out of the air as they passed by. Now I was taking it out of page thirteen. And there was something about that that I felt suspicious of, so I couldn't write it down. But I just *remembered* it. And I would resort to it as I was writing the songs.

It's a very cinematic tale. Have you thought of using it as a movie?
It was strictly for this purpose. So now I can throw it away, forget about it, because it has certainly fulfilled its purpose. Or I can now write it down. Or I can explore different avenues with it. I just don't know yet. I just now finished this album. I thought of writing a condensed version of this and putting it in with the record. But I couldn't boil it down to enough. And I didn't want it to ramble on and on. And sometimes some things are better left unsaid.

It's fine for *us* talking, it's something we don't usually get to talk about when talking about the process of making a record or songwriting.

Has your work in movies and with Scorcese affected your songwriting?
I don't know. I just *like* this stuff, myself. That's the only reason that I do it, because it *feels* good, and it could have something to do with a real connection that I made with movies when I was young. That instead of becoming a movie director or producer, I just applied that to what I did already. It could be that, but I don't know, I don't like to think it to death. But it's something along those lines.

You said that you didn't want to be restricted by a story when writing songs, so as to allow those ideas in the air to come to you. Where do you think those ideas come from?
Well . . . I think it's the muse. I think that she's totally responsible for anything that I write. So I'm completely indebted to this muse that I know.

Any advice on how to get in touch with this muse?
I don't have to get in touch with her. She gets in touch with me. Yeah.

So you're not the kind of writer who will go to it every day, and try to force a song when the muse isn't with you?
Oh, you can *try* all you want. But if she's not there, there's not much happening.

Can you tell when you hear a song written without the muse?
Yeah. It's like night and day.

When did you write your first song?
I can remember writing some silly song *very* young, like thirteen years old. But the first *serious* songwriting that I did was when I was fifteen. I wrote a couple of songs that Ronnie Hawkins recorded. At the time, Ronnie Hawkins had a couple of big hit songs and an album that was doing pretty well. It was playing on the big Alan Freed shows. So that was pretty thrilling for a fifteen year old kid.

And *then* he thought, if I could write these songs, maybe I could hear songs that would be good for him as well. So he took me to the big Brill Building in New York. I lived in Toronto. And he introduced me to Leiber and Stoller (who I'm *still* friends with, and I've worked with them on things over the years), and I met Doc Pomus and Mort Shuman, and Otis Blackwell and Titus Turner. And these people played songs for me. And I did my best to figure out what would be best for Ronnie to do.

So that was a big thrill, to go to the songwriter's headquarters of the world, to go to Tin Pan Alley, and to hear these people's songs and their *stories*, too. And Doc [Pomus] was a great storyteller. And Otis Blackwell, he was the first I heard from what a trick-bag this whole songwriting thing could be. He'd been really screwed out of his songwriting credits and money.

That's when I first became aware of that. And when Ronnie Hawkins recorded the songs that I wrote, there was my name under the song and like a couple of people's names that I'd never heard of before.

Listed as writers?

Yeah. Like Morris Levy was one of the names. And then there was another name and I don't think that person even *existed*. That's the way the game was played then. So I was learning about that at the same time. It made me see that this was a rough business. I thought it was going to be more glamorous. Although I was *very* impressed with meeting people and hearing their songs.

The next phase for me was when Ronnie Hawkins hired me to play guitar for him. His guitar player left and I got this job playing guitar. So that became a real *obsession* for me, because it was like, "We'll see what happens." I was sixteen years old. At that age, if I had any talent at all, it was in the *making*. I wasn't there yet. So I became guitar-obsessed.

Electric guitar?

Yeah. I really wanted to develop something special on the instrument. And songwriting wasn't that urgent to me anymore. And there was nobody saying, "*Write some songs, that's what we need!*" Nobody talked to me like that. It took a backseat for awhile.

And then I would write songs every once in a while. I'd think of a little something, I'd play it for the other guys in The Hawks, and that was about the extent of it. And then we left Ronnie Hawkins, and I started to write a little bit again, and then we joined Bob *Dylan*, and *then* it became a whole thing of trying to make this electric music work with this acoustic music, kind of experimenting. So that took some looking into, and in the meantime there was a whole thing going on. The doors were opening then, and there were certain people: John Lennon and Bob Dylan, were right there *recognizing* that Hank Williams' songs mixed with rock and roll songs, this was going to go the next step *further*. And that people, at that time, had open eyes and open ears. And you could *feel* it. There was a place for more profound writing of songs.

So I saw that kind of take place before my eyes, and I thought, though, that this can get carried away, too. It can get a little blabby, and I wish that it could say something, and be very *moving* and very soulful at the same time. When something tends to *ramble on*, that's not the train that I came in on.

Are your referring to early Dylan songs?

Anybody's songs that go on and on, and wait a minute, are you trying to *teach* me something? What's the catch here? I think this is *intelligent*, but it's not giving me *chills*. It's only affecting my *head*, it's not affecting my *gut* and my heart and my soul. I wanted a more complete thing. For *me*, musically. That's just the way I felt.

So then after we kind of discovered what we could do together, with people *booing* us everywhere we went. It was pretty bizarre. We deserve some kind of a medal for *persistence*. Because we never said, "Maybe they're right. Maybe this is just *awful* and we should stop and fix it, or do anything." Because we were listening to these tapes of the concerts, and we'd say, "This isn't that bad! What was all this fuss about? They're not *listening*. They're coming with preconceived notions." So, anyway, we persisted, and we were going to persist for more, but Bob had a motorcycle accident.

Then when we got to the *Basement Tape* thing, the songs started to take on another kind of charm, which I was really enjoying. They were shorter and more soulful. "I Shall Be Released." Okay? There was a *humor* and a charm to some of the things. It wasn't so *serious*. Serious in a way that *distracted* me from the reason that you'd ever *join* me to begin with. It would take itself too seriously.

So there was a nice balance happening there out of the stuff that we were doing. Kind of a carefree, soulful approach that *wasn't* like what we'd done before. And when we did *Music From Big Pink*, we explored that even more. And where everybody was getting louder and louder and louder, we were getting softer and softer and softer. And tried to do things that had a sensitivity, a musical sensitivity that was, to us, anyway, better than being beat over the head. It wears me out, and I stop paying attention. If someone is screaming in my ear all the time, I tend to move away. But if somebody screams and then *whispers*, then I'm curious.

Can you describe what those sessions for The Basement Tapes were like? It seems like the songs were just coming in abundance, and that it was the ideal atmosphere for writing songs.

One of the big things about that was that it was done on the basis that there was no particular reason for it. We weren't making a *record*. We were just fooling around. The purpose was whatever comes into anybody's mind, we'll put it down on this little tape recorder. *Shitty* little tape recorder. [*Laughs*]

And *because* we had that *freedom* of thinking, "Well, no one's ever gonna hear this anyway, so what's the difference?" And then we thought, "Well, maybe some of those songs would be good for *other* people to record." Like, "Here's one for Ferlin Muskey." There was this carefree attitude. A real luxury.

And as they piled up we thought, "Maybe these *would* be good for someone else to record." And at that time we needed to make a record. The Band. It was time for us to make a move. And nobody had any idea what the hell we were doing. We had just finished playing a tour with Bob Dylan that was quite *loud* and *dynamic* and violent. A very high-pitched attitude to it. And then to turn around and go in the other direction . . . we weren't even that *conscious* of it, it just seemed to be happening. Something was making it happen, but we didn't know what it was.

But it was good stuff. It led to *Music From Big Pink, John Wesley Harding* . . .

So many classic songs came out of those sessions. Would you all come in with song ideas to work on?

Yeah. Sometimes Bob would type up some words and Richard [Manuel] would take it, or Rick [Danko] would take it. *I* didn't do that, because I'd already been to the songwriting well. Because I had written when I was very young. So I wasn't really looking so much to *collaborate* as just to finish the ideas that I had. So I was writing songs on my own. Then I would collaborate with Richard on a couple of things, maybe he'd have something started and I would think of an idea for it.

Some guys were playing checkers, some guys were fixing the screen door, some guys would be at the typewriter, somebody would be building a fire . . . All this stuff going on. No real *importance* behind it. And it was a technique that we found to be, the *clubhouse technique*. Just like the Bowery Boys. Every day we'd all meet at the clubhouse. And we'd get together, and we'd talk about dreams, make a little music, cook a little food, throw a football around, play checkers. That's what life *was*. We did that every day.

And that was that, *The Basement Tapes*, these bootleg things, whatever you want to call them. And there's *still* stuff left. It's a very bizarre thing, too. I don't know where they are. But they're around somewhere.

Richard Manuel wrote about half of the songs on the first albums, but by the later albums you wrote all the songs. Why was that?

He stopped writing. Yeah. There was a need for songs to put on these albums, so I just had to do it. In those days you had to make records. You made a record and in a year you had to put out another record.

The Band was unusual in that it had so many great vocalists, unlike The Stones, for example, in which Jagger sings everything. When you wrote a song like "Stage Fright," for example, which Danko sang, would you write it with him in mind?

No, I could usually tell when I was writing it who it would work for. And sometimes we tossed it around. I'd say, "Why don't you try coming in on the verse there," and "You do the high part on the chorus," and "You sing the melody there," and "Why don't you come in out of nowhere on the next verse, and we'll see what happens." And we would just experiment, kicking the vocals back and forth.

Did The Band come up with the arrangements of your songs or did you bring them in with an idea for the arrangement?

When you write a song, you know more about it than anybody else. So you say what you think, and then you leave it to the musicians to help find a way to interpret this. A way that it sounds really honest.

Sometimes I'd come and I'd have part of a song or I'd have all of a song. Anywhere from one percent to a hundred percent. There was never any set way.

Sometimes they'd be there while I was working on them. I'd have something of an idea what we could do with this, and I'd sit down and I'd play them the song. And most of the time, one of the guys, or all of the guys, would say, "Oh, you should sing this one. It just sounds right with you singing it." But that wasn't the way this band should be. I really liked this set-up. I liked this idea of writing the songs and them imagining this guy doing this, and that guy doing that. And if I was singing the song, I'd be thinking about *singing the song*. This way I could sit back and say, "No, let's try this. Let's see what happens if you do that, you sing this. . . ." And that way we kept the *wheels* turning. It was a much more interesting musical *experiment*. And it was the only opportunity that I had to stand back.

It's interesting that you said that you didn't like long songs—
It's not that I don't like *long* songs. It's just that they weren't, for me, musically, going anywhere. And I'd find these sessions in which these guys were just kind of *flailing along* and the song kept going on and on, it felt that everything was staying in one place. He's just changing the words. This isn't *emotional* enough for me. What do we need musicians for if this is happening? And other things were appealing to me anyway. Other songs and other styles of songs. Things that I thought were *tremendously* effective, emotionally. And the *words* weren't particularly that amazing, but they were much more powerful. So I'm saying, "Let's find a place in the middle!" And that's what The Band was.

And do you think your feeling and The Band's music influenced Dylan?
Everybody had an influence. He had an influence on us and we had that influence on him.

Did you learn anything about songwriting from being with him?
With Dylan, the thing was, "Oh! I get it. Anything goes!" That songs don't have to be just this or just that. *Anything goes.* If it works.

Your songs are very much about America, both lyrically and musically. Yet you were raised in Canada. How do you think being Canadian has affected your writing?
There were two things. One thing is that coming from Canada, I got to come in at the age of sixteen, such a vulnerable, impressionable age, and things *hit* me, at just the right crossroads, and made such a large impression on me. And I moved to the South, when I started playing with Ronnie Hawkins. And that became headquarters. And I always thought, from the very beginning, that this music was born of this blues and country music, Southern stuff. The Mississippi Delta area, and the music came from down the river and from up the river and met, and it made something new. I always looked at that as kind of the *source* of the whole thing.

Almost all of the songs you've written over the years are in major keys, which creates a very American sound.
I've never noticed that, to be really honest. I've never paid attention to what keys they are in, or major or minor. I've written lots of songs in minor keys. Sometimes a song will start out in a minor key and then maybe the bridge will be in major, or the chorus will be major.

Open strings, sometimes, on guitar will cause me to start a song in a certain place. Sometimes just because they're easier to play.

When you wrote songs for The Band, did you have to transpose them to fit their ranges?
Ninety percent of the time, we'd do it in the key I wrote it in. Once in a while someone would say it's a touch too low or too high.

Recently you've done some interesting songwriting collaborations —
I did do quite a bit in the past, actually, with Richard [Manuel], and I've written with Van Morrison, and others.

With Martin Page, you've written two extraordinary songs: "Fallen Angel," from your last album, and now "Sign of the Rainbow" from *Storyville*.
There have been things that Martin and I tried to do that haven't been successful, but I like it with Martin. He's very good at coming up with musical things that get you stirred up. He's really good that way. His background leads him to some different chord changes than I would use, and that *freshness* is fun.

I noticed that both "Fallen Angel" and "Sign of the Rainbow" are in E Flat, which is an unusual key for a guitarist to use.
Oh, yeah? I didn't notice that. Maybe that's the only key that he can write in. [*Laughter.*]

His contribution is entirely musical?
Oh, yeah. We would figure out the music together. He would come and we would work on it until I would feel that it was something I could work with. Then I would write the lyrics and I would give it a shot and I would ask, "What do you think of the direction I'm going in?" Martin has never said too much about lyrics, except, "I like where you're going; I just think you should go the distance."

Is "Fallen Angel" a song that emerged from a musical idea that he had?
He brought to me, a long time ago, a vibe, as he calls it, that he put on tape. And there was the *germ* of an idea there. And we started to progress with that a little more, and when it became time to record, we took it to another place with musicians, and it just evolved into that. We would then try to get a structure for the song that felt right.

"Between Trains," which you wrote for *The King of Comedy* sound-track, was the first real solo Robbie Robertson we heard.
I sang lead on some Band songs: "Kingdom Come," "Out Of The Blue." "Between Trains," I haven't heard that in a long time. But when I did that song, I felt very good about it. The reason that it was to do with this *King of Comedy* thing was that there was this guy who worked for Martin Scorcese and myself one time named Dan. And he died all of a sudden. Just *died*. Like acute meningitis, just one day. Him and I, in New York, we went to a bar and we were just having a beer and talking. I was there doing music for *The King of Comedy* and he went back to his apartment and he just *died*. And it *struck* us so. It caught us off guard so much. And I was trying to exorcize this thing inside of myself. And all the time that he ever worked for us, he always said that it was temporary. He said, "I'm just kind of passing through." It went on for a long period of time, but he never ever changed his story, this was still just a stop-over for him. And I always thought of Dan as kind of being between trains.

Do you write songs differently when you write them for yourself to sing?

Well, yeah, it is different. There are certain songs I write now that I can't imagine saying to one of the other guys in The Band, "You should sing this song." It just doesn't apply anymore. It's either too personal, or something, but it is different.

Do you remember writing "Broken Arrow"?

Yeah. This is one of the songs I'm talking about. I couldn't imagine saying to one of those guys, "You should sing this song." It didn't strike me that way. Also, I was drawing on some of my background, on my heritage, and finding this way of expressing something.

How did your song "Ophelia" originate?

I had written these chord changes on this song. Now here's one that goes to all kinds of chords. And they're all major chords. A major chord with a 9th or a 7th, but they're major chords. It's an old-timey style, to use a chord progression of this sort. The idea was to use these chords and to do something for that time that was unusually modern. And I think that we accomplished that.

Another song of yours in that old-time style is "The Night They Drove Old Dixie Down."

This was another one that took me *months and months* maybe eight to ten months to write this song. Because I only had the music for it. I didn't know what the song was about at all. And if everyone would go, I would sit down at a piano and I would play these chords and go over it. And then one day, the rest of it came to me. But it took a long, long time. And sometimes you have to wait it out. And I'm glad I waited it out.

I had other ways to go with that song. I don't remember them now, exactly, what those directions were lyrically, but it could have ended up being a completely different story, if I hadn't had the patience.

For *Storyville*, you based all the songs on a story you wrote. Have you ever done that before?

I've been wanting to do this for a long long time. I toyed with the idea and never followed it through. Different things would throw me off the track, like writing a song that has nothing to do with the story. But I liked the song so I would abandon the story idea.

But this time I said, "I'm gonna see this through. If I don't do this sooner or later, I'm going to always be walking around mumbling to myself that I should have followed through with that idea." Like I should have never given up my piano lessons. [*Laughs*]

Is there anything that you think songs can't contain?

Well, you're limited timewise. You can only *ramble on* so long, and then it isn't interesting anymore. To me. Or else people would be writing symphony length songs. They don't seem to work in that context.

I wanted to experiment with this a long time ago. I wanted to write a piece of music, like an opera, a whole record that is one thing and it evolves through all these moods and places. And yet this album is kind of like that, except that you stop and you start, you stop and you start. But it wouldn't be that. It would be . . . And I don't mean sticking things together. I mean that it really follows a thread, musically, all the way through. The reason people don't do this is because the evidence is in that it gets old. Why didn't somebody do it? Maybe somebody will do it. There's certainly an opening there. If somebody's looking for a way to shuffle the deck. Write a song that is *an hour long.* But it's interesting enough to hold our attention for an hour.

There's a challenge for you.

* * *

Carlos Santana
San Francisco, California 1993

It's San Francisco in the early sixties. A guy goes up to Bill Graham one Sunday afternoon before the weekly jam session at the Fillmore and says, "I know this skinny Mexican kid who plays blues and loves B.B. King. Will you let him play?" The kid borrows Mike Bloomfield's guitar, jams with members of the Grateful Dead and Jefferson Airplane. And when he gets to his first solo he blows everybody off stage with the immaculate intensity of his burning guitar lines. Afterwards Bill Graham says to him, "Do you got a band?" The kid says "sure" and Santana is born.

"My tone was there from the start," Carlos says on a sunny day some thirty years later in the Bay Area. "It was a marriage between the tone and the rhythms and that's why Bill believed in it from the beginning." Music has been in Santana's blood since he was born in the little town of Autlan, Mexico. His father Jose Santana was a famous mariachi musician who taught Carlos how to sight-read when he was only five years old. When he was six and the family moved to nearby Tijuana, his father gave him his first instrument, a violin. Though he enjoyed his father's fame, concentrating on his own music was often tough, as it is for most kids. "I was enthused by how people received my father in the streets," he said, "but like most kids you want to play hide and seek or spin the bottle, not do-re-mi-fa-so-la-ti-do. But I'm grateful to my dad. He taught me that with freedom comes discipline. And he taught me discipline."

It was also tough for Carlos to put any time into learning music that didn't connect with his own life. "I didn't want to learn European Anglo-Saxon classical music. If I grew up on the border in Tijuana why would I need Beethoven and Mozart? They don't play those guys in the street. What I wanted to learn was Muddy Waters and John Lee Hooker. "

What he wanted was a guitar. His father, who had introduced Mariachi to Oakland, California, had become so popular that he couldn't return home. So he sent Carlos his guitar in the mail: a big hollow-bodied Gibson electric that Carlos played without an amp. "But I didn't care because it was something for me to put my fingers on."

It was as if he already knew how to play. Since he could sight-read and sound out music from the radio, it was not long before he could easily articulate the music in his head on the guitar. At first it was pretty easy, simple songs and blues. But when jazz entered his life, everything shifted: "I could sound out anything I heard. That is, until I heard Charlie Christian and Wes Montgomery and Gabor Szabo, people like that. Until then I thought I was the best guitar player on the block. Coming to San Francisco was a real lesson in humility for me because instantly I became aware of people like Jerry Garcia, Jimi Hendrix, Mike Bloomfield. In Tijuana I was the rising kid who played the guitar."

In time he found his own style, a beautiful melding of his pristine, zealous guitar lines with the Latin and Mariachi rhythms of his youth. It didn't arrive overnight, however, and Santana paid his dues by playing the blues and what was known as "Cut & Shoot" music. "That's music that you play in places where they cut and shoot you if you don't play right. Like John Lee Hooker. John Lee Hooker was our Sex Pistols. When you hear a guitar playing and it cuts you. That's what we wanted to hear."

He spent five years avoiding being cut or shot, playing the blues, and evolving his style. In 1966 he started the Santana Blues Band and all of his work paid off. Their music spilled out with an undeniable spirit of hope that engulfed San Francisco first and then the world. Their performance at Woodstock in 1969 was one of the true spiritual highlights of that historic festival. Their self-titled debut album and the landmark *Abraxas* album were both released that same year, blowing minds around the globe with classics such as "Evil Ways" and "Black Magic Woman." The psychedelic/erotic album art for *Abraxas* rivals *Sgt. Pepper* as being one of the most stared-at album covers of the sixties.

"It's the place where the spirit meets the flesh," Carlos explained about the meaning of "Abraxas." This union of the physical and the spiritual has been at the heart of his work since the beginning, though he often fought it. Bill Graham urged him to embrace the union, but for years Santana felt that the flesh could only lead him away from the spirit. And the lifestyle of a rock star, especially in the late sixties, was very much about the flesh. So Santana rejected it and walked away from his band and from the astounding success he had achieved.

He moved instead towards the music that moved him the most, the cosmic later work of John Coltrane, and made one of the amazing albums of his career, *Love Devotion and Surrender*, a collaboration with Mahavishnu John

McLaughlin. It would have been an extraordinary album for any musician to make, but to have come from this rock guitarist at this time was a true revelation, and the sign of things to come. The following year he recorded with Coltrane's widow Alice Coltrane for the *Illuminations* album and he also made a live album in 1972 with Buddy Miles.

Santana reconstructed the Santana Band, and managed to meld the spiritual aspirations of his jazz forays with the soulful rhythms of his heritage. In 1976 he made *Amigos* which featured one of the most beautiful and soaring guitar instrumentals ever recorded, and one of the most perfect examples of Santana's union of rock and jazz, spirit and flesh, "Europa." He details the suprising and humorous origins of this song in the following interview.

Throughout the years he's released some 27 albums, most of which have zesty one-word titles: *Caravanserai, Barboletta, Moonflower, Zebop, Shango* and *Milagro*, which is dedicated to the memory of two of the most important people in his life, Miles Davis and Bill Graham.

Both Miles and Graham were often impossible people to work with, as Santana remembered. But, he insisted, they both had the spirit of divine love in them. "God loves rascals and kooks," he said.

Do you remember writing your first song?

Yeah. I was sixteen or seventeen. It was one of those first sweetheart things. It was called "Confidential Friend." I never put it out. It made me feel good because it was my first actual achievement where I sat down and I had a melody, an intro, the verses, the bridge. It was the first time I had completed a whole song myself, which gives you a real feeling of accomplishment.

After that I kept writing songs and trying to make songs different than just the three-chord blues. To this day sometimes I write songs that don't even belong for Carlos or Santana. Sometimes it's like, "Oh, this song should be for James Taylor." [*Laughs*]

I don't sit down and say, "I'm going to write a song like this." They just come out and when they come out a lot of times they don't belong to Carlos or Santana and sometimes it definitely does sound like a Santana song because of the rhythm and the melody. I'm happy that it's not like shackles, that you don't have to write in just one way.

Are you the kind of writer who is always writing something?

Sometimes I'd try to write a song a day. But now that just doesn't happen because I've got a zillion things going now.

I have known from experience that most musicians really suck at raising kids. Most musicians are only into their thing and consequently they leave a legacy of some really disturbed kids. Mommie Dearest, Daddy Dearest. To me that's not the route I want to take.

So I spend a lot of time listening to my kids. So I don't write as much as I like to. But I do have a guest house that I use and sometimes I can turn it on. It's like Billie Holiday said: sometime you can turn it on like a faucet and other times there's nothing. If I don't hear anything, I don't force it. If I don't hear a damn thing, rather than pick up a guitar and play licks that sound like dirty dishes that are three days old, I'd rather just not play. I'll just listen to Trane or dismantle my guitar.

Because when I do hear it, I don't hear nothing else. I don't hear anything except the music that wants to come out. Like when you're pregnant, you don't care what the state of the world is, you just want to give birth. So it's like that.

You hear melodies in your head?

Melodies, a rhythm, a lyric—all of them. I can't even hear television or the radio, I just hear what I hear. And then I have to put it on a tape or write it down.

So you feel that when it comes it comes and it can't be forced?

Yeah. When music pops into my head it's undeniable because I'm not into sitting down and writing jingles. That's what you have to do when you're writing jingles, you have to force yourself. But when it's the other kind of music, it's an emotional, psychic release and mostly the best songs you write are the ones you write on stage and nobody knows what the hell you're going to do until it's over.

That's what Miles used to say. You'd ask him what the name of this song was and he'd say, "I'll tell you when it's over."

That's the essence of jazz—improvisation.

Yeah. And Indian music also. They improvise a lot. It's all about jamming.

On guitar you have such a distinctive, pure tone. Did you have that from the start or did it evolve over the years?

The tone was there. That's why Bill believed in it. There was a marriage between the tone and the rhythms already. I think it developed more as I started listening to Miles Davis, Jimi Hendrix, people like that. I think even in the beginning, like most of us, we copied B.B. [King] and people like that but we had a way of making it our own.

If you drink orange juice, once you sweat it it's your own. That's the only way to describe it. Oranges really don't belong to anybody. [*Laughs*] B.B. would tell you that music, we can play it but we can't grab it and put it in a bottle and say it's ours, man, because it just goes through you anyway. But the articulation is fascinating, the way B.B. or Miles articulates blues. How do you go about saying less but affecting more to the listener? So you play three notes and people say, "Damn, those three notes, they've got me intoxicated and in a trance all day." As opposed to a guy who plays a zillion notes and you just walk away. That is something I learned from people like Miles and Wayne Shorter and people like that.

Was John Coltrane an importance influence at that time?

I didn't get into Coltrane until a year after he passed, in '69. The first time that I remember that I heard "A Love Supreme" it just totally fried my brain. Wait a minute, I'm running on 110 and you're giving me 220 volts! I'm not ready for this. Give me a converter.

Then a friend played me some albums of Coltrane when he was playing just blues. He wasn't going into orbit. Because in the end, most people, when they heard him, they would go outside in the middle of the set and grab a parking meter and hold on [*laughs*] because their brains were just fried. Then they'd go back and get some more. But nobody could stay in for a whole set and digest it.

So that part was too much for me. But once I got into the blues, now I can listen to all of it. And he is my main man. Out of all the musicians, he and Bob Marley to me, along with Jimi and Miles, but especially Coltrane and Marley are the most powerful on the spiritual thing. They're all spiritual, man, but for the one who is the champion of the inner world, I definitely would go with John Coltrane.

Do you feel that this inner world is the source of music and songs?

Yeah. People are flowers, music is water and the musician is the hose. When you look at how Beethoven heard "Da-da-da-*dum*" it wasn't from the radio. There is an inner radio that is happening all the time. And the dial to turn it on is that you have to shut up. You have to shut up your mind, you have to shut up your mouth. And just listen.

I don't know if you've ever been to a place where it's so silent that it's loud. The silence is loud. Since I have learned to meditate, sometimes out of meditation you get the songs and you go, "Oh, now I see where Trane was getting this stuff, or where Jimi Hendrix was coming from." Because silence is like a radio itself and the way you tune in is to make yourself more silent and then you hear the songs louder.

But you have to still your mind. To get the real, real music that is going to last the longest, you have to be very quiet and be very gentle with how you write them down. This is why I admire Keith Jarrett so much because that's where he's coming from.

Is meditation the way to get to that place?

Sometimes. Sometimes when you wake up in the morning, sometimes late at night. Sometimes you're taking a shower and the water is hitting you in your face and you hear the song. Sometimes you stick your head out of the window on the freeway a little bit and that motion of the air can do it. There has to be some kind of motion to create emotions for me, whether it's a shower or that. Or completely the other extreme, which is silence, which is not motion at all.

One of the most beautiful melodies that you've written, or that anyone has written, is "Europa." Do you recall writing that one?

This came in 1967. We were in this lady's house and we had all taken peyote. Everyone was playing the Stones' *Satanic Majesties* and Procol Harum. It was that era.

When they finally turned it off, this lady started bugging out. She started having a bad experience. So I grabbed my guitar and I started playing that melody. I called it "The Mushroom Lady." And I never used that melody until later on, in 1975, Earth, Wind & Fire were opening up for us in Europe. I hadn't played that song since I did it that day and called it "Mushroom Lady." So I sat down and played it and the band said, "Man, this is a beautiful melody, we should record this on our next album." So I took the title out and called it "Europa" because we were in Europe. But it came from trying to cool a lady down from a bad trip.

People don't talk about drug use much these days, but did you find that there were times when certain substances opened creative doors for you?

We're in a stage now where people can't tell the damn difference between drugs and medicine. That's a shame because before the Anglo-Saxon man came here from Europe, there was a lot of medicine utilized for spiritual purposes. Now everything is like a Christian witch hunt and if you're not watching T&A with a bible in your hand, you're not a Christian. Which is a really false way of looking at religion. Religion is still a business no matter how you look at it, where spirituality is one on one with the creator.

I have never ventured into cocaine or heroin because I always felt that those things were destructive to my being. I don't know about Charlie Parker or somebody else but for me, the few times I have tried it my body felt like I was on the freeway and then I shifted into reverse. My body just said, "No. No." I said, "Okay." My body did not like it: my brain, my heart, my stomach, nothing liked it. So I said, "Okay, this is not something I want to fool around with." My inner voice said that this was a prison, it will shackle me. I don't know if it's because I'm vain or whatever, but I don't want to be slurring or stuttering. If I have an IQ of 9, I want that sucker to be 9. Clear.

When I was in high school, a lot of people were listening to your album *Abraxas* or just staring at that amazing cover. What does "Abraxas" mean?

I think the closest thing is the relationship between the divine and the flesh. To my knowledge, I never read the book but from what I gather, when you look at it from your mind, it's a contradiction. It's like a spiritual whore. But when you look at it from a spiritual point of view, Mary Magdelene was exactly that. I tend to lean more towards the spiritual to look at things and say, "God uses this for that. "

I know in my heart that God loves rascals and kooks. People like Miles Davis and Charlie Parker, it's always been known through history that people who are the rascals, when they turn to the spirit or the lord, they count for fifty men. John Coltrane and Charlie Parker, before they turned to spirituality, apparently were very greedy. And Miles was the one who said, "Those guys—forget it." But when Coltrane made an about-face and embraced spirituality, he had the same force. God loves kooks and God loves characters. That's really all I'm saying. A person without character is a boring person. I'm not saying you have to be evil but you do have to have some kind of character, that you can charm a room, that you could sell a fan to a guy in Arabia. Character. I'm not talking about con-artists, I'm just talking about character.

Was there something in your character that made you want to switch directions after *Abraxas* to make *Love, Devotion and Surrender* with John McLaughlin?

Basically, by that time I had peaked with *Abraxas* and everything. Fortunately, or unfortunately for me, I wear out things real quick. After a year of *Abraxas* I had had enough of that lifestyle. I had had enough of the band that I grew up with. I was fed up and they were fed up with me. Their lifestyle and my lifestyle was becoming repulsive to me. I started listening more to Mahalia Jackson and Aretha Franklin and Coltrane and less and less to music to sell beer or shake your booty to. Not till later on I discovered Elvin Bishop and I wanted to shake my booty and combine spiritualism.

Before Bill Graham died he said, "Your music is the perfect balance of the spiritual and the sensual. And I think you should face it. I don't think you should run away from it. After all these years I think you should face it."

Going to *Love, Devotion and Surrender* wasn't like running away from all that. I just had enough of the indulgence. When you're on top, you get bored with it. It becomes predictable. Having so many platinum records on the wall collecting dust and the band doesn't rehearse anymore, everybody walks around like they're prima donnas and it was boring.

So I got really hungry to learn to articulate the music of Coltrane. That kind of music, like Indian music from India. So John McLaughlin was the perfect outlet to seek out Eastern philosophy and religion. We decided to do an album that had John Coltrane songs and that direction. We didn't do it for any other reason than to please ourselves. It was almost being spiritually egotistical. We didn't care whether the Rolling Stones or anybody liked it or not. Because that's what we wanted to do.

We're very grateful that to this day a lot of people identify with it. To the extent that they say that I discovered my first love in the backseat to *Abraxas* but then I discovered divine love to *Caravanserai* and *Love, Devotion and Surrender.* People have told me that they discovered their inner self through this music. And I'm grateful that I can touch their life in this way.

I'd rather process things in my heart than in my mind. I've never seen a shrink or a psychiatrist or a therapist. The closest thing was having a guru but I never talked to him about my problems, I just meditated and read his book and that was it. So I haven't had the need to have some emotional catharsis. I just do it through my music. And I'm really grateful that after all these years people can identify with my sound and my purpose.

Do you have any sense of the lasting quality of your music, that it has a life beyond your own?

With God's grace, the things that I'm writing today are to get rid of the flags and the borders. I think there's only one enemy. There is only one race which is the human race. So I'm going the same way that Bob Marley and John Coltrane were going, to unify people and heal people rather than make you feel inferior or superior. Since I grew up in the sixties, I can see through governments and all that bullshit and I don't need it or want it. I'll bear it and pay my taxes. But I don't see the world going to a better place by rehashing and regurgitating the same principles that are outdates.

Trane's music is the closest thing to you and I being on a space-shuttle and going around the world three times. And by the third time you realize that there are no flags or borders, just one beautiful womb which is this planet, and we're all the baby. And that's what I want to do with my music, make people aware of that.

So many songwriters today approach songs from the commercial rather than the spiritual side. Do you have any advice for them?

It depends on the individual. To a starving man, God is food. To a person who aspires the way John Coltrane was aspiring, God is the only food. People have to wake up to that on their own. You can pinch them to help them wake up but people have to do it on their own time.

Are you optimistic about the future of songwriting?

Yeah. Because there are more good people than bad people. The bad people get more publicity. The good people don't get that much publicity. Look at Mother Theresa or President Carter, who is still helping people with his hands.

Yeah, I'm a very positive person. Like John Coltrane and Bob Marley thought, one positive vibration creates millions of postive vibrations. You create your own heaven and hell.

Have you created a heaven?

Yeah. I'm just very grateful, man. I could still be in Tijuana tonight, hiding in the bushes, trying to get in.

* * *

Jackson Browne
Santa Barbara, California 1996

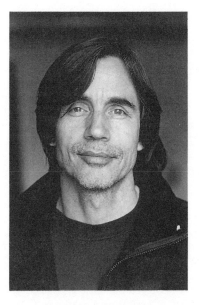

"Depending on the waves," he said, "we can talk tomorrow." Though the condition of the ocean doesn't usually figure into these things, for Jackson Browne it was of chief concern when arranging this interview. In Santa Barbara just steps from the Pacific, he was on a short respite in the midst of a long concert tour to promote his most recent album, *Looking East.* On this day, though, he was mostly looking west, towards a horizon of pure ocean, wondering about the waves.

Though only a couple years shy of fifty, he's in top shape—especially compared to the ravaged condition of many of his peers—and would not seem out of place riding the big breakers. So I figured he was probably talking about surfing, and didn't ask. Later it occurred to me that maybe I was wrong—after all, the use of symbolism is central to his songs and his thoughts—"Everything is metaphor," he said in our interview, even mentioning Joseph Campbell's concept of water as the universal metaphor for rebirth. And the symbolic sea comes into play over and again in his work, from early classics "Rock Me on the Water," "Jamaica, Say You Will" and "Before the Deluge" through more recent masterpieces such as "Sky Blue and Black." So I suspected that maybe the waves he was waiting for were of a more inspirational than recreational nature, more suited to songwriting than surfing.

This suspicion was partially confirmed as he described the sensation a songwriter experiences while connecting with pure inspiration, and his metaphors started to turn physical. "Sometimes, when it's happening, it's wild—it's like riding a wave," he said. "It's like having your finger in the socket. There's a current running through you. Great ideas occur to you and the last thing you want to do is sit down and shape it. You just want to ride."

"Rock me on the water,
Sister won't you smooth my fevered brow,
Rock me on the water
And get back to the sea somehow . . ."

So Santa Barbara by the sea seemed like the perfect place to talk to Jackson, who has often been thought of as kind of the quintessential Californian. In fact, if you look up the definition of "California singer-songwriter," you'll very likely find his name. In truth, he isn't native to the Golden State or even to America: Born in Heidelberg, Germany on October 9, 1948, he soon moved stateside with his family to the Orange County suburb of Fullerton, California. Though his most famous work is forever linked with the seventies, his consciousness as a songwriter was shaped in the sixties, thanks to his older sister and her friends, musicians like Steve Noonan and Greg Copeland, who became his mentors.

"Growing up in the sixties," he said, "music was more than entertainment, it was a form of education." He became politically active before it became popular—as a kid he used to get kicked out of class frequently for asking pointed questions that angered his teachers. Copeland, Noonan and the others introduced him to the issues of sixties—Viet Nam, civil rights—and he sometimes joined them on road trips, such as a 1964 trek to San Francisco to protest both the war and the candidacy of Barry Goldwater. When he saw first-hand the way folk music merged with activism to unite people, it changed his life.

"In San Francisco we met a lot of people and started making connections," he recalled, "and that was the opening of the floodgates." His first song was called "Happy Woman Blues" but was more of a "ragtimey kind of thing," as he recalled, than a real blues. Influenced by the "San Francisco Bay Blues" and the songs of Jesse Fuller, it was written just for the fun of writing a song. But he soon began writing songs directed at specific girls, usually with successful results. He sang at open mikes—known then as "hoots"—but never considered doing it professionally, and was surprised when people starting offering him gigs. "It's not something I had been aspiring to. I just sang my songs so that people would hear them."

His style then was an amalgam of influences—primarily Dylan, but with a healthy dose of Tim Buckley and others. "It took me a long time to find out how to sing and be myself," he said. "You sing in different dialects with different stances and tones and attitudes, and it all becomes part of your palette."

That palette gradually enlarged over the years, encompassing a visceral blend of folk, rock and gospel. Of all artists working in this genre, he's always been one of the most soulful, counterpointing his poetic lyrics with rich choirs of backing vocals. Adept with all the traditional aspects of songwriting, such as intricate and perfect rhyme schemes and meters, he also embraced the abstract lyrical explorations of John Lennon, with whom he shares a birthday, and others.

In 1967 he started getting his songs recorded by other artists: Nico, Tom Rush and even the Nitty Gritty Dirt Band all recorded them. The next year, along with Steve Noonan and other friends, he contributed songs to an album of local artists that was set to be released when the record company decided it should be unified under a single band name. The chosen name—Baby Browning—was found among the headstones in a little California cemetary. Like their namesake, the band died before it ever got very far.

Despite the fact that he's one of the first artists to define the term "singer-songwriter," he always yearned to be part of a group. "I would have rather have been in a band all along," he said, "but I didn't think I had the chops."

His own debut album was released in 1972—the ideal time for his heartfelt songs, as both James Taylor and Carole King had recently emerged. His first album—with its famous Henry Diltz photograph on the cover—was eponymously titled but often wrongly referred to as "Saturate Before Using." Fueled by the hit "Doctor, My Eyes," the album became a hit. With Glenn Frey of the newly formed Eagles, Jackson wrote that band's first hit record—"Take It Easy"—establishing him as that rare songwriter capable of crafting radio hits as well as confessional, artistically powerful statements such as the unbelievable trinity of "For a Dancer," "Fountain of Sorrow" and "Before the Deluge," all from his landmark 1974 *Late For The Sky* album.

> "And in the end they traded their tired wings
> For the resignation that living brings,
> And exchanged love's bright and fragile glow
> For the glitter and the rouge.
> And in a moment they were swept
> Before the deluge."

from "Before The Deluge"

In 1976 that dual songwriting ability merged in the song "The Pretender" which managed to be both a serious statement and a hit single simultaneously. But like Joni Mitchell and others at the time who ventured outside of an introspective outlook in their songwriting, Browne was berated for moving beyond the content of his previous songs. Like Dylan, Jackson showed that he was able to write about the moral emptiness and injustices of the world without abandoning the craft and energy of fine songwriting. And he was criticized for it.

Unlike Dylan, though, who generally limited his political activism to writing, Jackson became personally involved in many political issues, and was forefront in the protests again nuclear energy, and in his support of Amnesty International. In 1984 he released *Lives in the Balance*, a powerful song cycle that directly examined the result of America's involvement in Nicaragua.

His most recent albums have been a return to less topical content—1993 marked the release of one of the wonderfully inspirational *I'm Alive*, which emerged after months of turmoil triggered by his longtime relationship and subsequent breakup with actress Daryl Hannah. At the time of our interview in the spring of 1996, he had recently completed *Looking East*, and was about to embark on a world tour that would take him first to Japan, and then around the world.

Before leaving, however, he carved out ample time in his crazed schedule to devote many thoughtful hours to this discussion, generously digging deeply into the origins of many of his songs. Unlike other famous songwriters who are hard-pressed for details about past work, Jackson happily recounted with great clarity the often romantic roots of even his earliest songs. His estimation of his past wasn't always favorable, however: When I told him that I always loved the line in "These Days" about "sitting on the cornerstones and counting time in quarter-tones till ten," he laughed and said it was the only part of the song that was meaningless. After I explained the specific meaning I had brought to that line for years, he laughed even more heartily and said, "That's the great thing about writing songs. People bring so much to them."

Did you write "The Barricades of Heaven" around a title?

No, I had to look for that. I wrote many versions of it. Finally I even had a friend who's a screenwriter and a poet, and sometimes I enlist his help. But, in this case, I was looking for the word "barricades" but I didn't know what that word would be, and I was all over the place, looking for the word.

When you're writing a song, you're intuitively searching for something that will fit. It's like this great story by W. S. Merwin about a guy that keeps waking up in the middle of the night and confronting this empty place in the middle of his living room. He gets up in the night and he looks at this place; he perceives it to be empty, in other words, missing something. And finally, he realizes that there's a huge boulder out in his front yard, and that's where it belongs: in the middle of his living room. And so he goes and gets it and then everything seems complete.

And that's a little bit like trying to find the right metaphor for a song. You're looking for something that will fill that place that you only sense is empty. So, for that title alone, I could show you a list, several pages long, of words that I looked for for that.

Is that common in your work?

Yeah, sure. But, in this case, I asked this friend of mine to help me hunt this word that I was looking for, but I also misled him. And when he found out what I came up with, he liked it very much but he said "C'mon, that's nothing like what we were looking for." We were in the wrong place. We were prospecting one canyon over.

Is there a sense with something like that that you're finding what's already there, that it is already written?

Yeah, you're finding a way of describing something that you recognize as being true.

Is it a sense that you're reaching beyond yourself?

I think it's beyond me in that I think it's true of other people's lives, too. It's not like I'm looking to describe something that is only true of my own circumstances. So, yeah, it's beyond. It's way inside, you know. It's reaching inside to something that you have in common with many.

There's a lot of leeway and you can get away with a lot. I think it depends on how intently you hold your feet to the fire, as far as what it really means for you.

You described the process of consciously searching for a word. Do you sometimes take a less conscious approach?

I think it's both. It almost feels like I'm not there, when it happens, so it's hard to talk about it. Yeah, there's sort of a descent into a place below your conscious mind, a place where words have resonance and they have meaning and they don't necessarily make a kind of conscious sense. It's like your dreams. The sort of things that—if you're able to actually write down—don't really make a lot of conscious sense.

Sometimes it becomes a conscious thirst, because the song has become very developed and you're still missing a part. I think the finishing of a song winds up bobbing around on the surface and you're examining it. Or sometimes you simply see that it's not complete, and there's something that it needs.

Songwriting is like building guitars. You save wood for many years until it's ready, until you want a piece of wood like that, and you make an instrument. Or you may have the back and the sides, but you don't have the wood you want for the face of the guitar. The metaphor is beautiful because a song is like an instrument in that it can be played by somebody else, and it can lay around for years and somebody can pick it up and play it again.

And the good ones really age well.

Right. The best ones get better with age.

Your songs certainly do that.

Thank you. You know that I've always thought that they should, and I think that comes from folk music, from appreciating songs that are visible in all of their incarnations. Like a song like "Stagger Lee." I think it comes from learning songs that way and thinking of them as something that could age well. Something that could be worthwhile later, or something that's timeless.

Your song "These Days" certainly has that quality for me. Was it one of your very first songs?

That was among my first songs. I think I wrote that when I was about 16. That song changed a lot. I wrote that song on guitar and it was pretty folky and sort of quick. And it became musically a whole deeper thing when Greg Allman sung it. He slowed it down, and I sort of copped his phrasing—the way I sing it now. And the way I did it on record was very much influenced by his version of the song.

Do you remember writing "Doctor, My Eyes?"

I had a really severe eye condition. My eyes were so red I almost couldn't open them. Couldn't close them. And I didn't know what it was. Probably some sort of drug-induced condition. So it was a song about life in which the metaphor took over and it became about the loss of innocence. What sparked the song was having had this near-blinding experience where I literally could not see. I could not use my eyes.

I wrote the song after I got better. I didn't write that song while I had problems seeing. But it was really within a month or two months.

You've written so many great songs over the years. Do you find, as you go on, that you learn anything new about songwriting, or that it becomes easier at any point?

No. I think that I hope to learn something new all the time. Whether something I write is really new or whether it's something that is similar to what I've already done is not really something I worry about at the time. I think I'm motivated to try not to repeat myself too much and to try to uncover new territory for myself, because that's part of the pleasure of doing it and it's part of the search. You're sort of excavating for something you don't know consciously. You're looking for that resonance. Something uncovered that you recognize as being true.

How do you avoid repeating the same musical patterns you've used in the past?

I have probably played the same stuff over and over again on the piano. I was doing a concert and I sat down at the piano and started playing a new song in D, and the crowd started clapping even though they'd never heard this song, because what I was playing in D is what I always habitually play in D on the piano and they thought it was a song they'd already heard.

I have to play for hours to try to go to new places and develop something different. I think singing while playing is such a big part of writing for me.

Generally, when you go to work on a song, do you find that you have the creative energy it takes to see it through?

[*Pause*] Yeah. When it's going on, you know, it's going on. I always think it's just a matter of time; it's just a matter of whether you've given yourself the room, or gotten yourself to the proper reflective place. I know that you write songs with the same thing that you make love with, or that you receive music with. The same part of you, the same creative center. The Greeks called it "Eros"—not just meaning erotic, but love of beauty and the appreciation of beauty. It's the same thing you read a really great book with, or that is engaged when you see a fine movie. You can squander it, you can piss it away. You can waste it. And I think there are times when you're tapped out.

I used to think that drugs were a big help, but eventually I realized that they were the opposite. It seemed to be that anything that would keep you up for days would help you finish a song. People couldn't talk to you because you were three sheets to the wind, and had been up for two days, and they'd have to wait until you've slept. So you carved out some space to do the work, but unfortunately the work was worthless. And eventually it took twice as long to unravel what you'd been working on because you had to be in that state to get back to what you were doing.

So you have to be in form. That is you have to be used to doing it, to get the most out of the inspiration. Although, I wish it was just like a big old huge voltage switch that gets switched on, and keeps you completely caught up in what you're doing until you're done. It's been that way many times, but it's un-reliable. If you wait around for inspiration to happen and are not conducting a creative life where you're involved with your music and your instruments, then that inspiration will happen and you'll have a couple good ideas and it will be gone before you can respond to it.

So I relegate everything to the creative act as being what I'm here to do. And so anything that helps is something that I incorporate into my lifestyle.

Does that mean when you get an idea for a song, you stick with it and try to write the whole thing at once?

I usually put it on tape so that I can forget about what's happening and I don't have to try to engage my conscious mind in order to remember it to shape it as it's happening. I can just let some stuff happen and sometimes, when it's happening, it's wild: it's like riding a wave. It's like having your finger in the socket. There's a current running through you and it just feels great. It's a wonderful thing. Great ideas occur to you and the last thing you want to do is sit down, at that moment, and shape it. You just want to ride.

So I usually record it and then listen back. And for the most part, what you remember of it is the memorable stuff, but if you go back and check it you almost always find something that you would not have remembered because it was odd.

Are you generally working with words and music at the same time?

Oh, yeah. A lot of time I'm just making up music and singing nonsense, but there is a flavor to it; there's a certain emotional flavor and meaning going on that has to do with the sound of the instrument and the voice and the feel-ing. And ideally it's all going on at the same time. That's when it's most clear or most present. It's something that's all happening at once.

Have there been times when you got a whole song—words and music—at one time?

Yeah, that's happened for me a few times. I can't wait for that to happen cause there's too much else going on in my life. I have to agree that the sim-plest things tend to come that way. A lot of times it happens that you think of something in the car—especially living in L.A., you're in the car so much of the time. Or exercising or running and you're nowhere near anything and you have this whole idea come, and you try to remember it. That's usually to do with the lyrics, or a turn of a phrase or an idea, and it's usually when you're doing something else. It requires a certain amount of your attention.

It's like you're going from one place in town to another place in town. You have to take the road that will get you there. And you have to handle traffic. And there's this whole other thing going on in your life that has nothing to do with your physical location, because this stuff will sort of emerge and come up in the middle of a seemingly ordinary task.

Do you ever get a melody first before you think of any words?

Yeah, that's happened. That's actually very hard to write words to a mel-ody that's already formed. I almost remember the first time I tried doing that. It took me so long. I think "The Fuse" was like that—this whole melody, this whole piece of music that I had to write words to.

Some part of it usually comes fairly quickly. A lot of times it's just a groove or it has to do with the guitar or a piano.

You write on piano as well as guitar?
Oh, I almost always write everything on both.

You go back and forth?
Yeah. Even if it's a guitar song, I'll go sit down and work on it on piano to see what else is there. It's not something I do routinely, but I think that it takes me so long to write a song that, by the time I've finished it, I generally have logged a certain amount of time on both instruments.

Sometimes I'll start a song in a tuning and then I'll try to figure out how to play it in regular tuning, if I can. Or it's in the singing of it, in the abandonment of singing, and letting the song sort of live in you.

If you don't mind, I'd like to randomly name some of your songs to see what response or memories you have about them.
Okay.

"Sky Blue and Black" [from *I'm Alive*].
[*Long pause. Deep breath*] I decided I needed to write songs that I could play acoustically by myself, without the band. So I started writing by myself a lot and I wrote that song with this sort of tumbling rhythmic cadence.

I vaguely remember thinking that this sounded a little to me like Van Morrison in the stuttering, cascading, kind of free-falling cadence. I wrote this very descriptive first verse and it sort of existed by itself for a long time. And I didn't really have the rest of the story. I never quite knew what I was describing, although it did, at a certain point, seem like the story was somewhat doomed [*laughs*] by the time I wrote the end of the first verse. But, really, it got written over, literally, a period of two or three years. And the final thing to happen was that I had it half-written and I started playing it with the band and lines sort of occurred from playing it.

So we made up this bridge, musically. And then I had to figure out how to say what I needed to say in eight lines instead of the real long form that I'd created for the verse. And like you might imagine, sometimes the most compelling and far-reaching thing is said in the fewest words. What it didn't need was another long verse. It needed to go someplace really directly. And I took the advice of a Jungian therapist that I know: "You have to ask yourself what you want. You must talk about what you want. Say what you want." And then I was able to get to the heart of the song in the bridge.

Writing it became a colossal thing [*laughs*] that was so hard to finish. It was like painting the ceiling of a chapel. You spend three years on your back three inches from the ceiling, trying to get a perspective. I could never get enough distance from the relationship that I was writing about to really write about what was going on. I could never tell what the hell was happening. And so that whole beginning verse was written one year and the rest of it written in pieces in a couple of years that followed.

And finally I was writing the bridge in the studio as the song was being done. I left enough room to sing this third verse and I realized that if we had to listen to another verse that we're all going to cut our wrists [*laughs*]. We'd better go someplace else.

"Jamaica, Say You Will."

That was the first song I wrote on the piano. I remember writing that song for a girl I was seeing who lived nearby the ocean. She worked for this old, Italian guy in a garden. An organic vegetable farm overlooking Zuma Beach. And I used to go visit her. [*laughs*] And it was a pretty idyllic time. She was very beautiful, and ideologically she was into yoga and vegetarianism and organic gardening. I was really crazy about her, but I wasn't into any of those things. And I'd go hang with her because it was so beautiful in that garden, and she'd be picking figs, and I'd feel transported into some sort of Maxfield Parrish landscape—that sort of dry fig orchard with this very beautiful girl. I spent a lot of time talking with her and I wrote this song for her. It was sort of a metaphor.

Later I realized that that song really wasn't about her. As much as she inspired me, what I was really talking about was a relationship which I'd just concluded a few months before, and which had been going on for two or three years. I was in love with a girl and wanted to hide in the relationship, and not really deal with the world or with my obligations. And the girl that I was in love with was also unspeakably beautiful and was the object of the attentions of a lot of older, and really accomplished people. And she was really drawn to an adult world, a real life. An adult life was calling to her. And I just wanted to stay indoors with her. [*Laughs*] I wanted to stay in the beautiful cradle of this relationship and make love. But I was eluding my own career and my own obligations to myself and eluding my future, in a way, just wanting to retreat.

So that's what that song's about: a girl who's going to go sailing away with her father and go into the world, and a guy who wants to stay there in that idyllic place. It's something I think I've never quite figured out, how to reconcile the demands and responsibilities of an adult life with that pure, idyllic, beautiful, creative life of a child.

"Rock Me on the Water."

It's very much from the same place in my life. "When my life is over, gonna stand before the father / but the sisters of the sun are gonna rock me on the water . . ." It's sort of an ode to sexual pleasure and enjoyment and peace and love in the midst of a sort of apocalyptic scenario. I used to read a lot of Eldridge Cleaver and Bobby Seale and political stuff then, having to do with the inevitability of revolution. And I saw that, by that time, the late sixties, that there had been a lot of upheaval. I think that that stuff came from the very center of me: the desire for love and peace and release and reconciliation with the spiritual.

The song has a biblical tone to it.

Yeah. There was so much going on in the sixties, it sort of catapulted into all this stuff—the civil rights movement and Black Panthers and the Vietnam War and all that stuff going on. And, at the same time, people were exploding the cultural mores with the sexual revolution, and looking for spirituality in

Eastern thought and in drugs and all kinds of things. There was a lot going on all at once.

"My Opening Farewell."

It's another one of those songs that is about a specific relationship. I think I probably wrote it after I was there, but it's about this point in time in a relationship, and a place where we were living. Elektra [Records] had this recording ranch up in northern California and we stayed at this old hotel. And a train ran by it. So: "there's a train every day, leaving either way," the whole idea that you could go one way or the other.

And this relationship was struggling. There I was in this recording situation, but all I wanted to do was be with this girl [laughs].

You know, it's hard to make a record. It's really hard, and if you let yourself, you'll go do anything else—anything but toe the line and find out what you're really about. I was kind of using that relationship to hide in. That song is about the particular moment when you really recognize that the person you love wants to be anywhere else. Wants to be gone, wants to move on.

It's almost like the first good song I wrote—the first time I wrote a song I thought was really good. I remember the song. I remember my part of it and I was very proud of the guitar piece.

"For Everyman."

That's the first song I can remember having spent a really long time writing. I think I started writing that song one night at Glen Frey and Don Henley's apartment. They had some neighbors next door and they had been playing Grand Funk really loud and there was some one-line thing that was repeating on and on and on and on. A really thick refrain to the song. I started writing that song then and it seemed to me that, a year later, I was still writing the song. I had just made my first record and it seemed like I was still trying to ask myself what was going on in the song.

I'd write these descriptive first lines that sort of set the stage. They set the tone. I wrote that first verse: "As the evening descends, I sit thinking about everyman . . ." And the whole thing about "each with his own ticket in this hand. " It's so pregnant with promise [laughs]. It promises to be about something. And then I spent about a year trying to figure out what the hell I promised [laughs]. What was I going on about?

It's funny that you weren't sure what you were saying with that song, because in that lyric you say, "Long ago, I heard someone say something about Everyman . . ." Even in the song you weren't quite sure what it was they were saying.

They refer to somebody as an "everyman," that character. And I guess it's that vague reference to the thing that makes us all the same—the thing that is the thread that runs through every life, the human experience. Joseph Campbell talks about this in a book that I was reading at the time, *The Hero with a Thousand Faces*. He talks about water as the universal metaphor for rebirth. He talks about the "monomyth" and the idea that the story of the Buddha and the story of Christ are really the same story: they spring from that wellspring of spirituality that exists in each person, that myth that is formed by the life experience.

But I never wanted to answer that question because it sounds evangelical, if you do. It sounds like you know the way. As a matter of fact, that song had that disclaimer: "Just walk away if you don't agree." Because I think that we're all very suspicious of anybody talking about answers. We all instinctually know that the answers are for each of us to find ourselves.

John Lennon had done a great deal of demythologizing his own myth and the myth of the Beatles in the song "God." I think we really, in so many ways, have been instructed by his example to be suspicious of anybody who's carrying around the answers or says they have the plan: how to be, how to live, what to do.

You have reservations about preaching in songs and yet in certain songs you've taken on specific subjects effectively, such as the Latin America situation in "Lives in the Balance." Do you feel there are times when a kind of preaching in songs is appropriate?

Yeah, I think there are times, if it's a matter of trying to avert a calamity. There are times where you have to put aside your preference for being smooth or hip, and simply shout "Fire!" [*Laughs*] If it's a matter of something like whether your country's going to war, that's important. At the time, I just thought it would be worth it. I value my career, of course, but I don't value it so much as to preserve it at all costs. Like to be quiet during a Holocaust. I felt that I needed to say what I knew.

And I also believed—and I'm not sure that this is borne out by events at all—that if you told the American people what was going on, that they would do the right thing. I'm not sure that it's as simple as that anymore. I can't say that I have the certainty that I had, at the time, that that was possible. People have a huge capacity for self-delusion and it's no longer a given that if you show them the truth, that they'll do the right thing.

In "Lives in the Balance," you balanced getting a message across with writing a good song. Is it hard to do both?

Well, that's the challenge. You risk turning people away. For one thing, if you write about matters that they're not very well versed in, you won't connect. I don't think that the vast majority of people that heard that song were familiar with what I was talking about. So it can't be considered a hit in the same way that "Running on Empty" was.

"Fountain of Sorrow."

The opening is nice. I like that line: "I was taken by a photograph of you." Because not only is it just a play on words, but the double entendre of the word "taken," to be taken by something is to be attracted to it. But also it reverses itself again and you think, I was defined in that moment by this relationship to you.

I sing that song now and it's sort of resonant and as poignant now as it was then, for a variety of other reasons, too personal to go into. But it's one of my favorites.

You know, just saying to an audience right now, "You had to hide some-times, but now you're all right / It's good to see your smiling face tonight." So people cheer, you know? Because it's suddenly about me and them. Right in the middle of this story about two people, suddenly it's me and the audience—just for a moment. Great thing about songs.

I want to ask you about "Looking East," which reverses the Kerouac-inspired American westward tradition we've had for so long.

Well, you get as far west as you can go. It's similar to Kerouac's idea. He was sort of making an assessment, as he went across the country traveling west. There's also the added connotation of Hermann Hesse's journey to the east. Which is really a metaphor for a journey to the self. A spiritual journey. So I like that added connotation to the one of simply looking back and taking stock of the country.

Did the title of that come to you prior to writing the song?

The title was actually the first thing. [*Laughs*] And the title came when Luis Conte, our percussionist, walked into this African store and put on this feathered crown—it was made of ostrich plumes and beads. He looked like a king, and he turned his profile to us and said, "Looking East." Like he was some historical figure, like Hannibal looking towards the Alps.

I remembered the phrase "looking east" then. And it became sort of a catch phrase. That doesn't explain why the song turned out to be about what it's about. But that's the case with so many of them. That's how it happens: there's some phrase or some combination of words.

"Late for the Sky."

That's a perfect example of what I mean. That was another song that started with the title. As a matter of fact, I said that to somebody I was saying good-bye to and it was a ridiculously dramatic thing to say to somebody when you're leaving. [*Laughs*] Meaning, "I'm late. I have a flight to catch. And I have to go." And that was like an early morning flight. It wasn't even light out, and I said "late for the sky." And I just remembered it. It became a song.

To me, writing a song is very often a search for all the other imagery and the creative context in which that one phrase will then have an even greater resonance. Or it will mean all those things when you say it.

With a song like "Looking East"—do you really think about the com-plete meaning before you write it, or is that something you realize when you're writing?

No. I just start writing. With that song, the first verse was written on a plane. And I thought it was a pretty good first verse, because it really sets the stage, and sets a theme. It promised to be about a journey, in which I did not know where it was leading. So it was very promising. I didn't know where it was going and I had that first verse for a long time. Quite a few months before I could get the rest of it going. Because I had a problem there with how not to just start writing a very detailed assessment, or a real long list of things that are wrong with the world or wrong with society.

You have the lines about hunger, but also about where power can be found. You show both sides.

Well, this song is about hungering for a connection with real power and real meaning. The hunger is not about poverty. Because I say "hunger in the mansion." It's a kind of hunger that's there even with great wealth.

I love the line about "the power of the song that is sung alone."

Yeah. It's a great thing about humans, in that everything is metaphor. So, a song sung alone, it could just mean somebody living alone. It could mean somebody living their life, or working alone. It could be about somebody continuing on a project that somebody else has left and it has that kind of resonance because of the way our minds work.

I remember in an interview with you from a few years back, the writer complained that you were always the guy that could rhyme "world" with "unfurled," and yet you'd stopped using perfect rhymes. And you said. "Well, you can only use 'unfurled' so many times." And you were stressing that the meaning is more important than getting a real rhyme.

I don't think it's important to rhyme perfectly. I used to be pretty obsessed with it. I didn't even want to rhyme a singular with a plural. So it would be perfect. I would go to great lengths to change the line so that it would be. So that it would rhyme with "time" instead of "times." But I'd say that most great music is just fine without that kind of obsessive detail. And I tried to get beyond that.

Was there something that caused you to change your mind about that being important?

No one thing. Just appreciating a lot of songs that don't necessarily rhyme very exactly at all—especially blues. And there are songs that don't have to rhyme at all. They don't have to rhyme. [*Laughs*]. It's just something we do. It's almost like a crutch.

A song will sound fine, if it rhymes, even though it doesn't say a thing. That's the thing about songs. There's a lot of forgiveness in the medium because people are used to hearing stuff that doesn't necessarily mean anything, or make a lot of sense. It doesn't have to.

You can open up the whole structure and form by choosing to rhyme less often. Sometimes, when I've been writing a song and kind of aware that I didn't know what the hell I was writing about, I tend to rhyme way too much. Sort of like a stepping stone—like you're going from rhyme to rhyme trying to get something going.

To create some kind of structure to hold it together.

Yeah. And it seems to me that if you really had something to say you wouldn't need to do that at all. You would be saying what you have inside you that's dying to come out. So, there's that kind of inspiration, that seance-type of inspiration where you're kind of holding hands with yourself in the dark trying to have something appear.

Does that seance quality occur frequently?

I don't even know how to comment on frequency. It happens all different kinds of ways. Usually, what happens is in the middle of working on something, where your conscious mind is engaged, as a relief you sort of start goofing around—your body starts playing music. Your guitar. Your hands start playing music, or the piano is sort of playing while you're thinking of this other thing. And suddenly you're playing something that's pretty good. It's probably not something you can use right at the moment and you have to make yourself say, "Okay, stop working on this other thing. Stop whipping this horse. It's dead. And what is this other thing, though, that is sort of prancing around in me in my imagination? What is this little thing?" I think I have to constantly tell myself, "Okay. Stop working on what you know you've got to finish, and take off and follow this other thing and see where it goes."

It's possible to be a great craftsman, and to craft a great deal of beautiful work and architecture. There are people who spent their life learning to cut stone and how to make a certain kind of joint in woodworking. And then to employ that craft to create art is the goal.

It's like that metaphor again of making a guitar. When you find a guitar that transcends all of its beautiful craftsmanship and is also really an amazing instrument, it can change the equation for people. Because it's capable of creating some truly beautiful, meaningful music. So that is the most powerful combination, when the craft contains so much commitment that it becomes art. When those two things come together—craft and art—that's where the magic comes from.

* * *

Todd Rundgren
Santa Paula, California 1989

"Todd is God." It's a rhyming mantra spoken reverently by his devoted follow-ers around the globe. For them, there is no other but Todd; they're as steadfast in their loyalty to him as are Deadheads for the Grateful Dead. When a Toddhead chooses an album to play, the question of which artist to select never comes into play, only which period in Todd's multifaceted career to choose.

He's a musician of so many extremes that music writers seem to be thrown for a loop as to how to describe him. Called "rock's most outspoken maverick curmudgeon" by one, another referred to him as "Pop's ultimate hyphenate, a singer-songwriter-multi-instrumentalist-producer-videographer-programmer."

In real life Todd is a thoroughly thoughtful, spiritual man.

Born on June 22, 1948 in Upper Darby, Pennsylvania, he got his start with the band The Nazz, who scored a huge hit with his song "Hello, It's Me." In-fluenced by the songs of Laura Nyro and Goffin & King, he showed back then an ability to write both the catchy pop song, such as his hit "I Saw the Light," as well as real rockers. In time he also branched out into the world of progres-sive rock, and explored that vein of his creativity by recording albums with his band Utopia. Eventually, all of these musical tendencies fused in his albums, which became increasingly less commercial over the years as they became even more creative. Concert tours have featured him without any other musicians, interfacing for hours with only his voice, a guitar or a piano, and a computer.

The result was remarkably warm, intimate and spontaneous. On his *A Capella* album, there were no musicians at all nor any instruments. It was all Todd's voice, used in a myriad of wondrous ways to interpret a collection of amazing songs. Again, the result was full of warmth.

When we spoke, Todd was at work on the album that became *Nearly Human*. He recorded it live, without any overdubs, abandoning modern technology to capture the oft-forgotten magic of musicians making music together. In a business where most people are busy playing the game, Todd Rundgren makes up his own rules.

Maybe the reason he can is because he doesn't have to be a recording artist to make a living. He does it out of love for music and the need for expression, able to support himself easily in other ways. Not only is he one of rock's most influential producers, having produced albums for everyone from Patti Smith to Jules Shear, he's also a gifted engineer who recorded early albums by The Band and who still engineers his own sessions.

So when it's his time to make a Todd Rundgren album, he's freed of commercial restrictions. "I haven't painted myself into a corner," he said, and it's true. With an enormous built-in audience around the world hungry for his next musical adventure, Todd always comes up with something new, something we haven't heard before. Listen to "Miracle in the Bazaar" (from *A Capella*), replete with its authentic Middle Eastern chanting, and you know you're hearing a song nobody else could possibly have written.

The greatest songs are often those that are written by a combination of conscious and unconscious creation. Todd, who has written songs in almost every style on almost every subject there is to write about, spoke at length about both methods of creation, even admitting that some of his strongest songs were born in the land of dreams. The trick, as he explains in the following interview, is in the remembering.

Many of your songs, such as "Blue Orpheus," seem unlimited in their ability to express emotions with only words and music. Have you ever found the song form to be restrictive?

I don't have the same restrictions that other people do because I never painted myself in a corner in that respect. I've always done things that didn't necessarily fit the form. So it's more unusual for me to do a whole album full of songs that fit the so-called modern form than it is for me to throw in a couple things that are different. So I've never felt limited in that respect in terms of songwriting.

Do you have any kind of regular writing routine? Do you work on songwriting every day?

No, I don't. I usually spend a whole lot of time thinking about a song before I ever attempt to work with it.

Well, I have two methods: [*Laughs*] One is if I have to write a song consciously, then I spend lots of time ruminating on the idea that I want to convey and the musical mood that I want to create. Then when it comes down to writing the song, it usually doesn't take that long. But I may spend months thinking about a song before I actually sit down and start working it out.

And then, alternatively, I have this tendency sometimes to dream songs completely written. And then it's a question of just remembering them when I'm awake and transcribing them.

Other songwriters, such as Randy Newman, have said how that kind of thing, dreaming songs, never happens to them. Where do you think those songs are coming from, the ones you dream?

Well, to explain that you would have to explain where your dreams come from. [*Laughs*] That gets into something totally beyond songwriting. And it may be a myth to Randy Newman, but it's absolute reality to me, because I can name the songs. And all I had to do was teach myself to remember them, and get up and write them down.

When you wake up, do you go to the piano and find out what the chord changes are that match the song, or do you dream those as well?

Well, what happened was I used to dream these songs and lose them because I wouldn't remember them. And what I did was to get into an almost lucid dream thing and run myself through this discipline of waking myself up or putting myself in a semi-sleep state and actually working the song out; visualizing the song in my head, what all the changes were and their interrelationships. And playing it over and over again in my head so that I remember it and don't forget it.

There was one song on *A Capella*, "Lost Horizon," which I dreamed fully realized when I was in Nepal at the time. I had to remember it for three or four weeks until I got home. So that was kind of like the ultimate in that discipline. It was beyond just the dreaming part of it; I had to teach the song to myself so completely and without the aid of any kind of audio feedback on what the song was like, and then remember it until I got home to transcribe it, that it was a little scary. I was afraid I was going to forget it.

But you managed to get it home intact, without losing any of it?

It's pretty much the way it was when I dreamed it. The thing that's the vaguest is usually the lyrics. Sometimes there'll be a line or two that sticks out, and the rest of it will be just too much to remember.

Does that give you the feeling, then, that you are writing these songs, or are they coming from beyond you?

Even when I'm coming up with musical ideas consciously I don't know if it necessarily means I'm really writing them. [*Laughs*] There's no proof of that. There's no proof I'm not. There can be an argument either way.

From my standpoint, sleeping or awake doesn't make any difference. It's a question of being attuned to a certain thing. Even if you're consciously writing a song, you've conditioned yourself mentally to do things in a certain way.

It could conceivably be that the conditioning gets so complete that your subconscious mind continues to generate music while you're asleep. Then again there's the argument that you're actually only hearing things when you're awake that are somehow transmitted to you. Therefore, it's no different when you're asleep. They're getting transmitted with less resistance, perhaps, when you're asleep. So it's hard to say one way or another. It's curious to me when I dream these songs, they're so completely realized, that so much of the whole song is there.

Do you have a technique for consciously tapping into that unconscious source?

[*Pause*] I don't know whether it has anything particularly to do with song-writing, but when I get involved with something I get completely immersed in it. If it happens to be music, then it's music. If it's some other thing, then I think about it constantly and to that extent it just conditions my entire thought processes, conscious and unconscious. . . .

"Lost Horizon," which you dreamed, has a beautiful melody. Do you think composing a melody spontaneously, apart from your own internal critic, is a more effective method than doing it consciously?

I think I'm much less open, when I'm conscious, to that sort of thing than when I'm asleep. I think when I'm conscious I'm much more aware of trying to craft something, and to consciously avoid cliches.

There's also a certain dependency on stuff that you've already learned and habits that you've acquired. You're always trying to get this balance between the things that you feel comfortable with and lapsing into some kind of hackneyed re-hash of things you've done already. So there's a lot of conflicting stuff going on when you have to consciously write a song. When it comes subconsciously, I think most people would say that's the ideal way to come up with a piece of material.

And in your experience, have most of your strongest songs been created unconsciously rather than consciously?

I think the ones that have resonated the most, the ones that have struck a chord in other people . . . for instance, "Bang the Drum" was one of the songs that I dreamed. [*Laughs*] And that was the last time I had anything re-sembling a hit record. [*Laughs*] A song like "I Saw the Light" was a song I wrote in fifteen minutes. I didn't dream it. I just kind of blurted it out. And that got a response out of people.

Your song "Blue Orpheus" is about that process of expressing yourself in song and creating something timeless in the face of all that we lose in time. Was that a song that was created unconsciously?

Oftentimes I'll get a title that will suggest the entire rest of the song. I think I was watching the movie *Black Orpheus*, and for some reason the title "Blue Orpheus" popped into my head. It kind of spun off the whole story of Orpheus and the fact that he was supposed to be a singer, and that when he expressed himself, the gods were so moved by it that they created special dis-pensations for him.

And then this whole dark and light thing; the idea of the overworld and the underworld which is in the Orpheus myth. And the idea that no matter how black it is, black is just one side of the coin. No matter how dark it is on one side, there wouldn't be any darkness without light.

In "Blue Orpheus," are you singing about yourself or about the role of the songwriter in general?

I think, ideally, music is not self-limiting. That's the problem with when you consciously try to write a so-called hit record, that you are trying to read other people's minds and you're not necessarily writing toward an *ideal*. And most of the material that I write is moving toward some ideal that hopefully is transcendent of temporal things like what style is popular nowadays.

I'm really looking to create music that I can also respond to myself, and my presumption is that if I respond to it, then people whose opinions [*laughs*] I respond to and care about will respond to it in somewhat the same way, with their own particular individual slant.

Do you find that your lyrical ideas are generated by your music or do they come at the same time?

I often come up with words and melody simultaneously and usually the last thing in the process.

Historically, a lot of my song production has been to go into the studio and interactively work with the machinery and flesh out, almost, a complete track without vocals on it, and then come up with the words and melody.

I'm looking for as much of a musical form in the underlying structure as I am in the melody and words that go over the top of it. And once I have something and I'm satisfied with the infrastructure, that suggests to me a whole other range of things that I can do. It also helps to constrain me in a certain way; to refine parts of the song.

I think that, in one sense, the opposite of that might be a song like "When Doves Cry" [by Prince] which has like two notes in the whole melody. [*Laughs*] A lot of songwriters write out the words first and then set them to music. I never do that. Except in a case where I might have the title or one or two lines that I think have to be in there, and then I'll schmooze things around to make them work. But most of the time it's simultaneous, and the melodic elements come first.

How about a song like "It Wouldn't Have Made Any Difference"? That song has a gorgeous melody and the words fit it perfectly; was that a song in which you created the track first before the words and melody?

No, I had that song. That was actually written in the same period as "I Saw the Light," the *Something Anything* period. It was another one of those songs that probably took a half an hour or forty minutes to come up with.

I would usually come up with the basic structure of it, and then the rest of it just seemed to come naturally. The most difficult thing has always been lyrics, and that is what takes so long nowadays in terms of songwriting. I want all aspects of it to have equal importance. I want there to be a certain poetry in the lyrics and that requires, for me, that the music be structured in a certain way. And in that sense, with some songs you just get lucky.

At the time I was writing *Something Anything* I thought that I had a formula for myself, in terms of songwriting. And that's one reason I took such a radical departure after that. It's because I envisioned myself writing songs without thinking about them. And they were losing their depth in a certain way.

Lyrical depth?

Just overall. Because any kind of music, no matter how much it impacts and meshes with the time, if you continue to do it constantly without evolving anything, then you become sort of baroque; you become passe and, in some cases, irrelevant if you're just copping to a style.

I think nowadays I'm spending a lot of time on that almost as a reaction to disposable music. Which is what prevails generally in the industry. But there are a lot of times when I just take an experimental approach and do things that I'm not absolutely sure are working but which help me to break out of crystallized thought processes about the way music should be written.

Do you remember writing your first song?
I remember writing songs that didn't actually attain song, but I also remember writing my first songs that actually sounded like a song.

How old were you then?
Eighteen.

Do you remember what it was at that time that inspired you to write songs, and made you feel you could write songs?
I don't think I felt I couldn't write songs. But it was a tendency of mine never to finish things, previous to that. I guess at one point I just got it together to actually finish something.

I've spoken to artists that you have produced who have told me that you were very critical of their lyrics.
Lyrics are the hardest part almost for any songwriter. There are a few people—like Patti Smith, who was a poet first and then became a songwriter, so she always had a lot to say—but for most people they have firm musical ideas and very vague lyrical ideas. And they will spend a lot more time on refining the music than they will on the lyrics. They'll get lyrics that rhyme and don't seem *too stupid* and that'll be good enough.

I think that material that is meaningful in the long run, that has greater impact on people, is material that avoids cliches. And it also avoids picking a subject and abstractly filling in the lyrics for it without having any emotional impact behind it, without having any *real feeling* for the subject matter.

There's such a pressure for some people to be original that they lose the warmth in terms of being original. To think up a unique subject is not enough. You have to still put it in some relevant human context. Some songwriters tend to be observational; stand outside of the situation and talk about it without ever being in it. And to me that's not satisfying. It's much more satisfying to have someone relating what they feel to you than just being a narrator.

You mentioned disposable music, and I wonder if the record companies are responsible for that. You produced Jules Shear's album *Watchdog*, which is a truly great collection of songs. And the record company never released a single on it, thereby causing it to be disposable.
My personal feeling is that a record company can break any record they want. The record business is basically corrupt. And they can make the public conscious of anybody they want if they spend the money to do it. And it's just who they choose. Most of the people working in the record industry have no imagination or integrity. And that's why [*laughs*] things are the way they are. They're looking for repeats of previous formulas.

Given that, what would you say to the songwriters out there who are trying to break in—

Well, I've never given advice about breaking in, because that guarantees some success. [*Laughs*]

Well, how about someone who is just trying to make their living—

Well, I can't guarantee that, either. I would say, don't attempt to make a living and consider yourself an artist at the same time. If someone wants to be an artist, then get a job that pays and you can depend on, and don't be any less devoted to your artistry and hope at some point that it will happen for you.

Okay. But what if your goal in life happens to be to get a record deal—

Yeah, well, that's a pretty pitiful goal at this point in life, as far as I'm concerned. It's like saying that your greatest goal is to be an accountant. There are some great accountants [*laughs*] in the world, but most accountants are drudges. And most people making records are making mediocre music. And if you aspire to something that's basically mediocre, I would say that's not the point.

The point of being a musician is to go out there and create music and communicate it to people. And it's an illusion that the only way you can successfully do that is with the record companies.

So it's one of two things: it's either luck or prostitution. You've got to decide, "If I'm going to be a songwriter, I'm going to have to devote myself to that craft, you know, and not try to depend on making a living on it." Because if you depend on making a living on it, you have to do one of two things: You have to go out, find a connection, schmooze them, and try and get in that way, or you have to consciously prostitute yourself and write whatever is the currently acceptable style of music.

A song of yours that many songwriters can identify with is "Honest Work"; that feeling of simply wanting to work as musicians.

It wasn't meant to be limited to that but it certainly doesn't discount that concept. Many people think it had to do with money. At no particular point in the song do I talk about material reward as being the object. The object is doing something that you feel good about. Something that you can devote yourself to that doesn't make you feel degraded. There's always ditches to dig. [*Laughs*] But for many of us, we need to have meaning in the work that we do.

Was A Capella harder to put together than you had originally thought?

I kind of jumped the gun in terms of available technology. I was using the very first sampler made, which was the Emulator. And that made it a little more difficult to do some of the stuff that I was trying to do. But most of the album wasn't sampling; most of it was overdubbing of vocals. So I never thought it was going to be easy.

A wonderful song on that album is "Something to Fall Back On" which has a joyful melody and a lyric that is not at all joyful; it's an interesting contrast.

Yeah. That was actually the first one I ever recorded, and I was self-consciously trying to make it sound like a band. By using all the vocal sounds and seeing how close to a band I could make it. It was actually the first thing that

I recorded for the record. Then I went off into more sort of bizarre and traditional things.

In general, do you feel the state of songwriting has diminished as of late?

If I have any right to judge, [*laughs*] I would say, definitely. I suppose a lot of people would say, "You're talking like our parents talked when Big Band music went out." But I thought that the music as it evolved through the sixties and through the seventies actually *improved* on Big Band music. It wasn't this moon-June-spoon crap. People were writing about new ideas. And trying to actually open up people's consciousness through the vehicle of music. Not just entertain. And now it's back to wallpaper again.

Do you find that songs come out differently based on what instrument you write them on?

I usually only write on one of two instruments. Mostly I write on piano and occasionally will write on guitar. I usually know which because of the kind of song I'm writing. I'll very rarely write ballads on the guitar. Or those kind of harmonically complex songs; you can only get six notes out of the guitar. It really depends on what you can do with your fingers and the tuning of the instrument. The piano is just much more flexible in that sense. You have more options.

Do you find you usually pursue melodies based on chords that you play, or do you do it more in your head?

It's really hard to divide what's happening. But the melodies are often suggested by the changes. But I don't usually just play block changes. I'm looking for a certain flow and movement within the changes as well.

Do you have favorite keys to play in?

No, not really. If I have a melody in my head, I'll find the key that goes with it. [*Laughs*] I have a tendency to go for keys that are easier to play for me, like C or F. But if the song demands that I start playing all over the black keys, that's what happens.

Do you have any preference for major keys over minor keys?

I don't think so. I don't often write songs that are patently minor. I don't write a lot of those angsty, Irish, U2, Echo and the Bunnymen kinds of songs. [*Laughs*]

One of my favorite songs of yours is "When I Pray" [from *Faithful*].

That's a wacky one! [*Laughs*]

It's one of the most direct songs ever written to God. And you don't ask anything of Him except to be there, to listen to your prayers.

I'm always writing to God. I'm writing to whoever will listen. [*Laughs*] In some ways it was being a little cutesy and naive, because I don't feel prayer is a special situation. At least not for me. I'm constantly seeking communion with creation in general. And I don't consider that there are special hours when you talk to God. Or even that there's a special state of mind.

It also seems like a prayer to the world, to be there and to listen to your songs.

There's a lot of things in there. I think the real concept is that you put so much behind your belief systems that you don't want to be disappointed in them. You don't want to feel that your life has been completely misdirected in that sense. So even if it's just talking to yourself, you want to believe that what you're doing is not for nothing. You want to believe that there is meaning in what you do.

I think, in the particular sense of that song, I didn't look at the concept of prayer the way most people do, which is you get down and you ask God for something, and you do it on a daily basis, or you check in. I looked at it almost as a last resort. I really want to take responsibility for myself as much as possible and this is hoping for some dispensation when I'm broken down and I can't do for myself anymore.

I don't believe in a God that appears as a bearded old man and makes pronouncements to you. I believe it's there all the time, pronouncing to you all the time.

* * *

Walter Becker
North Hollywood, California 1989

Walter Becker is a mysterious guy for a number of reasons. As the nonsinging member of Becker and Fagen, the core of Steely Dan, his contributions to their songs were never certain. More than a decade now since the release of their last album, *Gaucho*, it's still difficult to go back over their records and distinguish Becker's ideas from Fagen's.

This mystery was fortified by the fact that for many years, Steely Dan existed only in the studio, so fans had no way of seeing Becker in action. And looking at the album photos didn't help at all: Donald and Walter made a point of appearing as distant as possible by wearing shades and never smiling, a tendency that led even Rickie Lee Jones to believe that they simply weren't very *nice*. (In fact, they were just trying to look cool, as Walter explains.)

Then there are the songs. Since they met at Bard College in New York, Becker and Fagen shared an enthusiasm for expanding the potential of the song both in terms of lyrical and harmonic content. Since Donald's nasal New York voice was better suited for irony than sincerity, they veered off the well-trodden path of introspective songwriting others were taking in the seventies to create brilliant oppositions of words and music: succinct, sardonic lyrics set to the slickest, tightest jazz a pop song could hold. They shared a passion, bordering on obsession, to push the limits of what songs can do while staying within the realm of rock; they explored previously unexplored lyrical areas with a wit and literate ingenuity few others possessed at the time. And they stretched the harmonic potential of the pop song (partially via the use of their "Mu chord," detailed herein) without ever abandoning the visceral rhythms of rock.

They also swam against the current of spontaneous, haphazard rock recordings to set a new standard in terms of record productions. Disbanding their original lineup after the third album, they evolved to the essential core of Becker and Fagen only, surrounded by the brightest satellites of the rock and jazz worlds.

Gaining a reputation as studio tyrants (which Walter dismisses as inaccurate), Becker and Fagen cooked up tracks that are at once burning and pristine; hot, sizzling jazz textures with the tightest, most precise rhythmic foundations imaginable.

Steely Dan, whose name was derived from a sexual toy out of William Burroughs' *Naked Lunch*, started in 1972 and immediately established a sophistication in their songwriting starting with their first album, *Can't Buy a Thrill* and continuing through *Countdown to Ecstasy*, *Pretzel Logic*, *Katy Lied*, *The Royal Scam*, and culminating with *Aja*, their last album of the seventies. Anyone who ever decries the lack of good music in that decade need only read that list to be silenced.

In 1980, their last album of original material, *Gaucho*, was released and the Dan was done. Fagen released *Nightfly* in 1982, a solo album that had the sound of Steely Dan (since it featured Donald's distinctive voice and many of the same musicians) but lacked a level of darkness and irony in the lyrics, a possible clue to the Becker influence.

He was born in New York on February 20, 1950, and knew Donald Fagen for a couple of years before they decided to become partners in 1969. Their first collaborative effort was a score for the film *You Gotta Walk It Like You Talk It* starring Richard Pryor. Attempting in vain to peddle their songs around New York, they eventually landed jobs as support musicians for the band Jay And The Americans, most famous for their hit "Cara Mia Mi." They met producer Gary Katz at the time as well as guitarist Jeff "Skunk" Baxter, and Katz used his connections at L.A.'s Dunhill Records to get them a songwriting gig. Even then, though, their songs proved to be too unique to sell to other artists, and Katz interceded again to get them their own record deal. Along with Skunk, they enlisted guitarist Denny Dias, drummer Jim Hodder and a lead vocalist—David Palmer—who was eventually completely replaced as lead vocalist by Fagen. Their debut album, *Can't Buy a Thrill* was a success, fueled by the hit "Do It Again," and Steely Dan was on its way.

At the time of our interview, Becker mentioned that he didn't have "the luxury to wish" he had a better singing voice, and openly contemplated recording his own solo album. "I saw how much fun Rickie had making her album," he said of *Flying Cowboys*, the Rickie Lee Jones record he produced, "and I've been wanting to do it myself."

Since then, he carried through with that promise by recording the glorious *11 Tracks of Whacks*, his first and only solo record, and it's shed a lot of light into the mystery of Walter Becker. Since Steely Dan's songs were all projected through the Fagan persona, it was easy to assume he was the guiding spirit of their songwriting. This record proves them wrong; brilliantly inventive songs like "Surf and/or Die" and "Book of Liars" make it evident that Walter Becker has the goods to guide the Dan every bit as powerfully as Fagan.

These days he makes his home over the horizon in Hawaii, though he keeps a little office in North Hollywood, and it's there that we met. He's a soft-spoken, intellectual man who was willing to discuss Steely Dan at length, giving us a rare perspective into the interior of one of the world's greatest bands.

When working in Steely Dan, you said you would sugarcoat subversive elements in your songs. Was that a conscious aim to mask the message of your songs?

Not so much messages, but using jazz harmonies in pop songs. At that time the people in the rock audience, if they were aware they were hearing something that sounded like jazz, weren't too happy about it. This is something that Donald [Fagen] and I always had to struggle with, to incorporate some harmonic elements that were more sophisticated than rock and roll and still have it sound like rock and roll.

So I don't think we were deliberately trying to hide things, but we were trying to combine disparate elements in a way that would make them work. So one of the things we would have to do was to make these little moments of harmonic density more palatable, integrate them well into what was going on. And also there were sometimes very strange lyrics for a pop song; rather than make the setting reflect the strangeness of the lyric, it would seem to work best for us if the setting was relatively polished and flowing.

When you began your collaboration, did you ever discuss the kinds of things you wanted to accomplish in your songs?

Sometimes we'd have an idea for a bizarre thing we wanted to do in advance. I think we both knew we wanted to write smart, sophisticated, witty kinds of songs.

Was there any artist the two of you were emulating at the time?

Not as writers, no. Looking back, the songs that we were writing were influenced by the overall tenor of the times. Like everyone else, there was a Bob Dylan influence and there were some folky things we did, The Band was happening, that kind of stuff was influential.

Jazz was always a big influence because Donald and I were both jazz fans.

It's surprising that you mention Dylan and The Band, whose recordings seem so spontaneous compared to the precise tightness of Steely Dan.

That's something that just evolved. Coming from a time when people just threw things together and went into the studio and let things happen, that seemed like a logical progression to us. To get some of the tightness and precision that certain kinds of jazz had.

That influenced us in that kind of perfectionism . . . and then, you know, pure neurotic *drive* took over at a certain point, and we ran on that pretty well for a few years.

Is there any way of musically explaining how you achieved that tightness? Does it mostly have to do with the lock between the bass and drums?

Yeah, we would spend many, many hours just trying to get things to be rhythmically precise. And especially when you're overdubbing things, layer after layer, that's very important. I would say that was a general trend in the seventies in record production up to and culminating in drum machines, where you have absolute and utter precision, although in many cases you have absolutely no groove because it's a machine.

Back before the days of drum machines, how did you communicate your ideas to drummers?

I'm kind of a drum freak myself so I would always have a pretty good vision of what I wanted. We would describe what we wanted to a drummer, listen to what he did, and then take it from there. But in the case of Bernard Purdie there was no point in having any ideas because he was going to do something that you couldn't really imagine. And he was the kind of a guy who could look at a chart and see a record in his mind's eye. He would put it together and make it orderly, make the transitions work. If he found something he liked, he would use that over and over and give it structure in that way.

That's also surprising to hear, because you and Fagen have a reputation for being studio tyrants and telling each musician exactly what to play.

Not at all. We would go in with a piano chart that showed Donald's chord voicings, and Donald would usually go through the keyboard chart with the keyboard player. The keyboard parts, in most cases, were so integral to what we were doing that a lot of the ingredients had to be there in that way. But then the keyboard player was free to articulate and add things to that, so there was a lot of just blowing. And that's basically what was written. No bass parts were written.

The guitar players had nothing written for them and they would come up with their own parts. We would listen and suggest things but there certainly wasn't any score.

Would you record bass, drums and keyboards simultaneously?

Yes, usually bass, drums, keyboards, guitar. Yeah.

You mentioned writing out the chord voicings for your songs. I've been intrigued by what you and Fagen called, in your songbook, the "Mu chord."

Yes, the "Mu chord." Probably the less said about that, the better.

Why?

It was kind of a joke, that name. In the late sixties when we first started writing together, we would write or play very simple tunes and the way that we came up with hopping up major triads was to add a second, usually right under the third. This was one of the few alterations that you could do to a major chord and still have it sound like a major chord and not a jazz chord.

I don't remember why the name [laughs] "Mu chord." I'm sure there was some very important reason at the time.

It's much harder to play on guitar than piano. Would you do it on guitar often?

That's something that I did where available on guitar. It's always available on piano. We had Denny [Diaz] do it on the guitar because he had far greater dexterity. But whole-tone dissonances like that are quite awkward on guitar except in certain open chord positions.

When you started using that chord, did you make a decision that it would be a signature chord for Steely Dan?

We just did it so much that it ended up that way. And as time went on, we developed other chord alterations that became associated strongly with what we did. And [Fagen] continues to explore the fringes of tonal organization; harmonic stuff that still sounds tonal but is as expanded as it can be.

Are there other chords you can name that defined the Steely Dan sound?

The particular chord that people have mentioned to me is a chord where you have, in the key of C, an E in the bass, a D, a G and a C on top. It's an extension of the "Mu chord," if you will, but you move the third, the E, into the bass. So it's a C-major chord with an E in the bass. [As well as the major second.] I've been told that in some circles this is known as the "Steely Dan chord." It's a chord we used over and over and now it's become kind of a generic fusion cliche harmony. There's a lot more sophisticated harmonic stuff going on now than there used to be, so a lot of this stuff is in the public domain.

Do you see Steely Dan as being responsible for that progression?

No, I think that was inevitable, and I think that the fact that keyboard players are so important now is responsible for that, because those are all things that are more likely to be outgrowths of keyboard structure than fretboard structure, as you well know as a guitar player trying to deal with some of these things. It's very hard.

You don't feel that Steely Dan set a higher standard than people were trying to reach at the time?

I think we were trying to be as musically sophisticated as we could and that wasn't really a priority for a lot of people and still isn't. A lot of people want things to be as rootsy and gutsy as possible, which is very valid, too.

In most songwriter collaborations, it's clear who wrote what. With Becker and Fagen, it's a mystery who contributed what to each song. Why is that?

We were writing together for such a long time that we really adapted to one another. We had a tremendous rapport from the very beginning of our collaboration, where we knew what we wanted to do and we weren't working at cross-purposes. That became more and more the case. We developed a way of working together that really combined our sensibilities. There were a lot of things that I never learned because Donald already knew how to do them. I could manipulate elements of his technique without having to master the same things myself. A lot of the themes that we developed, we developed together. Over the years, just bouncing things off of each other in ordinary conversations we'd be having, and I still find this when I talk to Donald; it's very stimulating. Also he and I will be thinking along similar lines and we'll start to talk about something and say, [*shouts*] "Yeah, that's right, yeah, yeah."

I think that our collaboration was so well integrated that we weren't sure ourselves where one guy's contribution ended and the next guy's picked up.

Did you usually work on words and music at the same time?

Usually we would get a melody first and then stretch it or do what we needed to do to accommodate words.

You'd come up with a whole melody without any words?

No, typically we'd get a chorus together first with lyrics. Ideally. Not having a chorus was a real pain in the ass. Once you had the chorus, then you could construct the music for the verse, and then the melody for the verse, and then actually write the verse. Try to make sense out of the chorus, if at all possible. [*Laughs*] Or otherwise illustrate it.

Did you two ever work separately on songs?

Yeah, we'd get little pieces and then bring the pieces in. And put them together.

You mentioned how the music will suggest the words, and yet with Steely Dan the words and the music would often oppose each other or work on different levels at the same time. When you were working on songs, were you trying to achieve a marriage between the music and words or did you try to have the two elements set each other off?

Even if they work together by opposing each other, that's a marriage too. The one thing underscores the other. Either by making it sound funny or making something that does sound funny sound serious, by ironically combining things, which we did often enough, I think.

Often songwriters experience ideas simply arriving. Do you have an idea where they come from?

No, but that is my experience. Maybe we're channeling Jeff Skunk Baxter. [*Laughs*]

Do you feel that ideas come from beyond you?

Yes, possibly.

Any advice as to how to get in touch with that source?

No, I think it's a matter of paying attention and diligence. And practicing at what you do and *doing it and doing it* until the moment of relaxation comes when you can be in touch with something like that.

When it's not flowing, do you stay there and work or do you leave it alone?

In the past when I was working with Donald I had the discipline to stay there and keep going. Even on days when you get absolutely nothing, and there are many of them, it's important to do it. You have to do that seemingly nonproductive work to get to the point [*snaps fingers*] where things suddenly click into place. You have to lay the groundwork for that.

And in your experience do the best melodies seem to be generated by an instrument or separate from one?

Most of my ideas are when I am playing an instrument rather than, you mean when I'm walking down the street? I have great ideas when I'm walking down the street, but they're gone from moment to moment.

If it's okay with you, I'd like to name a few of them and see what, if any, response you have to them. Let's start with "The Boston Rag."

I always think the nice thing about "The Boston Rag" was that it took place in New York. So "The Boston Rag" was part of a state of mind. I haven't seen Lonnie in a long time. I wonder how he is. Hi, Lonnie!

"Aja."

"Aja" had parts of another song in the middle of it that never made it that was called "Stand by the Seawall." The little chunk in the middle. "Aja" is kind of a song with a little suite in the center of it, and some of that were parts of that song and other miscellaneous bits and pieces that Donald had laying around in his head; things he was going to write and never did and it just all got assembled that way.

"Time Out of Mind."

Well, we both wrote that lyric. I remember writing that at Donald's house in Malibu. We wrote that before we moved back to New York, most of it. All of it. So we must have had that one sitting around for a while.

"Any World (That I'm Welcome To)."

I think we wrote that, believe it or not, for Barbra Streisand. [*Laughs*] Or Dusty Springfield. We had three or four songs that we wrote for some female vocalist that somebody we knew was producing. The key change in it seemed like a good idea at the time.

"Rikki Don't Lose That Number."

It wasn't written for Rickie Lee Jones. Nobody had any idea that there *was* a Rickie Lee Jones at that time. Well, obviously, some people did. It was just a pop song.

"Kid Charlemagne."

It was kind of an Owsleyesque figure that existed in our mind's eye. I think he was based on the idea of the outlaw-acid-chef of the sixties who had essentially outlived the social context of his speciality, but of course, he was still an outlaw.

"Through with Buzz."

[*Laughter*] The less said about that one, the better, I think.

"Your Gold Teeth," Parts 1 and 2.

That seemed like enough, to do two versions of it. We couldn't think of any other way to use that. [*Laughs*] I might add that the second version much more closely resembles the original version, which we never recorded. It was just a simple sort of waltz.

"My Old School."

Folk-rocky. Lots of fun.

"Any Major Dude."

I think that was the second take. That was great. It was almost over before anyone knew they were recording it.

"Midnight Cruiser."

[*Laughs*] Jimmy Hodder's vocal. Old song.

"Babylon Sisters."

Very spooky song. I still like that one a lot. Some of them I don't like. That one I do.

Rickie Lee Jones told me that she was a little scared about meeting you at first because you looked so tough in your photos and never smiled.

I think it was just that we were trying to look cool, you know?

[*Laughs*] It seemed like a good idea not to smile. But as Rickie found out, I'm actually a very jovial guy. We had a lot of laughs.

She said you turned out to be quite nice, but that you are simply too intelligent for the rest of mankind.

[*Much laughter*] That's very flattering.

But not true?

I think that's up to the rest of mankind to decide.

* * *

Loudon Wainwright III
New York, New York 1987
Hollywood, California 1995

There's an old joke about a songwriter who breaks up with his wife but is happy that at least he got some good songs out of the experience. It's a joke that applies many times over to the life and times of Loudon Wainwright III, who has amassed a bounty of great songs from his own failed marriages and from the broken union of his parents.

Yet he brings something to these songs that few songwriters can: an irrepressible sense of humor. And unlike others who have mastered the art of original comic songwriting (besides Tom Lehrer and Dave Frishberg, there aren't many), Loudon's work is distinct because of his penchant for writing funny songs about unfunny situations. Though he's penned many purely farcical songs—such as "Dead Skunk," which remains, absurdly, the biggest hit of his career—in recent years he's been effectively using his gift for comedy to illuminate the darker aspects of his own life.

To make a song funny isn't easy, and to maintain that humor over repeated listenings is especially tough, as any joke gets old fast. Loudon has learned to use humor in songs not to get an easy laugh, but to allow us to laugh at ourselves, and in doing so, to see ourselves more clearly. Even his most somber songs are punctuated with humor. "Thanksgiving" is a heartbreaking elegy to his family that begins around the traditional happy holiday table before moving back to reveal the unrosy realities of life. "Yet even 'Thanksgiving,' which is deadly serious, has two jokes in it," he said. "When writing it, I didn't intend to have jokes in it. But in the process of writing the song, the jokes emerged." In going for the laughs, however, he adds to the poignancy of his songs, creating a sense of needing to laugh so as not to cry. In "Thanksgiving" and other songs he's attained a beautiful wistfulness, especially about the passing of time.

He was born September 5, 1946 in Chapel Hill, North Carolina, and raised in both New York and Los Angeles. At 13 he became a musician when his father, an editor for *Life* magazine, was given a nylon-string guitar by the songwriter Terry Gilkyson ("All Night, Marianne") and passed it on to him. For eight years he played folk songs and imitated idols such as Pete Seeger and Dylan before ever attempting to write a song of his own. When he started performing in 1968 he was frequently referred to as "the new Dylan," which he hilariously detailed in his song "Talking New Bob Dylan." So intimidated was he by the greatness of Dylan's work that he was unable to write for decades. "What [Dylan] was doing was so amazing that the thought of me doing it was too audacious," he said.

So rather than follow Dylan's lead towards lyrical abstraction, he decided instead to write songs that were concrete and clearly linear, something he's continued throughout his career.

His first song, "Anchor," was a tale of a Rhode Island fisherman. Influenced by his father's work, he approaches his songs with journalistic accuracy, fleshing them out with telling details, physical images, and solid narratives. "I have a certain editorial sense," he said, "which causes me to keep my songs relatively uncluttered and clear."

He writes about everyday life, mostly: his triumphs, relationships and obsessions. And he's able to translate these subjects into song in a way that neither obscures nor trivializes them. He accomplishes in almost every song what many writers struggle a lifetime to achieve—making the personal universal—and he does so with all of the pathos and warmth of real life intact.

Sometimes, and this is an unfortunate reality of this business, our greatest songwriters only gain mass acceptance with a song that is a fluke, a novelty, and is in no way representative of the greatness of their work. Such is the case with Randy Newman's "Short People" and certainly with Loudon's "Dead Skunk in the Middle of the Road," which received ample radio airplay. But, against the wishes of his record company, which was urging him to create some kind of "Skunk" follow-up, he abandoned all future attempts to make a "radio record" and decided to enjoy himself instead, writing the songs he wanted to write. It's an enjoyment that is reflected in all of his songs, reminding songwriters that songwriting can be fun. "When a song is really happening for me," he said, "it's better than eating ice cream or having sex or whatever."

I know Dylan was a huge influence on you, yet your style from the start has been quite different than his.

I write much differently than Bob Dylan, it's true. There's nothing cryptic about my songs; they have a beginning, a middle, and an end. They're understandable and clear. That might be where my father influenced me the most, being a journalist. Clarity, detail, description, exploring a theme.

But you did enjoy Dylan's abstract songs?

Oh, I *loved* them. I admired songs like "Visions of Johanna." Is it "The country music station plays soft" or is it "The country music station plays *Sartre*"? What is he talking about? The mystery of it was a lot of fun as a listener.

When you started writing your own songs, was it something that came easily to you?

Yes. When I wrote the first couple songs, I thought it was pretty interesting. I had opened a door to a room I didn't even know existed. When I started writing, I was writing all the time—three or four songs a week. I think that's not uncommon when you start.

I had originally intended to be an actor, and I studied acting at Carnegie-Mellon. I loved performing and I realized that I could combine performing with writing. Getting up onstage and performing my own songs kind of got that rock off.

I also loved American musical theater, guys like Frank Loesser, Rodgers & Hammerstein, Lerner & Loewe. I loved all of that, but I didn't go in that direction because of Dylan and that school of writers who were writing about themselves. [The songs were] connected to who they were, and that was really powerful. That was so specific. It was rancorous and angry and personal. And when I wanted to be a performer, that played right into it.

And you're such a funny and natural performer. Did the onstage performances inspire you to make your songs funny?

Yeah. When I discovered I could make people laugh, too, I jumped on it. I started to write more novelty songs. The third album had 'Dead Skunk' on it, and then I was definitely into the serious jungle of comedy songwriting. Now I'm trying to bounce the two off of each other. And in some songs, you can do both.

Is it hard to be funny in songs?

I've always enjoyed making people laugh and I love to laugh myself. When I first started to play and sing, I sensed that people were amused by what I did. I went for laughs and I've been criticized for it. It's almost involuntary on my part. I love it when people laugh. And if there's any chance to elicit any laughter, you can be sure I'll go for it.

It seems you put more work into your words than your music. Often your melodies are very simple. Is this so as not to get in the way of the words?

Yes. For me the melodies are like train tracks—the songs ride on them. But I think that's a shortcoming. Quite often my melodies will be an old folk thing, or a standard blues or a country thing. I don't have a lot of confidence in my ability to write great melodies so usually they're just merely serviceable.

Do you have any kind of songwriting routine?

Not really. I don't have any form for it. I get an idea and I think about something.

It's kind of like fishing: If you get a nibble, you hang in there. And if nothing happens after a while, you just shelve it.

I know people who get up in the morning and sharpen pencils and sit down and write a song. I don't do it that way. There's a gestation period where I think a lot about it and then something pops out. I don't like to analyze it too much. It's a mysterious process that I don't really understand too much myself. But I'm grateful when it happens.

Any hints as to how to make it happen?
No. There isn't really. And I used to worry when it wouldn't happen for a while, but I don't do that either. It comes when it feels like it.

It's hard to do but if you can enjoy the process—whatever's happening—that's what I like, and I think the best songs come that way.

Your songs sound like they were enjoyable to write. Your verses always grow richer and more interesting as your songs progress, rather than grow tired.
Either that or I take the tired verses and throw them out. You have to remember about that editorial sense.

But songwriting is generally fun for you?
When it's going good, yeah. When the flow's on, when it's good, when the muse is there, it's a lot of fun. I can really feel something ready to come through, like waiting for a fax to come or a picture to develop. You watch it take shape, and you can actually feel it. It's hard to talk about, because it's something I don't understand. I don't want to dwell on it too much, because it's too painful when it doesn't come through.

So after all these years, you haven't found a way to control the process?
Not at all. I think I have less control of it. I realize more and more that it doesn't really have much to do with me. It has only to do with me in that it's filtered through me, my experience, my style of writing, and what I bring to it. And that's craft, working, having a style, doing it 25-plus years, having an audience to write for. But the actual *stuff* it mysterious.

Your songs seem so truthful. Is it important to instill truth into songs?
You have to write what you know about. And I don't know a lot about working on a cattle ranch or in a factory. I know about conducting my life and the relationships I've had. I'm very focused. I'm focused on me. It's a selfish kind of thing. I like sometimes to get out of myself. But, yes, I certainly do write about my swinging life.

Most of us aren't cattle ranchers either, so your songs reflect our lives as well.
Yeah, there aren't a lot of cattle ranchers in the audience. People can relate to the songs. Because the songs are about things that happen to just about everybody.

Do you think it's possible to write great songs and also be commercially successful?
It's possible to make a living. There are people who are writing great songs who are incredibly successful. I'm marginally successful. I've been able to make

a living at it for twenty years and I've got an audience. I enjoy working and I'm happy and grateful about that.

Do you spend any time while writing songs thinking of commercial considerations?

No. I let myself off the hook. In the seventies, when I was on major labels, there was always pressure to make what I term loosely as a radio record. A record that is designed and intended to be played on the radio. And that's what everyone wants to happen.

Obviously, it affected production values; what you would put on an album. But I also think it seeps into the writing of a song. And for me, personally, it made me very unhappy.

What was happening was that I happened to have written one song in fifteen minutes that happened to be a successful single—"Dead Skunk in the Middle of the Road"—but I'm really not that kind of artist. You know, a guy who makes great radio songs. And if I do worry about that, the quality of what I do diminishes.

So what words of advice, if any, would you offer to songwriters?

It depends on what kind of songwriter it is. If it's a guy or gal who wants to write hits—if we're talking about a young Carole King—then go ahead and work on that.

I think my ambition and abilities were just to write what I'm obsessed by, what I'm amused by, what makes me angry. I just take my temperature, so to speak, and blurt it out in a song.

If it's that type of thing you want to do, ignore everybody else and do what you feel.

But if it is that type of thing a songwriter wants to do, how best can he survive in the business?

You've got to be good, first of all. You've got to stick to your proverbial guns. You've got to know who you are, and have confidence in it. All the great people do that. You have to believe in yourself and trust your own instincts.

When you were working to write a radio hit, did that bottle you up creatively?

I started worrying. I was always looking over my shoulder. And it's hard enough not to do that anyway.

One of the reasons that people's first records are so impressive invariably is because they haven't been looking over their shoulder. If people notice you or write about you, you are affected by it. You absorb and store those reactions. And after a little while you become a vessel of other people's reactions. [*Laughs*]

I wanted to ask you about your song "How Old are You?" which is a tremendously funny and somewhat caustic song about being interviewed, with questions in it like, "How come you didn't get big like Bob Dylan? Why didn't you get big like Springsteen?"

Interviewers usually are a little shy of that song. They assume that it's totally about them. But these are not only questions that I am asked by interviewers. These are questions that I ask myself. It's a combination of the inter-view thing and my own doubts about my career.

Are you still asking yourself these questions? I thought you let yourself off the hook.

I put myself back on the hook when it feels like it might be a good idea.

Your song "Out of This World" is essentially about death and yet is an affirmative song, about leaving this world for a better one.

Well, I've written about the subject before; it's something we can all relate to. After all, we all die.

But it is an affirmative song, as you said. It's a hopeful kind of feeling of release, of getting out of the body. That song kind of came from outer space.

Is that where most of them come from? Do you have any idea where your ideas originate?

None whatsoever. And [*laughs*] I don't want to know!

When I write a song and it affects people, in whatever way, I'm grateful. I don't want to make any demands about where it comes from.

But is there no method of tapping into that source?

The only way to do it is by trusting yourself. And that sounds so impossi-ble. [*Laughs*] I don't know what kind of advice that is. I try to tell myself to do that all the time.

* * *

Townes Van Zandt
Nashville, Tennessee 1990

He often made fun of death, which is one of the reasons it's still so hard to accept that he's gone. Years before his actual death on New Year's Day, 1997, he made an album memorializing himself as "The Late Great Townes Van Zandt"—not to mention the countless songs he wrote in which he openly scoffed at death, though concluding that at times it seemed highly preferable to life. What he died of is still uncertain—it might have been a blood clot or a heart attack, nobody's sure—but what is known is that he died on the same day his idol, Hank Williams, died, and there's a poetic rightness in that which Townes would have appreciated. Like Hank, Townes left this world a better place than it was when he arrived, enriched by the beauty and brilliance of his songs.

Born on March 7, 1944, he was called a "derelict, a rambler and a rowdy, and more or less the greatest living songwriter in America." The songwriter Steve Earle went even farther when he said, "He is the best songwriter in the whole world, and I'll stand on Bob Dylan's coffee table in my cowboy boots and say that." He was a songwriter who was both mythic and obscure, a mystery to most of the world, yet considered one of the greatest by the greats themselves, by artists such as Willie Nelson, Doc Watson, Emmylou Harris, Waylon Jennings, Jerry Jeff Walker, Mickey Newbury and more.

He made eleven albums of miraculous songs.

"Won't you lend your lungs to me
Mine are collapsing.
Plant my feet and bitterly
Breathe up the time that's passing.
Breath I'll take and breath I'll give
And pray the day's not poison.
Stand among the ones that live
In lonely indecision."

from "Lungs" by Townes Van Zandt

When he was a kid, his sister had three girlfriends over to the house to watch Elvis on the Ed Sullivan show. As soon as the King came on the air, all four girls went into hysterics, screaming madly. "There must be something to this," thought the young Townes.

His most famous song is the elegiac "Pancho and Lefty," which has been made famous by Emmylou Harris and others. It's a tale of two bandits in the old west told in telling details and precise language: "Now you wear your skin like iron and your breath's as hard as kerosene." He wrote three verses for the song, felt that it was finished, realized it wasn't, and then wrote the fourth verse, effortlessly jumpcutting into the future to look back at these bandits with a mythic overview:

"Now the poets tell how Pancho fell.
Lefty's livin' in a cheap hotel.
The desert's quiet and Cleveland's cold;
So the story ends, we're told."

from "Pancho and Lefty"

His father, an oilman, told a ten-year-old Townes that he could have a guitar if "Fraulein" was the first song he learned. They lived in Fort Worth till he was ten, then moved to west Texas, then Montana, Colorado, Illinois, Minnesota and back to Texas. He heard music constantly in the car with his dad, going from oilfield to oilfield with the radio on. It was mostly the music of singers such as Hank Williams and Lefty Frizzell until Elvis burst into his life. "All of a sudden, Elvis hit when I was eight or nine, and that was a whole different ballgame. In the long run, Hank Williams and Lefty Frizzell probably inspired me more, they probably went in deeper to my consciousness."

Somebody dared him to perform at an Illinois sockhop, and he accepted. His mother drove him to the gig, where he played three songs. She told him later that she left the car and got on her hands and knees in front of the windows of the subterranean cafeteria to watch. When he sang, as in his dreams, the girls started screaming, "because it was in vogue at the time." He played songs by Elvis as well as ones by Ricky Nelson and Hank Williams, showing then the same blend of influences he still brings to his performances. It was a gig that brought him immediate fame: "I went through the crowd, everybody patted me on the back, and I got instant acclaim in my Junior High. I fell in with all the best guys and girls immediately. And I didn't play again until about 1964 in Houston."

He started listening then to a lot of jazz and Lightning Hopkins; later came Bob Dylan and Phil Ochs. "Dylan more than the rest. When I heard him, that was the direction I took." He played in a lot of rough spots, bars full of rowdy beer drinkers, and to arm himself he started writing funny talking blues. Then one night, out of nowhere, he wrote his first non-comic song, "Waiting Around to Die." It's an extreme song: you can't get much more serious than this existential tale of a gambler and a thief who gets addicted to codeine after getting out of jail.

Soon the serious songs began to outnumber the funny ones, and he started writing some real love songs as intense as real love itself. He plugged into the pure, constant current of creativity, and at times the connection was so electric that it hurt. "It felt like my right arm was going to fall off." He dove headlong into the frenzy of pure, spontaneous creation, an energy that is frozen forever in the freely cascading lines of his songs.

He was one of those songwriters that other songwriters regarded with reverence. When I interviewed Rodney Crowell a few years back, he said, "You really shouldn't even be talking to me. Go and talk to Townes Van Zandt if you want to talk about songwriting." He then proceeded to give me Townes' home phone number in Nashville.

Yet he remained a well-kept secret in most circles, and this was partially his own fault. "My personal behavior has been sporadic and erratic," he said. Content for years with the life of a traveling folksinger, he went from club to club and city to city, earning just enough to get him to the next town, taking the summers off to camp out in the Colorado mountains and gamble with the miners. He claimed he didn't even know Nashville from Seattle when songwriter Mickey Newbury brought him to the Music City, and got him a publishing deal.

But maybe his distance from the music industry was precisely what enabled him to write such organically beautiful songs in this day and age. His songwriting was the antithesis of all that is industrial. He kept himself on the outside of the machine, and for that reason, his music remained untainted by the influence of the marketplace. It might have meant that the majority of his songs went unheard by most people. But it also meant that he was able to keep writing them.

Your songs manage to be both simple and complex at the same time.

I know what you mean, but that just happens. The one priority that I have for that sort of song is to keep it simple. To keep it as perfectly bare and simple as possible. And get it down. I never consciously try to do both at the same time.

You said "Waiting Around to Die" was your first serious song. You can't get much more serious than that one.

I have a few others like that that I don't play all the time. I have to watch that when I do shows. I have to stay away from that side, because nobody wants to hear blues on blues on blues.

You mentioned that some of your songs, such as "Mr. Mudd and Mr. Gold" came to you so fast that it was like a frenzy.

I have songs of every degree, from pure craftsmanship to inspiration. Of all my songs, "Mr. Gold and Mr. Mudd" was closest to just coming out of the blue. It was back when I was doing a lot of drinking and gambling.

It was three in the morning in South Carolina. I was with a bass player friend of mine and a couple of girls, and they were all asleep in the other room, and I went out to the kitchen and brought my guitar and here comes this song.

It felt like my right arm was going to drop off. I had yellow pages from a legal pad crumpled up and thrown all over the floor of this kitchen, and I finished it, put down my guitar, it came to its own natural conclusion, I went into the bedroom, crashed, woke up in the morning, reread it, might have changed a couple of things, but other than that, it took maybe three and a half hours to write it. That was quite an experience.

Another strange experience came with the song "If I Needed You." I was in Nashville cutting *The Late Great Townes Van Zandt* album, and I was staying with Guy Clarke and Susannah Clarke, old friends. They had this little bitty old house in East Nashville and we all got the flu. It was such a little place that if one person got it, we all got it. Serious flu. We were all taking antibiotics and cough syrup.

And because of the cough syrup, and the fever and everything, I'm sure, my dreams that week were blazing technicolor vivid dreams. And one night I went to bed and had a dream about being a folksinger. And I was on stage somewhere and I played this song. And it was so vivid that I remembered it, woke up exactly after it finished, turned on the light and reached for this little pad and pencil, and wrote down the verses in the middle of the night, and remembered the guitar part exactly, and rolled over and went back to sleep.

In the morning I woke up, got some coffee, went to Guy and Susannah and said, "Hey, you all, listen to this." I played it and it seemed like my fingers knew the guitar part. It took one second to figure it out.

I played the whole song through and they went, "Hey, Townes, that's a great song! When did you write that?" I said, "Last night." They said, "No, you couldn't. You went to bed before we did. Did you wake up or what?" I said, "No, I wrote it in a dream and I just had time to write it down before I went to sleep."

That's the only time that ever happened that I can remember. I remember playing songs in dreams before that I didn't know, but it was never clear enough to write them down.

Does that make you think there's a part of you always writing songs?

Well, it must be. The subconscious must be writing songs all the time. I've heard a lot of songwriters express the same feeling, that that song came from elsewhere. It came *through* me.

Is that your feeling?

Oh, yeah. On songs like that, it was a definite feeling that anyone could have been sitting in that chair at that time in South Carolina with a pencil and paper and a guitar and had the ability, that kind of mind that was in tune with that, with songwriting, it felt like anybody could have written that song. And I know that I wrote it. But to take credit for it . . . It's a hard feeling to get across.

That song was there. I've had that feeling with other songs, certain Guy Clarke songs or Bob Dylan songs, John Prine songs, I feel, "Man, why didn't I write that? That song was *out there* and I didn't get it." You get that feeling the first time you hear it: "Man, that song was in me, too."

Was it the sickness and the cough syrup, do you think, that enabled you to get that song so fully?

Well, I've gone to sleep in much worse condition many times since. [*Laughs*] I can see myself going to a doctor and asking for a year's supply of codeine cough syrup so I can write some more songs. [*Laughs*] I don't think he'd go for it.

One thing about that song, "If I Needed You." There's one line that I changed. There's a line in there: "Lady's with me now, I want to show her how to lay her lily hand in mine." When it came in the dream, it said, "She lowed like a cow, when I showed her how . . ." Right? So when I got to New York— I've spent a lot of time in the country, you know—the city boys weren't exactly ready for "lowed like a cow." So I changed that line.

The main question many songwriters want to ask is how to get to that place, when you're awake, to connect with a song like that?

You have to be alone. You have to be ready for that. I've had a lot of songs that kind of intruded on whatever is going on. They usually come in the form of one line, which you might remember and go get alone later. Just allowing yourself quiet time to be alone to think.

I usually just sit down somewhere and tinker with the guitar. I have lines come at many different times that can turn into songs. Whole songs come, melody and words, when your mind is free. You can be thinking about the utility bills and the rent and write a certain kind of song. But you can't think about the utility bills and write "To Live's To Fly."

There's all different types of songs. I've got a new song that hasn't been recorded yet called "Marie" that's the first seriously topical song that I've ever written. It's about the homeless. That came from just spending some time in a hotel room changing strings in L.A. Just boom: the first line, the first verse.

You have to be alone.

The thing here in Nashville now is cowriting, to the degree where people make appointments to co-write. I have about two or three songs that I've co-written over the years and they came totally just from being out on the road with some friends.

Some writers approach songwriting like a job, going to it every morning. Do you think there's value in that?

Well, there are some cowriting arrangements that come out, some of the strongest ever, everywhere from Lennon & McCartney to Lerner & Loewe. And it was who and Hammerstein?

Rodgers.

Rodgers. And Richards and Jagger. They all seem to be the same two people over and over and over. Two people that relate to each other over a period of years. Now it's gotten down to cowriting with Mr. X. from 4:30 to 5:30, cowriting with Mr. Y. from 5:30 to 6:30, cowriting with Mr. A. the following morning. I don't know if that'll work . . . but it might get you in the proper gear to go home and write a song.

Have you read a lot of poetry?

Yeah. I studied a lot of Shakespeare and Robert Frost. I always considered him, Frost, among my biggest influences. Some people don't know what to think when you tell them your two biggest influences are Lightning Hopkins and Robert Frost.

But with you I can understand it, because your songs have a roots feeling, as well as being poetic and beautiful.

On a good night. [*Laughs*]

You mentioned Shakespeare and Robert Frost. Do you think that that's important for songwriters, to read great poetry?

Maybe for a certain brand of songwriter . . . everybody's different. I'm sure Hank Williams never read any Shakespeare. Blind Willie McTell never read anything. It's hard to say.

Some writers lean more naturally towards the poetic. It's a murky territory because you can't say that Hank Williams isn't thoroughly poetical. And Blind Willie McTell, too. And Lightning Hopkins, too. But there are many that do come from that angle. A bunch of them: Eric Andersen. Loudon Wainwright. A whole bunch of them.

When you work alone, do you find that if you stay there and keep at it, something will happen? Can the process be forced at all?

I've done that on a couple of occasions . . . At home I've made my number one job getting my son Will to school. I don't go to Music Row . . . When I'm off the road, I'm pretty much a recluse.

I have done that with songs. A few years ago, I got a motel room here in Nashville. I brought my guitar with the express purpose of writing some songs. And I got two or three songs that way.

When a line for a song comes to you, do you sit down and write the song then, or do you store away the line and write it later?

If it's a good line and I'm driving, I'll store it away. If I'm around a guitar, I'll do it right away.

Sometimes it can be a whole song and a whole verse. The core of the song will come through all at once. When that happens, I get some paper and a pencil and write it down.

Do you remember writing "For the Sake of the Song"?

That was done in one night. By candlelight. It came all at one time. I had just awakened from sleep and was in bed. I had a guitar and I did the whole first verse real quietly. Then I put the guitar down and finished it.

Was it written for anyone in particular?

Must have been. She was in bed next to me.

I love your song "Lungs."

That one came together pretty quickly. The guitar lick and the vocals all came at once.

The song starts with an unusual line: "Won't you lend your lungs to me?" Do you like that, when you get into an area where no other songs have been?

I like that kind of stuff the best. But I have a lot of respect for the closer to home stuff. I do have a strong streak of that. The not so close to home stuff.

Do you think those are less effective?

It depends on the song, and what you're trying to do with the song. Some of them are just like shock value. Like "Won't you lend your lungs to me?" If you sing it right, people hear it right and it gets their attention.

They are all different, except for the talking blues, which are all the same song but on different topics.

Do you usually write your songs from the beginning to the end or do you change the order later?

Usually. Sometimes they get real changed around. Then there's always changes to be made, even little changes, like putting an "s" on a word.

That's where my poetic background comes in. It seems a lot of people in Nashville write by the phrase, or by the line. As opposed to writing by the word. A lot of my best songs are where every single word is where it's supposed to be. Whereas a lot of country songs are more like everyday conversations. It's like a paragraph that rhymes as opposed to words that fit, and come to form a big rhyme. I have a lot of songs that are written that way.

"For the Sake of the Song" was written by the word. I once sat down and wrote out the rhyme scheme for that song, and it was amazing. Pretty complex. But it didn't seem that complex when I was writing it.

I have a song now that I wrote on the train over in Europe. I just wrote it to see if I could sustain the weird rhyme scheme.

Is rhyming enjoyable for you?

Yeah, it is enjoyable. But I don't care for goofy rhymes. It should say exactly what it's supposed to. I don't believe in bending over backwards to make something rhyme.

Musically, Tim Buckley did it pretty good, writing blank verse songs.

Do you remember writing "Pancho and Lefty"?

Yes. I was in Dallas. In a hotel room. That one kind of came from not having anything to do and sitting down with the express purpose of writing a song. I took one day and then I played what I had that night at a gig. And a songwriter told me, "Man, that's a great song. But I don't think it's finished." So I went back to my hotel room the next day and wrote the last verse. The only thing I remember thinking about while I was writing it was consciously thinking that this is not about Pancho Villa.

Also a friend of mine who is an artist pointed out one time that there's nothing in that song that says Pancho and Lefty ever knew each other. I had never thought of it.

It's a fun song. I've never gotten tired of that one. I think of it in a lot of different ways. But it's fun to play.

Did you like how Emmylou Harris did "Pancho and Lefty"?

You bet. And Willie and Merle, too. Though when they did it, you can tell they're reading the words. Hoyt Axton did it once, too.

Emmylou Harris has made the song famous. Is is strange for you to have one of your songs lifted up above all the others like that?

Not particularly. The one thing I've noticed about that song is that it's a very learnable song. Some great songs are and some great songs aren't. It's got an identity of being accessible. I've heard folksingers in country after country learn that song. And I get a whole bunch of young people come up to me after concerts and mention that song.

You said once that "To Live's To Fly" is your favorite of all your songs.

It's one of them. I kind of said that because I had to say something. But it would really be impossible to really pick one. There's one called "Snow Don't Fall" that might be it. It's a little short, simple song that I wrote about a girl who got killed. I went into a room that day in Kentucky. It was snowing, and I picked up a guitar. She'd been killed the previous summer. And I just sat down and wrote this song, and it's about the purest song, melodically and lyrically, that I've written. And I don't sing it. Ever. I recorded it once on the Late Great Townes Van Zandt record. I recorded it perfectly and then they changed it around.

They also changed "Pancho and Lefty." There's some Spanish trumpet that got mixed down. It seems somebody's been doing some creative mixing. It's one of those things.

Do you remember writing "Columbine"?

Yeah. I wrote that on the banjo. I had just come back from a summer in Colorado. Spent about two years of my adult life there. I'd quit gigging around May. I'd go up and catch a horse, live in the wilderness areas up around Aspen and Crystal Butte. All those mountains. And I'd camp out, go down to town, get drunk, gamble with the miners, go back up. I did that for a few years.

A lot of those songs came from that, although "Columbine" came a little earlier than that.

Do you find that the songs don't come if you stay in one place too long?

Yeah, you need to shake it up. It's not just the inspiration not coming. I start getting, you know, kind of crazy.

You've been a secret hero for years, writing songs that are on a much higher level than most of the music we hear. Some people have said you're simply too good for the mainstream. How do you feel about it?

The record companies and the radio stations all aim for a certain age group, and that's the age group that buys the most records. And they're concerned with selling records.

I've often thought about seriously trying to sit down sometime and figure out what it takes to be a Nashville hit, the hook and the tag-line and all that stuff. And write one. But I just can never get interested enough to do it.

You think you could do that and not hurt yourself artistically?
I think so. Because I don't think I'd take it that seriously.

You know, a lot of the Nashville songs are really good, class songs. 90 percent of them are interchangeable. But the top ten percent are really good songs that anybody would be proud to write.

Plus, my personal behavior over the years has been pretty sporadic and that includes, sometimes, erratic. I haven't been a professional.

Mickey Newbury brought me to Nashville for the first time and I was a serious traveling folksinger, with a guitar and a suitcase. Traveling around Texas, Oklahoma City, up to Colorado. That doesn't happen anymore. It used to be you could audition somewhere on a Wednesday night and play there on Friday for twenty or forty bucks. Which was enough. But that doesn't happen anymore. Now you need an album. You have to have gigs booked months in advance.

Mickey Newbury heard me and called me in Houston and told me I had to come to Nashville. I had about thirty, forty songs. And really, this is true, I had no idea what he meant. I didn't know about going to Nashville, making a record, getting a publishing deal, or anything like that. He could have said, "Come to Seattle" and it wouldn't have made any difference to me. And I got here and just kind of fell in, and I didn't have to knock on any doors or anything. One day we made a record, I got a publishing deal. I guess it would have occurred to me eventually. That that was what I was supposed to do, pursue it.

My third wife, she takes care of all of that. It's just not my concern. My concern is trying to capture a little bit of the essence in which we live. On paper. I'm not even sure what that entails, but I know that it's my job to do that and put it out for the world.

Other than that, I'm really not interested in hanging around Music Row or anything.

Is there a part of you that wouldn't really want that mainstream acceptance?
I wouldn't mind it, for sure, as long as it's just me and my guitar. I've tried it with bands before but it's just that on certain songs it works great, and on certain songs it doesn't work at all.

Have you heard many good songs lately, besides your own?
Yes. And I'm sure I don't hear nearly all the good songs out there.

You're known for not giving much time to the business end of songwriting. How much time do you think should go into non-musical, business efforts?
You might spend a little time just making sure you don't get totally ripped-off. Other than that, in my case, I just spend amazingly little time worrying about that stuff. When I write, it's just between me and the cosmos. The only person I have to answer to about my songwriting is myself.

* * *

Dan Fogelberg
Los Angeles, California 1993

He's a guy who likes to be alone, leaving the world behind whenever possible to sequester himself in the precious solitude of his ranch high in the mountains of Colorado or his home in rural Maine. His friends have said that even after his concerts he prefers to hang back in his dressing room rather than face the throngs waiting for him in hospitality suites. It's in Maine that he wrote most of the songs for *River of Souls*, the album he completed shortly before our interview. After months of constant touring, during which he gets no songwriting done, he returned to his peaceful Northeastern home and wrote five new songs in a fortnight.

Weeks after absorbing myself in his music from his first album, the timelessly beautiful *Home Free*, through *River of Souls*, many melodic and lyrical phrases from these songs would spring up in my mind unexpected. And this was in the midst of soaking in other songs from other sources and the chaos of life itself. Yet there is something so pervasive about his songs, something between haunting and heartening, that causes them to linger in the mind and spirit long after others have evaporated. Throughout all his albums, Fogelberg has consistently written songs as gracefully beautiful as his own singing voice, and the heavenly harmonies he creates in the studio.

Home Free, his 1972 debut, begins with one of the most timelessly touching songs ever written, "To the Morning," which immediately established Fogelberg as not only a master tunesmith, but also a purveyor of harmonies so sweetly and powerfully conveyed that they seemed miraculous. He achieved on his own the magic that Crosby, Stills, Nash & Young, The Eagles, and many others worked hard to achieve: a soulful blend of perfectly tuned, heartfelt vocal harmonies.

In 1974 he recorded *Souvenirs*, an album as melodically beautiful as *Home Free*, while also moving into areas of real rock and roll, such as "As the Raven Flies," which features Fogelberg burning on electric guitar along with Joe Walsh. Throughout the seventies he continued to release one powerful album after the next, including *Captured Angel, Nether Lands,* and *Phoenix*. 1978's magical collaboration with flutist Tim Weisberg, *Twin Sons of Different Mothers* featured "The Power of Gold" as well as a couple of extraordinary covers: The Hollies' "Tell It to My Face" and "Since You Asked" by Judy Collins.

In 1981, sparked by his own thirtieth birthday, he created an inspirational double album, *The Innocent Age*, which featured an unprecedented three hits: "Leader of the Band," "Same Auld Lang Syne," and "Hard to Say." This was followed by *Windows and Walls* (1984), the bluegrass-tinged *High Country Snows* (1985), *Exiles* (1987) and *The Wild Places* in 1990. In 1991 he released his first live album, *Greetings from the West*, which was recorded that year at the Fox Theater in St. Louis.

Born August 13, 1951 into a musical home in Peoria, Illinois, he traces much of his musicianship directly to his parents. "Both my parents are very musical," he remembered. "My mother is a studied singer, and that lady can still sing. My dad was a hell of a musician. Anything that I am came directly from those two."

He wrote his first song, he recalled with great amusement, at the age of eleven. "It was a really bizarre thing called 'A Strange Occurence at Edenshire Park.' It was influenced by the Beatles who were just going into their psychedelic period."

He played guitar and sang in rock bands from grade school on, but exchanged his electric guitar for an acoustic when he attended the University of Illinois. "I became regionally famous in Champagne/Urbana," he recounted. "I played the Red Herring there a lot. It was just the time. The singer-songwriter was coming around. James [Taylor] had just had *Sweet Baby James* out and all of a sudden everybody was a bloody singer-songwriter. And fortunately for me, I was able to maintain it. All of a sudden I was getting a following and people were paying me money to do this. And I thought, 'Jeez, I love writing songs.' That's when I really started taking songwriting seriously, from sixteen on. And I became known."

He's a songwriter who has had more than his fair share of commercial success, but he recognizes that the best songs are not always hit material. Though his most recent albums have not been the blockbuster hits that his albums from the seventies were, his urge not to repeat himself far outweighs any desire to repeat past glories. "Metaphysical songs ain't gonna sell on top-forty radio," he said with a laugh.

Many of the songs on your new album seem like a departure from your usual style. Did you approach these songs in a different way than your past work?

No, not in any way. To me the process is always the same. It's just, perhaps, the angle or the shading that changes. But mostly it's just like the kind of music that I happened to be influenced by on one song or another. The process still is exactly the same.

If the songs are in any way different I guess it's just because of influences. I've been doing a lot of listening to some other people: Johnny Clegg, Bruce Cockburn. And I just started adopting more of a world feel and a rhythmic feel. It's not new for me, really. It just kind of shows up. You kind of take what you can get, is what I'm trying to say. [*Laughs*] I don't think consciously, "I'm going to write a piece with a Caribbean solo in it." That just happened. I was working on a track and I had a guitar solo that didn't really kill me. So it's playing around with synthesizers, and boom, there was this steel drum and I said, "Well, I like that. [*Laughs*] It seems to fit better." So a lot of it was trial and error on this record.

You said that the process is exactly the same. Can you discuss that process? Do you work with a guitar normally?

It depends what I'm around, basically. For instance, if I'm up in Maine where there's very little electricity or heat or anything like that—it's a very spartan and simplistic life that I live when I'm up in Maine, as opposed to a very sophisticated, technological one at the ranch where I have the recording studio, right? So if I'm in Maine all I can do is acoustic guitar, so I have a tendency to write acoustic songs there. At the ranch I rarely pick up an instrument and try to write a song anymore. It seems that I go down to the studio and program something or go to the piano there and write. So it's kind of what's available to me. I keep telling myself that this winter I want to go into my music room [*laughs*] which I built for writing and which I haven't been in for *years* since I built the studio, and get back to writing, to actually writing some acoustic guitar music. Put the machines away for a while [*Laughs*].

When you program something in the studio, do you mean you start with a rhythm track and build it up from there?

Oh, no. It's always different. Sometimes I'll hear a song idea that's not really fleshed out, and sometimes I'll just grind away at it in a room with a guitar or piano. Sometimes I'll say, "Well, it might help me here, since I hear a groove here to program the groove and then work on it." Instead of having to maintain that in my head while I'm trying to work on lyrics or melody. So a lot of time it's been a good tool.

Is it unusual for you to write a whole lyric at once?

Sometimes yes, sometimes no. It depends on the song. "Same Auld Lang Syne" took about a year and a half. Something like "Blind to the Truth" I wrote over quite a few days but I had so much stuff I couldn't use that I had to edit it. Every song is very different. They come in a different way. I don't want to limit myself and say I'm just this or just that. I can't sit down in a room and say, "Okay, I'm going to write a song now." Or make an appointment with another songwriter, which I find absolutely *ludicrous*. But I know a lot of people in Nashville make their living doing that. That's not my style. My stuff has to come from the Creator. It has to come from an inspirational source.

And therefore I've gotten very patient and learned to wait. And when I force myself it usually doesn't work.

So you work only when the inspiration is there for you?
Absolutely. Yeah, something clicks on and I go in there.

Is there anything that affects that or allows inspiration to come easily?
Well, obviously when I'm alone. I really can't have any distractions around. It's hard for me to write even when my wife is in the house. Sometimes I do, but sequester myself in the studio when I have to get something done. But most times when I have a *little* time to myself just to be alone, say, in Maine or at the ranch or something, or wherever I happen to be—and these days, because I travel so much and tour so much that those times are pretty few and far between—so last summer I hadn't written anything because I was working on the album and touring and doing all this other stuff and finally got to Maine for a couple weeks alone and I wrote half the album in five days. It was like, *bam!* So it's in there and sometimes it's just dying to get out. You're not even thinking about it. It demands to get out. I love *that*. [*Laughs*] I hope that happens more often. Because I really am not thrilled about grinding away songs anymore. If I can avoid it. I still have to do that, obviously. Everybody does. But it's really nice when things start flowing quickly. Sometimes it's like you just have to close it up for a while and it forces its way out.

Do you keep notes, or record ideas in any way when you're not actively writing?
No, I don't. No, I don't keep a notebook of any sort. If there's something I like, I generally remember it. I keep it in my head. But I'm not one of these guys who keeps a journal and works from it. Basically when I go to write a song, the melody happens and then that suggests something to me, lyrically. And then I just go after it.

And you will generally finish a melody before finishing the lyric?
Oh, yeah. I can write melodies at the drop of a hat. I can give you a bunch of melodies today, if you want them. That's not the hard part. The hard part is always the lyric. Once you get the melody, and even the track, you can hear the finished thing. And then you have to go in and slog away at the lyric.

Do melodies ever come to you apart from an instrument?
Yeah. A lot of times I'll just be driving. While I'm driving my truck I've gotten a lot of melodies and ideas. I don't know why. So there's times when it's just straight out of the air without an instrument. And other times you may sit down with an instrument and just start fiddling and find something that's interesting. Find a little riff or a progression or something and that starts it rolling.

When you're writing a lyric to a finished melody, do you try to follow where the music leads you to discover the words?
Yeah. I think it's one of the best things I do, actually, the symbiosis of the melodic structure as it integrates with the words. I think that's one of my strongest suits. I think that the melody has always suggested very pertinent sounds. Just sounds, and you have to make more out of that. And I think I've

been pretty successful at, instead of just stringing together sounds, like what Paul Simon's doing these days a lot of, when you just take a train of thought or notebook stuff to string stuff together to create impressions. I think one of my strongest suits is that I have been able to use the melody to create stories with.

Most of my songs have all had a very cohesive story and imagery. As opposed to more of an impressionistic feel, which Joni [Mitchell] does, or Paul [Simon].

Does that kind of writing work for you?

Not much. I still believe in storytelling a whole lot. I appreciate that gift in a writer. Sometimes it's a lot of fun. Cockburn will sometimes go off on a tangent and just string words together that are just brilliant. Because he'll create these incredible, random images. But I don't seem to have that gift. My gift lies, I think, in writing stories.

Many writers have suggested that songs come sometimes like gifts, and seem to come from somewhere else.

Absolutely. I would feel the same way. I just feel like I'm a medium for this stuff to come through.

Is there anything else, besides being alone, that encourages songs to come through?

No. That's the key one for me. That really quiet time when you can be receptive. There's people who say they can write on the road. I've never written on the road and I couldn't even begin to think about it. It's so overpowering to be on the road.

I think of your line, "the audience was heavenly but the traveling was hell."

[*Laughter*] Still is. It's not gotten a whole lot better. But that to me is the best time, those are great times when you get a chance to sit and write.

You're a songwriter who seems equally good on guitar and piano. Do you find that it vastly affects the song, what instrument you write it on?

Absolutely. Sure. I have a tendency to write more of my up-tempo and rock and roll stuff on guitar and more of my introspective ballad material on piano, certainly. That's just the nature of how I play. Although "Power of Gold" was written on piano. The root of the song is that riff on piano through the whole song. I've written some fairly rocky things on piano. But I'm not a real rock piano player. I don't do a lot of that. I'm more comfortable playing in a neoclassical ballad mode on the piano.

Do you find that there are patterns that you tend to repeat?

Yeah. And you try consciously to avoid them. Every time you go back to one you say, "That's too typical, try something else here." But I don't have the chops to really be able to say I'm going to write a Dave Grusin piece because I'm a guitarist first. So I think I have pretty decent technique so I can keep it from getting *too* trite, but there's definitely a style to my playing. Which I think most songwriters have, which is fairly simplistic. If you're a writer you don't really have time to devote to being a really technical player. So for me, piano is always a second instrument.

On guitar are there any set of chord changes you would consider a signature of your work?

Some people say that. I don't know what they are. I remember somebody saying when Richard Marx had a song out, a ballad, "God, he ripped you off! Listen to this!" And I didn't hear it. I guess that's for other people to judge. I try to avoid that type of thing. There's a certain Floyd Kramer influence in my [piano] playing. It's country piano. I have a tendency to do those type of riffs [*laughs*] maybe too much in my songs. But I like them.

Much of your earlier work is more musically complex than your more recent songs—

Yeah. Around the time of *Nether Lands* and *Twin Sons* I was playing a lot of piano and composing a lot of neoclassical stuff. I went back to some of those recently and tried to relearn them, and I went, "Jesus, this stuff is not easy!" [*Laughs*] I think I've simpified my writing a lot since those days. Either by necessity or whatever, I find the simpler the better. I went through a complex period where I really wanted to be grandiose and move in that direction—very wordy, complex lyrics—and as I've gotten older I've realized that simpler is better. If you can say something simply and still have it be eloquent, that's more towards poetry than the wordiness of it. I used to think that the amount of words you wrote defined how good the poem was. And that simply isn't true. In a Zen way, less is more.

Was it listening to something in particular that caused you to change your idea about that?

No, if anything I was listening to all the wordy guys. [*Laughs*] I don't know what it is. Perhaps it's a desire to communicate more directly in songs. And perhaps some criticism. From some critics who said it's too floral, it's too Victorian. I remember somebody in the New York Times wrote that word, "Victorian." I happen to like that style of writing but I could see what he was talking about. So I thought maybe I'd try to get more direct here but still keep the elegance of language. But make each sentence more of an importance in itself. Make it simpler, a little more Zen, a little more direct. Say more with less, basically.

I'm trying to do that. I still get mighty wordy a lot of the time. [*Laughs*] Some of the tracks are still seven minutes long, a lot of them. When I finish them I go, "Jesus, how did that happen? I thought I was being concise here." So that's kind of what I desire but at times you just get kind of carried away by the verbosity of it all.

Your song "Illinois" meant a lot to us who grew up there. Most songs were about New York or Colorado or California back then. So thanks for that one.

[*Laughter*] I'd kind of like to remix it. But it's a pretty good song. I like that too. For anybody who relocated, especially to California—that's what I had been through, the year I had moved to California to try to get a record deal, I missed it so badly. I missed my family and that lifestyle.

"Leader of the Band" is one of the great father-son songs.

One of the earliest ones too, which I'm proud of. It's being done to death these days. Especially in Nashville, there's always somebody crying about his dad. At least to me it was a really honest revelation. Because there wasn't much of that. It was the only song at the time to be saying that. Especially on Top-40 radio where it became such a big hit. I was *astonished*. I never expected that song to do anything. For me it was something I was going to tuck away on *The Innocent Age*. It was Irving [Azoff's] idea. He heard it and said it was a number one record. I said, "You're crazy."

You felt that the subject matter wasn't commercial?

Well, that plus it was an acoustic guitar and three stacked vocals in the age of disco. I really didn't see anyway that this was going to be a hit record at that particular point in time and Irving's instincts were amazing.

It was a great contrast to what was going on.

Sometimes that works and sometimes it doesn't. It was very risky but at that point I didn't care. We were rolling pretty good and [*laughs*] he seemed to know what he was doing. So I said, "You go right ahead." [*Laughs*]

Your first album, *Home Free*, is a true classic.

That's funny to me now. That record to me now is kind of an embarrassment. I just wished I could have had it back. I was *so* young.

Yet it really holds up—

For me, I can't listen to it. It gives me the willies. [*Laughs*] It's just so young. I think it showed some sort of promise. But it amazed me that so many people loved that record. That it meant something to people at that time and I can understand that. But as a musician and an artist myself, it's like putting the first drawing you ever did in a gallery. I kind of wish I had waited a few more years. To me I kind of like to think my career started with *Souvenirs*. I'm always amazed when people say to me, "I like *Home Free* the best."

A song like "To the Morning," though, which is the opening cut, is just a timeless, beautiful song to this day.

I don't have a problem with the songwriting. I just wish I was a little more mature when I performed it. To me, my voice just seemed so high and so young.

The harmonies on the first album are gorgeous.

[*Laughs*] That's great to hear. I don't think I'm convinced.

Do you remember writing "To the Morning?"

I do remember that. That was the first good song I had written. That's when I thought maybe I'm going to be good at this. Because the other stuff was really pop for rock bands and such. When I wrote "To the Morning" I thought, "Okay, maybe I'm going to be able to stand up there with Joan and Jackson and James. And Lightfoot and Paul Simon, the people that were there before me." "To the Morning" felt like a really good song. I wrote it at my mother's piano in her house. I can still see it exactly, that place, where I wrote that.

Any memory of writing "Souvenirs?"

No. No, I remember vaguely writing it in Champagne because I was about to leave for California for the first time and the house I was living in was going to be torn down. It was a really final thing. This big old Victorian house that a bunch of hippies and students lived in, and it had already been slated to be torn down. And we had already demolished most of it ourselves. And I remember writing the thing about the key being unreconciled. Because I was leaving this place and there was no place to go back to. That's all I remember about that. Those days were pretty foggy. We were doing a lot of drugs in those days. Everyone was.

[*Laughter*] Pretty crazy town.

Do you remember writing "As the Raven Flies?"

That I wrote just after moving to California and I was really pissed off at my girlfriend. The person I perceived to be my girlfriend. I got a lot of mileage out of that fantasy. This girl in college I was mad for. My first love. She didn't even give me the time of day. It was an absolutely fabricated childhood crush, basically. But that broke me into the pangs of romance, of unrequited love. And I just revelled in it. [*Laughs*]

Was that written on guitar?

Yeah, it was written on a Gretsch. I think.

Did "Same Auld Lang Syne" take a long time to finish?

Yeah, about a year and a half.

Any memory of how it started?

Just joking and playing around with the "1812 Overture" by Tchaikovsky. That's the riff. Then I threw in a VI-minor chord and thought, "That's really pretty funny. I'd love Tchaikovsky to be able to hear this." And I figured that if he can't, I'll work this up a little bit and throw this back at my musician friends for a little fun. We're always noodling in the studio and throwing musical jokes at each other. I figured that would be mine. Because I found it very funny to put that chord there. No one else would. [*Laughs*] But it struck me as very funny.

So just as an exercise I said, "Let's write a song around this. Just to play with words." I didn't have any specific idea of what I wanted to write about, at all. And that little occurrence had happened to me the year before, of meeting my girlfriend at a grocery store, and her dropping her purse. So I said, "Okay, let's see if I can write a song about something as trivial as that."

I remember doing that. It was an exercise, a joke. I was having a large time trying to make something so small into something so large. See what I'm saying? It was really like a songwriting exercise. I'd work on it just for fun when I was bored with something else and then put it away for a month. But for some reason it just kept wanting to coming back. I didn't take it seriously until about halfway through it when I had this song half-done and said, "This is really pretty darn good here." It was meant not to be anything but somehow this is turning into something good here. And I think what happened is that when I came up with the title, "Same Auld Lang Syne," which I think is a terrific pun, then I said, "Uh oh, this is something here, this is good." And then I came up with the idea of toasting our innocence and time and all this. That's when it took a turn for the worse. It got serious. But I'm glad that it did.

It seems that those small details, what you found to be trivial, can often be the strongest thing in a song.

Sometimes. It was such an unconsequential time. But it had become such an important song to so many people. That blows my mind.

That one also suprised you when it became a hit?

Yeah. I knew it was a great track when I finished it but I didn't think [radio] would play it because I wouldn't cut it. They told me to cut it. It was over six minutes long. And I just said, "No" and I stood my ground on that one and radio went along. I was amazed. But there was no way you could cut that song and make sense. It just wouldn't make sense if you cut it. So I stood my ground and in those days Irving had such power with radio that he made them play it, probably.

With your okay, I'd like to name some of your other songs and you can offer any response you want.

Okay.

"Netherlands."

That was a great period of inspiration. That was when I just moved to Colorado and I moved into Chris Hillman's old house. It's way up, like 9,000 feet up, in the middle of nowhere, as bleak as can be, *beautiful* but, I mean, major weather. But it was such a great adventure. I picked up from Nashville and just took my guitars and moved to Colorado. Living alone. It was a great winter. My first winter up there. Learning how to run snow-plows . . . And I was just so inspired by Colorado. That song just floated up. It was not hard to write. It was very high to write that one.

That was a piano song?

Yeah. I bought a piano and moved it up there in my living room so I could sit in front of my windows, stare at the mountains and write. And that's where that album came from.

It sounds nice.

It was great. That's one of my fondest memories, of writing that stuff.

Did you write "Dancing Shoes" at that time?

Probably. That might have been written before I got there. That might have been a Nashville song. Because I was dating a girl in Nashville who was a dancer.

"Part of the Plan."

That's a funny song. That was the same girl. I wrote it and it was the first song I wrote and said, "That's a hit. That's an undeniable hit record." It was the middle of the night and I went over and knocked on this girl's door and said, "You've got to hear this!" I sat down and played it, and she just yawned and went back to bed. [*Laughter*] And I went home. But I was right. I just felt that was the one for me. It had that commercial thing.

It's a very affirmative song: "All the answers that you seek can be found . . ."

Yeah. I like to keep hope in music in some way. I think the new version of that is "Magic Every Moment," which is the new single. It reminds me of an updated "Part of the Plan." It's really upbeat, it's got a great groove to it and it's got some very positive lyrics, some philosophical lyrics.

Did it come fast?

It's about two or three years old. Yeah, it did. That's really true. I was kind of in a writer's block and we were up in Maine at the house. My wife and I were asleep at dawn and we heard this huge crash, like a shotgun, and we said, "What the heck is that?" And we went down and found this dove laying there. We are both serious animal lovers and we were just heart-broken by this. Especially out of a sound sleep. Your mind starts putting together what had happened here. *Glass everywhere.* It shattered a huge picture window. The bird couldn't possibly have survived: its neck was broken. So she took it outside and put it on the porch and we went back to bed and the rest is pretty much there. I woke up and went down and said it would be a miracle if the bird survived. And we went down and it's gone. We forget how close we all are to that window.

So that just broke me loose and I started writing all these songs because of that event. It's very strange how little things like that can just turn the faucet on. It was amazing. And I started writing a whole bunch after that. So I give special thanks to the dove on the album.

"Longer."

I remember beginning it. I actually saw my sheets of it recently. I thought I wrote it all in Hawaii but I actually started it there and finished it in Colorado. I remember laying in a hammock on vacation. With a guitar, just strumming around. And I kind of remember that thing just coming down from the sky. [*Laughs*] I jokingly say, "This song was floating around looking for a good home and decided I was the one to give it to it."

"Be on your Way."

Oh, yes. The great tragedy of youth. That one was about that same girl. She didn't give a fig for me. She fueled a lot of records for a while. I remember I finally realized that this was not going to happen. I had done a concert at the Red Herring and she showed up and just devastated me. And I remember being *so* sad that I thought I was going to die. And I remember just going home and writing that. It was me saying, "Okay, this is not going to work." It was the first time I had to confront that in my life. It was pretty heavy. That's a very, very sad song. Extremely sad. Then I put a cello on it, for God's sake. What was I trying to do, kill people?

It is a well-written song. I think it was kind of a precursor to "Longer." It was the first song I wrote in that vein to take me there.

"The River."

Yeah. I was on acid at the University of Illinois. They used to have this great music school with aisles and aisles of rooms with pianos. I used to hang out there all the time when I was high. It was *just great!* And you'd listen to this cacaphony because everyone was rehearsing at once. I wrote "The River" in that room.

Did acid contribute to any other songs?

Acid? Oh, I think it must have. I think "Heart Hotels" was an acid song. I didn't do a lot of it or I'd be too trashed to write. I certainly wouldn't consider doing that today. [*Laughs*] But those were great days, wonderful days.

Do you find the process of songwriting to be similar to painting?

[Songwriting] is certainly more mystical because in painting you kind of conjure up a finished thing before you start and go after it. Unless you're an expressionist who is just flowing with paint. That's not me. I'm a guy who sits down and paints portraits. So I generally have to have a subject in mind. So that's a more concrete expression. And I hope later in life to be able to bust out of that and find a way to put more of that mysticism and emotion into painting. I'd love to be able to do that, but it's going to take years of work to break me out of my traditional mode of painting.

Is painting more fun for you than songwriting?

Writing I kind of dread. I know what writing is and it's such hard work. I've been doing this for twenty-five, thirty years. If they come easy, great. But I don't look forward to struggling. Tim Schmidt said a real good thing to me the other day when we were rehearsing: "Songwriting is great at the beginning and at the end." [*Laughter*]

It's that middle part that's tough.

Yeah. I don't know many people who like that time.

Many songwriters say that they like songwriting as soon as it's over.

Exactly. Yeah, when you've got it finished you say, "Oh, man, that's great." Man, that's a weird, weird place. A bizarre space, not very healthy.

When you finish one, does it give you a feeling of satisfaction?

Absolutely. Absolutely. If I think it's a good one. In my criteria. I'm pretty tough on myself. A lot of stuff I'll let go if I don't think it's worth the time. When you do get a good one and it's finished, it still feels good. It still feels great. Songwriting to me is still the ultimate reward, and ultimate thing I do. It's the most mystical thing I've ever experienced—I don't know what this is about—I do it and I don't understand it and it's just so *amazingly* unconscious.

And as the years go by, you don't get closer to what it's all about?

No, I sure don't. It's given me a little more faith in a greater being, certainly. But it's still unexplainable. And at some point you've got to make that leap from the intellectual process to blind faith, basically. You've got to learn to trust those feelings. You've got to use the force, Luke. [*Laughs*]

I don't know what it is. I imagine you can interview every songwriter on the face of the earth and they wouldn't know what it is. It's great that you're trying, though.

* * *

Lindsey Buckingham
Burbank, California 1993

He comes to songwriting the way a painter comes to a painting. "You start putting strokes on a canvas," Lindsey Buckingham said, "and the colors will lead you in a direction you didn't expect to go." His paintings formed the heart and soul of Fleetwood Mac for many years. Now he'd gone his own way, leaving behind the corporate machine the Mac had become to devote his artistry to solo work, such as the wondrous *Out of the Cradle*, which was released on the day of our talk.

Imagine if after recording *Sgt. Pepper*, The Beatles then returned to the style of *Revolver* instead of moving forward towards *Abbey Road*. It wouldn't have been much different from the way Lindsey Buckingham felt in Fleetwood Mac after being able to stretch creatively on the brilliant *Tusk*, and then being instructed by the band to return to the safer, less-experimental pop he crafted so expertly on their previous album, the megahit *Rumours*.

It has to do with the folly of making artistic decisions based on commercial motives. It also has to do with the impossibility of ever matching the sales of such an extraordinary commercial success as *Rumours*. Lindsey's songs and production techniques on *Tusk*, influenced by the raw energy of the new wave, burst through all barriers and became the creative peak for this unit comprised of three singer-songwriters (Lindsey, Stevie Nicks and Christine McVie) and the rock solid rhythm section of bassist John McVie and the monumental Mick Fleetwood on drums.

"If you isolated my songs from *Tusk*," Lindsey said, "it's kind of like my first solo record." Had he been creatively unleashed to build on the momentum he started with *Tusk*, he could have furthered Fleetwood Mac's evolution as a major force in pop music. Instead, they musically regressed in an attempt to repeat their past success, and, according to Lindsey, "it took the wind out of my sails. It was a moment and we lost the moment." The band vetoed his desire to continue to break new ground and ignored the possibility that maybe the reason *Tusk* didn't sell as well was because it was a double album and fairly expensive. And that it had nothing at all to do with the music, which is some of the greatest they ever made. Not only are many of Lindsey's most powerful songs here, such as "Walk A Thin Line," "What Makes You Think You're the One?" and "Tusk," there's also his generously soulful productions of some of Stevie's best songs, including the haunting "Sara."

The band began to become so corporate and unresponsive to his creative needs ("We had five lawyers and five managers") that turning solo became his only viable avenue. It wasn't a decision he took lightly, delaying it for years and continuing to rob his own solo albums of their best songs in order to donate them to the band, as he did with "Big Love," which he had finished on his own, and then allowed to be used for *Tango in the Night*. It was the only song that was a major hit from the album, and the only one that was created outside of the confines of the band's corporate sensibilities.

He initially attempted to balance his solo career with his life in the Mac, but as he was not only one of the songwriters, but also producer and guitarist, he had no time or energy left over to devote to his solo career. He recorded albums, such as *Go Insane* and *Law and Order*, but was unable to tour, as was Stevie Nicks. So he eventually left Fleetwood Mac altogether, and they replaced him with two singer-guitarists. It was an attempt doomed to failure; you can't take the heart out of a band and replace it with mere musicians.

Now he has the luxury to spend years in his home studio with his main collaborator, Richard Dashut, writing and recording albums with little interference from the outside world. This is how *Out of the Cradle* was born, and the reference in the title happily alludes to the artistic rebirth he was experiencing, free from the creative constraints of Fleetwood Mac. Adapted from Walt Whitman's "Out of the Cradle Endlessly Rocking," the double-meaning appealed to Lindsey. "The gist of that poem has to do with the child that is rocking inside all of us, and I liked that and the irony of a 42-year old man leaving his band and finally getting out of the cradle."

He's had a fascination with guitars since he was a child, even before his older brother brought home the first Elvis album. Lindsey loved them not just for their sound, but for the whole idea of them, their various shapes and sizes and colors. "I can remember drawing guitars when I was about five. I used to spend hours and hours in my brother's room listening to 45s. I was the black sheep in that way."

He was born on October 3, 1947 in Palo Alto, California, and raised in Atherton, just south of San Francisco. He joined a band after high school in which he played bass "because the guy who played lead guitar had all the gear. That was pretty much the logic back then." It wasn't until he left that group and had known Stevie Nicks for a while that he began writing songs. Growing up he always knew he wanted to be a musician but for years followed the athletic tradition of his family, which spawned one Olympic athlete and proudly referred to itself as "The Swimming Buckinghams."

Playing music was always more important to him than writing songs, and to this day he says he can't wait until the song is finished so that he can get into the studio and start producing it. His prodigious talents as a producer and a guitarist have maybe distracted him from songwriting throughout his career, and for that reason he finds it the most difficult stage of the record making process. At times he finds himself producing the record before writing the song, as he acknowledges. "I could produce all day standing on my head, but the writing is hard."

We met up in Burbank, in the crowded confines of a windowless Warner Brothers room. Lindsey was a little nervous about the release of his new album, and about the fact that he had the urge to tour, but no band to back him up. Mostly, though, he projected a quiet calm behind serene, reflective blue eyes, and seemed happy to truly be out of the cradle, musically, for the first time in his life. "I think I've grown a lot in the last three years, certainly emotionally, having left one situation. And now I'm in a situation where I'm taking more responsibility for my happiness. And for everything, really."

When writing songs, where do you start?

A lot of the time I start off with a feel. Just a few chords. There has to be some seed that has a musicality to it. My whole process is like painting. On my own. With Fleetwood Mac it was more like movie-making, I think. [*Laughs*]

Working on my own, you know, you may start off with a certain intent and you start putting strokes on the canvas, but because it's so intuitive and one on one, the colors will lead *you* in a direction that you didn't expect to go, so you may have a preconception of what the song is going to be, melodically or otherwise, and you may end up in a totally different place. And that is probably more the norm than the exception, I would think.

So it's more a sense of following the music than leading it?

Yes. You're allowing the unexpected to happen, basically. Again, whatever your intent starts out to be, more often than not it's not that it gets dashed, but it certainly gets redefined. You may have a certain part of the canvas that you know is right and that might totally change what you thought an important part of the structure was going to be. In some ways, it does write itself, I guess you could say.

Do you generally work on lyrics after finishing the music?

Sometimes. Not always. There are certain songs, such as "Soul Drifter," that was kind of blocked out and completed, wordswise, before ever committing it to tape. It was done with a Tin-Pan Alley sensibility in mind.

It does have a good, old-fashioned melody.

Yeah. Actually, Lee Hirschberg, who used to work with Sinatra a lot downstairs here at Warners, he was making some copies for us. And when that song came on, he said, "Oh, a real song!" [*Laughs*] It's also the song my mom likes the most. You've got that tradition there, which is a nice thing to be able to do. And it seems kind of fresh against the non-melodic things you're hearing nowadays.

Generally the lyrics would come after there's a pretty strong structure.

Is that how you wrote your songs with Fleetwood Mac as well?

Most of the time.

Did your mom like "Street of Dreams"?

[*Laughs*] Uhh . . . yeah. I think so. I mean, that sort of thing might be a little dark for her. David Lynch might like that one. [*Laughs*]

It's a beautiful song, and very haunting. It's one of those melodies that sticks with you.

Great. That's nice with all the rain. Some people didn't like the rain, but the whole cinema of that is nice, and on the end almost using this rain like a ride-cymbal. It's like a musical instrument.

Most of your songs are in major keys, and that one has such a strong minor-key melody, using that minor-second note a lot.

Yeah. That's interesting. That song was written in two parts. The verses were maybe two years ago, and the center section was from about eight years ago.

"This Nearly Was Mine" was one of my father's favorite songs, and my father died a long, long time ago. And after he died I used to go and talk to him, and that's what that whole center section of the song is about, talking about following your illusions. It's interesting how you can have a piece laying around for so long and suddenly have it click into something that's current.

That song is more intimate than most of your work, with lines like "shadow on Daddy's stone."

It's true. There are a few moments like that that are kind of raw. And I'm sure just as many obtuse moments.

"All My Sorrows" also has a really beautiful melody.

Yeah. That was an interesting thing because that started off being an adaptation of this old folk song. The Kingston Trio and a lot of other people did it in the late fifties, and many of them took credit for it. [*Laughs*] A lot of those folk songs were pretty much up for grabs back then. So I, in the spirit of that, changed the melody and changed the chords and kept the words the same. So it's kind of a hybrid. And of course, it was too late for me to take credit for writing it.

Speaking of the Kingston Trio, I did an interview with John Stewart recently, who told me that he was astounded by your guitar playing on songs he had heard. And that when he eventually met you and told you this, you told him that a lot of it was learned from listening to his playing on old Kingston Trio records.

That's true. All of my style came from listening to records. I started at six or seven, and I didn't take any lessons. And the Trio was a really accessible group. Not only to get a song sensibility, but to continue developing my guitar playing. That was kind of ironic.

I just talked to John the other night. And he's kind of pulled away from the L.A. life, which is probably not a bad thing to do.

You mentioned that working on "Street of Dreams" took many years. Is that common for you?

No, that was the exception. "Soul Drifter" came sort of in a flash. Most of them come relatively quickly. Not all in one sitting, although some people say the best things come all at once.

And the other people say that never happens.

And I'm more in that vein. You know, you've got to go back and pound it out over and over. And that's something I'm still working on. The actual *writing*, the words, that's what I need to concentrate on the most. Telling a story.

Because the writing is so tied into the process of recording, it all becomes like strokes on a canvas. The work isn't really just sitting down at a piano or guitar and rewriting the verse. The work is going in and *making a record*. In that sense, it's a hell of a lot of work and you can spend six or seven months just on one song.

Does the song evolve in the studio?

Sure. The form becomes something that you want to hold onto that may define what you're singing, or even how you're singing, or even the jazz of the words, to some degree.

When you're writing, do you work on acoustic guitars?

Most of the time, sure. Whatever seems to be in tune.

Do you ever use a pick when you play?

I use a pick in the studio. Because for some sounds that you want to get, a very light pick with very light strings can create a delicate sound.

Live, never. Mick [Fleetwood] tried to get me to use a pick for years but I could never do it.

It's always seemed like such an integral part of your sound, that you use your fingers on the strings. It's more human sounding than a pick.

Yeah. But out on the road, I lose these [nails]. Maybe it's because I'm a little over the top on stage. So I play just with my fingers.

Your guitar playing over the years has been so distinctive. Often it seems as if passages are way too fast to have been played that way. Do you ever speed up guitar parts?

Sometimes for the sound. Not necessarily for the facility. For the solo in "Countdown" I wanted it to sound like a violin. So we took it down on a Telecaster and it came out sounding like a bee-sting. So I do it sometimes not to gain speed, but it's a form of EQ you can't get with just EQ.

I do it with voices. Say you want to get a block of voices with four part harmony, and you think of that as a unit. That, with four or five male voices is going to take up a lot of space. But if you slow that down, and you don't have to get into the chipmunk area, but there's a whole lot of space in between where you can deal with the spacing of that and bring it back up and it will be that much more contained.

I use it on drums, too.

I noticed that there's no drummer listed in the credits of the new album. Did you use drum machines?

Yeah. And some of them are not drums at all. I just saw a review in the *L.A. Times* [by Jean Rosenbluth] and one of the things she said was that the guitars were so aggressive at times that it sounded like the drums were recorded behind a sheet. And I think what she was thinking of was some of the tunes that didn't have drums on them. They were just cardboard boxes. [*Laughs*] "Don't Look Down" is trying to avoid the kit altogether.

You played boxes on it?

Yeah. Found sounds. It gives it a garage-y sound.

That's interesting, because in Fleetwood Mac, Mick's drum sound was such an important factor—

I know. That's one of the reasons I was trying to get away from that.

Mick always seemed like such a great drummer for a songwriter to work with. His energy is such a big part of those tracks.

He's great. See, Mick was never the one who was in making the music, per se. But he was a great overseer. I learned a lot from Mick, from his sensibilities about what works, and about the pocket of the feel.

Would you describe to him how you wanted the drum part to be for a certain song?

Oh, sure, yeah. "Go Your Own Way," that weird rhythm—[*plays rhythm on table with hands*]—actually, mine was weirder than that.

I was listening to his part on "What Makes You Think You're the One" from *Tusk*—

Oh, yeah, that's one of the classic drum tracks. I love that. That's one of the great drum tracks that I've ever heard. That's up there with "Instant Karma."

That was a great moment. That was just Mick and myself late at night in the studio, me at the piano. We put a cassette player that has one of those really cheap mikes in it, we put that right under his snare, and it was so explosive the way he heard it in the cans, he got off on it, and *he just turned into an animal.* And it was just two-piece, there was no Christine or anybody putting any constraints on what could or couldn't be done. That has to rate as one of my top-five moments with the band.

Was it tough to produce your songs without him?

Not really. I had done it anyway, I had worked on solo records. The solo records were kind of a way of carving out an esoteric side that wasn't as workable in the band. Although the *Tusk* album was much closer to the solo work. You can pull my songs out from that album and it would almost make sense as a first solo album.

Yes. I listened to only your songs from *Tusk* and was overwhelmed by how great they are.

I heard them the other day and I was really happy with how they held up. For me, even.

It was dismaying to realize that you expressed that kind of experimental freedom in those songs and then felt the need to return to a more mainstream approach with your next album.

It was a political thing. That's why I made the solo records. You had a company in this building here who, rightfully so, had just come off this astounding success with *Rumours* and they had no choice but to market it in a way that would reach the audience, who was expecting a *Rumours II*. And they were confounded. It wasn't the album, per se, it was the *timing*. We would have been better off to do *Rumours*, to do *Mirage*, to do *Tango*, and then to do *Tusk*. It was a really enlightening and exciting time for me. I felt as if I had taken a little bit of a risk and was coming up with some really surprising things. But they were a little too surprising for people. At least that seems to be the case. I over-estimated the number of people who were willing to look at that in the spirit in which it was intended, and maybe thinking of it as a ballsy move and a move of integrity and not doing a *Rumours II* just for that reason, and not following that cliché that if it works, run it into the ground.

So you come off of *Rumours* and you come off of *Tusk* and maybe *Rumours* sells sixteen million and maybe *Tusk* sells four. That's perceived as a failure. Not only from the company but at some point within the group. So there were elements that maybe had dug the way it was being done when it was being done, and yet when it was clear that it wasn't going to be another sixteen mil, there was a certain backlash. It was almost impossible for me within the group to say, "I don't care, I'm going to keep doing that" because it was like hitting a brick wall. And there was really no place to go but back.

Was that stifling to you as an artist?

I don't know. Things started to get crazy anyway. It did take the wind out of my sails. I felt I was onto a great thing and that it was a good thing for the band. Yet within the group, the priorities seemed to be to keep the machine greased. It was a moment and we lost the moment. After that there was no going back to *Rumours II*. But there was no going back to *Tusk* either. And that was really my high-point in the band for me feeling a sense of discovery and explosion. But, hey, that's band politics. This is nothing new.

Yet many bands have progressed and continued that progression. It's almost as if the Beatles had done *Sgt. Pepper* and then went back to *Revolver*.

[*Sadly*] I know, I know. The beautiful thing about them was that they did it slowly. They didn't make this whole non-sequitur thing from one to the other. They took the audience with them slowly and the other great thing about them is that they were growing with the technology. They were in the right place at the right time.

Fleetwood Mac is unusual in that you had three great songwriters all equally writing songs for the band. Was that tough for you as far as how many songs per album you could contribute?

[*Laughs*] No. No, not at all. In fact, it was kind of a relief. That was never my strong suit in the band. I guess I was the one who added the edge to the songwriting as the other two people were maybe bringing the softer side. But my main contribution was taking raw material and fashioning it into records.

And some of your treatment of Stevie's songs, especially, have been so brilliant. I think of "Sara" and "Gypsy," for example, which you turned into amazing works of music.

Yeah. Something that could have been pretty mundane otherwise. Those two I do throw together. "Gypsy" I like a lot. That's a really quintessential meeting of Stevie's strong points and potential foibles and me being able to fill in the gaps and make it work.

Was it as satisfying for you to bring your talents to someone else's songs like that?

Oh, yeah. In a way, it's more so. It comes easier.

It always seemed extremely generous of you.

[Laughs] Yeah, that's the way I felt about it. Mick might argue that point . . .

Well, you know, you're in a position and you may be ambivalent about certain aspects of it, but if you have a job that you do well and you've chosen to be there to do it, you might as well do it as best as you can. I tried to.

If it's okay with you, I'd like to mention some of your songs to see what response you have to them.

Okay. You may strike out with some of them but let's give it a shot.

"Big Love."

"Big Love." That was going to be for my third solo record. That was pretty much done. I had very small windows and time-frames to do solo work, never any time to tour or anything. Stevie had more of a luxury to do that.

That was the beginning of a third solo album and the band came in and said we had to make a record. And my choice was to keep making the solo record and walk in as a cameo and have cameo producers, or just surrender to the situation and say there will be more songs along later. And I chose the latter.

"The Chain."

That started off as—jogging the memory here—it was really Stevie's and mine to begin with in the verse: [Sings] "Listen to the wind blow . . ." And my ever-present psuedo-blues riffs in there. And at some point I think Christine fashioned the feel of the chorus, and the chorus was certainly Stevie's lyrics. And then at some point there's this bass line which came in at the end that's kind of a hook, and there was some case to be made for it to be a valid enough contribution as to deserve songwriting credit. I can't honestly say that Mick had anything to do with writing the song. But we did give credit to all members of the band.

Were you thinking of the band with the line "never break the chain"?

You'd have to ask Stevie. For all I know I think she was talking about me. Some of those things, I didn't know what the hell she was talking about. [Laughs] As late as Tango where I thought maybe that was about me, but there had been so much water under the bridge I don't know how it could have been. I never asked her much about that stuff.

"That's Enough for Me."

Oh, yeah. I like that. Yeah. That's like Stray Cats meets something from outer space. That's a really heartfelt thing. I don't know what to say about that. Sometimes it's hard to comment on subject matter because it may have a specific reference for you and you sort of compose that over somebody else's and it may just take away . . .

That must have something to do with Stevie. This was something that was done in my bathroom. I think I had just gotten the bug from the New Wave stuff that was coming over. It wasn't any particular artist but just the spirit of that, which is why *Tusk* came out the way it did.

I don't know, that's an interesting song because it's so fast. It couldn't be any faster. And it's really raucous but it's sad. That was kind of a reference to a rockabilly sensibility that had gone all wrong, kind of bubbling over with guitars.

"Go Your Own Way."

I remember putting that together on our first tour. We were still staying at Holiday Inns back then. I remember writing it and playing it for the band and I remember having Mick respond to it right away. We were in Florida. God knows why. And I also remember the first time I heard it on the radio, which was kind of funny. There was a DJ down here named B. Mitchell Reid who was very established. That was out as the first single and we were still mastering the album. And I was driving to mastering on the 101. And B. Mitchell Reid comes on and said, "I'm going to play the new Fleetwood Mac single." He plays it and says, "Well, that was the new Fleetwood Mac single. Uh, I don't know about that."

[*Laughs*] It's probably not something I would do today, but I got to Capitol for mastering and I called him up. And I said, "B., hi, this is Lindsey Buckingham. I just heard you say you didn't like 'Go Your Own Way.'" He said, "Well, I can't find the beat." And I realized that it has this guitar going on, and four-beat back-stroking guitar leading you without a clue until the first chorus. Which, I think, turned out to be something appealing about it. But at the time that would have never even occurred to me.

And then it became a big hit.

And obviously B. was way off the mark.

"Shadows of the West."

Oh, boy. That was kind of weird. I guess we were thinking Sons of the Pioneers or something. That whole album was like a variety show. That whole album [*Law and Order*] had a touch of the camp and tongue-in-cheek to it, and this one is more of a cathartic thing now. That's one of those things that was almost a cartoon, in a way.

"Trouble."

Yeah. That was the hit, the obligatory hit. That was Mick, actually. That was a loop of Mick, actually, maybe two bars. I think he was having a bad night, actually. We couldn't get a full take, so we made a loop. That happens! The bane of a drummer's existence is having a bad night. Because it's so microscopic what you can get away with live and getting a real tight drum track in the studio. Especially the way he plays, cause it's always a little bit behind, he's got that little hesitation like Charlie Watts, and that tends to open you up to be a little more sloppy.

That was just one of those things that we thought we should put on an album, otherwise it would have never seen the light of day at all. [*Laughs*]

You're not crazy about that one?

No, I like it a lot. But it's really poppy. It is very well crafted, as I recall.

"Walk a Thin Line."

Oh, yeah, I like that too. That was one where we were trying to get almost a march even though it was a ballad. That was me on the drums. Mick was appalled. He was appalled that these drums were going out and people would think that it's him because it offended the finer points of his sensibilities. And I understand that. I was really going for slop. And trying to cut through the slickness in some ways. And if you listen to old rock records, they're terrible but they're appealing in some way.

They've got a real spirit, an energy.

Yeah. They're left and right drums, and the kick and snare on either side, and these military press fills, which is really what the song is built on. Yeah! That worked out well, too.

"Save Me a Place."

Yeah. That was bordering on the Hawaiian, even. It had these great harmonies: [*Sings*] "Save . . . me . . ." These really wide things that Gabby Pahinui used to do.

I was thinking more of Peter, Paul & Mary in those harmonies.

Good. That's good, too. I remember Brian Wilson was kind of hanging out then; he had a crush on Christine, and was not doing too great then. I think he's doing better now . . . He came in and listened to "Save Me a Place" and said, "Bob Dylan would like that." And I figured he was referring to "I Shall Be Released."

That harmony is similar to Beach Boys harmonies in that it has the major-seventh note in there.

Yeah. It is. Very much. I should use those things more. I was thinking in terms of having a folky, organic sound, and maybe even being a little campy. It was somewhere between Hawaiian and some of those fifties things. Constructing harmonies is like engineering. You turn the knobs until it sounds good. [*Laughs*]

Do you have favorite keys to work in?

No, not at all. Maybe I should but I don't. I don't think about it. Often I'll use a capo on the guitar in the studio.

I was wondering if you used capos. I noticed that the song "Never Going Back" was in F#, which is an unusual key for a guitarist to choose, but with a capo it makes more sense.

Yeah. That was in standard tuning but with the E tuned down to a D. So in that tuning I would have to use a capo. Because I wouldn't be able to play that in any other key.

Do you have a favorite song of your own?

Well [*affecting the voice of an old man*], they're all my children you know. I don't know. I like the stuff off of *Tusk* quite a bit.

I love "You Do or You Don't" on *Out of the Cradle*.

Right. That's on the mature side. It's amazing that we can get songs like that or "Soul Drifter" and in between that you've got "This is the Time" which someone my age has no business doing whatsoever. [*Laughs*]

You did that one really well, though. It didn't sound like you were out of your arena or anything.

I know. It's bizarre how you can put your stamp on something that's that adolescent. I guess it isn't really. The verse is not adolescent. But it's got those elements where you go, "Hmmm. I think somebody's kid might like this one."

Was "You Do or You Don't" written to yourself?

I think it was a composite. I'm sure some of that has got to be touching on myself. "Wrong" is the same way. It's a composite of three or four people who have all lost their perspective and maybe acting inappropriately because of that. And we all know people like that and to some degree have been there. I've been there a little bit myself at times. It's about generic types and maybe laughing at yourself a little bit.

You wrote the song "Mystified" with Christine McVie. Do you recall how that collaboration occurred?

Yeah. A few of the things on *Tango in the Night* were done in a little bit of a different way. I took a bunch of the raw material home and Christine's basic drum track and worked at home on that and on a couple of things that weren't really the band. One of the reasons we did that was because it was really hard to get everybody together. At this point in time we had five managers and I think we saw Stevie for about ten days during the making of the record. We had to scramble a little bit. So a few things of Christine's I took home to re-work. So I think the melody of that was her seed and whatever I put over it.

When you started writing songs, did it come easy to you?

No. It's never come easy. It's the hardest thing for me. I could produce people all day standing on my head. All that stuff is just playing to me; it's pretty easy. But writing is very hard.

* * *

Rickie Lee Jones
West Hollywood, California 1989
North Hollywood, California 1991
Burbank, California 1993

There's a fragile melancholy in her singing, a heartbreak quality that brings a spacious depth to the sad songs and a sense of triumph to the happy ones. She talks in much the same way, often in a half-whisper, as if on the edge of tears. She paused at times during our discussions to collect her thoughts, and after explaining in detail the potential anguish involved in writing songs, she confessed her reservations about giving away too much in her answers, and reconsidered the wisdom of making public this most private of processes. (A few weeks later, after reading the transcript, she okayed its publication.) "Some songs you write with your eyes closed," she whispered knowingly with her eyes wide open, and laughed.

Rickie Lee Jones was born in Chicago on November 8, 1954, and moved with her family to Phoenix when she was very young. She wrote her first song in the eighth grade and never stopped writing them, a passion that led her in time to the western slopes of Los Angeles. Playing gigs around town, her songs reached the ears of Lowell George, who recorded her "Easy Money" (though he didn't "discover" her, scrapping a romantic rumor), as well as Tom Waits, who took her under his wise and ragged wings and wrote "Rainbow Sleeves" and other beautiful songs for her.

A sped-up demo version of a song she wrote for her friend Chuck E. Weiss called "Chuck E.'s in Love" caught the attention of the folks at Warner Brothers. Her first album, *Rickie Lee Jones*, revealed an amazing maturity and a vast range of expression, from the jazzy jubilance of "Chuck E." and "Danny's All-Star Joint" through the wistful, almost unbearably beautiful reflections of "Company" and "On Saturday Afternoons in 1963," through the soulful intensity and urban snap of "Night Train" and "Young Blood" to the spectral, longing humor of "Last Chance Texaco."

It was a debut unparalleled in popular music, but she knew "you can't debut twice," and to move forward she went back to her old hometown and sequestered herself in the choir-room of an old school, a room thick with ghosts, ideal for writing the songs that would become her second album, *Pirates*. "I responded by writing as deep and moody and personal of a record as I could," she said.

Pirates emerged from this seclusion a full-blown masterpiece from the first moment to the last, its songs seeming to have spilled out of her heart and mind in an abundance of riches —multidimensional suites like "We Belong Together" and "Living It Up" expanded the songform with dynamic expressions of sorrow and joy, a rainbow of harmonies, and a rich blend of acoustic drums, percussion, horns and harmonicas—its dark colors and rhythms shifting like shadows on the desert. Struggling for a comparison by which to define the harmonic richness of her music, critics likened her to George Gershwin.

"I think that album, more than any other I've made," she said in the softest of soft voices, "contains a spirit and a world that's just . . . unrelenting."

Girl at Her Volcano came next, a little record (literally; it's the size of an old 78) of cover songs that brought new levels of passion and poignance to pop gems like "Under the Boardwalk" and "Walk Away, Renee." It also contains a heartrending rendering of Rickie's only recording of a song by Waits, the beautifully sad "Rainbow Sleeves."

"That is the picture I see," she intoned softly on 1984's *The Magazine*, an orchestral excursion that moves through the dark narcotic streets of the present into carnival dreams of the past, with songs of love beginning and ending, and a final suite called "Rorschachs" that connects remembrances and reverberations from Van Nuys to Paris.

Years went by. And then some whispers started buzzing around town that Walter Becker of Steely Dan had left his Hawaiian home to come to Los Angeles to produce Rickie Lee's next album. And at the end of autumn in 1989, *Flying Cowboys* was released. We spoke in the summer of that same year.

She's recorded four more albums since then: an acoustic collection of jazz songs called *Pop Pop*; an acoustic collection of her own songs, stripped down to their most essential core, called *Naked Songs*; in 1993 *Traffic in Paradise*, which features some of her most magical songs to date, such as "Albatross" and "Altar Boy"; and in 1997, *Ghostyhead*. The release of these albums allowed me the opportunity to interview her two more times. At the time of *Pop Pop*, however, she was conflicted about her songwriting and understandably distressed about her record company's dearth of promotion for her albums. But by 1993 she had moved to a new company, and seemed renewed in her estimation of her own

songs, speaking about some of the early ones with a surprising and happy candor.

"The days go by like glasses of water," she said, downing them with an ease
she never knew when the days were still whiskey and hard to swallow. At the
time of our first interview in 1989, she was full of familial bliss, having recently
given birth to the beautiful and beloved Charlotte. She had left her old wild
ways to live with her family in tranquil Ojai, a little town surrounded by mountains about an hour north of Los Angeles. With Charlotte in her world, instead
of the possibility of a future, it became a certainty.

Like many songwriters I've spoken to, her answers were as often musical as
they were verbal. When I asked her if she remembered writing her first song,
she answered by singing it for me. Although she wrote it in the first grade, her
distinctive stamp of heartbreaking hopefulness was unmistakable. In softly
sweet tones, she sang: "I wish, I wish wishes would come true / And then I'd
know that it would be alright . . ."

**Have you ever had any qualms about sharing as much as you do in
your music?**
[*Pause, and then softly*] Well, no. There's no choice. That was just the way
it was. If anything, I had to learn to write happy things because the thing that
naturally came out was a real sad thing. It was real fun; it was like school and
lessons, learning to write a happy, nonpersonal type of song. One that I can do
pretty well.

By nonpersonal, you mean—
A story about somebody.

Are those fun for you to write?
Yep. They're easy. I shouldn't say that [*laughs*] because then I'll never be
able to write one again. They're fun. They're a lot more fun than needing to
write about something that you feel. Or that second sight you have that sees
something happening in your life and needs to write about it, unbeknownst to
you, and when you're done you learn something from what you've written.
Those are all songs you kind of write with your eyes closed.

[*Louder*] And I've gotten better at it, but as you write you go, "Gee, that
doesn't really make sense. *Okay, I'll write it*, if that's what you want, but . . ."
[*Laughs*] And then when it's done, you find out, as long as you don't interfere,
somebody knows what they're writing. You know what I mean? You just listen.
'Cause your logic will tell you, or your rhyme scheme will say, "You know, I want
this to be this other way," but you mustn't interfere with the spirit that's writing.

Once in a while, I write one. But [*laughs*] most of the time . . . [*very softly*]
most of the time I don't write them.

**How do you get to the place where you can let that spirit come
through? Is there any technique?**
I always admired those old thirties movies where they show a couple of the
really classic, great songwriters whipping out a song in a night. And I'd think,
"Why can't I do that?" [*Laughs*] And the times I've co-written, it's kind of
been like that. It's been a frenzy of do this, go over there, oh, God!

But I don't have a technique or a method of getting there. I just keep learning in my life a different thing. A few years ago, I didn't have any ideas for a few years. And a few years before that, I had ideas all the time. So it's just always changing. I think one of the most important things that's happened to me is to not get scared of writing a song, and not second guess yourself.

Since I became a professional, it's been hard for me not to critique my work while I'm doing it. And that can destroy it. 'Cause it really is a spirit being born. It's a living spirit. When people hear it, a spirit happens to them. And you have to be really quiet and careful with it when it's first being born, and you can't tell it it's wrong, 'cause it will just die. For me, they do. If before they're done I start to think something is wrong with them, they just won't get done. You have to keep going back and playing 'em over and over again and listening to them.

You have to go *into* them. And that's, I think, where the torment is for a lot of songwriters. You have to go into the thing, and it takes a lot of hours and you have to separate yourself from the life you know.

It's really alchemy. [*Laughs*] Did that answer your question?

Yeah. It did. Does that mean that you stay available to songs, or do you ever sit down with an instrument and try to force the process?

Sometimes. Lately I've been feeling that I want to write a song so I'll make myself available. Now I can do it and it doesn't have to be a song that's going to be recorded. Let's just write some *songs*. We're here 'cause we like music. You don't have to make everything the thing that's gonna be on the record. Just write some songs and enjoy writing songs and sing some songs.

Because I get to where, [*in a low, raspy voice*] "Oh, this isn't a good idea, I'm not even going to try it." And then it becomes brutal and *it's not fun anymore*. Everything has to be real important.

The thing that started to happen to me in the last year, being around Walter [Becker] and my husband, Pascal, who sit around and play music a lot, is that I remembered how it is to sit around and play! So I got myself a banjo again. It's my favorite instrument to play. I'm really comfortable holding it. I love it. I just sit and I pluck on that and I made up a song or two and I'm playing old songs I knew, and that's really reminded me of just sitting and playing. 'Cause that's really what it's about, and you can get really lost trying to make a great statement and trying to write not even a hit song, but to write a song. Just write the song at that moment and forget it.

You said that for a while you had many ideas and then you didn't. Do you mean concepts for songs, melodic ideas or—

Lots of songs. Lots of songs, and then I just kind of ran out of confidence in the songs and in their function . . . I feel like that's part of it, but maybe I just didn't have anything that I wanted to talk about. I didn't have a point of view. And that's okay. I just said, "Well, maybe I'm done." [*Laughs*] Maybe I've written and that's all I have to say. And I was really accepting of that. That's all right, I'll go do something else. And it's still okay. I'm prepared at any time to run out of things to say. If I don't have any more to say to the world, I've said enough. My ego isn't in this so much so that I have to keep proving myself each year that I still have something to say that will interest everybody.

Here's what it was: I had a couple of ideas and I could kind of feel the rumbling of something forming. But it seemed so distant. And it seemed like what I wanted to do or what I started to see was so *beautiful* and so perfect, I thought, "How am I ever going to write this?" [*Laughs*] I mean, I can't see it, I can only kind of sense it. I can't write that—How am I going to write that?

That's how it happens in me. It's almost like a smell. I just kind of feel the first images of the spirit of something. So . . .

[*Then very softly*] I have to tell you, I think it's dangerous for me to talk about that. That stuff is really private. The problem with interviews is that these are real private things people go through, and the problem with when you talk about them is that you automatically disengage them. You violate them and you interfere with them, and it's really hard to go back and readjust everything and say, "Okay, we'll be private again." [*Laughs*] I enjoy talking about it, but it is a dangerous thing to talk about, how you write. 'Cause I really feel that there are spirits and you have a sacred obligation to just be clear and quiet and if you put your ego into it too much and talk about how you do it, you mess yourself up.

But it's an education for us, for songwriters, to understand that even the greatest songwriters aren't completely in control of where songs come from.

Do you think that's true?

Yes. Most of the people I've talked to admit that they don't feel in charge, and that when it happens, it happens.

It probably depends a lot on the kind of songs somebody writes and what kind of person they are, if that really happens to them. Or how much they want to admit to themselves that that happens.

I think the listener can sense when a song comes through as a spirit as opposed to when it's fabricated and forced.

I really think that there's no doubt that music is dealing with alchemy and magic things. It does things that speak to us in ways that are like a living, other-world thing. I can't explain it and my words are going to diminish what it is, but it's really clear to me that it's a higher thing than any singular person.

And those songs are timeless. Unlike us, they never age or change. Your song "Saturday Afternoons in 1963" has the great line "years may go by," which was so beautifully sad the first time I heard it, and now I realize that it was ten years ago when that came out. And years have gone by.

Yeah. I had that feeling too, recently. I know what you mean. [*Laughs*]

That first album was incredible. Was the pressure pretty strong after that to match it with your second album?

Yeah, but I kind of knew that one. Following an incredible debut is impossible. You can't follow it. Because you can never debut again. It's not just the album that was great, it was the debut that was great. It was the arrival.

I responded to that by writing as deep and moody and personal of a record as I could. Not consciously, that's just what was happening to me. Also, I was real insistent with the producers about what songs I wanted to do and how I wanted them done. "Western Slopes" was a big fight. They just didn't relate to it at all. They tried to support me in doing it, but I could see it was just a blank in their faces until it was done. And even then it was scary to them because it was a real long and strange journey.

But when it was over, and it was a real torture to do, I think that that album [*Pirates*], more than *any* I've made, contains a spirit and a world that's just, from the moment it begins, unrelenting. It's really, really neat. It really *caught* something.

If you could take a picture of it, it's like a [*laughs*] little green light that's shimmering and every time you put it on, it fills the room.

Is it true that you went to your mom's house and wrote most of the songs for that album on a piano there?

Yeah. There's a little Catholic college in that town and they have a small music room. And it seems like nobody is ever in it. So my friend got me the key and I'd go in there at night and I wrote the songs in there.

I finished "We Belong Together" there. I started "Pirates" and I came back and wrote some things for *The Magazine* there as well.

Good room for you.

Yeah. It's an *old* room from the forties or thirties. They do the band rehearsals there and the choirs. It's very heavy. It's very thick. The minute I walk in there [*laughs*] there's a lot of things in there, you know? Yeah, I like it. But I'm not really interested in going in there for a while. [*Laughs*]

"Living It Up" from *Pirates* is such a miraculous song.

[*Laughs*] I can see that forming. I remember very well how that was written. It was over a few months. I remember the things that went into it. It was just a little picture of my life at that time. It just takes time to write down ideas again. I say, "Oh, that's a great idea, should I write that down?" [*Laughs*] I just never write them down.

Another miraculous song is "Company," which you wrote with Alfred Johnson. What was that collaboration like?

You know, I had just met him and we developed this wonderful, *strange* friendship, based on songwriting, getting together for the *purpose* of writing a song. With a black man, with no sexual interest. A *fabulous* and unusual thing to happen. And I guess I indicate that he's black because people won't know that, and I think that's an important part of seeing the dynamic of these two strangers meeting, and how close we are, and we became.

Writing "Company," for us, was like having a complete relationship in the evening we wrote it, [*laughs*], a complete love affair, a complete relationship, and when the song was done, we were done with each other. We were absolutely done. We were exhausted; we were finished . . . with each other. And we didn't see each other for years. [*Laughs*] And then he quit his job and decided to come out, and start playing and writing again. Because he's really dramatic, you know. He pissed me off because he's so talented, and he wouldn't keep writing.

That definitely has your signature on it. One of the themes of *Flying Cowboys* is a wistfulness for lost youth and time gone by. Is this something you've been thinking about lately?

[*Pause*] You know, I think I'm more in the now than I've ever been. I often find myself thinking that I'm glad it's right now and not then. But in the writing of the album, gathering together the picture, it's looking back and looking forward.

Flying Cowboys has a lot of western imagery—is this from looking back at your childhood in Phoenix?

Yeah. [*Pause*] I think it must be looking at the future, because it's what I'm going toward. A real simple answer would be that, obviously, it's pictures from the past.

The Flying Cowboys are coming. They're arriving. It's not something I'm thinking about that was. It's something that [*softly*] comes now.

How did "Rodeo Girl," also from *Flying Cowboys,* come together?

"Rodeo Girl" started with a different melody in the verse, but with some of the same images but in a different order. It had a line in it originally about somebody who was crazy, but I ended up editing most of that part of the story out. So I wrote the first version, and then I didn't get the response I had wanted and I felt I had tried too hard. So I rewrote it with a lighter verse. And I still like both of them. The first one was more western feeling. That was the syndrome with all of Flying Cowboys.

There was another one about a girl that I rewrote so many times. It was called "Wild Girl" or "Rodeo Girl." I had all these girl titles. It was really great and I really liked the verse, but then I started rewriting it a lot. It took real courage after writing and recording them [*laughs*] to rewrite them.

Do you remember writing "Horses"?

I think that "Horses" came out of a song that, in spirit, I'm writing about Charlotte. I think that I just sat down at the piano. I remember making the demo but I don't remember writing it.

Are you a writer who is writing constantly?

No. It's really different every time. As it becomes your career and then you're expected to write and you're supposed to write what you want to write, there's a lot of adjusting to "supposed to do it" and "have to do it for a living." So that answer is always changing. . . .

In your song "Skeletons" there's the line, "Some girls listen to records all day in their room." Were you one of those girls?

Definitely. When I was a teenager and preteen, that was pretty much all I lived for. [*Softly*] My records. Yeah. I didn't come out much. [*Laughs*] Did you?

I was listening to records a lot, too. What did you listen to?

I listened to the Beatles only until about 1968. Then I had a Buffalo Springfield record and I started buying *other* records. I bought *Surrealistic Pillow*. I practiced guitar on "Today" and "Coming Back to Me." I tried to sing "White Rabbit" [*laughs*] but it was pretty hard. She [Grace Slick] has her own voice. It's pretty hard to imitate it.

I heard Crosby, Stills and Nash and I loved them. So when Stephen Stills made a record, I bought his, and when Neil Young made a record, I bought his. And learned their songs.

You said it was tough for you when making an album to translate your musical ideas to a producer and to other musicians. I know, from experience, how hard just getting drummers to do what you need can be. How do you do it?

One thing you have to do when you invite anybody else into your life in any capacity is to open up to what they're going to do. And understand that your vision will be altered. No song I've done is ever the way I heard it when I did it. Otherwise, do it all yourself.

In a marriage or a friendship or anything, you've asked another human being to come in and contribute their point of view and what they are hearing. And you can instruct them, and be as animated as you can, tell the story and describe it in any way you can, do a dance for them, whatever it is to bring them as much to your vision. But eventually, you're going to have to send them home or you have to accept this other thing that's taking shape. And listen with another ear that says, "Oh, this is very good. It's not exactly what I had in mind but it's very interesting."

It might contain some of your intention, but it's not going to be what you hear in your head. 'Cause your head is not in the physical world. This isn't your dream world and you can't ever translate that into this. Never. Don't try; it won't happen.

The molecules change when they take physical shape. If you've ever had a dream and remembered a song or remembered a line, written it down and then looked at it later, it's not the same. Even as you're writing it down. It just doesn't translate. So you can come as close as you can, but for me, if I'm going to work with living musicians that I think a lot of, I'm going to give them room to do what they do.

Most of the time I've succeeded. Sometimes I've failed and it's really disheartening, because you bring together a big bunch of people and if they don't care, it's really hard. It happens to me and it happens to anybody.

One neat thing about not paying people to do it is that they're really there, involved in your song. They're really trying to figure out *their thing* in your song. And that's nice. That's what creation is.

I was never good with drums because I know *nothing* about drums, so I always had a really difficult time as well. [*Laughs*] And that's where a producer would help me a lot. And it's really ESP, because I can't tell him much better than I can tell the drummer. [*Laughs*]

I'm thinking about "The Ghetto of My Mind" [from *Flying Cowboys*]. It was really, really hard.

That's a real up song.

Yes, it's very up, but if you listen to the percussion and the drums, they're just as wild as animals. So it sounds very simple, and you feel very happy when you hear it, and it was a lot of work to get that there. Because other grooves and other things were much easier to fall into.

It's a lot of work, recording. And staying true to what you know it can be and also staying open. I used to be a lot tougher: "It has to be the way I hear it." I'm just not that way anymore. I enjoy, now, playing with people more and the experience of gathering them together.

I'm pretty impressionable, though, especially at the beginning of a record. If somebody says, "Oh, that song sucks," I go, [*laughs*] "Oh, okay. I won't record it." Unless I say, "This is my anthem. I don't care what you say about it." But that's hard. And when that happens, the song ends up carrying so much weight for you, it's really hard to enjoy it, because you had to fight to get it on.

I don't think people realize how deeply songwriters take these things.

[*Whispered*] I know. They say some really crass, *terrible* things. [*Pause*]

I probably shouldn't mention any names, but I had somebody say to me really early in the writing of a song, "Well, that's fine, Rickie, but what will somebody in Illinois think of it?" [*Laughs*] And I went, "Oh, God." And it caused the song to mutate. I wrote, like, six different versions of it. It was a really good song as it was. I thought, "But I'm from Illinois. What kind of thing is that to say? You think everybody in the middle of the United States is an idiot?"

It was like he dropped a rock on it and it shattered. It was really weird. I never saw it happen to a song before. But I couldn't stop writing it. [*Laughs*] "Atlas's Marker." I have so many "Atlas's Marker"s!

It's really important, when it starts to come, it's like you're in a trance and a frenzy all the time. Even when you're not writing for a month, you're still in it . . . And I'm very susceptible to the things, especially the negative ones, that people say. It's really easy to cause them [the songs] to mutate.

Are there any certain chords that you go to on the piano that are your favorites?

There are ones I gravitate towards. I like those whole step things against each other.

One of my favorite musics I've written is "Deep Space" [from *The Magazine*], especially the bridge. To me that bridge is really like somebody else wrote it because I have no idea what it is, and each time I play it I have to stop at the bridge.

And once I figured it out, [*laughs*] and I remember thinking, "Naww, that's not it, because you can't play like that!" Later I realized that I had done that, I had found these other chords, voicings. So it surprises me what I actually come up with. 'Cause when you do it, it's like you put on the other coat, you know, and she knows how to play a lot of things that I have no idea she knows how to play. [*Laughs*]

Are there certain harmonies you usually choose?

Songwriters have a thing, a basic couple of chords that they are, and they usually gravitate around those. I'd say there're probably harmonies and types of chords and intervals that are of me and I always like to play them.

Do you have favorite keys to work in?

I like to try to keep finding new keys and new things that I haven't used before and see what happens in them.

I think, on guitar, I find myself in G a lot and in B, oddly enough. My singing tends to often go to B. There're a lot of Ds in there too.

Was your song "Danny's All-Star Joint" about the place on the corner of Hollywood Boulevard and Cahuenga?

Yeah. I used to write in the building above that hamburger joint. It's called the Hollywood Building. And it was really Phillip Marlowe land up there. I'd go in there and nobody would be there, the lights would be burned out in the hall, and it looked out on an alley.

"Danny's All-Star Joint" I wrote there. It was really thrilling to go there because you never knew if you were going to get out alive. [*Laughs*] The thrilling feeling of the empty sound of your steps on the stairs and no one else there, and opening the door, and it's so old and the smells . . . looking out at the alley . . . . It was a really neat place, but I don't think I wrote very much there. [*Laughs*] I just kind of went and dreamed a lot. Got "Danny's All-Star Joint."

We've spoken about the ways songs have their own spirits. Do you always feel that spirit when you perform them? Do they move you the way they move us?

[*Softly*] Absolutely. I think of them as houses. I think that's the best way to describe them, so you get a sense of me being contained in the spirit. It's always the same with me. And it's complete. I don't know how you could sing something and not be completely in the song. So when I'm asked that, it's kind of odd to me, because how you could sing a song you weren't completely overtaken by? That's how I feel when I sing. That automatically happens. If it doesn't happen, I wouldn't sing it.

But certainly you've heard singers going through the motions, and not being moved by the spirit of a song. We hear that frequently—

Not from me. [*Laughter*] I just can't imagine it. I don't know why they would sing and why people would listen. But I guess maybe people do like that kind of singing.

"Altar Boy" is an amazing song—it covers religion, spirituality, sexuality, desire—

I know. It was really a gift. It came all at once in about one hour. And it was just perfect.

The music and the words came together?

Yeah. Everything.

Is that unusual or does that happen frequently?

No. That's unusual.

It's funny the way some of the best songs come the fastest.

Yeah. Let's see now. I don't know, I was going to say something general like that probably the best songs come all at once, but I don't know.

Did you write "Altar Boy" at an instrument?

The guitar. Yeah, it was just on guitar. I was sitting in my little writing room I had made with guitar and a pad of paper early in the morning.

Do you have any ideas about what allows a song like "Altar Boy," which is such a completely realized song both musically and lyrically, to come through all at once?

Well, that just seems like God to me. I mean, so you could say you are assimilating things all the time, and if you just listened, you could find you have a wise point of view about things in your life. But I more enjoy thinking that I'm just listening to somebody else's ideas and then just write them down. It's probably a little of both. I like to think that spirit speaks through all of us. And at moments like that, you say, "Wow, thank you so much, that was really beautiful." That's my favorite way to look at it.

Were you surprised when "Altar Boy" came out all at once?

No. It was an assimilation of great feelings I had at the time. I really loved it, but it didn't surprise me. Maybe it was surprise. It just seemed perfect to me. It's a perfect expression of what I can't speak.

The way that song came about was that I was with my friend and I was talking about being celibate. He said, "Well, what would be the use of being celibate if you don't have desire?" I said, "Oh, you mean like a monk with a hard-on." That must have just sat in there until the morning, when I wrote it down.

That's quite an opening line.

Yeah. But that's kind of what we're all like. We're striving really hard to be the best we can be carrying around this great ache and passion which can lead us down a path that is impulsive. I don't want to diminish it by explaining it, because all of its meaning is contained in the poetry. A discussion of it really makes it less than it is.

But it's always fascinating how a songwriter got to the place to write a great song, or to allow one to come through.

For me, I don't think you can give me credit for it. I wrote it, but I just listened.

But that seems like the greatest accomplishment of all, to get out of the way.

It is. [Laughs]

You mentioned that you felt that song is perfect. Do you feel that that is an exception among your songs? To me, so many seem perfect.

I think there's great writing. But the simplicity of this text makes it perfect. To state it quickly and simply is a great thing to do. So, would I say anything else is perfect? I get perfect feelings singing them, but I think they are more abstract. I don't know if I'd say if anything else was perfect.

An example, in my mind, would be "The Last Chance Texaco."

Yeah, that's really a great one. It is similar to "Altar Boy" because it also plays with humor and great sorrow. Beautiful landscapes and a classic kind of melody. "Texaco" is weirder. Yeah, I guess what's exciting about both of them for me is to play really hysterical lines against great sadness and beauty. And leave you to decide what you'll go with. You can sing "a monk with a hard-on" to one audience, and if you smile as you say it, they'll giggle. You can sing it another time and look into the light, and they're not sure what they should think. They'll listen seriously. So if they only hear it, what do they think? I can't tell. It's almost as if you have to tell them how to feel about things. And I like not doing that. So I like saying, "He tried to be Standard and he tried to be Mobil . . ." And that kind of kooky metaphor in the context of desperation is really exciting, dangerous, confusing thing to do. And if it works, it's really good.

Yeah. It's a very sad song but with jokes in it. And I realized how beautifully American a landscape it is.

Yeah. It is. I wrote it in a coffee shop and I got most of it in one afternoon. I don't remember getting all of it, but I think I wrote the whole thing in a day.

Are you amazed when songs like that come through you?

[*Very softly*] Yes.

One of the saddest songs you've ever written is "Skeletons." Which also seems pretty close to perfect. There's so much in it, musically and lyrically.

I wrote that on piano. That was an instance of great sorrow happening in my life and leading me to express terrible sorrow. Maybe I confused two stories, I'm not sure.

My memory is that these two people were driving on the freeway, and they were pulled over by the police with an All Points Bulletin for a robbery. The police got scared as they approached the car and they shot him. And again, I don't know if I made it up. I can't tell, because I'll just weave reality into me and in the end I won't know which one was my fantasy.

My memory is that she was pregnant. I don't even know if they were on the way to this hospital—did I make that up? Was that really happening? I can't remember anymore. So I feel—obviously, because that's what I wrote—she was pregnant, they were on their way to the hospital, cop walked up and shot him in the head. End of story. [*Laughs*] So how much of that is true, I'm not sure.

You took that story and then added the verse to it about "What do birds leave behind of the wings that they came with?" Which elevates the whole song and resolves it in such a beautiful way. Do you recall if the words and music to that one came together?

It did. That was one of those, too. You know, sometimes you can just hear how the melody said those words.

Do you tape yourself while working?

No. That's why I've got to work fast, so I don't forget. I used to. You know, it's always different. It's been a couple years now, so every record and every song I do it differently. You know, the longer ones, probably I taped. [*Laughs*] And the shorter ones probably I didn't. Like "Stewart's Coat" floating around for many years. Basically the verses, but I didn't have the chorus. My friend Sal said, "You should do that summer song." It was a summer song then because I hadn't written the September verses yet. I said, "Okay," and I made up the chorus right away.

If you're in the groove, you can probably write whole songs. If you don't want to struggle with them. I think some of the songs are things you want to say to yourself. So you don't let them go, because you have things to learn and to work out in the writing of them. So, probably, the ability to write a song is understood, and if it didn't have a therapeutic purpose, I could probably write them really quickly.

You purposely take longer than needed to write them so that you can spend more time with a song?

Yeah. I think I like to swim in them, and work them out, and think about them.

Is it the writing itself that is therapeutic?

It must be. I don't know, I don't think about it.

Do you have to cut yourself off from all distractions, and be completely alone, to write?

Pretty much. You get a slightly zombified air. Because once it begins to happen, it doesn't say, "I won't let anything come through while you're feeding the baby." So, ideally, you have someone else around. I probably would wait to leave the doors open until it was safe to write. Again, it depends on what happens in your life. I wrote [*Traffic In Paradise*] mostly in about one month when Charlotte went on vacation with her dad. [*Laughs*] I just wrote everything. And wrote for a couple of weeks after she got back. So I think you take the opportunity when it comes.

So songwriting is not something you are working on all the time?

No, I'm not. I think I'm thinking all the time. And within a year there might be one or two themes that return over and over, either lyrically or musically. And then, maybe, when I want to start writing, I start taking little notes. But I don't do it all the time.

In some of your songs, the structure itself is complex. Many are suites, with more than just verses and choruses.

That's right. Where did I get that? Probably Beatles stuff. And *West Side Story*.

Crosby, Stills & Nash?

Yeah, they did that, too.

How do you take a compound song, like "Living It Up" which is complex and quite tender, and translate it into a record, and produce it with other musicians without wrecking it?

That was hard to do. We had a band there, and they had to listen a lot, because they are telling a story. So they have to become really intimate with the text, how I'm moving, and how to bring it about without interfering with what I'm saying. It happens live. But it's really hard. I always start with a live thing. Because my time is too poor. If I'm going to record with a band, they have to be there with me. I never do voice-overs or over-dubs. I can't.

You never over-dub vocals?

Never.

Do you always play an instrument while singing?

Yes.

Joni Mitchell talked about how in the past she had trouble communicating to musicians about how they should play her songs. That she might be too abstract and they wouldn't understand.

I think Joni Mitchell is more abstract musically and lyrically than I am. And I think, as of lately, I'm not into controlling the musicians at all. I'll control them moodwise, or sexually. That I want a track to be sexual. But I'll just do that by my behavior and they'll follow suit. Because I don't explain my songs to musicians. You can play it yourself. But if you want to invite people to play with you, then you're inviting their point of view. That's how I see it. Let them play. And if it doesn't work, then it doesn't work.

Your music has often been compared to Tom Waits when you first emerged, and of course, you were romantically linked with him for awhile. Were you influenced by him, or were you both influenced by the same things?

Well, you know, we were lovers. So I think that when you're together, you can't help but not be influenced by each other. I think I was seriously influenced by him onstage. Not so much musically. Well, I think they just bled into each other. For a year or two. But what was most imitatable were things he did onstage. To be real honest.

Both of you had a lot of urban, street imagery at a time when not many other songwriters did that.

Yeah. That part, actually, I don't think of it as much in terms of imagery as with music. Actually melodies started to bleed into each other. We had a thing that happened once. We were talking on the phone and I said, "I'm working on this song and it goes, [sings] "Blue . . . horizon . . ." Which is the same as "Hang onto your rainbow . . . " [from "Rainbow Sleeves," by Waits] So I changed my note in my melody and made it a flatter note so it wouldn't be the same as his. [Laughs]

Melody is a profound spirit. I mean, who can say what it is? And you just make the same chords about you, have the same music about you. Your presence together is a mood, and perhaps if you're a musician, then you have the same music. Or if you're close friends, you're influenced by the same things so the same types of things will come out of you. I think a lot of it is kismet. I think then you perhaps purposely steal from each other the things you like. Or they happen accidentally. The point is that some things happen automatically. They just are.

It's interesting that you then mentioned "rainbow sleeves" in "Pirates," which was really touching.

Yeah, I did. "Rainbow sleeves" came up in "I'm still holding on to your rainbow sleeves." So yeah, we were speaking to each other.

You wrote that after he wrote his song.
Absolutely.

And then, of course, you recorded his "Rainbow Sleeves" on *Girl at Her Volcano*.

There you go. [*Laughs*]

Your version of it is heartbreaking.

I think that's a great song. I think it would be better if he did it. If he was the one to sing it. More than a girl. I think he wrote it for a girl's voice. Because it's a man's point of view: Hold onto me. I'll take you there. It would be more touching if he could sing it.

"Chuck E.'s in Love" is the biggest hit of your career. Does that affect in any way how you feel about it?

Sure it does. I didn't do it for a long time. It made it hard to sing it. I think, for many years, that it diminished the song. But now I've come to terms with it much better. It's not as completely at ease as some of the others. But I can sing it now, and almost look at it like another song. Because being a good songwriter, it's hard having one song that the radio played. And I just have to forget about the radio. The people really like hearing that song. We like hearing things we heard on the radio. I do too. I love hearing Van Morrison do "Domino" or "Blue Money." And it probably drives him crazy. But they signify points in our lives. And it's not necessarily that the song's better, it might not be. But it has meaning. So you can acknowledge that, and that's okay.

It's true for so many songwriters, that their best songs are not always their most famous ones.

Yeah, that's right. Well, it's a different kind of thing, the single. That single, that was such an unusual song. It's an unusual song, anyway, but really, really outside for its time.

So it was a huge hit. It was *huge*. And that was hard to live with. But it's okay now.

Was there ever any pressure to try to repeat that success by doing a similar song again?

Not that song so much. But, yeah, everybody—well, not everybody, but certain record companies I was at—would have liked to have seen that happen. Not realizing, of course, you can never duplicate anything. You have to respect an artist. If you like what they do, great things will come to them. If you just want them to duplicate something and you don't really love what they do, you'll curse the songwriter. It's really important for a songwriter to be around inspired, intelligent people in the business, or you'll be destroyed.

How do you generate melodies? Do you play chords to suggest melodies?

On the piano, I just play little chords. I don't play the melody, but I hear the melody with the chords. It's always different.

When you are working with chords, do you think in terms of which chords they are, or do you just experiment with the sound?

I don't know music well, so I'm not thinking what the chord is at all. I have no idea what the chord is. [*Laughs*] I just pick them out by sound.

And do you think that frees you up somewhat?

Absolutely. Not knowing if I'm playing the third on the bottom and if I'm supposed to do that or not. In some cases, that's really helped me. That's what I have to work with, so that's what I do.

Some of your piano songs are really difficult to figure out, musically.

Me too. That's why I can't play them later. Because it's totally inspired, and I memorize what I'm doing, and then if I don't play it for a year or two, I have no idea what I played. I have to relearn it. I have a way I play, so hopefully once I lock in, I remember what I would do. But I've actually done things where I felt I couldn't have played that. But I did know how to play like that. In that moment I played in a way I didn't know I could. I didn't know I could voice things that way. And I've been very pleasantly surprised when the spirit's on me, that I'm a much better writer than I would think I was when I am uninspired. Do you know what I mean?

Yeah. And you're quite a fine piano player for—

For someone who doesn't play, yeah. [*Laughs*]

The Magazine album opens up with that long, beautiful instrumental passage with you playing piano which is really wonderful, and pretty complex.

It's okay. The chords are nice. The piano technique isn't great, but the music is beautiful. It's kind of Satie-esque, I think. What I write well are these odd-voicings. Simple, but odd, haunting things. They come from me very naturally. And I guess I feel validated in Satie's existence, because he's a respected classical musician. When I hear him, I know his voice very well. It's not exactly mine, but I understand it.

Do your piano songs come out a lot different from your songs written on guitar?

Yeah. For a while I preferred piano, because I wanted a piano in my life and I got one. [*Laughs*] So for a long time, I just played on the piano. Now I'm back with string instruments again. Yeah, definitely, there's a different kind of music that comes out of the different instruments.

When you play chords on the piano, do you try to make up chords you've never played before?

Yeah. I often just sit and hit different things. I didn't study. I took some college piano course so I learned a little bit in a semester but I don't know how to play. I can just read really slowly. I still aspire to having lessons. Probably will one day.

So I just kind of let it go, and those are my favorite songs, the ones I just play. The wild, no-time, instrumental things that I make up on the spot. They just come and then they evaporate in the moment. Nobody's ever heard them. I love those! [*Laughs*] Those are my favorite things.

* * *

David Byrne
Hollywood, California 1992

"What is happening to my skin?
Where is that protection that I needed?
Air can hurt you too."

from "Air"
by David Byrne

The air over Hollywood is as hazardous as ever at high noon, and on the Sunset Strip the sun is blazing unforgivingly through the palms. At the Ben Franks coffee shop, which is always open and immortalized in song by Tom Waits ("Now he sits at Ben Franks every day / waiting for the one that got away"), the beautiful Iranian hostess says she's operating on only four hours of sleep, causing her to over-smile. People at the counter eat sandwiches and pie, drink coffee, read newspapers and surreptitiously watch each other.

Into this setting walks David Byrne, wearing blue jeans and a gray T-shirt, carrying an electric guitar in a black case. "I have to bring it to get fixed," he explains, and stashes it under a booth in the back.

"Electric guitar gets run over by a car / This is the meaning of life."

from "Electric Guitar"

He's in town in the middle of an American tour to support his solo album, *Uh Oh*. It's his first solo tour since the sad announcement that Talking Heads have officially broken up. It's a break-up entirely triggered by Byrne, who realized it was the only way to quell the battles being waged within the band. "As it happens with a lot of groups, there was a fair amount of griping and grumbling," he said, over a lunch of corn chowder and a tuna sandwich. Friends tried to persuade him, telling him that many bands made their best records while hating each other. But for Byrne that wasn't enough. "It just doesn't seem like a very good way to live your life."

Today he says that he doesn't want to exclude the possibility of a Talking Heads reunion, but quickly adds, "If it ever did happen, I'd want it to be a surprise rather than something everybody waits for."

Spying my tape recorders rolling on our table, a young crew-cutted waiter begins to ask Byrne his own questions: "Have you heard the new album by Morrisey?" Byrne politely listens and says no. "Well, you should check it out, man." "Okay, I will," Byrne promises, sipping herbal tea.

He has instant, even emphatic answers to some of the most abstract questions I ask, while pausing awhile to think about some of the simplest ones, such as if his first guitar was acoustic or electric. He was born in Dumbarton, Scotland and raised in Baltimore. He's married to Adelle Lutz, and they have a daughter named Malu Abeni Valentine. A photographer, film-maker, and composer, he was heralded "Rock's Renaissance Man" by *Time* magazine in a cover story on him. He's left-handed but plays guitar right-handed. "That's the way they sold them," he explains. "I didn't know you could turn them around." His first song was written when he was fifteen, establishing even then the twisted perspective he's employed through the years: it was called "Bald Headed Woman." Reticent then to go public with his music, he kept the song a secret. "I sang it in the basement. It never went anywhere. I didn't like it."

At about the same time, he became aware of strains of world music creeping around the corners of pop music, intriguing him then as it still does. He would go to the public library in search of international albums, such as the Balinese Gamelan records or Ravi Shankar's sitar music. It gave him an early understanding of music's potential to express itself in a multitude of ways. "In the late sixties there were all these other kinds of music that were finding their way into rock, whether it was Stockhausen or Page, who influenced Beatle stuff, or Ravi Shankar. It was hip to be aware of more than just the Top Ten. I heard a lot of that stuff, and it kind of blows your mind. It makes you realize music can be pretty much anything you call it."

At the Rhode Island School of Art, Byrne met fellow art-students Chris Frantz, who played drums, and bass player Tina Weymouth. "I opted for art school," he said, "because the graffiti was better." When he opted to move to New York, Chris & Tina soon followed. All of them could have easily gone in several different artistic directions, choosing music as somewhat of a lark, and this gave their music a carefree, unlabored freshness. Early songs such as "Uh Oh, Love Comes To Town," and "Happy Day" had weirdly appealing chord sequences and melodies that jumped in and out of keys, matching the happily quirky quality of Byrne's singing. The first song they ever wrote together, the now famous "Psycho Killer," was written entirely as a joke. To this day Byrne wonders why people love it.

Their debut album, *Talking Heads 1977*, was released in a signal orange sleeve, announcing in bold strokes the arrival of a band newer than the newest New Wave. They had something few of the other New Wave bands had: a sense of humor. They also projected a real warmth, unusual in the context of coldness then in fashion. In "Don't Worry About the Government" Byrne wrote, "I'll be working, working, but if you come visit, I'll put down what I'm doing, my friends are important." Here was a band that was not only funny and smart, but also friendly.

From that first album on, the Heads exhibited a real spirit of experimentation, always eager to push the boundaries of rock and roll. Byrne's endless imagination and willingness to expand propelled the Heads through more than a decade of groundbreaking music. Starting with this initial core of four musicians, Talking Heads expanded exponentially over their course of albums, both in terms of music and musicians.

Byrne has always gone against the current in his songwriting, and on the landmark *Fear of Music* album, released in 1979, he continued to defy the rock tradition of writing heroic songs about big abstract issues to focus instead on specific, elemental topics usually left unaddressed in songs, such as "Air," "Paper," "Mind," "Cities" and "Drugs." In these and others, such as the urgently dynamic "Life During Wartime," a distinctive perspective began to emerge that became more fully developed in later work. It's the outlook of an outsider, an alien confronted with our culture for the first time.

That perspective was crystallized in 1980's *Remain in Light*, a masterpiece of record making and songwriting inspired by the evangelical exhortations of radio preachers and influenced by the guiding spirit of Brian Eno. Structurally, the songs actually became more minimal, centering around single chord grooves. This was a reaction to what Byrne referred to as the "convoluted chord changes" of his first songs. These new songs were based not on chord changes but on rhythmic beds of instrumental tracks revolving around a single tonal center. In some he contrasted spoken verses with sung and chanted choruses, as in what is probably the quintessential Talking Heads track, "Once in a Lifetime."

Though it seemed as if the band might have peaked with the unprecedented power of *Remain in Light*, they succeeded in expanding on that open-ended, experimental energy in following albums, from the powerhouse *Speaking in Tongues*, featuring "Burning Down The House," through the charmingly low-tech *Little Creatures* (1985) and culminating with the Brazilian-inspired *Naked* in 1988.

In his solo albums Byrne has been continually moving in Brazilian directions. In 1990 he released *Rei Momo*, an album of songs based on Brazilian grooves, and 1992's *Uh Oh* continued to reflect this tradition, integrating these Latin rhythms into songs that are pure Byrne, both quirky and new.

The album opens with "Now I'm Your Mom," a song about a transsexual explaining her sex change to her son. Byrne considered dumping the entire subject and writing a whole different set of lyrics for the tune, finding the content too bizarre even for his sensibilities. But friends urged him to keep the original words, saying it was a song that only David Byrne could write. So he left the song unchanged. Yet after all these years of looking at the world from the outside, he seems tired of this alien outlook, and sitting at this beige booth in the back of Ben Frank's, thoughts of normalcy were appealing to him. In an industry where songwriters struggle daily to do something distinctive, David Byrne yearns to be conventional. "Sometimes I wish I wasn't so unique," he says with no trace of irony. "But then who would I be?"

When you write songs, do you attempt to consciously guide the meaning, or is it more a sense of following it where it goes?
I follow it where it goes. Often I don't know what it means until the song's finished. Sometimes months later. I don't think that's bad. It implies that I don't know what I'm doing but I don't think that's the case. I think that if you're able to follow your instincts, then that is knowing what you're doing. And being able to interpret the results is a separate skill altogether. It almost should be left to someone else to do.

After finishing a song, are you always able to completely grasp the meaning?
Some I'm not sure what they're about. But they have a kind of resonance. They say something to me, or they touch something, but I'm not sure exactly what it is.

You are the person who introduced the idea of "Stop Making Sense," which is a liberating thought for songwriters, that we can be freed from linear, logical thought in songs.
There was a lot of stuff I heard when I was growing up that was like that: Beatles songs, Rolling Stones songs, Bob Dylan songs. Even a lot of R&B and James Brown songs. If you took the lyrics at their face value, it was just a series of non-sequiturs. But in context, in sound and in the way they were said, whatever the gut reaction was to those particular words, it made sense on a non-logical level. It skirted your logical or rational facilities and struck a different level. A level which you can say, "That's reality." The rational way of thinking is only a gloss that you put on reality, and if through whatever means necessary you get at what's under that, you're touching something more basic.

And it seems that with those kinds of songs, which you have written and which have been written by others you've mentioned, such as the Beatles or Dylan, tap into an area bigger than the songwriter, and for that reason the song has an unlimited quality.
Yeah. It's almost like a cliche, that the writer taps into something universal. Some people call it a gift from God; some call it messages from the subconscious.

How do you see it?
I tend to believe that it comes from something within myself. But I comes from the collective unconscious, from a part of myself that's also very similar to other people, so it becomes a part of myself that's no longer me. It's not I any longer.

It doesn't reflect my petty concerns or desires or problems. It's tapping into something universal.

On the *Speaking in Tongues* album and others you did with Talking Heads, you wrote the songs to tracks that you made, allowing the track to guide the writing of the song. The phrase "speaking in tongues" suggests connecting with a source outside of yourself. Was there a sense that something outside of yourself was guiding the writing of those songs?

Yeah, I thought that that phenomenon of people speaking in tongues, in a religious context, was somewhat analogous to what happens in the songwriting process. Especially in that record where most of the songs, maybe 80% of them, the words don't make any sense on a literal level. So I thought it was almost like the jottings of somebody who was speaking in tongues. Glossalalia they call it.

I think that when you get real inspirations you are tapping something outside, beyond your normal consciousness. A lot of people drink or do drugs or whatever to try to loosen up to achieve that. I've got to admit I've tried those as well. [*Laughs*]

With success?

Well, sometimes. Kind of limited success. It kind of works for awhile and then after awhile you're too high to write [*Laughs*].

***Speaking in Tongues* has such an infectious spirit that it's hard not to dance while listening to it. There was a sense that you were inspiring your listeners to get to that altered state through the energy of the music itself, and from dancing.**

Yeah. Most of the times I would put on the tracks and blast them pretty loud and see what happens.

That album captured such a happy spirit; people were dancing and moving to it through that whole summer. Was it created in that kind of happy spirit?

I think so. It was pretty loose, that record. We felt, by that point, that we knew enough about our craft and how to make records. It was the first time we had worked without a producer, so it was loose in that sense. We weren't self-conscious about what we were doing.

In a past interview, you said that you listened back to early Talking Heads songs and were surprised by how convoluted the chord changes were.

We got more and more minimal as time went on. *Remain in Light* was the culmination of that in a way. Most of those songs have no chord changes whatever. The whole song has one tonic note through the whole song. And there's chords that change around that. But it's one of the things where the same bass line gets played through the whole song. We did that again a little bit in *Naked* but I found that I could add a few more chord changes. I found you kind of limit yourself as far as melodies go when you've only got one chord [*laughs*].

Yet it's remarkable how beautiful some of those melodies are. "Once in a Lifetime" is so beautiful because there are no chords, really, until the chorus, which is only two chords: D major and G major, yet that simplicity is

498 SONGWRITERS ON SONGWRITING

so moving, especially in contrast to the non-chordal, spoken context of the verses.

I felt that came out of the church preaching tradition. Where they do the same thing. They start with a sermon and then the organist or drummer starts to put a beat behind it, and it segue-ways into a song. There often isn't a clean break between the sermon and the song. There's a middle-ground in the sermon where the pronouncements and the shouts are so rhythmic that it verges on music.

And like a sermon that deals with the mundane, specific aspects of life and then reminds us that there is something bigger, that song does the same thing. The verses deal with the specific questions of existence, such as "How did I get here?" and the chorus emphasizes the timeless quality, of letting the days go by like water flowing.

It wasn't that conscious. It was only conscious in that once I had a couple of lines for the chorus, I knew that that direction was going to work. I knew I needed something in the chorus that would comment on, or balance, the words in the verses. Almost like stepping outside of the song and commenting on it. I knew it needed something like that but I didn't know what.

Was it a surprise for you when "Once in a Lifetime" emerged?

Yeah, it was kind of a surprise. Almost died a few times when we were working on it. On that record, the tracks started with a lot of improvisations. There was a guitar lick that I had and some other stuff. We ended up layering loads of stuff on tape. You could play it all at once and get this cacophony, but it would all be in the same key, more or less. D or G or somewhere in between.

We'd create sections in the song by punching in different tracks. Basically, we'd say, these eight tracks come in at the chorus and they come out again when the verse comes in, and then bring in these instruments. But basically, those instruments are playing the whole way through. The structure gets created at the mixing board.

There was quite a while when that particular song was going to be thrown out because it wasn't going anywhere.

Before you had the chorus?

Yeah. Eno had come up with the melody for the chorus. He just sang some gibberish. And I thought that was a great melody. But we couldn't get any further than that. So I took it home and worked on it and one day brought it in and I thought I kind of had it. I had most of the words for the chorus and the verses at that point. So that kind of pulled it back, because it almost had been dumped off. It was nice. It was one of those things where it was worthwhile to persevere.

One of the lines from that song that haunts me is "There is water under the ocean."

Yeah, it was kind of a stupid line. It was so obvious.

But in a song, supported by music, an obvious line takes on a bigger meaning. And in the context of this song, that line seemed especially meaningful.

Yeah. It does make this thing that is so dumb sound real profound.

It's a quality that's in many of your songs. Not the dumbness, but making an obvious statement about our world, as if you're an alien seeing it for the first time. And in the context of a song, it can be really powerful. It makes one look at the world in a fresh way.

I know. [*Pause*] I don't know what to say about that except that the world *is* a weird place. Although we all get used to it, it's a really weird place.

Songs are one place where our world can be re-examined. You've asked questions in your songs most people never deal with.

I guess even in a straight-ahead love song people can say things they would never say in normal conversation.

T Bone Burnett told us that he doesn't feel songwriters are being heard the way they used to. Do you agree?

I don't know. I'm still hearing stuff. I just picked up his record. There are a lot of songwriters I pick up who I get excited about, whether it's here or other countries or whatever. I'm still hearing stuff that's getting me off and that's really great writing. Not all of it is new. Some of it is stuff that I missed and went back to.

Which is a great thing about this art form, that the work is there for us any time we want to check it out. Although the industry tends to emphasize only new product.

Yeah, that's true. It would be a great shame if some stuff goes out of print. Which tends to happen. Maybe that's what T Bone Burnett was talking about, the emphasis on music as a commodity, as a disposable kind of thing. Which it kind of is. Which is kind of great about popular music, that it is disposable. But it also does have a lot of meaning.

Do you consider your own work to be disposable?

Sort of. I hope it has meaning. But it's basically also something that you can buy in stores and pop it in.

At the same time, I can hear *Remain in Light* today and it has the same power as it did when it first came out. It's not altered in any way by time.

[*Pause*] I am aware of my own past. My own stuff with Talking Heads. I don't dwell on it all the time. I don't want to repeat myself.

You said you realized at one point that you didn't need so many chords, that you could build a whole track on one chord. What triggered that understanding?

I don't know if it was one specific thing, but it might have been at that time, disco music was really hot and a lot of disco tracks were like that. Some of them would have real melodies in one section of the song, but the dance mix would take one vamp and stretch it out for five minutes. Which would be sometimes really great to listen to. And it made you realize that if there's a good groove you can throw a lot of stuff on top of that kind of bed. You're working from the bottom up instead of from the top down.

It's ironic to me that disco was an influence on you, because in the late seventies when Talking Heads emerged, your music was such a relief from the incessant disco music that was so popular then.

Yeah. Yeah, it got a bit tedious. It was weird how the whole idea of dancing kind of went out of favor for awhile. Maybe it was just the association. We went to the rock clubs and the discos and there were lots of innovative stuff happening in both places.

Of the first songs that you wrote with Talking Heads on *Talking Heads 77*, many of them, such as "Happy Day" and "Uh Oh, Love Comes To Town" had such a happy, fresh spirit. Do you remember what inspired those songs?

Yeah. "Happy Day" I was trying to write like an Al Green ballad. By the next record, everybody realized that we listened to Al Green. That was kind of my demented take on one of his ballads. It came out, of course, completely unrecognizable [*laughs*]. The other one, I don't know where it came from.

There was a sense on your early records that you could have gone in many different artistic directions, and that music was almost an arbitrary choice.

Almost. We kind of felt that we lucked into it. We felt like that it wasn't the only things in our lives that we could do. But that it was something we really loved to do, so we should at least give it a shot and see if anybody liked what we were doing. I think that was Chris' attitude; I think he expressed it in those terms.

So it was: Let's give it a shot, and if nobody likes it we'll find employment elsewhere. [*Laughs*] Once, whatever, twenty people liked it at CBGBs, that was enough. Everything else kind of fell away pretty quickly. We focused all our energies on it. I guess later on, after we became a little more secure, we managed to get back to some of our other interests. I know I did. Which, to me, always felt like it injected some kind of freshness into the songwriting. Whether it may just have been the break from it, you come at it added a new perspective that you've gotten from working in another area.

Is it true that your song "Heaven" from *Fear of Music* was inspired by a Neil Young song?

Yes. The chord changes and the melody. The lyric doesn't exactly sound like something he would write.

On that album, it seems as if you gave yourself an assignment to write on all these elemental topics. There's "Cities," "Paper," "Animals," "Air" and more.

After a few of the songs seemed to have one word titles, it became a kind of thing. Around that time we were getting into the third album syndrome, having to come up with all new material. And I remember one of the directions I took was that I did make lists of possible song subjects for future songs. Some of those may have been on that record, I don't know. Some of them probably never got written.

You'd start with a title?

More of an instruction: Kind of like a Yoko Ono thing: *Write a song about air.* That was it. That was the instruction. Well? What do I do now? [*Laughs*] It kind of left it wide open but it sounded great on paper.

Did you write these songs by yourself, away from the band?

Some of them. Maybe 75% of them, I'd written a good enough part of it, enough to come in and have something to play. And the band would flesh it out, change a few things, make some suggestions. Some of them came the other way. Maybe this was the first album in which the songs were coming out of jam sessions that the band would do. "Life During Wartime" was a two chord jam. "I Zimbra," of course, was something like that. There were a few songs like that where I wrote the songs later. But most of them were written in a slightly more conventional way.

When you write on your own, do you work first on words, and then on a musical idea?

I try anything. And some of them seem to have slightly different results. Sometimes I'd take a little tape recorder like this and just start singing words into it, one line at a time. If I liked whatever the emotional resonance of the way that particular phrase and those particular pitches, like if I like the syllables and words that that emphasizes, I try to figure out what notes those were and I end up with some pretty odd chord changes and some convoluted melodies. Because they weren't based on a chord pattern or a groove, they were just based on singing out those words.

Many members of the previous generation of songwriters have told me that they prefer to work on melodies that way, apart from an instrument, because it's not restricted by the chords.

Yeah. Recently I picked up a Burt Bacharach songbook because I always thought those were great melodies. I figured I'd learn how these songs were constructed. And I was thinking that they couldn't have written these based on chords. These were really weird chords to come up with unless you already had the melody.

Are you a writer who will work on songs on a daily basis, regardless of whether you're feeling inspired?

Yes. I still think you have to wait for the inspiration, but unless you're there, waiting at the bus stop, you ain't gonna get on the bus. If you're doing other things all day, a song ain't gonna tap you on the shoulder and go, *Pull the car over. I've got a song for you right now.* That can happen but I think it's pretty rare.

I find that you have to get into the mode and hope that something comes. It doesn't always.

How do you get in the mode?

Lately, I get in a room by myself. No telephone, no TV, not much to look at. I usually start by writing down random phrases. Maybe I'll start writing about a certain subject and there's a phrase that strikes me, so I'll spin off from that.

Sometimes I turn on the drum machine and program a groove that I like and play guitar along with it. I play chord changes and sing along with that, gibberish or maybe some words. Sometimes I'll record that onto a little 4-track cassette thing and try to improvise a melody onto that. It's usually pretty basic stuff. It's pretty low-tech, in other words.

Most great writing is low-tech, isn't it?

Maybe. *Remain in Light* really required a recording studio to be able to make all those tracks and create all that stuff. Other people have worked that way. Peter Gabriel and Robbie Robertson. Unless you've got your own studio, it's pretty expensive.

That's when I think you get songs that have a strong atmospheric quality. I don't mean that they're New-Agey sounding, but with an emphasis more on the texture than on the lyrics or the melodies or the chord changes. It seems that way to me.

It's nice that there's more than one way to skin a cat. And that you end up with a song either way.

At this point in time, do you lean in one direction more than the other?

At this point in time, I'm kind of buying that Burt Bacharach book! And some of the others, some of the old bossa novas as well. I think [Bacharach] must have listened to those.

I can school myself. Try to learn some new chords, some new changes. I can get to some more interesting melodies so I don't just keep coming up with the same changes and the same melodies. That's been keeping me excited. Is that what you meant?

Yes.

For a lot of people that might be old, but for me it's new and exciting.

You've expanded your musical vocabulary constantly throughout your career. You've never been content to stay with one style very long, while there are many songwriters who write in one style their whole life.

Yeah, and some people really write great songs that way. I don't want to put it down. It's kind of a blessing that way. To find your niche and be comfortable in there and just write within that thing. That's great if you can do that.

Do you get bored with styles quickly?

I guess, I guess. It's a curse, I guess.

Or maybe a blessing. It ensures that your work is always evolving and expanding.

Yeah, but often I wonder if I stayed at it a little while longer if maybe I'd get better at one thing or another. But it's all right. It kind of all mushes together eventually.

Your last two albums have been Brazilian. Will you continue in that direction?

I think I can take more. I'm a fan of so much stuff that I hear from so many different places. It might be Texas or L.A. or Santiago or Italy or wherever. When I go into a record store, I don't judge it on where it's from but if I like it, if it gets me off. And that's great. What am I saying? I'm sure it's all gonna fit. Whatever I hear becomes part of my vocabulary. Just like it always has. And it's not always a real conscious effort. Whatever you listen to, it becomes part of what you do. Sometimes it may be more conscious than other times. Sometimes I try to focus on one thing more than another. I think the

Latin American stuff I did on the *Rei Momo* record has been kind of fused into other things that I do. I'm sure that process is going to continue.

It means that now I have a wider variety of moods to grow on that I feel comfortable with. Instrumentation or whatever, all those kinds of things that are part of your aural universe.

You wrote a lot of Talking Heads songs, as you said, with the band. Do you miss that collaborative approach to writing songs?

At the moment I've been collaborating with arrangers a lot. Angel Fernandez has been very instrumental in doing a lot of the arranging of the songs. He's been writing middle sections of the songs that are maybe different from the verse or chorus that I write. It's a different kind of collaboration.

"Now I'm Your Mom" from the new album has that great transformation section with that whirlwind of woodwinds.

That was kind of a collaboration. He certainly wrote it. But I think I was kind of pushing him to do something. I remember saying to him, "Write something like if Philip Glass wrote me rengues. What would that sound like?" He came up with something I thought sounded like something I had never heard before.

It almost sounds like Klezmer music.

Yeah.

Do you recall where the idea for "Now I'm Your Mom" came from?

That one, we had cut the track. We had a melody, structure, everything, but I didn't have words. So it was improvising words to fit the existing melody. And that was some of the words that came out. I think the first verse. Or maybe it was the line, "I was your dad, now I'm your mom." Some kind of line like that triggered the whole thing, and the song spilled out. [*Laughs*] I figured I would finish this verse before I put it aside and try to write something more straight-ahead. So I wrote a completely different version. And sang them both for friends on guitar. And everybody said, "Well, the other one is good. But the one about the sex change is much more interesting." Everybody said, "The other one is a good song, it's a good song. But only you could have written that one about the sex change."

What was the other one about?

I think it was about escaped criminals. People on the run.

You're lucky to have good people to play your songs for. And that quality of writing a song only you could have written is something all songwriters want to do. To write something entirely unique to you.

Maybe it seems odd, but often I think you're writing something and you're trying to make it sound like some songs that you love by somebody else. You kind of emulate somebody else. And you go off the mark and come up with something that's really good, that's really you. But what you really wanted to do was to get one that sounded like something else. [*Laughs*] That's happened to me.

Dylan talked about writing songs in areas where you know no one else has been, which is something you've done. Do you like that feeling of getting in those areas?

Oh, that's great. Yeah, yeah. Because then it makes you feel that the songwriting tradition is open-ended, like they haven't all been written yet. There's still a few avenues to explore here.

You do feel that songwriting as an art form will continue to evolve, and that there are new places for it to go?

Yeah. It's something that in some ways is confined by what it is. It's really something for people to sing, whether it's the artist or somebody else. With the odd exception, most songs are just a few minutes long. Those kinds of things don't seem to change that much over the last few centuries. But there seems to be a fair amount of leeway within that. It still seems pretty fresh to work within those parameters.

In terms of content, can a song contain anything? Is there any subject that you've been unable to deal with in a song?

I haven't thought about this. I've never wanted to write a song about being on the road because I think there are too many songs about being on the road. There's some pretty good ones but they've been written.

I've tried to write songs about sex. I've tried to write sexy songs, songs about sex. I've touched on it but it's not one of my big themes.

"Little Creatures" deals with sex.

Yeah. That's one where I touched on it. I'm really happy with that.

I love the line, "I've seen sex and I think it's all right."

It's all right. [*Laughter*] But I've never written any of those songs where I talk about how great it is or how wonderful it feels, or any of that kind of stuff. Just kind of a human emotion. But it's just not my thing.

Your writing, like Randy Newman's, seems to distance yourself from the subject. It seems as if you'd rather write about a character or an observation of the world than about yourself.

Yeah. I've been thinking about that, too. I've been wondering if maybe I should try to bare myself more, write about myself more, see what comes out. That's something I thought I'd try.

I really admire the writing on the last couple of Lou Reed records and some other people's records as well, where you're not as aware of the songwriting so much as you're aware that this person is telling you something that he feels deeply about.

I may make a crack at it, but again, I'll probably be pretty wide of the mark; but maybe something will come out of it.

In many songs, like "Psycho Killer," you've made the odd slant of the narrator the point of the song—

Why do people like that song?

Why do they like it?

Yeah. Is it the chord changes? Or is it that it's kind of sick?

It's got a great combination of these psychotic lyrics with this happy melody. And on a purely aural level, the sound of these words with this tune is wonderful. When my nephew was only two, this was his favorite song, and of course he didn't understand the words. He called it the "Fa Fa Song" and responded to it purely musically. So it's one of those songs that can work on many levels.

[*Laughs*] Yeah. That's true. If the words and the music are both saying the same thing you feel like, hey, what's the point?

Are you surprised that people like that song?

Sort of. But, on the other hand, I think there are other songs that are more moving or more personal. So I can't figure it out.

Do you find that different musical keys have different meanings?

I think it's just however my voice reacts to it. Probably not surprisingly, when I first started writing songs, I didn't consider what key they were in. I didn't even think that you could move a song to a different key to make it more comfortable to sing. That didn't occur to me. Now I realize that if a note is too high, you can move the whole thing down a little bit. Or vice versa: if you want the thing to have a little more urgency, you can move it up.

It's probably a little late to learn this but it's something I learned in the last year or so [*laughs*].

At the same time, not having an awareness of any of those concepts can give you a real instinctual freshness.

Yeah. You just end up having to make it work somehow. With whatever resources you have at hand.

When I started writing songs, I always ended with an E chord no matter what key it was in. I thought that was how you had to end them.

[*Laughter*] Yes. Somehow we have to get back to that ending chord.

One of your most haunting lines is from "Houses in Motion" [from *Remain in Light*]. "She has closed her eyes / she has give up hope." I remember you saying you heard a woman say that, "I have give up hope," and there's something so touching and real about that weird grammar.

I remember that, again, it was influenced by the preaching tradition. Radio preachers. Recordings of church sermons that they put on the radio.

That grammar on "She has give up hope" combines the past tense and the present tense. So it almost says that the past is happening now. That's kind of what it does to your mind. It takes the past and shoves it up in your face. I might be stretching things but I think it does that a little bit.

Did you have an image in your mind for "Houses in Motion?" It's one of those phrases that can be seen in many ways.

I meant houses in a metaphorical sense. But I'm not even sure exactly what I mean. But I didn't mean a split-level or a mobile home heading down the highway or anything.

As a songwriter, I sometimes get superstitious about what allows good songs to come. Do you have any superstitions about songwriting?

[*Pause*] I do some little funny things. For a long time I've tried to write my lyrics on graph paper. Partly because the lines are smaller apart than on notebook paper, so I can often get a whole song's lyric on one sheet. Or at least a lot more ideas down because I write smaller. That's sort of a superstition.

Is that how you always do it?
I have for a long time. To the extent where I think I've got an idea for a song, and I'll look for some graph paper. Which is kind of stupid, because you can write on anything. [*Laughs*]

And if you don't find it, will you write on something else?
Oh yeah, I'll write on something else. But I'll think, damn, if I had some graph paper this would be much more organized. [*Laughs*]

Any other superstitions?
Things like that, like pencils. I like mechanical pencils. And if the lead is too thin or too thick, or too soft or too hard, it's like, *God, this is not working for me.* [*Laughs*]
It could be one of those things where [I'm looking for] any sort of excuse to get out of the room and go down to the stationery store. [*Laughs*]

Does exercise matter?
I exercise, but not when I'm on the road. I haven't noticed if it affects the writing.

How about eating?
I get drowsy when I eat. After dinner I get drowsy.

Do you eat meat?
Not often. I find that that makes me really drowsy. Unless I'm kind of drained, for some reason, I'll eat meat and it does give me some quick energy sometimes. But maybe that's a superstition, too.

Are you already thinking of songs for your next album?
I'm doing one song now that I haven't recorded that I wrote a few months ago.

Do you generally sit down and write all the songs for an album during one period of time?
Yeah. I think I'm always working out ideas but they don't coalesce into songs until I really sit down and work at that. Right now I'm really enjoying learning other people's songs. We do other people's songs on the road. We learn them out of songbooks or figure them out. I think that's probably some kind of unconscious preliminary process, preparatory process as well.

Do you think you'll continue to record with this group of musicians?
I have no idea. We only have another month and a half to go and at some point my mind is going to start being occupied with that: What sort of format do I want to work in?

Another one of your songs that goes into a new lyrical area is "Nothing But Flowers" [from Talking Heads' *Naked*]. I love the idea of being in an ideal future, surrounded by the beauty of nature, and feeling nostalgic for

the trappings of our modern times: the Dairy Queens, Burger Kings and 7-11s.

That was one of those things where I was talking again, improvising lyrics. I had the melody and was improvising lyrics into a little Walkman-like tape recorder. I was driving on a highway in Minnesota, outside Minneapolis. I was visiting or just hanging out, and I would just go out driving. I think it was summertime. I'd go out driving because it was a good way to free my mind and try to get some lyrical inspiration. I guess I was driving down some strip where all the Dairy Queens and all that stuff was. I think it was also the kind of song where once you had three lines, boom, that's it. All right. I get the point-of-view in about two or three lines of the chorus, and the rest of it kind of writes itself. It's like crosswords. You fill in the blanks almost.

Is that song true to you or a joke?
It's true. It's true. I remember the first time I came out west when I was an adult. I was hanging around with friends up around Sonoma and Napa, that area that's just *beautiful*, it's just beautiful. And after a couple of weeks I started getting really itchy. I wanted some trashy magazines to read. I wanted to hang out in the street or whatever. But there's nothing, just trees and flowers all around. [*Laughs*]

I was wondering if around the time of that album, Naked, if you were spending a lot of time in nature, because many of the songs, like that one and "Totally Nude" are about being immersed in the natural world.
That's right. That was more or less the same period I was writing orchestral stuff for *The Forest*—that film that never happened. And a lot of stuff had to do with that theme. Man and nature. Man versus nature. What's natural, what's not. Those kind of themes. A lot of that stuff was just on my mind and I guess naturally found itself into some songs as well.

One of your most magical songs is "And She Was" [from Talking Heads' Little Creatures], in which a woman levitates into the air set to this wonderful, simple melody.
The words to that were kicking around for a while. I tried to use them on a track for *Remain in Light*. I don't think that track was ever used for anything. Completely different melody. I think the words were slightly changed as well. And I think at some point when I was writing songs for *Little Creatures* I was going through old jottings, lyrics and stuff, and pulled those out and went, well, those are still good words. I started playing some chords and it came out pretty quick. Almost in a couple of days. It was almost too quick. I thought I'd put it aside because it came too fast, it might not be any good.

You mistrust it if it comes too easily?
Yeah.

Are your best songs the result of a lot of work?
No.

One of my favorite lines is from "Don't Worry About The Government": "I'll be working, working, but if you come over I'll put down what I'm doing, my friends are important." Which was such a friendly, warm sentiment in the context of the New Wave.

[*Laughs*] Yeah. Enough of this bad attitude. [*Laughs*] In a way it was maybe slightly conscious of going against the rock and roll pose in those kind of songs. Although they're true and they're honest. There is an awareness that, hey, this is not what the rock and roll attitude is supposed to be.

Do you have any thought about why we have music at all, and what the purpose of music is?

It can serve so many different functions. It can be therapeutic, it can be rabble-rousing, it can be a form of communication, telling news and what's going on. It can be something for dancing. It can be something for contemplation, meditation. It can be about a collective experience, about an individual experience. This is not all the same piece of music, obviously. Though one piece of music can do a few different things, it can't do all that. But music as an entity seems to do an awful lot of different things.

The difference between different kinds of music is sometimes so great. How can it all possibly be under the same umbrella and still be called music? It's almost like we need more words for it.

* * *

Tom Petty
Encino, California 1995
Encino, California 1996

He's crazy about Elvis. Standing on the deck of his L.A. home, looking out over a yard that has been deluged by about a century's worth of recent rain, Tom Petty is remembering back to childhood days in Florida, when he got to see Elvis in action. "My uncle did some work for the movies, so when Elvis came to film in Gainesville, I got to go," he says, peering into the past. "And I saw all these people just going crazy around him, all these girls screaming through the fence, handing him records to sign."

Since Tom had no records for Elvis to autograph, he immediately set about to remedy the situation. He sold his Wham-O sling-shot to a friend for her full collection of Presley 45s. "And she had *all* the good ones," he happily recalls. Although he never got a chance to go back for a signature, this closeness to the King forever changed his mind about what the future might hold. "I saw all those people going crazy, and then I heard this music. And I realized this is something I could do. And this could be a way for me and for my friends to get out, to get out of Gainesville for good. And it worked. "

These days Petty is the guy often on the other side of the fence as hysterical fans clamor and scream for his autograph. But for someone with nearly two decades of solid success under his belt, he takes it in quiet stride, continuing to revel in the process of writing songs and making records as he has for years. He's a songwriter whose work crosses over every demographic, especially after the enormous success of the undeniably appealing *Full Moon Fever*. He gets included with the older acts on VH-1 and the new ones on MTV, and persists in almost every radio format, whether classic rock, hit radio or album alternative. "I get a lot of letters from little children," he says with pride. "And I really like that, because little kids don't lie." Yet he avoids any commercial considerations when making his music, and doesn't talk of demographics. "I don't even like the word," he insists.

The following interviews took place a few weeks after the release of *Wildflowers*, a brilliantly eclectic album brimming with the beaming energy of pure creation. *Wildflowers* was the perfect title for this colorful collection of songs that emerged almost of their own accord, sparked by the gentle guidance of their creator. Real wildflowers don't grow just anywhere—they need a wild place to flourish freely, a place untrampled by the hordes, and unhindered by concrete and urban sprawl. Petty discovered this wild place within, and nurtured more than two dozen songs into existence for this album alone. [After honing down the album to an essential 15 songs, Petty used many of the others for his next album, songs for the movie *She's the One*.]

"I don't want to be one of those people who are miserable even when they're successful," he says. "That's not the way I want my life to go." He's one of the rare ones who has managed to find happiness in the heart of huge commercial success, and has done so by staying in touch with the thing he loves the most, the music.

This love of music has been a recurring theme in his life since he was a kid. Born on October 20, 1953, Petty started playing guitar at the age of 14, proudly mastering "Wooly Bully" by Sam the Sham. Mostly he was self taught. "I learned chords in the key of C," he says. "I learned C, C7, F and G. I got F right out of the way, because F is really tough. It will hang you up for a long time." Though he's got more insight into songwriting and record making than most, he's never taken an academic approach to music; from the start he rejected formal music education in favor of learning from friends, a pattern that continues to this day. "My mom paid for me to take a [guitar] lesson," he says, "but I could see that it was going nowhere. [The teacher] kept telling me to keep my thumb on the back of the neck, and I'd see these guys on TV and their hands were all over the guitar. Then I met this neighborhood kid who *really* helped me a lot. He'd come over and sit down and I'd learn things. It was fabulous. We had a great time."

Later in life, having achieved years of consistent success, he still learns from his friends. Attributing much of the easy-going greatness of his *Full Moon Fever* album to the contributions of Jeff Lynne, he says that their collaboration "had that happy feeling of a friend showing another friend some new chords." And when talking about his time as the youngest member of the Traveling Wilburys, joining Lynne and legends Bob Dylan, George Harrison and Roy Orbison, instead of concentrating on his own unique contributions to their music, Petty happily talks of soaking up all he could learn from the others—absorbing chords from Harrison, melodies from Orbison, and spontaneous brilliance from Dylan. In a field where most artists figure early on that they know everything, Tom Petty has had the wisdom to keep learning.

He started writing songs almost as soon as he could play the guitar. "My first song was called 'Baby, I'm Leaving,' or something like that," he recalls. "Which, looking back, was probably a blues. Although," he adds with a laugh, "I was hardly seasoned in the blues." Though songwriting was not a major priority among his friends in those days, Petty kept churning them out then as he does today. He played in bands from high school on, the first thrown together in a day to impress girls, which it did. Mostly they would perform the hits of the day, learning songs from records—a great education for any songwriter—with Tom mostly keeping his own songs to himself.

In Mudcrutch, his first real band, Petty was chosen to sing all Dylan and Byrds songs because of the obvious, though unintentional, vocal similarities. Never wanting to get identified as the guy who sings like Dylan, he nonetheless found himself professionally propelled in this direction. "I remember playing in a bar," he says, "and the club owner came back and said, 'You really ought to let that kid who sings the Dylan songs sing some more. Because those sound really good.' But I really wanted to sing like everybody at the time. I wanted to sing like John Lennon and I wanted to sing like Elvis."

The vocal similarities to Dylan and The Byrds continued to be prominent on his first albums with the Heartbreakers, first emerging in the midst of the "New Wave," 1976. Though often linked with many of the now-defunct New Wave bands, The Heartbreakers wisely followed Petty's heart, avoiding all trends to create an American music all their own. "I am profoundly American," he says with pride. Still, the influence of Springsteen has crept into Petty's music—as in the use of long, lyrical lines compacted into small phrases, a style that both artists simplified in later years. Careful not to rip off someone else's style, Petty purposely avoided listening to any music by the Boss while writing songs.

Today Petty exudes an almost Zen-like contentment, inspired but unburdened by the legacies of Dylan, Springsteen and even the King, Elvis Presley. Wearing blue jeans, a grey cardigan and fur-lined boots, he's in the music room of his home, drinking coffee, surrounded by guitars, Elvis memorabilia and other souvenirs of a musical life. On a big wooden desk is a gold crown adorned with giant faux-jewels. Asked if it had anything to do with his own desire to become king, he laughs and explains that a friend recently sent it to him. "But it doesn't fit," he quickly adds. "My head it too big for it. Which I think is somehow appropriate."

It seems like you've been on a songwriting roll for a long time, and that the new songs came easy.

Yes. They did. They did come out in an easy way, though they came out of a long period of time. Some of them appeared really naturally and quickly and some I had to wait on. But, truthfully, I wrote a lot more than I put on the album. Yeah. We did 25 that we finished records of and there were a few more that never got recorded. So I was in this constant state of composing, you might say. [*Laughs*] Or decomposing. For a year and a half. Almost two years, really. So some came really quick and some didn't. Some were really elusive for awhile.

When songs don't come easy, do you continue to work on them or do you put them aside to come back to them later?

Probably it depends on how intrigued I am by the bit I've got. If I know I *really* have got something, I'll stick with it and chase that thing down, you know? But if not, things can lay around for a long time.

Is it tough to reconnect with them after they have laid around for awhile?

Yes. I think it's preferable to finish them as fast as possible. It's just that it doesn't always work that way. Usually, unless it's an extremely strong segment or portion of a song, I'll just discard it and move onto something else. But if it's really strong, I'll keep coming back to it. But they're hard to come by. [*Laughs*]

Do you work on songs with your guitar, and work on music and words at the same time?

I try to, yeah. I work mostly with the guitar or piano. I've found, especially with this last album, that I really prefer getting the melody and music at the same time as hopefully a chunk of the words. I think this is better—mo' better—for me than trying to marry the two together at different times. I think I was always happiest with stuff that I wrote that came alive all in one try. But, you know, honestly, you do anything you can to make it work.

Is it unusual for something to arrive in one piece, with words and music together?

It's not unusual for most of it to arrive. For the whole song to arrive instantly is really strange. Really unusual. I don't think it's ever happened to me more than once or twice. It happened to me once on this album, the song "Wildflowers." I just took a deep breath and it came out. The whole song. Stream of consciousness: words, music, chords. Finished it. I mean, I just played it into a tape recorder and I played the whole song and I never played it again. I actually only spent three and a half minutes on that whole song. So I'd come back for days playing that tape, thinking there must be something wrong here because this just came too easy. And then I realized that there's probably nothing wrong at all. [*Laughs*]

Did that one come in the midst of writing the other songs or was that the first one for this album?

No, it was kind of in the middle. It really surprised me. And I was really nervous to play it for anybody. Because I thought maybe I'd stolen it. Maybe it came from somewhere else. I played it for Rick Rubin and he said, "Oh! I love this." So I figured I'd do it then, and we made the record.

It's such a nice, gentle opening for the album, as opposed to starting with a big rock single.

I really searched my soul a lot for what should open, and this always kept coming back as the opening song. Because it sort of sets the mood, I think. It's a long album and there's a lot of different stuff to come, but for some reason that song would only work first. Like I said, I had to cut ten songs out, and I really didn't want to cut that one out. But I didn't know where else to put it in the sequence except first. So I put it there.

Did you think of making it the title song later, after finishing the album?

No. After writing the song. I didn't have the title, obviously, until I had the song. And I thought it was a great title for the album. But it still didn't necessitate making it the first song.

Did you write "Wildflowers" with somebody in mind? It's directed to a person: "You belong among the wildflowers."

I don't know. It just appeared. Maybe in retrospect I can piece together who it's about. I just write these songs. And then I hope there's some sort of truth and some sort of timelessness to them. And if it feels like there is, then I feel, okay, that's a song. But it's very hard to get that, too. It's easy to say it. But it really takes a long time to get that. I kind of try to play until I go into a semi-subconscious space. And then things start arriving. And then you get so caught up in the process that you don't want to look much deeper at the time because it could really make the whole thing disintegrate. I feel that way. I don't want to look too far behind the curtain.

I'm just glad that they're arriving. And then suddenly, like a bolt of lightning later on, I see, oh, I know what *that* is about. I would never have written *that* if I had known what it was about. [*Much laughter*] Never would have wanted that revealed.

But you're careful not to question them while writing—

No, you mustn't. You've got to let them just arrive. [*Pause*] Yeah, you can't question what you're doing, because that could really get in the way of what's trying to come up.

Is it more of a sense of following it than leading it?

Or just letting it happen. On this album I didn't do any second drafts, either. Which is something I've always done. I've always sat and refined the thing after I've done it. But there's zero refinement [*laughs*] on this album. I just felt like I had to write whatever comes out—*then.*

How did you get to that trance state when songs begin to happen?

There are some days when you pick up the guitar and it's very friendly to you and it sounds very beautiful and you can just play C and it sounds great. Some days you pick the thing up and it's just not friendly. It's not ringing. It doesn't want to respond. That's kind of how I know, "Oooh, it's being friendly today!" [*Laughs*] "Oooh, I feel very musical and things are coming." But when it's not, I just close down.

I could *write* a song *now* if I had to. But I don't think it would necessarily be good. You've got to have some real, very real, inspiration. But to look for it too hard is ridiculous. If it feels like music, then probably some level of inspiration is working. Then you just start to play. Play "Walk Don't Run" for half an hour, or whatever has come into your mind, and from there you'll move off that into something. You'll find a couple changes, or a lyric that comes into your own mind.

It's a funny thing about songwriting, that you can work hard on a song for months, and then a really great one will pop up almost on its own, like

"Wildflowers," with hardly any work. So it's not an activity where work equals achievement.

Not really, no, because you're dealing in magic. It's the same with any other imaginative work—painting or filmmaking—it's this intangible thing that has got to happen. And to really seek it out too much might not be a good idea. Because, you know, it's very shy, too. [*Laughs*]

But once you've got it, you can work on songs and improve them. Once you've got the essence of them. You see if there's a better word, or a better change.

Is part of getting to that place building up a momentum in writing by doing it a lot, and getting on a roll?

I was certainly on a roll for a long time. I felt like I was on a roll for this album because I wrote so many songs. I must have written thirty songs. Which, for me, is unusual, to write that much in that period of time. But it doesn't always happen like that. Each experience is different. I tend to find that the ones I like best usually are the ones that appear pretty quickly. They just pop up, and maybe going through all that hell helped to make one suddenly pop up. Maybe it didn't, I don't know.

And, generally, the best ones came easily?

Most of them, I think, came easier than harder. There are exceptions, of course.

I've gotten the feeling with much of your recent work, starting with "Freefalling" and the *Full Moon Fever* album, that you were having a lot of fun writing and recording these songs.

Yeah, that was a tremendously fun record to write. The whole *Full Moon Fever* album in general was written extremely fast. The fastest one that I ever did. Though I had Jeff Lynne to help me a lot of the time. It's kind of like that exhilaration you get from new people being around, and I was suddenly in a whole different environment. I lived in a different house and I had a whole different circle of friends around, and I had been through this really long tour with Bob Dylan all around the world. I had just gotten off that and I felt really liberated.

I wasn't even thinking about writing an album or anything, it just started to happen. And I was twice as much in a hurry because I thought Jeff would have to go to England in nine days. So we literally wrote a song every other day, and we'd spend the next day to make the record, and then *right* back to writing the song. And we didn't take it seriously in the least. I think that was kind of the spirit of that album. It was an entertaining album.

And that was much different from how you approached writing other albums?

Well, they're all different. I had been in the same band a long time, and the band starts to influence the songs. You start to write for the band, because you know from doing previous records how they play and what they do well and what they don't. On *Full Moon Fever* I hit another place. And I was really relieved when it happened. And there are some people that don't like that place. There are some people who wish I'd never gone to that place. [*Laughs*] But I don't care, you know, because I think it was good work. [*Laughs*]

"Freefalling" seems like that perfect symbol for that kind of song, as if you allowed yourself to freely fall into it.

Very much so.

I recall you giving Jeff Lynne a lot of credit for helping you write that one.

Yeah. He sat beside me as I wrote that song. Actually, I think "Freefalling" was his line. I think it was the only thing he said.

It was a good thing.

Yeah. Thank-you very much, Jeff. [*Laughs*] I was just playing on a keyboard and Jeff was listening to this song. And I played that lick. And he said, "Whew, that's good." And I said, "Really?" And he said, "Yeah." And then, almost to make Jeff laugh, I ad-libbed the verses. And he's there with his tape-recorder recording it. And then I got to the chorus and I didn't know what to do. And I remember it very well. He said, [*imitating Lynne's low, British-accented voice*] "Freefalling." And I didn't even know what that meant, but I just sang it. And he said, "Go up! Go up! Go up an octave." So I went up an octave, and there it *was*. You know? It was done.

I think I wrote the last verse after he left. But the chords never change through the whole song. It's really just the same three chords, all the way through. And we went in to make the record the next day immediately at Mike Campbell's house. And Mike was saying, "When did you do this?" I did it yesterday. "Wow. Gee." He was actually kind of weirded out. Because we had just come back from being on the road, and had only been home for a few days, and songwriting wasn't high on the list of priorities, like "Let's dig in and make some records." We were going to relax for a little while. [*Laughs*]

I've always loved that line about "all the vampires in the valley move west down Ventura Boulevard." It really captures that kind of spooky feeling the valley gets at night.

I think I had once gone down Ventura Boulevard and I kept stopping at all those red lights. And it was night, and on the side of the road you'd see the post office or these different buildings. And there would be these teenagers in these big clothes. Kind of stepping back into the shadows. I don't know what they were doing there but I saw them as vampires. It was really late and there are these shadowy people standing off the street. And I think that's where that image came from. But it's hard to be sure. Because you write the song in three or four minutes. But in reflection I think that's probably where that image comes from.

You said that working with Jeff had that happy feeling of a friend showing a friend a new chord.

It was. He showed me a couple of chords and it opened up a whole new world for me. For me it was a revelation. Nobody had ever showed me a diminished chord. [*Laughs*]

It's the great thing about guitar. As long as I've been banging on it, I can still find something I didn't know. That fascinates me. I never knew that. Well,

shut my mouth. So through that whole Wilburys experience I really kept my eyes open. And memorized [*laughs*] how they did a lot of things. Because there you had a lot of writers and they all had their own little chord tricks. And I tried to learn as many of them as I could.

Was Dylan the biggest influence?

It was really all of them. They were all really good in their own way at what they did. George Harrison has an amazing bank of chords in his mind. He really knows a lot about playing the guitar and writing songs, and I learned a lot from him. Bob, of course, is just miles beyond all of us. But you sit and try to learn with him. It was a really valuable experience for me.

I was wondering if that easy approach to writing was inspired by Dylan. He seems to have generated a lot of that kind of spirit in the approach to writing.

Well, it's tough with Bob because he's been such a profound influence on me. Since I was a teenager, it's mainly been awe that I feel for him. I almost try not to be influenced by Bob because I'm so influenced by him I try to al-most stay away from anything that sounds like Bob. Then when you can be-come friends and work together for all those years, you know that it's still rubbing off on you.

I did really enjoy the opportunity to work with him. He's just so damn transcendental. He's just the absolute depth. That's what he really is. And it becomes really apparent [*laughs*] when you're working with him. Damn, he's good, you know? He's *really good.*

He certainly never carried himself that way or presented himself like that. If anything, he's really one of the boys. But he's so good, you know. He'd take the simplest thing and it would become such a marvelous thing. I really wish I had film of some of that. Because with the Wilburys, it was more like an ex-perimental band, where you didn't show up with anything. There were no songs when you showed up. You simply showed up. And then *everyone* sat down to-gether. And *had* to knock out a song. So, you know, some times different peo-ple would take the lead and then the others would follow along.

I remember, we did one song, called "If You Belonged to Me," it was on the second album, we were all *there*, and we were all working with Bob, but really he wrote the song. I think I got a few lines in that. But you would con-tribute a line, and then he'd take the line and say, "Oh, that's good," and em-bellish on it like you *would not believe!* And I'd feel really proud, like, "Wow, I'm really glad that I helped him get to that place." Because I never would have gotten there. I really admire him a lot. He's a really terrific writer.

We spoke about song openings before, and one that is very strong is "Crawling Back to You": "Waiting by the side of the road / For day to break so we could go / Down into Los Angeles / With dirty hands and worn-out knees."

Yeah. Well, I saw the "worn-out knees" having a double meaning of crawl-ing and the way you see these people with no knees in their jeans anymore. The same with "dirty hands"—it can be a matter of conscience, or maybe you were just changing a tire. [*Laughter*]

There was another verse I took out because it was too long. It was a reflection on this trip I took a long time ago to Birmingham, Alabama, with Mudcrutch. The first gig we went to fell through because we were wearing tennis shoes, and we got fired before we even played a note. So we went out on the street and we just started going into bars and asking to sit in. So that we could get a gig. And we finally landed this gig at this place called the Crazy Horse, which had topless girls. It was this really wild trip. Part of the song was reflecting on that trip. I kind of moved it to Los Angeles. [*Laughs*] Later on.

It's also such a nice lead-in to the verse that starts, "I'm so tired of being tired, sure as nighttime follows day / Most things I worry about / never happen anyway . . ."

[*Pause*] I was very pleased when that line appeared. [*Laughs*]

Do you remember that happening?

I remember that line. I was very pleased with that line. That's when I realized that it was a song. It's often like that. We're going on and on but where are we going? And suddenly, that's where we're going. And all of a sudden, it all makes sense.

It's a great feeling to have written a song. Still, to this day, I get excited and it just lifts my mood immensely. It's hard work, sometimes, it's really hard, just to have one that feels great.

Yeah. I was very happy when that line came up. That was luck. Or divine intervention or something. It's just sometimes that you get to the end of a verse, and *pow*, there's that line. It's a good feeling.

You wrote "You Wreck Me" with Mike Campbell?

Yeah. That's mostly Mike's contribution.

He came up that with chord pattern and gave it to you?

Yeah. Well, he actually gave it to Mick Jagger. [*Laughter*] He never even played it for me. And I guess Mick couldn't come up with anything. And Rick [*Rubin*] remembered it and asked him to play it for me. So when he played it for me I took the tape home and learned the lick, and wrote the song to it.

So he had just the guitar part?

No, he really had the whole idea, the whole chord structure and everything.

But no melody or words?

No. And it just sounded kind of like a jam, you know. I don't know. That was another one that was done pretty fast. And I really liked that one. You see, I thought it sounded very much like an old Heartbreakers record. So I thought it would be interesting to have a throwback suddenly, where you go back in time. A nostalgic one, almost.

Did the title emerge immediately?

No. It took me forever to get the title. That was one where I had the whole melody sketched out and most of the words, but I couldn't figure out that title for a long time. I was singing "You rock me," but I knew that wasn't going to fly. I was using it as a dummy line to get to the next one. And then the next day it hit me. Because I didn't want to change the phrasing. I could change "rock" to "wreck" and this whole picture emerged. It's amazing to me how *one word* can *completely* change the entire thing. It's the hardest thing. Because if you've got one word wrong, you've got to be so patient. And I've learned this from experience, that one word can mean so much. It can change the entire thing. It can really lift the whole trip and elevate it if you're patient enough to get that, that one little word or key line. Very important.

And it's quite a difference from the vibe of "You rock me."
Yes. But I was smart enough to just go ahead and sing "You rock me" because I *felt* it. I felt the same emotion, really, and I felt the same melody and the same timbre in the voice. So I'm glad that I was smart enough not to just quit.

Does that kind of experience lead you to believe that the song is already there, and that you need to uncover it—
I had to find it, yeah. It's almost like it's there and I just have to keep digging until it reveals itself.

With your indulgence, I'd like to name some of your songs to see what response you might have to them, starting with one of your most powerful songs, "Southern Accents."
I started with the title. I thought at the time I was going to do an album based on southern themes and southern music. I wrote it at the piano. Very late at night, about four or five in the morning. I still think it's probably one of my best two or three things that I ever wrote. I thought it was very personal, so that was one where it just took me over. [*Laughs*] I don't know *what* happened there. I do have a vague memory of being extremely glad when I hit the bridge. I actually woke up my wife and made her listen to this song.

"Refugee."
Mostly Mike [Campbell] had the whole track down, the whole chord progression. It's one of the first things that we actually wrote together. It took minutes. Literally, just a few minutes. I remember walking around the room, singing it, just circling the room. The words came very fast, and there are only two verses. And that was it. Finished.

"Learning to Fly."
That was inspired by the Gulf War. I remember that line about the rocks melting and the sea burning being directly inspired by seeing this whole thing on TV. I think that was the jumping off point. It became something a little more substantial than that but that is how it started.

"Breakdown."
I wrote it on a break from recording at the Shelter Studio in Hollywood. I think we took a break because we had recorded everything we had and I made up "Breakdown." I wrote it on the piano. I still have that piano. I bought it. [*Laughs*]
Many years later, it's sitting in my living room.
I wrote it very quickly. It's a very short song. I played it to them, and they really dug it, and we made the record.

I think we got the drumbeat from a Beatles record, "All I Got to Do." We just varied it. That was the idea, to have that kind of broken rhythm on the highhat.

The next night I wrote "The Wild One, Forever" on the same piano at the same circumstance, where we took a break. Because we were so naive I thought, "Great, I'll just write another one." So the band played cards and in an hour I wrote a new song.

The next night, though, it didn't work. [*Laughs*] I realized, oh, I'm not going to be able to do that every night.

"Two Gunslingers."
Oh, I love that one. Thanks for noticing that one.

It's one of my favorites. The whole idea of a gunslinger questioning his existence is great, saying, "I'm taking control of my life."
It really cracks me up, still, that song. [*Laughs*] I was tremendously pleased with that one. That was one of those rare moments when I actually got to say something and entertain the people at the same time.

Did it come together quickly?
Yeah, it did, in a couple of hours. Written during the Gulf War. Almost all of that album [*Learning to Fly*] was written as the war was going on. Which I think, whether I liked it or not, influenced the writing.

"Mary Jane's Last Dance."
That was one I wrote during the *Full Moon Fever* sessions. I wrote all but the chorus. I just had the loop going around and around and really had most of the words and everything. And I played that tape for Rick [Rubin] and he liked it a lot and suggested I write a chorus. So I tried to finish it up while I was making *Wildflowers*, and there were maybe five years between the writing of the verses and the chorus.

Is Mary Jane a marijuana reference?
I don't think I was writing about pot. I think it was just a girl's name. I can't imagine that I'd write a song about pot necessarily. I don't think there's enough there to write about. [*Laughs*]

"The Waiting."
I remember writing that one very well. That was a hard one. Went on for weeks. I got the chorus right away. And I had that guitar riff, that really good lick. Couldn't get anything else. [*Softly*] I had a really hard time. And I *knew* it was good, and it just went on endlessly. It was one of those where I really worked on it until I was too tired to go any longer. And I'd get right up and start again and spend the whole day to the point where other people in the house would complain. "You've been playing that lick for hours." Very hard.

It came in piece by piece. First the chorus, which was pretty easy. And the verses took a long time, and the bridge even longer. I knew, when I had gotten that chorus, that I was *definitely* onto something very good. And I just couldn't, *for the life of me*, figure out where to go with it. Eventually I did.

It's one of those special songs that people can easily adapt to their own lives. I think of that line frequently: "The waiting is the hardest part."

It's one that has really survived over the years because it's so adaptable to so many situations. I even think of that line from time to time. Because I really don't like waiting. I'm peculiar in that I'm on time, most of the time. I'm very punctual.

Roger [McGuinn] swears to me that he told me that line. And maybe he did, but I'm not sure that's where I got it from. I remember getting it from something I read, that Janis Joplin said, "I love being onstage, it's just the waiting I hate."

"American Girl."

I think the original inspiration was Bo Diddley. If you listen to the beat, it's a Bo Diddley beat. And it's forever being equated with the Byrds. Even Roger thought it was the Byrds. But we honestly didn't think about the Byrds at the time. But it *must* have been influenced by the Byrds in some way, but I didn't realize it at the time. There's also no 12-string on that record. It's just two six-strings playing off of each other.

"You Got Lucky."

That came from a riff that Mike had. It was almost a throwaway. Almost just tossed off. And the next thing we know, it's the single.

"Don't Come Around Here No More."

I was always very partial to that one. Odd song. That was an idea that Dave Stewart had, this tom-tom thing going. I think it was my idea to take it double-time when it got out a little ways. We really went nuts. We worked on that record for a long time. We wrote it very quickly. We were doing stuff like grabbing the tape and pulling it off the reel. There's one part, if you listen where the piano does this *r-r-r-v-v* thing. And we did that by literally grabbing the tape and *yanking* if off the reel.

Did the two of you write the song to that beat?

Yeah, I think he had a drum box playing the beat, that tom-tom thing. And then [on the record] we put Stan Lynch playing real drums along with it. Yeah, we wrote it with that little beat playing again and again. That was actually the day we met. We met and we wrote that song.

Did you write "Stop Dragging My Heart Around" specifically as a duet to do with Stevie Nicks?

No. I wrote it with Mike. And cut the track for *Hard Promises.* And that would be an interesting tape to hear, because it's the same track. But with me singing it, it sounds more like a blues. It doesn't sound like a pop song at all. She wanted a song really bad for a couple years. She kept coming around and saying, "Please, I'm trying to do a solo album, I need a song." And I don't know if I really wanted to. I kind of wanted just to write my own songs, and I kept politely declining.

She got pretty adamant about it, you know, and I didn't really know Stevie well, but she would come around and visit some times. I thought she seemed kind of strange. And I kind of liked Stevie, I still do. In there is a wonderful person [*laughs*]. And we would sit and sing with an acoustic, and *boy*, you know, she can really sing. So I said, "Okay, I'll write you a song." And I wrote her this song called "Insider." And I *really* liked that song. I wrote it for her with her in mind.

So she comes and I played her the song. She says, "I love it. Can you put it down for me?" So I put the track down and I sang a vocal for the track. And she immediately wanted to sing along. I had pictured it that she would take my voice off of it. She didn't want to take the time to do that. She wanted to sing right then. So they put a mike up and she sang a harmony to what I was doing.

I listened to it the next day and I really liked the edge. She came to the session the next night and I said, "You know, Stevie, I don't really want to give you this song. If you don't mind, I'd like to keep this song." It was really a low-rent thing to do, when you think about it, because I'd written it for her and it really probably should have been her song. But I really wanted to keep it. [*Laughs*]

I said, "Would it really sound totally lame if I said I wanted to keep this one and write you another?" She said, "No, not at all. I completely understand, if it's something that's personal for you and you want to keep it. But I do want you to give me something else." So I said, "Let me play you what I have." I had a few songs that I didn't think I was going to use for the album, and "Stop Dragging My Heart Around" was one of them. I played it and she said, "That. I like that." And I thought, "A blues? It's the last thing I would ever dreamt that you'd go for. " And she said, "That's what I want. Really I like this *better*. I'm looking for a rock and roll kind of thing." So I said, "Great. Knock yourself out." [*Laughs*]

And so I gave her that tape, and they took it. And they made it the duet—Jimmy Iovine and Stevie. Because my vocal was already on it. And so she filled it up with all this harmony and girl singers and made it much more of a pop song. And the next thing I know, it's a big hit record. It probably wouldn't have seen the light of day if she hadn't done it.

You wrote "Jammin' Me" with Dylan. Was that similar to working with him in the Wilburys or was that different?

It was different in that it was just me and Bob just sitting there with a piece of paper trying to come up with stuff.

Again, it has that joyful feeling, as if the writing was a lot of fun.

Yeah, we were having fun. And Bob always seems to me that he writes a lot of verses. Long after you think he's done he's still writing. And he's still do-ing more verses [*laughs*] and then he gets convinced "I don't like this" and then something better shows up in that ninth or tenth verse than what you had before. And you go, "*Oh.*"

"Face in the Crowd."

I wrote it one evening with Jeff Lynne. Just strumming our guitars. He had a musical idea for that one and I worked on the words. Because it's very hard for me to sing other people's lyrics. Jeff is a melody guy. And he's very good at that. He would do a lot of editing. One good thing about him and the whole Wilburys experience is that I became completely unashamed. I would spout out anything. And that was really good for me. Because it was literally four or five people sitting there going, "Handle with care." [*Laughs*] "No. Yes." Spout out whatever I thought and it would immediately go to committee and it's knocked out or it's approved. And then that line would lead to something else. But that's a different way from how I usually work. But it really loosened me up. I'm not inhibited by trying anything lyrically just as you wouldn't be inhibited to try anything on the guitar. You just want to keep letting your mind go and seeing what falls out. [*Laughs*]

When you're making an album, do you give any thought to what will be the single, or try to write a hit single?

I think I may have thought about that in the late seventies when we first started making records, and we needed a hit single to sell the record. "Don't Do Me Like That" I thought would be a hit single. But I never have got caught up too much in it since then because you just can't anticipate a hit record, or a hit song. I think a hit song is a really good song. I think it's very simple. You can break it down to that simple of a thing. It may need some other aspects. But usually a really, really good song is going to be a hit on some kind of level. And that's what I go for. To write a good song. If it moves me and has some kind of feeling of timelessness to it, then you do it.

But I think that's the difference between your songs, and many others, in that a lot of the others don't have that sense of timelessness, and then don't stand up to the test of time. I listened to "Breakdown" today and it sounds as good as ever.

We were lucky in that we never got into any particular trend or fad. You try to avoid it as much as you can. And I've just been fortunate that way. Because I didn't know that starting out. [*Laughs*] I didn't have a master plan. I was just going day to day. I'm still very pleased when I hear my old records. You hear them on the radio and they really don't sound too bad. They really don't. So that's nice. I feel very blessed with that. I'm really very blessed.

* * *

Richard Thompson
New York, New York 1994

If Bob Dylan was born in Britain, raised on Celtic folk music rather than the songs of Woody Guthrie, he might have become a lot like Richard Thompson. Like Dylan, Thompson is a genius of the English language, a poet inspired by the indigenous music of his native land as well as by the electricity of rock and roll. What Dylan did was called folk-rock. And Thompson's contribution—first made as a founding member of Fairport Convention—was simply called British folk-rock. But it's more than just a merging of musical forms. It's the union of poetry and the popular song.

He's too good. It's what some "industry insiders" say about him. His songs are too literate, too brilliant, and too eclectic to ever connect with the mass public in a mass way. But some things aren't meant for the masses. And those who know better, to quote Marilyn Monroe, know better. They know that every year or so, Richard Thompson releases another brilliant collection of beautifully crafted, finely detailed, heartfelt songs. The masterpiece at hand during the time of our interview was *Mirror Blue*. It's an album that does everything albums should do: lyrically it's about love, romance, fire, desire, joy, disappointment, humor, memory, crime, marriage, divorce, birth, death and more. Musically it incorporates folk music—both American and Celtic—blues, rock, reggae, jazz and funk, and fuses them all with Thompson's visceral singing and fluidly expressive guitar playing.

And if this weren't already more than enough, the icing on this musical cake is the happily inventive production Thompson concocts with Mitchell Froom (Los Lobos, Latin Playboys, Elvis Costello) that rises consistently to the creative level of the songs. When Thompson connects rock verses with ancient Celtic-sounding riffs—almost a signature of his work—Froom embraces the opportunity to flesh out these diversions with an acoustic smorgasbord of medieval sounding instruments: shawms, concertina, fiddles, flutes, pipes and more. As Thompson searches for fresh avenues of expression within a song, he and Froom share the urge to discover alternatives to routine methods of record production.

He's in New York City today to publicize the new album and to perform on the David Letterman show. On a gray Manhattan afternoon prior to the show, he takes time out in his art-deco hotel room to divulge some of his songwriting secrets. But he doesn't offer them up readily. When asked how he stays open to inspiration for songs, he laughs, and with thick British-accented derision, says, "I'm not telling you in any case. I don't see why I should help other songwriters. There's far too much competition anyway. So I curse them all."

Persistence wins out, fortunately, and eventually he reluctantly succumbs, sharing thoughts on the process that led to the writing of songs from his time with Fairport Convention (1969 to 1971) through his duo days with former wife Linda Thompson (from 1974 to 1982) and ultimately to his work as a solo artist.

He's an exception among songwriters in that he's also a great instrumentalist. Like Mark Knopfler, Lindsey Buckingham and few others, Thompson's a true guitar innovator who speaks volumes with the controlled fury of his solos, adding extra layers of depth and dimension to his work. He's a player who sings through the instrument, creating a sound both raucous and tender but always intimately human. It's a vibe many artists have attempted to capture for their own records; Bonnie Raitt, Crowded House, Suzanne Vega, Shawn Colvin, Robert Plant and many more have all succeeded in getting Thompson's unique solos on their tracks.

But his greatest gift might be his way with words. He weaves formal, rich lines of lyrics with elaborate meters and rhyme schemes that challenge and celebrate the conventions of songwriting. Like Dylan, Thompson fuses the energy of poetry—the sense of "endless possibilities" that he discusses in the following interview—with a solid respect for the purity of song craft, employing feminine rhymes and interlocking rhyme patterns few writers ever even attempt. On the page, one of his verses might appear haphazard, with the rhymes falling in funny places. But once you hear it sung you see that it's structured ingeniously, so that the very play of rhymes and rhythm adds to the emotional momentum of the song. His songs are all structured on an inner skeleton of essential singability, so that the words and music lock together with an undeniable inevitability, giving them the timeless essence of old folk songs.

The facts: He was born in London on April 3, 1949. John is his middle name, black is his favorite color and Leonard Cohen's "Famous Blue Raincoat" is his favorite song. Asked by an especially inquisitive reporter what animal he would choose to be, had he the choice, he answered, characteristically, "Ring-tailed lemur."

When asked about the meaning of "Mirror Blue," the newest album's title, he quoted Tennyson's poem "The Lady of Shalott":

"And sometimes thro' the mirror blue / The knights come riding two and two / She hath no loyal knight and true / The Lady of Shalott."

"The lady is someone who is cursed," he explains. "She can only see reality in reflection. If she looks directly at the world, she dies. The same could be said of music. Not that you die, but that it's a reflection of reality."

You've written so many great songs over the years that it seems like you must always be writing. True?

I probably sort of fret away at it all the time. When I'm on the road I can't, so maybe I just take notes. I jot things down. And even when I'm at home, homelife can sometimes be too chaotic to have a routine. So I probably jot there as well and when I have time to get to an office and do a regular shift of writing, then I can get things finished. So I'm probably nibbling away at it all the time.

When you're taking notes, are those musical ideas as well as lyrical ones?

Yes, I write down musical ideas as well.

Do you approach songs both musically and lyrically?

Yes, yes. I think an idea is an idea. I don't have any particular thought about which should come first. Hopefully, if you keep open-minded about it then it comes all ways. Because I think the possibilities are endless. You have to be open to things coming to you.

Does songwriting get any easier over the years?

Yes, it gets easier. I think you can refine what you do. And I think you can get more consistent. And you can get better. You can definitely write better songs that have a better shape and a better feeling. You can go through phases thinking what I write's too simple, or what I write's too complicated. You know—am I really communicating what I want to say? There are different things that you go through.

What you can't have is a checklist, where you say: Spontaneity, check, Depth of Meaning, check. [*Laughs*] It really changes because human beings go through different stages of life and different emotions. So what might be a good song or a good approach might not hold up a year or five years later. You kind of evolve in and out of different things and hopefully you generally improve. Sometimes you go around in circles.

You said that you question if you are communicating in your songs. Does this questioning come while writing or does it occur after you have gone with the flow of an idea, and looked back at it afterwards?

Perhaps while you're writing. You are spontaneous. I think most of us song-writers write for enjoyment, write for fun. I think that's the main thing. You write to be musical. So the point of the exercise is probably enjoyment. And music. And then perhaps, if you look at it quite well, I think there might be something more in the song, or if I tweak the song a certain bit it will mean something a little more, or it will fit my moral outlook or something. So I think it's something that you do instinctively.

It's in you and it has to come out, and you might self-critique yourself or censor yourself—later. And say, "Well, is this really true to my feelings?" or "This isn't a true reflection of human nature," or "This isn't truly what I think about this . . ."

Do you do a lot of rewriting and editing?

Well, I do. I suppose some songs just seem to stay the way they're written. And those songs are good songs. Some songs get written very quickly. Some of the songs get written in fifteen minutes.

Are those good ones, the ones that come that quickly?

I think so. A good song or a really, really bad one. And I've also definitely tweaked songs for years. There are songs that I haven't recorded that I'll take a few years to get right. Where I'll go back and rewrite them a lot.

Do you rewrite the music as well as the words?

Sometimes. Or sometimes certain musical components don't fit, like a bridge that doesn't fit and you take a bridge from another song that does fit. So you can swap components of songs.

And then for recorded stuff I've written extra verses or gone back or changed lyrics that could be fifteen or twenty years old. And I think that's also fair enough because sometimes you write something that's junk. And sometimes you find words or phrases or ideas that, in maturity, seem out of balance.

I noticed that even on the new album some of the lines have changed from the way the lyrics are printed to how you sang them.

I think some of that has to do with singability. Sometimes you write something and then you can't actually sing it, so you change it. And with some of the stuff on the record, it hadn't been sung in. Maybe only half of the record had been performed live. And performing live is a good place to soften up the rough edges.

One of the great things about your songs is that singability. The lines are devised rhythmically that they roll in very pleasing ways, such as "Beeswing."

Good. I'm never sure of that. [*Laughs*]

Wasn't "Beeswing" the name of your publishing company years before you wrote this song?

It was. I wrote another song called "Beeswing" that was never published. Actually because it wasn't that good of a song. I always liked the name. It's the name of a little town near where I grew up. I just liked the sound of the name.

It's a beautiful song, a long narrative all wrapped around that delicate image.

Too long for rock and roll. It's a song that some people feel is two verses too long. But if you can hook people with a story, then it can work. In performance there are ways you can get people's attention.

Did you write the story in that order?

No. I don't remember, actually. I wrote a lot of versions of it. That song is a good example of something that took about three years to finish.

Is that unusual for you?
To work that long, yes. I do tend to put things away and then come back to them. You keep getting frustrated.

Many songwriters, such as John Lennon, have said that writing songs for them is almost a form of channeling, as if they are bringing in the song from another source. Others say that they are completely and consciously in control of the writing of the song.
I think Lennon was right. [*Laughs*] Yeah. I think you do have some control. Sometimes it seems to be conscious, and sometimes unconscious. Sometimes it's intuitive, sometimes it's intellectual. You go back and forth between the two.

Sometimes you definitely just step outside of the process and say, "That rhymes with that," or "that's three lines in, I need another line to make this verse." So you're making conscious decisions about the structure and about the theme. Then there's another side of you, or there's the itch, the bit that writes itself, that's somewhat independent.

It is hard to analyze. Perhaps it shouldn't be analyzed.

Do you remember how old you were when you wrote your first song?
Sixteen. I was trying to write stuff like Dylan.

He was your main influence at that time?
I suppose. Dylan, Phil Ochs.

The form and structure and mood of "Beeswing" reminds me of Dylan's "Tangled Up In Blue."
Yeah. A heck of a song. [*Laughs*] You've just named one of the top-ten songs of the twentieth century right there.

I agree. Did you play guitar for a few years before you began writing?
Yeah, I started guitar when I was about ten.

Acoustic guitar?
Acoustic and electric.

Who were your musical heroes at that age?
I suppose people like Buddy Holly. And The Shadows. Scottie Moore. And Les Paul. Django Reinhardt.

In your own music there is a mixture of rock with traditional folk music. Was there much folk music in your home growing up?
Yes, there was. Particularly dance music played with traditional instruments.

Most great songwriters, it seems, are not also great instrumentalists. Of course, there are exceptions such as Hendrix or Mark Knopfler—and you certainly are one—but most seem to have spent much more time working on songs than working on an instrument. Did you put in as much time playing guitar as working on songs?
Yeah, I do. I mean, I practice.

And that was always the case?

Yeah. I probably used to think of myself more as a guitar player. Especially in the beginning, that was the description of me. Yes, among guitar players it's more unusual but look at pianists, there are a lot of great pianists who are accomplished writers. People like Mose Allison.

Do you generally play in standard tuning on guitar?

I hardly ever play in standard tuning. I play usually in modal tunings: modal D, modal G, modal E.

Do you use capos often?

Yes, a lot of the time. When I'm playing solos, a lot of the time.

Do you use a pick when you're playing lead?

I play with a pick and fingers.

When you write, do you write on electric or acoustic?

I write on acoustic or nothing. I write without an instrument. About 50% of the time I use no instrument. I hear the whole thing in my head and then I can go back and work out the nuts and bolts.

Do you find that writing without an instrument encourages freer melodies?

Yeah. You're much less of a slave to habit. Because inevitably you fall into habit every time you reach for your guitar. It can really free you up.

Are there signature chord changes on guitar that you frequently go to?

God, I hope not. There probably are, I mean, everybody has them, but I'd hate to think what they are.

Do you write to titles, and collect titles?

Yes, I love titles. I'm obsessive about titles. I love to find a good title. You know, a title can paint a picture.

"I Can't Wake Up to Save My Life" is quite an evocative title. Is that one in which the title was first?

No. [*Laughs*] I'm not sure where it came from but it wasn't first.

Another great title—and song—is "Dead Man's Handle."

That came because I'm a real train fan. Since when I was a kid I knew about the dead man's handle. I don't know in America if cigarette cards were much of a big thing. I used to collect cigarette cards. I had a set of railway safety cards. Quite a bizarre idea. They were an amazing educational tool because you would look at them and read them, whether it was football or sports cars or something, you'd look at each one and read it. So the dead man's handle came from that.

Did your song "Wall of Death" come from an actual carnival ride?

Yes. It was two different things, really. In the 1970s it was a motorcycle daredevil stunt. Where there was a bowl-shaped area around which you would ride a motorcycle horizontally. You'd build up to speed around the bottom and then the faster you got, you'd keep going and actually be horizontal. A friend of mine claims to have done that.

That's one thing. But it's also kind of a generic name for a certain kind of fairground ride. Where I grew up in London, there's a very old fair, the Hampshire fair which had been running consecutively for hundreds of years. And they have a Wall Of Death. It's one of those things like a gyro thing where the floor drops away and you're stuck to the wall by centrifugal force.

It's interesting on that album [*Shoot Out the Lights*] that you printed the lyrics in all different patterns, in circles and vertical columns.

I got a lot of flak for that, actually. People thought I was trying to be e.e. cummings. Actually, I was trying to slow down the process of reading the lyric.

It does force the reader to look at it more carefully.

Yeah. Because I hate the fact that if you wanted to, you could take out the lyrics and read them first. Before you hear the music even. And that's something that always seemed like putting the cart before the horse.

Because as a songwriter you don't want your lyrics read separate from the music?

Exactly. So I asked the record company if it would be possible just to send people the lyrics later. Put them in a postcard or something. Or could we stick these lyrics in the next record? They felt that wasn't practical. So I thought if we could print the lyrics geometrically and move them around a bit, then they'll be harder to read without hearing the music. Because the meter of the lines won't make sense of their own. So that's really what I was trying to do.

An interesting title, which isn't used at all in the song, is "King of Bohemia."

Yeah. It's a little misleading and maybe a little obscure. I thought about that song and there wasn't an obvious title from the lyric. And I thought, this song is never going to be Top Ten, it's never going to be a hit. So I think I can indulge my own whim and call it whatever I damn well please. It's named after a pub, actually. Near my house. Which is the setting for the song. But I realized it's a little obscure. And I had people try to read strange things into the song. There was one journalist who thought the song was about Dylan. They thought that Dylan was the King of Bohemia. They had this whole theory which I thought was quite good. I was almost encouraged to take it up.

Sometimes those kind of interpretations can be the best.

Yes, that's quite true.

That song is in E flat, an unusual key for guitar. Why did you choose that key?

It's the easiest key to sing it in, actually. It doesn't fall easily on guitar. It's a capo thing.

Do you sometimes write songs and them transpose them into keys that are best for singing?

Yeah, a bit. And also, I'll perform it anywhere from E to D. Depending on the concert. If I'm warmed up I'll do it in E. If it's the morning and I'm on a radio show, I might do it in D.

Can you tell me about "Shane and Dixie"?

Yeah, it's another song where I've written a lot of verses that I didn't use. Actually, I've got a version now, different from the one on the record, which I think is better. It's a little different. It's not so dark. Which I kind of prefer.

Does the new version have the verse about Shane's grave getting vandalized?
No. In the new version, nobody actually dies. It goes in a whole different direction.

So, like Dylan, you continue to rewrite your songs even after they've been recorded?
Not often. I was just kind of noodling around with it and it just happened.

When you used to make records with your ex-wife, Linda, did you write some of those songs specifically for her to sing or did you make that decision afterwards?
Sometimes I would just write them and we would divide the spoils later. Other times I would actually try to write from a woman's viewpoint. And that was quite difficult, but it was rewarding. And if I failed, I could always just sing it myself. And sometimes we would swap songs. Songs I'd write songs for Linda that she wouldn't end up singing and songs I wrote for myself she *would* end up singing. It was actually quite loose.

Do you recall writing "Civilization"?
Yeah I do. I suppose I was thinking that I wanted to write something like the Rolling Stones. Even though it came out like something quite different. I'm not totally happy with that one. It's the arrangement I'd like to change. And the lyrics, actually. It just seems a little rushed. It was rushed.

Do you mean in terms of tempo?
No. Just how fast we recorded it.

Are you generally critical of your past work, or do you enjoy it?
Some songs seems to last and other really don't. They don't have much of a shelf-life. And tend to get discarded. Some songs it is possible to revise and find new things in them. And some songs it's possible to tweak and change lyrics around.

Do you find in your writing that your ideas are always flowing, or are there periods when you run dry?
Yeah, I think it goes through stages. I find that sometimes I can work away at things for a long time and nothing really very good comes out of it. I find that the more work I do, the more days I string together and then weeks I string together and then months, the better it gets. I get more productive with it. If I'm able to have that kind of time I find that I don't have any writing blocks or anything. It just steams away. It's hard to keep up.

When you have that kind of time for work, do you go to it routinely, at the same time every day?
Absolutely, yes. I'll have a minimum amount of time every day I'll give myself to work and then if it's going well, I'll just keep on.

When writing, do you tape yourself?
I don't use tape at all. I don't trust tape.

Why is that?

Because I tend to lose it. If I get something really great, sometimes it's hard to get back to that feeling. It's the same thing with demos. I don't like to do demos. Just because I like the first recording to be the last recording. So whatever excitement you get out of a thing the first time, it becomes the final thing. What's the sense of doing the demo and getting that adrenaline rush you get the first time if it's only the demo?

That's interesting. You've recorded many albums now with Mitchell Froom producing. When you start a project with him, do you sit down and play him the songs on acoustic guitar?

Yeah.

And then do you try to cut live tracks or do you record piece by piece?

I've never recorded anything piece by piece. I've always recorded as much as possible live. With Mitchell, that's always been the approach. To try and get everything at once. And to record as fast as possible. We usually only take a couple of takes on any particular track. Two takes, three takes.

Your tracks always have the energy of a live performance. Are you singing and playing guitar live as well?

Yes. Sometimes we'll fix the vocals later. But I'm actually out there doing it.

You do the guitar solos live?

Yes.

You said recording fast is part of the approach?

The approach is to have fun. In the recording process. And not make it a job or a chore. Or a perfect thing. We'll leave perfection to God. So we try to keep that spark and really have a good time doing it. I think there are people who can spend a long time making records and do it bit by bit and make it sound exciting and spontaneous. And that's a kind of gift. And I really don't have that.

At the same time, it seems many have lost the ability to record live and capture a live energy in the studio.

Sometimes, yeah. Sure. But I think there is a trend to reverting to a live approach. People are realizing that your career is not always on the line if you make a few mistakes.

Are you going to continue to work with Mitchell Froom?

Well, I'd hate to say yes and I'd hate to say no! [*Laughs*] I love working with Mitchell because it's so exciting. Excitement in the music is a very important ingredient. And I think in terms of a team, it works very well. Because we don't agree on everything, but there is a mutual respect. We have creative disagreements and although we might be pulling in different directions, generally it's in a creative way. So I would always want to work with Mitchell. And I'm a great admirer of the other records he's done.

Do you like having your work on CDs as opposed to vinyl LPs?

I suppose I have affection for vinyl and probably I think vinyl sounds better, to tell you the truth. But for consistency, you can't beat CDs. I got tired of complaints about the vinyl quality on my stuff. And I got sick of the stuff I bought jumping, skipping, scratching. So it's a quality thing.

Do you remember writing "Did She Jump or Was She Pushed?"

Yes, I do. I think that song started with a guitar riff. Which I think I came up while I was in the studio just noodling around. I discovered that riff and started from there.

How about "Jenny"?

That's one that started with the first line. I think that's another good place to start, with the first line of a song. If you can nail that, you're in good shape.

And so many of your songs start with great lines. "For the Sake of Mary," for example, starts with, "For the sake of Mary, I kicked the reds / Junked the juice, drink coffee instead . . ." It launches you right into the song.

Well, there isn't a lot of time in a song to get stuff across so generally you have to jump in with both feet.

Also, "Easy There, Steady Now," has a powerful opening: "Jackknife with a precious load / Spills its guts all over the road / Excuse me, I had to smile / Lost my grip there too for a while . . ."

[*Laughs*] That's funny. That was a song that started with lyrics. It was just lyrics on a page. And I wrote it down very swiftly while I was trying to write something else. I hadn't even really realized that I had written it and I found it later. And I thought it was interesting.

There's a great bass part on that one.

That kind of evolved in the studio, the bass guitar arrangement evolved into what it is by doing it live, and if we didn't have that opportunity, I don't think that would have happened.

Another wonderful song is "The Way That It Shows." It has such an aching melody.

I'm glad that it worked. [*Laughs*]

Usually in songs, the tension is in the verse and the chorus is a release. But in that one it's reversed and the musical tension is in the chorus.

Yeah. [*Pause*] I wasn't really conscious of that. I know it changes tempo and it holds tension. But I wasn't really aware of the mechanics of it. Unless I think about it. The chords in the chorus cycle. And the way it cycles, it doesn't ever really resolve. It's the kind of chord cycle where, in a sense, you can keep building and you can keep solos rising. And the fact that there's a keychange also helps to keep the tension. It moves a fourth down.

That ending is so explosive, with the swirling organ part.

Yeah. It's a real handy sequence to play guitar over. The possibilities are really great. It's a really great sequence.

Do you have a favorite song of your own?

I find if I perform a favorite song it ceases being a favorite song. So it goes in cycles.

Do you have many songs you haven't recorded or even finished?

If I do, chances are I'll plunder those songs for spare parts. So if you have a good bridge somewhere that is in a song that otherwise is not particularly distinguished, you might remember that and use that for something else. I'm sure there are many songs made of bits and pieces. And many songs that are unfinished as well. But there's a reason that they don't get recorded, usually.

And do you have new songs already since making this album?

Oh, yeah. That was recorded almost a year ago. I've got some songs for what I would think of as the next two or three records. Yeah, I've definitely got more songs.

* * *

Bruce Cockburn
West Hollywood, California 1995

He talks fast. Unlike other thoughtful songwriters who pause often and speak slowly to collect their thoughts, Bruce Cockburn's thoughts are already thoroughly collected. Verbally bounding into the interview before a first question was formally asked, he could have easily filled the hour on his own—as the following will attest—with no pressing need for a series of questions. He succeeded in squeezing more recollections, reflections and information into sixty minutes than most people relate in a week, speaking in precise, comprehensive paragraphs, quite ideal for print yet uncommon in conversation. And he's much the same way with his songs—condensing as much complex emotion and depth into lyrics and music as these delicate elements can hold.

For many years he wrote poetry and music and never thought about putting the two together. His poems were abstract, influenced by Beat poetry, Dylan Thomas and T. S. Eliot. His music was instrumental, inspired by Coltrane, Miles Davis, Ornette Coleman and Charles Lloyd. He studied composition at music school with the intention of being a composer. But the thought of writing lyrics to match his music didn't occur to him for years.

"I hadn't quite figured out that you could take the poetry that I was fond of and put that sensibility with music," he said in the late purple afternoon of Hollywood, in a hotel room overlooking the city at sunset. "I hadn't quite figured that out."

Though he was inspired by great songs, he gave little thought to their origins. "Nobody knew who wrote the songs then," he explained. "And nobody cared. They were just there. It wasn't until the Beatles came along and John Lennon and Bob Dylan, that I remember being struck by the fact that you could write a good song. That you could have lyrics that say something."

It's been a long and winding musical path Cockburn has taken since his childhood in Canada. Long before he ever wrote his first song, he was eager to absorb every kind of music he could find, moving hungrily from one to the next. "I was listening to Mississippi John Hurt and Big Bill Broonzy and those blues guys. I started out taking guitar lessons thinking I was going to play rock and roll, and then I got introduced to country swing—Les Paul and Chet Atkins and stuff like that—then I got heavily into jazz and I thought I was going to be a jazz player. Then I got into folk music and heard country blues for the first time. And then I went to music school to study jazz but I was playing in a jug band at the time."

Attending the Berklee School of Music in Boston to study jazz and composition, when he wasn't in class, he was soaking in the sounds around him. "The Cambridge folk scene was still really intense then and there was all kinds of fantastic jazz coming through town, Roland Kirk and Coltrane, I saw all those guys. And that Chico Hamilton band. It was a fantastic period of fermentation in life for me. The jazz people were especially influenced by Arabic music, so when you walked up and down the alleys around the school you would hear all these people practicing and listening to stuff coming out of their windows. 24 hours a day there was something going on."

After leaving Berklee in 1965, he wrote his first song, "It's Not You Who Is Leaving Because Baby, I'm Heaving You Out." He'd heard Dylan and thought, "Maybe I could do that."

He returned to Ottawa and formed a rock band called The Children with some old friends. "We were convinced that we were going to be the next Beatles. England had had its day and the States had had their day and now it was going to be Canada's turn! Of course, it didn't quite work that way."

What did work out is that Cockburn learned how to write songs. After the first few, which were essentially imitations, he realized that there was a lot to be done with the form. He wrote a lot of songs and performed them in a succession of bands, and eventually realized, towards the end of the sixties, that the songs he liked best were the ones he could perform on his own. So he went solo, and started gigging at coffeehouses and folk festivals. In 1970 he released the first of some 22 albums.

He's written songs about the spirit and songs about the earth. One of his most memorable and moving albums is *Stealing Fire* in which he took on the subject of war, specifically the civil war within Nicaragua. For this album he took a journalistic approach to songwriting, traveling to Nicaragua and presenting the real images and actions of his travels as if recorded in a diary, capturing the true intensity and immediacy of Nicaragua, 1983. His most famous song, "If I Had a Rocket Launcher," came from this album, and remains to this day one of the most forceful anti-war songs ever written, a statement of pure rage rarely achieved in song: "How many kids they've murdered, only God can say / If I had a rocket launcher, I'd make somebody pay . . ."

Cockburn feels mixed about his Nicaraguan songs, appreciating the accomplishment but disliking the sad, temporal quality of the lyrics, the sense of something lost. It might be what has led him to dedicate himself in more recent albums to his own inner landscapes—focussing more on journeys of the spirit than of the earth.

His newest album at the time of our talk, *Dart to the Heart*, is a song cycle approaching the subject of love from diverse angles. He'd been quoted as saying that he didn't intend to write about love for this record, but when that path became apparent to him, he followed it. So I began by asking him about that path. Speaking quickly and with a happy intensity, he started answering my question before I'd asked it. And I did my best to keep up with him.

BRUCE COCKBURN: Saying I followed that path was an attempt at putting things in convenient terms. Because people ask you what your album is about. How do you answer what your album is about? At least in my case it's a difficult thing to do. So it's necessary to try to condense the truth into some phrase.

I don't approach an album with a concept in mind. The songs are written over a random period. It might be a short period or a long period. It depends on circumstance and many different factors. So when I describe the album as an album that's about love it's because the word love occurs in almost all the songs. And more than average for me are what people would actually think of as love songs.

After the fact, when I was looking at the body of material that was going to constitute the album, it became apparent that these facts were true. And it was, in fact, an album more or less much about love. [*Laughs*] But it's about love from many points of view. A song like "Scanning These Crowds," for instance, is in a sense about love but it's also kind of a call for armed revolution in Canada [*laughs*] or at least insurrection. It's a cry of frustration with the status quo for a return of the revolutionary spirit that's crept up every now and then in Canadian history that generally we don't think of as our national makeup.

You said that you don't approach an album with a concept in mind, but do you approach a song with a concept in mind? With that song, did you decide beforehand that you wanted to deal with that theme or did that happen after the song began to flow?

I almost never say I want to write a song about anything in particular. Almost the only exception to that which immediately comes to mind is "If a Tree Falls" where I actually remember hearing a radio program on the subject of the destruction of the South Asian rainforest. The particular information and the way it was coming at me triggered something and I thought, I have to make a song out of this.

But most of the time if I get that kind of sense, it's just barely on the edges of consciousness. There's a lurking intent back in the back of my mind somewhere. But it's not a deliberate plan to sit down and write a song about a given

subject. The imagery starts to come or the motivation starts to well up and
that produces an image or a verse or some statement of something that can be
built upon. And if the energy is really intense at that moment, it will be built
upon right away. And the whole song will start to come out in a few minutes.
At least a set of lyrics which can then be edited down into a song. Other times
it takes a lot longer. You'll get an idea and the idea will have to sit on the page
of the notebook for weeks, maybe, before I think of something to go with it.

You mean lyrical ideas?

Lyrical ideas, yes. I'm speaking of lyrics now. Because I don't generally
write anything until I've got lyrics. The music is almost always designed to
carry the lyrics so the lyrics have to be there first.

I thought that you wrote sometimes to a guitar riff or pattern.

I don't write lyrics to that. I may have a guitar thing in mind that will sit
around for a long time waiting for a suitable set of lyrics. But in the case of the
instrumental pieces, that's obviously a different thing because there's no lyric
element there. So those things develop in a different kind of way.

**And when you think of those, it's usually clear that it should stay an
instrumental?**

Yeah, it's usually intended that way from the start. I'll discover some little
thing when I'm fooling around, warming up in the dressing room or sitting at
home playing. It will be something that suggests that it could be part of a larger
piece. It's actually a lot like what happens when I'm trying to find music to
carry a set of lyrics. Except that the parameters are different. With a guitar
piece you can do anything you want. With a piece that has to be at the service
of lyrics, there's obviously the restriction that the lyrics themselves impose on
the music that has to be taken note of.

When working on music to carry a lyric, do you always work on guitar?

Almost always. Occasionally it'll be another instrument and if it is another instrument, that's what will be on the record. Charango on the song "Bone in My
Ear" for instance. And occasionally other instruments. But generally it's guitar.

In those cases, do you generally play chords to generate melodic ideas?

Usually. Or just a rhythm, one chord with a drone effect. It's hard to gen-
eralize about how the guitar affects things. It could be any one of a number of
things. It might be a little lick that triggers something else. Or it might be a
rhythm or it might be a set of chords. I'm looking at the lyrics and I'm going
"Hmmm . . ." I just start fiddling with it. And sometimes it comes out very
quickly, and sometimes it takes a long time. Sometimes a song goes through
several kinds of music before it settles in one place.

**Do you mean that you finish the entire lyric before thinking at all of
the music?**

Usually. Actually, the truest way to put it would be that there's a potentially finished set of lyrics. Once you start putting the music to it, the music
may then demand that you add a word here or there to make it scan or fit the
melody. But the lyrics usually are in a state where they could be left that way.

And you're able to write in meter and with rhyme without any music in mind?

That's the most common thing but there are songs like "If a Tree Falls" where it's just talking. It's free verse, there is no rhyme scheme and it doesn't have to scan. I have a few songs like that. I went through a period in the late eighties in which I tried to expand the songform as much as I could, to push it this way and that. I had some songs with hardly any words and some songs with a lot of words and hardly any music. Now I seem to have gone away from that and I'm writing in a more traditional form.

You said at one point that you wanted to write more singable melodies.

That started with the last album, actually, *Nothing But a Burning Light*, and I definitely had that intention then. I don't know why, it just seemed time to do that. And that trend seems to be continuing on.

Did you feel that your earlier songs didn't have singable melodies?

A lot of them don't. At least not to me. There are bits of pieces of things you can sing along to. And some of the songs do have that. But through the eighties there were a lot of songs where there is a kind of droning effect in the lyrics too. Something where the melody is not the main thing. It's rhythm and words. Like "You Pay Your Money and You Take Your Chance." If you try to whistle it, there's not much to do. That depended, to a great extent, on an instrumental performance to make it work. A song like that doesn't sound very good when I play it by myself. Because there isn't much melody and it really needs some other melodic element provided by the other instruments. The little counter melodies that the other instruments play are in there for that reason. It would be kind of dry without them.

I guess the idea with the more recent songs was to stay away from that kind of thing and make them structurally simple. So that people sitting around could sing them at parties, if they wanted to. I mean, I've had the experience of an audience singing along with "If I Had a Rocket Launcher." But it's not the obvious thing. I'd like to make songs that people who aren't musicians could actually sit and sing.

There's many really nice melodies on the new album. Especially "All the Ways I Want You." That one keeps occurring to me. It's always interesting, after listening to an album, which songs keep coming back.

Which ones haunt you to distraction? [*Laughs*] Very interesting. It was a fun album to make. Because there are two ways you can approach a song in a musical performance. The performance can be designed to enhance the song, or the song can be a vehicle for another kind of performance. Like in jazz, for example, where you can play anything you want and the song is just an excuse to be there playing. And there's a common literature to play with each other even if you don't know each other and you haven't rehearsed.

And the other way is a way that T Bone Burnett is particularly gifted at doing, and that's putting the song right in the middle. Which is one of the reasons that I wanted to involve him with both of these albums as producer. Putting the song right in the middle of things and having everything else there to enrich the basic song. Which is something I hadn't really understood until relatively recently. I don't like resorting to cliches of breaking things down into decades, because I've never trusted that. But it's true, in hindsight anyway, looking at my old stuff, it looks like it does break down that way. And through the eighties my own music was characterized by something more like the jazz approach where I had a lot of great players working with me. And they did a lot of playing in the songs. And that provided some really interesting and intense moments in terms of performance, but it wasn't necessarily the best way to get the song across to people.

I discovered when I did a solo tour at the end of the eighties, that this was true. When I went out onstage by myself, after all that time of not doing that, suddenly the song was just there, bare naked, in front of everybody. And it had a different kind of intensity all its own that I actually really liked. And continue to like. So I've kind of made a point of keeping things that way without resorting to the solo context to do it. So the albums have been done with that in mind. And the shows are performed with that in mind. It still allows for jamming and for points where things can get really out of hand musically if we want to. But not while the lyrics are happening. And not while the song melody is there.

It's true, in T Bone's productions, that the focus is not on the track but on the song.

Exactly. That's his thing. Working with him is a real instructive thing for me. Because he's very conscious of that and understands how to make that work. So I've learned a lot about that from him.

Did you feel that with earlier songs, such as "Rocket Launcher," that the track overshadowed the song?

I don't think that track did, no. I think that track worked well with the song. There are lots of cases where it worked just fine. But there are other cases where it didn't work as well and where there was too much playing.

It's not like revisionism, exactly. It's not like I would take back anything we did before. It's just growth and a realization that we can improve on that. By simplifying things and keeping the song essential.

How do you and T Bone approach producing a song? Would you play him a song on guitar and discuss it?

Yeah. Or, in the case of this album, he had a demo tape of the songs that I made, just voice and guitar. Because we didn't have a chance to get together much before we started to work on it. He gets to hear the songs and we talk about them, talk about where we want them to go, he'll start talking about who is a good player to fit this direction, and where is a good situation to work in that will allow us to pursue this direction. Then we discuss that and arrive at a conclusion.

"Burden of the Angel/Beast" from the new album has an incredible guitar solo.

It was so much fun to play that. We had a great band. Jerry Scheff on bass, Mickey Curry on drums, Richard Bell on organ. We cut it all pretty much live. We did some overdubs but most of it was straight off the floor.

Many songwriters have said that they feel songs come through them from another source. Does it feel that way to you?

Yeah. Certainly the feeling that something's coming through. In the initial process. Not in the revising that might go on. And certainly in performing too. You want yourself as well out of the way as you can to be a vehicle.

Is there anything that enables you to do that?

I used to think drugs did. Actually, what you don't want is to be stuck in a particular habit or mode. And periodically I find that I have to do something to kick me out of my particular set of habits at the time. And usually it's travel that does that for me. The exposure to new things and new ideas and new people. Sometimes dangerous things, sometimes not. But newness, anyway. Newness can do that. Following the same set of circumstances for too long, I can feel static and need a jolt of something from somewhere.

I think drugs do the same thing for some people. Probably for everybody for a short period. But if they then become a habit, then of course you've defeated the purpose. I wouldn't want to go around promoting the use of drugs. But I'm also not afraid of it. The important thing is to keep your mind active and open. That's the simplest way to put it is the openness. That's part and parcel of having something come through you.

After writing songs for all these years, has your approach to songwriting changed in any way?

Yeah. I mean, it's not so much a conscious thing but I know it's different now than when I started. I'm a lot more particular about what I write than when I started. The first few years that I was seriously writing songs for myself to sing, I kind of wrote whatever came out and left it at that. And if it didn't happen right then and there, it didn't happen at all.

Over the years I started feeling like this could be worked upon a little bit and more and more of an editorial process went into it after the fact and now there's quite a lot of that. I want to get things exactly as I want them and shape them. Particularly the lyrics. I mean, the music too but the whole process is different with the music. For me, anyway, it is. I know from working with various other people that some people will hear music the way that I hear lyrics. With that kind of particularity. But I don't, really. I'm less critical, perhaps, of the music than the lyrics.

Does that editing of the lyrics happen before you bring music to it?

It's both. Sometimes the music requires that kind of editing. Sometimes I won't even think of it until much later on, after singing the song for a while.

But there is a long period in which you work only on words?

It may be long or it may be only about twenty minutes. Depending on the nature of the song and the particular energy of the moment, how undistracted I am and things like that.

Are the ones that come quickly often the best ones?

Yes, I would say that tends to be true. The best ones in hindsight. I like all of them when I first write them. And then some of them die within a matter of weeks. And most of them persist and get recorded. It's hard to be objective about that. I end up disliking songs sometimes just because I've sung them too much. Or because I don't agree with what they said anymore. That happens occasionally.

Does anything affect those periods when songs come easily?
I'm sure something does but I don't know what it is. Blood-sugar level [*laughs*] or something like that.

Do you have any kind of everyday routine for writing?
No. I did that in 1970 for a few months. And that was the only time. And it didn't produce anymore of those that I could keep than just waiting for them to come. Which is what I tend to do. You go through dry-spells and then the juice starts flowing and all of a sudden these songs come out. Sometimes you get three or four songs in a very short time. And then wait a few weeks before there are any more and sometimes even months. I went through one period of a year and a half. All of 1989 and the back half of 1988 were totally dry. As far as songwriting. And I actually kind of quit the whole thing at the end of 1989. I figured that even I'm not going to write any more songs, or I'd better change my way of living and see if I do write more songs. So I kind of put myself on sabbatical. And within a matter of days of actually having done that, songs started popping up. And that's all of what is on *Nothing But A Burning Light*.

Were you worried about writing during that dry spell?
Yeah, I was, actually. Because it was so long. I had gone through other dry spells of a few months. And usually after a certain time I'll start to feel real antsy and think I'm never going to write again. And start to feel real frustrated. And as soon as I feel like that, I know I'm going to start writing soon. But in this case, I was feeling like that for a year [*laughs*] and nothing came. So I started thinking I'd better be looking for another line of work. But I didn't know because that was right at the end of five years of real intense work and travel. I was exhausted and burned-out, and I thought that might be the problem, so I just decided to quit everything and see what came out. And the songs started coming immediately. So I had a year where I didn't do anything but write songs, and I had a great time, and then we started working on *Nothing But A Burning Light* and we were back into it again.

When you are writing, do you enjoy the process?
Yeah, I do. When I'm writing—it can be on the tour bus or the year I described when I don't have anything else to do but that. Usually it isn't that free. I'm in a hotel room or in my rehearsal room at home. But when the actual writing is going on, it's a rush, yeah. You're so focused and all this energy is flowing through you. It's the creative thing, I guess. It's like somebody painting.

Do you write on acoustic guitar?
It depends. Half and half. Whatever you hear the song played on on the record is what I wrote it on.

It seems most people don't write on electric guitars.
I think that's part of the issue of whether I'm playing chords or not on the guitar. It might be just a rhythm. It might be like a fuzzy wall of noise. Which

guitar I'm playing definitely affects which direction the music takes. So to that extent it's a deliberate thing. I may decide to write an electric thing. Or the lyrics will demand it. Like "Scanning These Crowds." To me, it's just obviously an electric song, a rocky song, just from the tone of the lyrics.

Do you work in standard tuning on guitar?

It varies. Most of the time I'm in standard tuning but I use a lot of drop-D (tuning the low E down to a D) and occasionally I'll drop other strings. There's several songs with the G string dropped to F#. I just stumbled on that one day and it comes up every now and then. I haven't written a song with that in a while but the last one was a song called "Understanding Nothing." Actually there's two on that album, *Big Circumstance*. The other is "Don't Feel Your Touch." You get a nice ringy thing with that tuning.

I have a skepticism about relying on open tunings because most of the people I hear using open tunings a lot use the same fingerings from tuning to tuning and so you end up with a certain sameness in the music even though the tunings themselves are different and the keys are different. The patterns are the same so it's a little predictable. And I don't want to subject myself to that—I have enough problems. So I try to keep the tunings just a little different, with just little alterations here and there. With the exception of an open-C tuning that I use for a lot of stuff. Almost all of it is sort of spiritual in nature. On the new album, "Sunrise on the Mississippi" is in that tuning.

I noticed when you were writing that you're left-handed. But you play guitar right-handed?

Yes. I do lots of stuff righty. I became more ambidextrous in the last few years. When I started taking guitar lessons the teacher said, "You're left-handed, do you want to play left-handed?" It looked to me like the left hand is going to do most of the work anyway, so it seemed like the normal way would be the proper way. And it worked okay. I know other left-handed people who can't put any rhythm in their right hand so they have to turn [the guitar] around. I learned it that way because it seemed like the right way to do it. In the end, it all comes down to work.

Do you tape yourself while working on songs?

Not really, no. I've done it from time to time but I don't really bother. It usually seems like too much of a hassle. I'd rather just play the thing over and over until it gets fixed in my mind.

When you traveled to Nicaragua, did you do so with the intention of writing songs about it?

No. I always go everywhere thinking maybe I'll get a song out of it. But I don't go intending to particularly. Or looking for the song in what I'm seeing. A good analogy would be the photographer who takes photos all the time and spends all their time looking at their camera. So they come away with a lot of nice pictures but they don't understand what's in any of them. And the song-writing thing is similar that way.

I've got a lot of good songs out of travel. It's those intense emotional moments that produce songs. Where your feelings are liberated with some contact with something. "Nicaragua," "If I Had a Rocket Launcher," "Dust & Diesel," those songs came out of my notebook from notes I took at the time and they're very photographic. I wrote down what I was looking at and made it into a song. Or my own feelings, in the case of "Rocket Launcher."

In those songs—especially "Nicaragua," which is a real masterpiece, there's a kind of journalistic writing that is very powerful and which few songwriters have used. They include the writer in an interesting way, like the lines about the old women in the town laundry.

It's a kind of documentary songwriting. I think of it as cinematic, it's like putting cinematic images in a sequence with music. Only instead of being visual images, they're verbal images. You get a shot of this and a shot of that, and the sum of that makes a whole song. Even though the verses might not be directly related to each other, you get many scenes like a movie and together it makes a plot.

Dylan will do that in songs, jumping from scene to scene.
He's got a lot of songs like that, that's true.

"Nicaragua" was a song in which you wrote the lyrics first and then set it to music?
Very much so. If I looked at the notebook it was written in, I could tell you right away if it all came at once. I think it came about from bits and pieces. Scenes that I did write down in a book while they were happening. Like the women in the laundry.

When you're doing that kind of travel, you don't write everyday. The opportunity is not there. But sooner or later you're bound to be sitting somewhere waiting for something to happen and that's when the writing comes out. There may be things in your mind from the day before that you didn't get to write down, or it may be what's right around you at that moment and you start documenting. In that case, you don't really know whether those are going to become songs or not. You just don't want to lose the image. With that song it was probably a case of going though the notes and saying, "Here's an image, here's an image."

With "Rocket Launcher" it wasn't like that. It was instantaneous. I wrote that in quite a short time. The lyrics. The music didn't happen for quite a long time.

It's interesting to have those two songs, "Rocket Launcher" and "Nicaragua" follow each other on the album because they're both about the same situation, but they are such different songs.
Yeah. The situation is a human situation with all of the facets that human situations have. The media, in their various guises, will try to paint things in black and white terms all the time. But, really, we all know life isn't like that. It was important for me, especially with that issue, to make sure that what I produce could cover as much of it as I could grasp.

The song "Nicaragua" has such an uplifting and beautiful chorus: "In the flash of this moment, you're the best of what we are, Nicaragua."
Yeah, and it felt like that. It's weird to sing it and I haven't sung it for a long time. Because I don't think that that's still true. It is for some people.

What I was writing about at that moment was something I discovered about the human spirit at that time. Most of the time most of us live in a gray zone where we have our peaks and valleys but most of it is not extreme. In terms of our own spiritual state and in terms of moral transcendence. But every now and then the situation that we're confronted with requires more of us and produces more from us. And it seemed to me that somewhere in the world at any given moment, that spirit is just burning like mad. And at that moment, Nicaragua was where it was. I didn't expect that it would always be there and it would be naive to think that it would be anywhere for more than a very short period. Because humans are what we are. But that's what I was getting at.

It wasn't to say that Nicaragua was better than every place else on earth. Because obviously that isn't true. Nicaragua is a beautiful country. Or it would be a beautiful country if various parties would let it be. But in that moment there was an *incredible* feeling of forward movement and of hope in the face of adversity, that was free of desperation even though people were living in pretty desperate conditions. It was just a magical thing to be next to.

That comes across. And it seems like a tough thing to have translated into a song, but you definitely pulled it off.

Well, I'm glad. It's weird to sing it now because it's a memory now. I don't know, it feels funny. People ask for that song all the time but I've been hesitant to do it because it's sort of heartbreaking to sing it. And sing it in the present tense but have the fact be in the past.

Now it's a piece of history.

Yeah. But it wasn't meant to be that. And it's regrettable that it is that. So it's not attractive to want to wallow in that.

That will always happen when you write such a topical, specific song.

Yeah. I think that's true. It's there for the moment. And it is a piece of history, whatever anybody thinks of the song or whatever they think of me, that was a true statement of how I felt and how I saw that place at that time. And it's true as anybody's. Yeah. I think that's true. It's there for the moment. And it is a piece of history, whatever anybody thinks of the song or whatever they think of me, that was a true statement of how I felt and how I saw that place at that time. And it's true as anybody's photographs of the place or anybody's journalistic reports of it.

"Rocket Launcher" is an unusual statement of pure rage, something we don't hear much in songs.

No we don't and I think that's probably a good thing. I don't think it would be good to have a fashion of songs like that. But in a way, the punk movement was full of stuff like that but it degenerated into a fashion statement after a fairly short time. But in stuff like "Anarchy in the UK," somebody's spitting out some serious rage there.

That song is exactly what I saw there and exactly the way I felt. You're listening to these unbelievable stories of atrocities that these people have survived and witnessed and hearing the helicopters in the background. It was like a B-movie from the forties: crummy hotel in a little Mexican town and I was drinking a whole bunch of Scotch and I was crying, writing that song. It all came out in a lump.

It's a great recording, an amazing track.

The guitar part was there and John Goldsmith, who produced the record, came up with that beautiful vibe part—it's a synth playing it—that really went beautifully with the guitar. And everybody got into it.

I'd like to name some songs of yours to see what response you have to them.

Okay.

"Wondering Where the Lions Are."

I have a relative who is involved in one of those kinds of government jobs where they can't say what they do. The part you can say involves monitoring other people's radio transmissions and breaking codes. At that time China and the Soviet Union were almost at war on their mutual border. And both of them had nuclear capabilities. I had dinner with this relative of mine and he said, "We could wake up tomorrow to a nuclear war." Coming from him, it was a serious statement.

So I woke up the next morning and it wasn't a nuclear war. [*Laughs*] It was a real nice day and there was all this good stuff going on, and I had a dream that night which is the dream that is referred to in the first verse of the song, where there were lions at the door, but they weren't threatening—it was kind of a peaceful thing. And it reflected a previous dream that was a real nightmare where the lions were threatening.

"Mighty Trucks of Midnight."

That was written during the sessions for *Nothing But a Burning Light*. It was the last song written for that album. We were getting ready to mix the record and I got the idea, while sitting in the Shangri-La Hotel in Santa Monica, in my little apartment there. The image came from home, "mighty trucks of midnight," because where I live is a junction of a couple of highways and there's a truckstop right there and there's a lot of these big rigs going back and forth. They get spooky at night when there's this huge machine with lights on it and you can't really see anything but the lights. But there's this incredible roar.

It reflects the downturn in the economic scene around home where, partly as a result of the free trade deal between Canada and the U.S., all these little single industry towns started losing their industry. A lot of Canadian industry has traditionally been branch plant operations of American owned companies. And when the free trade was there, they didn't have to have the branch plants anymore, so they shut them all down and all of a sudden there are whole towns of people with no work. My whole life I don't remember ever meeting anybody out of work except someone who wanted to be.

And all of a sudden every second person you met was out of a job. So that was kind of where the song jumped out of and then it moved onto reflections of more spiritual things and the need to move on whether you wanted to or not.

"Burden of the Angel/Beast."

It's an observation of an aspect of the human condition. The inability to grasp where we are at any given moment and go with it. Which is unfortunately too common a problem.

"Cry of a Tiny Babe."
I wanted to write a Christmas song. I went at it like trying to tell the bible story but put it in modern terms. Like the Godard movie *Joseph and Mary*. I thought the story in the bible is such an interesting story but you forget how interesting it is because it's held up as a cliche so much to us. And over the years people have lost their humanity who are in the story and they've become larger-than-life figures. And I just thought it would be interesting to play at putting them in a human context. So Mary becomes a little bit shrewish and has a little bit of an attitude. The classic Mary figure, the Madonna—the original Madonna—is a far cry from any young Jewish mother I've ever run across. [*Laughs*] So I wanted to get it into something that people could relate to.

"Fascist Architecture."
That was when my marriage broke up. And that fact broke a lot of things in me. The image "fascist architecture" came from Italy. It was stuff that was built during Mussolini's period that was a particular style where the buildings are really larger than life and what is supposed to celebrate the greatness of humanity actually dwarfs humanity. And makes you feel tiny and helpless next to it. And everybody hates this stuff. It seemed to me a suitable image for the things in ourselves, the structures we build that are built on false expectations or pretenses. The things we pretend to ourselves. And then when some catastrophe comes your way, like a marriage breaking up or some other thing, those things crack and you get glimpses through them, the light comes through them. It's not a comfortable thing.

"Planet of the Clowns."
I had just finished reading *Shikasta* by Doris Lessing. I was in the Canary Islands sitting on the beach. That book is a work of fiction, which the author is very careful to point out in the introduction to the book. It's a beautiful myth that is built out of the myths of all cultures. The origins of the world and its short future. It's very poignant and disturbing but beautiful at the same time. Somehow that all went together with the imagery of the place, being on the beach under the moon.

"Planet of the Clowns" is a song I've always really liked, actually. There's that sense of standing on the edge of space, when you're near to the ocean. But a person standing at the edge of the ocean is kind of comparable to the world on the edge of the galaxy. That sense of being on the edge of something so much bigger of which you are an inescapable part but which will engulf you if you don't keep yourself together.

"Closer to the Light."
That was written addressed to the late Mark Heard who died recently. He was a fantastic songwriter. His death sent a shockwave through our whole community, and what that did in me was that song.

"Lovers in a Dangerous Time."

I was thinking of kids in a schoolyard. I was thinking of my daughter. Sitting there wanting to hold hands with some little boy and looking at a future, looking at the world around them. How different that was when I was a kid when, even though we had air-raid drills, nobody took that seriously that the world would end. You could have hope when I was a kid. And now I think that's very difficult. I think a lot of that is evident from the actions and the ethos of a lot of kids.

It was kind of an attempt to offer a hopeful message to them: You still have to live and you have to give it your best shot.

* * *

Los Lobos: David Hidalgo & Louie Perez

Los Angeles, California 1988
Burbank, California 1992

In Los Angeles, if you take Sunset Boulevard west as far as it goes, you reach the Pacific Ocean. If you take it east as far as it goes, and then some, you end up at Phillipe's, Home of the French Dipped Sandwich, as well as a great ten-cent cup of coffee. It's there that I first met up with David Hidalgo and Louie Perez of Los Lobos to talk about songwriting.

Unlike Bob Dylan, who began his career in folk music before "going electric," Los Lobos began as an electric band, performing other people's songs at weddings and backyard parties. But they soon realized that they had music of their own to make, and to find it, instead of "going electric," they went acoustic.

For eight years, the members of the group—David, Louie, Cesar Rosas and Conrad Lozano—put away their Hendrix and Cream records and delved deeply into their collective roots, the world of traditional Mexican folk music. It was a music that had been playing in the background for all of their lives, but unlike their contemporaries, they made the decision to bring it to the forefront. "It was like we lifted up this rock and there was this incredible life teeming under it," Louie said. To connect with that life, they spent months learning how to play the traditional instruments that this music requires: button accordion, bajo sexto, mandola, harp, mandolin, violin and more. They played only acoustic for eight years, and released an album, *Just Another Band from East L.A.*

Eventually they combined all the fruits of their labor in folk music with their first love for rock and roll and became an electric band again, integrating the traditional instruments they had worked so hard to master with their electric ones. Their music was eclectic, to say the least, mixing up traditional Mexican with surf music, samba, blues and soul. They started playing at punk clubs, where their sheer musicality must have seemed like a blessed relief. Opening for the Blasters at the Whiskey in Hollywood, the band was signed to Slash records and released an EP entitled . . . And a Time to Dance.

But it was the next album, How Will the Wolf Survive?, that signaled that Los Lobos was more than a fun party band. Sax player Steve Berlin joined as a permanent member, and in songs like "Wolf" and "A Matter of Time," David and Louie began using their immense writing skills to illuminate some dark areas. They carried this even farther on their next album, By the Light of the Moon, for which they wrote seven of the album's ten songs, including the soulful "Tears of God" and "Is This All There Is?"

With a Beatlesque combination of writing styles, David and Louie collaborate on the band's serious songs while Cesar Rosas writes the rockers. Not to say that the songs David and Louie write are somber. In fact, David's happy, romping, major-key melodies provide a stark contrast to Louie's images of persistence and hope, a process we discuss in the following interviews.

The second time I interviewed Los Lobos was four years later, and Louie alone came to speak for the band. In the interim they had carried through with their promise in our first interview to put out a "little album of folk songs." Entitled La Pistola y el corazon, it's an intimate collection of acoustically-rendered traditional songs. Since then they've released three more albums, The Neighborhood in 1990, followed two years later by Kiko, and Collosal Head in 1996. They also compiled a CD set called Just Another Band from East L.A. A Collection, which traces the evolution of Lobos from a party band who played traditional Mexican folk songs such as "Volver, Volver" and the beautiful "Anselma" at backyard weddings, to the songwriters who created "Will the Wolf Survive?" and more.

While conceiving the songs and circus-scape of the colorfully dreamlike "Kiko," Louie and David locked into such a charged songwriting groove that they kept writing and began creating pieces that transcended normal song structures, moving into a John Cage-inspired zone of sound paintings. Realizing that the fruit of their labor was falling outside the realm of Lobos, they devised a new band as an outlet for these pieces, quickly dubbed the Latin Playboys, consisting of themselves, their engineer Tchad Blake, and their producer Mitchell Froom.

Lobos has stretched the limits of conventional songwriting while simultaneously honoring the beauty of conventional songs. They are that very rare band that started out great and became greater, expanding their songwriting and record making with a fearless spirit of experimentation. One of the highlights of Head is "Mas y Mas," a rhythmic rollercoaster of a song in which Hidalgo belts out an urgent slice of life in Los Angeles in both Spanish and English, before emphasizing the constant clash of cultures by exploding into a furiously unrestrained electric guitar solo. Speaking volumes about life in a modern Babel, it's one of the most essential tracks Lobos has yet recorded, wildly accentuated by his primal screams.

It's the work of a band unafraid of experimentation and spontaneous magic, extending their music into a myriad of new areas without abandoning tradition. While reflecting much of the turmoil of modern times, they also represent a ray of hope, harmony, pure creativity, and the significance of honoring one's roots. Now raising their own kids in the same peaceful, tree-lined neighborhoods where they themselves were raised, they are musicians who have never wanted to move too far from the music they were raised with. It's that music which has sustained them, allowing the wolf not only to survive, but to prosper.

How do you two collaborate on songs? Is it true, Louie, that you primarily work on lyrics and David works on music?

LOUIE PEREZ: People assume that, but it usually goes a little beyond that. Often David will come up with a lyrical idea and I'll finish it. David sings the song, for the most part, so he'll make some adjustments for his voice. It goes back and forth.

Once we have a song pretty much in a finished stage, at that point we'll sit down together and work out exactly the songform, where the introductions will go, the possibility of a solo . . . We'll get everything pretty much laid out before we're done with it, before we present it to the band.

Have there been any Los Lobos songs in which you finished the whole lyric before giving it to David?

PEREZ: "One Time One Night" was that way. It had the whole lyric thing done and David had a whole music thing and it just seemed to come together.

It's not like a really set pattern. The only thing that is pretty routine is that David will have four or five ideas, just melodies and chords, and put them down on cassette, give them to me, and I'll sit down and listen to them and see what comes up from there. I might have a few lyrical ideas floating around, and I'll see if they fit in any of those different formulas that David has come up with.

The ideal thing for us to do is to sit down and write together. Guitar, pad of paper, pencil, and you come up with something. But because of scheduling and trying to spend time with our families and all—the time at home is really valuable—we have come up with this system of cassette communication.

How did you two first meet?

PEREZ: We met in high school in an art class. We started collaborating musically right after high school. We started writing in a real informal way. We'd write these satirical, silly little songs about people we knew and stuff like that. There was no real content to it.

DAVID HIDALGO: Those were the days of progressive rock. So just to make fun of it, we put together this long instrumental piece. We played a thirty-nine dollar Magnus organ on it; that was our Mellotron. We made up our own percussion using a ceiling fan. It was a thirty minute opus and we called it, like "Space." [*Laughs*]

PEREZ: Every now and then we run into somebody who's playing the same kind of progressive stuff and we realize we were ahead of our time.

Do you remember the first song that you wrote together?

HIDALGO: That was "How Much Can You Do" which was on the first EP [. . . *And a Time to Dance*] It was during that time that we were out of school and pretty much goofing off. I had a few songs and Louie had a few songs and we put them on tape. And when this band started, we started getting into folk music. At that point we just kind of put writing aside for a while.

PEREZ: We were having a lot of fun with that; we were concentrating more on interpreting traditional songs than actually writing our own.

HIDALGO: Trying to search out the old songs.

How long did that period of concentrating on folk music last?

HIDALGO: I guess it was about eight years. We didn't do much performing during that time. We spent most of our time with the instruments. You know, playing . . . researching the songs. It was a lot of fun and it occupied a lot of our time.

PEREZ: We were so involved with that that we took time off from the song-writing. It was like the kid who suddenly gets a mini-bike for Christmas and he forgets about everything else for about six months. So we took eight years off just to fool around with all this regional music from Mexico.

Did this study of traditional music affect your songwriting?

HIDALGO: I think it taught us a lot in the way of songform. Before that there was a lot of jazz, or a blues shuffle in A that would go on for two hours, all that kind of stuff. And when we got into folk music, it was all like three-minute songs with *arrangements*, and real choruses and verses and everything. I think it just seeped in, you know, these ideas of form.

I noticed that almost all of the songs you have written together, with the exception of "Is This All There Is?" are in major keys. Does this stem from your folk music background?

HIDALGO: Yeah, I guess it could. For me, it's very hard to write in minor keys. It just sounds too melodramatic. It's nice when it's done right, but sometimes it comes off too heavy or too dark. I have nothing against it, but it's easier for me to think in major keys.

Some writers have expressed the opposite to me, that writing in a major key is more difficult when dealing with a serious theme. And you have done this in many songs: "How Will the Wolf Survive?" for example, is a dark song in major key.

PEREZ: I think it does have a lot to do with the folk music. During the time we were listening and learning Mexican folk music, it opened the doors to all kinds of other music—international music, folk music from England and all over the United States, the South, American folk idioms—and those things are mainly all major key tunes. And they, too, had this real lightness of melody and structure but this sort of hillbilly mentality about death and dying and everything else. It was real lighthearted. It's not like, just because it's a major key, it should be happy.

That quality of darkness and lightness together definitely comes across in your songs. "One Time One Night," for example, has a breezy, upbeat melody while murders and other tragedies are going on.

HIDALGO: [*Laughter*] Yeah. A lot of Mexican songs are that way, too. Like the song on our first EP. It's got this very up-tempo tune, but this guy's talking about shooting up a girl's wedding. It's pretty cool. It's fun. And there's a lot of stuff like that.

PEREZ: The ballads of the Mexican revolution were pretty much a standard form, but lyrics were usually done about heroes and villains. And that has a parallel with American folk music, too; you know, things about bank robbers. . . .

Was it hard to carry on a tradition while still retaining your vision?

PEREZ: No. I think what happened is that after so many years of learning and being involved, it doesn't take too much thinking, it's just there. It's sort of like a language. It just seems to come together without too much concentration on the delicate balance between the cultural thing and contemporary music. We've learned enough that it just seems to happen.

You know, songs for us, we don't spew them out like some people do, who just turn on a faucet and songs come out. It takes us a while to work on a song.

Some songs *will* happen like that. Some songs will take a long time.

David, beside guitar you also play lap-steel, accordion, and many other instruments. Do you ever use any of these instruments for songwriting?

HIDALGO: It's mostly guitar. Maybe, sometimes, something will start on accordion. It happens different ways. Like with "One Time One Night," I was listening to some Cajun steel player and this guy had a real fast staccato style. And I just got the guitar and tried to imitate some of that, and that's how I came up with the melody.

PEREZ: We were working on a lot of things for the *Light of the Moon* album. And I just decided to write something. I didn't know what it would be. And one night coming home from rehearsal, David talked about an idea he had and I talked about this idea I had. By the time we got halfway down the freeway home we decided, "Hey, this is something that just might work."

It was one of those that you run into every now and then that you know is special. So with that one I said, "Okay. This one is a real keeper. I'm going to spend some time on it." I spent a long time refining it. I went backwards and forwards substituting things until finally it got to be something where we wanted it.

Was there the feeling, after writing "Will the Wolf Survive?" that you were swimming in deeper waters?

PEREZ: Yeah, that was kind of like the turning point, actually. It was kind of leading to what was coming up next. That was one of the last songs we wrote for the album.

At that point we didn't have any idea what to call the record or anything. Searching for an album title we came across this idea and we both got excited about it. The song came up, and it brought everything together; and at the same time it signaled what was coming next. Songs like "Will the Wolf Survive?" and "A Matter of Time" were heading in the direction of giving more thought to making a statement.

Where did the idea come from for "Will the Wolf Survive?"

PEREZ: We were trying to find ideas to name the record. And we knew it had to be something to do with the wolf. We wanted to use that as a symbol. I remembered the *National Geographic* that my father-in-law had. I flipped through it, and I found this article that was called something like, "Where Can the Wolf Survive?" or something like that. It was this whole thing about wolves being misinterpreted. And the fact that they were getting pushed out of North America.

We started getting these ideas about drawing a parallel between that and American culture. In the same issue there was a thing about the cities pushing out the smaller people, the smaller beings, and they had a picture of this one guy thumbing a ride down the road with a suitcase and a dog, all this visual imagery that suggested a parallel with the wolf story.

I talked to Dave about it, he got excited, drove out to the place where I was staying at the time and dropped off the beginning of a lyric.

HIDALGO: We talked about it. I got really excited about it, and I just got the guitar and started shouting, hoping that something would come up. And I got to the melody and then jotted down a few lines just to get it started, and then I ran to his place, dropped off the tape, a few lyrics, and that was it.

That great opening guitar riff on the G chord really gets the song going.

HIDALGO: Oh, that came way later. The chord changes were there and the riff was the last thing we added to it, trying to figure out something to put over that.

Though the song asks the question, "Will the Wolf Survive?" it seems to imply the answer "yes." You say, "He will find his way by the morning light." Will the wolf survive?

PEREZ: Well, it was like a hopeful sort of thing rather than painting a picture of something bleak and hopeless. It's a song about hope. "One Time One Night" has that same sort of feel to it. There's all this dark imagery, but ultimately it talks about survivors; people bouncing back from the worst sort of things that could happen to them.

In that song we were using the wolf as a metaphor for American culture. I guess that song was specifically about America.

I think a lot of people assume you were raised knowing traditional Mexican music. And in truth, I know Jimi Hendrix was a major influence.

PEREZ: Yeah. We grew up like anyone else grew up in America. But what was different about us growing up is that we did go back to the tradition. For kids our age to get into that kind of stuff was very unusual. Other bands we played with all thought we were crazy.

How did you have enough vision at that time to know it would work?

PEREZ: We didn't. At that time, we were just getting satisfaction from playing that music. Before that we had been spending all these hours trying to sound like a song played on the radio. And it just seemed pointless to us. We were moonlighting as a Top Forty band at night. And we started doing this on the side. We'd get together during the day. And it got to be so much fun that we decided that *that* was not fun and that this *was* fun.

There was no sort of vision of where it was gonna go. We just said, "We enjoy doing this better than that so let's do this for a while."

We were just doing it for fun. It wasn't until a friend of ours who was involved with the community heard what we were doing and he said, "Hey, you know that would be great for an afternoon get-together at the VFW hall," or something. At that point we knew eight songs or so and we decided "Hey, people liked what they heard." And we got a big kick out of hearing people respond to us positively in that way. And we just kept going from there.

The song "Is That All There Is?" seems to me to be in a slightly different style than your other songs. And, as we mentioned, it is one of the only ones in a minor key [C minor]. Do you remember writing that one?

PEREZ: That song had been around for a while before we started to make the last record.

HIDALGO: It was one of the first songs we wrote for the *Moon* record. I think I wrote the music first for that one. I had the verse. I played it for Louie, and we just sat in our hotel room and talked about it for a while and figured out what we wanted to say. And when we had the time, we went in our corners and finished it up.

It started out like an Otis Rush song. That was what I had pictured, something that Otis Rush would sing. That was kind of the feel that we wanted.

That song has such strong imagery: the mountain top, the ocean, the woman at the sewing machine. Are you someone who jots down images and ideas when they occur to you?

PEREZ: No. I don't write things down too often. I should. [*Laughs*] But I remember things. Little things. I feel like half a person; there's been a song in my head for about six months that I haven't written down yet.

Yeah? You can use my tape recorder.

PEREZ: [*Laughs*] Thanks. See, David and I usually talk about songs even before there's an idea of a melody or a lyric. It will be just the basic idea of what a song could be. It might come from just a line or a title that we might have, and from that point on, we'll talk more about it.

We decided not to restrict ourselves to writing songs only for the band. We wrote a couple of country songs that are flat-out country songs. We weren't really thinking of the band to do them, we were thinking more of George Jones or Merle Haggard—people like that.

Do you remember writing "The Breakdown"?

HIDALGO: That song we were playing live for about a year before we recorded it. But we were doing like a completely different arrangement. The reason it got the name "Breakdown" is because when we did it live it had this Zydeco breakdown in the middle of it. And we were recording the drums, and that was just not going to work at the time.

PEREZ: When we got into the studio with it, we changed it. T Bone [Burnett] had a lot to do with that.

HIDALGO: We were recording it the way we did it live. And it didn't work, it didn't sound right. So we just sat in the studio and took it back to the acoustic guitar, and said, "Okay, this is where it started, okay?"

We slowed it down and made it more of a New Orleans type of groove, and so Conrad started playing the bass line and everybody just fell into their parts and it just happened, it clicked.

The two of you co-wrote a song with T Bone, "All I Wanted to Do Was Dance." How did that come about?

HIDALGO: We had talked about it before we ever did it. Same thing with "The Breakdown," we had written the whole tune and we got to the last verse, and that's where we got stuck. So T Bone stepped in and we worked it out together.

PEREZ: We were writing and recording at the same time. At that point we were really burning the candle at both ends. I was working on two other things and they were already doing a dance song. T Bone kept calling on the phone and saying, "Do you have that other verse done yet?" And we'd say, "No, not yet." And finally he figured that he would work on the part himself. I think the bridge was his part, except for the last verse, which was a combination of our ideas and T Bone's ideas.

HIDALGO: When you get into a rut, T Bone's good at getting things rolling again. Just because of his personality. He starts jumping around. He's a silly guy, you know. There were a couple of times we couldn't do anything, we just couldn't think anymore. So he'd go and buy a fifth of Scotch. And that helped a great deal. [*Laughs*] We got a couple songs out of that.

PEREZ: Yeah. I think "Prenda Del Alma," the traditional song on the *Moon* record, the whole song is completely under the influence of Glenlivet.

HIDALGO: And "River of Fools" was also done that way.

PEREZ: Oh, yeah, it was that evening where we all got into one of those things where we were hugging each other in the parking lot and saying things like, [*loudly and drunkenly*] "YOU'RE MY BEST FRIEND IN THE WHOLE WORLD!!!" [*Laughter*]

"Tears of God," which you said was the last song written for the last album, is a very powerful song. I especially like that deceptive cadence on the end of the third chorus, where it shifts into a blues feel on that D7th chord.

PEREZ: Yeah. That was David's idea.

HIDALGO: I was watching that gospel movie, *Say Amen, Somebody.* I saw it on PBS, was watching it. And I was just listening to this song and it was real beautiful, like a soul ballad. But at the end it just got—

PEREZ: Lowdown. [*Laughs*]

HIDALGO: Lowdown, yeah. He just dug into it and that was the idea I was trying to get.

Is it hard to write songs with the family around?

HIDALGO: I wait until they're asleep. Or if my wife's going to the market, I'll say, "Hey—why don't you take the kids with you?" [*Laughs*] You know, just for a few minutes of quiet.

PEREZ: I wait until everybody crashes out. Once the dogs are fed and the trash gets taken out, I get to work.

I get ideas when I'm active, like when I'm raking leaves. And I'll make a mental note of them. But to actually sit down and work on things, I don't throw the rake down and run into the house and jump into the cassette player. During the day is my kids' time. I belong to them during the day. After they go to sleep, then it's my time.

Last time we spoke we discussed the different methods that you employ to write songs. You said back then that David would often bring you musical ideas that you would then bring lyrics to.

PEREZ: Yeah, we would go back and forth. We still, to a certain extent, do that. We exchange ideas. Unfortunately we don't have the opportunity to spend much time sitting together. But when we worked on the songs for *Kiko* we set up shop. We rented a little back room in a bookstore, midway between my house and his house. And we'd meet there every morning and work on songs. That was a change in the formula. But now since we're back to touting and all, we still communicate via cassette or we'll exchange ideas whenever we have a minute together, in a car or whatever. It's a conversation that's ongoing.

When we're home, we're completely consumed by our families. But I'd run into him at the market or picking up the kids at school.

On *Kiko*, were all those songs written face to face?

PEREZ: A lot of them we did, yeah. We'd work up ideas and have homework, and come back the next morning and try things. Ultimately all of the songwriting is done eventually together. When we would exchange ideas like that, we would eventually sit down and finalize everything together. Since then we got a little 4-track machine to work up more fleshed-out ideas before we take them to the band. Before it was just Dave with a guitar and everybody would just have a go at it. As a matter of fact, for *Kiko* we put everything on this 4-track machine and we'd have the song all done. It was kind of like the Little Rascals' school of studio techniques. We had no rehearsals for *Kiko* or take the songs on the road. We thought we should put less distance between the performance and the song.

We'd use the 4-track sort of as the first impression. Then we'd go into the studio and start chipping away at it to see what reveals itself. It was very spontaneous.

Some of the songs have unusual rhythms. Did you write any of them to a finished track?

PEREZ: Thanks to Tchad Blake, our engineer, who collects sounds, we used unusual sources of rhythm. Like the Octagon. We used a lot of weird stuff like that to establish the rhythm. Or it could be just an idea that Dave had on a track that we would start from. The accident was a big pan of it. We'd stumble onto things and say, "What was that?"

There's some moments of dissonance that are wonderful.

PEREZ: Yeah. Like on "When the Circus Comes to Town," the guitar solo on that was from Dave trying to find a setting on his amplifier and he just kind of did one pass and played along while adjusting the knobs. And when he was ready to do the take it was already finished. A lot I owe to Mitchell [Froom, the producer] for the kind of atmosphere he created in the studio, which was real free. Which was one of those real fortunate things to happen, because when David and I first started working on the songs, we went in and we felt that nothing should be affected by anything, that whatever comes through the pipe we should put down. All of those peripheral pressures that go along with this business, we left all that behind. And when we finally took these songs to the studio, Mitchell was keen enough to pick up on that vibe and follow through with the way he conducted things in the studio. Nothing was hard-pressed. We didn't do basic tracks and add vocal later. We'd move across the song.

The entire *Kiko* album, including the title, is much more surreal and dreamlike than your previous work. Did you decide to do it that way or did it evolve?

PEREZ: It definitely just evolved. Something came out of what we were doing. Because we started in a very free place where we didn't let anything affect or direct what we were doing. There were a whole bunch of songs. We could have gone on forever. We went in with a whole bunch of songs and continued to write through the whole recording process.

On "Kiko and the Lavender Moon" and "Angels with Dirty Faces" you can kind of tell things were going in that direction and you go with it. We didn't try to redirect things. If that's the way it goes, you follow it. Kind of an expressionistic way of making a record, I guess. You just wait for something to reveal itself and go with it. John Cage did a lot of that stuff. Things that just happen for a reason. You can find music everywhere. It's a healthy way of looking at things.

Where did the name "Kiko and the Lavender Moon" come from?

PEREZ: We had some time off. A few months, believe it or not. I paint and am a visual person. I kind of became a musician by default. I started out as a painter and still consider myself that. So I started doing all these paintings and one of the paintings was "Kiko and the Lavender Moon." The title just jumped out at me. I liked the way the name "Kiko" is irreverent and "the lavender moon" is poetic, and I liked the juxtaposition of those two things. Then Dave came up with the rhythm of the song, a style from Colombia, and I had an almost Duke Ellington-like introduction for it. I had been writing all this stuff that wasn't directly connected with any song and I said, "I think these two ideas might be connected together," and it worked. I had written all the lyrics first almost as a poem, and Dave had been working on the music separately on the 4-track. And we put them together.

Which is a way we have been working together lately. And as a result of that song "Kiko," in which we let the text dictate the melody instead of the other way around, where you have a melody and kind of fill in the blanks. Which I think restricts you a little bit. We let the words indicate the structure of the melody.

Last time you said that "One Time One Night" was the only one in which you wrote the lyric first. But now you do more of that?

PEREZ: Yeah. As a matter of fact, David and I just finished this Latin Play-boys project where we ended up with 14 songs. And he'd go home from being on the road and he had the 4-track set up and work into the wee hours. He had all these song ideas on 4-track, a lot of them were just sounds. And he played them for me and I said, "Why don't we turn these things into songs?" A lot of them had a rhythm track or a groove. And we decided on trying something.

So he'd work on that and I wrote all these stream-of-consciousness lyr-ics. I'd play them back and these songs would give me an image and then I'd just write. So when we went into the studio we had all these musical ideas on tape and I had a stack of lyrical ideas. And at that point I had some ideas of what lyrics should go with what musical idea, but I threw that out right away. But he had other ideas. And when we went to the studio some of the lyrical ideas ended up with musical ideas I never thought would go together.

Mitchell laughed one day and said, "Working like this could probably drive any other producer crazy." After a while he realized exactly what we were do-ing, which was that we didn't know what we were doing. We went in and transferred all of the 4-tracks to multi-track, so basically the stuff that was done in David's kitchen is pretty much what the record was made of. We put everything on multi-track and added to it.

So many of your songs make strong visual statements.

PEREZ: A lot of things come from a visual place. Something that I'll see will trigger a lyrical thing. I see it in my head before they become words. Folk music and plainsong has been an incredible influence on me. And at the same time Hendrix's lyrics have also influenced me. I like the stark minimalism of folk music, and a lot of that affects how I approach lyrics.

I love the line in "Dream in Blue": "I flew around with shiny things / And when I spoke when I spoke, I seemed to sing." It's almost biblical.

PEREZ: I didn't think of it as being biblical but I guess it could be. That came from this image of an angel with wings that were like grand piano lids. I kind of imagined Bird or Coltrane as this angel. This was part of a dream. I wrote this little piece quick about this angel with piano-lid wings and then I went with the idea of this person who almost, in a dream, gets to see what the meaning of life is. Or enlightenment or whatever this is that we're all trying to find. And in this dream he gets real close to it. But maybe he wakes up before he actually gets there. That's why in the lyric he talks about how he kind of peeked into a door. His eyes almost focused. He got so close. And then the refrain says, "I can almost see it." But not quite.

I don't dream a lot but when I do they stay with me. "Peace" was a dream. We were on the road and I had this dream of seeing Dave alone on stage on a stool playing the guitar. And I could remember some of the lyrics he sang. I told Dave about it and he said, "Wow, cool," and he came over. And I was trying to think of how it went and I could remember a couple of the verses. I kind of sang the melody to him.

Does that experience of dreaming a song give you the sense that these songs are gifts?

PEREZ: Definitely. They are. They definitely come from some place else. I'm not going to claim anything on this stuff. I'm very grateful that these ideas come but they definitely come from somewhere else.

Does anything in your experience make the process easier?

PEREZ: I get ideas when I'm doing something else. I think it's when your waking mind is addressing some physical issue, like driving or whatever, that the other part of your brain, where your imagination lives, is going wild. Neil Young talks about how he jumps into the back of his car and writes songs because he just gets them.

I was talking to a painter friend of mine at length about the problem of feeling that every time you sit down to write it has to be a masterpiece. Which is a syndrome I think a lot of painters and writers and songwriters have to deal with. It's so terrifying, that failure. But he told me, "Hey, it's only paint. You can always get some more. It's only paper. You can always get some more." You've got to keep writing it.

Some songwriters have expressed their need to write a song all at once, because it can be hard to reconnect with an idea. Do you feel that?

PEREZ: I can always think of a way I could have made it better after it's already done. But I don't spend too much time with that because you can beat yourself up too bad.

Some of the early songs, like "One Time One Night," I spent forever on that song. Because I had to make sure that every little article and preposition was perfect. It wasn't too meticulous. That's part of the songwriting craft, when you sit there and make certain decisions about a song, lyrically or musically. And that's okay but I don't put a lot of stock into that either. I think they just have to come out. Hank Williams said, "If it's takes you longer than a half hour, it ain't worth a shit." [*Laughter*] But some of the songs come in an instant, and some take a little longer. But lately I've putting them down real fast. I just wrote one the other day that has six words. And there's a thing on Latin Playboys where I took a line and started to move the words around, like Burroughs cutting up words and coming up with "Vanilla Chrome Gear" or something like that.

I tried that on one song and it came out pretty cool. It's all based on one word, "shining" and in experimenting with the words it started to tell a story. And I added a refrain to it and it actually became a real song that way. I saw Ginsberg do a reading in which he used one word as the source of the piece, and everything else did an orbit around this one word, which was "bomb." So when listening to the musicality of the words in that piece, I was inspired to write this song called "Dumbo." I had heard this Mexicano, this Mexican dad telling his little kid at Disneyland that Dumbo was coming down for the parade. And I heard this thing with "Dumbo . . . Dumbo . . ." and it was wild, so I wrote this piece that was just this father telling his son about Dumbo. He was saying in Spanish, "Look at Dumbo, here comes Dumbo . . ." So I wrote this and sent it over to Dave. And he had this other song which was a merengue, just two guitars on the 4-track.

So we took it into the studio and put it down. And Tchad Blake had some sounds of a brass band playing at a wedding in India. So we took that and put that on top of it and it started to have almost this circus feeling, like a parade. Then we set the mike up out in the parking lot to get ambient sounds. And I brought out my sheet and just started reading his thing off. And then it started to sound like being on the sideline of a parade. So we brought more people out there to talk and whatever. Then on the top of this whole thing I just kept yelling this thing, "Mira Dumbo . . ."

When you and David write a song together, such as "Dream in Blue," do you discuss it beforehand?

PEREZ: Yes. We do a lot of talking about songs before they are even written. He came up with the song "Angel with Dirty Faces." He wrote the whole thing. He said, "I like that old movie title, *Angels with Dirty Faces* and it kind of connects with the idea of homelessness." So he brought in the song and kind of played it. And he had words that he thought we could improve on. He sang it and when he finished the song he said, "What do you think?" And I said, "I think it's done." The lyrics were really great.

Yes. "Broken window smile / weeds for hair . . ."

PEREZ: Yeah. Sometimes things just come. They just pour out on the page and other times it's like getting blood from a turnip. But we live for those days. And you know what? You've got to be grateful for the little things you get in any day.

Do you remember writing "Wake Up Dolores"?

PEREZ: Yeah. We had finished the whole record. And everything was already loaded out of the studio. And Dave came over and he had this idea and played it for me. And I said, "Whoa. I think we're on to something else here. It's got this feel like almost an indigenous sound." He first played it on a 12-string and it sounded almost African. And I had this idea about writing something about indigenous people who were displaced by the wars in Central America and how they had gone back to reclaim their homeland. I told Dave I had this idea about people traveling back home again.

So I wrote the lyric based on that idea of a husband and wife who are heading back down that road back home and it's a long walk. It talks about "the stones are hard on this endless road . . ." Then the idea of the plumed serpent and all that imagery played in with this idea of native people in South America and Mexico. That's where the chorus comes from: "Quetzal Plumes, dying suns and purple moons . . ."

Man, I wish I could write a song like some of those indigenous songs of the North American native people. Some of those lyrics are just incredible, the way they just use a few words. So I tried to do that on this song, to keep it very sparse and to the point. And I took one of the lines from an Aztec codice: "Our houses are broken and the streets are red with our blood." That related somehow to the conflict in Central America and how many people are affected by that. So we took those lines—that's what it was translated to but it was in the language—so that's what the chorus sings in "Wake Up Dolores": "Ocuiltin / Moyacatla / Otlica / Auh in caltech."

When David gives you a melody to work with, do you write to the tape, or play it on guitar?

PEREZ: I'll work to the tape or kind of learn it and keep it with me for a long time and wait for something to come out. I work in the evening when the kids are asleep and I'll sit down and bang out some lyrical ideas.

And when writing to a melody, do you try to allow the music to suggest the words?

PEREZ: I find that melodies suggest a lot of words. Lately I'm trying not to think so much about it. A lot has to be said about subconscious stuff. I'll just write a lot and then I'll go back and I'll see there is a thread, or I'll find meaning later. And sometimes in editing I'll go with that certain thread and try to follow that.

It's more a sense of following than leading?

PEREZ: Yeah, I think so. I find that if you can let it take you, it's usually the right direction. Instead of trying to correct things along the way. I had a friend who told me he would write himself a little note that he would keep by the bed and when he woke up he would look at it. And it said, "Dear Paul, I won't be needing your help today. Signed, God." [*Laughs*] And sometimes we just have to jump into the shotgun side and let someone else do the driving.

Where did "Reva's Home" come from?

PEREZ: That was sparked by a story by a Southern writer named Reese De-japancake. Who took his life when he was 26 years old. He had one story with the character Reva, who is a little bit disenfranchised, desperate. One of those American dreams unfulfilled kind of things. I had the line, "Knock down the door to Reva's house." Then I got the rest of the chorus: "The dogs were barking late last night, something's going on . . ." At that point I didn't know what was going on. It was something that maybe the neighbors were saying. A lot of people have read into that song and felt that it was about abuse. I tried to tie in a dysfunctional relationship. I saw the male character was an alcoholic. I've been in recovery myself for four years so I went with that. One journalist wrote that she heard that song and all these red flags went up. Which made me feel that maybe the song did what it was supposed to do.

Kiko definitely was a record that you can put away and put on again and it's like a living thing. You find new things in it. I guess as a songwriter making a record it's kind of an over-and-done thing and all your ideas should be clear-cut and finalized. But I always go back, especially with *Kiko* and find that there's something there that's still generating every time I listen to them.

In Bill Bentley's liner notes to the Lobos boxed set, he makes the point that when Lobos first started, along with many other L.A. bands, it was clear that your songs and music were here to stay. Is it at all surprising to you now, looking back, that Lobos has lasted this long?

PEREZ: Well, as you know, we don't plan too much. Things just kind of happened. Twenty years looking back it shows you how fast time flies. It's hard to believe how fast it's gone. Seven albums in ten years is not that prolific. I don't know how we managed. There's always the sense of discovery. Trying new things all the time. We all play many instruments and move things around. Dave plays drums and I'll play guitar.

Twenty years. It doesn't mean there's that many records sold. I wish we sold more records. We weren't going to have one smash hit and then break up. We decided early on that we were here to stay.

* * *

Suzanne Vega
Hollywood, California 1992

"All the mysteries of life come in A minor," she said, curled up on a couch in Hollywood. It was a statement she made to the guys in her band who were urging her to use more chords in her songs. Hoping not to antagonize them, she had been struggling with ways to harmonically expand her music, despite her faith in the omniscience of A minor. It's a struggle she's known for years, wanting to write songs that uniquely express her own soul and reveal the mysteries of life, while also wanting to please other people. "I'd like to be a poet," she said with a smile. "As long as I still get to mingle in society."

She drinks milkshakes. She even eats meat occasionally. Though the common perception of her is that of an ascetic poet, one who only eats when nature absolutely demands it, she's actually quite earthly. While on tour in Texas, she shocked a record exec by saying she wanted to go shopping. "I'm so glad you're a regular girl!" the exec said happily. "I have a reputation for being pacifistic, vegetarian, Buddhist, ethereal, and frail," Suzanne said with a smile, "and it's not like that at all."

We met in my Hollywood office, where she was extremely serious about her songwriting, but surprisingly humorous and light-hearted about herself. Expecting her to be as somber as many of her songs, I was happy to find that she's quite funny, and broke up into laughter countless times during our extensive talk, her entire face lighting up with mirth.

She was born on August 12, 1959 in New York, and raised in Spanish Harlem by her mother, a musician, and her step-father, a Puerto Rican novelist. Dreaming of being an artist since she was a kid, she studied dance seriously, and attended New York's High School for the Performing Arts. She soon realized, though, that it was music more than motion that mattered most to her, and refocused her energies on being a musician. "I started to realize it was the music that made me want to dance," she said. "All my instincts were moving me towards music, even though all my training was in dance."

Songwriting was something she took seriously from the start, spending three years working on her first song. She was inspired by artists like Dylan, Joni Mitchell and Joan Baez, both by their music and the spirit that they represented. "These people had a very mystic significance to society," she said, "It wasn't that they were just pop stars. They had an almost religious responsibility. I wanted to be one of these people who had that responsibility. I wanted to join them."

Her first effort in that direction, completed after three years, was written for her brother Matthew and called "Brother Mine," beginning with the line "Sonny boy, you need some new sneakers." She taught herself to play the guitar by learning songs from songbooks containing hits of the day, such as Jobim's "The Girl From Ipanema." But when people asked her to sing out loud, she'd shrink with terror—an experience that nearly kept her from music permanently. "I just wilted," she recalled. "I'd say, 'Sing out loud—are you crazy?' I was very shy and withdrawn, and I couldn't do it. These big guys with their big stomachs singing 'Barbara Allen.' I wasn't into it."

It was hearing Lou Reed that transformed her ideas about songwriting: "I started feeling I could be experimental. You could write a song with no chorus or melody. All the restraints were off." Her second song was a long tragic ballad entitled "The Silver Lady," and it inspired her to keep writing. She sang in a gentle, unforced style, wanting to capture the easy spirit of children spontaneously making up songs.

Her eponymous debut album was released in 1985, and with luminous songs like "Cracking" and "Marlene on the Wall," it quickly established her as a leader of the "New Folk" movement, a movement that seems to happen about once a decade when great new songwriters surface. But it was a song that she wrote years before but didn't record until her second album called "Luka" that really introduced her to the world. A simple, haunting song that managed to touch on child abuse in the gentlest way possible, written from the perspective of a child who has learned to not say too much, "Luka" became an enormous hit, and Suzanne Vega was soon known the world over.

Having such huge commercial success with such an uncommercial theme made life confusing for her: "When a song like 'Luka' becomes a hit, what does one write next? After a while I just gave up and decided to write what felt right."

What felt right was to write the songs that wanted to be written, ambitious works such as "Men in a War," which revolves around the idea of a phantom limb, and "Predictions," a lexicon of fortune telling techniques. Her song "Book of Dreams," is a collection of dreams about the future rather than the past, unlike the Kerouac book of the same name. "Yes, the future," she said, "things to come. That was a theme I found emerging from a lot of my songs, leaving the past and going toward the future." These songs became the foundation for her third album, *Days of Open Hand*.

We met up with her soon after she had written all the songs for *Days of Open Hand* and was in the midst of thinking about what to do next, and wanting to musically expand her writing. We spoke for a long time, during which she shared her ideas about being an artist in the world, and the ways to be selective about the voices one listens to during the rush of creation. Afterwards we took a walk down Hollywood Boulevard, a constant circus of manic humanity that she took in pensively from behind rose-colored shades, slipping quickly and easily through the throng.

Bob Dylan said poets don't drive cars. You don't drive, do you?
[*Laughs*] Well, that's because I grew up in New York City where you don't really need one. Although I was considering today maybe I should learn. Yeah. For a sense of freedom.

Do you think of yourself as a poet?
That's always a tricky question because I love poetry and I would love for my songs to be as poetry. But the word 'poetry' has all these strange connotations of preciousness and aloofness. I love words and I love what they do and I love poetry. I'd like to be a poet.

I get my inspirations from things that are very ordinary and not precious at all, like children's nursery rhymes, and games that kids play in the street. Things that I had played as a child; sing-song rhymes and rhythms that you make up to amuse yourself while you're jumping rope, or if you're teasing somebody else. To me, it's all one and the same. As a child we had things that we played, and that's where I first got a sense of words, what they were about.

But I also use other things. Medical textbooks, science textbooks. Pieces of information. Wherever I can get information. Whatever rings true to me is where I'll find it.

Your songs are often very ambitious, sometimes concerning something quite abstract, such as "Small Blue Thing." Do you ever find that you can't put across an idea in a song?
It depends how you go for it. I usually don't start out with the idea of being abstract. I usually, honestly, try to be as simple and clear and as straightforward as I can. A lot of people say [*laughs*], "Oh, yeah? Why don't you just say what you mean?" I honestly am trying to say what I mean, it's just that the things I'm writing tend to be really dense. I think, because of my childhood experiences, that my perspective is somewhat unusual, maybe. So I'm coming at it from a different perspective.

So to me, "Today I am a small blue thing" is a very straightforward statement. Whereas other people are saying, "If she loves the guy, why doesn't she just say so?"

Sometimes I pull it off and I'll sing them for a while and they just won't hit the mark for me. To me, "Cracking" really hit the nail on the head. "Small

Blue Thing" hit the nail on the head, and "Luka" hit the nail on the head. But other ones didn't. "Marlene On The Wall" always seemed a little wide of mark, somehow.

That's surprising to hear, because it's such a great song.

[*Laughs*] Well, it's accessible and people do like it, but for me, personally, inside myself, I feel I had something in mind, and I kind of did it. It was stylish, it was interesting, but I didn't feel it was quite the bulls-eye that some of the others were.

The idea of using a poster as a reference point is a very pop idea. It's a song about Marlene Deitrich. You kind of get that from it, or it's a song about a relationship. As opposed to "Today I am a small blue thing" in which some people think I'm speaking in code, or it's a riddle they have to break. It's more like "Let's pretend," like a kid's game. If you were a small blue thing, what would you be? Well, you'd be like a marble or an eye. It's pretty straight-forward.

It's a straight-forward way of expressing a feeling. But that's something people don't often manage to express in songs—

[*Laughter*] I love songwriting. To me, there's all these elements that are mixed into it, of magic, spells and prayers . . . as I said before, children's games . . . science . . . I like to brings all these things together so it's all one. You can draw from any source.

Do you write songs as poems, finishing the lyric first before working on music?

I'm still working on that. I wouldn't say that I have one set way of working. It's usually that it comes together. Usually I have an idea. With "Cracking" I knew that the title came first, and after that I would try different lines and it just wasn't working, and sometimes it will take months for the thing to line up correctly until it seems to fall right in the right place.

"Luka" was that way, also. It takes months of kind of fingering it in my mind, while I'm walking around or doing something else, it's just like a problem that my mind goes back to. It wiggles. It's like you're trying to get the right angle, and once the angle comes, I can write the song in two hours. Like "Luka" took two hours. It took months of thinking about it and lining up the shot, in a sense. Like if you're playing pool and you want to clear the table, you line it all up, and then you just hit it and everything clears. It's very satisfying, but it takes months of preparation.

With "Luka," you had a character in mind?

Yes, but I wasn't sure what the character would say. I knew what the character's problem was, but I didn't know how to get the listener involved. I wanted it to be from the point of view of a person who is abused. Now the problem that that person has is that they can't say it. So how do you get the problem out if you can't say it. How do you involve the listener? Well, you introduce yourself: "My name is Luka." And "I live on the second floor, I live upstairs from you," and so therefore you're engaging the listener. "I think you've seen me before," so you start to listen. You're drawing the listener into this world with very simple, basic information. And it then proceeds to state the problem without ever saying what the problem is. That was my problem as a songwriter: How do I give this information without ever giving it?

It's easy to point a finger. It's easy to say, "Child abuse must stop" and everybody knows this.

And so much tension is created with the line "just don't ask me what it was," that this person is holding a lot inside, and doesn't want to talk about it.

Or can't talk about it.

It's a technique that Randy Newman often uses, though few others do, of using a character to make a point by what he doesn't say.

Yeah. The listener has to work a lot. It's true. There's no getting around that. [*Laughs*]

Was Randy Newman an influence on your writing?

For a long time, one of my favorite songs was "I Think It's Gonna Rain Today" because it's not sentimental at all. There's so much feeling in it; he just gives you certain images. It's a very moving song but it's not sentimental. I think I was aware of a few other songs, but that one, I remember feeling that I'd like to write like that.

I was thinking more of his character songs. Not a lot of songwriters write in character, as you did in "Luka."

I guess I got that idea from studying poetry, and from T. S. Eliot. "The Love Song of J. Alfred Prufrock." If you just read it flat, it doesn't make any sense. When you realize that this character is revealing information, then "The Love Song of J. Alfred Prufrock" makes sense if you look at it through his eyes. Whereas if you just read it flat as a poem, it just seems to just lie there, it doesn't really do anything. And once I realized that, I started thinking about how you could use that, like a camera. So it was something I was playing with.

Are there other poets besides Eliot who have influenced you?

I'd say Sylvia Plath because of the way she uses language, the way she puts words together. She uses language almost sculpturally. She'll pick words for what they sound like as well as what they mean. That was very impressive to me. It seems to pack more into it. It's almost like code.

And, of course, Dylan.

You think of him as a poet?

The way that he used his images. To me, they work as well on the page as when you listen to them.

I don't mind being a poet as long as I get to mingle in society. I don't like this idea that to be a poet you have to be aloof and you can't walk in the street. Poetry should be part of living. Everything should be all mixed together.

On one of the tours I was down in Texas and the woman from the record company said to me, "What would you like to do?" because we had an afternoon off, and I said, "Let's go shopping." And she goes, "Oh, I'm so relieved to find you're a regular girl. I thought that you were a poet. I thought you'd be no fun, that you'd sit in your room and look out the window." She was relieved.

I think, yes, I probably am a poet, but I really feel the need to be among people and to watch them and talk to them and be on a regular basis.

Do you get a lot of song ideas from observing people?

A lot of people say I'm very observational, but I'm really much more involved than I pretend. These are not just clinical observations about people. There is a direct connection between me and the person that I am writing about. There was a boy named Luka but he was not abused. He's probably shocked to death that I put him in this song. [In] the things that I'm writing about, I'm revealing some facet of my own life. It's something that I've seen or been involved with. It's not just a question of reading a paper and saying, "That's a good topic. I think I'll write a Gulf War song." That to me is too academic. I think, in order for it to ring true, you have to know what you're talking about. It's not enough just to *look* and say, "This is what I deduce." You have to be involved.

Do songs gain more resonance if they are true?

I think so, yeah. To me, it's really important that a song be true because you have to stand on stage every night and sing it. And you have to force people to listen to it. And if it's not true, they're not going to want to listen to it. You can fool yourself for a while, but after a while you will lose the urge to sing it because it won't have any resonance anymore.

So with a song like "Marlene on the Wall," you actually had a poster of Marlene Deitrich on your wall?

Yeah. Oh, that was a truthful song. The lines came out of my life. But you want to be careful, too, because you don't want to get into "Oh, my boyfriend left me . . ." I have a problem with specifically confessional songwriting. I think you have to craft it in some way. I don't think you can come on stage and blurt out your innermost feelings. My niece can blurt out her innermost feelings. She's four years old. I wouldn't want to pay $25 [*laughs*] to go see her do that. You need to put it in a form. Although it is truthful, you have to give it some respect, or a certain kind of dignity, by putting it into a kind of form because these people are not my friends. They're paying to see a show, some form of entertainment. So I'm not gonna sit there and talk to them like Ronee Blakely in Nashville. [*Laughter*]

I had breakfast with Leonard Cohen once and I asked him, "What do you think of confessional songwriting? Is it better to be confessional or not confessional?" He said, "You do whatever you have to do to make the song work. Whether it's confess or lie or make it up." And that makes sense because that's what his songs are. Some of them are confessional; some of them you're *sure* that he's lying. [*Laughs*]

He is extremely business-like about his songwriting, working constantly on his songs every day. Is this how you approach your songs?

I find that I do work on it everyday but it's in my mind. I find that it's more like a problem that's unsolved. My mind will wander back to it if I'm in a good frame of mind. I'll say, "Well, that last line just isn't working" or "That just doesn't seem to be the right thing," so my mind will wander back to it, but it's not the formal thing of sitting working on my lyrics.

Do you mean that your mind keeps working on songs even when you're doing other activities?

Yeah. Usually when I'm walking. Walking from one place to another. Or sitting on a bus or thinking or talking. My mind will keep going back to that one song and go, "Well, those last two lines, I just don't know . . ." And it'll start fingering it and eventually the whole thing will just fall into place.

Lots of songwriters have said that their problems get solved while driving—

Yeah. Your mind is occupied, so your other mind is left to play. You really need that time to do that. I was under a lot of pressure for the third album, and everyone was kind of stomping around and going, "Where's the rest of the songs? We can't finish the album without the songs." I started to feel that I just wanted to get out. I just wanted to go for a walk or go anywhere. And it *looks* as though I'm avoiding it. And I'm *not* avoiding it. I'm just going to do my work in the way that's the best way that I can. But it looks like I'm avoiding it, so everyone goes, "No, you *can't* go to the health food store. You must stay here and finish the song." [*Laughs*] But you need that time to approach it obliquely. For some weird reason, that's where the answers come from. Sort of a left-handed approach.

It would seem that your material would demand that kind of approach, as opposed to songwriters working to write radio hits, that go to it every-day—

It's never worked for me. [*Laughs*] I've tried it a couple times, and every time I write a song to be a hit, it doesn't even sing. It doesn't work for me.

Pete Seeger, who encouraged us to interview you, said that he agreed with Woody Guthrie that anytime you try to write songs commercially, you can harm yourself artistically—

Well, you see, everyone knows that, and I knew that. I knew that when I was fourteen, and I knew that when I was 26. But somehow you forget, and you start thinking you can dabble in it just a little bit and twist it just a little bit and aim it in this direction. But for me, that kind of stuff just doesn't work. So I'm strict with myself now. I'm only going to do the things that are satisfying artistically. Because I realize that my own standards, when I'm left to my own devices, are very strict. And I have a whole system of rules for myself that are satisfying to me. So for a song to really ring true, it sort of has to go through this filtering process within myself. It's much stricter than what the record companies expect. [*Laughs*] I realized that's really what's going to make it satisfying. Not trying to get a Top 40 hit. I learned a lot in the last year, from the last tour and the last album.

What did you learn?

[*Laughs*] I learned that it's not good to try to force a hit. I mean, as a pro-ducer you have to be aware of this thing because your record company wants a single. I feel that it's better to not go for the pop thing if that's not what you're going to be. I mean, for a while I was confused cause "Luka" was a hit and I was never expecting it to be one. So I became popular, which made it pop. So this made me confused. Am I pop, am I folk? And the journalists were doing the same thing. Now I see that it's pop if it's popular, and other than that, it doesn't matter. I wrote "Luka" three or four years before it became a hit. I wrote "Tom's Diner" ten years ago. It wasn't pop then, but now it's pop.

You actually wrote "Luka" before your debut album. Did you consider putting it on your first album?

No. I needed some time for it to settle into the bag of songs. I needed some time to get used to it as a song. A lot of people felt it was catchy, and I used to feel insulted, because I'd say, "Catchy? Obviously you missed the point of the song."

And yet it is. Musically, it is a catchy song.

I guess it is. I think because I was aiming at such a complex subject that I was aiming for the simplest line to get there. Simple melodies, happy chords. I felt I had to make it accessible because it was such a dark subject. So I went all out. But I also tried to write in the language of a child. So that's probably why it worked, because it is so accessible.

It's an upbeat song, and the melody is a happy one, as you said, especially for that subject matter.

I'd been listening to the Lou Reed *Berlin* album that Sunday when I wrote the song. And you can really draw a straight line between "Luka" and that album. That *Berlin* album is filled with references of domestic violence and all kinds of violence. The songs are all in major keys. They're all done on acoustic guitar. So for me, ["Luka"] is like the extra song on the *Berlin* album. [*Laughs*] To me. Stylistically, it almost belonged there.

I never would have drawn that line.

No one ever draws that comparison.

Did the record company choose it to be the single?

I think when we produced it, everybody felt that it was going to be the single. I said, "Well, good luck. Knock yourselves out." Cause I had no expectation for it.

When making the third album, did you then try to make one of those songs a radio hit as "Luka" was?

The most obvious one, obviously, is "Book of Dreams."

That was your intention while writing it?

When I wrote it, it was just an interesting idea. And I thought, let's do this with the chorus. I had been listening to a lot of XTC at that point. Production. Somewhere in the back of my mind I was thinking, this will make everyone happy. Which, of course, it didn't, and it doesn't. [*Laughs*]

It made me happy. That's a great song.

Well, that's good.

What was it that you did to the song to make people happy?

You repeat the chorus a lot of times. You make it bright. You put the hooks on it. You decorate it with riffs and hooks. But even so I think my idea of what a pop song is is different than a record company's. Because they weren't sure at first what the single was going to be. I was thinking "It's obvious!" I don't think they heard it.

I think it's a good song but most people seem to feel it's *very* obscure. And, again, it's one of those things where people say, "What did you *mean* by 'Book of Dreams'?" I said, "Well, 'in my book of dreams' is a phrase, like 'in my wildest dreams, in my imagination.'" That's the way I meant it. I didn't mean it as in my journal where I put my dreams that I dream at night. People think of it very literally.

That's how I took it, that you were referring to an actual collection of dreams. I took it as a reference to Kerouac's *Book of Dreams*, which is a very faithful record of his actual dreams.

Someone gave me that. I read some of it. I've never really been into Kerouac, though my brother is. You know, "Tired of Sleeping" is about night dreams. "Book of Dreams" is about day dreams and the future.

The thing about Kerouac's book is that it's so revealing to write down, uncensored, your actual dreams. And he wrote in the introduction, "what shame I'd feel to see such naked revelations so stated, because the subconscious does not make discriminations between good and bad." Which seems very similar to the process of writing songs, and expressing those interior ideas without the conscious mind getting in the way.

Right. See, that's the hard part, when you start to have a little jury of critics: journalists, record company executives, boyfriends, family members, fans. When you start to have those people speaking up and going, "Hey, that won't work!" You have to work through that. Cause if you're really a songwriter in your blood, your instincts will take over. And once you're on the right track, there's no stopping you, really. Regardless of how famous you are and how much money you have. I think if you're really a songwriter, once you start, your instincts will really guide you. But you've got to get rid of the critics.

How do you do that?

Hide. [*Laughs*] You withdraw for a while. Reading other people's stuff helps me.

Songs?

No, just other people's writing. And so you can kind of *catch* it. It's catching. It's contagious. You can catch the spirit again. But you have to be careful about that, to go towards those things that will help you and not make you judgmental towards yourself, or critical.

So when you're writing, are you able to suspend that critical voice or does it still enter into it?

Sometimes it still enters into it. But I find recently that if I'm writing about something that really interests me that the subject itself just draws me in and I'm not thinking about what the newspaper is going to say. So that helps.

When you're writing, do you actively guide the meaning of the song or do you follow it?

I try to do more following. I find if I try to lead it, then you get something that is stiff or contrived. Whereas if you go back to the original thing that provoked you to write the song, there's some answer in there. It's outside of yourself. It's in the situation that you're writing about. That's where the answer is if you get into trouble. I find that I feel more that I'm following something that is already there. There's a way of arranging the information so that it will make sense and be beautiful. And so it will be all in harmony and everything will feel right. And it's a question of wiggling it around until it falls into place. A song, when it is really well done, it feels balanced and it feels right. It's a question of manipulating it a little bit here and there, a little bit everyday, for months, until it falls down, falls into the music. That's the way it feels to me.

You have to write about something real in the world. You can't just say, "Oh, I'll write about this." It has to be based on something actual.

In your own life?
Yeah.

When you mentioned the way songs will fall into place, I thought of your song "Men in a War"—
That was hard [*laughs*] to write.

I can imagine. It revolves around the idea of a phantom limb, that one would still feel a leg or an arm even after it is cut off, which isn't the easiest idea to get into a song. And the song is so perfectly balanced.
That was a weird one, because I was not paying attention. I was driving somewhere in a car and it appeared almost like a telegram in my mind. Men in a war. And that's basically a medical fact. I thought, "I'd better write this down, because it's such a strange idea." And I thought, "Well, what are you after? What are you trying to say?" I wanted to bring the comparison of violence to your body. Whether it happens through a war, or whether it happens through sexual violence. The woman in the song is experiencing sexual violence. Some people don't get that, and they think she's getting an abortion. To me, there's a parallel between the two experiences. To me, that was a valid enough reason to write the song.

But it was very hard. People listen to it, and it's not a clear anti-war song. It's not "We must end the war." Some people listen to it and they don't know how to feel. Except that when you sing it live, it really has a strong impact. And everybody just seems to start getting up and jumping around. Not dancing with joy, but just moving. The rhythm of it and the intensity of it just seems to *hit*.

When I heard it, I didn't even think of war as much as how we have to deal with reality, that we still feel things even after they're gone.
Yeah. When you receive a bulletin like that: "Men in a war who have lost a limb . . .", you start to think, "What am I trying to say and what is the reason for it?" And it's not so important that you state it in a song but that you know what it is. Because that's what forms the secret heart of your song.

People, when they listen, want to know what you're singing about. And if you know what it is, they'll know what it is. Not even that you have to say it, but if you know what it is, then they'll know. Because it will be there in the structure.

That one I don't know if I pulled off. That one took a long time for all the pieces to fall into place, and I still wasn't sure. I think if it were a perfect song, I probably would have edited out some more and done something else.

It's a challenging idea to get into a song, and that seems like a signature of your work, that you will get some pretty ambitious concepts into a song, things most people wouldn't try.

I try. Those things are interesting to me. If I'm going to write a song, I might as well try to write something that hasn't been heard before.

Although my *ideal*, and I have to say lately, I've been listening to Elvis Costello, all of his songs over the last ten years, and the great thing about what he does is that he still writes about love, thwarted ambition, jealousy, all these basic things in life that aren't particularly ambitious. Everybody writes about love. But at the same time he'll do it in a way that it's his and it's distinctive. He's not afraid to use long words, he's not afraid to use his vocabulary. He's not afraid to say, "I want you," and say it over and over again for five minutes. And it's still unmistakably Elvis Costello. As a songwriter, I need to be able to say those things that are a part of everyday life: I need you, I want you. War must end. How you get to say them without sounding like a jerk or sounding simplistic, that's my next challenge. Because everyone says, "Oh, she's so intellectual." But I *am* trying to communicate. How do you say it but say it in such a way that it seems as if they haven't heard it before?

It seems that you answer that question in your work by your use of images. You use pictures that show us something that allows us to feel for ourselves, rather than be told something.

That's what I find beautiful. I found that to be one of Dylan's strengths. Not that he said war must end, which he did, but when he said, "A hard rain's gonna fall," and used the images of "white ladder covered with water and white man walking a white dog." All of these images have mystery in them and *they* say racism must end and all men must be brothers. But they don't come out and say it. They have it within the images, which we recognize from our own lives. And that to me is where his strength was. Not that he was a great politician, but that he was a great poet and he used those images to reveal those basic messages. Because it's not about messages. If it was just about printing messages, you could write a pamphlet or a bulletin on index cards and pass them out. So it's obviously not just messages that we're trying to give. It's got to work on some other level.

You said that "Men in a War" came to you like a bulletin. Do you have any idea what the source of those kind of ideas is?

It's like I hear a voice. Yeah. It sounds a little spooky: "Oh, she hears voices." But the best songs are just like that. I'd say it comes from your subconscious. A mystic might say it comes from God, but I don't want to say God because I'm a Buddhist and I don't believe in that, necessarily. It's when you are connected with something outside of yourself. It's when you are connected with something happening in life. It relates back to paying attention to the situation that's outside of yourself. Does that make sense to you? In other words, it's not enough to just invent it. It has to be connected to something real outside of yourself. In life. I don't know how else to describe it.

When receiving it, do you think it's a bulletin you are sending to yourself?

It doesn't feel that way. "The Queen and The Soldier" was one where, again, I had been circling for months. At first it was an "Alice In Wonderland" kind of song with a red queen and a white queen, and they were living in the same castle and they were going to have a fight, and I thought, "That's the stupidest thing I've ever heard. I will not tolerate this scene anymore." So then I got rid of one of the queens and had the queen by herself in the castle. Again, this takes months of circling.

Then when I had the soldier come to the door, the whole thing seemed to happen in front of my face, as though I had nothing to do with it, and all the details were right there and you know you've really got it when everything starts to rhyme of it's own accord. And the rhythms and the rhymes just seem to be right there. And it seems inevitable. And you're kind of held in the grip of this for a few hours. For two or three hours, you're just held by this and you have to finish it. You can't just leave it. You're completely absorbed by this thing. And it seems to be taking place in front of you as though you're watching it. It's a very peculiar thing. And it's wonderful when you feel it. And later you look back and think, "How did I do that?" And it's almost as though you didn't do it. And it's very scary, because you're sure it's never going to happen again.

I was watching a special on JFK. And I noticed that people, when they are very moved by grief, that their language became very condensed and would start to rhyme. And they weren't being poetic. They were trying to express something that meant a lot to them. And I noticed that the quality of their language changed. Suddenly they started to speak in that way that you speak when you're writing songs, if you're close to something truthful. It was very eerie to watch and see that.

You mentioned people in grief. Do your songs come at times of grief and other emotional turmoil?

Usually there is some feeling of fighting my way through something very hard. I keep hoping that I can write happy, joyful songs, too. I'd like to write something like Stevie Wonder. He has such pure, joyous feelings that it hurts. I'd *love* to write something like that.

Is writing for you a playful experience?

At its best. There's a feeling of relief when it's finished. It's like doing a puzzle. At its best. That's when no one's pressuring me, or looking at me, or trying to get me to finish writing, or trying to get me to face some deadline. That's a *really big drag*.

You get a lot of that?

I've gotten some of it, just because we're all still learning how to balance the artistic thing and the business thing.

You mentioned that phenomenon when things start to rhyme of their own accord. Does that make you feel that these songs are already written, in a sense, and that what we have to do is uncover them?

It used to feel that way to me. Now I feel, maybe with just this last batch of songs, [that] they feel more contrived. I can see where the cracks are and where the seams are and where I've pasted things together to make them whole.

At its best, I feel that it's like you described. "The Queen and the Soldier" seemed that way to me. "Luka" was kind of like that, although I was aware I was doing something I hadn't been doing before in quite that way. It's kind of dangerous to fall into that because then you lose control. You feel like, "Well, it *came* that way," so I have no control over it. Whereas I'm trying to teach myself more about melody and crafting a song, so you have to know when to step in and manipulate it a little. If you just give up to it and say, "Well, that's the way it arrived," then it's kind of absolving yourself of responsibility. [*Laughs*]

Sometimes it seems it can arrive wrong, if you've got a faulty connection, and you have to keep digging to get it right.

[*Laughs*] Right. Or people will go, "Why did you kill the soldier?" [*Shrugs*] That's just the way the message came. I didn't kill him. It just had to be done. [*Laughs*]

Is it necessary for a songwriter to have a complete grasp of the meaning of a song?

You can't possibly. I don't think you can ever really know. And if you think you do, I think you're mistaken. Some people go, "If she doesn't know what it's about, who's supposed to know?" But the fact is that it will make sense in a certain way. It might not make logical sense and at this point in time, but it makes sense. . . . in a sense. [*Laughs*]

Leonard Cohen's songs are like that to me. A lot of the songs, I don't know what he means, but you get a sense of what he's talking about, pieces of his life, but you don't know what the whole story is. But it's okay, to me. I still feel that I know this man from the pieces that he's given me. And when I met him, it was confirmed. I felt I knew him as though he were a friend of mine. Which is not always the case.

I think of your songs "Big Space," which I feel that I understand to a point, but there seems to be something bigger about it. I love the line, "All feelings fall into the big space / swept up like garbage on the weekend."

[*Laughter*] I think a lot about feelings, which is unusual. Most people feel their feelings and I think about them. I'm constantly trying to become more articulate with them. And to feel them as well. I think for a long time I did not feel them, as a way of protecting myself. You learn to disassociate yourself, so that your feelings seem to be out there somewhere. As I get older and more comfortable with myself, they're coming back into me as opposed to being out there. As opposed to "Small Blue Thing" where it's something abstract that can float around. It sounds *terribly* abstract, but it does make sense.

That's why I love that garbage line, because it mixes the abstract with something that's very down to earth: sweeping up the trash on the weekend.

Yeah. I am interested in real life.

And that seems like the real challenge, to translate abstract feelings into language people can understand.

That is the challenge. How do you make it accessible to people? That's why I'm always pleased when kids like my songs. They like "The Queen and

the Soldier," they like "Luka," or "Tom's Diner." They'll send me pictures of the
diner, or the queen sitting in the diner. They mix it all up. It makes me feel
that I've done a good job if I can reach people from all different levels. That's
why I was pleased that "Tom's Diner" did what it did, cause suddenly all these
black kids in the neighborhood where I grew up in New York were listening to
my songs. So it had this impact, and I'm happy when I feel that the songs can
go into all different levels of society. That's what I'm aiming for.

**When writing, do you ever feel that something is too abstract, and that
people won't get it?**
Sometimes I feel that way, but then I think if I censored myself everytime
I did that . . . I used to go on a long, rambling apology that nobody will understand what this song is about, but, oh, well. They are kind of code-like. A lot
of them are kind of knitted-up, crocheted, and bundled up. "Knight Moves"
was stolen from bits of conversations. But some people love that song. They
love the chorus. They don't quite know what the verses are about, but it
means something to them. It resonates. So I just throw it out there. If they like
it, they like it, and if they hate it, they hate it.

**Your song "Fancy Poultry" is great, and it seemed really brilliant the
way you use the image of chicken parts and relate it to people.**
Yeah. It was about the women in Ironbound. Obviously, if it was just about
chicken parts, you could put in words like liver or gizzards, and it would never
work. But the breasts and thighs and hearts, that's a while side of life. Some
people don't get that *thing*. There's the words, and the thing behind the words.

**It's one of those areas, like "Men in a War," where no one has been
before in a song.**
That's where I'm most comfortable. If I feel no one else is around doing it,
then I feel happy. I feel like I must be in my own spot. Occasionally I think
people will really hate this, because they'll just think I'm being morbid or griz-
zly. But I do have a tendency to want to bring things down to the facts of life,
and the physical. Which kind of goes counter to the whole idea of being ethereal and poetic. I really am interested in the world as it is.

**Some of your images are extremely physical, like the line in "A Room
Off the Street," ". . . her dress is so tight you can see every breath that she
takes." It's like a Raymond Chandler line.**
It was one of those things, like "The Queen and the Soldier," where you
feel like you're seeing the whole thing: the dark atmosphere, the color red, the
red tapestry, the red dress, something's gonna happen but you don't know what
exactly. I never thought of the similarity between those two songs until now,
but there is a similar feeling. You feel as if you're watching it. I was originally
going to call it "Cuba" because that seemed to be what Cuba might be like.
But then I thought, well, my last name's Vega, everyone's gonna think that I'm
Cuban, and then I'll really get into trouble.

Any advice as to how to best get in touch with the source of creativity?
Be attentive. Don't listen to people who try to make you do things. Don't
listen to advice. [*Laughs*] Don't listen to advice, and pay attention to your
moods and your visions and your weird ideas and the things that seem too

weird for other people to understand. There's usually something in there that's good if you listen to it and let it come out.

I guess it's really a question of how you want to spend your time. I realized also that for a long time I was spending my time on how I wanted to look, and shopping for clothes and whatever. And you can still go shopping for clothes and all that stuff, but just be attentive to the little voice that comes into your mind saying, "Men in a war . . ." You might have to stop everything and go, "What? Why should I pay attention to this?" But there's something in there.

Are those voices coming all the time, or—
You get on a roll. Sometimes it seems as if they're there all the time. Other times you're just as dry as can be and you can't hear anything. And that's when you need to fill yourself up with people that you love. For me, it's Lou Reed and John Cale, Leonard Cohen, Bob Dylan, Rickie Lee Jones, Natalie Merchant, R.E.M. All of these people have something vital for me.

I was wondering if you liked Rickie Lee.
I really admire her a lot. She really moved me, especially with the *Pirates* album. I would just listen to that like crazy. I also feel that I know where she's from, with her background and her family history. Whenever I read an interview with her, I'm very interested in her as a personality. I empathize with her a lot. I feel a connection with her. I have no idea if she feels any connection with me. I met her last year, but I just sort of feel that I know something basic about her from her music.

It used to be Laura Nyro that I used to get that from. So you go back to those people and fill yourself up. And you get yourself excited about writing again.

Is that excitement harder to connect with now that you are an established artist in the industry?
No, I find it doesn't have anything to do with it. When I met Rickie Lee Jones, my mouth was completely dry. It has nothing do to with being in the industry at all. [*Laughs*] It's very basic. You sit in your room like you did when you were a kid, and play the records. Maybe now you can be a little more analytical and other times you can be more business-like and think of marketing schemes. But that shouldn't have anything to do with how you feel when you're sitting alone in your room the way you did when you were a kid and it meant the world to you.

Those records, to me, were my lifeline into the world. Even when I was a receptionist, I would go and look at records, and figure out how much money I could save to buy whichever record I could get, because I could only get one. See, then you get the *Berlin* album and take it home, and you can't listen to it all day everyday, but you listen to it twice a year and that's enough.

Being known can create its own pressure. But I really believe it's in my blood. I think if I were not famous I would still be writing. I've written songs since I was fourteen. I got my record contract when I was 24, so I had ten years to figure out what I wanted to do. I would still write.

Are you always working on songs?

I'm always writing something and working on something. People think I have writer's block, but I don't really have writer's block. It's just that my filtering process is really long. It takes months to work on something until it's right. I still have songs that I was working on for the last album that never came out. Some things will lurk around for eight years. So I'm always working on something.

Do you feel that there are new things to be done in songs, and that the song itself will continue to evolve?

Yeah, absolutely. The songs come from the time, and every time has its own form of folk song. Like "Bonneville Dam" by Woody Guthrie, that's nostalgic now. But there are songs that will speak now and new songs to be written about now, and stylistic experiments to be made. Because it's not just the information. It's not just "I love you" or "we must all be brothers" but the style and the way that you sing it.

Songs, as opposed to other artforms, are not physical. Unless you record them, they don't exist outside of yourself—

It's temporal. Which is why they have to be truthful. If it's not truthful, you'll forget it and it will disappear. You have to call it up and tell the story again, which means that you have to have the need to tell it. And that's the nature of songs. The chorus keeps coming back. It's a part of life. You have breakfast every morning. You wouldn't say, "I don't want breakfast today because I had it yesterday." Most of life is cyclical.

I think that's why songwriting is so primitive, and why children understand songs. They say that people with brain damage, for example, can remember song lyrics even when they can't remember how to speak. They can't put together linear information but they'll remember the lyrics to something.

Pete Seeger recently said that he'd rather put songs on people's lips than in people's ears.

That's Pete. That's been his lifework. I listened to him as a child. That's what he does. It's visceral. Whereas with me, I always wanted to put songs in people's ears. [*Laughs*] I'd try to get people to *stop* singing along, *stop* clapping. It's like, I'm singing now, you be quiet. Which is not exactly the spirit of folk music. People ask me if I think I'm a folksinger, and most folksingers tend to bring people together and I tend to make people feel alienated. So I don't know how much of a folksinger I am. I do like to think that people are listening.

* * *

Jules Shear

Universal City, California 1988
Los Angeles, California 1992

"When you hear a piece of music that you really like," says Jules Shear, "it hits a place that nothing else ever hits. That's the reason I got into music, to get back to that thing." It's the thing that makes the songs he writes so special, whether performed by him or the legion of singers who have recorded them. It's the same thing that causes his fans to become fanatic about him. They're never complaisant in their devotion for Jules: they record and collect rare performance tapes, compile archives of articles about him, gather and swap new recordings of his songs by other artists, and happily gush for hours, when allowed, about the glory of his greatness.

Of course, I'm one of them. And I'll forever be celebrated by them for including Jules in this book of great songwriters, most of whom are more famous than him. And maybe it's because he isn't more famous that incites us who know about him to be even more fervent in our reverence for him. As Dylan said, "I prefer secret heroes," and Jules is one of the most beloved of these secret heroes.

Like his idol Jimmy Webb, Jules is a great example of a "songwriter's songwriter," in that his songs are the kind other songwriters aspire to write. He organically fuses the best aspects of all previous pop music in his songs—the rhythms and catchy hooks of Motown and R&B, the lyrical dynamism of Dylan and Simon, the melodic prowess of Jimmy Webb, Brian Wilson and McCartney, the craftiness of Tin Pan Alley and more. It's why so many other songwriters—including Susanna Hoffs, Rick Danko, Natalie Merchant, Marshall Crenshaw, Dion, Maria McKee and more—have enlisted him to collaborate on their songs. Ian Matthews paid tribute to Jules by recording an entire album of his songs, the wonderful *Walk a Changing Line*.

When I tell Jules about the depth of devotion that his fans express, it ruffles his feathers. Like other great artists, blatant evidence of such direct adoration can be unsettling. "That sounds like the kind of person who will say, '*Jules, I love you!*' and then shoot me," he says, only partially joking.

He first got into music in Pittsburgh, at the age of five, when he wrote his first song, "Oo-Eee," drumming on a tabletop. "The lyrics were surreal. I still remember it to this day." He wrote mostly "ditties" until the age of thirteen when he picked up his brother's guitar, turned it upside-down to play it lefty, and invented a strange technique that he still uses to this day: an open tuning that allows him to form chords with his right thumb.

At the time he loved Top Forty radio and listened religiously, memorizing the Top Ten songs each week. This inspired the writing of two or three songs a week all the way through high school, "much to the detriment of my schoolwork." He kept writing songs, many songs, and started a band called Funky Kings with Jack Tempchin, who went on to write songs with the Eagles.

After that Jules formed Jules & the Polar Bears, recording two albums and a pair of EPs, the latter of which was produced by Peter Gabriel. Next came the first of many great solo records, the great *Watchdog*, produced by Todd Rundgren, followed by *The Eternal Return*, *The Third Party*, *The Great Puzzle*, and *Healing Bones*, his most recent at the time of our second talk, in 1996.

He's a songwriter always looking for new ways to express himself musically and lyrically in songs. Unhappy with stale metaphors, he invents fresh and unusual ones, as in the song "Love Will Come Again" from *Watchdog*: "Wishing your life would set like thick cream gravy in a bowl / but how to keep the bowl from spoiling?" He saw that lyric scrawled on my list of questions and laughed, mentioning how Todd Rundgren said that the song had "a high caloric content." He's a serious songwriter who doesn't take himself seriously and still seems to have a lot of fun writing songs, a fun that is reflected in the solid joy contained in every one of his records.

"Get in here, you," he said with a sleepy smile when he saw me, beckoning me into a conference room where we were surrounded by stacks of albums. He mentioned that he had picked up *SongTalk* in the past to read about Jimmy Webb, with whom he collaborated on an unfortunately unproduced musical.

JULES SHEAR: It was going to be a real musical, where people were talking and then they'd break into song. So I wrote one song that Jimmy wrote a countersong to. Which was a *big, big* thrill for me. You know, because I used to go crazy as a kid when he used to do that kind of stuff.

It's interesting that you worked with Jimmy Webb, because he's one of the great melodists of our time. And like him, you write incredible melodies; melodies that have a big range.

It's his influence, I'm sure. I think one of the biggest reasons he was an influence on me is that I never had the feeling that he was trying to write a hit. He was just writing something that he thought was amazing. And they [his songs] happened to coincide with the time period where that was just what people were looking for.

I don't know, I guess melody isn't as important as it used to be. Do you think that?

No. I think when people hear a great melody, they are relieved by it. There's not enough of it.

I wish that would be true, 'cause I'm certainly not going to change. For the first time in my life I would see someone listen to a song—not one of mine but maybe something I like—and the reaction would be, "Well, it's kind of melodic . . ." And I wonder, What's wrong with that? Is that something bad?

I just don't think melody is as important to people as it used to be. It would be very strange for that to be a sociological phenomenon, but I think it is.

How do you pursue melodies? On the guitar?

On my own, I play guitar. But when I was working with the band, Reckless Sleepers, I played nothing and we all wrote the music together. They played, I came up with melodies, and then I went to work on the lyrics.

The whole idea of having the group was to draw some of the creative juices from them as well. I have a tendency to be introverted, and I'm not really that crazy about that part of my personality. One way I can be more out-going is to share the creative process with other people and force myself [*in sarcastic voice*] to come out of my shell.

I'm trying to do that in all sorts of ways. One way is by living in New York City, where you're forced to do that. And the other is by working with a band. It's an effort to not be so isolationist, to not be so cut off, to be more at one with the world.

But to write great songs, you do have to isolate yourself, don't you?

No. I think a lot of great things come out of collaboration. Though it's very difficult for me to write words like that.

There are a lot of musicians who aren't good songwriters. But they have a lot of great ideas. And I can put these ideas together, not because I'm such a great craftsman but because I do it so much.

One thing definitely happens, and that is that the songs become a lot more rhythmic because we're dealing with live drums and live bass playing loud in a rehearsal room. And another thing it does is to keep me from writing so many chord changes. To keep things interesting for me, I'll write a lot of changes. If we're in a room and everybody's playing loud and a groove is happening, I don't really need that as much.

One of the great things about your work, especially the album _Watchdog_, is the great range of styles, from rock and ballads to folk and funk. So many records nowadays have such a narrow spectrum, with every song using the same sounds.

Todd had a very, very eclectic bunch of songs to choose from. He chose the songs from about twenty-five I had. And his idea of selecting songs for a record was sort of a one-of-each idea. Like, "We'll have one of those and one of those . . ." And so that was his input.

In the song "Deliver Love," from *Demo-itis,* the verse is in a minor key and the chorus in a major key; it sets up a great contrast.
Yeah, I'm really attracted to that minor sort of thing. But once again, it seems like it was much more popular to do something like that in the late sixties. And it's not as cool these days to write a real minor thing, but I love that kind of stuff.

Do you care much about what's cool?
Obviously not! [*Laughs*]

Is it easier to write a melody in a minor key?
Maybe. I don't like to use minors that much because it seems like there's a danger of using them up. [*Laughs*] I try to be sparing about it. Then when you go to it, it has much more of an effect than keeping everything minor all the time.

Your song "If She Knew What She Wants" is in a major key, but it's that movement to the relative minor chord which makes the melody so strong.
Yeah. I don't really think about these things consciously. As you mention them, I'm thinking about if unconsciously I'm really thinking of these things. And it's just a feeling, really, that you get when you go from one chord to the next. But I don't really think about if it's major or minor.
When I wrote "If She Knew What She Wants," I wrote it on one string of the guitar. And so it's sort of like what the bass would be. So I was totally unaware if the chords were major or minor until I wrote out the lead sheet.

Have you written other songs this way?
Yeah, I've gone through phases of it. Because the way I play, in open tunings, I can't always play all the chords I want, like if I want G with B in the bass. But if I play the bass line, I can do that.

So you often generate melodies simply from a bass line rather than from whole chords. Do you think that frees up the melody somewhat?
Yes. You know how sometimes somebody makes those really beautiful chords on the piano and you go, "Wow, that's such a beautiful chord there." And then you realize it's not the melody that's any good and it's not the chord changes that are any good. It's just a beautiful chord. That's why I kind of like the idea of keeping it really basic. As I said, "If She Knew What She Wants" I wrote on one string on the guitar. I think, if you do that, anything you add to it can only make it better. Because you know, at that point, that it sounds good to you with only one string. Then you've really got something and you don't have to depend on somebody making unusual weird chords.

Do you still have the method of playing guitar lefty with your thumb barring the chords?

Oh, yeah, I'm not giving up on the method, Paul. The world's going to have to come around to me on that one.

And you still always use an open tuning?
Yeah. It's a G chord with E in the bass. So if you play everything but the E, it's a G chord, and if you play the E, it's an E-minor chord.

Do you sometimes write songs to titles?
Yeah. I dread to say. Because I have gone through these stages of not wanting to work from titles. Purposely not wanting to.

Why not?
Because I know a lot of songwriters who have a bunch of songs that have the most amazing titles in the world. And the songs are awful. People who write around titles. People tell me they've just written this song with this outrageous title. And you say, "Whoa. That sounds great." And then you hear the song and it's terrible. Because they just had an idea that they were not able to turn into a song. And so as a reaction to that, for several years, I've never written anything to a title. But I've gotten over that. I try to get over all those weird things and try to be able to write a song starting anywhere. Whatever makes it easier.

I've been writing with Susanna Hoffs, and she was saying how the hardest part is that you can write about anything. What do you write about? When you have so many choices, where do you begin? So by starting with a title, you can be instantly directional, and you can have a way to go with it. Getting started is really a key.

Did you write "Human Bones" to the title?
No. I didn't know what it was going to be called. It was just me and Rick Danko [of The Band] sitting there with guitars. He had these chord changes and I tried singing over those chord changes. And I sort of had the feeling that that was where the title went. I might have been singing something syllabically that sounded a little bit like that when we were messing around. And then later on, after he left, I thought of it.

I love the musical contrast of the verses, which are in a minor key, and the chorus, which is this great heroic progression of four major chords.
[Laughs] Yeah, I know. I know. When it finally hits that last major chord, it's got a little bit of that skies-opening-up quality that I really like. Well, Danko, you know, he's connected to all those kinds of feelings. When he makes up stuff, he's got music dripping off of it.

Speaking of minor melodies, one of my favorite songs is "I Didn't Know Your Smile" [from Demo-itis], which has a great melody and real cool phrasing.
Oh, I'm glad you like that! Nobody ever mentions that song. I really like that one. I guess it started out as being kind of Marvin Gaye influenced, but as with all of my songs, they started out with me thinking of something else, but by the time it's done it sounds like another one of my songs. [Laughs]

You said that you don't mourn for songs that don't make it on your albums. Do you ever mourn for songs that do get on your albums but that people don't respond to much?

I always think somebody notices them out there. Even if nobody mentioned "I Didn't Know Your Smile" to me ever, I would probably think that somebody out there really liked that song. Because I know what that feeling is, loving songs. Or really loving songs that are obscure album cuts, songs you just happen on for some reason or other. You love it and you know nobody else in the world knows it or maybe five people know it. And something about that makes the love for the song even stronger. It makes it a little more special for you.

I think it's good if somebody out there has that relationship with one of my songs. I'm really happy about it. I don't have to know about it, but if you mention it, I don't mind.

You've been collaborating a lot recently with other writers—and I think about what you said about how songwriting decisions such as whether to use "a" or "the" can be bad enough to make when alone, but truly terrible to have to discuss with somebody else in a collaboration.

Oh, it can be kind of stupid. But the whole dynamic has to do with who you're working with. Somebody else changes the dynamic dramatically. Because all those inner dialogues that you have when you're trying to write something all become *outer* dialogues, all being voiced. Like, "This lyric—is it weird? Is it creeping you out or not creeping you out? "

You always have such distinctive and unexpected metaphors in your songs. There's that great line about the thick cream gravy from "Love Will Come Again." And I love the line about pea-pods in "Never Again or Forever."

[*Laughs*] Yeah, pretty good, wasn't that one? "It was harvest at the Hazeltown farm, and in the fields we'd meet / I could feel the pods and know the peas inside were sweet."

And in your song "Make Believe" from *The Great Puzzle*: "The skim milk of human kindness stinks, I flush the whole thing down the sink . . . ." Lots of food imagery.

Yeah . . . Food imagery. What do you think *that* means?

What do you think it means?

[*Laughter*] The psychiatrist. "What do you think it means?" I don't know. I don't ever think about it.

The song "Leave Town" from *The Third Party* is one of my favorites. It starts with this verse about Pericles and Aesop. Where did that come from? Does it refer to a myth?

[*Laughs*] No. Because the song was about people having to leave the place where they live, I figured I would do it historically. So I had the first verse about ancient times, the second verse is sort of depression times in America, and the final verse would be like Pittsburgh today. Which was, at that point, about steel mills closing and people leaving. So I thought up some good ancient names, and I just made them up. That one was the ancient one.

Really? I always figured it was a real fable you had adapted. It's got that line about the potion made of bark and all. That's some good stuff.

[*Laughs*] Yeah. I was just making it up. I'm sorry to disappoint you.

I also love the line in "By and By" about the neglected garden. That's such a strong and sad image.

Yeah. "There's cobwebs on the window, there's the garden you neglect/you don't want to get it fixed up, you don't want to get mixed up, with anything you might have to protect."

You always manage to come up with a good physical image to show something. Is that intentional or just intuitive?

It just sounds good to me. [*Laughter*] I don't know what that is. It just seems like for some things, you need something concrete, and you want to set an actual picture in somebody's mind. If you end up using too many abstract things, the whole thing becomes abstract. And then you have to face the possibility of losing somebody. A lot of people don't care if they lose anybody. "What's the Frequency, Kenneth?" [*Laughs*]

I really try to have it make sense. I guess I empathize with the listener. But it doesn't work, because people end up not understanding them really, the way I understand them. I don't know what anybody thinks the song "Healing Bones" is about, but any of the stuff that I've read about it has not been about the stuff that I think it's about. So I wasn't able to really get it across to people, what I was singing about. But the intent was there. I tried. And people still hear the song and think it's a great song and they still love it. And I tried but I didn't do it. People didn't understand it.

It seems that way with any song, though, that people have their own interpretations based on their own lives. And those can be valid.

I think so. That's why it doesn't really bother me that much, but it's a fact that they get it wrong.

How so? What did they get wrong?

[*Laughs*] It's a story that I created in my mind to write this song. There was a movie I saw in Woodstock. And there was this scene of a farmer and his wife working out in the field. She is running this thresher, and—this is a lovely story [*laughs*]—she falls backwards into the thresher in slow motion. And he is in the field, and he turns around and watches this happen. And I used that. I have no recollection of the rest of the movie. But I figured "Healing Bones" would be the story of that guy and what happens to him, and his reaction to this happening. And most people think it's just a "she left him" song. It was much more, if you read the words: "You couldn't see my face, you had your back to me / I watched the unbelievable symmetry . . ." I was writing all this stuff and it didn't get across. It wasn't concrete enough for anybody to understand.

Now does it matter? I don't know. If people like the song, it can be "she left him." Maybe that's what it should be about! She does leave him. But there's so much more to it, the way I was thinking of it. I pictured him going to the city and moving away from the farm because he couldn't stand to be there. He's obviously feeling desolate. I guess it feels depressing. Like you say, it has that minor thing in the verses, which makes it feel kind of dark.

But the chorus is very uplifting —
Yeah, because it's a pleading kind of thing and then it opens up with his wishing for her return.

Do you think that, generally, people do understand your songs as you intend them?
I don't know. I do know people hear songs in really different ways. People hear songs in ways you really can't imagine. I hear songs in different ways than writers. I think it's just a fact of life.

Is songwriting a fun process for you?
It's fun to have them done. [*Laughs*] There are those moments. They don't last too long, but there are those moments when the sparks go off. When you overcome a hurdle.

Generally, it's fun. But it's an odd kind of fun. Work is the best thing for me, the most important thing.

That reminds me of your song "Standing Still" [from *Watchdog*] with the line, "I want to be working now, don't leave me standing still."
Yeah, definitely. I was definitely having a lot of that. "Standing Still" was written while I was going through all those problems with the record company. And working on my songs was the only thing that was real to me. That's definitely what that song is about.

Another favorite is "Mary Lou" [from *Big Boss Sounds*]. The opening is so evocative: "She blew into town with the summer corn / Sweet and golden freshly from the farm." It's a great set-up.
Yeah, I always liked that line, too. That one is a real throwback to days when I first lived in L.A. I used to hang out around the Troubadour bar. And a new girl would hit town, you know, and everybody would fall in love with her immediately. Mary Lou was just the name of a friend of mine; she wasn't the person in reality, but I thought it would be good for that sort of person.

Was there a real minister's daughter, as mentioned in "I Know I Know"?
[*Laughter*] No, there wasn't actually. I wrote that song in Todd Rundgren's guest house in Woodstock, New York. All the musicians were there, and I was thinking, "We have all these songs to play and I want to play them, but I want to play something down but rocking."

I'd been driving around Woodstock, and there are all these old churches, so I got the idea to write something about someone who lived up there where Todd lives. I had never been there before, so it was kind of a raw impression of something that might go on. But I don't think it was really very accurate.

It is a hard rocking song but the chorus is so melodic.
Yeah, I always liked that bridge/chorus thing. And Todd plays a good solo on that one.

You know, when you mention these songs I have to actually go through them in my head because I don't really think about them much.

I guess I listen to them more than you do.

[*Laughs*] Probably. But I'm probably about due. Before a record comes out, it probably wouldn't hurt me to go back and listen to things.

Yeah. Do some research, Jules.

That's right. Except most people aren't as familiar with the stuff as you are, so I can get away with it.

I know quite a few people who are major experts on your work. Do you have any sense of how much people know and appreciate your work?

No, I don't think I do. Because I'm not famous in my everyday life. I just go about my business. And I live in New York City where I don't really stand out much. I take subways and nobody ever goes, [*in a high voice*] "Jules Shear!" Or anything like that.

Do you remember writing "All Through the Night"?

Yeah, very well, actually, because it was a very odd situation. I was in London with a couple friends of mine and we had rented an apartment in Palmer's Green. They wanted to go out and have fun, but I was feeling bad because I hadn't written anything in a while.

So I decided to write a folk song—just so I could write something that day, and it wouldn't take up too much time so I could go out and have some fun. It was really a strummy sort of song. I wrote it all in four hours or so. Then went on with the purpose of having fun. And I had no idea that would ever become a hit song. I thought it was really simple lyrically.

Did Cyndi Lauper choose it for herself?

Her producer heard it and played it for Cyndi and she flipped over it. He called me and told me she wanted to record it. I said that that was great. He said, "Do you want to meet her?" I said, "No." He said, "But you know what? She really wants to write with you." And I said, "No, I don't want to write with her, that's okay. If she wants to do the song, that's fine."

Because I was enjoying life in Woodstock writing songs and I didn't want anybody to bother me. But he kept coercing me . . . so we hung out for a couple of days, and we wrote a couple of things together. We wrote the song "Steady" and a song that ended up on her record, "Kiss You." That was kind of an update on "Love Potion 9."

Was she fun to work with?

She *can* be fun. She has a lot of really great attributes as far as writing songs. One is she's really outgoing. And she doesn't mind at all if I say, "I'm going to play on guitar and you make up something while I play." And she'll say, [*in a Lauper-like voice*] "Okay!" [*Laughs*] And I'll play and she'll go, "Whaaaaaahhh," and this *voice* will come out, which the whole world knows as being Cyndi Lauper. And it is. She isn't shy or demure. She's totally game and open to doing what needs to be done.

When you're working on a song, do you have any technique for getting the ideas flowing?

I don't know why, and I don't feel bad about it, but I seem to really have a lot of musical ideas. So when I sit down to write a song, I can usually get something going pretty quickly. It's bringing it to fruition, finishing it, that's the hard part.

Lyrically?
Yeah, lyrically, and making all the parts fit together musically. But the first burst of inspiration is probably the most fun part.

One way to make it happen is to do it so much that a momentum is created, and you get on a roll with it. Do you do that?
I like that idea. I like that. I think you can get on a roll. But then there's the other side of that, when I'm doing something like now, and I have a record out, and I have more than one job. I'm a recording artist, I have to meet other people, I have to go out and do a lot of other stuff, I have to play shows. And you can't get on a roll. And after a while you start thinking, "I can't write a song today. Even though I have two days off. I won't be able to get on a roll. Because I have to go to Cincinnati next week. I've got to play a show in Denver, or something." So that can also subvert your discipline.

Yes. Because it can take a couple days just to get it going. You need some extended time.
You can get lucky and get it the first day. But a lot of songs, I think, are just stepping stones. You write it to get yourself to that real one.

So if you're working on something that doesn't seem great, you keep working on it and finish it?
I do. I finish them. I try to finish them all. I don't feel right until they're done. And I don't care whether they're not as great. I think it's good to. Because then you don't have to start second-guessing. You're not second-guessing, "Should I finish it, should I not finish it?" You just know, "I'm in here till the quick. I'm going to battle with this thing until it's done." And then that's one more doubt that you don't have to have in your mind. But that one doubt is taken care of. You know you're going to finish. But I'm pretty good at finishing. I know a lot of people who have a hard time finishing things. It can be a terrible torment for them to get things done. It is for a lot of people, I think.

When you're working on a song, do you generally finish the melody first and then work on lyrics?
There's not any rules anymore, I don't think. And I have gone through phases of having rules. Recently, when I work by myself, I've been starting with words, actually. Four or five lines. Maybe six. And then they wouldn't even be, maybe, in any form of rhyming or poetry. They would be just what the song is going to be about. And then write the music, and try to fit those words in there somehow. It's kind of a weird way of working. Once I'm done, then it's like filling in the blanks. But by then I know what the song is about, so it really makes filling in the blanks really easy.

Do you find, when finishing a new song, a sense of validation? Some writers have said that period of happiness gets shorter as they get older.
Really? I don't know. I get excited when I actually hear it back and I think it sounds good. That's it. Then I put it behind me and say, "I got it. It's there.

It's on tape or in the notebook." And I don't think about it again until I make the demo. And then when I hear it in the demo studio, I get excited again.

Loudon Wainwright said that he doesn't listen to other songwriters when working on his own songs. Do you feel that?

[*Laughs*] I listen all the time. I like to hear stuff. I like to always try to find stuff I like. It's hard. I always feel like the person who likes the most music wins, basically. I feel like I'm always looking for something to like. And so that constantly is happening. I mean, it never can be bad. If you hear something that's terrible, you go, "Oh, geez, I'm so much better than that." And if you hear something that's great, you go, "Oh, God, I'd really like to write something as good as that." So whichever way it hits you, if you have the right attitude, I don't think it's going to be bad.

I think it's really good to hear a lot of stuff. That's me, though. I've always really loved listening to music, to records in particular. Not so much live shows, even. I love to sit with the headphones on and listen to a record. I like it. Always, whether I'm working or not working. In the hotel, I got a pile of CDs over there. I like to listen all the time. I'm glad that I can find stuff that I like to listen to, so I never really stop.

I know one of the fears is that you will be overly influenced by something.

Yeah. But I don't think it rubs off in any noticeable way. I've never noticed it rubbing off. It might go in there somewhere and then come out five months later, sitting in a room, and an idea comes out, and I say, "Oh, that sounds a lot like that Grassroots record I was listening to the other night."

Do you have any idea where your ideas come from?

Things get inside; you don't really know how they do. They tend to pop out at the oddest times. And lots of times when I'm working on something, I'll get excited about it because I really dig what I'm working on.

In the back of my mind, I think I'll probably even know why I like it, probably because it's reminiscent of something that I liked when I was a kid. Or maybe something I heard a month ago, I don't even know.

When you hear a piece of music that you really like, it hits a place that probably nothing else ever hits. Because music is so unspecific, it can worm its way into places I think words can't. And I'm sure that's the reason I got into music, because as early as I can remember that's a feeling I wanted to experience over and over again.

And that's always what I'm looking for, to get back that thing. And knowing what that feels like, you can do it for yourself, if you write something really good. And you can think, "If there's someone out there in the world who's at all like me, it will do it for them, too."

* * *

Bruce Hornsby
Burbank, California 1996

Bruce Hornsby is burning. We're at NBC in Burbank, on the set of "The To-night Show," about six hours prior to the taping of tonight's show. Jay Leno is nowhere to be seen, and Bruce and his band are burning through a spirited re-hearsal rendition of "Spider Fingers," the opening cut of his album, *Hot House*. It's a great performance, and even the usually jaded crew is impressed. Horn-sby's not the kind to go through the motions, and he sings in full voice and full heart. Music is what matters to Bruce Hornsby, and when there's a chance to play—be it a rehearsal or the actual event—he's completely, joyfully there, totally inside the music.

And when the time comes to play on a major TV show for an audience of millions, he chooses the song that most inspires him at the time. Though his record company would have greatly preferred that he perform his current sin-gle, the inspirational "Walk in the Sun," he's much more jazzed about jamming with his band than pushing his hit. And "Spider Fingers" offers him the oppor-tunity to really jam out. Here in this famous TV studio, with millions of dollars of technology surrounding him designed to propel his image to every corner of America, he's cooking on the keys. And he's smiling.

"It's the first time we've gotten to play a song on TV that wasn't a single," he says moments later, having bounded up the stairs to his brightly lit, plaid-dominated dressing room. "And we really reveled in that. Because we got to show more of what we are about as musicians. It's sad that the apparatus of the music industry is set up to really preclude music like that from getting out there."

It's an apparatus that isn't really prepared to deal with the totality of a musician like Bruce Hornsby. Because he's more than a gifted singer-songwriter, he's also an accomplished and inventive jazz pianist. And the industry isn't set up to support someone who crosses over so drastically between the commercial world of pop and the artistic world of jazz. Yet Hornsby refuses to stay in only one world, and in each album he has opened up his music to allow more playing, more jazz, bringing in great musicians like Pat Metheny and Branford Marsalis, while never abandoning the powerful appeal of the simple pop song. Rather than choose one over the other, he simply does both. Though he humbly says that he's a "jack of both trades and a master of none," in fact he's both a great songwriter and a great jazz pianist, and his combination of the two has created a great hybrid that really is unlike what anybody else is doing.

It's a world of his own creation, a place where a kind of bluegrass jazz country soul music makes sense, where Bill Evans and Thelonius Monk can sidle up besides Bill Monroe and Hank Williams and no one seems out of place. Where Bela Fleck's banjo and Pat Metheny's electric guitars and sitars blend effortlessly with Hornsby's sparkling piano solos and spider-finger dances across the keys. The best way of describing it, we both agreed, is simply to call it "Bruce Hornsby music."

It's a kind of music he had on his mind many years ago, before anyone else had ever heard it. Born in Williamsburg, Virginia on November 23, 1954, Hornsby and his wife moved to Los Angeles in 1979, where he intended to break into the music business. They shared a little tract home in L.A.'s San Fernando Valley. "Our house had a view," he recalled. "Unfortunately, it was of McDonalds." It was in the garage of that house that he wrote a song about the small-mindedness of people in his home-town. Revolving musically around a haunting piano riff, it was called "The Way It Is."

This wasn't a time of great confidence for Bruce Hornsby. For seven years, he submitted tapes to every major record company and got shot down by each. In his little studio, though, he was coming up with a sound that was close to his heart, a sound propelled by the rhythms of rock and anchored by the beauty of the acoustic piano. He made work tapes that he never let anybody hear. But when he finished "The Way It Is" and put it down on tape, he had to share it with somebody, and took it inside his house for Kathy to hear. She wasn't crazy about it. Her cool response threw him into a funk that lasted for months. Stashing the tape in a drawer, he concluded it was worthless, and moved onto other things. Three months later he listened to it again, felt it deserved another chance, and recorded it for a demo. That was the demo that got him signed, and that was the song that made him famous.

"I thought that maybe it was nothing. Because you're writing it but you don't really know. So that's a good example of this whole fragile emotional and psychological mindset that is songwriting and presenting your songs in public."

Since that time, he's learned a lot about the public presentation of his songs. "The Way It Is" became a huge hit, and he won the Best New Artist Grammy in 1987 for his debut album. He's also been nominated for six other

Grammys, as well as being named by Keyboard magazine as their #1 Rock Piano Player for four years in a row. Besides collaborating on songs, as he and Don Henley did on "The End of the Innocence," he's collaborated instrumentally with artists in every genre, adding his distinctive pianistic magic to records by Branford Marsalis, Bob Dylan, Willie Nelson, Bill Evans and more. He also became the unofficial official keyboardist for the Grateful Dead, playing with them for nearly two years prior to the death of Hornsby's good friend and fellow expert on rare folk music, Jerry Garcia.

We are interrupted in the middle of our talk as Bruce's publicist slopes into the dressing room to introduce his "segment producer." "She needs to talk to you about what you are going to talk about on the couch." "I thought we weren't going on the couch," Bruce responds, somewhat annoyed. "I thought I was just going to come on and say 'Hey.'" It's the only time Hornsby has appeared exasperated all day. He's happy talking about his music, and very happy playing it, but the idea of talking about what he might talk about if they happen to have enough time to talk doesn't interest him much. But as soon as they leave, and he's free to focus on music again, Hornsby is happy.

Do you have one main approach to songwriting?

I write songs two different ways. Sometimes I write the songs lyrics first, sometimes music first. I think you can generally tell the songs written lyric first, because the music tends to be really simple. And the songs that are written music first have music that is a little more elaborate, a little more involved, maybe more instrumental sections in the song.

Sometimes in my songs the main memorable section might be an instrumental section. A melody that I'm playing on the piano.

So it comes different ways.

The cycle is writing, recording, touring. We just finished the recording cycle of it and went right into the promotional and touring aspects. I'm on the road a lot, hotels. It's hard for me to focus on completing a song. So what I end up doing is that, just living my life I get a lot of ideas. I get little bits, little germs. Maybe a story that I've heard that sounds like a song to me. I'll go as far with it as I can. Usually it doesn't go more than six or seven or eight lines before I know I have to work at it.

Now comes the work, the inspiration only takes me so far. I carry a notebook with me at all times. I read your Tom Petty interview and I was interested to see that he has all his old notebooks. Well, I do, too. Somewhere.

I started writing songs in 1978, after being intensely into the piano. I got my degree in jazz music from the University of Miami. You can actually do that—you can get a degree in jazz at American universities. What a concept. And since '78, there have been about nine notebooks.

Sometimes—like I saw Petty does—I go through [them] if I'm kind of barren, kind of dry. Because there are a lot of things in there that never became songs. I go through there, and generally I don't find much. But every now and then I have found something that sparked. Something that mildly and emotionally gets me in some way.

So I accumulate a bunch of different bits. Practicing a lot can't help but give you song ideas on the music first level. Something that feels great to you and feels like something you can really develop. When I get a germ of a melody, I press record on my little box, and accumulate a cassette of maybe twenty thirty-second little bits. It could be a chord progression, it could be a groove.

So you don't keep the tape running all the time?

No. Because usually I'm not trying to write. I'm basically an improviser as a musician, because I'm terrible at playing the same thing every night. It's always composing on the spot. I make up new words. Like on "Valley Road," for instance, I'll come up with an entirely different thing. Instant writing. Very stream of consciousness.

So I accumulate this tape, and when it's time to write the record, I go to this little wealth of information that I've accumulated, all these hopefuls— hopeful ideas—and I'll listen to the tape and a lot of the time I'll wonder what it was I thought was good about something. Because it's in the moment, and sometimes something in the moment is really truly special, and sometimes it's just a feeling, a vibe that happened then, and not really that great. I'm not good at identifying at the time something that is really the business. The real thing. So it helps me to have a little distance and to go back. And that is the beginning of the editing process.

From there, I'll try to develop something. Sometimes I'll get real lucky and the whole thing will come to me. The whole idea of a song will come to me. For instance, "Rainbow's Cadillac," which is one of my favorite songs on the record. Very simple. I think you can tell it was written lyric first because it's only three chords.

You're quite unique as a songwriter because—as you said—you're a jazz pianist as well as a songwriter. And the melodies of your solos are quite different from the melodies of your songs. It's like you have two melodic approaches going on at once.

Right. One is a much freer approach. In a solo setting, you want to be melodic but you also want to create intensity and energy, and it's not about what is singable. Sometimes I do want to be very melodic in my solo playing. Other times I want to be very rhythmic and intense, and create an excitement with the piano. To me, though, some of the best and most memorable melodies that I've written have been melodies written on piano, rather than melodies that came in my head.

There's a song called "Long Tall Cool One" on the last record. [*Sings melody*] It reminded me of a melody from an old musical. Rather than some pop thing. It's a jazzy melody. That's one I wrote on the piano. Same with "Walk in the Sun" [*hums verse melody*], that's something I wrote on piano.

Do you mean you write the melody by itself, or do you generate it with chords?

I'll have the groove and some chords. On "Walk in the Sun," the progression is very stock—I, flat-VII, IV. How many thousands of tunes have that, from "Sweet Home Alabama" to "Taking Care of Business," "Human Touch" by Springsteen. There's thousands of them. It's very stock. It's as generic and typical chord progression in pop or rock music as I-IV-V. So there's not too much that is interesting going on in that chord progression. And when you sing a melody to it, you might sing something very ordinary.

So, sometimes for me, it helps me melodically to write the melody on the piano. I tend to play, perhaps, more interesting melodies than what I hear in my head.

It's interesting that as a jazz pianist that you would choose that progression, which is a folk-rock progression.

Well, you have to realize that when I started playing I was into Elton. Listening to Top 40 radio. I have Dave Clarke Five records and James Brown and Wilson Pickett. That's my real roots in music. It's very generic, ordinary, typical. I love old Drifters records and Sam Cooke records. So very often jazz music has absolutely nothing to do with what I'm about as a songwriter. The jazz consciousness has only really come into my music really intensely only on the last two records. Before that, the jazz flavor was really only in the soloing on my records. From "The Way It Is" on. Where I got away with "blowing" on a pop record. Which doesn't have much to do with the songwriting, except that here is this section that I am going to blow over.

The jazz consciousness comes into my songwriting later, when I wrote some swing tunes and chord progressions more influenced by that.

It's a great sound, and what makes your music truly distinctive, this cross-current of pop-rock with acoustic piano jazz. Very few have done it.

Joe Jackson has. And Steely Dan, of course, is the most well-known example.

But you have a much more country-folk flavor to your songs that they don't have at all.

Also, certainly now, most groups are much less about improvisation in songs. They're not as much long soloing. Steely Dan's music borrowed from jazz harmonically and melodically and compositionally, but it did not at all borrow from jazz at all in the musical approach, the looseness and spontaneity of jazz. Those records are very much not spontaneous. As everyone knows. And that was their thing. And it's truly great; I was a big fan. But the playing consciousness is not coming from jazz. It's very studied.

That's not where our thing is. It's mostly about a bunch of guys who are into playing. And sometimes those two attitudes conflict. The songwriter's consciousness and the player's consciousness. Sometimes they're diametrically opposed.

Yet you bring them together in your songs, combining folk, rock and country progressions with an overlay of jazz. I wonder which ones appeal to you most, or if they all do.

I guess it's all about what moves me emotionally in harmony. My harmonic knowledge is fairly broad for this area of music. I know a lot of chords. But sometimes the progressions that I really love can be I-VI-IV. As opposed to something very involved, where you're writing a B flat over A, polychordal things.

It's all about what moves you coming up. You talked to Tom Petty—what really moved him coming up? I think it's fairly obvious because he sort of wears his influences on his sleeve. He's carved out his own sound, but it's very easily identifiable who his interests are. And I think most people are like that. Certainly, Springsteen seemed to be very influenced by those old classic Phil Spector records. That's what I hear.

So, for me, I have a disparate set of influences. But as a songwriter, my influences are not Harold Arlen, Johnny Mercer. They're not people who wrote standards that jazz players play. I'm not so moved by a III-VI-II-V-I progression with the flat-nines and all that jazzish standard tune type chord progressions. That doesn't move me as much in my soul, frankly, as I to IV.

It's just all about what I loved coming up. As a piano player, I was really into all these jazz guys. But as a listener, I loved those early Elton records—Elton's version of The Band. Very much an American sound and feeling. I loved the Byrds. So I can definitely get into some more extended harmonic language, which I have gotten into more lately. The last records, especially *Harbor Lights*, are harmonically more complex in a lot of areas. But generally, the harmonic language of my songs is not complex.

On some songs you combine the two, as on "Harbor Lights," where the second section goes into that syncopated rhythm and the melody is very jazzy.

Right. And I'm all for that. You've got to move on. So I'm really glad I went to music school, because I think it really broadened my horizons. I'm just a guy from a small town in Virginia. Wasn't turned on to a whole lot of interesting music there. But at school there were a lot of like-minded, kindred, searching people, looking to do things. So consequently I got turned on to everything from Stockhausen to George Jones. So if I want to move my music into another place, take a left turn, I don't have a problem doing it, at least on the knowledge level, because I've studied a lot of different kinds of music.

Whether it's successful as a song, who the hell knows? That's subjective. That section in "Harbor Lights," those kinds of chords, people who don't know much about me would think I was learning some new music there. But this is what I have been knowing for a long time, I just wasn't putting it into songs.

So I'm interested in pushing the music, trying to open up, trying to be freer in the music. So it's the odd combination of trying to write songs that are open and conducive to more playing, rather than some straight, strict pop song. I can't help but have been influenced by my time with the Dead, by the great freedom in their approach to music. I love the combination of really good songs, and their approach, which let the songs evolve. And move to new places. So that's sort of where we are in records now, and we are live.

You said that sometimes you start with a lyric and sometimes with music. Do you mean you write an entire lyric before writing the music?

Every now and then I've had the whole set of words, yeah. "Talk of the Town." "The Way It Is." Once again, very simple songs because they were lyric first.

How about "Walk in the Sun"?

"Walk in the Sun" was music first. I had this melody on the piano. I was going for a Drifters-ish feel on that song. I always loved what we called in Virginia "beach music." And there are three beach music songs on this record: "Longest Night," "Swing Street" and "Walk in the Sun." It's a little beachy. Beach music is regional soul music in the Virginia–Carolinas areas and Georgia. So I had this kind of Calypso-Latin feeling in the groove. So, yeah, it was a musical area that I went to.

You had the entire melody?

Yeah, I had a track. Sometimes I'll just write a track. "End of the Innocence" was a track. Sometimes I'll have a notion for a chorus. The chorus usually comes to me first. Not always. But often I'll get a chorus—lyrics—that has the idea of the song. And then where you go from there is like filling in the blanks.

And does the music then suggest what the lyrics should be?

Maybe. I don't know. That's sort of an intangible area. I'm not sure what suggests what.

The words and music of "Walk in the Sun" go together so well, as if they came together.

That's the trick. To work hard at something to make it sound easy. So it flows. And that's definitely what I try to do. So much of this is about writing words that are singable. Singability is so important. I've got to feel comfortable. I think everyone can tell when something is awkward. That's really what I work for when I write words.

I usually have a story in mind. I came to feel that I wanted this song to be about a guy who works in a strip joint, and his girlfriend's one of the strippers. Comes from our old days playing bachelor parties backing up strippers. And sometimes the stripper's boyfriend would be there. Sort of acting like her manager and making sure that nobody messed with her. And also to collect the money at the end of the night.

It was always so strange to be sitting there playing the Fender Rhodes on "Brick House" or "Play That Funky Music, White Boy" while this guy watches these other guys watch his girl. That's a very strange psychological scenario. So all these years later, it seemed like a good idea for a song.

So once I got that, you have to write a good version of that that sings well, and puts across the meaning, but not too obviously. I want it to be so it's not so obvious but you can get it if you look at it. I don't want to be too obtuse.

You mentioned "The End of the Innocence," which was written by Don Henley and yourself—was that a melody you wrote and gave to him?

Yes. I can take absolutely no credit for any lyrical content in that song. That's all Don. The music is mine. I had written my own set of lyrics to that music but I didn't think it was strong. It was just there, waiting for something else to come along to complete the picture. And the complete picture came when I got the phone call from Henley. He came over. I cut this track for him and he responded to it. I think he wrote the lyrics very quickly. I think it really hit him right away.

Do you recall what your original title was for that song?

"Lonely Town." It seemed a little too uninteresting. Too straight, too ordinary. It wasn't special to me. So I threw it away, but I liked the music. And Henley's lyrics took it to a whole different level, and I thought that was great. It's a song I'm really proud of. I do it on my gigs, and we just did it the other night on my PBS special. Don and I did it together.

Do you recall writing "The Way It Is"?

Yes. I had the lyrics first with that one. Inspired by intolerance and the narrow-mindedness of the small town that I grew up in.

My memory of that is a little hazy. I wrote it in the fall of 1985 in my garage in Van Nuys. Little tract home on Heartland Street, every house looks the same. Could see the golden arches from our house. I'd write and put things down on cassette. I had this song I was working on called "The Way It Is." I put it down on cassette and felt really good about this song. I really liked it. I never had any notion that it would be a hit or anything. I had never played any of these work tapes for anybody. But I brought the tape into the house for my wife to hear, and said, 'Hey Kathy—listen to this.'

I played her this tape, and she listened to it, and all she said afterwards was, "That's pretty funny." Pretty funny? What a reaction. It was just something perfunctory for her to say to have something to say. And that lack of enthusiasm and saying that inexplicable statement sent me into months of self-doubt about the song. I thought that maybe it was nothing. Because you're writing it but you don't really know. It took me three or four months to recover from that and come around to the other side of thinking it was good. And then I ended up recording it for a demo that ended up getting me signed. So that's a good example of this whole fragile emotional and psychological mindset that is songwriting and presenting your songs in public.

Did she ever revise her opinion of that song?

Well, sure, after it was a hit, which is pretty easy. In hindsight, everyone said, "Oh, I knew that would be a hit." But they didn't—they said it was a B-side if anything.

One of my favorites of your recent songs is "Fields of Gray," which is really a beautiful song.

Oh, thanks. It's one of my favorites, too. That's also coming out of the Drifters, Sam Cooke groove. I've always loved that music and I just wanted to write my own version of it.

I never wrote too many personal songs, about me. I guess I always thought it was a little pompous to think that anyone would be interested in your own woe is me tale. I don't like wallowing in self-pity songs. That's not an angle I find interesting. But every now and then something very personal will come, and this was one of them.

I wanted to write a song for my boys. My sons. And that's what "Fields of Gray" is, it's a song about how it feels bringing these kids up into this world of uncertainty, which is the fields of gray. As you get older, you realize I grew up as this cocky-assed kid, everything was black and white: this is good, this is no good. As you get older, you realize that it's not so simple, that it's mostly gray.

And so trying to guide your boys through that is sort of a daunting proposition for me, and it's a song about love for your kids, and your uncertainty about hoping you can do the best for them.

Did you write the music first for this one?

I think this was an example of something that came into being all at once. I probably had a basic lyrical idea first and then went to the piano. I don't quite remember. At the exact moment of creation of a song, there's a zone that you get into, and it's not like a zone that you're into for a definite period of time. It can be a zone that you come in and out of for a few days or a few weeks. It's very nebulous, really.

The process of writing, for me, is not very cut and dry. One thing for sure, it's one long process of self-editing and self-critique. I think a lot of people who have problems with writing, I don't think they're tough self-critics or self-editors. You go into the record stores and hear the young pontificators spouting out about something, like "Man, have you heard the latest Paul Simon record? Man, it just sucks, doesn't it?" And you go, "Man, let's hear your record. Let's hear what you can do. You're sitting here spouting off about this amazing person." You feel like saying that if you would apply the same scrutiny that you apply to other people's records to your own music, you might find that it's sorely lacking. So I think a lot of time people are tougher on others than they are on themselves.

For me, it's really a process where you get into a zone with a song and you're always thinking about it. There are certain problems that you can't seem to resolve. For instance, I'll have a couple of verses and a chorus, and I'll get to a bridge and think, what haven't I said? This is not finished. I haven't said everything I need to say here. I haven't tied it all together. All I've got is a bridge left. You have all this information you want to get into a short section. Unless you write an eight-minute opus, which I try not to write. What are you going to write? It's a constant strain of self-criticism and self-editing.

The bridge on "Fields of Gray" is an especially nice one.

I like to write bridges. I don't know what it is about them. Some of my songs don't have them.

I've tended not to be as adventurous in my pop songwriting. Some of my songs are a little bit more adventurous and more obscure and not stock, not standard. Yeah, I particularly like that bridge.

You mentioned how sometimes songs will just appear—

Rarely. But it has happened to me.

It's funny how the best songs often come quickly without a lot of work.

No doubt. And sometimes the best things come with a lot of work. So for me, I try not to have rules about songwriting. I used to say that I wasn't very good at sitting down and writing a song. Well, that's sort of a rule I was making, a restriction I was applying to myself. And I found that I could do that. Not every time. But it wasn't a bad thing to try to do and I could do that. Every now and then I would come up with something I really liked.

I wrote two songs that way that I really like: "Country Doctor" and "The Changes." So I've learned, hopefully, to not have any rules about songwriting.

I'm surprised by how many rules about songwriting people try to enforce. Because for every time a rule is right, there's a song that totally breaks that rule.

Have you found in your experience that anything affects the process, and can allow those great songs to come through?

I wish I could find the magic little formula. But I can't. I think deadlines and having to do it is as good as anything. It's not cosmic and esoteric and interesting. But, at least for me, it is pragmatic and it is a reason. It is something that can force inspiration: I have to write this song for this particular thing.

There have been times I tried to force it and it didn't work. That I did write a song but it wasn't very good. So I guess the best scenario for me would be a deadline that wasn't etched in stone. So if what I came up was no good, I could retract and write a new song.

Do you find that to write you have to separate yourself and cut yourself off from everything?

Definitely. I get ideas everywhere. I can get an idea on the bandstand. But as far as really working on it, it's too personal to do it unless I'm alone. I definitely need my own space.

Do you have any kind of routine for songwriting?

No. No rules. There are no clever tricks in songwriting that work for me. No little tricks for me.

Does time of day affect it at all?

No, it doesn't at all. It may affect the type of song you write. But not necessarily.

Do you always work on acoustic piano?

Generally. But I write lyrics first lots of time. I wrote some songs on accordion years ago and I liked that. Because it takes you to a different place. It's good to get away from your typical trip. But I don't really think I have a typical trip as a pianist. You just heard me play "Spider Fingers." That sounds nothing like "Mandolin Rain." There's very little that they have in common. And neither of them sound like "Talk of the Town." So I guess one reason why I might not feel the need to write on other instruments is that I'm always conscious of trying to take the music to other stylistic places. On the piano, as I was saying, I'm versed enough in different styles that it's not like it's a stretch for me to go from a jazzy context into a folk context to sort of a rave-up thing like we were doing today [on "Spider Fingers"].

Some songwriters have said that songs feel like gifts, like they come from another place.

I've had a few of those, as I said. But not too many.

Where do you think those come from?

That's the cosmic question. Who can say? I don't have a sense that they're gifts. But I have a very personal feeling about my songs, that they are like friends of mine, and some of them are better friends than others. Some are friends I've grown closer to over the years and some I've fallen away from. I know that's odd, but that's how I feel.

Many of the songs on the new album are written from the perspective of a musician in a band, and are about the experience of being a musician.

Yes. That's definitely my background. Like the song "Changes," being an old jazzer at heart, I was always one of the guys trying to get away with as much jazz as I could play. Much to the dismay of the crowd.

That song is especially nice, and such a musician's song, using the word "changes" in terms of chords as well as life changes.

That's right. A lot of people won't get the double meaning of that, because they don't know the musical definition of "changes." But that's all right. I write these songs for me.

I like the progression of "Changes," which is a really nice jazz progression.

Well, actually the progression is not so jazzy as the sound of it and what we bring to it. You could sing "Hit the Road, Jack" over those changes. It's that same type of thing, A minor, G, F, G. Just that walking bass line back and forth. So chordally, to me, it's very simple. At the end it goes to an Emaj7#11. Which is way out of the diatonic scale.

Are you extending the chords at all?

As far as the voices I'm playing, I never play just an A minor. Very rarely. It's probably an A minor with the added 9th and 11th. Like a big cluster. Like if you took your fist on all the notes from G to E, those white notes. That's the chord.

And that is quite different from most rock and pop music, in which you hear triads, often with added sevenths, but not extended like that.

No. My harmonic background is really coming from that area, influenced by Bill Evans and the way he played chords. And, really, he got it from the French impressionists, really, Debussy and Ravel.

Which is what gives your music such a unique sound. Even among pianistic songwriters, like Randy Newman, Elton John and others, their chords are mostly triadic, and not extended like jazz chords.

Yeah. That's maybe why some of their music is more accessible than mine. [Laughs] But don't get me wrong here, I've definitely had my triadic moments: "Fields of Gray," "Walk in the Sun." And they tend to be the singles. They tend to be the ones that everybody thinks sounds like what sounds like radio.

I like complex things but I think it's really hard to be good being really simple. Some of my favorite songs that I've written are three and four chord songs. "Rainbow's Cadillac" is a perfect example.

You mentioned that you learned a lot about songwriting from working with Leon Russell. What did you learn?

Leon has a very unique approach to songwriting. [Laughs] He engages in automatic writing. He writes a song right there, instantly. Sometimes he'll take an old track of a song and write a new song over the old track. Sort of like the rappers do. But not in as blatant a sense as that, where they take the actual track. He'll take the chords and write another song over it.

He'll steal from himself. For instance, we were in [the studio] and he said, "What's a song you like of mine, Horny Man?" I said, "I like 'Alcatraz.'" He said, "Why don't you play it?" I said, "Okay." So I played "Alcatraz" on the piano. He recorded that and wrote another song around it. Called "No Man's Land." [*Laughter*] And that ended up on the record. It actually was a pretty good song. So that's a good example of the unique approach he would take.

The song "Anything Can Happen," which we wrote together, came about this way: Leon said, "Horny Man, write me a Barry White track." So I did my best version of Barry White. He had this book of lyrics of his that he had written out, and told me to pick something out of there for him to sing. So I looked through. Hell, I didn't know—what was I supposed to pick? I didn't have any idea what would go with this, but okay. I randomly picked out this one song, this one set of lyrics, he studied it for maybe three minutes, said to turn on the tape, and sang this great, great version of these lyrics over this track. [*Laughs*] And there was the song. So that was really something.

Sometimes he would say to me, "Give me a title, Horny Man." So I would come up with something like "Dirty Pants" that I thought would be Leon-esque. [*Laughter*] And he would write some lyrics to that and store it in this notebook of his.

It was an amazing experience working with him. He doesn't get enough credit for being a true original and an amazing artist. He's very idiosyncratic; his thing is very unique.

Talk about someone who is hard to categorize. He and I share a duality in our musical personalities in that Leon has always been two different things for people. On pop radio, he was this balladeer: "Tight Rope," "Lady Blue," "This Masquerade." But when you went to his concerts, he would rock your socks off. Pure gospel rock and roll. The greatest shows I ever went to were Leon's shows. And in a similar sense, the people who listen to the radio know me as a pop balladeer, because those are the kinds of songs they play on radio. But people who really know me, they know more about "Spider Fingers," "White-Wheeled Limousine" and "Tango King."

You were talking about the importance of self-criticism. Does that criticism come during the process of writing, or is it something that you bring to it afterwards?

To me, it comes throughout. Maybe I overdo it. Maybe I should write the whole thing and then look at it. I can't help but judge it. Music is a very emotional experience. It's like if I play you a demo of a song and I say that it's rough, so just listen through it, that doesn't matter. You can try all you want to listen that way but in the end, it's an emotional reaction: either you like it or you won't.

That's to me the same as with writing your songs. You can't help but judge it. You can't help yourself. If you play something, you like it, yes or no. You don't even ask the question; it's natural, it happens. I think it's just human nature. So, for me, I'm judging it instinctively as I go. I mean, it's only natural. I'm judging everything.

* * *

k.d. lang
Hollywood, California 1992

The sun is shining for the first time after what seemed like an eternity of rain in Los Angeles. k.d. lang is gazing out the window of her hillside Hollywood home, wondering aloud if the sun will stay. In an old manual typewriter on the windowsill is a page of lyrics, yellowed and faded by months of the formerly blazing sun. It's the first draft of "Constant Craving": "Constant craving has always been . . . ."

She made the decision to abandon country music as instinctively and abruptly as she made the decision to embrace it. After recording many country albums, she knew she had to move on, but to where? She had a sound in mind: a rich blend of accordions, guitars, violins, vibes, piano and more. Constructing new songs around sounds and moods, she and her partner Ben Mink crafted elegant, sophisticated melodies, inspired by a rainbow of influences: 1940s movie musicals, spiritual hymns, Russian folk music, American jazz, Joni Mitchell-like tunings and harmonies, Indian music and more. And channeled through the Nashville-inspired Canadian soul of one of the most gifted vocalists to grace the airwaves in many years, the resulting album, *Ingenue*, emerged an instant classic.

"Constant Craving" was the last song finished for the album, and the last song on the album itself. Besides being a brilliantly crafted song, it's also a wonderfully produced record, with all of the instrumental ingredients she had imagined beautifully and subtly interwoven into the mix. It's also one of her most genuinely hopeful lyrics, maybe the reason she still keeps it tucked into her typewriter. "Always someone marches brave here beneath my skin / Constant craving has always been."

Kathryn Dawn Lang was born and raised in Consort, Alberta. She started singing at the age of five, mostly old folk songs like "The Water is Wide." Her older sister had a lot of records that she liked hearing, especially Delaney & Bonnie, Rita Coolidge, Leon Russell, Joe Cocker, Maria Muldaur, Emmylou Harris, Linda Ronstadt, and Anne Murray. As she got older she started buying her own records, mainly those by Joni Mitchell, but later Kate Bush and Rickie Lee Jones. "And then I just exploded," she said.

She started playing guitar at the age of ten and wrote her first song at fourteen on a theme she's returned to many times in her writing—emotional yearning. It was called "Hoping My Dreams Will Come True." "My first song came easily. My second song was 'Conclusion to Love' which was much more advanced." She went through phases when she considered being an actress, a professional athlete and a cinematographer. But ultimately she knew that music was to be her life.

What kind of music, however, still hadn't been determined. Country music didn't matter much to her until she was twenty years old, at which time it became her whole world: "I totally submerged myself in Patsy, Loretta, and Kitty and George and Lefty Frizell. When I realized I appreciated country, that's all I did. I went very deeply and totally into it."

Prior to this country conversion, she was a performance artist who had moved far from her Canadian roots. But after a few years of being away, she gained a new perspective on Alberta. "I realized that I kind of dug it and understood it, and that sort of triggered this loving the salt of the earth thing. But I had removed myself from it. So I had this really leftist side loving the really right side."

And that's how she approached country music, from opposite perspectives. One day she made the decision and said, "I'm going to do country." And all of her art friends said, "How are you going to do it?" and she said, "I'm just going to do it. You'll see."

She never felt actual acceptance in the country world but never sought it. After the abstract openness of performance art, she was drawn to the challenge of being expressive within the narrow confines of the country genre. "It turned out perfectly. Country music was restricting to me but that's exactly what I wanted at the time. I came from being a performance artist and there are no limitations. It's almost a competition to see who can be the most bizarre. I was a little bored of that at the time. I found the challenge to rework and be creative within the structure of country music—lyrically, thematically and musically. I was limited. I had to use these tools and I found that really interesting and challenging."

Today she's sitting at a small table in this sun-strewn room with little else around save for the typewriter, a CD player, some stacks of CDs, and a little TV covered by a towel. She has another home in Vancouver and goes there often to reconnect with the beauty of nature, but here on the top of this hill above Hollywood, surrounded by tall sycamores and pines, it's surprisingly peaceful. For a few moments, anyway, until our serenity is shattered by the sound of a shotgun echoing through the canyon. She regards it peripherally. "Living in L.A.," she says, "it sometimes sounds like a war outside."

After the interview, with the sun now shining victoriously through the branches, she thanks me for talking about her favorite subject. "You mean you?" I ask. "No," she laughs. "Songwriting. Thanks for talking about songwriting. People ask me questions about a lot of things. And songwriting's usually not one of them."

Was the switch to this style of songwriting on *Ingenue* a conscious shift of styles, or did these songs simply begin to emerge?
It was all of the above. It was a conscious switch, because I knew I couldn't write another country record. I just wasn't into it. I just didn't want to face another country record.

Why?
It just wasn't in me. You know, it's sort of like when you have a lover and you go, "Look, I'm sorry. It's just not in me anymore. And I have to leave." And then it was really just . . . completely open, and it was like option anxiety because we had a completely open structure. And no idea of where we were going to go. I knew the instruments I wanted to use: I like vibes and I still love [pedal] steel. I will probably always have steel. I love accordion and piano and upright bass and Ben [Mink's] strings, which are just mind-blowing.

So I told him these were the instruments I wanted to use, and then we went CD shopping and bought thousands of CDs, skipped through them, and started mixing different styles. Like we'd mix Kurt Weill and traditional Hawaiian music together. And we just started experimenting with what was coming out. We'd do the stupidest, stupidest little things on the guitar, and if it made us laugh we would take it and then work it from there.

"Still Thrives This Love" went from a joke to being a beautiful song. That's one of Ben and my assets, that we can see the beauty in the stupidest things and work them into beautiful songs. We don't give up.

So you had a sound in mind but not a style?
Right. We had no idea what style. As a matter of fact, even into the middle of the writing, maybe five songs had been written, we still didn't know exactly. We knew that we had all these songs and as we demoed them, we used the same instruments so they became cohesive. But by the fifth song, all of a sudden, *wham*, it came, almost like tunnel vision. We realized it was like a new vocabulary in music we were creating. So then we started to really mold it into that one sound.

Did you always know that you would eventually move beyond country music?
Absolutely. Always. I mean, it's not planned. But I've always been very, very intrigued and impassioned by so many different kinds of music that I assumed I would move on.

When you and Ben write together, do you start with a musical idea, or do you ever come in with a lyrical idea?

Very very rarely. Generally what happens is that we will sit down and we'll discuss, emotionally, what is going on with us that day. Like we just start off like with "How are you?" and have coffee or something. And then we pick up whatever instrument is sitting around. Because we always usually just doodle when we talk, when we're in writing mode. I might be playing mandolin, he might be playing guitar, whatever. Either we come up with a guitar lick, or melody line, or sometimes we just totally tune our instruments to something completely different from each other, but which is harmonically cohesive. But we don't know what we're doing [in these tunings] so then we write the song making up chords that work together, though we don't know what each other's doing. And then he deciphers them after. So that we get all these really extended chords after. It's really nice for me because then the melodic options are so vast. I get to have all these different inlets into the melody, where I can go with it.

So the two of you are working just on chord changes at first, with no thought or words or melody?

Kind of chord changes first, and feel of the song. And then what happens is that after we get the skeletal structure of the song finished, he will start to demo it on whatever machine we are using. He will build a platform for me. And then I get a cassette and I go away and write the melody and lyrics. And then when I come back, he has an arrangement. The arrangement is finished before the melody or the lyrics are put on. So it all is very intricate. All his string lines are almost in before I write. It's like two pieces fitting together, so that's why the arrangements are very specific.

When you're inventing those skeletal structures, do you designate verses and choruses?

No. "Constant Craving," as a matter of fact, wasn't finished until a week before we actually finished the record. I struggled really a lot with that song because I wasn't sure if the melody was the accordion one or the one I picked for the melody. The accordion part is [*sings accordion melody*] and that's a counter-melody to [*sings verse melody*]. So I decided on the latter.

I wasn't happy. I was fighting with the structure of the song right up to the last minute and finally I decided to take a verse out and put a guitar solo in, and Ben came up with that wonderful guitar solo, and it started to really fall together. But really at the last minute. It was a real tough tooth to pull, that one. It was really hard.

"Constant Craving" is a great title, and so many of your songs have wonderful titles. Do you ever have a title idea before beginning the writing process?

No, it's sort of all interconnected because when we're writing the song we talk about what emotions are being conjured. We talk about what the melody and what the chords seem to evoke in us. And then when I go away and I start writing the lyrics and I start seeing what kind of lyrics fit, it's all swirling, it's never really a pattern. It's whatever happens. It's not really ever a consistent formula.

Do you remember writing the lyrics to "Constant Craving"?

Yeah! [*Gets up to get typewriter with lyrics still in it*] They're faded, they've been in the sun, but there they are.

See, I struggle with tiny little words like "here just beneath my skin" or "just beneath my skin." Every little word. I take hours sometimes on one word. It's *horrible*. I hate it.

It's not a fun process for you?

When I'm finished it's the most rewarding thing there is. Well, you have a baby. It's what you do. You've given birth to a song. Yeah, I remember writing it, sitting here . . . I almost feel ill sometimes when I'm writing lyrics. Like "Season of Hollow Soul." I was physically ill from writing it because it's from such a dark place.

What were you going through while writing it?

Well, love. The difficulty of love. And how you have to remember that you're not always given what you think you need or want. But it was really about the process of losing lovers and how the experience of losing a lover is like a leaf that falls and then it turns into mulch and fertilizer for the next love. I was walking a lot in the forest during that period and I would see these trees, there would be a dead trunk and then a tree would grow out of the top, so you'd have a dying trunk and roots and then a tree growing from it. It was so amazing because of what I was going through.

I feel nature is my biggest text-book, my biggest reference.

And you can stay in touch with it even here in Hollywood?

Well, I make an effort at going to it. Mostly in Vancouver I was inspired, and then came here.

Why here?

I don't know why but this place has been really magical for me.

There does seem to be a concentration of creative energy in this area.

Yeah. Well, there are a lot of artists here, which is kind of fun.

"Season of Hollow Soul" has an interesting structure. The whole verse is on an A minor chord, and then the chorus moves to F, and revolves around two chords, the F and B flat. Do you recall constructing that structure?

"Season of Hollow Soul" was derived from a lot of very diverse songs. I don't know if it's wrong or right to tell you what songs we were emulating. It was derived from songs like "Those were the Days" and "Is That All There Is?" and the chorus was a little bit from "Annemarie's the Name." But we never try to steal. But songs like that are sort of put together and we love a lot of different types of music.

That one has such a triumphant refrain, yet the title, "Season of Hollow Soul"—

Is so morose. Yeah, I know. [*Laughs*] I think every song on *Ingenue* is about contrast. And I think *Ingenue* in itself is a contrast. It is about the balance. It's about the pain and the glory of love. If you summed it up, that's what it's about.

Another great contrast of verse and chorus is "Outside Myself" in which the verse could easily stand on its own musically, and then the chorus is such a beautiful contrast and complement to that.

"Outside Myself" is really interesting because I actually wrote the melody and the chorus in Berlin during the filming of "Salmonberries." I was actually writing the song for "Salmonberries." And I never even really sang it to Ben. Until he came up with some chords or something and I sang "Outside Myself" right over what he was doing. And it *worked*. And it was just so amazing. Then I went to the piano and played [*sings connecting piano part*] because I'm a horrible piano player and that was really naive and primal. And it worked.

Do experiences like that make you think that there is a magical source for these songs?

Well, there's never any doubt that that's what is happening. Yeah. There's just no doubt. That's just a given. They're gifts. And it's just a matter of clearing yourself and being able to channel into where it's going.

My whole thing right now is that I am faced with the challenge of remaining extremely committed after being faced with success. It's all about the reciprocity of the muses. To me being completely giving back to the sources that give to me is what my goal is. That's what my goal is, to stay creative, to stay completely full of integrity. Because it's so scary when you achieve your goals, your material goals, or the goals of being nominated for Album of the Year. I mean, it's beyond my wildest dreams. But when you achieve something like that, you go, "Oh . . ."

Now my commitment is even deeper. And it's even more severe. It's a real time to really reflect on your spirituality and how it's connected to music and success and all the things that come with that.

How do you keep yourself clear?

Through nature. Through friends that are really grounded. Through music itself. Through Ben. Through God.

Do circumstances affect when you're open to the source, or is it a question of luck?

Both. Luck is a part of it but it's also how much energy you put into it. Probably I think the biggest, biggest ingredient is integrity and honesty with it. Not compromising to yourself. And you could have the biggest pop record in the world, but did you compromise to yourself? That's the main line.

Does being famous get in the way?

Sure. The challenge is there. Not necessarily the outside forces. But I'm talking about the inside. You have all these rungs that you want to reach, and the closer and closer you get to the top, the harder I think it is to keep yourself inspired. That's what I mean. I don't necessarily mean that the record company pushes you more and more and more. That's not what I'm talking about. I'm talking about the inside desire to stay challenged.

Now, with the success that *Ingenue* is experiencing, I'm right now going "Oh, God, [*laughs*] what is the next record going to be like?" I can't *imagine* writing anything as beautiful as *Ingenue*. But I have to do it. I have to trust that whatever is going to come out is what is something that needs to come out. It's probably going to be totally different . . .

And you have no idea—
I have no idea right now. No, none.

Because we're all curious, too.
Yeah, I know. Well, who isn't?

What is the key to your collaboration with Ben Mink?
I have a real hard time writing because I'm not a technical writer at all. I'm a completely guttural and emotional writer. I don't know what I'm doing. To this day I could barely tell you if it's a G chord. Even when I produce, I do it completely on an emotional and instinctual level. And that's why the collaboration works. Ben is very musical and I'm very emotional. So every area is covered.

Many of the greatest songwriters, such as Lennon & McCartney, had no knowledge of music theory and this seems to have freed them from musical restrictions. Do you think not knowing theory is a blessing?
Absolutely. I studied music in college and I think there might have been a conscious decision not to retain what I learned, not to absorb it. Because I studied everything, and I just went and I didn't listen and I didn't learn it. And I don't know why, maybe I was stubborn, maybe I was stupid, but the results seem to be okay.

Can you easily communicate musical ideas to Ben?
Well, no. That's the whole seed to this story. I need someone who understands me, and Ben understands me on an emotional level *totally* when I'm talking about music. I can look at him and go [*gestures with hand*] and he'll know exactly what chord I mean. There's this one chord we call lime sherbet because it's sweet and sour and clean, and exactly like lime sherbet.

When you write on guitar, do you always use open tunings?
Not always open tunings but different tunings. Different than . . . normal. I just find that, because I do have a little knowledge of the guitar, that it is a block. Then you're thinking C-D-G . . . You're thinking of all the structures and how it's supposed to go. So when we're completely lost in a world of instinct, you have to be so set on your instinct that you can't apply your knowledge.

You want to get away from thinking about it too much?
Yeah. We write on instruments that we don't know how to play. Like "Outside Myself" I wrote on a keyboard and I have no concept at all how to play keyboard.

Playing chords?
Yeah. I picked out the melody first and then I started to put chords on it. I knew the melody, but a melody sounds completely different until you put the harmony with it.

Are you able, when working on a song, to keep your critical voice outside of the process?

No. Ben and I edit each other constantly. We've gotten to a point where we just check our egos at the door. We're at a point where we're not afraid to go, "You know what? That *stinks!*" And even if it stinks so bad, we can sometimes make it work. Like "Still Thrives This Love." Cause it really stunk. It was such a joke, and when something is so obviously a joke, you know that something is good about it. But if it's so bad, we'll throw it away right away. We only wrote ten songs for *Ingenue*. We actually wrote eleven but we got rid of one right away.

It's interesting the way you say that you and Ben go for things in songs that are jokes, or that make you laugh.

Oh, well, we're such jerks. We have such a jerky sense of humor that we understand that the *worst* songs can be beautiful. It's just a matter of how you do them, and how you arrange them and how you approach them.

"Tears of Love's Recall" is another wonderful song. The words to the chorus are quite haunting: "The tears . . . like blood to chocolate fall . . ."

It's the whole bittersweet thing of love. When you're thinking about somebody that you've lost or you've let go and you cry about it, all the blood and all the guts and the passion that went into it, when you're remembering it, the blood falls—but it's sweet, you're not bitter about it. It begins bitter but it ends up sweet because you're sentimental about it, and you think, "Maybe I'll get back with that person" when you know you're not going to. It's the process of bitterness turning into sweetness.

The melody of that one, and so many of your melodies, are very beautiful, and employ big melodic leaps. "Save Me" has that great leap of a major tenth, which is not something we hear much in popular music.

A melody has to move me as a singer. I think that I'm fortunate that I'm a singer because a melody has to really mean something to me as a singer. When I write a lyric or a melody or a phrase, it really has to fit my personality as a singer. And it has to move me as a singer. So the writer really has to put out to turn me on as a singer.

And as a singer you have a really big range. It must be three octaves at least.

It's three or three and a half. Yeah, I do like those big melodic skips, and I think a lot of that comes from people like Roy Orbison.

Do you recall writing "Trail of Broken Hearts"?

[*Long pause*] It came from East Indian influences. Then I kind of just went [*sings main riff*] when Ben was playing the chorus, and we had our signature lick.

How about "Pullin' Back the Reins"?

We wrote that real close to "Trail of Broken Hearts." We realized that we had tapped into something: sort of a New Age country. Very linear and open and wide. With very long, sustained steel parts and very smooth, acoustic patterns.

Another great title of yours is "Diet of Strange Places," which is also about craving, a "craving that wears you thin . . ."

[*Laughter*] There you go! It's about the same thing. ["Constant Craving"] is exactly the same song. It's written ten years later.

I woke up from a dream and I was in Japan and I actually fasted that day to help me write the song, and I wrote the song. I guess I was feeling very much in shock of the culture. I was really young and just being around all these strange things and strange people and strange culture and feeling, as much as traveling fills you and feeds you, it makes you feel empty at the same time. It's a weird paradox. That's what it's about, really, that you can travel and travel and travel looking for something but you'll never find it unless you find it inside. Which is exactly the same thing as "Constant Craving."

So you fasted to help you write?

Yes. It's just sort of this weird thing. I thrive on discipline. I'm a little bit of a martyr.

And did that give you the energy you needed?

Just for that song. I guess it's kind of like acting. You act out the emotions while you're writing. Like when I wrote "Mind of Love," I was here and I can remember getting up from the table and I would walk back and forth like a pendulum, in an emotional fight between two positions, which the whole song is about, fighting with your consciousness or fighting with your reality. And I can remember very well walking back and forth in this room. I think when you're in the middle of lyric crafting, it's about acting. I act it out. My whole day is spent acting out the song.

In that song you sing to a woman named Kathryn, which is your name. Are you singing to yourself?

Yes. Which is kind of funny because, apparently, when Warners released it, it had a really limited air time. They just put it out to see what would happen. And people called in and said, "I don't want to hear a woman singing a song to a woman." And I felt like, "Excuse me—listen to the lyrics." Yeah, I'm Kathryn. My name's Kathryn. It's really about fighting with your own consciousness.

Do you address yourself as Kathryn?

Yeah. I think that stems from when I was in trouble with my mother. [*In an authoritarian tone*] Kathryn! And Kathryn to me is more feminine . . . Kathryn is sort of what I want to attain. Kind of the older, more mature woman inside myself that I'm trying to attain. You know how you have different personalities?

We spoke about the formality of your writing. When writing country songs, did you find the formality to be a problem?

Yeah, but that was another one of the challenges. You see, to me, country had this list of requirements of what it took to be a country song. Whether it was instrumentation, chord structure, lyric—all these different requirements. And to me it was about balancing them out. To be traditional and progressive at the same time.

Do you remember writing "Save Me"?

"Save Me" was the first song that Ben and I wrote together for this album. "Save Me" sits at the beginning of *Ingenue* and was the first song we wrote together because it sums up the paradoxes that *Ingenue* presents. It has a country lag to it but it has all these new directions in it musically. Lyrically, again, it's "save me, save me from you but pave me the way to you." It's all about this trepidation that you feel in love. It was just like a door that we walked right through. It was a door. It was this new door.

I love the melody. It's kind of reminiscent of Joni Mitchell, in the harmonies especially.

God, I would never say that I wasn't influenced heavily by her. That's a tough thing, when you've been so influenced by someone. When I hear people who have been really influenced by Joni, I get really turned off. It's a really tough thing. I try to acknowledge by a tip of the hat and say, "Thank you. This is who I've listened to." But not steal their stuff. I'm really aware when writing something with Ben of "Does that sound too much like Joni? Does that sound too much like Rickie [Lee Jones] or Peggy Lee?" I really keep that in check because I don't want to copy them. But I do try to acknowledge them.

How do you stay in shape?

I hike. Or when I'm preparing for a tour, I weight train.

Does the exercise affect your writing?

Yeah. When I'm writing, hiking is the answer. Uphill is always questioning, the top is knowing, and back down is like going, "Why am I questioning?" [*Laughter*]

* * *

Madonna

Los Angeles, 1989

"The image gets in the way," she answered, when asked why people don't generally think of her as a songwriter. It's an image she's worked hard to establish in people's minds, taking her from the Midwest to Manhattan and to a home high in Hollywood's highest hills. Today she's more than famous; she's gone from the musical to the mythic while still alive, as much a part of our collective awareness as were Marilyn Monroe, John Kennedy or the Beatles in their day.

It didn't happened by accident. She's been wise since the start to the notion that it takes more than talent and charisma to shoot a star beyond all others into this pantheon; it takes controversy. "People are asleep," she said, "and you've got to do what you can to wake them up." She awakened more than her share of sleepers in a variety of ways, from dancing before burning crosses and sporting stigmata on her hands in the video of "Like a Prayer" to visually fusing, in her "Open Your Heart" video, the madonna/whore dynamic inherent in all images since her first appearance wearing lingerie and crucifixes.

Beyond this rainbow of shifting images and calculated controversies is a serious songwriter who writes or co-writes the majority of her own material, starting with first singles like "Lucky Star," which she wrote alone, through "Like a Prayer," written with Patrick Leonard, to "Take a Bow," which she co-wrote with Babyface.

Born in Detroit, Michigan on August 16, 1958, Madonna Ciccone wanted to be a dancer most of all, and studied dance at the University of Michigan in Ann Arbor. In 1982, after moving to Manhattan, she started attracting attention by dancing and lip-synching along to her single, "Everybody," at New York's Dancetaria. Her penchant for mixing her music with dance and visual flair coincided perfectly with the dawn of the video age, and she soon dominated the medium with videos for all her hit singles, from "Lucky Star" through "Like a Virgin" to "Take a Bow." To this day she's had more videos played, and played more times, than any other artist in the history of MTV.

Which is not to say her success hasn't been equally phenomenal on radio: during the last fourteen years, she's had 29 Top Ten singles, eleven of which went to Number One. "Like a Virgin" alone was at the very top of the charts for six weeks in 1984.

Her inevitable transition into movies began with *Desperately Seeking Susan* and has included Warren Beatty's *Dick Tracy* as well as an extremely intimate look at her life both onstage and off, *Truth or Dare*. And 1996, the year she gave birth to her daughter, was also the year of her starring role in *Evita*.

We spoke on a typically bright Angeleno afternoon during a break in the filming of *Dick Tracy*. She seemed openly relieved to be asked questions about her songwriting—a topic rarely broached during most of her interviews—and remembered clearly the exhilaration she experienced writing her first song.

MADONNA: I don't remember the name of my first song but I do remember the feeling that I had when I wrote it.

And it *just came out of me*. I don't know how. It was like somebody *possessed me*. It was like I wanted to run out in the street and go, "I wrote a song! *I WROTE A SONG! I DID IT!*" I was so proud of myself. [*Laughs*]

And then after that, they just kind of gushed out of me. Because I always wrote poetry in free-form verse and kept journals and stuff, but to be able to put it to music, that was a whole different thing.

How old were you then?
About twenty-one.

It's interesting to learn that you have written so many of your own songs. I don't think people realize that you're a songwriter as well as everything else you do—
You mean they don't realize I'm a songwriter as well as a slut? [*Laughs*]

It's the image that gets in the way. What am I supposed to do? The information is on the label. If they don't read it, that's not my problem. I'm not going to put a sticker on the outside of the album that says, "Listen—I wrote these songs!" You know, they pay attention to what they want to pay attention to.

This album, *Like a Prayer*, seems to be the most honest album you've done. Do you agree?
I didn't try to candycoat anything or make it more palatable for mass consumption, I guess. I wrote what I felt.

Have you candycoated things in the past?

It's not that I candycoated it. I just chose to write in a certain vein. It's like anything—it's like movies: There are brutally honest, frightening movies and there are really slick, commercial films, and I like both of them as long as they're well made.

In the past, were you writing more about a character than about your-self?

A side of myself. And a character. I'm constantly inventing scenarios that are a combination of something I know and something I imagine. But it's just a side of myself that I chose to show. I definitely have that slick, glamorous, manufactured side that I feel very comfortable with showing to the public. But there's the other side to me, too.

Is it harder, in songs, to reveal your inner self?

No, it's not harder. In the past I wrote a lot of songs like that, but I felt they were too honest or too frightening or too scary and I decided not to re-cord them. It just seemed like the time was right at this point. Because this was what was coming out of me.

When you say, "what's coming out" of you, do you mean that you're the kind of songwriter who is always working at it, or do you wait for inspiration?

I wait for inspiration. I set out to record an album and that was my state of mind at the time.

How does your writing process work? I know that many of your songs were written with Pat Leonard. You've mentioned that sometimes you'll come up with a melody and bring it to him and let him figure it out—

Yes. In my very retarded fashion I will sing it to him. Or hum the melody line to him, and he will put it into a chord progression and we'll come up with the song that way.

These are melodies that just pop into your head?

Yeah. And I start singing them just from my head. Or if I think of a lyric, like a hook or a line, I'll just put it to a melody and he'll bang it out on the piano for me.

You must have a great working relationship to be able to connect with him at that stage of the process.

We have a very good working relationship because we both come from the Midwest, and we both worked our butts off to get where we are. But, you know, he's the one who studied music. He knows how to read music, how to write music. I don't know any of that. I'm completely instinctual and he's com-pletely intellectual. So it's a really good combination.

Does he ever give you a finished melody to write words to?

Yes, he does. But inevitably we fashion it to me. I don't think he's ever written a melody that I just *took* and said, "Okay, that's finished, I'll just slap some words on it." It always needs to be worked.

One of my favorite songs on the album that you two wrote is "Oh, Father." It's one of those songs that has a near perfect marriage of words and music.

That's the great thing about Pat. I mean, Pat puts together these really strange chord progressions and these really great time signatures, and I'll listen to it and I won't even think about it. I'll just *put it on*, and I'll just keep playing it over and over again; it's like free association. I'll start singing words to it and making them fit. I don't think of structure. I don't think of first chorus, first bridge.

Did you come up with the melody for "Oh, Father"?

No, no, Pat thought of that melody.

It's interesting that you were free-associating on that song and yet the words are so specific and thematic —

Yeah, well, we definitely plugged into each other. I know, because I've tried to work with a lot of people. It's really a relationship. It's a relationship that works. There's definitely a chemistry.

You mentioned how melodies will pop into your head. Do you have any idea where those ideas originate? Do you feel that they come from beyond you?

[*Laughs*] I'm such a sponge; and I love so many different kinds of music, and I've listened to so many different kinds of music all my life. You know how you just keep memories in the back of your head all the time? I'm sure it's everything that I've ever heard. And then it comes out in my own bastardized fashion. What I am is what I've digested throughout my life. What comes out of me. I don't think it's *beyond*, I just think it's all stored up.

Have you ever experienced writer's block?

Sometimes, yeah. Oh, yeah, definitely. And when that happens, you just have to stop and go out or something. Go to a movie.

Some writers say that when nothing is flowing, they stay there anyway and try to force it—

I do that, too. Sometimes me and Pat will sit through it. We'll say, "Let's write a crappy song today." But then there are times when you just have to let it alone. And go get some inspiration. Ultimately, you can't force it. But there is a certain amount of discipline required. When I have to write an album, I sit down and say, "This is it." I sit down and write the album. I give myself a block of time. But once every once in a while, it's really tough.

Do you have any technique for staying in shape creatively?

Yeah, just living. Just experiencing life, being really open and observant.

Is it tough for you, being one of the most famous people in the world, to stay open and observant?

You can be open and observant in any situation. I mean, in a work situation, watching people on a set of a movie or whatever. I mean, humanity is everywhere. There are endless possibilities of ways to absorb the information.

You and Prince wrote "Love Song" together, which is a wonderful song. Did you and he work together or did he give you a track?

No. We did "Promise to Try" first. Pat and I. Once again, he just sat down and started playing. And I started singing. And we built it from there. We'd start stuff and we'd come back to it.

With "Oh, Father" he wrote the tracks, and I was doing the play in New York [*Speed the Plow*]. He came to New York and I was in a very, very dark state of mind. We got together in this really dingy, awful little studio in the garment district in New York. It was grotesquely dirty and cramped, and that's what came out of me.

The song "Cherish" is incredibly joyful. Were you in a happy mood when you wrote it?

I was, actually. It was before I went to New York. Absolutely. It was right before I left.

Was "Promise to Try" written for the little girl in you?

[*Softly*] Yes. It was . . . yes, it was. I mean, it's not just one thing. It's my father talking to me, it's me talking to me . . . and "Oh, Father" is not just me dealing with my father. It's me dealing with all authority figures in my life.

Does that include God as well? You say, "Oh, Father, I have sinned."

Absolutely.

In that song you also say, "I lay down next to your boots and I prayed . . ." Which kind of reminds me of Tom Waits. Are you an admirer of Waits' work?

Oh, I *love* Tom Waits. I've always loved him. He's great. He's a great performer. I love watching him.

What other songwriters do you enjoy listening to?

Prince. He never ceases to amaze me. I've heard all the tracks off of his next album that he hasn't released yet and they're incredible.

Stephen Sondheim, who I worked with for *Dick Tracy*. I never really appreciated his stuff because I didn't pay that much attention to them [his songs]. And having to learn his songs, which are *unbelievably* complex. I just have the utmost respect and admiration for him. An incredible songwriter. Incredible.

Complex musically and lyrically?

Oh, yes. There's not one thing that repeats itself. It's just unbelievable. When I first got them, I sat down next to him and he played them for me, and I was just dumbfounded. And then, forget about making them my own, just to learn to sing them—the rhythmic changes and the melodic changes—it was really tough. I had to go to my vocal coach and get an accompanist to slow everything down for me. I could hardly hear the notes, you know what I mean? So it was a real challenge. And they definitely grew on me.

So you eventually mastered them?

I *think* so. When we ended up recording them, I think Stephen was very pleased.

You're an actress, a dancer, a singer and a songwriter. Can you say what the most powerful art form in your life is?

God, it's tough. I like visual arts. I'd have to say music even though I love movies and dramatic arts. Music is the most accessible art form. And I think *everybody* relates to music. It is completely universal and therefore the most powerful for me, too.

Do you have a favorite song of your own?
[*Pause*] No, I don't like to say that. It's like having ten children and saying I have a favorite child. It's not fair.

You wrote "Lucky Star" alone. Did you write it on guitar?
No, I wrote it on synthesizer.

You say you're not a musician and yet you play guitar and keyboards.
I know, but I'm lazy and I don't practice because I've gotten involved with so many other things in my life, and I just had to make a sacrifice. Of course, Stephen Sondheim encourages me to start playing the piano again. Maybe I will.

Do you remember hearing "Like a Virgin" [by Steinberg & Kelly] for the first time?
I thought it was sick. I thought it was sick and perverted and that's why I liked it.

And that appealed to you?
Yeah! Sick and perverted always appeals to me.

And it sounded like a song you could pull off well?
Yeah. Because there were so many innuendoes in it, I thought, "This is great. This will really screw with people."

And you enjoy controversy.
Yeah, controversy. I thrive on it.

You've certainly generated a lot of it. After "Like a Virgin" there was "Papa, Don't Preach" and, of course, all the controversy surrounding your video for "Like a Prayer."
It's not really that I thrive on it. It's that I think it's necessary. I think art should be controversial. I think it should make people think. About what they do believe in and what they don't believe in, and if they don't believe in it, that's good too.

I mean, everything is just kind of opium for the masses. It puts people in a trance. I think it's good to hit people over the head with this stuff and make them question their own beliefs.

Is it hard to get an album scented with patchouli?
[*Laughs*] Yes, it is. I had to work hard for that.

* * *

Stan Ridgway
Los Angeles, California 1989

He's got a voice like a carnival barker, one of those sideshow guys who always sound like they're talking through a megaphone even when they're not, imploring you to pay a quarter to see the two-headed baby. Then when you go in the tent and see what looks like some rubber chicken floating in a bottle, the guy's glee, his perverse delight in showing it to you, makes it all worthwhile.

Such is the way Stan Ridgway leads you into the dark, derelict world of his songs; worlds that entail a vivid, palpable squalor that few other writers have captured in song. From a dilapidated Hermosa Beach bar ("A Mission in Life") to south of the border ("Mexican Radio") and beyond, he lures us into the shadows of his own sideshow with a sardonic mirth that makes it worth the price of admission.

He started writing songs in high school, where his affinity for the underbelly of urban life began to surface. "You work in opposites," he said. "Growing up in a clean, happy neighborhood can create an attraction to things in the dark." That darkness has been incorporated into the songs he wrote for his band Wall of Voodoo and for his own solo albums, including *The Big Heat*, *Mosquitoes* and *Black Diamond*.

"I rarely *think* about songwriting," he said at the end of an unusually long and thoughtful interview. "Mostly I just think about trying to get something to hang my lungs on." Earlier he expressed his aversion to the "cookie-cutting mentality" of songwriters striving to make hits, as well as his larger problems with talking about songwriting at all.

Then, like other songwriters thoughtful enough to harbor reservations about revealing too much, he divulged many of his songwriting secrets, even touching on his "paper bag" technique, a conscious method of delving into the unconscious that shines a light, albeit an inconstant one, into the shadows.

STAN RIDGWAY: Talking about songwriting to me is really an ambiguous thing. I honestly don't know how you can do it. [*Laughs*] How you can talk about songwriting with almost everyone without a level of self-consciousness creeping into it for a while? Even an interview about songwriting kind of gives me the willies.

Why is that?

I think you're in danger, possibly, of just knowing too much about it all. And what I think is interesting about the songwriters who influence me is that there's a certain level of primitivism. Or almost a level of their own academy of craft; it's not learned.

It's not something I really want to put my finger on. It's like creativity is some bird on a twig, and you don't want to get too close to it or it might fly off.

How do you approach it, without scaring it off?

What I do now is to collect a lot of words. I free-associate on a number of things.

Apart from music?

Completely apart from music. I find music to be at times a distraction. Music is such a powerful pull; depending on what you're playing or what you're listening to, it can make what you're writing maybe fall out too evenly or put it into a corner where it's not interesting to me.

I do something that some people call clustering. This sounds like something that goes on underwater with crabs, but it doesn't.

I'll sometimes start with a blank piece of paper and I'll think of a word. Just one word like "bend." And I'll put that in the middle of the page. And I'll circle it. And I'll just stare at that for a while. And other words will soon come to mind. Maybe "walls." Bend walls, I don't know why. And I'll draw a line from that circle that says "bend" to the circle that says "walls" and circle that. Now after a while, maybe "walls" says "paint," so I'll write "paint" and circle that and draw a line from "walls" to "paint" because that's where "paint" came from. Then I'll go back to "bend" and think of "rubber" or something, draw a line from "bend" to "rubber." And I'll just keep building this out.

What this enables you to do is to get away from the idea of "What do I write?" You're actually playing with words. And once this cluster builds up to a degree, you can pull back from it and something will shift in your imagination. And then you immediately go with that line.

It's a lot different than sitting there. It's valuable because you are drawing from an unconscious state instead of a state that says, "Now I am going to write a song about unwanted pregnancy." It doesn't offer up any *questions*. It just gives these answers: This is the way you should feel, this is the way you should think about this issue.

So you look for unconscious connections first.

Absolutely. Because to me that's more entertaining. Then I'm surprising myself. You don't know what's going to happen. You're basically tossing dice into your subconscious and seeing what pops out. And if you get to a point where you know that no one's looking over your shoulder and you're uncritical about it, a lot of things will tumble out. A little bit like a songwriting Rorschach test.

Do you try to write every day, or do you wait for inspiration to arrive?

I make an appointment. With my muse. Try to do it every day, at least for one period of time. It doesn't always mean that my muse will show up. But I'm there.

I have a series of shopping bags that I dump things into. I mark them like "February-March." And then I stop there, because it'll get too confusing, and I get another bag. Then I dump everything I have into there and it's kind of like a grab bag. I fool myself into thinking maybe I have an organization here, but I really don't. And when I'm just playing around, I'll pull out a bag and put my hand down in there and just pull out something. And say to myself, "I don't care what it is, but it's going to work." Then I'll just kind of fit it in without thinking to myself that I'm going to judge it.

It's a little like alchemy. You can alchemize from certain areas of your consciousness to have out what kind of new combinations can be had from that.

[*Laughs*] So I've got all these bags that I hate!

I've never heard of the bag technique. That's a new one.

It's good to always know that when the bag is filled, then it's time to start a new bag. I don't throw out anything for quite a while. You're building up a lot of bricks. Usually you have to sit there and go through it and say, "This is not very good. But I have to keep going." And if you think too hard on it, you'll stop.

Something I read last time in *SongTalk* that Van Dyke [Parks] said that I remembered was, "It's important to maintain one's composure." I think that says a million behind just one line, but you know what that means is that you've got to stop from going insane. [*Laughs*] From really hitting yourself in the head and saying, "I can't write."

So when you find something in a bag that you like, do you then take it to an instrument?

I have another series of bags. That contain cassette tapes. That have nothing to do with words or with lyrics. They're just feels and grooves. They're unrelated from the whole idea of having it be a so-called song. And then I'll alchemize the words against that. Then it's a matter of finding something that will be an interesting juxtaposition to that.

Countless songwriters have expressed that for them, the ideal situation is when the words and the music emerge together at the same time.

I've always found that to be extremely boring. Because it just falls into a sound that sounds like a lot of other things I've heard. It doesn't interest me as much as finding a surprise. So it's very rarely that I'll sit down and sing against chords.

How about your song "A Mission in Life"? The chorus of that is so majestic and moving musically; it seems as if the words and the music of that came together.
Well, the music was there first. Although it was like a strain of chords. It sounded very noble to me. And I did put it on a tape machine, and I'd just run around the house and sing, free associate. And out came a line about somebody sticking out their hand. As if pulling someone onto a lifeboat.

As I worked on that a bit, the chorus came about. Probably after I'd gone down to some bars in Hermosa Beach, I think. I was in this rundown old place that had probably seen a lot better days. I think it started out as a high-society bar about twenty years ago . . . but now it's just a dive. It had a lot of aquariums around that were real dirty. Nobody had cleaned them in a long time, so you had all these fish kind of belly up floating around. The irony of that struck me, and I went home and wrote the rest of it: "They drown in the tide" and stuff. So once I had that, that was the chorus, and then the rest of it came from a lot of things I had written. From some of the bags.

Where did the name Wall of Voodoo come from?
It was a play on Phil Spector's Wall of Sound. I had a collection of all these old rhythm machines and I was in a studio doing a track of five or six of them all hitting together; I turned to a friend of mine and said, "Joe, it's like a wall of sound." And he said, "No, I think it's more like a wall of voodoo." I never wanted a band called Wall of Voodoo. I thought, "My God, what are we going to do with that? Shouldn't we call ourselves the Dots or something like that?" But a band's name kind of becomes a sound.

First we were going to call the band Drunk Cops and we put it on a flyer and I woke up in the morning and realized that was really bad. I called the other guys and said we couldn't be Drunk Cops, so we said, "Okay, we'll be Wall of Voodoo." After six months it sounded perfect.

You said that you'll make an appointment with your muse but you weren't sure if he would show up. Do you have any method of getting the muse to arrive?
I'm reminded again of what Van Dyke said in *SongTalk*: "It's always important to maintain your composure." It's a little bit like Zen. I've had my share of interest in other religions, ways of thought. I was always a watcher of those Joseph Campbell shows ["The Power of Myth" on PBS] and the link-up of all kinds of manner of subconscious stories. So I try to trust it. Sometimes that's hard. I do what I can. I'm there and what's important is to keep it coming out.

Then, after that is over, you have to get enough distance from it for a couple of days and then look at it as if you haven't written it.

You put it away for a while?
I put it in a bag. Yeah. Once it's there and it's allowed to get away from having just done it, it's much easier to judge it. To not make it as personal. So then you get into a spot where you're looking at it fresh. That's hard to do the day you write it.

Do you remember writing "Mexican Radio"?

That was something that I think I wrote out in about an afternoon thinking about Mexico but only having just been in Tijuana. As I was writing it I was thinking to myself about a kind of person who is kind of flippant with what the culture was about. And I was also thinking, "Gee, this is really dumb. God, this is dumb with a capital D." And I was really enjoying that. It's really just a fun song.

I hardly ever write from inspiration. I don't have the mind for it. Sometimes I wish that I did. There's a certain price for anything. And people who aren't interested in paying those prices, I don't know what kind of material they're going to come up with. Nothing's for free. How can you possibly communicate to anyone if you don't have some experience on your own besides just sitting there and trying to write a song?

I spend half my time feeling really good and the other half feeling really bad. It's a balance and I think it's natural. I don't really know what *happy* is.

* * *

R.E.M.
Hollywood, California 1991

Michael Stipe's earliest musical memories start in Texas, and revolve around a spectral cow skull called Clyde that he kept on top of an old piano in his bedroom. Clyde scared him away from music for years, but he overcame his fear and returned to music at the age of eighteen, inspired by punk music, and by an invitation from a new friend to sing in a church.

It was 1980 and the new friend was Peter Buck, who lived in an old Episcopal church on Oconee Street in Athens, Georgia. It had great vibes, lots of space, and was perfect for parties. Just for fun, Buck decided to form a band to play there. He played electric guitar, and invited Stipe, an art student at the University of Georgia, to sing. He also invited Bill Berry to play drums and Mike Mills to play bass. They learned a lot of songs from the sixties—considered unhip at the time—but it enabled them to master the architecture of popular songs, wisdom they later applied to their own music. They called themselves R.E.M.

In 1991 their song "Losing My Religion" is the number one song in the nation, but they are no longer playing in churches. Today they're staying at a Sunset Strip hotel in Hollywood, where they are giving successive interviews to the press. Among other distractions, Cindy Crawford is in the midst of a photo shoot at the pool, easily visible from our windows, prompting the bandmembers to leap up frequently from the couch and monitor the modeling.

"Isn't she going out with someone famous?" Stipe asked to no one in particular as he surveyed the black umbrellas being shifted at poolside. His hair was cut short and he was days unshaven, wearing a raggedy Salvation Army jacket and baggy green jeans. A vegetarian, he ate salad while we spoke, and seemed initially uncomfortable with the focus of my questions. When asked about poetry, he first said he hated it, and then laughed, admitting he was lying. It was as if he made the choice to talk about himself rather than create fiction, and he chose the truth, a choice that also arises when writing songs.

"I found something that was secret, it was dangerous and it was exciting," Stipe said of the punk-inspired music he discovered at the end of the seventies. For a long time, R.E.M. too was a secret, known only to those in the know. They were secret heroes of the underground, "alternative" artists embraced by college radio for their jangly folk-rock sound, and the plaintive, yearning voice and poetry of Michael Stipe. They released a series of remarkable albums: *Document, Reckoning, Murmur*, and *Fables of the Reconstruction*. Like Talking Heads, who started only three years earlier, the combination of gifted, instinctual musicians and an eccentric lead singer/writer with a perspective as unique as his voice, R.E.M. exhibited a limitless potential in their ability to create songs both original and inviting, songs that could belong to no other band: "Exhuming McCarthy," "Seven Chinese Brothers," "Welcome to the Occupation," "It's the End of the World As We Know It," "The One I Love," "Harborcoat," "Finest Worksong," "Orange Crush" and others are all pure, and distinctively essential R.E.M.

Out of Time became the number one album in the country within a week of our discussion. Yet despite its commercial clout, it didn't iron out any of the wrinkles that make R.E.M. unique. Staying true to their "alternative" roots while scoring commercial hits, they changed the sound of the Top Forty. "Alternative" music became mainstream, and mainstream turned alternative.

In "Radio Song" Stipe swaps vocals with rapper KRS-One to decry the lack of meaningful music on the airwaves: "The world is collapsing around our ears / I turned up the radio but I can't hear it . . ." "Losing My Religion," though, was a exception to this rule. It's a song the record company didn't want to release as a single, but the band insisted, defying the conventional wisdom that singing about religion in a minor key with mandolin instead of guitar isn't radio-friendly. The band's instincts were right; the song flew to the top of the charts not by imitating the contrived sounds and structures of other hits, but by offering an alternative. Stipe's clear voice, his longing lyrics, and Peter Buck's acoustic mandolin all provided a welcome relief on the radio, especially in the context of sampled and synthesized sounds. They broke down the distance created by the cold surfaces of most radio songs. It's the sound of real people making real music together.

Part I: Michael Stipe and Michael Mills

You said once that you were a child prodigy?

STIPE: That might have been a stretch. [*Laughs*]. I was having a good day that day, I think. Prodigy is a strong word. But I did play well as a child.

I think it was when my parents bought a piano and put it in my room and I had this cow skull . . . I lived in Texas at the time and I had this cow skull that I carried with me all the time. I shouldn't say that. I had a cow skull up on top of the piano and one night I woke up and the piano and the cow, whose name was Clyde, were staring at me. From that day on I never played piano again. Till I joined the band.

[To Mills] Never knew that, did you? I got rid of Clyde really quickly. [Laughs] The piano stayed there for about another year haunting me like a Bruno Shulz book.

MILLS: Haunting you like a benevolent 88-toothed ghost. [Laughter] Sorry.

STIPE: That's okay, it was good.

When the big success comes for some artists, they have to tour and do promotion and no time is left for songwriting. How do you connect with the part of you that writes the songs while being so public?

STIPE: You make decisions like not touring behind the best-selling record you've ever made. [Laughs]

MILLS: It doesn't get in my way, personally, because I can't hardly walk past a piano or guitar without sitting down and picking it up playing. And everytime I do that, there's a one in fifteen, or twenty, chance that part of a song is going to come out. It depends on whether the creative muse is sitting on your shoulder that day. And if it does, then in just the time it takes to play something, you can have the genesis of a song.

Other times, we made it a point last year, to give ourselves plenty of time to write songs. We took six months to go into the studio, five, six days a week. We would guarantee ourselves at least going there. That was our discipline. We would go in there and we would sit down and think about it. Nine times out of ten we would pick up instruments and play something. Sometimes we'd just go in there and say forget it and go out for beer.

Sometimes if you get into a little routine, sometimes the creative ball will just get rolling. You know, we'll play for two weeks and not get anything done and then in one week we'll write seven or eight songs. Or in three days we'll write six songs.

Do you always write the songs with the four of you together?

MILLS: We put them together that way. Everybody sits at home and diddles around. Sometimes you'll come up with little ideas and sometimes you'll come up with a huge part of a song. And then you'll take that into everyone else and piece it together until you get a song. Other times, things just come out of, literally, just the four of us sitting around making noise. All of a sudden it will reemerge into a song. It's really strange.

And do the lyrics come during this time of it?

STIPE: Yeah. There's no real set way that it happens. Sometimes I have an idea for a melody or I've got this stuff written and I'm trying to figure out what to do with it.

You write lyrics on your own and bring them to the band?

STIPE: Yeah, or I'm inspired by a song to write something. There's no real method.

Do you listen to the music to suggest the words?

STIPE: Yeah, a lot. A lot of times the words can really change the music. We would have a song like "Shiny Happy People" that was originally like a stomp rock kind of song.

MILLS: When I first wrote it, it was a quiet, little acoustic ditty. That's the weirdest thing about it.

You wrote it on guitar?

MILLS: On acoustic guitar. It was finger-picked, quiet, four little chords. The chords that comprise the chorus now. It sounds nothing like the song. And that's the way things go. When you start to get input from everyone, you start to use more instruments that you have at your disposal, and the songs evolve. They turn into final songs. Sometimes they still remain little acoustic numbers but sometimes they become "Shiny Happy People." There's no way to tell.

Did those lyrics for it emerge because it had a happy sound to you?

STIPE: Yeah. It's a real happy song and it was written as a happy song. A few people have taken it to task for being extremely cynical, or reading cynicism, or negativism, or irony, into it. And it's really not intended that way at all.

MILLS: They're not willing to believe that it's a happy song.

STIPE: Except they happen to be right. With my past, I can see where someone would feel that. With something like "End of the World As We Know It" under our belt, I can see where someone could look at it that way; there's a degree of irony or cynicism involved. But I think that distinction is fairly obvious.

Is it hard to write a happy song?

STIPE: Yes, it's very difficult.

Why?

STIPE: Happiness, true happiness, the feeling that you get from real happiness, is just difficult to describe. Real sadness, you can find examples of sadness that are very real and tangible. Happiness, true happiness, just is kind of silly. There's not really any way to describe it without going into the usual stuff, and everyone has surely heard that.

Anger is much easier to write about in music.

MILLS: To write happy that hasn't been done to *death* by people who don't bother to think beyond the most obvious analogies and similes for happiness ... People who write happy songs often haven't delved into what really *means* happy, or what really makes someone happy, and it's kind of superficial.

You recorded that song with Kate Pierson singing a duet; was that part of the original conception?

STIPE: Yeah.

MILLS: When it got to be four-piece, putting the song together, we felt that we needed it.

You've mentioned how sometimes songs will just appear out of nowhere—

MILLS: I'm sure every songwriter in the world feels that.

What's your feeling about where the ideas for songs originate?

MILLS: Since we tend to write the music first, I think it's just about impossible to say. I mean, I went to see a Midnight Oil concert and there was a song that had a great beat and a great feel, and I said, "Dammit, I'm going to go home and write a song that feels like that." And I couldn't do it. Because once I left the concert, I lost the feel.

I wouldn't know how to say where musical ideas come from. They just click in your head. Maybe you hear some rhythm of nature. Literally, the sound of a hubcap rolling down a street might set you off. Or a birdcall, or someone yelling something at someone else from an upper-story window.

STIPE: This sounds real silly as an example of that, but do you know the band Suicide? They made this some really industrial, grungy, noisy music that was *incredible*. Very melodic, very beautiful. They're from New York, and I was a fan of theirs in the early eighties. Their music was always real foreign to me, not having lived in large cities all my life. And the first time I went to New York and I was sitting on the subway, it just *hit* me. This is where Suicide is from. This is it. It's a subway.

Does songwriting ever seem magical to you, to come up with something together that seems almost perfect when it's complete?

STIPE: It seems uncanny, sometimes, but I think it's more of an interpretation of someone else's stuff, very much like your interpretation of this conversation. Or a director's interpretation of your song that winds up as a video. It's not exactly what I meant, but it's an unusual take.

If I give these guys a set of lyrics and say, "Set them, I'd like to have a song," they might not write a song exactly to those words, but they've read them, and then, by some wild symbiotic relationship, [*laughs*] they seem to fit. Six months down the line.

Or I'll hear a song that these guys have put together that's still very bare-bones, very skeletal, in its arrangement and get an idea for it and move the elements that enter into it around to suit the vocal. Peter does that a great deal and we all do that.

So, if you want to separate the words and the music for the sake of conversation, the sake of example, then there is a point where they meet and then everything kind of evolves from there.

We've dropped entire verses and choruses as we've gone because it was just unnecessary or because it was really important that there be another element coming in. We've dropped entire songs; we've rearranged songs to fit the meaning.

When you said interpreting, do you mean the way you're interpreting what is coming through?

STIPE: I mean interpretation on a very one-to-one level. It's very different once the record is made and it's out to the general public. The listener is outside of the creative process. Actually it becomes a peripheral force of that creative process because they enter themselves into the music and they interpret it to fit their lives and to fit their needs.

And I think that is what music is all about, whether it's pop, or rock and roll or any other type of music that you can imagine, whether it's Bulgarian voices that for all we know could be singing about housekeeping duties at an airport Holiday Inn, it's up to the listener to interpret that and really pull what they *need* from the music.

That's what makes music such a strong force, such a universal force. And that's a cliche, but it's really important. Some cliches are there for a reason.

Some songs seem like they've been around forever, and it's hard to believe someone wrote them. Does it ever feel to you that you find songs, rather than write them?

MILLS: There's no way to deny that what you write musically is a synthesis of everything you've ever heard in your life plus the way that you hear music. You can't have lived your life in a musical void; it's impossible. And I'm sure those ideas get channeled out eventually through you if you're a songwriter.

But I still feel that they're pretty much mine. These songs are mine.

STIPE: As an idea, I can't disagree with that.

I think I have an unusual approach to writing.

How so?

STIPE: I just don't think that other songwriters really work the way that we do as a group or the way that I do. People I've spoken to, or people I've compared notes with, outside of R.E.M., have worked in very different ways from me.

The song "Country Feedback," for example, was not even a song. It was words on a page that hadn't even been put into an order. And I went into the soundbooth, strapped on the headphones, sang it, and that was it. That was the version we kept.

MILLS: The song has only been performed once. By any of us.

STIPE: The words were written down on a piece of paper. But I had no idea how many times I was going to repeat a certain line, or that "it's crazy what you could have had," would be used over and over again. There was no set order. I just—

MILLS: Winged it.

And it worked.

STIPE: And it really worked. [*Laughs*]

And then other songs I've worked on for three months, picking apart each syllable and making sure of its exact order.

When writing, how conscious are you of guiding the meaning?

STIPE: I think we tend to work as a band, and individually, very intuitively, and often I'll write a song and not know exactly what it's all about. And I think that's fine. Other times I'll have a topic in mind or a point of view.

With this record, particularly, I've chosen a certain point of view, or character, that I want to get across. For instance, in "Me in Honey," the idea of pregnancy from the father's point of view. Which, as far as I know, has never been seriously addressed in music. With the dubious exception of Paul Anka's "Having My Baby." [*Laughs*]

"Me in Honey" is a wonderful song, and it's got a great title.

STIPE: Just the phrase itself is so open to interpretation. It could be very loving, or it can be kind of nasty. Which is exactly what the song is. A diametrically opposed emotional thing can and does occur. ,

MILLS: Yeah, that's either a real loving or a real nasty song. Depending on how you look at it.

Was that track done before the words?

MILLS: That depends. [*To Stipe*] Did you have an idea when you worked out that bass line that you insisted that I keep playing against my better judgment? [*Laughs*]

STIPE: Yeah. It just rocked. It felt great, over and over; the riff, the repetition of it was beautiful. To me.

I like really dumb, repetitive things.

That song only has two chords, and it's in C#, which is a weird key.

MILLS: Yeah. I was just messing around on the bass and I started doing that riff.

STIPE: I was in the corner.

MILLS: I just happened to be there on the fretboard and played it in that key. And we kept it in that key. And it's good to change keys. Not just to do it, not just to say, "Hey, look, I can play in C sharp," but—

STIPE: Is that a weird key?

MILLS: [*To Stipe*] Well, C# minor is what "Moonlight Sonata" is in. It's a very, very beautiful haunting key that lots of classical composers use, because it has a lot of flat keys in it.

The song really shows the power of simplicity, because when you finally go to the second chord, the V chord, it's so intense.

MILLS: Yeah, it's very effective. It's gratifying. See, songs like that are very hard to write and make them work, because when it sounds so simple, but it has to be right to be powerful. You can't just have two chords and assume it's going to be really powerful and strong and correct. But that one worked out.

I used to think that to make a great melody, it took a lot of chords.

STIPE: It's really the other way around, I think. I think it's much easier to write a good melody over simple chords.

MILLS: Yeah, see, that's why you like those broad songs.

STIPE: Yeah, because I can really control the melody, and dig deep into it when it's very simple and steady.

MILLS: Yeah, and that's the thing that made our songwriting different a lot in the early days. Because often our verses are catchier than the choruses. Or were. And had more chords in them.

Generally, when people are trying to write hit songs, they have a very simple one or two chord verse and then a three or four chord hook chorus. But we would have five chords in the verse and then three in the chorus. But we would have a whole lot going on before the vocal melody. There's the bass melody, there's the melody that's within the guitar chords. There's even a melody in the drums, because they're tuned. So you have all this melody going on before. So when you add on the vocal melodies and the harmonies, you make a very nice tapestry of the song. The listener has a lot of things to listen to and to choose from.

When I hear chords changing, I hear melodies moving. When I hear one chord going on, it's hard for me to come up with a melody, which is why it's really great that Michael can do it. I would be hard pressed to come up with a melody over a one chord drone.

STIPE: But you've got it in you. Look at the melody of "Texarkana."

MILLS: Yeah, but that's not a one chord song.

Another formulaic way of writing songs is to build up to a title in the chorus. But you'll have songs in which the title is not even used, such as "Texarkana."

STIPE: [*Laughs*] Poor example.

MILLS: Yeah, that's a very extreme example. It is from a previous attempt at lyrics that didn't get finished.

STIPE: That was a work song we had been working on and never got right.

MILLS: So when I did the new words and melody, I tried to put other titles to it, but they wouldn't stick. "Texarkana" just *was* the title of that song.

Now I don't believe in channeling. I think our songwriting talent comes from within us and nowhere else. But that song took a title of its own and wasn't going to let it go.

How has changing instruments while writing changed the songs?

MILLS: It made a big difference. You can hear it on *Green* on things like "Hairshirt" and "Wrong Child." *Green* had this incredibly weird juxtaposition of "Stand" and "Orange Crush" and then "Hairshirt" and "The Wrong Child." This album isn't quite so far-flung, although I think it moves very well from song to song. It's not repetitious. But I think it's a little bit more of a piece, this record is. Because the mandolin's a little bit more prevalent, and the keyboard is more prevalent, because we wrote on them rather than added them later as overdubs.

When we wrote in the rehearsal studio, we had mandolin, organ, and acoustic guitar. That was generally how we started. If we could come up with something in that configuration, we would. If not, we would see if we could come up with something in a more traditional vein, and we would switch to guitar, bass and drums. And that doesn't always mean Peter playing guitar, either. Sometimes I would play guitar. Or Bill would play guitar and I'd play drums. Anything to keep us interested.

Everyone in the band has songwriting ability. There's no reason to keep Bill on the drums because he writes great songs on the guitar and mandolin.

STIPE: He wrote "Perfect Circle."

[To Stipe] Do you write most of the melodies?

STIPE: Well, my part of the band is more in the arrangement. When they're just fooling around, I'll say, "Hey, play that over." I'm good at arranging from a very non-musical point of view. I have a musically dumb standpoint that I'm looking at the song from. That Mike doesn't have, because he's musically trained and knows what's too stupid. And I'm not.

You're known for doing lots of songs in minor keys. Yet it seems that there are as many major key songs that you do.

STIPE: Again, it's probably the minor key-ness of my voice.

MILLS: "Losing My Religion" has both.

It's all in A minor, isn't it?

MILLS: The verses are all A minor and E minor, but the chorus is F and G and A minor.

Minors are very powerful keys, and very powerful chords. My favorite chord is a seventh. Whenever there's a chord and I think it's boring, I play a seventh on the bass. Like on the song "Fireplace" on *Document*, it's not a very popular song, but in the chorus [*sings melody*] I throw in the seventh, and it's a good linking chord.

I'm going to name a few of your songs we haven't mentioned yet and you can give any response to them that you like.

STIPE: R.E.M. songs? Okay.

"Harborcoat."

MILLS: That was our first dual lead vocal. [*To Stipe*] As far as I'm concerned. Yours was louder.

Is that song about Nazi Germany?

STIPE: Yes. From a Jewish viewpoint.

MILLS: Don Dixon helped with the arrangement of that one.

"Seven Chinese Brothers."

STIPE: Kiddy tale. From the book. But I got my facts wrong. I think there were five Chinese brothers.

"Welcome to the Occupation."

STIPE: That's a song about Mexican guest workers. Big fish eats small fish kind of thing.

MILLS: With a great turnaround coming out of the bridge.

"Finest Worksong."

STIPE: Protestant work ethic.

"Stand."

MILLS: Big and dumb. What more can you say?

STIPE: It's basically a call to action.

Do you like that show "Get a Life" that uses it for a theme song?

STIPE: I don't mind it. I've only seen it one half of a time.

Do you have a favorite R.E.M. song?

MILLS: "Fall on Me" is pretty close.

STIPE: Yeah.

MILLS: The vocal harmonies on the chorus are incredible. Some of the passing chords are beautiful.

STIPE: I like "Losing My Religion" a lot. It's a nice song.

Part II: Peter Buck and Bill Berry.

Did you write your first songs with R.E.M.?

BUCK: Michael and I wrote a few before the band started. We wrote like forty songs in two months and only two of them get recorded. I think the first song we recorded was "Guardian Night" although "Just A Touch" was written then, though we didn't record it until our fourth album.

Was it surprising when you first got together and all those songs emerged?

BUCK: Yeah. That's why we stayed together. We wrote three songs all in the first day. They were all pretty imitative of someone else. When we started writing together, most of the songs were in A because that's the key I was most familiar with.

A minor?

BUCK: Major, actually. I think I discovered minors a month into the band.

So most of your songs then came from jamming with the band?

BUCK: I think in those days we used to bring in more completed stuff. We'd write in tandem: me and Mike or me and Michael or Bill and Mike or Bill and Michael. And show it to the other guys. And after two or three months we started writing all together. All of us can write songs on our own. But having the four of us all do it has really made the difference.

With us, songwriting is real organic. I don't know anybody else who works like us.

When Michael comes up with words to fit your music, do they usually sound like the right words when you first hear them?

BUCK: I almost never have any objections.

BERRY: We'll change a word or two here or there, but that's all.

BUCK: We all have veto power. We'll change lines a little.

BERRY: But his *melodic* sense is just uncanny. We never have a problem with that.

BUCK: It's weird. He'll hear a riff in the bass or a riff in the guitar. And we'll say, "The melody should be like this," and he'll come up with this real weird phrase. His phrases go over lines and over repeating patterns a lot. We'll be doing a repeating pattern of four and he'll do six, and then stop two and do four. So he'll never be where I think I would be if I was singing the song.

It's funny, if you analyze the songs, Michael's melodies will come a lot from the bass. In a different register. We'll be playing and Michael will say, "You know, Peter, that's not the right chord." And I'll say, "Oh, yes it is, because I'm the one who put it there." And the bass will be playing a note that Michael's following and it won't work with the chords. So I change my chords.

A song like "Me in Honey" has only two chords, yet the melody is soaring, and has a large range.

BUCK: That's a real example of Michael pulling something out of nowhere. "Me In Honey" was not even a song. We were just hanging out playing and Michael puts on his little tape deck, records everything we do and then goes home and works on them. So we laboriously would work out songs to present to him. We played the riff for "Me in Honey" for maybe a minute and Michael said, "Oh I have a song for that." We said, "For what?" He said, "Oh, that thing." So he had to play us the tape recording of it. It wasn't even a song. It was just a jam, one of a hundred things that day like that. And he just happened to hear, in that one riff, the song.

Where do you think songs come from?

BERRY: It's something that people can't control. There are songs we labor over and other ones that just appear in the room out of nowhere. And in our case, that's from the interplay of four people. And we've been playing together so long that it's almost unconscious. We can come up with a song when we're not even looking at it.

It seems like the good ones just kind of appear.

BERRY: And the thing is that we've gotten better at it. It's not something wholly other or beyond. It's something that's in you. It's just how good you are at pulling it out.

BUCK: When we were starting out, we didn't know anything technically, and it was all "How do you write a song?" Now it's maybe three quarters slob work. Like knowing what keys are. And I still can't tell you the notes of keys, but I can kind of figure out how to go around them. And figuring out arrangements, knowing if you need a chorus or something here. And the other quarter is inspiration, hoping it hits. Which is why we practice everyday. No other band in the *world*, I think, does what we do. No matter if we've got a project lined up or not, we practice five days a week. I mean, we'll take a week off to go to Mexico or go on vacation. But we worked eight months on this one.

There's a huge amount of songs that are totally unplanned. We don't know what they are or where they come from. It's just being in the room there all together helps it occur.

How did the mandolin affect the way the songs came out?

BUCK: I don't know. It felt more homey. I bought one, decided I was going to write on it, and learn how to tune it, which took me about a day. With mandolin, you tend to use more breathy, wooden instruments, so there are acoustics and strings and stuff.

I go for chords I wouldn't normally go for. Like in "Losing My Religion," I don't know if I would have an F in there.

When you're writing, do you guide the music or do you follow it?

BERRY: Both.

BUCK: Both. When I'm sitting at home, I'll have the TV on and play to the TV, so I won't have to think of anything. I'll watch an old movie and just strum away to that.

In the studio, it's the same thing except there's no TV. I'll come up with a riff, and sometimes the band won't follow it but sometimes the band will go *boom!* and that's it.

Did you have that mandolin riff for "Losing My Religion" before you wrote the song?

BUCK: I worked that out later on mandolin, because I'm so bad on mandolin that I had to have some kind of basis. The riff was the first thing I came
up with.

On guitar, an F to a D major, which is "Half a World Away," that's not a
good chord change. But on mandolin it is a good chord change. I don't know
why. I guess because the chords are upside-down on mandolin, it's not that big
of a step so "Half a World Away" has F to D major on mandolin and it sounds
okay. You can have F to D minor, or F7 to D7, but F to D major on guitar just
doesn't sound good.

Do you still buy a lot of records?
BUCK: I've already sent home a huge box of records. You should see my
room. I just heard they put out Leonard Cohen on CD so I bought that.

You're a Leonard Cohen fan?
BUCK: Yep. Always have been.

**Your songs often have unusual titles. Do you name them afterwards
sometimes?**
BUCK: Sometimes afterwards. Sometimes you just know what it is and
sometimes not. Something like "Texarkana" doesn't mean anything. That's the
title of the song before we changed the lyrics. But what would you call that
song?

"Catch Me If I Fall" is the main line of the song.
BUCK: But, no. I don't like that. I like "Texarkana" a *lot* better.

**That's the great thing about R.E.M., that you won't choose the most
obvious title, and that you go against those formulaic ideas.**
BUCK: Yeah, well, you know, we're not trying to sell our songs to anybody.
They're there for whoever wants to listen to them. Michael always says you
should save a little bit of mystery for yourself. I think it's neat not to have it
given to you. You pick up most records and you can look at song titles and
know what they're going to be about immediately. I always hate that.

Some of your titles are super intriguing. Like "Exhuming McCarthy."
BUCK: Yeah, that's a great title. Being that that kind of McCarthyism is
coming right back.

**And your album titles are always intriguing as well. People usually
choose the name of one of the songs on the album as the album title. And
you've never done that.**
BUCK: Yeah. We considered using "Near Wild Heaven" from this album.

**But when you do that, it changes that one song, making it the title
song.**
BUCK: Yeah, it makes it more important than it is.

Where did the title *Fables of the Reconstruction* come from?
BUCK: Michael was really interested in the oral tradition of storytelling,
and was reading about the stories of the slaves. Those songs were personality
and character-oriented, like "Old Man Kensey" and "Green Grow the Rushes."
"Wendell Gee."

I love your song "Seven Chinese Brothers."

BUCK: I like that one. I must have ten videos of the cartoon. And I used to get the book every year.

BOB MERLIS: Weren't there five Chinese brothers?

BUCK: Well, we didn't realize that. I thought it was seven. And Michael thought it was seven. But it's five.

Seven sings better.

BUCK: Yeah. We needed that extra syllable so it's a good thing that we mis-interpreted it.

Do you have a favorite R.E.M. song?

BUCK: I always liked "Perfect Circle" a lot. From the new record, I think "Losing My Religion" is really good. "Perfect Circle" was the first one we ever recorded that actually sounded like, wow, a real song. So I guess that's nostal-gia speaking there. As a collection of songs, I like this one the best. I like the selection of songs and the way they flow together.

The sound of it is great.

BUCK: Yeah, it's a real live, human sound.

* * *

John Hiatt
Los Angeles 1987
Nashville, Tennessee 2000

"Sooner than the dogs could bark
Faster than the sun rose
Down to the banks in an old mule cart
She took a flat boat 'cross the shallows"

from "Crossing Muddy Waters"

These are happy days for John Hiatt. Just a few days short of his forty-eighth birthday, he's a happily married father of three happily living on a farm in Franklin, Tennessee, and happier than ever to be a songwriter. "Right now I really like where I'm at as a songwriter," he said over coffee on a bright August morning, a trio of dogs barking in the distance. "I like the way it flows when it flows. I like the way I don't have to force it. I like the way I don't get nervous if I haven't written a song in a month or two. I just don't have those worries anymore."

It's a contentment contained in the ageless simplicity of the songs on his newest album at the time of this interview, *Crossing Muddy Waters*. Inspired by the pastoral splendor of life in the country, far removed from the chaos and clamor of his early L.A scuffling days, he's written new songs like "Lift Up Every Stone" and "Before I Go" that shimmer with the authentic essence of old spirituals and blues. "When we played some of these songs," he said, "it felt like we were seeing a ghost come riding up in the pasture."

"Ghosts on the trees, there's ghosts on the wires
Asking questions and showing signs
Shivering with truth, they're lighting fires
Lighting fires all down the line"

from "Before I Go"

Hiatt produced the album himself (although he considers that tantamount to having no producer at all) and kept the tracks as pristine and unforced as the songs themselves. He sat in a circle with two Davids (David Faragher on bass and tambourine, and David Immergluck on mandolin and twelve-string guitar) and cut each song live, overdubbing only the harmony vocals later. To ensure no tracks grew stale, he only let the Davids hear each song once before laying it down. "I don't believe in *too* much rehearsal," he said, laughing. "Of course, we have a musical dialogue we've gained from playing together for three years. And that's good advice for the kids at home: Play together, play together, play together."

To evoke the backwoods timbre of these songs, Hiatt suggested various visual guides. "I told them all to picture themselves on a porch outside in the woods somewhere, playing these songs."

"Red tail hawk shooting down the canyon
Put me on that wind he rides
I will be your true companion
When we reach the other side"

from "Before I Go"

Born in Indianapolis August 20, 1952, Hiatt played in a string of hometown R&B bands, most notably The White Ducks. At eighteen he moved to Nashville and was hired as a staff songwriter at Tree Music. It was the first and last "real" job he ever had, writing songs that were cut by Conway Twitty, Tracy Nelson, and others. Three Dog Night had a hit with his "Sure as I'm Sittin' Here" in 1974, the same year Hiatt landed the first of many record deals and made his debut album *Hanging Around the Observatory*.

He then went through an often torturous process that many of our greatest performing songwriters have also endured, getting bounced from company to company. Although he made one wonderful album after the next (such as the frenetically glorious *Two-Bit Monsters*) and was beloved by critics and musicians alike, his sales, at around 200,000 to 300,000, were underwhelming to his labels. After Epic he moved to MCA to Geffen to A&M and to Capitol.

"The problem," he said, "is that selling a couple hundred thousand records doesn't mean much to the big record companies. Unless you sell five million copies or more, it isn't worth it to them." But unlike the leagues of artists who've been diluted, derailed, or entirely decimated by their time in the majors, Hiatt emerged unbroken. His 1987 album *Bring the Family* sold in the millions, as did his next one, *Slow Turning* , while a diverse, ever-expanding amalgamation of singers sought some of that Hiatt magic on their own albums and covered his songs, including Bob

Dylan, Bonnie Raitt, Iggy Pop, Linda Ronstadt, Ronnie Milsap, the Neville Brothers, and Suzy Bogguss. Though Elvis Costello referred to him in a 1986 concert as "one of L.A.'s best-kept secrets," by 1987 the secret about John Hiatt was out.

"It's all opened it up now," he said. "Which is great. Because it is successful to sell 200,000 records. There are a lot of people out there who would take that success. So the major labels, by mainly just trying to beat each other up, have opened a lot of doors."

He's since put his days in the majors behind him. *Crossing Muddy Waters* was the first album he's made that he owns entirely. Rather than launch his own label, a prospect that doesn't jive with his slow-turning rural life, he licensed it to Vanguard, who can sell it for five years, after which ownership reverts to Hiatt. "I'm a free-agent now," he said happily. "Which is really exciting, because this record is the first record I own. It's like buying your first house, or your first car. And it means that I have the possibility of getting a record out every year. It was such a slow process with other companies, because they had to second-guess everything. And I always felt, hey, this is music. Let's get on with it!"

Free now to call his own shots, Hiatt's carved out an ideal songwriting existence for himself. Living legends such as Eric Clapton and B.B. King (who recently teamed up to record Hiatt's "Riding with the King" as the title song of their collective album) continue to cut his songs. Yet he spends no time targeting songs for artists, or badgering or being badgered by record companies. Instead he revels in the peaceful environs of his farm, drives the kids to school, and writes songs for fun rather than necessity. "I have no real complaints," he said. "It's not like I've got a record on the charts next to Britney Spears and I have to write the next one. So it takes a lot of the heat off."

"You gotta lift up every stone now sister
Gotta lift up every stone
Gotta lift up every stone now sister
Gotta clear this field and build that wall"

from "Lift Up Every Stone"

Do you still enjoy writing songs?
Absolutely. I love it. Of course, it can be something in which you get banged up a bit. I've got lots of cuts and bruises. But when inspiration strikes, off I go. Songwriting for me is pretty pleasant. It's something I love to do and have been doing for years, ever since I was eleven and living in Indiana. My general routine, when I'm not on the road or in the studio, is to get up in the morning and go into my office to write. I just pick up a guitar and start noodling away and hopefully something will come up.

What started you at eleven writing songs?
I picked up a guitar. I started strumming some chords. My first songs were mostly two-chord songs. At the time I was inspired by lots of great music: Mitch Ryder, the Young Rascals, and of course Elvis Presley. Later I got really into Ashford & Simpson, John Fogerty, Thom Bell, Linda Creed. Bob Dylan has influenced me greatly. Jesse Winchester, Guy Clarke. Randy Newman's a great writer.

Does songwriting get any easier over the years?

[*Pause*] No. I still feel pretty much the same as I always did when I write a song. When I'm playing the guitar and I get a little chord pattern or a melody, I still feel like I've never written a song in my life. It's the weirdest damn thing. There's a kind of emotional muscle memory you develop that can point you in the right direction. Finding melodies is like using physical muscle memory. It's like physically pulling melodies from a melodic stream that is always floating around out there.

What's the source of that stream?

I think it's God. Or somebody like her.

I used to think that I had to write all the time for it to happen. But I don't think that anymore, because I've found that it can be almost better for me when I don't do it for a few months. Then all of a sudden I throw myself into it. Sometimes when you feel like you don't know what you're doing, out of that comes some good stuff.

Do your songs always start with music?

Yeah, always. Maybe fifteen or twenty years ago, I might have had an ax to grind, or some brilliant insight that I was certain that you had to hear about. [*Laughs*] So I would write that first. But now lyrics, really, are the last thing I do. And they take the most time.

Do you finish a whole melody before working on words?

No. Usually I'll get a chord pattern going, and that will evoke a melody, and I'll start singing nonsense. And then the nonsense will actually start taking shape into words.

Are you shaping it, or are you following where it wants to go?

I'm not sure. [*Laughs*] I'm really not exactly sure about that. I guess I'm shaping it, to some degree. I think it's pretty similar to a lot of creative processes. There's a certain amount of getting on it and taking a ride. I mean, certainly you employ your skills, whatever they are. But I think it's like anything else—when you gain a certain level of ability to do it, you can start to do it unconsciously. It's like when I'm driving my race-car. I'm not thinking about how to drive a fast lap, I just do it.

Do you write more than you need and then edit?

No, not anymore. I don't edit much. [*Laughs*] I probably should. It pretty much comes out in a stream. I'll scratch stuff out, and jumble it around. But I don't write many verses and then go back and cut stuff. Usually when I get to the end, that's it. I try to write the whole song in one sitting. There are times when I will let something sit, but not very often. Because it can be very difficult to get back to it.

Some stuff is just shards and fragments. I used to sing everything I would write into a little $20 dictation tape deck. But I almost never go back and listen to those tapes, so I don't know why I do that. [*Laughs*] There are plenty of times when I've forgotten stuff. But I've always pretty much trusted that if I forgot it, it probably wasn't worth remembering. [*Laughs*]

Was "Have a Little Faith in Me" written on piano?

Yeah. I ought to write more on the piano. I like that song. This album is very guitar-oriented, so I didn't do any piano songs. I predominantly write on acoustic guitar and always have. I've written a few songs on electric guitar. In fact, one of the songs on this album, "Mr. Stanley," I wrote on a '57 Telecaster. I ran it through a little battery-operated Vox toy amp, and it sounded so cool that I started playing that riff. And the song came out. I had the amp up all the way, but it's not very loud. It was cool—it was at about an acoustic guitar volume level but it was all distorted. So that one was influenced by the sound of the electric, but all the others were written on acoustic.

Does the guitar you use affect the song?
Absolutely. There are songs inside guitars. For sure. The question is how you get them out of there.

And what's the answer?
For me, it's to kind of sit down and start playing, because it's fun to play. If I'm lucky, something will hit me. If not, I keep playing.

On guitar do you write with a capo?
Yeah. "What Do We Do Now" is in the C position with the capo on the 2nd fret. I like that, because it's different than a D chord. "Crossing Muddy Waters" is in A, but in G position with the capo on the 2nd fret. You can slap the capo on a guitar and hit a chord up the neck and it will evoke a totally different song. I wouldn't have written "What Do We Do Now?" if I hadn't capoed up. The whole thing comes from that—the weight of the C chord.

Do you also feel certain keys affect the song? For example, "The Love That Harms" [from _Riding with the King_] is such a powerful E minor song.
Yeah, there's something that happens when you go from that G to E minor. Any song that uses that chord change sounds good; something happens to you when you hear it. And certain keys definitely evoke different moods—they affect the way your body vibrates.

One of the great things about your songs is your use of small, telling details—
You remind me of this rap from the movie _Lost Weekend_. There's this writer talking about love and he says, "It's the details. You have to get the details." But it seems when I'm writing, not that I get more vague, but as I get the song down and get more direct, I weed out a lot of the details. I try to get it down to its simplest form.

It seems that the songs I work on most sound that way—overworked. They don't come out in one sitting, necessarily. I let them take their own sweet time. I do get a kick out of the craft, out of the rhyming. Sometimes I have too much fun with my own cleverness, and that doesn't work out too well. The thing you have to do is try to get some real emotion that you feel, and hopefully that's what people will feel when they hear the song.

Is it hard to write about yourself and have those feelings translate to other people?
It's not about writing about myself as much as it is about writing more from the heart than the head.

You've written many hits. When writing, do you think in terms of what will be commercial?

Oh boy. I don't think so. I'm not sure what is commercial. But basically I feel it's important to write what you feel like writing; I don't believe in *trying* to write a hit single. I don't want to be corny, but you do have to be true to yourself.

Is it tough to be true to yourself and still satisfy record companies' expectations?
Well, you know, the world is full of adversity. It presses in at you from all corners. Where is it written that it was supposed to be an altogether pleasant experience? It goes up and down, but you can set yourself on a certain path and say, "What am I up to, what am I all about, how can I function at my optimum, and what do I have to give?" You have to deal with questions like that. You have to do it your own way, and if you do, what are they going to do—put you in songwriter's jail?

Crossing Muddy Waters **reflects a certain contentment—**
Well, I'm glad you can say that, because I'm married and most of these songs are about breaking up. You can't really write that stuff all the time—you're either breaking up or you're happily married. You can't be in-between and write those kind of songs. So in my case, I'm happily married. These songs are inspired by that.

They also have a lot to do with living out in the country. We live a rural existence, and it affects you physically and mentally. That feeling is what I like about the album. "Crossing Muddy Waters" is a perfect example of that. I have a fondness for those kind of old-timey, almost Appalachian type songs, where the music is almost ebullient. It bubbles along with the story, while the story tears your heart out. I love those kind of songs.

It's like the idea behind blues, which is that it hurts like hell, but it feels real good going down. These songs kind of work like that.

Has it been surprising to you how many of your songs have been covered?
Yes. It's been a real nice surprise. I'm so glad so many people have wanted to record my songs. I'm proud of that. But it was not by design. It was just because I write. I've never written for someone. I've tried, but those songs are just never very good. I'm not that kind of writer. I'm not a Brill Building-book-an-appointment-cowrite-with-somebody-have-a-hit-the-next-day kind of writer. And not being that kind of writer, I'm very fortunate to have had so many of my songs covered.

Your songs were always great, but suddenly everybody seemed to notice.
Yeah. Before that I had never really been able to separate the songwriter from the performer. I kind of started to get it together with the *Riding with the King* album. My personal life was still a complete mess. But once I got healthy as an artist, I got healthy as a human being. Or healthier, I should say. [*Laughs*] And when that happens, you start firing on all eight cylinders and things start to happen.

Many songwriters have said they require some turmoil in their lives.
Yeah, that's bullshit. [*Laughs*] But let them think that. It will weed out the dabblers, the ones who really don't have the heart of an artist.

You've always been a storyteller in your songs.
I always felt that if you're going to sing words, why not tell a story? It's what holds my interest, too. This is really selfish, really. I want to enjoy it myself by discovering some new way of telling a story.

Do you decide what a song is going to be about?

No. Oftentimes, I don't even know that. A lot of times it will be just an opening line. Like "What Do We Do Now?" I had those chords, and they just sounded so sad to me. I had just had a fight with my wife, and this line came out. I sang it four times. And I felt, okay, that's repetitive, and that repetition can be the emotional center of the song. Who hasn't reached that level of frustration when you really don't know what to do? What do we do—do we take another breath?

So it just sort of happens like that. Or I'll get a verse, and I won't know what it's about until the chorus comes.

Do you need to understand the meaning of a song while writing?

Not necessarily. Sometimes I don't know what they mean until they're done. And some I still don't know. [Laughs]. A lot of these songs just come out of emotional shards that I hold onto. There's all these little pieces of shrapnel that you keep in your mind and piece songs together from them.

People always think these songs are autobiographical. And they're not, although I certainly draw from life experience. But it's fiction, for God's sake. There are some songs, like "Crossing Muddy Waters," that have nothing at all to do with my life. I didn't wake up one morning and have a woman gone like a rusty shot in a hollow sky. I knew nothing about mule carts and flatboats. That just came out, and it's every bit as powerful to me.

There's not a wasted line in any of these songs.

Yeah. I kind of wanted to steer clear of the whole smart-ass singer-songwriter thing. [Laughs] You know, the I-know-something-you-don't-and-I-want-to-tell-you-about-it kind of guy. I hate that. It's a popular motif, and I've been guilty of it. That's the only thing I try to avoid. Other than that, it's open.

Do you think that songs will continue to evolve?

Oh sure. I think so. Cool things happen. Melody is coming back into the picture, along with the hip-hop beat thing and the rhythm of the lyrics. People love melody. And you can go far out to get it. John Coltrane's whole thing was to take a melody as far out as he could, and yet he believed in that old saying that if the guy in the street can't hum it, that you don't have a tune.

Will you write songs your whole life?

I think so. I've been writing songs since I was eleven. And I'll be 48 on Sunday. That's 37 years of writing songs. I think I'm going to keep at it. Because there's just no telling what will come next.

Do you think people will always hunger for meaningful songs?

Absolutely. People recognize the ring of truth. It's just the middlemen who gum up the works.

Alanis Morissette
Santa Monica, California 2000

"I can't love you because we're supposed
To have professional boundaries
I'd like you to be schooled and in awe
As though you were kissed by God
Full on the lips
I'm in the front row
The front row with popcorn
I get to see you
See you close up"

from "Front Row"

"It's all about honesty," she says, absorbing the abundant sunshine streaming through the western windows of her Santa Monica home. (A Canadian in Southern California, she still delights daily in the incongruity of such springtime warmth in the midst of winter.) "It's about writing songs that are like snapshots of how I feel and who I am," she says. "Because if they are not real, it's impossible to sing them with any real conviction. And the audience always knows when it's not real. There's no fooling them."

And fooling them is not something that interests Alanis Morissette, who has elevated the expression of personal truth in songs to new heights. As a teen star in

Canada, she'd already sung her share of songs that were more about confection than confession. But when she discovered the capacity of songs to contain the real truth, it changed everything. "I can pull out different lines from those early songs that were *exactly* how I was feeling," she says. "And when I performed, I found that I would *inevitably* be able to sing those particular lines with more conviction than anything else." She knew that if she could write an entire song that reached that level of essential truth—or an entire *album* of these songs—that she could make music with such soul and substance that the entire world would notice.

And that is, of course, exactly what she did.

But first she had to find a collaborator. Which was no easy task, as previous collaborators objected to her desire to be fluid with songform, to change the lyrics of the chorus every time if need be, and to be spontaneously unbound in the pursuit of words and music. She met with "a huge handful of writers" before finding her ideal partner, capable of providing her with a firm musical foundation for the profusive freedom and frankness of her lyrics. That person was Glen Ballard, who had previously written hit songs such as "Man in the Mirror" (with Siedah Garrett) for Michael Jackson and produced hit records for Wilson Phillips, among others.

It was a match that couldn't have been more ideal. Because Ballard possesses not only prodigious musical ability—great melodic sense, keyboard and guitar prowess, and production chops—but also a hunger to reach a deeper and more personal level in his own work. It coincided with Alanis's inclination to explore the full freedom of unadulterated honesty in songs, and a great new songwriting team was born.

Their connection was immediate and electric. Rather than discuss what they hoped to accomplish, they simply started writing and recording, and the result astounded even them. "There was no need for any revision," Glen said. "The pure, raw energy of it was better than me going back and then refining it and overthinking it. This was completely *felt*. When we were in sync, it was like all the lights were green and we just kept driving."

And rather than consult a map or check a compass to determine their direction, they kept cruising at full speed. The songs kept flowing, usually one a day, with Ballard making musical tracks fast enough to capture the full heat of Alanis's vocals on tape while the creative fires were still raging.

"I didn't know what style this music would be," he said, "but I knew it needed to reflect her intelligence and her energy. So we went in that direction, but nothing was calculated. I didn't know who she was supposed to sound like. But as soon as I heard her voice, I said, 'Hey. You sound like you. And that's all I need to know.'"

Like Dylan and others who expanded the content of popular songwriting with a union of poetic energy and personal truth, Alanis and Glen embraced a spirit of spontaneous expression in their songs without abandoning the traditional aspects of songcraft—such as the use of strong melodic structures—that hold songs together. As stunningly provocative as the explicit carnal candor expressed in "You Oughta Know" was, it would not have been half as effective if not for its solid musical underpinning, which allows the words to explode with an unalloyed power and purity of purpose.

Asked if he had any reservations about the overt sexuality of "You Oughta Know," Ballard said, "No. In retrospect, I probably should have. I felt that I knew she was coming from a real place, and I encouraged her to go for it and not be afraid to say what was on her mind. She was so courageous to keep doing that. And if I was able to provide a sanctuary where she was able to do that safely, then I accomplished my mission."

So genuine is the wrath directed from woman to man in "You Oughta Know" that it's hard to fathom such a young woman writing it, and even harder to conceive of her doing so in collaboration with a man. But according to Glen, "It didn't matter if I were a man or a woman. What mattered is that Alanis felt safe and supported. My job was to provide an artistic free zone, a sanctuary, where she could do what she wanted to do and say what she wanted to say, and we would figure out the market later."

Not only was he stunned by her way with words, but also by her singing: "She has a tremendous range, but never uses it to show off. It's always in the service of the idea. Writing for that voice is a great gift. She can hit intervals most people would find challenging, and do it so naturally it's scary. She has remarkably good diction, and with *such* a clarity of expression. She's really one of the great singers."

Born on June 1, 1974, in Ottawa, Canada, Alanis was a child star by the age of ten when she joined the cast of a kids' show called "You Can't Do That on Television." Even then she had little interest in performing just for the sake of performing, and used her TV earnings to fund the independent recording and release of "Fate Stay With Me," the first song she ever wrote. "I started my own label because record companies were *deathly* afraid of ten-year-olds then," she says with a laugh. "And it was amazing. I wasn't invested in anything other than the process of doing it. It was thrilling."

She was happy to abandon her TV career when offered a record deal, and moved to Toronto in 1991 to record her debut album, a mixture of dance songs and ballads called *Alanis*. Though it wasn't the international hit for which she'd hoped, it was immensely popular in Canada, where she won several Juno Awards. Her second album, *Now Is the Time*, was also a Canadian hit, though not to the extent of her debut. (To this day those in the Great North tend to consider Alanis as a kind of Canadian Debbie Gibson instead of a songwriter who deserves to be included in the lexicon of Canadian songwriting greats, along with Leonard Cohen, Joni Mitchell, Neil Young, Bruce Cockburn, and others.)

Aiming southwest, she moved to Los Angeles, eventually hooked up with Ballard, and created the miraculous *Jagged Little Pill*, which raced to the top of the charts on the engine of "You Oughta Know." A remarkable record for several reasons, "You Oughta Know" broke through because of the voice, the music, the words, the maturity, the rage, the honesty. And perhaps even more astounding than the impact of this one song was the fact that the *entire album* contained songs at this level. This was clearly no fluke—here was a woman expressing anger, love, and desire with the passion of Janis Joplin, the authority of Chrissie Hynde, the expansive honesty of Joni Mitchell, and the unhindered creativity of her first idol, Carole King. Within months of its release, *Jagged Little Pill* generated as many hits as King's *Tapestry* did some two decades earlier.

By 1996, after much touring, and after picking up Best Song and Best Album Grammys, she and Glen reunited to commence work on the follow-up to *Jagged Little Pill*. But rather than rush or overthink the process, they wisely allowed the new songs to emerge organically, as they did with *Jagged Little Pill*, and again their creative bond was instant and electric. Inspired by the affirmation of near-universal acclaim, Alanis further broadened the scope and structure of her songs with great torrents of verbal virtuosity, creating visceral surges of zealous articulation, such as the awesome "Front Row," in which she furiously chants a combustible counterpoint of lyrics behind the words of the chorus.

> "We said, 'Let's name thirty good reasons
> Why we shouldn't be together'
> I start by saying things like,
> 'You smoke'
> 'You live in New Jersey'
> You started saying things like,
> 'You belong to the world'
> All of which could have been easily refuted
> But the conversation was hypothetical . . .
> I'm in the front row
> The front row with popcorn . . . "

from "Front Row"

"On *Junkie* there is an enormous amount of words," Ballard said. "But there is *always* a melodic through-line on every branch. And then her words are like leaves on that branch which infuse the melody. The way she takes that through-line and wraps the words around it is *amazing*." Once their creative floodgates were opened again, a river of new songs rushed in, including "Thank You," "Baba," "I Was Hoping," "That I Would Be Good," "Joining You," and more. But Alanis recognized that the world was getting impatient to hear this record, and she elected to stop recording and save many of the new songs for future albums. "I knew I had to finish this record that *everybody* at *every* check-out stand of *every* grocery store around the world wanted to hear," she says.

Many members of the press predicted that, like Carole King's inability to transcend *Tapestry*, Alanis would never surpass the phenomenal success of *Jagged Little Pill*. They were, of course, wrong. Far from the shallow sophomore effort many expected, *Supposed Infatuation Junkie* was a solid artistic and commercial success, and powerful proof that Alanis was much more than a one-album wonder.

MTV's *Unplugged* show was graced by a beautiful 1999 performance by Alanis, which spawned a live album that features outstanding alternative approaches to her many famous songs, as well as the previously unreleased "Princes Familiar," as well as her version of Sting's "King of Pain," which she makes very much her own. Recently she wrote two beautiful songs for movies—"Uninvited" for *City of Angels* and "Still" for *Dogma*, a film in which she plays the role of God.

Despite the international magnitude of her success, which could easily convince even the most earthbound among us that they possess some measure of genius and/or divinity, she's authentically humble in person. When we meet, she politely says, "Hi, I'm Alanis," instead of assuming the obvious—that most people on this planet already know she's Alanis. As someone who has existed in the center of a hurricane for years, her countenance is almost supernaturally peaceful, the polar opposite of a prima donna. She's as present and genuine with inquisitive writers as she is with fans, roadies, bandmates, and friends. Grounded in gratitude and spirituality, she's dedicated to the expression of an eternal truth in her songs, which is especially admirable in an industry that often celebrates that which is ephemeral and emotionally empty.

Although she recognizes that people often focus only on the rage and sexuality expressed in her work, in her soul the songs that matter most are the ones infused with the divine spirit. "There's divinity in all of us," she says softly. "But sometimes people just need to be reminded of it. And that's why there are songwriters. To remind everyone. That's our job."

Is being truthful in songs something that came easily for you?

No. I think on the first records that I did when I was younger, some of it was truthful. Some were pretty close to how I felt, but I don't think I was old enough consciously or emotionally to be able to actually share everything that was my highest truth in songs at that age. Because I would have had to back them up in the way that I lived and in performance and in the interviews that I gave. And I surely wasn't prepared to do that back then.

Has your songwriting process changed since the start?

I have come full circle. It's exactly the way I wrote when I was ten. Usually I start with a note that I hit, and that starts a melody and lyric all at the same time. Or I'll have a line written down that I know I want to sing about, and I'll sing it and then I will envelop the melody with whatever music is underneath. But the music and the lyrics are always written at the same time.

Are your lyrics always true to your own life?

Yes. I mean, they're snapshots of where I am at the time. There're songs on *Jagged Little Pill* that have lines that make me realize I have already altered that belief.

But then other songs that were written in retrospect, songs like "You Oughta Know," I think I could sing till I was ninety, because I was singing in retrospect. Songs like "Perfect" or "One" or "The Couch," because they're all my having looked back or my having summarized a different part of my life. And I could sing those forever.

The rage in "You Oughta Know" is so genuine. When you wrote it, were you still in the middle of that anger?

I was very much in the middle of it. I was in the middle of it up into right before *Supposed Infatuation Junkie* [laughs], really. I was in that space, definitely, while writing all the songs for *Jagged Little Pill*.

Some say it's impossible to write while in the middle of emotional turmoil, while others seem to require it—

I feel both applies to me. Sometimes I feel when I'm in the middle of it, I *love* it. That's the *best* time to write. And then other times, equally, I'll write in retrospect. But I can conjure up, or remember if nothing else, how I felt.

"You Oughta Know" is a rare example of a direct attack in a song, reminis-cent of Dylan singing, "You've got a lot of nerve to say you are my friend," in "Positively 4th Street." Was it directed at a specific person?

Yes. And it wasn't directed at him in the sense that I wrote it just to finally admit how I felt. It was written almost irrespective of the person and irrespective of their response to it. It wasn't written to elicit a response from this person or to seek any sort of revenge. It was to unburden myself with my now allowing myself to just admit how I felt. And in admitting how I felt by singing it so many times, I kind of *transcended* it, really. I was able to allow myself to admit all of this [*laughs*] and to go forth from there, instead of getting stuck there.

I think, though, that at times this may have been misinterpreted. I mean, if I were to listen to *Jagged Little Pill* now with the objectivity that I have, it could be perceived as a record very much about being a victim. But I think there's almost a footnote that needed to be given after that record, saying *these* expressions were ex-pressed in order to *transcend* them. As opposed to staying stuck in them forever.

The vocals on the album are amazingly passionate—

Yeah. I was letting a lot out. I did all the vocals in one or two takes. That was an incredible time, doing that. I consider a record successful when it really is a snap-shot of a period of time in my life. And singing "Your House," which is the hidden track at the end, was like sewing up, finishing up the record. I was excited and afraid and vibrating all the time right when that record was being finished.

Did you and Glen always write words and music simultaneously?

Yeah. All at the same time, really quickly. And if it became a belabored process at any point in the writing of the song, we would stop. Because if it wasn't channeled and it wasn't stream of consciousness, then I just didn't want to have to beat it out of me, because it didn't feel inspired. And that was the template we had, which was great.

To achieve that level with a collaborator is remarkable—

Yeah. Believe me, I tried to do it with a huge handful of writers. For the years prior to that, I wasn't actually able to tap into the proverbial source, because I felt limited or judged and any of the above things that aren't overly nurturing. And then when I was with Glen, just the songs that we wrote were such a testament to how open he was, and how nonjudgmental and excited he was about it, too.

Did the lyrics emerge in the order that we hear them?

Yes. Usually I start with the first line. And I've never rewritten a song. Ever. All the words come out exactly the way you hear it. I have definitely *edited* the lyrics. I have taken certain verses out. Because the song is 13 minutes long. But I've *never* rewritten a song.

And yet your songs are so well-conceived.

Thanks. It's like a conversation.

With who?

With God. Or you. Or Glen. Or myself.

What allows a song to come through that completely?

It's a hugely spiritual experience for me. Which I am humbled by in the grandest sense of that word. It's very channeled, and I oftentimes don't even feel like I wrote it.

Is it more a form of discovery than invention?
Absolutely. Yeah. Exactly. It is not something you can really control. But if you can kind of ride with it and not smother it, it can take you where you need to go.

Did you and Glen ever talk about it?
Sometimes we would talk about it. But a lot of times we didn't need to talk about it. It's just *so* obvious. So we just smiled and laughed. [*Laughter*]

Did it take time to establish a connection with Glen at first?
No. It happened within the first fifteen minutes. [*Laughs*] We wrote our first song, "The Bottom Line," within half an hour of having met each other. It was *so* great. I knew it was not something I wanted on the record, but I knew that if we continued and evolved together, eventually I would reach a point where I would tap into certain parts of myself that had been scary prior to that experience.

Writing with Glen was much like the way I wrote when I was ten. I'd be singing, and he would be following me, chasing me. Or he'd play a chord and I'd sing on top of it.

Besides your amazing lyrics, you and Glen also created amazing melodies with big ranges and unusual, appealing intervals.
Yeah, I love interesting intervals and movement. I like melodies that have a big range and open up slowly as you hear them.

Did you and Glen work equally on the music?
Yes. It was a total collaboration. I wrote the lyrics, but the melody and lyrics were always coming out at exactly the same time, basically.

Did you ever write a whole lyric before bringing it to Glen to work on the music?
Yes, twice. I did that with "That I Would Be Good" and also "Would Not Come."

Did that change the writing process?
Yes. It makes it easier. Because the urgency and the energy in the room when you're creating something out of *nothing* is more intense. When you're going into it knowing what you are going to sing about, it softens the energy.

How long would it take to reach the place where it felt the songs were channeled?
Sometimes it would happen within ten minutes of getting together, and other times three hours into it, it would be just floating around, trying not to get too frustrated, and then it would hit, and then we would know we had tapped in, and we would just go.

What allows that connection to succeed?
Not pressuring it too much. I think writer's block can simply be translated into pressure. Whether it's time or whether it's expectation. The best way to write a song,

for me anyway, is to have no expectation at all and to make sure you put no pressure at all on yourself.

Did Glen ever comment on lyrics while you were working?

Sure. I mean, he'll *comment* on them. Not in the sense that he says I should or shouldn't write something. But he will laugh. Or sometimes he will compliment. Especially during *Jagged Little Pill*. I remember him saying such sweetly flattering and complimentary things. And I had no objectivity at *all* on what I was doing. He would say, "*Wow*, you really have *no* idea how great this is." And I would say, "Thank you, and I don't *really* know what you're talking about. [*Laughs*] But thank you."

Have you ever found anything that you couldn't express in a song?

No. No. I remember when I was younger I was working in environments with people who would say, "Well, you *can't* fit this in," and "*This* isn't syncopated properly," and "*This* structure doesn't work." And I remember just *bubbling* with anger and wanting to say, "*Please*, just don't tell me what can't fit into a song." But out of respect for them and respect for the collaboration, I didn't push it. But I knew at some point I could gain a very unfettered view of songwriting and get to a place where I didn't have to worry about structure. Or I could adhere to structure if I so chose. But I didn't ever have to be restricted by it.

Did Glen ever discourage your readiness to mess with song structure?

No, he was *thrilled*. Because he was ready to mess with song structure himself.

Carole King also loves to play with song structure.

She inspired me since I was very young. I have *always* adored Carole King. *Tapestry* has been one of my favorite albums much of my life. It was kind of a staple for me throughout many years.

Like her, you play unusual structures against conventional ones, as in "I Was Hoping," which has expansive verses set against a normal chorus structure.

Yeah. I do that because I *love* the feel of that, the release of a chorus that I can hold onto musically, especially when I am trying to fit so many words into the verses. That song was originally twice as long as it was. We edited it down, because it just went on for, like, five years. [*Laughs*]

Though that chorus is regular, still you change the words to it each time, as in many of your songs.

[*Laughs*] Yeah. Right. Because I feel limited by repetition of lyrics. Unless they're *so* perfect. The chorus of "Baba," for example, is one I felt I could sing over and over. I felt it tied up *exactly* what I was singing about.

In "I Was Hoping" and "Thank You" and others, though, I felt that there was more to say and that I wasn't done saying it yet. So I just kept saying it till I felt it was done.

"You Oughta Know" resulted in your reputation as an angry young woman. But "Head Over Feet" is as genuinely happy as some of the others are angry.

Yeah. I wrote that at a time when I was willing to admit that in a lot of the other songs I may have felt like a victim of sorts. But in this song I kind of take responsibility, which was a foreshadowing of things to come in the future. Just seeing that a lot of times I was my own saboteur, you know? So that song is such a sweet, warm song. It's about the fear of health. [*Laughs*] About being with someone who would, heaven forbid, treat me kindly. [*Laughter*]

It has the line, "I've never felt this healthy before."
Yeah. [*Laughs*] Yikes! *Scary!*

"Ironic" sparked an ironic discussion in the media about the definition of irony.
Yeah. [*Laughs*] And a lot of what was in that song wasn't ironic at all. There was a bit of a non-sequitur-izing going on in that song. A lot of my songs are very literal, so I could understand if people are in a very literal head space, it would be disconcerting to hear things that weren't ironic to be followed with, "Isn't it ironic?" [*Laughs*] So I *totally* get it. But I wasn't being overly precious about it. I had to laugh myself, though, because I had always been the *queen* of malapropisms when I was young. [*Laughter*]

Recently you've written some beautiful songs such as "Uninvited" and "Still" by yourself. Is writing alone something you want to do more of, or will you continue to work with Glen or others?
I think I am going to do more writing alone. I may write with other people musically. Lyrically, I don't think I will ever write with anyone else. Or I may just do it all on my own. I would also be open to working more with Glen. The best thing about my working with Glen is that we're interdependent. He can do his own thing and I can do mine, and we can work together too. But there's no pressure to do any of those three.

After doing so much collaboration, how does it feel to work alone?
It feels beautiful. Yeah. [*Laughs*] I'm less afraid. Figuratively and literally, I'm not afraid to write alone. Whereas I think in my mid-teens, even though I had already done it so many times when I was really young, I was in environments that were kind of leading me to believe that without Mr. X, I wouldn't be able to do what I was doing. And I knew intuitively that wasn't the case, but there was a part of me that actually believed that it might be true, out of fear.

You've been great at coming up with provocative opening lines, such as for "Thank You," which starts, "How about getting off of those antibiotics?"
That is a funny one. [*Laughs*] It's true, though. I was on antibiotics, and I was talking to Glen, and I was just jittery all day and freaking out. And then an hour before writing I was saying that I had to get off of these. And then when he started playing the music [*laughs*], it was such a natural thing to sing.

Is "Thank You" another song that came fast?
Yes, it did.

In it you give thanks to India—
I was thanking the experience of my having gone there, and the space that I entered into and emerged from surrounding the time of my having gone on that trip.

You did one cover on your *Unplugged* album, Sting's "King of Pain." Why did you choose that one?

I didn't really choose it. In the sense that I actually had decided not to do a cover, because there's so much pressure on your proverbial *Unplugged* record with the proverbial cover, you know? So I was trying out all these different songs and playing some of them on the guitar. And none of them I was able to sing with conviction. So one day during rehearsal I turned to my bandmates and said, "I'm officially announcing that we're not doing a cover on this album." And they all said, "Okay, cool." And within seconds the keyboard player started tinkling a few notes on the piano randomly. And it reminded me of the intro to "King Of Pain," so I started singing it. So we all just looked at each other, and continued. And it was very obvious that it wanted to be on the record.

It almost sounds as if he wrote it for you—
[*Laughs*] Well, it was hilariously ironic. And just sweet. And those lyrics are great. Some lyrics that Gordon Sumner [Sting] has written are just so great. He's a fucking genius.

When I was a teenager, when I first got my license, the Police's *Greatest Hits* record was in my CD player in my car for a year straight. That's *all* I listened to.

Your song "Front Row" has that great chanting section behind the chorus, which gives it such a unique subtext of musical and lyrical energy.
Yeah. That is my favorite part of the song. I sang the original chorus, and then when I was playing it back, I started to sing the other section underneath it. So I just went in and recorded it over. It was really simple. But a *lot* of people tried to talk me out of that.

Why?
Because they thought that they needed to be able to focus on one lyric, and not have to split their brain in half and listen to two. And I said, "How exciting is it to split our brains in half? Don't underestimate people." And they are more subliminal, those lyrics. They're almost like a footnote to the song.

"Baba" seems directed at a guru gone bad, or a false prophet.
Yes. A whole lot of the environments I had been in over the years, not just in India or in Asia but in L.A. for that matter, had a foundation that was supposedly compassion and kindness and nonjudgment, and I found the opposite to be true. And it was really sad and wonderfully disillusioning. I was kind of disillusioned in the greatest sense of that word to begin with. So it was kind of affirming, the fact that we don't find this bliss and this sense of our higher selves outside of ourselves, it's something that we already are. If you are around people who seek and seek and seek, you will seek forever, because it's not outside of you.

It has the line, "I've seen them overlooking God in their own essence." Which is a theme you've touched on in other songs, as in "Thank You," when you say, "How about remembering your own divinity." Do you think people hear the fullness of what you are saying in your songs?
[*Laughs*] I think a handful of people do and a handful of people don't. And it doesn't matter who does get the message and who doesn't get it. What matters is that I have the power to express it.

I think the greatest thing about music is that it's such a choice for the people who receive it. No one is *forced* to listen to these songs. Or to agree with *anything* that I'm saying in them. I'd far rather present a record to someone and have them be able to turn it down or accept it, rather than stand on a soapbox and hammer away at all these ideas, preaching to people. I would *never* be able to do that.

I'd like to name some of your other songs to see what response they evoke.
Okay.

"All I Really Want."
That was one of the last songs written for *Jagged Little Pill*. It just felt like this song was my wanting to start again, wanting to close the chapter of *Jagged Little Pill* and start a whole new record right in that spot. But it was time to tour. So I had to stop recording, put out that record, and hit the road.

"Princes Familiar."
That was a song we wrote for *Supposed Infatuation Junkie*, but that record was already *really* long, so we couldn't fit it. I actually didn't like how "Princes Familiar" sounded when we first recorded it. Breaking it down in the acoustic form for the *Unplugged* record was exciting. Because I loved the song itself. I wanted to approach it from a different way. But a lot of people are furious with me for not having shared that version, because they loved it. And I might share it at some time.

"That I Would Be Good."
I actually had taken a break from writing the record for a few days, because I had gone into the studio one day and Glen could see I was under a lot of pressure, just time-wise if nothing else, to hurry up and finish this record. So one day I turned to him, and I said I was buckling a little bit here. And he said, "Go away." And I said, "Right on, see ya!" And so I was sitting in my house and I had roommates here for a minute or two. And when I write I need to be alone, for the most part. So I didn't want to kick them out of my house, but I needed silence. So I just locked myself in my closet and sat there and I wrote everything that I felt. And those were the lyrics for "That I Would Be Good." And a few days later I went in and wrote the music with Glen.

"Still."
Ooh, writing that and making that record was a juicy, *beautiful* time. I actually just listened to it today. I hadn't heard it in months. I was just really excited to be able to sing about who and what I thought God is. I was in Dublin, and I saw a rough cut of *Dogma*. I had told everyone that if I saw it and I was inspired, then I would write a song. And if I saw it and the song didn't want to come, that it wouldn't. And they said, "Okay." I saw the movie while riding on the bus somewhere through Dublin. And I went to bed that night and *couldn't* stop writing. I was writing everything I felt God was. And I woke up the next day, and I had sort of a pseudo-studio built in my hotel room, and I stayed in and wrote it and recorded the demo that night. And I produced the record at Abbey Road a few days later.

"Joining You."
It's one of my faves. And it is very true. It's a tough one. I hate being in a position where I have to preach or give advice. I oftentimes don't really even believe in it. But in this I was being asked just with my own self if I was actually going to call someone and give them any reason to not want to end this existence, what would I

possibly say to them? And that is what the song became. The person I wrote it for cried when he heard it. And he said to me, "I don't even understand half of what you are writing about. But I will one day." [*Laughs*] I said, "Right on."

How do you see your musical future?

I see that I will continue always making records that are snapshots of what I am thinking about and feeling at that time. And I'll continue stretching always, trying new instruments, working with different people in different environments, different countries, different flavors, and always evolving. It would be hard not to keep evolving.

Steely Dan:
Walter Becker & Donald Fagen
New York, New York 1999

We're in Manhattan, a couple weeks before the final Christmas of the twentieth century. Donald Fagen and Walter Becker have arrived together at the 12th floor Broadway office of their publicist. But not before going first to the fourteenth floor, where Fagen was sure the office used to be. It's the first time the two have ever been here together, as this is the first interview they are giving to herald their new album *Two Against Nature*. "It's pretty *bleak* up on the 14th floor," Fagen says darkly, clearly rattled by the experience. "There's *nothing* going on up there."

It's but one of the many struggles they've had to endure in order to create this, their first album of new Steely Dan songs since *Gaucho* was released some twenty years earlier. It's the reason they designated "Two Against Nature" as the title song: It has to do with their dual struggle against the elemental forces they fought to finish this album, as Becker and Fagen (hereafter referred to as B&F) explained in this characteristically spirited exchange:

> **Donald Fagen:** We made it the title cut because we thought it was descriptive of our condition at the present time. Because when you start to get older, you really are fighting nature all the time. And musically you're fighting nature, trying to organize atoms of sound. You're trying to manipulate or overcome obstacles in nature.
> **Walter Becker:** You're fighting to tame the forces and bend them to your will.

DF: Right. You're fighting lethargy. You're fighting—
WB: Chaos.
DF: And laziness. You're fighting—
WB: The ordinary.
DF: And other people, even if they're on your side. You're fighting your own sloppiness, or lack of patience.
WB: Your own internal economy of time, energy, money, ideas, patience—
DF: Trying to balance your musical life with other parts of your life. It's essentially a classic struggle.
WB: Think of the *Two Against Nature* album as akin to the building of the Hoover Dam.

Although no humans actually sacrificed their lives during the making of *Two Against Nature*, as during the construction of the mighty dam, the creation of this album was hardly less monumental. Stretching three years from the writing of the first song to the completion of the final mix, it was a period ironically delineated by the visible progress of other people in the proximity of Fagen's studio on East 95th, where much of the record was recorded. "We'd been working on the album for about five months," Becker said, smiling, "and we looked out the window and noticed that they were starting to build a large, high-rise, forty-story apartment house on the corner across from the studio. And we actually went back in the studio a couple of days ago to add a part to the album, and we noticed that the building was finished. And people were *living* in it already! And here we were still putting parts on the album!"

Truth be told, *Two Against Nature* might very well stand longer than the new high-rise across the street. Like all previous Steely Dan albums, it's been built to last. As their fans know well, B&F have never followed any trends other than their own, and for this reason, as well as the tremendously high standard of artistry and musicianship they bring to every project they take on, their albums possess a distinct timelessness.

Two Against Nature extends this magic into the new millennium. It's got everything that makes the Dan great: supernaturally tight, soulful grooves; lyrics that are elegant, mysterious, funny, sardonic, even perverse (such as the lecherous "Cousin Dupree"); melodies that are sophisticated and slinkily visceral set against tight textures of electric guitars, bass, and keyboards; and all underscored by a dazzling counterpoint of horns and harmony vocals.

It's a stunning level of accomplishment they've achieved by being intricately involved with every aspect of the creative process, as consciously careful with each word of every line as they are with each beat of the kick drum and the snare. Though the ongoing brilliance of their seamless and soulfully singable songs might often seem to be the product of some kind of spontaneous genius, it's actually the result of a lot of hard work, as B&F explained. Take the flowing chorus of "West Of Hollywood," for example:

"I'm way deep into nothing special
Riding the crest of a wave breaking just west of Hollywood"

It's a single sentence that evolved through a profusion of lyrical permutations before the ideal form was discovered. "One trick of writing is to use the mechanics of typing things over and over again as a way of exercising and developing an idea," Becker said. To illustrate this technique, he shared some of the variations he and Fagen generated for this line:

"I'm way deep into nothing special. . .
. . . coming from a place of power just west of Hollywood.
. . . with a base of support located just west of Hollywood.
. . . in a matrix with its nexus just west of Hollywood.
. . . situated as I am in the crescent just west of Hollywood.
. . . having as my target the citizens just west of Hollywood.
. . . in a cluster franchise operation just west of Hollywood.
. . . and business is booming in the triangle just west of Hollywood."

All of the songs on the new album went through this lengthy process of thought and revision, each the result of many pages of notes, character development, and explorations into the best ways to compel and conclude narratives. Each character emerges only after sessions of abundant B&F banter and discovery, resulting in a rich emotional subtext that serves as a foundation for all of these songs. In "What a Shame About Me," for example, they went through a series of variations before arriving at the appropriate climax for this tale of reminiscing college sweethearts. When the woman in the song boldly suggests a rendezvous at her hotel to rekindle their romance, the man sadly declines, admitting that any substance left to his soul is mostly spectral at this point. It's a confession that assures that this character, who takes his place now among Kid Charlemagne, Peg, Doctor Wu, Aja, and other fully-realized personages from the fertile fiction of B&F, shines with a spirit that is genuine and poignantly human.

"I said, 'Babe, you look delicious
And you're standing very close
But this is Lower Broadway
And you're talking to a ghost
Take a good look it's easy to see
What a shame about me . . . '"

from "What a Shame About Me"

B&F were both born on the east coast of an America darkened by the shadow of war: Fagen came first, on January 10, 1948, in Passaic, New Jersey, "amidst growing furor over Soviet acquisition of the atomic bomb," according to B&F's self-written and often hilarious bio. Becker's birth in New York on February 20, 1950, occurred "as war loomed on the Korean peninsula." Though they wouldn't meet for decades, like separated identical twins they developed acutely similar artistic preferences, simultaneously gravitating towards the music of classic American jazz masters Charlie Parker, Duke Ellington, Miles Davis, and others. At this point, according to their bio, "inexpensive saxophones were purchased forthwith."

At Bard they merged their love of jazz and black humor into songs, which they performed in a series of pick-up bands. After graduation they started peddling their songs at the Brill Building in New York, and succeeded in getting signed to two publishing deals, as well as joining the touring band for Jay & The Americans. They came to L.A. to work in a tiny office with an upright piano where they were expected to start churning out hits like Goffin and King. Instead they collaborated on a series of "classic but unrecordable cheesy pop songs" while secretly conspiring to start their own band.

With Fagen on vocals and keyboards, Becker on bass, Denny Dias and Jeff "Skunk" Baxter on guitars, Jim Hodder on drums, and David Palmer sharing lead vocals with Fagen, they rehearsed for a few months in an unfinished office wing before recording their debut album, *Can't Buy a Thrill*. They named themselves Steely Dan after a sexual device described in William Burroughs's *Naked Lunch*.

From the first album on, B&F shared an explicit musical vision, swimming against the current of spontaneous, haphazard rock recordings to set a new standard in terms of record production. Disbanding their original lineup of musicians after their third album, they evolved to the essential core of B&F only, surrounded by the brightest satellites of the rock and jazz worlds, including Michael McDonald, Steve Gadd, The Brecker Brothers, Phil Wood, Bernard Purdie, and others. Gaining reputations as studio tyrants (which both deem as inaccurate), they cooked up tracks that were at once burning and pristine, hot, sizzling jazz textures with the most precise and tight rhythmic foundations imaginable. And they created a succession of masterpieces throughout the seventies, following their debut with *Countdown to Ecstasy*, *Pretzel Logic*, *Katy Lied*, *The Royal Scam*, and *Aja*. In 1979 came *Gaucho*, and the Dan was done.

During the eighties, B&F went their separate ways. Donald recorded his own solo masterpiece, *The Nightfly*, a huge critical and commercial success. Becker moved to Hawaii to become "a gentleman avocado rancher and self-styled critic of the contemporary scene," but returned often to the mainland to produce albums for others, including the glorious *Flying Cowboys* for Rickie Lee Jones. (Rickie on Walter: "He's much smarter, you know, than most humans.")

The nineties found B&F at work on an assortment of solo projects and productions, including Fagen's second solo album, *Kamakiriad* and Becker's first, the triumphant *11 Tracks of Whacks* (which a Swedish magazine recently named the "Best Album of the Decade." "I told my son that we're all moving to Sweden!" Walter said). B&F also returned to the touring circuit as Steely Dan for a series of summer concerts, and in 1995 started writing songs for *Two Against Nature*.

> "Two against nature don't you know
> Who's gonna grok the shape of things to go
> Two against nature make them groan
> Who's gonna break the shape of things unknown"

from "Two Against Nature"

In person B&F project opposing personalities. Becker seems quite comfortable in his skin; bearded and beatific, he's happy to expound on any subject posed to him with a warmly gentle and somewhat professorial countenance. Fagen, who fidgets in his chair and distractedly pages through a book of photography on the desk before him, seems ready to ankle at any moment, but gets noticeably calmer as soon as the subject turns to music. Unlike other songwriting duos who have famously tired of each other after decades of collaboration, it's obvious that B&F truly enjoy each other's company. Rather than tune out when the other speaks, as is often the fashion, they seem as close as brothers—hanging on their partner's every word, finishing each other's sentences, even laughing at each other's jokes.

The following discussion is a combination of our initial talk in New York on the second day of December 1999 with a phone conversation that occurred soon thereafter, allowing us a generous measure of time to illuminate the perpetual mystery and marvel that is Steely Dan.

You've said that impatience is one of the natural forces you had to fight against to make this album. Yet you both must have a lot of patience to get your albums to the level that you have.

Donald Fagen: Well, it just means we're victorious over our lack of patience. I *am* impatient. I want everything to happen *now!*

Walter Becker: But on the other hand, having said that, you're able to work very patiently on something.

DF: Yeah. I'm more impatient about technical breakdowns.

WB: You're only impatient during delays. You're only impatient when you have to wait.

DF: Yeah, only when I have to wait. Yeah, when the band is learning a song, I'm impatient for them to already know it.

You have always had tremendously high standards, both in terms of writing and production. Does the struggle to get it right ever get easier?

DF: Mostly it gets harder, I would say. Some of your techniques might prove to make things a little easier, but those can have their downsides.

WB: I don't know if it gets harder in general. I can imagine making a different sort of record where it would have been easier instead of harder. But we decided to do something that we knew was going to be hard to do, and it was. And depending on what the musical context something is going to be viewed in may make it harder to make something mean what you want it to mean. It makes it harder to make things that have the real feel of real musicians playing instead of the mechanical feel of machine tracks, but that still has the same kind of consistency.

In most songwriting collaborations, it's usually pretty clear who writes what, yet in your work it's always been mysterious who does what, though a little less so since you have done solo albums—

WB: Although that might not be informative as to what we do when we are actually writing together. Because if we are writing separately, then each one of us perforce has to write the lyrics and the music and have the overall concept.

So the two of you actually do write the songs together, as opposed to bringing in separate fragments that you write individually?

DF: Usually, a lot of time, most of the time I will bring early music. I'll bring a chord progression or an idea for something. And sometimes Walter will have an idea for some music. A piece of something, and then we'll work on that together. And then we'll work on lyrics almost from the beginning together.

One of the things that has always been so impressive about Steely Dan is your chord progressions. Yet these would not be so effective without a strong melody over them. Do you come up with chords first, before the melody?

DF: Well, they sort of come in a piece, usually.

WB: Sometimes they come in a piece and sometimes we'll have—

DF: A riff.

WB: Or vampy sort of things where you set up a vamp, and then you have to develop a melody over it. Eight bars or sixteen bars over one chord, or over some sort of repeating figure—

DF: A lot of times we'll have music and a title. Sometimes not even a title but maybe just an idea, what the song is sort of about. And other times we'll have a title.

Do you always know what the song is about prior to writing it?

DF: No. But that's usually what we start with. We might have a *clue* as to what it's about.

By the time you finish it, is the meaning always clear to you?

WB: To us it is.

DF: In recent years. [*Laughs*]

WB: Listeners might argue otherwise. But to us we've usually got a pretty good idea very early on—these days—what we're writing about.

Was that different in the old days?

WB: Well, yeah. I think in the old days some of the songs were more, shall we say, more impressionistic. And so—

DF: But we knew what those were about, more or less—

WB: We knew what we were trying to do, but we didn't necessarily know what those were about.

Most songwriters write songs using existing idioms, but you two almost always invent your own.

DF: Well, it's cheating to just take idioms that are in the language.

Is it?

DF: [*Laughs*] Isn't it?

If the idiom is used in an inventive way, such as "Still Crazy After All These Years," it can work.

WB: That's a perfect example of cheating.

DF: I thought Paul Simon invented "Still Crazy After All These Years." But maybe I'm wrong.

WB: Then it's not cheating if he did. Then he's just doing what we're doing.

Your new album starts with "Gaslighting Abbie," which seems like a newly invented idiom—

DF: Right. Well, the slang word "to gaslight" is something I've heard used—actually, I've never heard it used outside of New York City. [*Laughs*] It usually was from a woman who is usually accusing me of gaslighting—

WB: [*Laughs*]

DF: The word "gaslighting" comes from the film *Gaslight*, where Charles Boyer tries to convince Ingrid Bergman that she's crazy. So it's kind of a synonym for mind-fucking—

WB: A certain kind of mind-fucking, where the method by which this was accomplished was by manipulating the physical reality in such a way that the person would be cold all the time, or by lowering the gaslights all the time making it so that the rooms were getting darker and darker. That sort of thing.

DF: Stealing clothes and things like that. Or denying that something happened that actually did happen.

"Jack of Speed" is another new idiom you've created.

DF: Yeah, that one represents the personification of a kind of demonic obsession.

WB: We just felt that "Good King Psylosibin" was too hard to sing. [*Laughs*] So we decided to go with "Jack of Speed."

I love that line about trading fours with the Jack of Speed.

WB: [*Laughs*]

DF: Yeah, that's scary. You know, the Jack of Speed is very competitive. If you're trading fours with the Jack of Speed, you'd really have to be on your toes.

WB: Yeah, talk about your cutting contests. [*Laughter*]

DF: Yeah, really.

The use of original idioms ensures that songs retain some mystery and don't ever seem dated.

DF: Yeah, they don't become dated that much. At least the greater part of them.

WB: Well, I guess they also don't become dated because they're not tied to the slang of twenty years ago.

DF: Yeah, though the slang of twenty years ago seems to have been completely recouped and is back in circulation.

WB: Some of it.

DF: I think maybe we got some of that, because when we were kids we were both big science fiction fans, and sci-fi writers, at least in those days, invent slang, because they're writing about the future. For instance, there may be some kind of technology that they're inventing, so they will invent slang words for the technology. Just the way we invent slang words for current technology.

You've often used words that originate in science fiction, such as in "Two Against Nature," when you say, "You've got to grok the shape of things unknown . . . "

DF: Yes, "grok" is also a pre-existing term.

WB: "Grok" is from *Stranger in a Strange Land* by Robert Heinlein.

DF: Twenty years ago that word was used more than it is now.

WB: Let's say thirty years ago. [*Laughs*] It was part of the sixties currency.

DF: "To grok" meant to understand something, to see its deeper meaning—

WB: At an intuitive level, yeah.

You said that using existing idioms is cheating, yet you both love Dylan, who has used existing idioms such as "a simple twist of fate" repeatedly through the years.

WB: Well, Bob Dylan started out, and in some ways never moved that far away from, the idea of being a folk musician. In which genre you sort of are permitted to recycle a chord change or a melody or a lyrical idea. I think that's essentially what it means to be a folk musician. You are going to be recycling musical and/or lyrical ideas. Or personalizing them in a variety of ways. There's something about the economy of someone like Bob Dylan. There's a great economy that allows him to focus his energies on what is really important to him. And I think that's probably part of his genius, and what made him so productive over the years.

His is the complete opposite of your approach in the studio. Not only will Dylan not write out his chords, he won't even say what they are—you have to watch his hands.

WB: Right. Certainly we couldn't get away with that. "Watch my hands" wouldn't work for us. [*Laughter*] Even in the best of circumstances.

Yeah, it is the opposite of what we do. And I think we feel that an integral part of what we're doing has more to do with the presentation and production, the sound of the record, perfected arrangements, and stuff like that.

Like Dylan, some of your lyrics are clear narratives and others are quite cryptic. Yet those songs also never age, because there are new possibilities in them. Is it sometimes better that meaning not be obviously understandable?

WB: No, I think, depending on what the song is and what it's about, it's more or less important that it have a very comprehensible narrative to it. And I think for example, a song like "What a Shame About Me" on the new record, I can't imagine anyone having any trouble knowing what that's about. Whereas a song like "Two Against Nature," people ask us about quite a bit and sort of wonder about it. And particularly foreign people who are sort of confused about what might be meant by the idea of "Two Against Nature" or who don't recognize any of the names of those demons. The figures of the voodoo pantheon there. Which must just seem like a lot of confusing names to some people, I'm sure. Or a song like "Gaslighting Abbie," if you don't know about the movie *Gaslight* and that expression, you're screwed, right? You have no idea what that's about. And yet if you do know that, then I think you can make sense out it.

But even if you don't, it's still intriguing and has a lot of resonance—

WB: Yes, it's still intriguing and it has a lot of resonance. And I think there's a lot of times when I will read something, and I'll like it and be taken with it before I completely know what it is. And then there's other cases, with Bob Dylan songs and so on, there's such a series of kaleidoscopic images and surrealistic imagery that it's hard to categorize in your mind what it is. It's something that you experience, and it sort of reinvents itself every time you hear it because it's so allusive.

I think there is something to be said for the idea that something can retain some element of mystery. That is very likable. And I think our new songs, generally speaking, are less obscure than they might have been at other times earlier in our career. It was the seventies back then, and the sixties weren't far behind. [*Laughter*] We felt free to take appropriate liberties. At the same time, I think what we're doing has gotten a little clearer, don't you?

Yes. And your use of the language and specific details, even when the meaning is not immediately obvious, such as "now you're the wonderwaif of Gramercy Park" from "Janie Runaway," is so great.

WB: [*Laughs*] We certainly were pleased with that. We probably sat there for two hours trying to come up with that line. We had all different parts of the city. We had "Another year of dogpatch would have done you in." [*Laughs*] Let's see: "My waif queen," "My waif supreme," "waif mistress," "the baroness of my Wall Street loft," "now you're the princess of Van Damme Street," "now you're the baroness of Elizabeth Street," "of Irving Place," "of Waverly Place." We had "Dixie Runaway," "Susie Runaway," "Polly Runaway," "Molly Runaway," "Annie Runaway."

We have notes which define the idea of certain songs. For "West of Hollywood" we had, "Ideal flatness of field, leveling, nulling out, zero potential, the tyranny of the disallowed."

When your lyrics get mathematical like that, or "the axis of pain/pleasure sheared the arc of desire," it sounds like some of the language in your solo album, Walter, as in "Surf and/or Die."

WB: I think when we hone in on something, it's hard to tell who it came from. The original version of that line was "The axis of pain/pleasure distended the calculus of desire." Which I actually liked better. But try singing it that way sometime. The one we came up with was a little more singable than that.

That smooth singability is a hallmark of your work.

DF: Yeah, well, it's hard to sing those tongue-twisty words. It has to sound good.

WB: Things have to meet a minimum standard of singability.

DF: There have been times when we couldn't figure out any way to say something, and so we moved up to rougher language. But generally speaking there is a way to do it when you get both the sound and the meaning.

When you're working on a song together, how do you go about it?

DF: In recent years we usually start out with me on acoustic piano and Walter on guitar. And then when we have something, it's transferred into some kind of sequencing program so that we have something to work with that sounds a little like a track. And Walter usually works the computer. [*Laughs*]

WB: That's true.

How conscious is your process when working to create new music?

DF: Sometimes it's not conscious at all. Sometimes it comes from just messing around with a cassette recorder on. And other times there are effects you hear in music that you try to store up in your mind. And you think about what will this effect sound like in a different context than you found it in.

A sound effect?

WB: A harmonic effect.

DF: A certain tension or atmosphere of a certain harmony and/or melody. Even down to the timbres. For example, there are things in Duke Ellington's music I know I've used. He was amazing at coming up with original pieces of sound. Because of the guys in the band and the ways it was arranged and the chord progressions and the melodies and the ranges that he put the instruments in. For instance, you will hear something in there and you will come to a certain place when writing a song and I'll play a certain thing that might remind me of that. And then I'll see what would happen if I used a similar progression or somehow assimilated that effect right here in this context.

When you are working on the lyrics, do you do it with the music?

DF: Generally. We have an idea of the rhythm of the melody and sometimes the melody itself.

WB: Usually we have the melody by the time we write the lyrics.

And you always write lyrics together?

DF: Yeah. Almost all of them.

What is your main objective when working on a lyric?

DF: Mostly it has to do with what's the most entertaining. If you can come up with something that's funny in some way or tells the story in an amusing way, that's best. Or little details. Someone will come up with a detail that is very telling about the character. It might be more like writing stories than actual lyrics sometimes.

Do you plot out the story before writing the song together?

DF: Yes, but sometimes we might not know how it ends.

WB: You get the general idea, and then you see where it takes you. I noticed on the songs we just wrote, for example, by the time we were finished with the song, we'll have a couple of pages sometime of lyric material and ideas and conceptual stuff about the character and the situation that we didn't use. Either lyrics that we rejected, or just back story, if you will.

DF: Yeah, sometimes we will have two or three pages of junk we came up with as notes about a story or a character.

WB: It's just like a short story writer or a novelist would work in some cases to develop an elaborate back story and a set of impressions that you then draw from—

DF: The reader doesn't have to know the whole back story, but we have to know it—

WB: We have to know it to write the song.

It's not surprising that you work this way, because these stories are so rich and real seeming, as in "What a Shame About Me," which is like a little short story with a surprise ending.

DF: Yeah, that's kind of like a five-minute play.

WB: That started with the title for the song.

DF: That's kind of a renovated blues idea. I think the ending of it was the last thing we wrote, I think, the ending.

WB: We had ourselves on the edges of our chairs until we got there. [*Laughter*] We just didn't know what was going to happen.

DF: We thought it was just too obvious for the guy just to go up with the girl—

WB: I would say, generally speaking, that songs on this album, we didn't know how the stories were going to end until we got there. Wouldn't you agree?

DF: Yeah, pretty much.

To be funny in songs can be tough, because jokes quickly get old. Yet your songs such as "Cousin Dupree" are funny without being jokey.

WB: Well, when Donald and I started writing together way back when we were in college and for several years after that, the songs that we wrote were humorous but in fact they were too humorous. They sort of, unfortunately, suffered from that very problem that you're describing, that they were just too jokey and sounded like novelty songs. But we realized that that was a liability and so we developed over time and we sort of tempered that idea, and honed into the idea of things having humor in them but a certain kind of humor and a certain amount of humor, along with other stuff. Because we were both definitely interested in humor as a central element of what we were doing, but we didn't want to write Tom Lehrer songs.

DF: "Cousin Dupree" is a song we had from a while back. That one had sort of been kicking around for a while. At one point we were talking about writing some country songs, and I think that one came out of the list of ideas for country tunes. Really, parodies of country tunes.

Musically country?

DF: Well, we were thinking of doing that at the time but we didn't. Although "Cousin Dupree" does have a kind of rockabilly, Chuck Berry-ish quality to it. It's mainly the lyrics that are country.

It's hard to imagine you writing country music, because the kind of expanded chords you use are never heard in country. Years ago you referred to the "Mu chord," which is a major triad with a major second in it. Musicians also know of another "Steely Dan chord"—did you consciously choose to use these chords, and are they still a part of your vocabulary?

DF: Well, I think both of us have maybe been to the College of Musical Knowledge since then. [*Laughter*] So we know a lot more about harmony now. Those chords that we used then were some of the more interesting chords that hadn't been used that much in beat music at the time. So, yeah, I think we still use those chords—

WB: But there are so many others—

DF: It's not like we ever said, "I'm going to use this Mu chord here"—

WB: That was just a joke. We made that up just for the songbook. We never referred to it, before or after that day, as the "Mu chord"—

DF: No, we never did, we never did.

WB: It was just an invention. [*To Donald*] Do you know what he means by this other chord, this "Steely Dan chord"?

DF: Yeah, it's a minor seventh with a sharp-five.

WB: Yeah, right.

DF: It is a major chord, but with the third in the bass, you can call it a minor-seventh. [*Laughter*] It's really an inversion of a major chord with an added second—

WB: Right. And no third.

You're famous for getting the tightest rhythm tracks possible. Musicians now have machines which can create that kind of precision, but they rarely get the soulful grooves that you create. How do you do it?

DF: It comes out of the arrangement a lot. And the drummer. And in the last couple of years there has been a certain manipulation of the rhythm track. We started with live drums on every song.

WB: But then we edit. Essentially it's an editing process.

DF: Yeah, it's not only a live drum track, but actually a live band playing. We have a quintet or a sextet.

WB: Some of the later ones we did with a trio. Sometimes on some of the larger sections I wouldn't play.

DF: Walter was actually producing when we were having the bigger bands. I was playing outside and Walter was inside—

WB: Ordering take-out food. [*Laughter*]

The horn arrangements on this new album are remarkable. Are they part of the original conception of the song?

DF: It's usually one of the last things we put on. Of course, you listen to a track and say, "Oh, we can have horns do that." Generally speaking it has to do with where do you need a kick in a song. And I think that's good, because it keeps it kind of minimal that way. So you don't overwrite. Sometimes just a little horn goes a long way.

That to me seems a key to your production and arrangement style, that you have a lot going on, but everything comes in at the right time, so that you can hear all of the separate components.

DF: Yeah, that's the advantage of working on tape.

WB: We try to avoid the abuse of the bourgeois football technique. Where guys are just playing chords and holding them. We want more emotion in there, more contrapuntal movement—

DF: More air in the production. There are a particular bunch of guys, especially guitar players, who just want to play a chord and hold it through the bar. Which is something we try to avoid. Because it weighs down everything.

It's also common to sustain keyboard pads through the bar, which is something you never do. And that does create a feeling of space in the music.

DF: Yeah. In fact, because we don't do that much, then when we bring in the horn section, then it can serve as a little pad there or sustain section. You can do it at the end of the song without gunking the whole thing out.

To keep that space, are you also pretty sparing when it comes to the use of reverb and echo?

WB: Certainly by comparison to other people I think we are. We are shooting for a different end result than what a lot of people are. In general, people, when they are making rock and roll records, want a big, powerful sort of massive sound. And we're thinking more in terms of being able to clearly hear the details. We're more influenced by good-sounding jazz recordings of the late fifties and sixties and some subsequent things as well. So I think our things tend to be a little drier and clearer sounding and more up-front in general.

Unlike most bands who develop a distinctive sound over a series of albums, you had your sound complete from the first album. Did you two discuss what you wanted to do in terms of sound, before you accomplished it?

DF: We had been working at studios a little bit, and by the time we made the first record we had met Roger Nichols, and Roger was also a hi-fi buff and had a very compatible concept, and certainly we had a pretty good idea of what we wanted to do. And Roger knew how to do it, essentially.

WB: Roger was totally into doing whatever we wanted to do in terms of experimenting. We knew early on that he was the guy for us. It was essentially working on the Steely Dan albums with Roger where we first had the opportunity to go in and fool around with things and try different stuff, and play around with equipment, and mix a record, and so on.

Do you have favorite keys to work in, and do you feel that each key has its own character?

DF: Yeah, I do, in a funny way. I don't know if I can define it, exactly. With different keys it's almost as if they each have different smells. [*Laughter*]

WB: There is some kind of complex, synesthetic effect that each key has—

DF: Yeah. At least in relation to other keys. I'm sure if something was in D and then it was in E, I don't know if that would make as much of a difference if you heard it out of context. But if you heard the D one first and then the E one, then you could compare them.

WB: And forgetting about if keys in the abstract have some kind of color, if you are working on some particular musical instrument, they certainly are quite different.

DF: Also the way that keys affect range and inversion. That's not anything intrinsic to a key, but it does affect the way it sounds.

As the lead singer, do you gravitate towards certain keys that best suit your vocal range?

DF: No, I just usually make sure the highest note of the melody falls within my range.

WB: Or very nearly so.

DF: If not, then we decide if it's possible to have that be some kind of background part, so that we can get up higher. Sometimes we'll take the melody and say that it is going to be falsetto or a girl singing. And that's cool. I'll sing the lower part.

WB: Sometimes the verse needs to be in a certain key or not below a certain key, because we are modulating a lot up to the chorus, and that would place the chorus too high.

DF: In "Two Against Nature," we liked the verse in a certain key for my voice and the way it sounded on the keyboard. And we actually had the chorus in another key, but it didn't work out rangewise for my voice. We tried to get the same effect by putting the chorus in a different key.

WB: Often we'll have a series of possible different key relationships between verse and chorus, and we'll have to decide on one that is the best in terms of ranges. Sometimes there will be two or three modulations in one song. I know that was the case with "Two Against Nature."

DF: Right. We wanted the effect of the chorus to have a lift in a certain way. What is it?

WB: The verse is in A flat and the chorus is in D.

DF: The first relationship we had was similar. Maybe it was a third up. But we knew we wanted that kind of thing, but the first thing we had just didn't work out from a range point of view. So we searched around for something that sounded pretty much as good that was singable.

The harmony vocals on *Two Against Nature* are wonderful. And more then ever you have a lot of counterpoint harmonies going against the melody.

DF: Yeah, I think that is one of the things we are doing a little different is the vocal parts. Because we used to do more block harmony. Now this is more interesting. I guess this is our classic period because we are going back to counterpoint.

WB: [*Laughs*] It's our Baroque period.

DF: Primitive counterpoint it might be, but counterpoint nonetheless. [*Laughs*]

You finished this album in 1999 to be released in 2000, which ensures that there will be good music in the next millennium. Any thoughts as to how your music applies to the next century?

WB: Well, we're still confused about how our music applies to the current century. [*Laughs*] We have been fortunate enough to do something that has always been out of the mainstream and yet have an audience for what we do. And I hope that continues to be true. I don't think what we are doing fits neatly into the context of what's happening now anymore than it did in the early seventies when we started doing it. We were fortunate at that time that radio was as wide open as it was that people doing something like what we were doing could sneak in there.

DF: We sneaked in a window of a couple of years when radio was willing to play something that didn't sound like something that had been played for the last forty years.

You are one of the only bands to never have been influenced by any trends.

DF: You know what it is: We're influenced by music from the last century.

WB: We're influenced by trends, but they are only trends that we know about. [*Laughter*] They're secret trends.

Will there be more Steely Dan albums after this one?

WB: There could be. It depends on how long we live.

DF: Depends on the sales, really.

WB: [*Laughter*] It depends on demand.

DF: They're not going to let us make another one, you know, unless somebody buys it.

Having listened to it thoroughly in both New York and L.A., I can attest to the fact that it sounds great on both coasts.

WB: [*Laughter*] Well, that's really nice to know, but it's really the *middle* of the country we're worried about. If you find anyone in the middle of the country that likes it, please let us know.

Mark Knopfler
New York, New York 1992

"I wish it was simple," Mark Knopfler said of songwriting, "just for the sake of talking about it. But it's not." We're sitting in a conference room at Warner Bros. at Rockefeller Center in New York, close enough to Christmas that the big tree has been lit for weeks. He flew in from London only the night before and was understandably weary, yet struggled nonetheless to define the indefinable and discuss his process of writing songs.

> "It's a mystery to me the game commences
> For the usual fee plus expenses
> Confidential information
> It's not a diary
> This is my investigation"

from "Private Investigations"

Like detective work, songwriting is often a process of checking out clues and piecing together a puzzle from whatever evidence is at hand. Sometimes it's no more than a few lines; sometimes it's a cheesy sound on an old organ. The songwriter dusts his own psyche for fingerprints, searching for that ever-elusive connection between words and music.

Such is the way Mark Knopfler has solved many mysteries for many years—from "Sultans of Swing" through "Money for Nothing" and beyond—and he's done so with an earthy, Dylanesque singing voice and an elegant, human sound on the guitar, a sound almost startling in these spurious times for its simplicity and grace.

He's brought that simple grace to the many movies he's scored, such as *Cal*, *Local Hero*, and *Last Exit to Brooklyn*, as well as the many albums he's produced for others, including two of the songwriters who have most influenced him, Randy Newman [*Land of Dreams*] and Bob Dylan [*Infidels*].

He wrote his first song at the age of eighteen, after having played guitar for years. Though his parents tried unsuccessfully a few times to convince him to study the violin, he always resisted in favor of learning the guitar. Though he's left-handed, he never inverted the guitar like McCartney or Hendrix, and this approach to the instrument might have contributed to his distinctive style. Unlike other songwriters who use their respective instruments basically as writing tools, Knopfler seriously studied all facets of the guitar for years while keeping songwriting on the back burner. It was on those six strings that he most fully expressed himself for many years, developing a tender, human style as eloquent as a singing voice.

"I knew I wanted to be a musician," he said. "I didn't know if I was going to be a songwriter or not. I certainly didn't think of myself as a singer. And I still don't. I thought of myself as a guitarist and sort of a half-baked songwriter, and then the songwriting just developed and things switched around."

It was a switch prompted by the fact that the songs he started writing were great. "Sultans of Swing," which is one of his first and most famous songs, is the tale of a jazz guitarist who, unlike Knopfler, "plays strictly rhythm / He doesn't want to make it cry or sing." It's a story punctuated with his own beautifully singing guitar lines, bending the notes with a tone so pure you can feel his fingers on the strings.

"Good morning!" he said when he was brought a much-needed cup of black coffee and softly began to answer questions while looking out at the murky Manhattan skyline. Later, when informed in the middle of our talk that the crew from *Entertainment Tonight* had their lights and cameras set up and were waiting for him, he slowly sipped his coffee and told me there was no need to rush. We were in the midst of reviewing specific songs of his, both famous and obscure. "It's alright," he said with a smile. "Take your time. I'm having fun."

Do you find that the process of writing songs is ever magical in any way, or do you feel you are always in control of that process?

You can't be in control. You can't control anything musically or otherwise, really. So you just have to watch for developments. There aren't any rules. The songs will dictate themselves, sometimes. Other songs will become what they become because of people's ideas.

People outside of yourself?

Yeah. If the keyboard player comes up with a certain kind of organ sound, you go, "I like that." The more you do it, the better you get at putting different sounds together, and it's really just from time spent doing it. That's all.

Do you usually go into the studio with a finished song?

Yes, usually. But that's still not the rule.

Do you have a main technique for writing songs, or do you have a number of approaches?

Yes, it's a number of ways. I wish it was simple. Just for the ease of talking about it. But it's not. I've always been attracted to certain situations that seem to provide possibilities. I don't know why it is, but every now and again a situation taps you on the shoulder and says, "song." Like the "Sultans of Swing" situation; it was there. The possibility struck me that it was there, for a song to work on a number of levels. I was actually in a physical situation. Same thing for "Money for Nothing." Same thing for "Les Boys."

When you actually see the situation happening, one thing that all those situations have in common is people expressing themselves in some way. And it's usually expressing themselves from a restricted situation, from a dire straits situation, if you'll excuse the term. Often that kind of expression is a liberating thing for them, for those characters. They find their means of expression, those characters, so I've always been attracted to people finding their own means of expression. So that's certainly true of *some* songs.

With "Sultans of Swing", was that a man you saw playing guitar?

Yes, exactly. It was a jazz band. But because there were some kids in there as well, they were coming from another place and didn't relate to what the band was doing, so the situation had possibilities.

Did you write that song long before you recorded it?

Yeah. Initially, the music for that I wrote on a National Steel guitar and it was completely different. I played it in open tuning and it had a different tune. It was more of a flowing affair; it had just two or three chords in it. Maybe four. But when I was fooling around with a Fender Stratocaster guitar, it became something else. Which again, is another interesting thing about songwriting: A healthy proportion of songs are stamped by the instrument that they are written on, or are developed on. Randy Newman's songs, for instance, are the way they are because Randy's a pianist and not a guitar player. Then there's the *type* of instrument that you're using. Most of my songs have been written on acoustic guitar. Once other people get to them, when you get keyboard players doing all their inversions and all, that's going to change bass lines and so on and so forth. As the thing becomes more orchestrated, it starts to change.

Did the writing come easily to you or was it a struggle at first?

[*Pause*] Some songs write themselves really easily. And other ones, you have to spend a lot of hours on getting them right.

Do you have a recollection of one that came easily?

Oh, yeah. Things like "Walk of Life" just come really quick. And you just hear the keyboard line, and the song is just there, and it has to go that way, and that is pretty much it. That song has that spontaneous feel; it doesn't feel labored at all.

Yeah. And kind of meaningless. [*Laughs*] But there it is. There's no law about it. There's no real rules.

Songs like "Tunnel of Love," you spend a lot of time writing lines. "Telegraph Road" probably took quite a while, too. You spend a lot of hours putting the bits all together.

When we first heard your voice in this country, people's first response was often how much you sounded like Dylan—

Yeah, well, it would. I'm not really a singing singer. You're not looking at Dolly Parton here. I listened to Dylan avidly from eleven years old on.

When you started singing, did you consciously imitate his style?

No, it just came out naturally that way. But probably, because he's *so* ingrained in the consciousness, that style, that you can't help but sound that way part of the time. But I was never conscious of trying to *be* someone else all the time.

Randy Newman discussed the use of the "untrustworthy narrator," which is the foundation of your song "Money for Nothing," as well.

Yeah, exactly. I'm sure that the seeds of that were put there in my mind from listening to Randy Newman songs.

You listened to his work a lot?

Oh of *course*. Again, from the very beginning. From his very first albums.

You wrote "Money for Nothing" based on a guy you saw in an appliance store here in New York City?

Yeah. I started writing it in the store, in a kitchen display area in the front window. I had a piece of paper and a pencil and just started to write down some of the lines that this guy had been coming out with. So they're pretty direct; some of those lines are pretty direct. They were written down two minutes after he said them.

Music came later in that case but I had some of those lines: "That ain't working . . ." and "maybe get a blister on your little finger" and stuff like that.

Was that an easy song for you to write?

Lyrically it was pretty easy because he said a lot of it. The store gave me the microwave ovens and the TVs. So that chorus, even though he didn't say the chorus, all the things that were in the chorus were there. The refrigerators.

Did that guy have any clue that you were the kind of person he was talking about?

No. I had to back up and actually spy through a little hole in the row of microwaves. 'Cause I didn't want to put him off and interrupt his flow.

Did you think of getting Sting to sing on that song while writing it, or was that an afterthought?

That was a fortunate thing, because I had seen the Police doing this MTV advert and other people saying, "I want my MTV." Those five notes happened to come out like "Don't Stand So Close to Me." So, in fact, Sting's publishing company insisted on a percentage of the royalties for the song.

When writing songs, do you consciously guide them? Do you attempt to be objective and subjective at the same time?

That's exactly what you're being. The trick is that. It's great working with a Synclavier now and a little home studio, because I can get sketches done now. And as they're going down, you can listen to it. And the next day you can listen to it and be much more objective.

And does that ever get in the way of the spontaneous creation?

You're probably right. [*Much laughter*] There's always a downside to anything you do.

You can end up overworking something far too much. But, if anything, I'm tending towards much more simplicity. The trouble is that when you have something of a musical vocabulary on your side, when you're dealing with simplicity, you bring that more sophisticated vocabulary to bear on it. Simplicity has its own complications. I'll describe them as being *delicious* complications. They're highly enjoyable to work with, but nevertheless they are there.

May I name some of your songs and see what response you have to them?
Oh, sure. Fire away.

I'll start with maybe my favorite of your songs: "It Never Rains."
High Dylan influence. I think of the Hammond organ, and the combination of Hammond and piano, which I've always loved. And of a scene which you can build up yourself. I'm pleased there have never been any videos of that to spoil it, because that's happened with other things that I've done. And videos, to me, always spoil songs, because they make particular what should really be there. Just the way the novel is always better than the TV movie of it.

"Lions."
I think of Trafalgar Square in London. It's just off there where I wrote the song. I also think of a Ted Hughes poem comparing the idea of "Where are the lions?" as opposed to these starlings, in terms of contemporary figures of strength who aren't there, who used to be there. An element of that. In London, when I was making London a focal point.

"Solid Rock."
Quick. I think of that as being quick. And same as "It Never Rains," it's an idea of people reaping what they sow. Taking responsibility for what they do. In other words, you make a bed, sleep on it, lie on it. That's an idea that seems to reoccur with me, I don't know why.

"Private Investigations."
I think of it essentially as just a little poem, and then a musical experiment where the character says what he says. It's a song about writing songs, actually; it's a song about the process of writing, that you make your own little private observations. Then I go into this spaghetti-like music. It's a soundtrack for a movie that was never made.

"Brothers in Arms."
"Brothers in Arms" I always think of as how much I enjoy playing a Les Paul. But I like the song.

"Private Dancer."
"Private Dancer," now, I think of Tina Turner. But at the time, it wasn't written *for* anybody. It was written about the same time that I was doing the *Love Over Gold* album, and, in fact, was recorded that way, and it was sort of with brushes, and it was much more cool.

"Wild West End."

Early London years again, just mooching around London. Don't like to hear it very much. It doesn't do anything. It doesn't go anywhere.

"Water of Love."
"Water of Love," written out of pain and frustration of earlier years after break-down of first marriage, I think. And now I think of it as the Judds, because they recorded it.

"Secondary Waltz."
"Secondary Waltz," I just found the words again recently. I think of schooldays. It's never been recorded. I should write a tune for it. How did you hear about it?

Someone told me about it, and it sounded really intriguing.
Yeah. It's about sadistic gym teachers. [*Laughter*]

Lou Reed

Denver, Colorado 2000

"Music was what bothered me, what interested me. I always believed that I have something important to say and I said it. That's why I survived, because I still believe I've got something to say. My God is rock and roll. It's an obscure power that can change your life."

—Lou Reed

"I don't know how to write songs," Lou Reed says. We're in a hotel dining room in Denver, where he is trying to cajole a decent meal out of a very flustered waiter, less than two hours before he is to perform with his band at the old Paramount Theater around the corner. "I really *don't* know how I write songs. But I *do* know how *not* to write songs. I know how to screw it up. So I spend my time removing the things that get in the way of it. The impediments that block it. The negative things, the attitudinal things. And since I know how to screw it up, I know how *not* to. Just don't do those things that get in the way of it, and then it can start."

And when it does start, what happens is not that Lou starts inventing the kind of astounding songs he's been writing since the sixties. What happens is that he starts listening. And what he hears is something he calls his "permanent radio," which transmits a non-stop broadcast of verbiage both serious and hilarious, specific and broad, narrative and impressionistic, full of comedy and tragedy, kindness and indifference, magic and realism, love and hate, sex and violence, set in present, past and future America and the world. It's a station that only Lou receives, but there's no guarantee on any given night that he'll be able to tune into it. ("I don't sleep," he says more than once.) When the reception is clear, what he hears, however, is not music but words. "Yes, words," he says. "And my job is just to write it down."

And what happens, I ask, if you don't write them down?

"They're gone," he says.

For good?

"Yeah, pretty much."

The real problem, as he explains in the following conversation, is not how to write the songs, but what to do with all the ones he receives. Many times during our talk, he said softly, as if confiding a long-kept secret, "Writing an album is nothing for me. *Nothing.*"

Nothing though they might seem to Lou as he creates them, they are certainly far from insubstantial to the legion of Lou lovers around the world, an extensive network of fans from Boston to Borneo and beyond that shouts "Loooouuuuu" with the same devotion that Springsteen's fans shout "Broooooooce." (Both, in fact, sound like boos to the uninitiated.) These are the ones who have hung on every one of his words, both spoken and sung, since his early days with the Velvet Underground, and through successive solo masterpieces such as *Berlin* (1972), *Street Hassle* (1978), *The Blue Mask* (1982), *New York* (1989), *Magic and Loss* (1990), *Songs For Drella* (written with John Cale, 1991), and most recently *Ecstasy* (2000).

Unlike other songwriters who struggle to write an album's worth of material every few years, Lou Reed—even at the ripe old age of 58—struggles with the frustration of not having an outlet for the full blossom of his creativity, and so channels it into other arenas: a gallery show of his photography, for example, or a musical (*Time Rocker*) written with Robert Wilson.

At an age when many of his peers are trying to summon up the energy to do another oldies tour singing their old hits, Lou is on fire, spitting out the words to the jazzy, metallic, "Ecstasy" or the breathtaking tirade of imagery in "Rock Minuet," maybe the most graphically violent song ever written in waltz-time.

"In the curse of the alley
The thrill of the street
On the bitter cold docks
Where the outlaws all meet
In euphoria drug
In euphoria heat
You could dance to the rock minuet"

from "Rock Minuet" by Lou Reed

The son of an accountant, he was born on March 2, 1942, in Brooklyn's Beth El Hospital and grew up in Freeport, a suburb of Long Island.

From an early age on, he had a passion both for the expansive poetry and prose of his teacher and mentor, Delmore Schwartz, and for the sound of pure, electric rock and roll. From his teenage years on, his one goal was to merge the two forces and infuse the unlimited expression inherent in poetry and fiction with the electricity of rock and roll.

And unlike Dylan and Neil Young, both of whom fell in love with the simplicity of folk music, Lou was steadfast from the start in his love for the electric guitar. At Syracuse University, he fell in with fellow guitarist Sterling Morrison, and the two found they both shared a love for exploring the electric edges of the instrument, experimenting with the use of feedback and playing off the droning dissonances they could coax out of thin air together.

Like John Lennon, Lou had been in bands since he was a kid, and was wise to the notion of only getting the best people possible. So it was a few years before he found another member for his band, classically-trained John Cale, a tremendously gifted musician who was fluent on many instruments, including piano, viola, and bass. Lou's choice for drummer was Moe Tucker, who managed to keep the rhythm going down on earth, even when the others went into orbit. They named themselves after a notorious paperback then making the rounds that detailed the dirty details of suburban sex, *The Velvet Underground*.

The VU, as they are commonly known, were never embraced by critics during their short span from '65 to '70, but they were warmly welcomed into the fold of the New York art community, attracting the attention of Andy Warhol, who decided he would produce their first album, despite his lack of any actual musical knowhow.

He also decided the beautiful model Nico, although she couldn't sing very well, should serve as occasional vocalist for the band. Warhol was already an international icon at this time, and his declaration of the VU as the house band of his own Factory gave them easy access to landing a record deal.

From the start, the VU made music together and Lou wrote and sang the words. While other bands sang songs of peace and love, his reflected the dark side of the sixties—the violence, sex, drugs—topics that had rarely been conveyed in songs, and surely never with the kind of defiant authenticity Lou brings to everything he touches. You know Lou has not only been there, he's survived. When he sings about heroin in his famous song of the same name, he does so with an unapologetic lucidity which is entirely unique to him, and with which the song makes perfect sense. "That's what it's all about," he says vehemently. "You have got to *believe* the singer."

The VU went on to record four albums: *The Velvet Underground and Nico*, *White Light/White Heat*, *The Velvet Underground*, and *Loaded*. All of them were roundly panned upon release, as were their live concerts. "When the Velvet Underground was around," Lou says, "we sold almost no records. Literally."

In 1972 came his first solo album, *Lou Reed*, which included some classics written for VU, including "Lisa Says." *Transformer* came next, produced by Lou devotees David Bowie and Mick Ronson, containing "Walk on the Wild Side," which is said to be based on remembrances of his time within the Warhol galaxy. To this day it remains Lou's most famous song.

Like Neil Young and Dylan, Lou has managed to step up to the plate almost every year with a new album of original material, and like both of those artists, every few years or so he hits one *way* out of the park and makes a masterpiece. While there might be some dispute among his fans over which albums deserve this designation, few will argue with the inclusion of *Berlin* (1973), *Sally Can't Dance* (1974), *Street Hassle* (1978), and *The Blue Mask* (1982).

Then in 1989 came the amazing *New York*, a tour-de-force of songwriting that succeeded in conveying the divisive results of the Reagan era, which split our nation into disparate parts as different as darkness from light.

> ". . . there's an opera at Lincoln Center
> Movie stars arrive by limousine
> The klieg lights shoot up over the skyline of Manhattan
> But the lights are out on the mean streets
> A small kid stands by the Lincoln Tunnel
> He's selling plastic roses for a buck . . . "

from "Dirty Boulevard" by Lou Reed

With *New York* and the albums that followed it—such as *Magic and Loss* and *Songs for Drella*, both of which delve into death in their own ways—Reed reversed the conventional rock pattern of writing one's greatest songs at the start of one's career. Good when he started, he's consistently gotten even better over the years, more in command of the language of rock and roll than ever. One of the shifts he's made is that he writes songs on computer now, a tool ideally suited to the rapid-fire transcription necessary to preserve the onslaught of words he receives. Before the dawn of the PC, he would just write them down anywhere and hope to collect enough when the song was done. "Yeah," he said, "Matchbook covers. Pieces of paper. Arrows with rewrites pointing to another piece of paper and it's written upside down. Now there's version one, version two, three, four, ad infinitum."

Lou is in great shape, both physically and creatively. At the age of 58, he's as lithe as ever, playing muscular, full-tilt rock for three hours every night on this current tour. And when Lou plays, he *rocks*.

He's a man of many contradictions. Or maybe they only seem like contradictions, because he has so often been portrayed inaccurately in the press. Said to be sullen and surly, he's actually warm and gracious. Thought to be darkly serious, he's in fact quite humorous, with a heartfelt respect for great comics such as Groucho, whose volume of letters he was in the midst of reading, as well as Chaplin, who he called "a phenomenally talented guy." Even Jackie Gleason received Lou's praise, both for his comedy and his composition of the "Honeymooner" theme.

Though he's surely aware of his immeasurable influence on a vast array of songwriters, from Bowie to Strummer to Cobain, he's a modest, unassuming man, much more interested in explaining the intricate schematics of his guitar rig than any rehashing of past glories and/or controversies. When discussing his friend Andy Warhol, for example, rather than celebrate his own role in Warhol's exclusive cadre, he mentions more than once that Andy felt he was lazy, and not productive enough.

> "There's a funeral tomorrow at St. Patrick's
> The bells will ring for you
> What must you have been thinking
> When you knew the time had come for you
> I wish I hadn't thrown away my time
> On so much human and so much less divine

The end of the last temptation
The end of a dime store mystery"

from "Dime Store Mystery" by Lou Reed

He's intimately and passionately involved with every aspect of his music, always striving to capture in a cold recording studio the heat of a live performances. And he goes out of his way when performing live to ensure that the sound in a cavernous concert hall or arena has the same clarity and warmth of a studio. Michael Soldano, whose custom-made amps have endeared him to Lou and other famous guitarists, said, "Lou Reed has the *best* ears in the business. He can hear subtleties in tone that most people never hear. He is *beyond* a perfectionist in terms of sound. He goes to a great extent, and spares *no expense*, to get the greatest possible sound he can get."

The one thing he doesn't like to make time for is interviews. Not so because he has colossal disdain for journalists, although he does. "All this stuff about me not liking journalists," he said somewhat apologetically after polishing off a couple of lamb chops, "is not really accurate. It's just that I don't like talking about myself. Why *would* I? I mean, that's *really* work. I don't listen to my own stuff. Why *should* I? I already know my stuff. I would much rather listen to someone else."

You once said, about your own songwriting, that you hear songs all the time, like a "permanent radio." Is that accurate—are songs coming to you all the time?
Most of the time, yeah. On a good day. I hear stuff, yeah. It's fun.

Fun to hear them, or fun to make them into songs?
Fun just listening. To whatever it is.

Do you hear words and music?
Mostly just words. Sometimes I just hear words just for fun. You know, just kidding around. I only write it down if I'm officially making a record.

Have there been times when you tried to tune into it and couldn't?
Yeah. Lots of times. Oh yeah. It used to scare me to death. Not that you can do anything about it. Particularly if I don't know where I want to go. I'm so happy when I hear the regular thing again. It makes me so happy. When I hear that stuff going on in my head, unbidden, I just love that. And when it happens that there is nothing, I walk away. I say, "Okay, not this week."

Do you have any thoughts about where that comes from, or what makes that happen?
Who knows? I don't have a clue. I just don't want to get in the way of it. And some of it is also being in shape, in fact. It does make it better. For me.

Physically in shape?
Physically, mentally, spiritually, emotionally.

Then again, Oscar Wilde did pretty good. And Orson Welles. I saw his *Othello*. Wasn't that made at the end of his life? It was *fantastic*. And he weighed 700 pounds. So I don't know.

You wrote many great songs during times of great turmoil—

Yeah, thank goodness.

Is it easier to write when there is no turmoil in your life?
It's easier to *live* when there's no turmoil. And I think that is the first thing you want to do.

Some writers almost require turmoil. To keep them going.
I've got enough. I've got enough stored up to keep me going for four hundred years. [*Laughter*]

Is writing more enjoyable for you than making records and performing?
Writing is agony. Sometimes, yeah. It's just awful. When it's not coming. That's really hard. It's like being emasculated. Then there's what you are writing about.

Do you know what you are going to write about before starting a song?
No. I don't have a clue. I might have a direction. I'm usually following.

Following it more than leading it?
Hardly leading. It's like being a recording secretary or something. I'm just *listening*. I mean, I *know* I'm listening to me. When somebody tells me that one of my songs is great, I didn't really have that much to do with it. It sounds stupid. That's why I don't like to talk about. It's something that if you publish it, other writers will make fun. Journalists.

Maybe journalists, but not songwriters—
No, not *them*. Of course not *them*. I write about seven hours a day until the record's done. And I do some major rewrites, we run over it, practice them, then we go and do it.

Is there sometimes more of it than you can get down?
Oh yeah. Oh yes. But I do it all the time. I do it in the hotel for amusement, out loud. It always use to amaze Cale that, *bing*, I could do it on the spot. A lot of my records I made up in the studio with the tape running. That was just another version of it. And then at a certain point I decided I would rather do just that exact same thing. And then go over it. [*Laughs*] If that makes any sense.

When you are writing music, do you write it down in any way—do you write down the chords?
No, I record it. Usually. Usually on something like this. [*Points to my portable cassette recorder*] Sad to say. That's the only equipment I have. It was like this one— only bigger and clumsier. I use it because it's quick. I mean, the thing has to be quick. It's easy coming, and really easy going.

So it's easy to lose stuff if you don't tape it right away?
Yeah. We have a lot of really, really miserable tape recordings. They are almost indecipherable.

When writing, do you always work with a guitar?
Well, sometimes, or I just sing it. That's how I did "Dirty Boulevard." We had the lyrics to "Dirty Boulevard," and I could not figure it out. And usually, if I can't figure something out, I'll make that the last thing that I work on before I sleep. Usually I'll wake up with it solved. I did that with "Dirty Boulevard." Because I don't

sleep. And I suddenly heard it clear as a bell, put it on a tape recorder. And me and Mike [Rathke] tried to figure out what was this strange sound on the tape, just what was going on there? And we finally did decipher it. But it was clear than and only then. It wasn't clear anymore after that.

You got the whole lyric for "Dirty Boulevard" but no music?
Yeah. *Well*, there was music, but of undetermined rhythmic tempo and approach. Nothing that sounded right. It just wasn't right.

That song, and the entire *New York* album, is extraordinary. There's content in those songs that no one has ever put into songs before—
I don't know that no one's ever done that before. Everybody does things differently. I haven't listened to everything that's out there, so I don't know.

A lot of songs don't have much going on in them—
Most things don't have much going on. Most movies, most everything.

Why do you think that is?
You have to see what's popular. My friend Doc Pomus always used to say, "Look at the source." When you get criticized, it's important to look and see who's saying that. I think people hear what they want to hear. People are doing that for money. If everyone ran out to buy this other thing, then that's what they would give you. Although they don't seem to up the ante very much.

Because they feel there's no need to?
Right. It's like *Mission Impossible 2*. There's a screenplay by Robert Towne. John Woo directs it. And they are aiming *so* low that the audience they think they are aiming at actually *laughs* at the movie. It's amazing to see people that good aiming that low. I think it's Number One.

That's so common nowadays, to do a sequel, and to try to repeat something that has already been done. Which is something you've never done—
You mean like doing *Son of Wild Side*? [*Laughs*] I think record companies were just hoping for a long time. That I would see the light.

Were they just hoping, or did they actively encourage you?
It's never really happened. I mean, when I was younger, before I had control over my career, there were manager types who tried to bring in producers to try to make you go a certain way. Certain players to make it go a certain way. And having to fight about that all the time.
You know, when we started out in the Velvet Underground, people didn't know who we were. Literally. They thought Andy Warhol was the guitar player. They said I would never write anything as good as "Heroin." And then they said that if I left the Velvet Underground, I would never be as good as I was in the Velvet Underground.

That's common with people's reactions to songwriters. They don't want you to change—
It seems this country, in particular, is geared to turning people into nostalgia acts. Everything moves really quickly here. It's really based around 14-year-olds, and that's kind of that. People get older and they stop buying records, really. And it's like a vi-

cious circle. They stop making records because there's nothing there for them. So they don't buy any records. And it's not on radio, so they can't hear it. So it becomes this insulated little thing. Of an endless series of things aimed at 14-year-olds. I don't have anything against 14-year-old people. I was 14. And I think that's great. It's just that music is so wonderful, it's kind of extraordinary to gear it only to children.

I mean, there used to be infinitely more eclectic radio. Like college stations. There's a station called WFMU. There's a station in L.A. called KCRW. That's wild.

What would you consider good radio?
When it's programmed by someone who really knows the music, and is turning you onto something. Whether it's Moroccan music or blues or rare Etta James recordings. Things you might not have heard. That's just fantastic. Usually you want to tape something like that.

You've played rock and roll since you were a kid—
Yeah. I was always in a band. I've been in bar bands since I was 14. I was always the youngest one in the bar. I played right through high school, right through college. It's kind of funny to look back and see, hey, there's a pattern! I had my first record out when I was 14.

You were a rocker, but also very involved with poetry and literature, which is unusual—
You don't believe that, do you? They are certainly not incompatible. I just thought it would be the greatest fun imaginable to put something like Delmore Schwartz or Raymond Chandler into a rock song. I'd say, "Can you imagine if you have that whole physical thing going on, the fun of that, and this other thing hitting you in the head?" Now I know there are people who say that if you engage the mind that way, the sexy, physical part of it vanishes. But I don't think that's true, the mind being the most erogenous zone of all. So I think you can have the whole kit and kaboodle. [*Laughs*] There's a phrase you haven't heard for a while.

See, this entire conversation is being affected by the fact that I have been reading Groucho's letters while on the road, and I'm starting to talk like him.

He was a great letter writer, wasn't he?
My God, yes.

When you had the idea of combining rock with great literature, where did that thought come from?
Well, I was studying with Delmore Schwartz. And he just hated any music that he heard that had lyrics. He just thought it was all shit. But he's not the person I would point to as someone would know anything about the kind of music *I'm* interested in. But it did pose an interesting thought. I think "In Dreams We Take Responsibility" is one of the greatest short stories ever written. Simple language, five pages, the most astonishing thing I have ever read to this day. It's just incredible. Imagine being able to do something like that with the simple language that is available to anybody. It's mind-bending. Now imagine putting it into a song. It's so simple, it's ridiculous. So it's not a major leap, like an illuminating thought. It was more like a log in the middle of the road that you could trip over. You know—hello? Hello? Hello? It's so obvious.

But many artists never venture into a place where no one else has been before.

But people had been there. Kurt Weill, for example.

Had you ever heard Kurt Weill back then?

No. [*Laughter*] That's in retrospect. My models were rock and roll songs. A lot of people were into folk, but I just liked rock. I liked creative writing and stuff like that, so it was natural for me to take that and put it over here, with the music.

Did you ever think of being a poet or an author?

No. Because I'm a guitar player. I mean, I like to think I'm a guitar player, and that I have some musical ability. My first record, I was in the background. I wasn't worthy. [*Laughs*] You've got to work your way to the front. You know, some people are naturals.

The Velvet Underground is considered to be a classic rock band, and is in the Hall of Fame—

Well, *now*.

Some stuff takes a while for people to catch up to.

Twenty years. That's just the way it is, and I'm very much aware of that. Things people say to me about stuff I do now means *nothing*. I mean, it didn't mean anything then and it means even less now. Like Doc said, consider the source.

I mean, I have a vision. I have a vision, an ambition. And it's words and sounds and rhythm and tone. On and on and on. Just 'cause I get off on that.

Is it a vision to always move beyond what you have already done?

Well, the sound gets better. And the writing ought to be improving. I should be able to write better now than I did then.

Rock has been a young person's game, unlike jazz.

I think I'm part of the first generation to refuse to be nostalgia acts.

You are more prolific than most songwriters—with a new album of new material each year—

It think it's pathetic to put out only one record a year. That's not very much at all. That's *nothing*. You could do ten a year, easy. I mean, it's nothing.

You could write ten albums of new songs in a year?

Well, I mean, while I did this album I did a play with Robert Wilson. I did the text and the music and lyrics for that. And that was just before I did the album. And then I had a photo show before that.

But, as you know, even one album of new material each year from many artists would be very difficult.

Believe me, it's really nothing. It really isn't. The hard thing is deciding what you want to do. Once you decide that, it's easy. When you decide what vision you have for it. I mean, this stuff is really easy. And, of course, someone would say, "Well, listening to your stuff, you're proving it by how bad it is." [*Laughs*]

Compared to Warhol, I will always consider myself lazy. Because Andy said I was, and he was right. And look at what he did. It's endless. I mean, look at that body of work. I mean, that's incredible. But Andy, he would have said it wasn't incredible, he was just working. And he always said I was incredibly lazy. He thought I should be writing more.

More songs?
Right. He was talking about ten or fifteen songs a day.

Do you think it would be possible to write ten or fifteen good songs in one day?
Sure. But then do what with them? That's what I mean. I mean, one album, it's like nothing. But the record company would never want any more than one album a year. They would say that that is way too much product. I've got a home studio. I could just record things and stock them up for albums. But I never do that.

Your albums reflect the fact that you write all the songs together. Often the themes connect—
It's like my vocals. I don't like to do vocals in pieces. I *hate* when people do that. I just think there's an intrinsic logic. I mean, *we* do it sometimes. Sometimes we'll have a great vocal, and I'll have fucked up this or that. And we'll search around to get the best thing. But we don't do a lot of them. I'm only good for a couple of shots.

Do you ever make demos first of your songs?
No, but sometimes then I would bring the guys in and sit in my home studio and get it down. I don't have a lot of equipment in my studio, but like Spencer Tracy said about Katharine Hepburn, what I have is choice. [*Laughter*]
So we would just play around with a song, do different versions of it, different tempos, different grooves and stuff. I usually sit down with Mike or Fernando or we'll bring Tony in, and we'll go over something. Usually a lot of it is on there, on the tape. Cheap date. It doesn't take much, you know. That's the nice thing about writing. I mean, pencil, piece of paper, fifty-buck tape recorder, and off you go.
You know, it's really funny, after you've done things for a while, people have this desire to learn new chords or to expand their musical horizons as though, I don't know, as though rock isn't big enough to contain some beautiful things. I mean, I'm always aiming for Otis Redding's "I've Been Loving You for So Long." Those horn lines. That incredible emotional peak. Yeah, let's see you do that. Before you go off sniffing around . . . I mean, everybody can do what they want. I just really like rock. I really, really like it. Good rock. Hard to find. I like the physicality of it.

Though you are not interested in nostalgia, many of your old songs are classics—they still sound great and are meaningful today.
See, that's never something I care about. People don't believe me, which I don't understand. Other than I wish that Clint Eastwood would make another *Dirty Harry* movie. I think it's kind of like that. I mean, I *admit* it. I love him. I really do. I go see *everything* that he's in. Not quite, but almost. I'd love if he made another *Dirty Harry*. A really good one, not like the last ones. And I think people, when they come to see you, they want you to do that thing that they really liked then. And if you don't do that, they're disappointed. And they don't really want to hear what you're doing now.
You know I was very, very careful, generally speaking, not to put language in a song that would date it. And it's kind of funny. When I did get interviewed, I would tell people this and they would not believe me.

What wouldn't they believe?

That you're *doing* this. That you're thinking about it. That there's tradition at-tached to it. That you're not just some thing bouncing off walls. That there's a concept behind it. That this is not a runaway car.

"Sweet Jane" is one of the very few songs from your past they you've been playing on this tour. Is that because it has meaning for you today that some of the others don't?

I have fun playing that because I love the lick so much. I mean, we played it the other night and we got into such a groove, it was a joke. I mean, it was my first great lick, and I really am enormously fond of it. [*Laughter*] And it makes the audience happy, which makes me happy. I mean, I want them to have a good time. I just don't want to be dictated to. I want to have fun. That's why I'm doing it. I'm playing and recording for me. First and foremost. I want to like it. I want it to be something I would run out and buy. Or a show that I would *kill* to get in and see it. That's what I want. How else could I do it? I'm gauging it for that. I'm not trying to make them like it. Although I certainly would like them to.

A song like "Sweet Jane" connects us to our common history with you. Like seeing Dylan, it can be great to hear both his new songs and old ones.

It's great as long as he still likes doing them. It would not be great hearing him do it when he does not want to do it. That would be very depressing for you.

Yes. And so to keep himself involved, he does new versions of old songs, which is something people don't always like.

But the thing is, that's just the way the song was on that day at that hour when it was recorded. If it was the next day, or two hours later, it could be different. It could be a little different or it could be very different. Certainly a month from now, it's going to be different. To ask you to just do it the way it was that one moment—why would you want to do that? Why wouldn't you want to hear the guy who wrote it do it the way it is? If you want it exactly the way it was, you could hire somebody to do that. Just mimic that.

Some artists feel that their record is the ultimate, perfect version of the song, as it should always be—

I think it's a work in progress.

Your records capture a moment in time.

It was that moment. You can't have that moment back. The head you were in. The age you were. You're not there anymore.

So for that reason is it important to record them quickly?

I want to do it while I know it. And I don't want to sit around. And things get majorly changed in the studio. Because I leave a lot of space in things. A lot of space in the whole way of approaching it. In the studio. I want to be able to try everything, and to really play loud. And try a whole bunch of different things. And things change. They're not written in stone, for Christ's sake.

People don't understand that.

I wrote it, by God. It's not even recorded yet. Besides, my live versions of things are always better than the album versions. Oh yeah.

Why?
Because there's an audience.

You've captured that live energy in the studio.
We're barbarians. I want to have fun. I'm in love with good sound. Great sound. I didn't always know that about myself, but I finally figured it out. I always knew that the live sound was important, I just didn't know how we were getting it. I certainly didn't know how to record it. What mic, what mic-pre, what kind of a board, what kind of cabinet, what kind of speaker, what kind of tape. It goes on and on and on. What kind of room are you in? I mean, when they say "paying your dues," this is part of it. Somebody says, "Put a carpet under that," and it sounds better.

Much of the conventional wisdom about recording seems to be wrong.
Well, yes. Because so many people are deaf. Engineers. Deaf. They can just read meters. But they don't hear it. It's better to ask a janitor. You know how musicians always say, "What do you think, what do you think?" Asking the janitor would probably be more informative than asking an engineer. Or a producer.

Unless that producer is someone like Hal Willner—
Now you're talking. There're gradations of things.

Will you always write songs?
Well, only if there was a place to put them. Or I would just listen to them in my head. A record, or a play, or a movie, or something like that. Or else I can just hear it in my head. I mean, my goal in life is to have my own bar and to hire myself. I don't really drink, though. Not anymore.

Your songs always seem genuine and uncontrived, as if you've lived through everything you write about. As opposed to some pop songs—
The *whole* thing is that you've got to *believe* the singer. You *believe* Edith Piaf. You hear Maria Callas, and you *believe* it. With certain people like that, you just go, "*Whoa!*"

They are both transcendent singers—
But they're also great actors. Make no mistake.

Does that apply to you as well? Does the aspect of performance affect the songs?
Yes. Because I'm writing monologues for myself. "It was you, Charlie, it was you." And there's lots of ways you can do it. That's why I can play around with the lyric of "Sweet Jane" for the next thousand years.
But, you know, I *love* pop songs. Really sentimental stuff. Sure. "Pilot of the Airwaves." "Stay with Me, Baby." Sure.

The old pop songs.
I'm sure there's stuff out there. I mean, I like the song from *The Titanic*. As a pop song, it's great.

Do you like the way that Celine Dion sings?
For that kind of a song, sure.

Enough to get the CD?

Oh no. It's meant to be heard in a car. Or in a bar. Or as party music. It's not meant to be actually *listened* to. It's cry-in-your-beer music.

I was listening to Merle Haggard before we left. He is *such* a redneck. *Oh my God*, it's unbelievable. You know, he's singing [*sings in low, Merle-like voice*], "My home has a neon sign above it . . ." Okay. Now in his case, you probably believe him.

He's written a lot of songs for other singers. Would that appeal to you?
Sure. In *Time Rocker* I was writing for the actors and actresses and their voices, and not me. And I found it was really interesting, because we were freed from the limitations of my range.

Does it seem like a limitation to you?
There are places I would go to if I could. I cannot do what Al Green does. But Jimmy Scott—who I worship—told me that I was right there. And he was startled that I didn't know it. And that meant a *lot* to me. Because I was trying to do certain things, but I hadn't earned the right to do certain things yet. I didn't do them in public. Not until I felt I really, really could do it. And that's pretty much what I am doing now. But it took a long time to get there.

Do you have any routine for songwriting?
Late at night. But I'm up anyway.

You say you don't sleep. Because your mind is always going?
No. I just don't sleep.

But you make use of those hours?
Sometimes. You know, I'm really lazy.

You said if you didn't write down your songs, that they would go away. Might someone else get those?
[*Laughs*] I'm not into any kind of mystical thing.

No?
No. I don't know how it works. You can use all the metaphors you want. I have thought about this a lot and I haven't made any progress. It's a mystery. Which is great, actually. I like that it's a mystery. It's not something I can unravel. It's like trying to figure out how we got here. It's involved with that. It makes no more sense that the rest of it.

Do you enjoy the unknown quality of it?
I might as well. It doesn't do me any good not to like it. I won't make any more progress if I don't. But I do know how to screw it up. So since I know how to screw it up, I know how not to. Just don't do those other things. Stay out of the way. For instance, when I write, I don't stop. I don't stop to haggle over a word or a form or a "this" or a "that." I don't stop. I go straight through to where the end is. Then I'll go back. If I stop, that's it, it's over.

But you do go back.
Yeah, I go back. I rewrite.

Do you get any satisfaction out of the fact that many of your songs are classics and have influenced and enriched a lot of lives?

[*Long pause*] I think they should build a statue to me. [*Laughter*]

In New York?

Yeah. In Central Park. Short of that, I'm not that interested. Do I know in my heart of hearts that it's good? Does it do *that thing*? If it does *that*, I get satisfaction out of that.

Songwriting is phenomenal. I get a major league kick out of it. That's the only reason I do it. I just want to have fun.

Merle Haggard
Nashville, Tennessee 2000

"I can always hear a train in his voice. His songs are made of wood and steel: tender, rough, and wise. Want to learn how to write songs? Listen to Merle Haggard."

Tom Waits

Merle Haggard is one of the true patriarchs of modern country music, having written many hundreds of songs, including classics such as "Silver Wings," "Mama's Hungry Eyes," "Okie from Muskogee," and "Sing Me Back Home." He's recorded over 65 albums, generated 41 Number One singles, and received 56 BMI awards. Many of his songs have been recorded by many different artists, such as "Today I Started Loving You Again," which has been cut by over 400 artists to date. At the time of our interview, he had recently signed with Epitaph Records, home to Tom Waits, who counts himself among Merle's fans, an ever-expanding league of devotees that also includes Johnny Cash, Elvis Costello, Dwight Yoakam, and even Keith Richards, who said, "There are only a handful like Merle. I can't remember a time when I didn't listen to him. And he's from Bakersfield instead of Nashville. *Big* difference!"

Haggard's life reads like the lyrics to an old blues song: Born on April 6, 1937, in a boxcar in Oildale, California, he wandered east to Texas, got arrested, incarcerated, and escaped, a pattern of behavior he repeated a few times till he got hard time at San Quentin. Eventually emerging as a powerful songwriter, by 1965 he was a hit recording artist with great records that reflected the hard times he knew well, such as "Lonesome Fugitive" and "Branded Man." His most famous song is probably the infamous "Okie from Muskogie," an anti-marijuana song that he dismisses now as the result of cultural brainwashing.

Today it's morning in Nashville, Merle's favorite time for songwriting and in-terviews, and he's got a lot on his mind. When asked about the inspiration behind his most recent album at the time of our interview, *If I Could Only Fly*, he expounds at length on the way almost everything was better in the past. "They used to treat you like a *king* when you flew the airlines," he says. "Didn't matter *what* class you were in."

Record companies and radio stations receive his rightful wrath. "They're all dic-tated to by programming. The bottom line is all that they're interested in. They're not interested in programming something which appeals to the entire listening au-dience. It's all about what they like to call 'targeting.'" Merle also has little love for modern studio recording, which can alter a vocal to make it sound on tune. "Some people even use it for live shows, you know," he says with dismay. "You don't have to be Frank Sinatra anymore. With this tampering, how can the consumer even know what they're getting anymore? How can the consumer say, 'Man, that Britney Spears can really sing.' How do we know?"

"I wonder," Johnny Cash said, "from where comes this newfound creativity? The answer is: It isn't newfound. Once you've had it, you always got it, and Merle has always had it."

What do you think of the state of modern music?
There's very little substance to anything anymore. I think it's due to the times in which we live. Dictated by several different things. The computer age, number one, the ability to make everyone sound like they can sing in tune. They got a ma-chine—it costs about $490—you can put in your studio that will make it sound like you're singing in tune. Some folks even use them on their road shows.

Then there's the dictation of programming. It's sort of an onion-skin deal. The bottom line is all that they're interested in. They're not interested in programming something which appeals to the entire listening audience. Everybody has a phrase they call "we're targeting"—as in "We're targeting Mexican broadcasting," or "We're targeting 13- to 24-year-olds." It's like we can't have a clear picture anymore. We can't have a little bit of this and a little bit of that.

There are no barrooms to play in anymore. The nightlife has completely gone away. You can fly over the entire United States in a Lear jet and the only thing you see are streetlights. You don't see no honky-tonks anymore. Even Las Vegas closes at 2:00. [*Laughter*] It's a time in which I'm sort of amazed. I'm amazed with how people will put up with the plebeian force-feed that they're going for in music. Nowadays most of us could turn it on and you couldn't tell any difference between anybody. You certainly couldn't pick out any musician playing on there. Even though there are only about seven of them that they use. It's exactly opposite of what I like. I don't know about you, but there are a lot of people like me who would like to have a little more selection in programming. For example, you can't combine talk radio and music anymore. You can't go in there anymore with a guitar like Arthur Godfrey used to do many years ago and play a song and then talk about politics. I tried to do that, but they wouldn't let me. You either have to be Art Bell or be on the hit parade during the daytime.

In America now, every city and town looks absolutely the same. There is not a bit of character to the entry of any city in America anymore. There used to be a time when I could wake up on the bus, look outside—if you were coming into Amarillo, you'd see a big old Santa Fe engine sitting off to the left, and you knew, well, this is Amarillo. If you were coming into Modesto, California, you'd see the big archway over the city that said, "Welcome to the Waterwell of the World." There was some pride in each city. Now it's an off-ramp with a Wendy Burger and those other things all sitting there, and they all look alike, and you could be anywhere in the USA and you couldn't tell. I wake up in a different world every day. Used to be fun. Now I don't even ask where I'm at. It don't make any difference.

This war against drugs is a joke. It's a big cycle that they depend on, and they encourage, and act like they're trying to stop. [*Laughs*] I think everyone knows it's a joke.

Radio music is kind of like sausages. You pinch off another one every time to start another one. You might as well just have kept the last one going. They're all the same. Being honest, you can't really tell what they're singing about. And if you take the time to investigate, then you're even more disappointed. My wife said, "It sounds like they're singing about air." [*Laughs*] I thought that was a good description. Because they really have nothing. There's not even a catchy phrase anymore. And there are no melodies anymore.

Do you feel it's tougher now to be a songwriter than it used to be?

Yes. It's a hard time now to be a songwriter. With the Internet now, and the ability to download music, there's really no way to protect yourself from copyright infringement. There is no respect at all in that area. There's not a lot of future right now for songwriting, unless they come up with some way to protect the things we're up against with that Big Brother. I know there are people who think all music should be free, like the wind. They don't understand, do they? They think it's all just something that everybody should be able to enjoy. And what's going to happen is that it's going to kill the incentive of people who have talent. If I had another lifetime left, I'd move to Australia. Yeah, I'd go over there. It's like a new country. They got that big old country over there and nobody's there. We went over in '96 and saw only two police officers. [*Laughs*] Isn't that the reverse?

When did you start writing songs?

It all started when I was about in the fifth or sixth grade. I started getting those bad report cards. It said, "This boy is capable of doing anything in school, but he won't pay attention." They said I was looking out the window. I guess I was trying to write songs then. I managed to get passing grades, but the things they were teaching didn't seem to be very entertaining, by any means. I think I must have started writing very young. it's been a hobby. I go through periods where I don't write something for a year. I started playing guitar the same summer. I think I was nine when I learned C, F, and G. My brother had a service station, and some old boy came through there and didn't have no money for gas, and traded his guitar for a few dollars worth of gas. It was an old Bronson. A Charles Bronson guitar. It set around there in the closet for a couple of years. Steel strings. One of them old Gene Autry guitars that you could put any name on. They probably sold new back then for about seventeen dollars. It sat there for a couple of years. When I got about nine years old, my father passed away. He played guitar, but my mother didn't really play. He had showed her as couple of chords, and she remembered them. She showed me C, F, and G. It was right about the same time that I started dreaming at school, and thinking about songs, and trying to write.

Have you had that dream where you can fly? Writing a song is the conscious version of that same dream. Every time you start to write a song, there's a chance that maybe you can fly with this damn thing. Maybe you can lift yourself out of obscurity. Maybe you can become somebody. Maybe you can become an Ernest Hemingway. You never know. Every time you start writing, it might be the one. I guess it could be called an addiction as well as a talent. It is something that is necessary for me to do to release anger and to express love, and it probably keeps me from going down to McDonald's and shooting all the hamburgers. [*Laughs*]

Music was just something I enjoyed at first. I never thought of doing it for work. Work was something you did outside with a hammer. I never thought I could make my living doing it. I certainly never thought I'd be a Frank Sinatra or somebody great. I didn't have any ideas like that. But I kept doing it until, when I was about thirteen, all the kids would ask me to come over to their house or go to a river party with them—we used to have a lot of river parties on the Kern river—and they'd always ask me to bring that guitar. About then I started to realize there was some power and clout in that. And also that I could do something that all those other kids couldn't do. Even the ones with better grades. [*Laughs*]

I had idols growing up, like Jimmie Rodgers and Hank Williams. Country records were called hillbilly records back then. They were on 78 records. My mother bought me an album that had four of those in it—a fold-out of Hank Williams. And one of Jimmie Rodgers. There was no television back then, and there was not a lot going on. And I think you paid a little closer attention back then. I got to looking at these records and noticing that some of them had Jimmie Rodgers as the artist, and then down underneath it was the name of the songwriter. I got to noticing that he delivered the songs that he wrote with more conviction. I started to realize that the guy who writes the songs gets more attention. I knew early on that the ability to take your feelings and things that occur in your own life and write about them, those same events were going on around the corner, too, and people identified with them.

I wrote "Mama's Hungry Eyes" about the days of the migration, the people from the Dust Bowl all moving west—there was many a mama who had hungry eyes. And many a dad who couldn't do anything about it.

When I was in jail, my mother bought me a guitar. We were a poor family, so for my mother to buy me a $250 Fender Jazzmaster guitar was a chore, and probably took her two to three years to pay for it. She sent that to me in the penitentiary. She came to see me every month. It was 300 miles, and she had to ride a Greyhound bus. That's a pretty good mom.

Do you recall writing "Sing Me Back Home"?

Yes. "Sing Me Back Home" was one I wrote on a trip from somewhere to somewhere in Ohio. It conjured up a lot of the feelings that took place around an execution. I had the privilege to talk to one of the condemned guys.

Songs don't take a long time for me to write, because I don't force write. Most of my writing is done in the morning. If something has offended me or affected me deep enough to touch my soul, sometimes early in the morning things come from somewhere and I write them down. Sometimes I'm as surprised when I write them down as anyone who hears it. There's a certain amount of talent you develop in writing songs. Methods and ways of proving whether a line should be there. The best songs I've written, like "Mama's Hungry Eyes" or "Mama Tried," came so fast I could hardly hold the pencil. I could hear the whole song, and I would just try to get it all down before I forgot it. There is no doubt that songs are gifts. People who don't believe in another dimension, a higher plane of existence, have never written a song. Or have never had songs given to them. I've read some songs back and *wept*.

The good songs are completely done when I get them. All I have to do is learn them. Sometimes I get a song with a great melody, but I let it slip away. And I have to go back and write a phony melody to it. I hate doing that. If they're not good enough to remember, it doesn't make it to the record.

Do you have any kind of regular routine for songwriting?

I keep a guitar close by, pencil and paper, and if something good comes by, I can catch it. I never sit down with an intention of writing a song. A song comes to me, and then I sit down to write it. It has to be good enough for me to pick up a pencil. And then it gets exciting—it can really be like someone sending a teletype to me from the other side.

I don't know where songs come from. If there's a force of good and evil that's represented just out of our vision, maybe there's subject matters that need to come across. Maybe they try to get it to me, or maybe they try to get it to Keith Richards. Or somebody else. Maybe it takes some time for them to find someone sensitive enough to realize it's *there*. Hank Cochran, who wrote "I Fall to Pieces," said, "If I hadn't wrote that, Harlan Howard would have wrote that the next night."

Roger McGuinn
Los Angeles, California 1999

They were known as America's answer to the Beatles. Their harmonies were every bit as sweet, and their lyrics, whether written by or influenced by Bob Dylan, were every bit as poetic. They were the Byrds, led by Roger McGuinn on lead guitar and vocals. The other Byrds were David Crosby on rhythm guitar and vocals, Gene Clark on tambourine and vocals, Michael Clarke on drums, and Chris Hillman on bass. And though Crosby is given primary credit for the arrangement of the group's harmonies, it is the sound of Roger McGuinn's electric twelve-string guitar that was at the heart of the Byrds' music. It was from this guitar sound—the combination of electric rock with finger-picking folk music—that folk-rock was born. It is a sound that still echoes through pop music in the music of Tom Petty and many others.

He was born James Joseph McGuinn III on July 13, 1942, in Chicago. Both of his parents were professional writers, with whom he toured throughout his childhood. In the fifties he studied at Chicago's Old Town School of Folk Music and became one of that city's most beloved folksingers before moving to Greenwich Village in the early sixties and joining that scene.

He went on to work as a backup musician for Bobby Darin, Judy Collins, and others. Working in the heart of Tin Pan Alley—the Brill Building in New York—he attempted to churn out hits on a daily basis. In 1964, he formed a band in L.A. that was first called the Jet Set and then the Beefeaters. It was at a Thanksgiving dinner that year, probably while tearing into some turkey, that they finally settled on naming the band the Byrds.

Do you remember writing "So You Want to Be a Rock and Roll Star"?

Yes. The inspiration for that song came from a guitar riff that Millard Thomas, one of the guitar players for the Belafonte singers who played behind Miriam Makeba, used to play. And I showed it to [Chris] Hillman one day and he liked it.

We happened to be looking through this teen magazine at the time and cracking up over how people turned over in this business. Like next week there'd be another batch of, you know, rock and roll people. And we thought, "Let's write a satirical song on that."

And at that time did you think the Byrds might be another group that would turn over?

Well, at that time we had already been higher than we were. A lot of people, as a matter of fact, thought we were coming from a very bitter, disgruntled place when we did that song. But we were really just kidding around.

I remember back when "Chestnut Mare" and "So You Want to Be a Rock and Roll Star" came out, they didn't seem like particularly good songs. It's funny how time has a way of separating things out. You get a better perspective over a period of time.

The sound of your Rickenbacker electric twelve-string really defined the Byrds' sound, and it has had a huge influence on the rock world. Was it a conscious decision on your part to use that instrument?

Not at all. Coming from a folk music background, I played twelve-string guitar and five-string banjo, and gradually when we got turned on by the Beatles and the whole British invasion sound, I bought a pickup for the acoustic twelve-string, and it made kind of a woody, very hollow sound that wasn't conducive to rock and roll. But it was loud. You could play it in a band, but it wasn't the sound. It wasn't until I saw "Hard Day's Night," and I saw George Harrison playing his Rickenbacker twelve-string, that I went out to the local guitar store to get one—it was one of the first Rickenbacker twelve-strings ever made, and I plugged in it.

I think another aspect of that style developed from my five-string banjo work. I played kind of a Scruggs-style, rolling, finger-picking thing and employed that on the twelve-string. Most people strum the twelve-string or pick certain notes, but they didn't do a finger-picking thing on it, which is what I did.

It's interesting that you mentioned seeing George Harrison playing a Rickenbacker before you got yours. How else did the Beatles influence you at that time?

I was working at the Brill Building, and my job was to listen to the radio and write songs like what I heard. The Beatles came out about that time. And I was up for that. I loved it. Because they employed a lot of chords and changes that I'd known from folk music—lots of passing minors and things like that. They weren't even conscious of it, but they had employed some folk music in their rock and roll—subconsciously, I guess. I started writing songs in that direction right away.

Was there ever a decision to make the Byrds an American version of the Beatles?

Well, we were just trying to be as good as that. I don't think we were trying to capture the American market in place of the Beatles. It was kind of a dream. We were out in the street, and we didn't think we could do anything like that. We just wanted to be able to keep a beat. Coming from a folk music background, there was no beat emphasized. We would just play what feels natural and not worry about the beat.

Was there ever a conscious decision to combine folk and rock into folk-rock?
It just sort of happened naturally. My experience working with Bobby Darin helped me out with that. I asked him how to get into this business, and he said, "The best way to get into this business is through rock and roll."

So I had that in mind, and folk music was getting to the point where it was boring. I think what really killed it was the "Hootenanny" show on TV. It just got to be too commercialized, and it just sort of fell apart.

I wanted to do something else, and the Beatles came along. So folk-rock just happened out of my folk music background and my desire to get into rock and roll.

Do you remember hearing Dylan for the first time?
Yeah. The first time I heard him was in Greenwich Village at Folk City. He had just come to New York from the West Coast. He only had a couple of songs that he had written himself. Mostly he was doing Woody Guthrie songs.

I remember the little girls used to like him a lot. They'd kind of squeal when he got on stage and get all excited. I didn't have any idea that he'd get as big as he did. But he was really good.

How did the Byrds happen to record his song "Mr. Tambourine Man"?
Dylan's road manager sent our manager a demo of it with Dylan and Jack Elliot singing it. Jack was a little drunk, so the harmony was a bit out of tune. Our manager loved it and thought it would be a hit. So we listened to it, this 2/4, four- or five-verse song, about eight minutes long. We auditioned for who would get the lead vocal line, and I got it.

Did you feel that the song was too poetic to be a hit?
It wasn't so much the poetry that I didn't think was commercial. I thought it was soft and ballad-like; it didn't have any punch to it. But we punched it up.

Do you remember writing "Chestnut Mare"?
Yeah. The middle part of "Chestnut Mare" I composed in Santo Domingo. It was in 1961. I was sitting on a cliff, and I was watching as the waves crashed against the rocks below. And I came up with a little melody in 3/4 time. [*Sings melody*] I just kind of filed that away. In 1968 I was working with Broadway director Jacques Levy on a country-rock musical based on Ibsen's "Peer Gynt." The lead character goes off searching for the truth, and it takes him out to the Wild West in 1840, following this horse. He's been looking for this horse for a number of weeks, and one day he sees it off in the distance. And this is the song that he sings. It's part of the play.

Do you have any idea where your ideas come from?
I think it's a spiritual thing. I think they come from out there.

Is there any way you know of tapping into that source?
Well, you can pray about it, but that's not what I usually do. I just sort of sit down and it happens. Tunes come to me, and then I work on them. Sometimes I get an idea for a song, and I'll make up a tune for it. I do that after I've developed the poem somewhat. There are a number of different ways. But I don't have a lot of discipline to go into a room and sit down and do it. But I do it. They mostly just come to me.

John Fogerty
Burbank, California 1995

John Fogerty is nervous. It's been some ten years since he released his classic solo album *Centerfield*, and he's anxious about how his first new album of material in a decade, *Blue Moon Swamp*, will be received. "You never know," he says about the public reception of his work. "Sometimes you hit, and sometimes you strike out." Today, to bolster his spirits, he's asked his beautiful wife to sit in on our interview, which is taking place in a big sunny conference room at Warner Bros.' Burbank headquarters.

He was born in Berkeley, California, on May 28, 1945, and grew up in the San Francisco suburb of El Cerrito, California. Introduced to music by his mother, he'd happily listen to her play standards such as "Shine on Harvest Moon" on the piano in stride style. At the age of 12, he picked up his mother's old Stella guitar and taught himself to play Jody Reynolds's hit "Endless Sleep," which consists of one E major chord repeated over and over, influencing his own songwriting, which started soon thereafter. Many of his most famous songs, as discussed in the following, find their strength not in a combination of many fancy chords, but in the vigorous repetition of one chord, over which his melodies swell and fly.

He started making up his own songs in the third grade while walking to school. He'd imitate sounds he heard in old blues records he'd started collecting, a habit that earned him the nickname "Foghorn." His first real song was a bluesy imitation of Muddy Waters's rendition of Willie Dixon's "Hoochie Coochie Man" that he called "Washday Blues." His next song was inspired by the songs of Little Richard and revolved around the rhymes of "lazy, hazy, and daisy."

In 1959 he formed his first band, The Blue Velvets, along with his brother Tom and classmates Doug Clifford and Stu Cook. They released three singles on the Orchestra label in 1961; in '63 they signed with Fantasy Records of San Francisco, changing their name to the Golliwogs. In 1967, at the urging of label head Saul Zaentz, they became Creedence Clearwater Revival. Though they lived in California, their songs reflected life on the bayous of Louisiana and came to be known as "swamp rock." John was the main songwriter, and still frequently hammering away on those single-chord vamps, wrote a string of standards for the group, including "Down on the Corner," "Born on the Bayou," "Green River," "Bad Moon Rising," "Have You Ever Seen the Rain," "Travelin' Band," and his most famous song, "Proud Mary," which was a major hit for Creedence and also, of course, for Ike and Tina Turner, who turned it on its head, cranked up its inherent funkiness, and made it an enduring classic.

In 1973 he left the band to form what seemed to be a new one, The Blue Ridge Rangers, though in fact it was a solo effort on which he played all the instruments. In 1975 he released *John Fogerty*. It wasn't a hit. "I recorded an album back in 1975 because I felt I owed it to the public," he said. "When it was done, it just didn't ring my bell." He didn't make another album for ten years.

From 1975 to '85, he spent much of his time struggling with writer's block and fighting for control of his catalog of songs with Saul Zaentz. "I was slowly drying up," he said. "I kept trying, and it kept coming out lousy. Suddenly, I began to feel like I could no more make a hit record than the guy out in the street running a jackhammer."

In 1985 he returned with an album that was a stunning success, rising to Number One on the charts, *Centerfield*, which featured the hit song "Old Man Down the Road" and an all-out attack on Zaentz called "Zanz Can't Dance"; lawsuits from Zaentz forced him to change the name on the second issue of the album to "Vanz Can't Dance." In 1986 came *Eye of the Zombie*, which was his last effort until *Blue Moon Swamp*.

He's clearly not the kind of guy who likes to rush the process. After having written dozens of classic songs, he knows that a song has to be of an extremely high level to earn its place in the echelon where his other famous songs reside. So when it's time to record a new album, he told me, he'd rather wait an entire decade to write a dozen new classics than release an album of inferior material. "I never write a song just to fit the slot between track one and track three," he says. "I write them to be great." It's the reason *Centerfield* took ten years to complete, and the same reason his new album took ten more. But once again—with the inclusion of brand new classics such as "Walking in a Hurricane" and "110 in the Shade"—it was well worth the wait.

When you write a song, where do you start?

I'll sit with a guitar and I'll be noodling: doing riffs, doing chord changes, whatever, to get a good rhythm or a good *something*. Since I'm such a rock and roll guy, I try to connect a song with a riff, and therefore an arrangement. Because I know I'm going to ultimately make a record.

I used to describe a great record as being four things, in this order: title, the sound, the words, and then the last thing—and all the great rock and roll records have it—is a really great guitar riff. So it might sound like I start backwards by coming up with a riff first.

But that's what gets me started. And then I think about the title. Because when you hear a song on the radio, it must have a good title. Like "Bad Moon Rising." That's a good title. And I've got a book of titles I've been keeping for a long time.

What makes a title good?

It should just sound cool. And then, if it is an image of something as well, that's great, but it doesn't have to be. "Blue Moon Nights" to me is a good title because it's evocative, it creates a specific mood. "Southern Streamline" works a little less efficiently.

"110 in the Shade" says what it is and brings you right into that feeling. I've had that title for almost twenty years. Before I finally wrote the right song to it.

After all these years of writing songs, does it ever get easier?

Writing songs is something that gets better the more you are currently doing it. I know I can write songs because I've written songs. I have a past of writing songs. Yet if I lay off doing it—for years, especially—oh *man*, it's like I'm not a songwriter. Because it's not an automatic button you can push and songs come out. When you lay off songwriting, it's not like riding a bike where you get on and go. You might work for a few weeks all day, every day and just get *garbage*. And I mean six hours every day, you're trying. You've got your guitar or whatever your little crutch is. And you're trying to be inspired, you're trying to get your voice going, *something*, and at the end of that time you think, *God*, how did I *ever* do this? I really mean that sincerely. It's *so* frustrating.

What busted you through that for this album?

Getting the riff for "Blueboy." I knew that was a good riff. So I said, "Okay, here we go." And then I started getting the melody. I have to have a valid melodic structure that can hold up over a whole song. And writing the words is the last thing I do in a song. Because they're so doggone hard. I agonize over words. If I'm going to put all that heartache into it, all that effort, it better be a decent song.

Songwriting is *hard* for me. It's not like they just come rolling out of my ears or anything. And the only difference between me and the other guy who is a songwriter is that I cull. I throw away a lot of stuff. I throw it away until what is left is good. I'm willing to do that work. I don't keep something until I think it's great.

You've said it's hard to be original with chords. Yet you've shown many times that you can be creative with how few chords—rather than how many— you use. You've written whole songs, like "Commotion," that vamp on one chord like a James Brown funk tune. Other times you'll have many changes in the verses and contrast that with a chorus that has no changes, such as "Walking in a Hurricane."

Right. You're hitting on the fact that rock and roll is about rhythm and sound. So, in other words, in rock and roll nobody takes note of that. It certainly isn't unique to me. You just mentioned James Brown. Back in the sixties, the boogie bands would hit that A or D for the whole song! The old Delta blues tradition, a lot of times, would have no changes. So it's an old form. And in rock, form is much more important that substance. The sound of it and the feel is much more important than what you are singing about or what chords you are playing.

Bruce Springsteen came up to me at the Rock and Roll Hall of Fame, and he said, "Any guy who can take an E7 chord like you did and get 'Green River' out of it is all right with me." [*Laughter*]

"Proud Mary" is another one where the main part of the chorus keeps rolling on a D chord.

Right. I wrote it in open D tuning, which probably led me to that kind of chord structure.

Was that a song that took a long time to complete?

It didn't take me a long time to write it, the way I view the world. Probably a month. It didn't happen in five minutes. "Proud Mary" is the first title in my book of titles that I told you about. I just wrote it down because I thought it sounded good. I didn't even know what it meant. I actually thought it might be someone who is a housekeeper or a maid. On that same page, as far as I can remember, are "Bad Moon Rising" and "Lodi." And on the other side is "Green River."

Good page.

There you go! I wish I could get back to that page. [*Laughter*]

Can you recall writing "Born on the Bayou"?

With that one, the feeling and everything was there first. We were on the stage at sound check at the Avalon Ballroom in San Francisco. I just started going into the lick and told Tom [Fogerty, his brother] to just keep hitting the E over and over. And I just started screaming syllables, which I do a lot when I write, just screaming sounds without any words. I worked out the whole song without lyrics right there.

The stage manager at the Avalon said, "You have to get out of here. You're not allowed to keep playing." We were only supposed to sing one song and then split, because the big heavy-duty headliner was coming. And this guy said something like, "Get out of here. You're not supposed to be wasting our time." And I looked at him and said, "That's not nice to say." And he said, "Why? You're not going anywhere." I said, "Listen buddy—wait a year. We're going somewhere, and you'll be sorry you said something like that!" And I went home and worked on it, and it became "Born on the Bayou."

It took a couple of weeks to finish it. I was writing many songs at once then in 1968 for the *Bayou Country* album. I remember because I was writing these at night, watching TV, and I remember that Bobby Kennedy got killed during this time. I saw that late at night live. And all night, because I had the TV on, they kept showing it over and over. Which was a chilling thing.

"Bayou" and "Proud Mary" and "Choogling" were all kind of cooking at the same time, kind of gestating during that period of time. If I had to go back, I'd say that that was when the whole swamp bayou myth was born. Right there in a little apartment in El Cerrito.

Why the bayou?

I don't know. It was late at night and I was probably delirious with lack of sleep. I remember that I thought it would be cool if these songs cross-referenced each other. And once I was doing that, I realized that I was kind of working on a mythi-cal world or a mythical place.

That creation of myth gave the songs a timeless quality. It's surprising to me how few people know that you wrote "Proud Mary." I think the reason is be-cause it seems that it has been around forever. And so many of the songs on your new album have that quality as well, that they're perfect and timeless.
That is what I go for in writing a song. I feel when you write a song, it should all work. There shouldn't be a part of it that is awkward, that makes you wonder why did he go there. It should all go logically. I try to make it be something that stands up by itself. And I don't rest until it's done. And I don't feel like I can say that it's a completed work until that little buzzing stops, the bell stops ringing and going, "Come on, attention! Do something!"

At that point, then when I feel it's all right, that seems to be when people tell me it sounds timeless. So that sense of rightness, that's what I search for. It's why I can work many years on one song. That's what it's all about.

Lenny Kravitz
New York, New York 2000

He's in his Miami recording studio working on his new album when he decides to take a walk with a friend. They're out on the street, getting some of that fresh Florida air, and suddenly sirens start to scream, flashing lights abound, and a trio of cops cars containing Miami's finest screech to a halt yards from where they stand, frozen. Guns are aimed at Lenny, he's ordered to the ground, handcuffed, and taken in for suspected bank robbery. Hours later, when a bank teller arrives to inform the police that it wasn't Lenny, but a different unshaven black man in green pants who had just robbed a bank down the street, he's released.

This is not the first time this kind of thing has happened to him. Getting arrested for DWB (Driving While Black) or even WWB (Walking While Black) is a common experience for a black man in America, be it New York City, L.A., or Miami. It's not something Sting, Stipe, and Springsteen have to encounter while working on their albums. But it's something Lenny Kravitz knows all too well.

Such stuff surely rattles him, but he doesn't allow himself to be derailed, and he's soon back in the studio immersed in music. It's the way he's dealt with other potential derailers over the years, such as the ongoing criticism that his songs are not original, but amalgams of other people's work—most prominently Hendrix, Prince, and the Beatles. But Lenny Kravitz is, after all, somewhat of an amalgam himself: both black and white, Jewish and Gentile, East Coast and West. The son of "The Jeffersons" star Roxie Roker and TV producer Sy Kravitz, he was raised in both Brooklyn and Beverly Hills adjacent, and fully absorbed the regional music from each of the opposite coasts. So the amalgamation of influences he brings to his music is a birthright, as natural as the Beatles' own mixture of British music-hall music with American folk and rock.

Now comes Lenny's *Greatest Hits*, and if he still hasn't received the respect for his music that he deserves, this collection might tip the scales at last. Taken in its entirety, this series of hits makes it pretty hard to ignore the singular voice and achievement that is Lenny's, including his own classic rock anthems such as "Let Love Rule," "Fly Away," "Are You Gonna Go My Way," and more, as well as his incendiary version of the 1970 Guess Who hit "American Woman."

Like most musicians, he's happier talking about music than other topics, and is justifiably weary of the media's obsession with his personal life, ignoring his music to focus instead on big questions like why he cut off his dreadlocks. ("Because," he was quoted, "it was time to shed them and grow some new ones. They went back to the earth.")

"There's a perception out there about me," he said. "I guess there's many perceptions. They never really want to see me for me, just Lenny the musician. There has to be all this drama and hoopla and hype and all this rock star shit, which I understand, but I am just a *musician* . . . Even though I play and I write and I produce, people just don't *grasp* that. They are more interested in the way I look and who I go out with, the rumors and what's going on, the clothes. It's very strange. They just want to know about all that rock star stuff."

Though some writers have characterized him as a man of few words, he's anything but when asked about the music and musicians he cares about. Mention Hendrix, and Lenny lights up. "Jimi Hendrix was just so *fluid*," he said. "His hands were connected to his soul, you know? His playing was just so emotional. You could feel the fire, you could feel the blues. You could feel the sadness. What did I *learn* from him? What you can do with an electric guitar. And how to blend rock and roll and blues all together in songs."

Born on May 26, 1964, Lenny learned to sing and play long before he started writing songs. His first instrument was the first one he had access to, the piano, which he promptly pounded on as soon as he was tall enough to reach the keyboard. There was also an acoustic guitar in the house—purchased by his mom for his dad, though he never played it—which Lenny also made his own.

More than anything he longed to play drums, but living in a small apartment in New York City with neighbors constantly in close proximity, his folks understandably refused to get him a set. When he moved to L.A., however, his dream of being a drummer began to be realized. He joined the junior high school orchestra as a percussionist, which allowed him instant passage to all the orchestral percussion instruments—snare, bass drum, timpani, and even xylophone. "We weren't allowed to play a regular drum set, though," he recalled. "So I learned how to play all those individual instruments, and I got really good at snare drum. Of all the instruments, I really loved playing snare drum. And then in high school, there was a stage there, and that was the first time I got a drum set happening. But drums came naturally to me. Drums is something I don't even think about."

It was during high school that Lenny also got his first electric guitar, a Fender Jazzmaster, purchased as a gift for him by his father. After that he was able to afford his own Les Paul, "a deluxe with smaller pick-ups. That saved me. I was happy." At eleven he moved with his family to the West Coast. It was his mom's idea that he audition there for the California Boy's Choir, then second only to the Vienna Boy's Choir in terms of international reputation. It was a tough audition, but his clean sustain and pure pitch got him in, and immediately he began to receive a serious and professional musical education.

"That's where I learned about discipline in music," he said. "Your craft and how you apply yourself. And it was great for my ears, learning harmony and also learning theory and composition, sight-reading, all that shit. That's where I learned the fundamentals of theory and harmony. We sang in ten different languages. It was an *incredible* experience. And through singing with them I sang with the New York City Opera Company, the Joffrey Ballet, the L.A. Philharmonic, I got to work with Zubin Mehta and all these incredible conductors. It was a really unexpected thing, and that was the basic foundation for everything I do."

Although his choirmasters felt that all forms of rock and R&B were inappropriate for their young singers to hear, the one exception they allowed was the Beatles. "The reason was that they thought [the Beatles'] compositions were very musical and worthy. Otherwise we heard only classical, but they thought the Beatles were sophisticated, so they let us listen to that. Which was funny. Because Hendrix was even more sophisticated in many ways than the Beatles. But that would have been *too* extravagant for them."

Of course, because of this ban on rock records, few things were more seductive to Lenny and his pals than getting their hands on this forbidden music. So they started to surreptitiously smuggle records into their bunks like contraband. "We lived in these dormitories, and it was like the military. We'd sneak in our Kiss records and Led Zeppelin records. It was *exciting*."

Though liberation from these barracks might seem like something Lenny would have been eager to embrace, in fact it was one of the toughest transitions he'd ever encountered. When he hit puberty, his once-angelic alto voice began to become baritone, thus ending forever his time with the choir. "Basically, I was asked to leave, although it's called *graduating*," he said sadly. "You graduate from the choir because your voice changes and that's it. It was upsetting when I had to leave 'cause it was like a family. I did it for three years, and it was just incredible."

Following his "graduation," Lenny circumvented further vocal pathways to focus instead on the language of rock and roll and the tools required to express it. Unlike the majority of songwriters who spend as much time mastering the art of writing songs as they do any specific instrument, Lenny became fluent on many instruments long before he ever wrote his first song. All he wanted to do was to *play*, and play he did, every instrument he could get his hands on, including drums, guitar, bass, and keyboards. Before long, Lenny had transformed himself into a one-man studio band, as adept as his idol Stevie Wonder in not only laying down all the parts in the studio, but in doing so with real soul.

"I didn't really start writing until I wrote the songs for *Let Love Rule*," he said. "I just wanted to be a studio musician. I played for other people and made demos for other people. Because I can play all these instruments, people could hire me to do their demos. And I would play everything."

His fusion of musical influences started to coalesce back then, when he moved from the heavily funk-inspired streets of New York City into the surfer-dude realm of Southern California. Never a musical snob, Lenny loved all of it. "New York was all about R&B," he remembered. "The first records that I listened to growing up were the Jackson 5, Stevie Wonder, The Temps, The Supremes, and Gladys Knight and the Pips. Motown, basically. And Stax. Al Green and people like that. And then when we moved to L.A., we went right from New York City to Santa Monica. Where everyone had straight, long blonde hair and surfboards and skateboards, and I wondered, 'Where the *hell* am I?'" He paused to laugh and then continued. "That's when I got into marijuana and Zeppelin and Cream and the Who."

This bridge between the music of the East Coast and West was the foundation on which he built his own style. "It's a direct reflection of my life. That is, obviously, what music *is*. I was always such a huge music fan. I would wait at the store for certain records to come out. I'd unwrap it, read every liner note, see who wrote what, who played what, who produced. Listened to it a million times. I was *into* it. I wanted to know *all* the information."

Though he did intend to actively emulate Stevie Wonder on his own debut album, Lenny never meant to take it to the extent of playing every instrument, a la Stevie. But when he and his engineer, Henry Hirsch (who Lenny called "my right hand"), began auditioning players, they could find none as fluid and funky on each instrument as Lenny was himself.

"I told Henry that I wanted to make a Stevie Wonder record," said Lenny. "Real dry, no reverb. And the initial plan was to assemble a band. But none of the musicians cut it." Simple as it sounds to create the kind of sound he did on his own, making a rhythm track work back in the days before drum machines and programming were prevalent was no easy endeavor. Like Stevie in the studio and very few others ever, Lenny would lay down real drums first, before any other parts were played, performing to arrangements yet to be recorded. It wasn't easy to do. "Yeah," he said, "that was a *bitch* to do sometimes. I would actually play the drum track while just singing the song in my head. You have to play like you're jamming with a band, but it's just *you*."

> "Machines for hearts, how warped a view
> Forgetting that they're human too
> Waiting like a branded steer
> Who first will launch the burning spear
> When every day may be your last
> You think we'd learn from our past"

> from "Living In Fear" by Lenny Kravitz

Let Love Rule, released in 1989, was the first of his five albums, reflecting his respect and passion for classic rock. He married "Cosby" star Lisa Bonet in 1990, which plunged him into the midst of media attention from which he's never emerged. In 1992 he wrote and produced the hit song "Justify My Love" for Madonna. Each of his subsequent albums extended his reputation as a true soul contender, as much of a commercial force as an artistic one, from *Mama Said* (1991) through *Are You Gonna Go My Way* (1993), *Circus* (1995) and *Five* (1998).

We spoke on a unseasonably warm autumn afternoon in Manhattan, a few days before Lenny jetted down to Miami to resume work on the follow-up to *Five*, which he characterized as "about the funkiest stuff I've done yet."

You played your own drums on your first album and following ones, which is something that very few people, with the exception of Stevie Wonder, have been able to do.

Prince did it, too. And I love Prince, and have been a major Prince fan since high school. But actually I molded a lot of my drumming after Stevie Wonder. People don't think of him as a drummer. They think of him as a keyboardist and a songwriter and a singer. And a harmonica player. [*Laughs*] But his drumming is *so* lyrical. Next to Ringo, I like him best. Both of those guys are very lyrical drummers. They're the kind of drummers that a lot of other drummers just don't get. Like I hear musicians say, "Yeah, Ringo can't play." Like you know what? *Fuck* you. Because you obviously have no ears at all. Ringo was *so* sick, it was ridiculous. I mean, nobody played a tom solo like Ringo. Those were the kind of things I was listening to.

Did you use a click track—

No, no. *God*, no. I can't play to a click track, man. It feels unnatural to me. I mean, I *could* play to it, but it just doesn't feel right.

Did it take many takes to get those drum tracks right?

Sometimes. Sometimes just one take. Sometimes I'd have to punch in on a cymbal crash or a break, you know. But basically I would get it in one take.

Did you record all of *Let Love Rule* before getting a record deal?

Yes. I just went in and made the record. That was my conscious decision to stop playing for other people and start concentrating on my own stuff. Because all of a sudden I felt this music coming out of me. That is the first collection of songs that I had written, that album.

That's quite a start. Did it come easy to you?

Yes. The music just came. Some songs came easy. Some required a lot of work. It all depends.

Is it true you didn't intend to play all the instruments?

Absolutely. I produced the record, but Henry [Hirsch] shaped the sound. He knew that I could play. So every time that these guys would come in to audition, he said that I sounded better. Nobody passed the damn test to play the way we wanted them to play. So I ended up playing all the shit. I *never wanted* to do that. It just became . . . It just became. I knew how to do that from playing all those demos for other people. So I just did it. And that became my sound.

That sound has evolved over the years, but was fully-developed from the start, as shown on this new *Greatest Hits* collection. Was it fun to put these songs together?

Well, because it was a greatest hits record, that limited what it had to be. I couldn't just pick a bunch of my favorite tunes. We had certain songs we had to deal with because they were hits. So basically what we did was to ask all the territories around the world to put a list together of what songs they needed to have, because certain songs were hits in different places at different times, you know. So once all the tunes came together, we put them in an order that we thought sounded good, in terms of a sequence.

Would an album of your own favorite songs be much different than this CD?
Somewhat. I mean, I *love* all the songs that are on here. But there are more obscure songs that weren't necessarily hits that might be some of my favorites.

Do you write all the time?
Yeah. Whenever I feel it. And that's the way it works for me.

Do you remember writing "Let Love Rule"?
Yeah. It was a phrase I had come up with before writing the song. I wrote "Let love rule" on the wall of my building on Broome Street. It was just something like, hey, let love rule. It wasn't a song, it was a slogan. I just kept looking at it, and one day I just wrote the song. I love that song. I think it's one of my favorites. It's so simple, and it says a lot.

It's in E major but goes to a G, which is a chromatic, Beatlesque thing to do. Do you recall getting that progression?
Yeah. I was playing on this acoustic jazz guitar that was laying around the house. And I just started playing it and those chords came out. And I knew I had hit something. It all happened kind of quickly.

Do a lot of your songs come fast?
It's always different.

Do you run a tape when you are writing?
Sometimes. But I am *so* disorganized. It doesn't matter how many platinum albums you have or anything. I still can't find a tape recorder when I need one. Or a guitar pick. But sometimes I just play it in my head. And if I forget it, I figure it wasn't good enough to remember.

Have you forgotten many?
I've forgotten several. Sometimes I'm dreaming and I'm in bed and I hear a song. I get just caught between that place of being awake and being asleep. And I can't get out of it. I've lost a few things that were actually good.

Have you been ever able to retrieve a song from dreams?
Yeah. "Can't Get You Off My Mind." *Boom.* There it was. Also "Don't Go and Put a Bullet in My Head."

Where does it come from?
From the music. It's floating out there. You pick it up. It's floating out there. It's the beauty of imagination. You imagine these songs. When I hear something that isn't created yet, I'm listening to it in my head as if I'm listening to a record. So it's great, you hear this thing that doesn't even exist—well, doesn't exist *materially*—until you put it down. And it's going on in your head.

And if you don't—
If you don't put it down, somebody else might get it.

Do you think so?

It happens. Things like that have happened. A certain vibe goes around. Some-body writes something which is really similar to something you've been thinking. Those things are out there. They're on whatever waves there are, out there.

And what's the best way to tune into them?

You just have to be aware. You have to be relaxed. And you'll pick it up.

Do you ever sit down with the intention of writing a song?

No. I can't do that. I hate that. I wait for them to come to me. And when they do, they let me know.

Do you remember writing "Fly Away"?

I wrote that in the Bahamas when I was over there doing the *Five* record. I was traveling along the beach in my jeep, cruising. That's the vibe of the song. I didn't mean to write a new song. I had already finished the album and turned it in. And I was in the studio messing around with this guitar amp and this guitar, a Les Paul. I plugged in this guitar. And certain sounds on certain guitars will inspire certain chord progressions. And that guitar sounded chunkiest right in that middle section. Just the combination of that Les Paul and this amp. I started playing those chords, and I liked the way it sounded. It was no big thing, it was simple, I just liked the way the guitar sounded.

And then I said, "Well, let's just put this down, what the hell." And I put down the drums and the bass and all, and an hour later here was this track. So I made a CD of the track, put it in my jeep, and just drove around with it, and it just came to me. So it was done in about a day or two. An architect friend of mine, the guy who built my studio in Miami, said, "You've got to put that on your record." He had heard me making it. I said, "No, the album's done, I'll probably just make it a B-side or something. It's just a simple song, no big deal." But he *begged* me. He said, "You've *got* to put that thing on the record." He just kept going on and on and *on* about it. So I said okay. I called Virgin and said, "I've got this other song. Can we stop the press?" They said yeah. And the rest is history.

So you just made the track for fun—

Yeah. I wasn't writing a song or anything. I was just messing around. Which, of course, is how the best stuff happens.

Because you get out of the way?

Exactly. Exactly. You think, "I'm not doing anything here." So you're off the hook. You're *free*.

Did "Are You Gonna Go My Way" also come fast?

Yeah. It came so fast and easy, the engineer said he didn't even think I should put it on the record.

Do you ever make demos?

No, I don't believe in demos. Because you can't beat them. There's always a great vibe that gets on the demo. You try to cop it again later, but you can't. You can only do it once. I had made a few demos at home during *Let Love Rule*. And even if the demo was shitty, there always was this vibe. Because you're putting it *down*, you're feeling it. Even if the recording of it is messy. But there's this vibe, this great sound, that happens by accident. So I just figured, *enough* of that.

Your cover of "American Woman" is great. And like the original, it has no snare drum—just hand claps.

Yeah, that's great. That's what made it funky, having those claps on the two and the four, and not having any drums, except for high hat and kick drum. That was fun to record. It happened quickly, too. They wanted me to cover it for the Austin Powers movie. So I went in and cut it just to see if I liked it enough to want to do this. So the version that you hear is like what I guess you could call the demo version, except that it ended up being a master.

That's a great tune. Very simple, to the point. The whole thing stays on one chord except for the solo, which goes down from a C to a B. But the original doesn't have that. I got to play a couple of weeks ago in Toronto with the Guess Who. It was very cool.

"Can't Get You Out of My Mind" is a great song.

Thank you. I dreamt that song. So I never really wrote it. It was just there. I was at the Royalton Hotel in New York. And I dreamt the song, and I called my friend to my room and I said, "Listen to this." And we both listened and I said, "It's a damn *country* song, what am I doing?" It's got that *vibe*, you know? But there it was.

It's got a really nice bridge.

Yeah, thanks. That's my favorite part. It's like this ultimate country thing with an Earth, Wind & Fire bridge.

That rich mixture of elements is at the heart of your music—

Yeah, it is. I'm always mixing it up. See, it takes ears to hear that. A lot of people don't have the ears to hear, within one song, the different elements. I may have five or six different elements within one song. People don't necessarily hear them.

Why do you think that is?

I'm not sure. Maybe because they're so used to hearing things one way. And they just don't want to really listen to something else. Even when it might be something good.

Do you go to one guitar to write a song?

Whatever is around.

Does the guitar affect the song?

Well, it affects the sound. It can affect the song itself, if I'm starting with just guitar, and I'm kind of jamming. Yeah, it can make me play certain things, the sound of it.

Do you recall writing "Always on the Run"?

That was written with Slash. He and I were just jamming. He played the main riff, and I played drums, and that's how we cut the track. Then I played the bass, and then I played my chicken-scratch guitar part on it, and that was it.

How about "Stand By My Woman"?

That's kind of a gospel, R&B thing. Wrote that with Henry Hirsch, playing around with those chord changes. That song just came. It was one of those magical moments where the song just materialized. The minute I heard the chords, I heard the melody.

Did you write "Justify My Love" for Madonna?

I brought it to her, and I told her it was a Number One hit. The track was laid, she had to just do the vocals. I knew that was a song for her, I never thought of doing that myself. She said, "Yeah, okay, pop it in." So I popped in the tape, she heard it once and said, "Let me hear it again," and then she looked at me and said, "Okay, let's go," and I said, "I'll see you in the studio tomorrow." We did it and it became Number One.

What's next for you?

I'm working on the sixth album. I take it day by day. I thank God for everything I have so far, and I pray that I can just keep going forward and keep making music, man. That's what I love to do. And I have so much more to offer. I'm just looking forward to that.

MeShell NdegeOcello
Hollywood, California 2000

MeShell contains multitudes. Multitudes of soul, that is: of passionate melodies, rich harmonies, funky basslines, dynamic rhythms, and words that speak directly to the heart. She's one of those rare musicians who seems to have a limitless capacity for expressing herself in song, and it's an expression unbounded by any particular genre, style, or even instrument. Fluent in funk, jazz, R&B, hip-hop, soul, rock, and folk, she sings and raps, plays bass, guitar, keyboards, and writes words that are poetic, provocative, political, passionate, and—especially on her newest album at the time of this interview, *Bitter*—heartbreakingly vulnerable.

In person she's shy and soft-spoken, and is not entirely at ease with the conventions of doing publicity. All of her albums have started with an instrumental, and in life she also seems to prefer to allow her music to speak for her. Wearing a T-shirt and jeans, she is ensconced within an immense royal blue couch in a Hollywood hotel suite, sipping hot chocolate from an oversized cup. When told that certain songs on *Bitter* are brilliant and beautiful and quite a departure from her previous work, rather than expound on the glory of her own greatness, she answers instead with a genuinely gracious, almost silent, "*Thank* you!"

But in her music her message is clear, and her voice is strong. And as reserved as she is in person, in her songs she doesn't shy away from any subject, and tackles tough ones directly and without apology. After exploring the politics of sex, race, and religion on her first two albums [*Plantation Lullabies* and *Peace Beyond Passion*], she delves deeply into the politics of love on *Bitter*. Songs such as "Loyalty," "Faithful," "Sincerity," and "Grace" speak to the elemental aspects of romantic love and the struggles of monogamy. And as in her previous albums, she does it with a kind of soulful candor that is disarming and tremendously touching:

> "I hear voices and I can't stand to be alone
> 'Cause emptiness is all I've ever known
> Soiled by my lust I feel no shame
> No longer forsaken when they call my name
> No one is faithful
> I am weak
> I go astray
> Forgive me for my ways"

from "Faithful"

Her name (pronounced *Me-shell En-deh-gay-o-chello*) is Swahili for "free as a bird," and it's this freedom that is foremost in her thoughts and her songs. In an industry where artists often revel in self-glorification, she yearns for greater anonymity and for the freedom to express herself musically without any emphasis on her own image and voice. "I would love to find a band," she says. When reminded she already has one, she says, "No. I mean a *real* band. Where everybody works together. And I don't have to be the singer. I would *love* to be in a band where someone else is the front person. I would be happy just playing bass." But wouldn't she miss playing and singing her own songs? "No," she answers immediately. "I like to *play*. And I make whatever music I play my own. It doesn't have to be my song. I don't have Sting-itis. [*Laughs*] You know, where he said to Stewart and Andy [of the Police], 'We're going to do all of *my* songs.' I don't need that. I'm happy just playing bass."

The daughter of a military musician, in 1969 she was born in Germany and given the name Michelle Johnson. Raised primarily in the environs of Washington, D.C., she lived for years in both New York and Los Angeles. She was roundly rejected by all of the major record companies until one of her homemade sizzling demo tapes was heard by Madonna, who wisely signed MeShell to Maverick Records. "I respect MeShell on every level," Madonna said. "As a songwriter, a musician, a singer, a performer, but mostly as a woman."

MeShell's debut album, *Plantation Lullabies*, was astounding for the maturity of its musical vision and the depth of its soul. Frequent comparisons in the press between MeShell and Prince, which might have seemed overblown before hearing her music, made a lot of sense when confronted with her prodigious musical range, swinging from the funny-sexy hip-hop of "If That's Your Boyfriend (He Wasn't Last Night)" to sweetly romantic piano ballads like "Outside Your Window" to full-blown ambitious jazz-funk suites such as the astounding "Two Lonely Hearts on a Subway."

Other artists heard this music and started clamoring to capture her magic touch on their albums: John Mellencamp sought her out to duet on a cover of Van Morrison's "Wild Night"; Arrested Development enlisted her as musical director for many live shows; and jazz legend Herbie Hancock collaborated with her on the song "Nocturnal Sunshine."

Her second album, *Peace Beyond Passion*, spins through various aspects of spirituality and sexuality, starting with "The Way," one of the most inspirational tracks she or anyone has recorded. "I was in a real searching period on that record," she said. "I was just totally trying to find my way. I'm glad I've gotten through that and I've gained some bit of understanding about what I need to be doing. Your spiritual path is such a personal thing. And I was thinking I was trying to find some groups to belong to, trying to *fit* in somewhere. And that's not really what it's all about. Now I just try to be thankful and to be a good person."

That sense of gratitude permeates the rich and peaceful textures of *Bitter*, her third album, which resounds with a sense of tranquility, even when exploring the battles and burdens of being human. It's a peace that's also permeated her life, inspiring her to leave the urban sprawl of Los Angeles far behind to live with her son Askia among the beautiful forests near Mendocino in Northern California.

"I was tired of the city," she said. "And tired of always being right in the middle of the industry. I'm on the same label with Alanis Morissette, who sold 28 million records. Candlebox sold 17 million. The Deathtones go gold. I haven't even gone gold. So I feel a lot of pressure. But that doesn't keep me from doing it. I don't let that feed into my insecurities. So this label might be my home for a long time. Or it might not be. We'll see how it goes. This business is great, but, you know, I'm someone who needs to have a *life*."

Bitter contains many songs addressed to elemental human topics, such as "Loyalty," "Grace," and "Sincerity." Was that your intention starting the album, to deal with these topics?

Yeah. I don't know what's wrong with me. I guess growing up listening to Pink Floyd's *The Wall*, I'm deep into the concept thing. I just get hooked on something and it drives me, and before I know it I have twelve songs on one topic. I was coming out of a relationship—a very important relationship—and I was learning a lot about just being vulnerable. I'm hoping that the record comes across with the message that it is okay to be vulnerable. And somehow talk about it.

One of the main themes of the album is forgiveness—especially in terms of forgiving yourself.

Yes. And that is so important, to forgive yourself. In any aspect of life—work, play, or whatever. We're so hard on ourselves sometimes. And I was. I was just the lash and the whip. It took me a while just to realize to let it go, to move on, to not have any regrets. To live for today.

You've written most of your previous songs on bass and keyboards. But these new ones you wrote on guitar?

Yes. I bought an acoustic guitar for the first time. Three years ago. After I did Lilith Fair. Because I was just in love with the way Amy [Ray] of the Indigo Girls would just sit and play the acoustic and sing songs. I'm a huge fan of Chris Whitley, who goes out with just acoustics and is just incredible. So I got an acoustic guitar and started fiddling around, and that's basically how this album came to be. I just wanted to write some stuff that had a lot of simplicity. And then a lot of lyric stuff came afterwards.

With "Beautiful," though, I think the lyrics came first. But a lot of the stuff I was just sitting writing on the guitar. That's what's really different about this album—that I wrote these songs on the guitar. And I would just go and show the musicians what I was playing, and the music came together that way in the recording process.

Have you played guitar before?
I play funk and rhythm guitar. But this approach was different. I'm not a virtuoso on any instrument. I can sort of play at it and write on it. And come up with cool parts. But in *no* way am I a guitar player. I can just play a lot of different things.

In past songs, did you work more from a rhythm track first?
Yeah, this one was very different. This album I have Abe Laboriel on drums, Lisa Coleman on piano, Doyle Bramhall—who is one of them most incredible guitar players in the world. And I would hum the drum parts to Abe, and he would make them sound human. I would show Lisa the piano part, and I would show Doyle the skeleton of the song we had, and we would just sit there and play it and put it together. And that was so fun, because that is so different than how I had done the other two records. It was usually just David [Gamson] and myself.

You started the album with him?
Yeah. I started with him. And he produced most of the vocals on the tracks. But Craig [Street, who produced] I have known since I was 17 years old. He was part of the Hendrix Foundation that I worked with over the years. We just get along really well, and we are always having this dialogue about music. So we were kind of on the same wavelength. And he came up with this idea of doing a record the old way. You bring in the people and record it in four weeks. We had a dollar to make it.

A dollar?
Yeah. A pretty low budget.

Sounds pretty good for a dollar.
I thank Craig so much for that. He was a great help and influence. He's great with colors and textures and guitar tones. So we had a great time doing the record together.

It was great to be with him. He's like an abstract painter. He doesn't really talk in terms of music. The most important things that happen while we're in the process is that he talks about art and film and how we are today, and just trying to find a good cup of coffee. Those are the most important things to talk about while working on the record. He just made me feel very comfortable.

In your press material, you said that this album is a testament to him and others who refuse to be pigeon-holed by genre.
Yes. It's for the great producer Tom Wilson who did the early Dylan albums and other things. He is a person of color. Or it's for people who don't just want to be seen as doing hip-hop or R&B. It's for Joan Armatrading, Richie Havens, Cree Summers, Lenny Kravitz, Ben Harper, Tracy Chapman. You express yourself differently. But you still have a black experience. You know, this is your music. And Jimi Hendrix, you know, what saddened him the most was that his own people didn't come out to hear his music. I just wanted to show that they're appreciated. That I appreciate them.

It's one of the most powerful things about your own work, that it doesn't neatly fit into one bin, but crosses over into so many kinds of music. Record companies, though, aren't really prepared to deal with artists that contain so much.

That's exactly right. So I'm hoping like MP3 and the Internet changes that and allows people access to a lot more stuff. You don't have to do the same thing every album.

Bitter opens with "Adam," and continues the tradition of starting each of your albums with an instrumental.

Yeah. The first songs I ever wrote were all instrumentals. I would try to get with people to write lyrics, and it never happened. And then I got really into avant-garde jazz. And hopefully in life I might do a jazz record, if I can find the right label who would let me do it.

"Adam" starts with a beautiful passage for strings. Did you write that on keyboard?

Yes. But it's weird how I did it. I wrote one string part at a time, instead of playing it all together. Because I just wanted to write in a contrapuntal way. Yeah, so I wrote it and came up with the percussion part later. And then I gave it to Steven Barber, and he arranged it to go with cello, viola, and two violins. And I'm very proud of that piece.

It's beautiful. And after hearing so much sampled and synthesized music, it's so nice to hear real humans playing.

Real is the way to go. [*Laughs*] It's really great.

When you are writing music, is there more of a sense of following where the song wants to go, or leading it?

Once I start on it, I hear it all in my head. Once I find it, it's there. And all of a sudden I just hear it, all of it, and I just try to get it to come through my hands. I enjoy writing. I enjoy writing something that's terrible, too. Sometimes I have to write five terrible things to come up with one good one. That's fine.

Do you finish those ones?

Everything I start, I finish. It may not be the best thing. But you want to be able to look back at it and say, "Okay, that's where I was at that time." I never throw away anything. I know Picasso painted a million things all the time. You just got to go with it.

I've done writing sessions with other people, and if it's not going well, they just want to quit. And I hate that. You've got to finish it, or else how can you know that it's no good? So I just finish everything.

Do you finish songs in one session, or does it take a lot of work?

A lot of work. Never just one session. I have a little studio in my house so I can go back and finish it. Or wake up in the middle of the night and go to it. I live with a writer. So it's usually 1:00 rolls around, and somebody is on the computer, or I'm in the studio. I guess that's when everything is quiet and still. That's when the best writing gets done. I do hear it all in my head, and then just work it out.

Do you have any theories about what causes that to happen?

I think because I listen to records all the time. At home or in the car, I listen to CDs. I still buy records all the time, and I just love music. I still enjoy music. I go to concerts and enjoy myself. And I'm not critical. David Gamson can't listen to music—he starts to break it down, deconstruct it, talk about the production. I don't do that. I just enjoy it, have fun, and listen to it. It's the best thing in the world. [*Laughs*]

I just bought some Miles Davis live imports, and I've been listening to those a lot. And I've been listening to *The Wall* [by Pink Floyd]. Just the guitars on that are *so* great. And a lot of Hendrix. I listen to everything. It goes in spurts. I listen to one thing for a month, and then move on to something new.

That joy of music is reflected in your own work—
Well, I'm very happy to hear that. I love it. I don't understand how people can get jaded. Or start writing schlock that all sounds the same. I love music too much for that.

There are so many people who work in music as a job, without any joy—
I *hate* that. I don't want to get like that. It's crazy. People complain to me that I wait three years between records. Yeah, it's because I go out and have a life. What can I write if I don't have a life? I just write when I feel like it. If I don't feel like it, I don't write.

Does that mean you wait for inspiration to trigger a song?
Yeah. I can go a year without writing.

Some songwriters feel they will lose touch with the process if they wait too long.
I know. And I know one day I won't be able to write. One day I won't be able to play. That might come when I'm 50 or 60, and that's okay. It's part of life. I'm not afraid about it. Who cares? Every day changes. I hope I write a lot. But I'm sure the way I play now I won't play ten years from now. And I think if I stop writing, I'll discover something else to do.

You could keep writing songs into your eighties and beyond. There's no reason you have to stop—
I know. But maybe I'll just write poetry. Maybe I'll just be a lyricist.

Would that be fulfilling for you?
Yeah. Because I'm always afraid that people are struggling to be hip. To write today's music. Instead of just writing what they feel. And that word "dated." I think that's more frightening than not writing. I just want to not have this fear that I'm dated. I just don't plan to be 50 and go out and perform "Boyfriend."

Well, you can play your new songs.
Right. And hopefully I'll have an audience then. My geriatric club.

The song "Grace" is great in that it has almost two choruses. There's "I never thought I'd fall in love again" and the part which has "Your love's my only saving grace." It's like an abundance of riches.
[*Laughter*] Someone was trying to teach me that the first one is really the B verse. [*Laughs*] I don't know. Yeah. That all came on guitar. And I had the guitar sec-

tions. And then the melody came. I am terrible with song structure. It is not my forte. 'Cause I just throw them together. Whatever fits fits.

That's why they work so well. They're organic.

Yeah. I agree. Though I have been told that I make weird song structures. David and I, when we first started working together, we used to fight over how the song should go. He'd say, "You can't do that," and I'd say, "Who's *telling* you I can't do that?" Eventually I got him to come over to my side. Songwriting is a free-for-all for me. I just write what I feel.

The great songwriters have all played with song forms. Carole King has done it a lot—

Yeah. I have so much respect for Carole King. I think she's great. I've been listening to *Tapestry* a lot. I love that record. Her melodies are so good. That's a dying art form—how to write a great melody. If I could write melody like that, it would be great.

"Grace" has that feeling of a classic melody—like something she or Bacharach would write.

Well, Bacharach is my *man.* I want to redo one of his tunes called "My Little Red Book." This group called Love did it. Love was from L.A. They were one of the first black rock bands. Everybody said the Doors stole from them. They did this version of "My Little Red Book." And I love that song. The melody is just great. So hopefully I'm going to redo that song.

How do you feel about the way your music has been promoted and distributed around the world?

I feel very blessed. Oh, yeah. I try not to take it for granted. I'm extremely blessed. I hope I can pave the way for other people who don't write formula songs to do other stuff and to get heard. It's just hard. There are so many great people out there who no one is hearing just because they're not flashy and pop-oriented and look a certain way. I'm hoping that changes. I hope TV just dies. And you don't have to be a slave to video.

You think video is the culprit?

Yeah. It's ridiculous. Okay, you have Britney Spears. And she's great or whatever. But you also have the Natalie Coles and Chaka Khans. But because they don't look a certain way in the videos, no one will take a chance on them. I feel that way, too. Just because I don't look like Tom, Dick, or Jane, why should I do a video? It doesn't get *played.* It's just hard. It makes you wonder—is the music more important, or whether I wear Gap or Versace? Who cares? Would Ricky Martin be so great if he didn't look that way? Maybe I'm nostalgic or an old fogey.

And yet people react to meaningful music when they hear it.

Right. [*Softly*] It's *hard to get it to them,* though. How do you get them to hear it? I am hoping the Internet's going to open the way to people being into music. Just going online and trying to hear stuff that they'll dig. It changes everything when you don't need the record companies. I think that they'll be obsolete.

And the new technology affords songwriters the opportunity to make their own records—

Yeah, I can make my own record. With the little bit of equipment I have. I have 24-track digital recording. I can make my own record, just take it to a CD manufacturer and make a record. It's not that deep anymore. It's a really great thing.

Does the industry make it hard for artists like yourself, or someone like Prince, who refuse to follow trends, to do your best work?
Money makes it hard. It's sad that the industry hasn't supported him. But it's all about making money. If they can't sell you to the everyday John in Iowa, they won't do it. That's become very clear to me. So I just had to redirect my focus. I just want to make things that I'm proud of, not just so they can make me rich.

You seem to have done that. As someone who started really young, you've seemed able to maintain your focus and never been distracted or derailed.
I guess because I try to have a life aside from the music business. There's so many other things going on in the world to worry about besides if I'm not selling a million records.

So even though this album is called Bitter, you're not feeling bitter these days?
No, not at all. *Bitter* just has to do with the music. It has nothing to do with me.

You once said bitterness is something we have to experience to know compassion.
Right. And to know *joy*. And *appreciate* those things. I called the album *Bitter* because I just wanted to celebrate pain for once. From pain I've learned so much. I'm tired of being afraid of it. I think the world is moving into wanting just entertainment, something that takes them out of their pain and misery. And just make them think that the world is this perfect thing. And I could never write like that. So I wanted this record to be a testament to being vulnerable. It's all right to be vulnerable and to have feelings.

Yes. These songs are all meditations on human weakness.
Yes. And human weakness, you know, is okay. [*Laughs*] It's *okay* to be human.

Paul Zollo is a singer-songwriter, author and music journalist. As the editor of *SongTalk*, the journal of the National Academy of Songwriters, he's been dedicated since 1987 to interviewing the world's great songwriters. Born in Chicago, he studied English and Music at Boston University and is the author of *The Beginning Songwriter's Answer Book*, a manual on all aspects of writing, recording and marketing songs. He has written about music for many magazines, including *Musician, Acoustic Guitar, Sing Out!, Billboard, Variety*, and *The Performing Songwriter*, and has contributed CD liner notes for artists including Paul Simon, Laura Nyro, Dan Fogelberg, Townes Van Zandt and Thom Bishop. He performed and recorded with his band The Ghosters for many years in Los Angeles, and has recently released his first album as a solo artist, *Orange Avenue*. He is the founder and original host of "The Acoustic Underground," a Los Angeles acoustic showcase, and "Bobfest," an annual tribute to Bob Dylan.